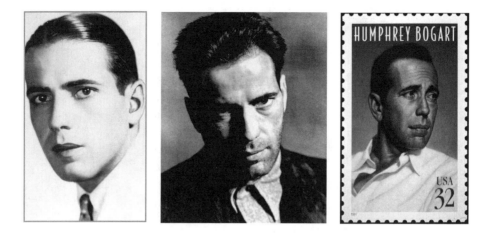

"In 1980, Darwin Porter inherited a vast but disorganized archive that had been compiled over a period of 50 years by eyewitnesses to the Jazz-Age shenanigans of Humphrey Bogart. Enriching it with information from players who either loved or hated Bogart (or both), Porter distilled this treasure trove of historic data into one blockbuster of a Hollywood read."

Danforth Prince

"Porter's biography is laced with gossipy gems. It also paints a sympathetic portrait of Bogart as a loyal friend who went out of his way to help others. He also had some scandalous skeletons in his closet."

The National Enquirer

"Porter's book uncovers scandals within the entertainment industry, when publicists from the movie studios deliberately twisted and suppressed inconvenient details about the lives of their emerging stars."

Turner Classic Movie News

"Humphrey Bogart was one of Hollywood's most celebrated lovers, his romance with Lauren Bacall hailed as one of the greatest love stories of the 20th century. But before they met, he was a drug-taking womaniser, racking up a string of failed marriages and broken relationships with some of the world's most beautiful women. Here, in an extraordinary biography drawing on a wealth of previously unseen material, veteran showbusiness writer Darwin Porter reveals the explosive truth behind Bogart's shady past."

The Mail on Sunday (London)

HUMPHREY BOGART

THE MAKING OF A LEGEND

History's Most Famous Male Movie Star
HUMPHREY BOGART
1899-1957

OTHER BOOKS BY DARWIN PORTER

Biographies
Howard Hughes, Hell's Angel
Steve McQueen, King of Cool, Tales of a Lurid Life
Paul Newman, The Man Behind the Baby Blues
Merv Griffin, A Life in the Closet
Brando Unzipped
The Secret Life of Humphrey Bogart (© 2003)
Katharine the Great: Hepburn, Secrets of a Life Revealed
Jacko, His Rise and Fall (The Social and Sexual History of Michael Jackson)

And Forthcoming:
Frank Sinatra, The Boudoir Singer
*
The Kennedys, All the Gossip Unfit to Print
*
J. Edgar Hoover & Clyde Tolson
Investigating the Sexual Secrets of America's Most Famous Men & Women
*
and in collaboration with Roy Moseley
Damn You, Scarlett O'Hara: The Private Lives of Vivien Leigh & Laurence Olivier

Film Criticism
Fifty Years of Queer Cinema (500 of the Best GLBTQ Films Ever Made)
Blood Moon's Guides to Gay & Lesbian Film (Volumes One & Two)

Non-Fiction
Hollywood Babylon-It's Back!, and *Hollywood Babylon Strikes Again!*

Novels
Butterflies in Heat; Rhinestone Country;
Marika (a roman à clef based on the life of Marlene Dietrich*)*
*Venus (*a *roman à clef* based on the life of Anaïs Nin*);*
Razzle-Dazzle; Midnight in Savannah;
Blood Moon, The Erotic Thriller; Hollywood's Silent Closet

Travel Guides
Many editions and many variations of ***The Frommer Guides***
to Europe, the Caribbean, California, Georgia, and The Carolinas

HUMPHREY BOGART

THE MAKING OF A LEGEND

Another Hot, Startling, and Unauthorized Probe
of America's Entertainment Industry from

Darwin Porter

HUMPHREY BOGART, THE MAKING OF A LEGEND

Copyright ©2010, Blood Moon Productions, Ltd.
ALL RIGHTS RESERVED
www.BloodMoonProductions.com

Manufactured in the United States of America

ISBN 978-1-936003-14-3

Cover designs by Richard Leeds (Bigwigdesign.com)
Videography and Publicity Trailers by Piotr Kajstura
Distributed in North America and Australia
through National Book Network (www.NBNbooks.com)
and in the UK through Turnaround (www.turnaround-uk.com)

1 2 3 4 5 6 7 8 9 10

THIS BOOK IS DEDICATED TO THE LEGACY OF

STANLEY MILLS HAGGART

AUTHOR'S NOTE

In the pages ahead, a description of the source of each individual piece of information is positioned very close to the spot where that information actually appears. Also, within the pages ahead, direct quotations have been transcribed "as they were remembered" by the witnesses who originally heard the remarks. They're presented with the same nuances, and with the same phraseologies, that were used when those remarks were originally transmitted.

CHAPTER ONE

It was an idyllic setting, a picture postcard of Victorian life that still thrived in America before its last vestiges were swept away by the coming of the Great War.

Ever since the final summer of the nineteenth century, handsome Dr. Belmont DeForest Bogart and his successful artist wife, Maud, with her frizzy red hair and strong jaw, had come to a manicured spot on the shoreline of Lake Canandaigua, one of New York State's Finger Lakes, to relax and go sailing on his deluxe yacht, *Comrade*, moored just two hundred feet from their gingerbread-decorated, two-story Victorian manse.

A local brewer, Jonathan Mulhouse, had built the house in 1871 for his rotund wife and their equally hefty brood of six very fat children. Although Mulhouse himself looked like a lean and mean Abraham Lincoln, his children resembled his blubber wife more than they did himself. The Mulhouse family was the scandal of Seneca Point. The children were ridiculed for their weight and for a physical deformity inherited from Mrs. Mulhouse. None of the brood had a neck. Locals called them the "no-neck Mulhouses." This genetic flaw also didn't come from Mr. Mulhouse, who had one of the longest necks east of the Mississippi.

The ridiculous appearance of the Mulhouses was not the only subject of local gossip. Rumor had it Mrs. Mulhouse allowed all her children to drink beer from her husband's brewery even though they were underage.

It had been with a sigh of relief that neighbors learned in 1899 that a New York doctor and his wife had taken over the Mulhouse home. "To judge from the size of Mr. Bogart's yacht moored on the lake, I think they are rich New Yorkers," the Mayor, Frank Schmidt, proudly announced at a private dinner of the Chamber of Commerce. "From what I hear, the Bogarts are a most respectable family."

The arrival of the Bogarts at Canandaigua and their departure every Labor Day was considered a news event to be reported in *The Canandaigua Gazette*.

On the particularly lovely summer afternoon of July 5, 1913, the spire of the tower room of the Bogart home still stood proudly after the Fourth of July fireworks. The lawns sweeping down to the lake were immaculately trimmed.

The crops were at full bloom in the adjoining farmlands, and cows grazed in the surrounding pasturelands. Even the woods seemed quiet except for a young farmhand sneaking into the darkest part of the forest with one of the local wives whose husband was in New York City on a business trip. From his bedroom window, the teenage son, Humphrey, nicknamed, "Hump," looked out at the weeping willows that fluttered in the wind so gracefully that their movements seemed to be the work of a choreographer.

When Maud had first seen the fluttery willows and a bubbling brook running alongside their property, she'd dubbed their new home "Willow Brook." She set about to furnish it with crystal, tapestries, classical statues, precious china, antiques, and Oriental carpets.

The Bogarts' neighbors were invariably from Boston or New York, and they'd come to Seneca Point, a rich community directly south of Canandaigua, to escape from the blistering summer heat of those two cities. Wealthy businessmen hobnobbed with bankers, newspaper columnists, presidents of colleges, and even a well-cared-for clergyman who was said to drink five bottles of wine a day.

Dr. Belmont DeForest Bogart and his wife, Maud Bogart

It was at Seneca Point that young Hump first met two men called the Warner Brothers. They were not the brothers who built a powerful Hollywood studio that would bring Hump his greatest fame when he was no longer called "Hump" but "Bogie." These Warner Brothers, Henry and David, designed and constructed steamboats, including some showboats that sailed up and down the Mississippi.

Even more fascinating was another pair of brothers, Frank and Arthur Hamlin, who lived next door to the Bogarts. Their father was the local banker. Ever since Hump rescued Arthur from the lake when the youngster fell off the dock, the Hamlins had told Hump he could consider "our house your second home."

Willow Brook, their summer house on Canandaigua Lake,

Although Hump enjoyed playing games with the boys, he mostly liked coming over to visit their mother, Mary Hamlin, in the afternoons where she gave him rich pastries and told him of her life in the theater.

She wrote religious dramas which played across the country. It wasn't Hump's type of drama but he loved listening to her stories about life in the theater. She knew all the great actors of her day and confided the most intimate stories about their personal lives.

"It's a world of make-believe," she told Hump. "You can lose yourself in the world of the theater." Mary urged Hump and his playmates to launch an impromptu theater at the lakeshore near the bandstand, setting up their own summer playhouse.

Until meeting Mary, Hump had never considered being an actor. When it was first suggested to him, he told Mary that it wasn't his kind of thing. "Father wants me to be a surgeon, but I'd rather be a sailor."

In time, breaking from religious dramas, Mary Hamlin would write *Alexander Hamilton*, a play that became a hit on Broadway. Warner Brothers, Hump's future studio, purchased the rights to it and filmed it in 1931. The movie became one of the most successful talkies of that time.

In his bedroom, a noise distracted Hump, who went to look out the rear of his window, from which he had a good view of the carriage road that ran over a one-lane stone-built bridge at the rear of their manse.

Their cook was receiving a load of fresh produce from a local farmer. From a horse-pulled carriage, he could see the unloading of the largest, ripest tomatoes he'd ever seen, along with peaches, potatoes, carrots, and grapes so fresh that the aroma of the vineyard rose to his second-floor open window. Maud always insisted that she get "only the best" of the local bounty before it was shipped off to the stifling city markets of New York City or Philadelphia.

Seneca Point in those days was a staunchly Republican enclave even though only that summer, a young Democrat, Franklin Delano Roosevelt, had arrived, ostensibly on what he'd told his cronies was a "hunting expedition." The daughters of the prosperous families of Seneca Point were said to have produced the loveliest single concentration of "female pulchritude" this side of Broadway. Roosevelt became enamored of one young belle, Beth Ferguson, whom he invited every afternoon to the lake for swimming. It was while showing off his prowess as a swimmer that Roosevelt had been stricken with a stomach cramp. When Beth saw his right arm go up into the air and then her boyfriend go under, she thought he was playing another one of his many tricks on her. Since meeting her, he'd always chided her for being so gullible. At first

Franklin Delano Roosevelt

3

she'd thought that he was only pretending to be drowning. When he didn't surface for a while, she grew panicky and screamed for help.

The family of Dwight St. Davids was having a picnic nearby along the shores of the lake. Beth screamed to them to rescue Roosevelt. Their youngest son, Peter, was home for the holidays from Princeton. Sensing what was wrong, Peter, an expert swimmer, dived into the cold lake and swam toward Roosevelt. Peter went underwater and emerged with Roosevelt gasping for air. Peter brought the body ashore and called for his other family members to help him carry the body to the nearby Bogart home.

When Dr. Belmont Bogart came out onto his front verandah, he encountered what he thought was a dead victim of drowning. He rushed to give the young man medical attention.

The commotion attracted the rest of the Bogart family. Hump, Maud, and the two daughters, Catherine and Frances, also came out onto the porch. They looked in horror as Belmont seemingly brought life back to the victim. When young Roosevelt was breathing properly once again, Belmont ordered that he be taken upstairs and put in Hump's bed.

Laid to rest on the soft bed upstairs, Roosevelt fell into a deep coma-like sleep. Belmont ordered Hump to stay in the room with the recovering victim in case he should experience a turn for the worse. "Make sure that he's breathing all right," Belmont said before heading downstairs to join Maud.

Hump resented spending the rest of the afternoon and evening guarding Roosevelt. A surly Irish maid arrived with a tray of food for his supper. She plopped down the tray telling him, "Eat it if you don't want to starve."

"I don't like turnips," Hump protested.

"Then throw the bloody things out the window," the maid said before going out and slamming the door.

With those turnips still uneaten on his plate, Hump had fallen asleep somewhere during the middle of the night. Before nodding off, he'd checked on Roosevelt. The young man was snoring loudly.

The following morning, it had been Roosevelt who awakened Hump. The doctor and Maud had departed on a shopping expedition, and had left Hump to have breakfast alone with Roosevelt after the doctor had examined him and had pronounced him fit.

Roosevelt appeared to be in his late twenties or even early thirties. It had been over the breakfast table where Hump finally got his favorite dish—ham and eggs—that he'd begun to learn who their mysterious guest was.

Even though innocent at the time, Hump soon realized that Roosevelt, who had quickly become "Franklin" to him, was not supposed to be at Seneca Point but had told his wife, Eleanor, that he was in Philadelphia on business. "Being an attorney allows me to go out of town on occasion," Franklin said,

4

"and seize the opportunity."

"Are you related to Theodore Roosevelt?" Hump asked.

"Actually, he's my fifth cousin," Roosevelt said, "but we're not particularly close. In fact, I married one of my cousins, Eleanor. A fine woman but a bit plain. Perhaps you'll meet her one day. If you do, please keep my visit to Seneca Point a secret."

Hump promised that he would.

After thanking Hump for the hospitality and leaving a note for Dr. Bogart, whom he claimed "saved my life," Franklin departed, planning to return to New York City. He told Hump he was heading for Washington, where he was going to become Assistant Secretary of the Navy. "Cousin Theodore held that post before moving on to become governor of New York and later president of the United States. Who knows? I might follow his trail." Before leaving, Franklin said, "Since we share a dark secret, young man, I want to invite you to come and visit me in Washington when you grow up a bit more. Washington may not have as many beautiful young girls as Seneca Point, but I'm sure to find a suitable debutante for you."

"That's a promise I'll hold you to," Hump said before shaking the young politician's hand.

"This is not good-bye," Franklin said. "It's just a temporary farewell until we meet again. Hopefully, under far better circumstances."

The strange visit of Franklin Roosevelt to Seneca Point had been the highlight of Hump's summer there. Otherwise, he found the days long, lazy, and slow. He craved action and wasn't getting any excitement from anywhere except from books. He loved to read.

Back in his upstairs bedroom following a big lunch, he felt bloated. He liked to lie down after eating to digest his food.

Maud always preferred to go with his father to sit on their large front verandah overlooking the lake. Over the lunch table, Hump had gotten mad at the mean family cook. Although the meal had consisted of two roasts, and a selection of seven fresh vegetables from the field, there was no ham

Bogie, Aged 2

on the table. He always complained when he saw no ham.

Going downstairs for a glass of cold water, Hump looked out through the French doors onto the porch where his parents were resting in a large swing. He wondered if he'd grow to be as tall as his father, all six feet of him with shoulders so broad he could have been a football player. Even on the hottest days, Belmont never appeared outside the house unless he was dressed in a heavy suit of dark blue wool along with a white shirt and a stiff collar. He always ordered the maid to "make my collars extra stiff."

Almost as tall as her husband, Maud was an Edwardian beauty. She invariably wore only mauve, lavender, or gray—mostly graceful silks that seemed to flow in the wind, or else heavily starched cotton dresses that were immaculately tailored. She had thirty pairs of high-heeled, high-button shoes, always with a lavender ribbon. The tiny shoes were like those of a little girl's. Almost daily, Maud commented on her size two and a half feet. "They're so tiny I don't know how they carry me around. Some six-year-old girls have feet larger than mine."

Remarks such as that always brought a compliment from Belmont. "In China I hear they bind women's feet to make them as small, tender, and beautiful as yours. I don't dare get you near a Chinaman because he'd kidnap you for his harem and make love to your feet all night."

Returning with his cold water to take upstairs, where he was reading Joseph Conrad's *The Nigger of the Narcissus*, Hump paused once again to look out at the bucolic scene of his parents sitting in the swing on their verandah on this perfect summer day.

From his black leather satchel, Belmont removed a syringe. Maud was wearing a long-sleeved dress in soft tones of mauve with gray accessories. She unbuttoned the pearl buttons on her left arm and rolled up her sleeve. With his wife's forearm exposed in all its porcelain beauty, Belmont very gently inserted a needle into her arm. She closed her eyes and leaned back in the swing as if enjoying a respite from the hot summer afternoon by a cooling breeze blowing in from the lake.

After having injected his wife, Belmont removed his jacket and rolled up the sleeve of his white shirt. He then injected the needle into his own arm.

Hump had seen enough. He didn't know exactly what was happening, only that his parents were injecting morphine into their arms. Morphine, he'd heard, was to be injected only into sick people. His parents weren't sick. They'd never looked better and healthier.

Placing the glass of water on a nearby antique, Hump quietly tiptoed upstairs. He didn't want his parents to know he'd been spying on them in a secret moment.

Back in his bedroom, he was deeply disturbed by that scene he'd just witnessed on the porch. He picked up his book and tried to resume reading it on his bed.

Somehow he knew that what his father was doing was not right, but he didn't exactly understand why it was wrong. From the safety of his bedroom, he tried to think this out rationally. His father was a surgeon and a leading heart and lung specialist, earning $20,000 a year, so Hump figured his father must have a valid reason to shoot morphine into himself and into Maud.

An awful reality dawned. His parents weren't healthy at all. They were sick and that's why they needed the morphine, perhaps to prevent some incurable illness.

He dropped his Conrad book to the floor and sat up in his bed. This idyllic summer home, and their grand life in New York City would surely come to an end if his parents died. Who would raise him and his sisters?

A paralyzing fear swept over him. He had to find out what was the matter with them.

His world as he'd known it was now in jeopardy.

***

Two days after Hump had seen his father shooting morphine into his mother's arm and his own arm, he went to Maud's studio and knocked on her door. When working, she'd left instructions not to disturb her for any reason, "even if someone is dying." Showing her displeasure, she threw open the door. "What is it?"

"I saw the needles going into your arms," he blurted out.

She pulled him inside. "You're to tell no one, especially your sisters. Certainly none of the neighbors."

"If you're sick, I want to know," he protested.

Very patiently Maud sat him down and told him that three years before he was born, his father had been in a dreadful accident after he'd earned his degree at Columbia University's College of Physicians and Surgeons.

"Your father was an intern being driven in a horse-drawn ambulance going at top speed. The vehicle accidentally overturned when it hit an enormous pothole. Belmont fell out of the ambulance onto the cobblestones. The ambulance turned over on him, breaking five of his ribs and his left leg. The leg was not set properly. It had to be broken again and reset by more competent surgeons. Ever since that day, your father's health has declined, and he constantly suffers unbearable pain. He doesn't want you children to know the extent of his pain. He puts up a brave front for all of us."

"I'm sorry to hear that," Hump said. "That tells me a lot about father. But what's the matter with you? Why do you need morphine?"

"I don't suffer as much as Belmont does, but I have this skin disease. The words won't mean anything to you. It's called erysipelas, a streptococcal inflammation. That means fiery hot, red skin that burns me so badly at times it's like putting my skin on a hot stove. Sometimes when I'm in here retreating from the world, it's because I can't show my face. Either my left or right eye will close completely. A whole side of my face will burst into flames. The condition will even spread to my breasts. Morphine is the only thing to cure it. Belmont thinks that the condition is so severe, the pain so unbearable, that I will be driven crazy if I don't take drugs."

"But won't morphine turn you and father into drug addicts?"

Enraged, Maud grabbed the back of Hump's stiff shirt and ushered him toward the door. As he stepped into the hallway, she said, "Don't you ever come into my studio again." She slammed the door in his face.

Humiliated, Hump rushed down the hall, colliding into one of the Irish maids, Jane Byrne, "Watch where in the hell you're going, you little shit," she cried out at him. She used the word "shit" all the time.

All the servants called him "the little shit," never Humphrey. It was "the little shit" this, or "the little shit" that. For the rest of his life, Hump would refuse to allow the word "shit" to be uttered in his presence.

He didn't understand why Maud always recruited from the lowest class of Irish servants, each of whom received $3.50 a week in pay. They had vile tempers, horrible manners, and terrible language. Without provocation, a servant would suddenly strike either him or one of his sisters. Complaints about the behavior of the staff to his parents went unheeded. They didn't seem to care.

When Hump had told Maud that the male servant, Liam Mangam, had taken off his leather belt and had beaten him severely, she'd said, "I'm sure he wouldn't have done that if you'd been behaving properly."

After Maud had ushered him from her stu-

(above) Maud with Humphrey
(below) Her illustration, later entitled "The Maud Humphrey Baby"

8

dio, Hump wanted to run away or at least escape from their summer house for the rest of the day.

He stood in the living room, not certain where to go. Over the fireplace mantle Maud had hung a baby picture he hated. It was an idealized portrait she'd painted of him in 1900 when he was only one year old.

Known as the "Maud Humphrey Baby," the portrait had been reproduced across the country, becoming the most famous baby picture in the nation. It later appeared on the label of the best-selling brand of baby food of its day, Mellins Baby Food.

Later in life, the man then known as "Bogie" would say, "There was a period in American history when you couldn't pick up a God damn magazine without seeing my cute little kisser in it."

Maud was a true Victorian illustrator, who believed that babies should be cherubic, their faces round, their cheeks evoking chipmunks. If they also had ruby-red lips, a long white starched dress, curly blond ringlets, large trusting eyes, and a frilly collar, so much the better.

On a wall overlooking the dining room table hung another Maud portrait of him when he was two years old. He was as chubby cheeked as ever but his slickly combed hair was revealed, no more baby bonnet. He looked like Little Lord Fauntleroy in side-buttoned overalls with rolled-up cuffs and a billowing white shirt, again stiffly starched.

Hump was determined that, if not today, maybe tomorrow, he was going to grow up to be a man and not some powder puff.

***

Later, on the same day he'd been banished from Maud's summer studio, Hump wandered alone around the tranquil lake. Except for the turmoil going on in his own home, the setting looked like the fantasy life his Dutch ancestors had sought when they'd come over to help settle New York.

Hump always felt that it could be a dreamy life for all of the Bogarts if only his parents were different. They were cold and distant and never gave him the love he needed, not even a kiss on the cheek or a warm embrace.

Even though they were his parents, Hump didn't know all that much about them, since they rarely mentioned their own childhoods. Both parents traced their lineage to Europe as far back as the early 16th century. Members of royalty were included among both Dr. Bogart's ancestors and those of Maud.

Decades later, one royal link would be leaked to the press. It was reported at the wedding of Lady Diana Spencer to Britain's Prince Charles, that his new princess was the seventh cousin of Humphrey Bogart on his mother's side.

Dr. Bogart's father, Adam Watkins Bogart, had run an inn for summer visitors to the Finger Lakes. Arriving from Holland in the 17th century, his family had farmed in Brooklyn, which until the 20th century had a "Bogart Avenue" in their memory. In 1853 the family moved to the Finger Lakes.

At Canandaigua, Adam had run a tough tavern, with a jailhouse in the basement. It was called Franklin House, and it was the only inn in Canandaigua, attracting men who smoked cheap stogies and wore muddy boots reeking of manure.

The woman he'd married, Julia, was considerably better off financially than Adam. After marriage, he moved with her to Jefferson House in the village of Watkins on Lake Seneca. There they ran a small three-story hotel with more than a dozen rooms to rent. It was here they gave birth to their first born, pretentiously naming him Cornelius Edward Bogart. Cornelius was killed at the age of six when he attempted to slide down the banister of stairs that led into the lobby of Jefferson House. He fell on his head on the black and white checkerboard Tuscan tile and died instantly.

Their second son, Belmont DeForest Bogart, was born in 1866, a year after the death of his brother. Julia was to live only two years after the birth of her second son. She developed a "mysterious" illness and lay in bed for five months, suffering. In her will, she left all her money to Belmont, and none to her husband, Adam.

In 1871, Adam sued her estate, eventually winning control of the money and his son. Julia had asked that Belmont be taken away from his father and placed in the care of either of her sisters.

After her death, Adam never remarried. Using Julia's money, he grew rich when he created a method of lithographing on tin plates, a technique later used extensively in advertisements.

Maud had been born about a year before her husband on March 30, 1865, the daughter of a rich shoe manufacturer, John Perkins Humphrey, in Rochester, New York.

Her family was wealthy enough to finance her artistic career, sending her to the Art Students' League in New York from 1886 to 1894 and later to the Académie Julian in Paris where she'd studied with James McNeill Whistler. There were rumors that she'd had an affair with the fabled American painter, who was in his 50s when he first met Maud. Throughout her life, Maud never confirmed nor denied the rumor, saying, "It's for damn sure I didn't pose for *Whistler's Mother*."

It was in Paris that she'd painted her first nude. The model was the well-built former prizefighter, Rodolphe Julian, who frequently modeled in the nude at the *Académie* he'd founded. Some of the art students jokingly said that Rodolphe had founded the art school only so he could "show off his ample assets" before the art classes, as he'd often confess that he himself "knew nothing about art. I know what I like—and that's that."

Even though aging when Maud had met him, Rodolphe still kept his body as neat and trim as that of an Olympic athlete. In those days, only male artists were allowed to paint male nudes. Most art schools didn't even encourage female painters and, if they allowed them entrance, did not let them paint nude models either male or female.

At his *Académie,* Rodolphe changed all that. It was said that many young women signed up for his classes just to see what a man looked like in the nude. Many women at the time saw a naked man for the first time on their wedding night, with virtually no prior knowledge of the male anatomy.

"After looking at Rodolphe, and painting him, it's probably inevitable that we'll be disappointed with our husbands," Maud confided to a fellow art student, Mary Fielding, from Charleston, South Carolina.

Maud was known for her razor-tongued wit, and she found a perfect match in the equally sharp-tongued Belmont. Each could take the other down with biting sarcasm. Both of them passed this dubious characteristic onto their son, Humphrey.

Bogie's future director, John Huston, said the actor was known throughout his life for needling people, or "sticking in the saber," as Huston put it.

What his parents didn't pass on to their son was their political conservatism. Belmont was a Republican and a Presbyterian, Maud a Tory and an Episcopalian. Humphrey would grow up to become a liberal Democrat.

Born on Christmas Day, 1899, "a Christmas gift to his parents," as later reported by publicists at Warner Brothers, Humphrey DeForest Bogart came into the world at Sloane's Hospital in New York, weighing eight pounds and seven ounces. He'd been born six days before the end of the 19th century, and in later life always referred to himself as a "man of the last century."

He'd had an elongated foreskin, and his doctor father had recommended circumcision. Maud had been adamantly opposed, claiming that "was a barbaric Jewish custom."

Until he'd gone into the Navy at the end of World War I, Humphrey had lived with this extended foreskin. After his military service, when he ran into his former classmate, Doug Storer, at a tavern, he confided, "I had a doctor trim it a bit, but he left enough for me to still have fun."

Belmont himself in 1901 delivered his second child, a girl named Frances Bogart. Because she was chubby as an infant, Hump nicknamed her "Fat." When she grew up and lost her excess weight, she was called Pat. Two years later, another sister, Catherine, was born.

In his early years Maud and Belmont had big plans and high hopes for Hump. Belmont, dining at Luchow's, his favorite German restaurant on 14th

Street in New York, boasted that his adolescent son would one day go to Yale and become a world-famous surgeon. "My wife says Columbia, but I definitely see the boy as a Yale man."

Hump's one and only attempt at performing surgery had ended in disaster when he'd attempted it when he was eight years old. His sister Catherine had developed a large boil with a pus-filled head. She begged her brother to puncture it, since Belmont was away on a hunting trip. Retrieving his father's first-aid kit, with its scalpel, needles, and cotton, he attempted to lance the boil with a needle. When it didn't work, he used his pocket knife. Immediately, a mixture of pus and blood shot with high velocity into his face. His screaming sister had to be rushed to the nearest hospital before she bled to death.

One afternoon, about a month later, Hump found Maud terribly depressed, revealing that she'd learned some "very bad news." She told him that she'd visited an itinerant fortune teller who was passing through the Finger Lakes that summer. "Your son will grow up to enjoy fabulous wealth and will know many loves," the gypsy had told her. "But both of your daughters are destined for tragic lives."

***

Hump was heartbroken to learn that Maud and Belmont had placed Willow Brook up for sale in August of 1913. If a buyer could be found, their summer home and their days at the lake would be over. Maud promised the children a summer cottage on Fire Island for the coming year.

She'd taken a position as an illustrator on the magazine, *Delineator*, and

The Delineator
November, 1900

needed to be close to New York City, the magazine's base of operations. "The pay is fabulous," she told Hump. "Fifty-thousand dollars a year."

Walking down by the lake, Hump recalled his happiest times here when Belmont took him sailing on his champion yacht, *Comrade*. It was on that very lake that Belmont had taught Hump how to sail, a passion his son would enjoy until the day of his death.

In time, Belmont purchased a one-cylinder motor boat, which Hump had called *Desire*, and he went out, putt-putting around the lake all by himself. In later life, Bogie would tell friends that sailing on the lake by himself was "the only time in my life I've ever felt free."

His sister, Pat, later told friends that her brother went through a typical adolescent period when he developed crushes on males. "It was just a period," Pat said, "and in no time at all he grew out of it. He certainly didn't grow up to be a homosexual, as many of his leading ladies can testify."

That summer Hump made Belmont the focus of his attention. Belmont was tall and good looking, a strong man and avid hunter, a real outdoors type, everything that Hump wanted to be, but wasn't. When his father would invite him sailing, Hump was thrilled to have Belmont to himself and not have to share him with family or patients.

But after Belmont met his neighbor, Mrs. Harry Lansing, he no longer invited Hump sailing. Although a bit hefty, Mrs. Lansing was extremely beautiful to Belmont. He pursued the married woman when Maud wasn't present. Her husband, Harry, the son of a railroad tycoon, was never at home. Rumors were that he was an alcoholic. When not drinking, he was said to chase after other women.

Sometimes Belmont would announce to his family that he was taking Hump sailing with him. But when they got to the lake, Mrs. Lansing would be waiting for the doctor. Belmont always gave Hump money to spend in town while he sailed away with Mrs. Lansing.

Out there alone on the lake, Belmont was surely making love to Mrs. Lansing, or so Hump suspected. They'd be gone for hours. Instead of going to town, Hump would often wait for him beside the pier, no matter how long it took.

Perhaps Maud learned that summer of her husband's affair, or maybe she didn't. All Hump knew was that during those final days on the lake, before they returned to the city, Maud moved out of the master bedroom she shared with her husband and took a smaller bedroom on the top floor.

"I'm still going to be married to your father," she told Hump, "but one phase of our relationship is definitely over. You'll have no more brothers or sisters."

That bitter rejection by his father was eased when Hump was introduced to Mrs. Lansing's daughter, Grace. Hump felt that she was the most beautiful girl he'd ever seen, even more stunning than Franklin Roosevelt's young mistress.

They'd met when Mary Hamlin had organized the resort's young people into the Seneca Point Players. Over his protests, she'd named Hump the producer and director and had cast

William A. Brady Sr.

him as the lead in the players' first production, *Sunset in the Old West*. Mary had cast the Lansing daughter, Grace, as Hump's romantic female lead.

Before leaving for Seneca Point that summer, Hump had met a patient of his father's, William Brady Sr., a handsome showman and promoter and the son of Irish immigrants. Living next door, Brady had called on Belmont, claiming that "my cook has given me ptomaine poisoning."

Hump had also been in his father's office that day, and had found Brady a fascinating man. He regaled Hump with stories of his former life when he'd gone from shoeshine boy to newsboy, from stage manager to actor, and from comedian to play director. "Now I'm a producer," Brady said. "I also manage boxers, none of whom know how to throw a punch. That is, except for two winners, both heavyweight title holders, Jim Corbett and Jim Jeffries. I have luck with boxers named Jim."

Before Brady had been called into Belmont's office, the producer turned to Hump. "I have a son about your age, William Brady Jr. I'll introduce you to him. I'm sure you'll hit it off real swell."

Hump had to go to Seneca Point for the summer, but he eagerly looked forward to seeing young Brady when he came back to New York. Hump was in dire need of a male best friend.

When Brady Sr. learned that a local theater troupe was being formed at Seneca Point, he sent some discarded Broadway costumes to the Bogart family. Brady had just closed down a show on Broadway, *The Girl of the Golden West*, and he had plenty of outfits to spare, including chaps, boots, and western garb.

Hump tried on a ten-gallon hat that practically drowned his head, but he wore it in his first play anyway. He played the star, a role that depicted him as a "good man gone wrong." He'd become a gun-slinging bandit—that is, until he met the heroine of the play who "sets him on the straight and narrow path once again."

Grace, the female lead, won his heart in the play and also won his heart in real life. The audience around the bandstand peacefully watched this farce. They'd paid five cents each for tickets, plus another one penny for a glass of cold lemonade.

Throughout the rehearsals, thoughts of Grace had consumed Hump. The day after the play closed, he bribed one of the Irish maids to pack a picnic lunch for him. He'd invited Grace to go hiking in the nearby woods, and she'd accepted.

After their picnic on a blanket, he leaned over and kissed her. Decades later, Grace said she kissed him back, even though she'd never let a boy kiss her before. "He was handsome and charming, and I genuinely liked him. But he got carried away when I kissed him. He wanted to go farther."

As a summer rain fell across the meadow, Hump jumped up and begged her to strip off her clothing with him. Even though she remained fully dressed, he pulled off his trousers, shirts, and underwear and danced around her in the nude, urging her to take off her clothes too. "I'd never seen a boy's penis before," Grace said, much less one erect, and I was terrified. I started running across the slippery meadow heading for home, leaving him standing nude with his erection on the wet blanket."

He later told his friend, Peter St. Davids, "I'm not much of a lover, I guess. I got the gal at the end of that stupid play, but not in real life."

Later when Grace Lansing had become Mrs. Gerald Lambert of Princeton, New Jersey and Palm Beach, Florida, she became friends with Bogie's first wife, Helen Menken, telling her of that summer on the lake with Humphrey. "I always regretted we didn't fool around that day," Grace said, "especially when he became a world famous screen actor. I could have claimed to be Humphrey Bogart's first love. But, alas, it was not to be."

***

With no buyer was found for Willow Brook, the Bogarts returned to New York City, where Belmont resumed his practice, and Maud took up her job as an illustrator for the magazine, *Delineator*, a position she would hold for twenty years. The sole purpose of the magazine was to sell dress-sewing patterns manufactured by its parent company, the Butterick Pattern Company, in an era when many women sewed their own clothing at home.

The magazine was one of the first to publish pictures of females in nightgowns, bathing suits, and underwear. Mainly, it featured women appearing in fashionable clothing. Its backers hoped that America's women readers would fall in love with the illustration, then go out and purchase the Butterick dress pattern.

In spite of its focus on sewing patterns, the magazine also had pages devoted to serious fiction. Its editor was the novelist Theodore Dreiser, who printed pieces by such famous journalists as H.L. Mencken. Maud was especially proud of the magazine because it published articles about her favorite cause, women's suffrage.

One afternoon, Hump's mother invited her boss, Theodore Dreiser, and the famously caustic visiting writer from Baltimore, H.L. Mencken, back to her townhouse for afternoon tea. Both men were ostensibly there to meet the "Maud Humphrey baby," even though Hump was a growing adolescent at that time.

The Bogart sisters were not at home. Hump dressed himself formally, as requested by Maud. He eagerly awaited his introduction to both men, even though he wasn't quite sure who they were. Maud had talked at length about their status as "literary lions."

Dreiser was the first to enter the house, firmly shaking Hump's hand. "My, oh my," he said, "how that baby did grow. They're still publishing Maud's portrait of you as an adorable baby, though. You're easily as famous as the Arrow Collar Man or the Schweppes Commander."

Dreiser had not yet written his masterpiece, *An American Tragedy* which wasn't penned until 1925, but *Sister Carrie*, written in 1900 when Hump was one year old, had already been broadly distributed throughout the country. Dreiser had brought an autographed copy as a gift for the boy. "Maud claims you read one novel a week. Try mine. I must warn you, though. Even my publisher tried to suppress this book."

With perfect manners, Hump accepted it with genuine gratitude. It would be the first of many autographed books that writers would present to him as tokens of their esteem. They'd eventually include men as diverse as Ernest Hemingway and Truman Capote.

At that point, H.L. Mencken arrived, with Maud on his arm, both of them having overheard the friendly exchange between Hump and Dreiser. Bombastically turning to Dreiser, Mencken said, "Your publisher didn't want to suppress *Sister Carrie* because it was racy; he wanted to suppress it because its style is so weak. There are lines in that novel that simply don't work, like 'he worked in a truly swell saloon.' Calling a saloon 'truly swell' sounds inarticulate and unsavvy, and sometimes I wonder how you got away with it. I could go on and on, citing other examples."

Averting his gaze from Dreiser's angry eyes, Mencken extended his hand to Hump. "Hello, I'm H. L. Mencken." Hump stammered his hellos.

Ignoring Mencken, Dreiser returned to his dialogue with Hump. "Please overlook the occasional unevenness in my style. I'm interested in bigger game, especially the expression of broader ideas. I write as a means of prov-

(left to right) Theodore Dreiser, H.L. Mencken, and a pre-teen Humphrey Bogart

ing that history does not dominate a man, but that it's actually an expression of mankind at its most creative. It is man who creates history, not history that creates men."

Taking off his coat, Mencken acerbically shot back. "Is that what we do?" he asked Dreiser. He turned back to Hump. "Be careful—reading *Sister Carrie* will stunt your growth."

Smiling grimly at the insults, but holding his tongue, Dreiser got up, supposedly to pee. Maud showed him down the corridor to the toilet. Mencken sat down next to Hump on the sofa. "It was my reading of *Huckleberry Finn* at the age of nine that changed my life. It was, in fact, the most stupendous awakening of my entire life. It turned me into a bookworm and eventually a writer. Do you want to be a writer?"

"Father wants me to study medicine and follow in his footsteps."

"Become anything but a shyster lawyer," Mencken said. "I detest lawyers, especially Jewish lawyers. They are the worst."

Hump silently noted that Mencken shared Maud's anti-Semitism.

"After you've read the important books, go out and learn from life itself, taking all the worldly wisdom you can glean from the saloon keeper, the cop on the block, even the midwife, or especially the midwife if she performs a few abortions on the side. I figured being a newspaper reporter was the best way to meet people from all walks of life. After my first story, a five-line report about a horse thief, was published in the Baltimore *Morning Herald*, I was committed to journalism from that day forward."

At that point, Maud came back into the living room with Dreiser, who looked over at Mencken. "Why don't you move to New York and leave that hick town of Baltimore behind you?"

"New York is but a third-rate Babylon," Mencken said. "I prefer the frowzier charms of Baltimore. Even that immense protein factory known as Chesapeake Bay."

Dreiser had to excuse himself again to go up to Maud's studio to look over some of her latest sketches.

Humphrey chose that moment to invite Mencken up on the roof to look at his pigeon coop. "Maud finds these birds disgusting and unsanitary. When I came down with pneumonia, she blamed the pigeons."

Mencken didn't much like pigeons either. But he was entranced with the view of the New York skyline from the Bogart roof. The bracing air delighted him, and seemed to spark some crazed ambition within him. Hump suspected that he'd had a few whiskies before arriving at the Bogart house.

Mencken waved his arms in the air and seemed to be speaking to the world at large, and not specifically to Hump. "I want to be the native American Voltaire," Mencken said. "I see myself as the enemy of all Puritans.

I will become a heretic within academia—a one-man demolition crew of Victorian morality."

Later, Maud called them for tea in her little garden in back, although Hump suspected that both of these men would have preferred whiskey.

Over tea, Mencken continued to lecture Dreiser, albeit more diplomatically. "There is only one way to make money publishing books. You can write about only four subjects. First, murder stories. Second, novels in which the beautiful heroine is forcibly overcome by the handsome hero. Third, books about spiritualism, occultism and such claptrap. Fourth, any book devoted to Abraham Lincoln."

"Speaking of Lincoln," Dreiser said, "Someone recently submitted an essay for publication in my magazine. It's written by Theodore Ward, a historian, and based on extensive research. It's an exposé of the sex life of Abraham Lincoln, but I fear I cannot publish it, although it's a hell of an interesting article."

"Is it too controversial?" Maud asked.

"That it is," Dreiser said. "It maintains that Lincoln was a homosexual and had a five-year love affair with another man."

"I don't think that article will ever be published," Maud said.

"Maybe in fifty years the public will be ready for it," Mencken said.

As Maud was pouring tea for Dreiser, a large butterfly flew from a flower bush, winging by her head. Dropping her tea pot, she screamed as if ten rapists had surrounded her. She ran into the living room and up the steps leading to her studio.

Both Dreiser and Mencken looked to Hump for some explanation of this erratic behavior.

"All her life she's been terrified of butterflies," Hump said.

***

It wasn't only Dreiser and Mencken who wanted to meet the Maud Humphrey Baby. The stigma of having posed for that illustration followed Hump throughout of his school days. He'd been mocked and ridiculed when he'd entered Delancy School, which he'd attended to the fifth grade. He still hadn't shaken the curse when, at the age of thirteen, he enrolled in Trinity School, which was housed in a sandstone building at 91st Street between Columbus and Amsterdam Avenues. An Episcopal institutional "for the training of young gentlemen," it was the oldest continuously operating school in the country.

Doug Storer, a classmate, recalled that virtually every day after school, a gang of bullies waited for Hump, calling him "sissy" or chanting, "rock-a-bye baby."

The confrontation sometimes led to Hump arriving home with a bloody lip and, on more than one occasion, a black eye.

At school, Hump had turned out to be a poor student, excelling in nothing, and with particularly low marks in German. Since Belmont, a classically educated descendant of the original Dutch burghers of New York, spoke fluent German, he had demanded that his son learn the language too.

Hump's grades in other classes were almost as bad. As the months went by, it became apparent to Belmont and Maud that their son would not follow in his father's footsteps as a surgeon.

"He'll be lucky if he graduates from high school," Belmont told Maud. To compound matters, Hump developed scarlet fever and had to repeat the eleventh grade.

Although Belmont had been a notable athlete, Hump did not willingly participate in organized sports unless he was forced to as part of the school curriculum. He told classmate Storer that he especially disliked wrestling. "I loathe such close contact with other guys. There's one fucking guy who gets a hard-on every time he pins me down on the mat. I can feel the God damn thing pressing up against me."

Storer remembers that there was a debate among some of the girls over whether Hump was "handsome" or "just good looking." His classmate recalls that, "His appearance was always neat. I never saw him when he wasn't well-groomed. He had a slim figure with very dark eyes and jet-black hair that was always plastered down to his head with some kind of cream. He showed up every day in a dark blue wool serge suit with a vest and a stiffly starched white shirt with detachable collars held on by gold-plated brass buttons. His black shoes were always highly polished. His ties were never garish but always in some somber color like navy blue or berry brown, the stuff bankers wore at the time."

In winter he'd appear in a Chesterfield overcoat with a velvet collar.

The author, Eric Hodgins, remembers that "Bogart always wore a black derby hat, rain or shine. It set him apart from the other boys. Many a time he would get that hat knocked off his head. But he always picked it up, dusted it off, put it back on his head, and went on his way."

Hump told Storer that he didn't want to get out of bed sometimes, knowing that at three o'clock that afternoon a gang was waiting to taunt him. He was not a fighter and had never taken on one of the neighborhood toughs in combat. If Hump defended himself at all, it was to raise his hands to protect his face.

One cold January afternoon, the toughest guy on the block plowed his steel-knuckled fist into Hump's face, breaking his nose. He'd run all the way to his father's office at 245 West 103rd Street. The office on the second floor of the family brownstone was covered in a thick moss green carpet with beautiful mahogany paneling rescued from a townhouse in Chelsea which had been demolished. It was one of the few houses in the neighborhood that had a telephone, a necessity because Hump's father was a doctor. Belmont had tended to his son's nose, making emergency repairs before taking him to the hospital. All the way to the clinic, Belmont had chided Hump for not defending himself better. "When I was your age, I could beat up any boy in my hometown. Maud's making a sissy of you. I hate the name Humphrey she gave you. That's a sissy name."

Even as Hump had moved into his teenage years, Maud had continued to dictate his dress. At formal school dances, she'd demanded that he wear white kid gloves and black patent leather pumps. "I was like a God damn teenage dandy," Bogie later told his favorite director, John Huston.

***

One afternoon Maud called her teenage son into her studio and revealed to him some of the male nudes that she'd painted in Paris. He was shocked because until then, he had known only her scenes of Victorian innocence.

For reasons not known to him at the time, she'd tried to explain to him when male nudity was acceptable and when it was not.

"When a man is nude and aroused, and is showing himself off, that is not acceptable," she informed her son. "But when a man in a flaccid state is posing nude for an art class, that is acceptable. The men and women painting him have no actual interest in his sex. They view the body as a whole, as an object from which they can make an artistic statement. It's the same when your father sees a nude man or woman in his office. He has them strip to examine them in detail. But as a doctor, he has the same disinterest in the nude body that an artist does while painting a nude in his studio. This is called sexless nudity."

After that rather detailed and pedantic explanation, Maud invited Hump to accompany her that afternoon to her art classes.

At the Artists and Models Studio on Manhattan's West 28th Street, Maud had been temporarily teaching classes to young illustrators who wanted to become working commercial artists like herself. Since she was widely known as a Victorian illustrator portraying an idealized fantasy life of home and hearth, she'd been an odd choice to teach classes with nude models, although her background in Paris had prepared her for such an assignment.

When she arrived with Hump at the studio, she still hadn't told him why he was here. It turned out that Maud had been filling in during a sick leave of Duane Edwards, the regular teacher. To an increasing degree, Maud had been leaving the house on mysterious errands. Hump had heard her talking over the phone several times with someone named "Duane," and he'd suspected that Maud was having an affair now that she was no longer sleeping in the same bed with his father.

In a back dressing room, Maud told her son, "Remember what I said about nude modeling. There is nothing about the nude male body that we have to be ashamed of. Our regular model is not here today. He's just a young boy who models for classes. The class has painted mature models, both female and male, in the nude. This week we are painting young boys. I want you to model nude and fill in for our regular model who is sick."

Horrified at his mother's suggestion, Hump wanted to bolt from the building. Except for a medical examination, he'd never pulled off his clothes before anyone, and certainly not in front of women. Since he had no real basis for comparisons, and hadn't seen any pictures, he had not been certain just how he measured up with other boys his age.

He'd always been curious about other male genitalia, but when he'd been at a latrine with other boys, he'd always looked away, afraid to be caught gazing at them. He'd feared that because of his reputation as a sissy, all he would need was to be spotted glancing at the genitals of other boys. He'd never showered with other boys and had never seen his father in the nude either.

When he revolted at the idea of the posing session, Maud taunted him. "Don't tell me you're afraid to take off your clothes in front of artists. Are you ashamed of the way you're developed? You don't have to be."

As he looked at her, he began to think that he hated her. Defiantly, he began to peel off his clothes. Before he'd taken his trousers down, she turned and walked away.

A school custodian came into his dressing room, finding Hump standing there looking pathetically naked. He handed him a white robe, telling him to wear it out into the studio. "When you go up on the platform in front of the class, drop your robe and sit naturally on the stool I put there."

Years later, Bogie recalled how he'd come into the studio so embarrassed that he didn't dare look at anybody. He was red-faced but he did as he was told and dropped his robe, going at once to a large stool in the center of the platform. There he had braced himself for a long sketching session, crossing his legs.

The custodian came out and pried his legs apart, exposing Hump's genitalia to the painters. His heart was beating so fiercely at that point

Humphrey Bogart
as an angst-ridden teenager

that Hump didn't much care what happened next. His only thought was that Maud was there, along with the others, looking at her son in all his shame.

As the artists painted, Hump tried to think of anything except what was actually happening in the studio.

The session ended exactly at noon. Hump put on his robe and retreated to the rear where the custodian brought roast beef sandwiches for the artists. He'd offered one to Hump. Because he was hungry, he accepted, only wishing that it had been a ham sandwich.

Maud remained in the studio evaluating the nude drawings of her son. At one o'clock, Hump was summoned back to the platform. The second time wasn't as traumatic for him. He still refused to make eye contact with any of the painters in the room, not even knowing whether they were men or women.

He was called back for a final session at three o'clock, and at exactly four o'clock, the day's work ended.

Fully dressed, he waited outside on the street for Maud. When she appeared, he was embarrassed to look into her face. "Now that wasn't so bad," she said. "You're to come back with me four more days this week. The good news is that you're going to get fifty dollars for your work. Imagine that. Fifty dollars, the most money you've ever seen at one time in your life."

She told him that he'd have to go home alone, as she had to visit a sick friend. She was obviously going to meet her new friend, Duane.

Hump stood watching Maud go up the street to her next rendezvous. A militant suffragette, she passed out pamphlets as she made her way along the crowded boulevard, calling on passers-by to give the vote to the women of America.

***

His parents' names had appeared regularly in *Dau's New York Blue Book* since 1907, but Belmont constantly attacked his wife for "trying to climb the social ladder." The son of a saloon keeper, he couldn't care less about the opinions of New York society.

Every night at their New York home, their arguments were virtually the same. "When you're not social climbing, you're driven by your career like some God damn maniac," he'd shout at her when drunk.

Matching him drink for drink, Maud always stood up to him. She constantly reminded him that her profession brought in more than twice as much money as his did.

She claimed that she was known among the very upper crust of New York society, and enjoyed a national reputation as an illustrator, whereas he "consorted with river rats."

22

Instead of accepting invitations into some of the finest homes of New York, Belmont preferred the company of saloon keepers, mechanics, janitors, and truck drivers. He'd frequent the taverns of blue-collar laborers, preferring those saloons along New York's waterfront where he'd find "men of the sea." If he'd had enough to drink, he'd invite sailors back to his home to spend a night or even a weekend.

That had led to some of Maud's most brutal fights with her husband. "These bums aren't coming into my living room," she'd shout at her husband in front of the Bogart children. She'd demand that the doctor take his newly acquired sailor friend up to the fourth-floor bedroom, which was usually assigned to a servant. "You can sleep up there with him," she'd said. "Don't come to my bed tonight."

That had seemed like a strange remark to Hump, because Belmont, at least to his knowledge, hadn't entered Maud's bed in years.

She had also insisted that this "waterfront trash" eat in the kitchen with the Irish servants. To defy her, Belmont would also take his meals in the kitchen with the object of that evening's fascination.

Usually, a "river rat" would visit the Bogart home only once. Belmont's interest in these uneducated specimens he would pick up rarely lasted more than two or three days.

The exception had been a handsome, ruggedly masculine, and well-built "man of the sea," Lars Schmidt. Depending on what day of the week you asked him, Lars claimed to be Norwegian, Swedish, or Danish, and during one particularly frank dialogue, German.

Because he spoke six languages, had incredible good looks, and always dressed nicely, Maud had at first been attracted to his charm and personality. Even Hump had been fascinated with Lars. He'd entertain the boy with tales of all the shipwrecks he'd survived. The most fascinating adventure, as he'd related, was when his merchant ship had almost collided with another in the middle of the Atlantic. This ghost ship had seemingly come out of nowhere, appearing mysteriously in the fog.

"It was definitely a Swedish man-of-war from the 17th century," Lars had claimed. "Our crew could actually see seventeen sailors standing on deck as the ship passed us by. They were as lifelike as you are sitting across from me. We were awe struck as we watched the vessel drift away into the dawn. I've never seen anything like that before or since."

Whenever Lars came to the port of New York, he always arrived unannounced at the Bogart home. His parents' explosion over Lars had come one hot, blistering August day as the entire city was melting under a record-breaking heat wave.

It was so hot that when Lars had to walk outside his bedroom to go to the bathroom on the second floor, he'd wandered down the stairs stark naked. One of the Bogart daughters, Frances, had seen him nude in the hall and had run to her mother in her studio to report on this.

Maud had been furious and had climbed to the top floor to see what was going on. The door to the bedroom where her husband had slept the night before with Lars was wide open. She'd looked inside and found Lars in the middle of the bed playing with himself. He'd invited her in to join him.

She'd screamed and had run downstairs.

That night when Belmont came home after a day's work at the local hospital, she confronted him. "Lars is not a man," she shouted in front of the children and the servants. "He's a freak of nature. That is no penis that belongs on a man. A horse maybe. Frances will be ruined for life having seen such a thing. For all that poor girl knows, all men are built like that. Because of this, she'll never marry, and if she does, she'll be afraid to go to bed with her husband."

That night had led to a Bogart family drinking marathon and more violent arguments. Maud threatened that, "If Lars darkens this door again, I'm packing up, moving out, and taking the children with me."

Despite the enormous pressure, that drunken night didn't end Belmont's friendship with Lars. Whenever the sailor came to New York, the doctor packed a suitcase and checked into the Hotel Marseilles with Lars. A then-fashionable address, it lay across the street from the Bogart home, which was at 245 West 103rd Street.

Like any hotel, it operated like a world unto itself. The beer kings, the Rheingold brothers, called it home, as did Sara Delano Roosevelt, mother of Franklin.

When Mrs. Roosevelt learned of Belmont's rescue of her son during the nearly fatal drowning incident at the lake, she sent a servant across the street with an invitation for Dr. and Mrs. Bogart and their young son, Humphrey. She may not have known about the existence of the two Bogart sisters.

As Maud rarely accepted any social invitation and attended almost no parties, she tore up the invitation without telling her husband. Maud was offended by the politics of Theodore Roosevelt and didn't want to seek any more intimate contact with the Roosevelts after she'd reluctantly sheltered Franklin for one night at her summer home.

When Lars had some time off from sailing, he would go with Belmont on a train to Canada. Up there at an address never revealed to his family, the doctor and Lars would stay at a rustic hunting lodge owned by Belmont. Sometimes for weeks at a time, Belmont would neglect his medical practice, coming back to New York only when his supply of morphine had run out.

On one particularly long trip, Maud had talked to Hump. "There are men like your father who don't have natural instincts. He'd rather be socializing with riff-raff than in a good clean bed with his own wife. We stay together but only for the sake of you children. In time you'll understand what a loveless marriage is. Perhaps you'll even have one or two of your own."

***

At one school dance during his early teen years, Hump asked Leonore Strunsky—nicknamed Lee—to be his date. It was the beginning of a friendship that would last for the rest of his life, because Lee in time would become famously married to another Bogie friend, the lyricist Ira Gershwin.

At the dance, just before Lee excused herself to go to the ladies' room, she'd asked for a glass of punch. While he was getting it for her, two older students in their senior year had deliberately bumped into Hump. "Still dressing like a girl?" one of them had taunted him.

Instead of trying to defend himself, Hump had escaped and fled to his school locker. Once there, he'd removed the Daisy Air Rifle his father had given him six weeks before. Belmont was a superb wing shot, and he wanted to pass his skill on to his son.

Running outside of the school hall, he'd taken the rifle and aimed it at all the red lanterns lighting up the night. He hit every one of them before the school custodian had found him, chasing him from the grounds.

He'd later walked in Central Park arm in arm with Lee, rather proud of his accomplishment. He'd known he couldn't take the boys on in combat, but in some way had felt he'd gotten revenge.

On a bench in Central Park, they'd indulged in some heavy necking. Lee not only let him kiss her, but told him that, "It'll feel much better if you stick your tongue in my mouth."

He'd done just that. She didn't object when he reached inside her dress and felt the firmness of her breasts. But she did not let him do any exploring below her beltline. "That's only for when we're married," Lee told him.

When he'd gotten home, after kissing Lee good night, he felt like a real man.

The moment he walked into the Bogart's living room, he knew that something was wrong. His father was there waiting for him, and he'd been drinking heavily. Maybe the doctor had also been drugged.

The principal from the school had already contacted Belmont about the lantern shoot-out. Coming up to his son, his father seemed to tower above his teenage boy.

Without warning, Belmont delivered several chopping blows to his son's face, loosening two front teeth and smashing his upper lip repeatedly until part of it was torn from the boy's face.

25

As he'd stood back, realizing the damage he'd done, the doctor seemed to sober up. Maud rushed into the room. Seeing her son, she screamed before turning to confront her husband. "You touch him again, and so help me God I'll kill you."

When the male servant, Liam Mangam, came up from the rear, having been aroused from his bed with one of the Irish maids, Belmont ordered him to carry Hump upstairs to his office.

Once there, the doctor sewed up his son's lip, but he was too drunk to do an adequate job. He ordered Mangam to summon a cabbie to take them to the nearest hospital.

In the aftermath of the injury, Hump's upper lip never healed properly. As every close-up in nearly every movie house in the world later revealed, Bogie's upper lip throughout his adult life bore the scar of that awful night. His lip was to remain partly paralyzed, giving him a slight lisp.

After surgery on his lip for the second time in five hours, Hump had been told that he'd have to go to the family dentist in the morning to replace those two missing front teeth.

The attending doctor at the hospital, John Kells, also gave the teenage boy a thorough physical examination. He recorded that he was 5 feet, 9 inches, weighed 110 pounds, had brown eyes, a fair complexion and light brown hair, his chest measuring 33 inches.

Belmont reported to Kells that his son had had a severe case of the mumps two years ago and that they had "fallen." That most often led to a temporary enlargement of the testicles, followed by a massive shrinkage to a withered pea.

Dr. Kells examined Hump's testicles, finding that he'd escaped from this curse relatively intact, although noting a swelling of the spermatic vein on the left side of the boy's scrotum. Both doctors agreed that this was a "congenital condition" and would probably not affect Hump's ability to father children at some point in the future.

At midnight, Hump, accompanied by a chastised Belmont and Mangam, was released from the hospital to return to the dismal life at 103rd Street.

During his first week home, Hump made one trip to the dentist, accompanied by one of the Irish maids. The dentist replaced Hump's two front teeth. Hump insisted on having his teeth in place before "my best gal," Lee Strunsky, came to visit him at the family brownstone.

Having never had a girl friend before, Hump was excited when Lee called to tell him that she was coming over at three that afternoon.

Maud ushered Lee upstairs to Hump's bedroom, where he was convalescing. From the look on his mother's face, Hump knew that Maud disapproved of this visit.

26

It wasn't until an hour later, after Lee had gone, that Maud stormed into his bedroom. "Don't you ever invite that stinking little tramp into my house again," she yelled at her son.

"She's a very respectable girl, and very nice," Hump protested.

"She's a slimy Jew," Maud charged. "I don't want a son of mine going out with a Jewess. These money-changers are the anti-Christ. They have no appreciation of the finer things of life. They're all about greed and chicanery. They are the bottom-feeders of life."

"Jews are just as good as anybody else," Hump said. "No better, no worse."

"You're a moronic fool if you think that," Maud said, her temper flaring. "If you ever again invite a Jew into my house, boy or girl, I will personally shut the door in their face. Is that understood, young man?" She turned and left the room, leaving Hump in total bewilderment. Since he didn't plan to give Lee up, he'd sneak away and see her in private.

Maybe, when he finished school, he might even ask Lee to marry him. That would really piss off Maud.

As Hump saw it, there was one major problem in their courtship. Lee wanted to wait until they were married before doing it.

Hump decided the time for seduction was at hand. In the days ahead, he was going to figure out a way to charm the bloomers off that pretty girl.

The way he saw it, a Jewish pussy could be just as hot as a Gentile one. Maybe even more so. Time would attest to the accuracy of that perception.

***

In ways that anticipated the plots of some of the movies he'd eventually make in the 1930s for Warner Brothers, Hump did not get the girl in the final reel. He never knew exactly what happened to his budding relationship with Lee, but it ended almost as suddenly as it had begun.

All Hump found out later was that Maud had placed a telephone call to Lee. He never knew what his mother had said to his young girl friend, but Lee never saw him until decades later, and he did not press her for the answer.

He even went to her house, but a servant informed him that Lee was not at home, even though he suspected that she was upstairs hiding in her bedroom.

He would meet Lee later in life as a political ally and friend. He always referred to her as "my first girl friend," even in front of her husband, Ira Gershwin.

A new friend had come into Hump's life that made him forget all about Lee. William Brady Jr. was the son of the showman and promoter, William

27

Brady Sr., whom Hump had met when this entrepreneur was a patient at his father's office. Brady Sr. had promised an introduction to his son, who was Hump's age, and in spite of the producer's busy schedule, he remembered and set it up.

The moment he arrived at the Brady house and met Bill Jr., Hump almost overnight transferred his crush on Belmont to Bill. Bill was a handsome, precocious young man, filled with facile charm and a manly grace. He'd grown up in a world of famous names in both boxing and the theater, and he had a sophistication that Hump envied.

Many young girls were captivated by this dashing man, but once Bill met Hump Bill had no more time for the females in his life. The two young boys became fast friends. Soon after they met, they pledged loyalty to each other and a devoted friendship "for the rest of our lives."

Friends and mentors of Bogie: Victorian actress Grace George, (*top photo*) and (*bottom photo*) her Edwardian stepdaughter, actress Alice Brady

When Hump was finally invited into the Brady home for chocolate milk and cookies, he was dazzled by the opulence of the parlor. Although Maud decorated her house elegantly, it didn't have the ostentation of the Brady home, which some guests had described as "a Victorian stage set."

Not only was Bill's father famous, but so were his mother and step-sister. Hump was especially intrigued by Bill's mother, Grace George, a bigtime star of her day who had appeared in many of her husband's films or Broadway productions.

A darling of Broadway's theater critics, George had gone from triumph after theatrical triumph that included appearances in George Bernard Shaw's *Major Barbara,* as well as *Divorçons, The School for Scandal,* and *Kind Lady.* She was also a major talent scout for her husband, encouraging him to offer breaks to such newcomers as Helen Hayes in *What Every Woman Knows.* She also picked out the then-relatively-unknown Douglas Fairbanks, Sr., from a cast of hopefuls, persuading her husband to cast him opposite her in *Clothes,* even though "he's not good-looking."

The daughter from Brady's first marriage,

28

born in 1892, was Alice Brady, a rising star in her own right. Seven years older than Hump, beautiful, and educated during a period of her life in a convent in New Jersey, she captivated Hump with her talent and charm. She had abandoned a budding career as a singer in grand opera, preferring instead a career as a Broadway actress. She had been appearing on Broadway since her debut as an ingénue in *The Balkan Princess* in 1911. Having made a name for herself in several Gilbert and Sullivan revivals, she had been in dozens of her father's silent films shot for World, his film company. She'd first appeared on screen in 1914 in a flick called *As Ye Sow*. When Hump met her, she'd just filmed *The Gilded Cage*.

The first time Hump appeared in her living room, Grace George was polite but distant, and soon excused herself to go and read a script sent over by her husband. Alice remained behind to have a cup of tea, but it quickly became obvious that she was not smitten with Bill's young friend the way Hump seemed to be with her.

As she recalled years later, "He was just too young for me when we first met. But when Humphrey came back from the Navy, he'd matured a lot. I became very interested in him despite the difference in our ages."

Brady Sr. always gave his son all the free passes he wanted to Broadway shows, both his own productions and those of his rivals. Bill's father had dreams of becoming a theatrical producer as well known and successful as David Belasco.

Paying a nickel fare, Hump and Bill rode to 42nd Street on the rickety Broadway trolley, headed for a vaudeville show at the Palace Theater. Hump had never been to a performance at a major Broadway theater before, and he was immediately captivated by the bright lights and bustle. The show they were headed for was noteworthy in that it included, on the same bill, both Sarah Bernhardt, the greatest dramatic actress of her day, and the comic actor, juggler, and drunk, W.C. Fields.

Decades later, Mae West, co-starring with Fields in *My Little Chickadee*, and herself a Broadway star at the time of Hump's introduction to the theater, dismissed the claim that "The Divine Sarah" and Fields appeared on the same bill. "I'm sure Madame Bernhardt has other things to do than appear on stage with a low-rent, drunken comedian," West claimed. "If Fields thinks Bernhardt was there, he'd had too many drinks, as usual."

But despite Mae West's denials, Bogie maintained through the rest of his life that he'd seen Bernhardt on the same playbill with Fields.

When Bernhardt was rolled onto the stage in a wheelchair, Hump was shocked. He'd expected to see some tall and statuesque figure of glamour and intrigue. Instead he saw a pale and very frail hospital patient in her 70s, with frizzy red hair. In an accident in France, she'd slipped and had fallen, breaking her leg. Gangrene had set in, and her doctors had to amputate her leg. For her first U.S. performance, she had turned that tragedy into an advantage. Wearing a *poilu* (the uniform French soldiers wore at the time), she'd appeared in New York playing a French soldier who had lost a leg. She'd held a battered flag in her hand while standing unsupported on her still-remaining good leg. Hollow cheeked and colorless, she emphasized her deadly whiteness with a dense coat of chalk-colored *poudre-de-riz* on her face. Looking like a consumptive wraith, she evoked the mummy of an Egyptian Pharaoh.

But when Bernhardt spoke lines from Dumas *fils' La Dame aux Camélias*, her beautiful voice radiated magic. Even from her wheelchair, she moved her body with the lashing grace of a panther.

Spellbound, Hump sat with Bill throughout the performance in a state of rapture. At the end, Bernhardt received a standing ovation that lasted ten minutes. Of her *voix d'or*, the writer, Maurice Baring, rhapsodized, calling her sound, "A symphony of golden flutes and muted strings, a silver dawn lit by lambent lightnings, soft stars and a clear-cut crescent moon."

After that day, Hump became addicted to the theater the way an addict is to heroin. He couldn't get enough of Broadway shows.

Back home that night, Hump poured out his enthusiasm for the world of the Bradys and his love of the theater. Maud was not impressed. "Not only are they in show business, they are Jews." Hump didn't care.

***

As days drifted into weeks, Bill Brady was becoming more possessive of Hump, who no longer planned his own life but allowed his best friend to do it for him. At plays or at the cinema, Bill took to holding Hump's hand. Hump never objected to this and enjoyed the camaraderie. Even when Bill put his arm around him and walked along the streets of Manhattan or Brooklyn, Hump did not object. A lot of schoolboys in those days did that.

The word "homosexual" was just coming into vogue in avant-garde circles, but in the minds of most people, if such a thing existed at all, it was never spoken about. Many indulgent parents, especially those as sophisticated as Belmont and Maud, assumed that a young boy went through periods of infatuation with another boy his own age. Even if extreme affection was displayed, it was taken for granted that this was just a "stage" a young man went through before meeting the girl of his dreams and settling down.

In spite of the domestic horror surrounding the shooting incident at school, and the subsequent injury to his lip, Hump had not lost interest in his Daisy Air Rifle. Nor had it been taken away from him by his father. The future actor, who would one day become a famous icon in a trench coat carrying a

30

gun, spent hours in his room dismantling his gun and reassembling it.

He even carried it in the leg of his trousers and took it with him whenever he went with Bill to the theater. After a show let out, they would find nearly deserted streets where no cop could be seen, then shoot out the globes of gas lamps before scampering off into the darkness of an alleyway to hide if anyone tried to chase after them.

One late summer afternoon, Hump tired of his air rifle and wanted something more lethal. Before going over to Bill's house, Hump went into the basement of the Bogart home and removed a .22 caliber pistol from his father's collection which he kept there.

Bill had been given tickets to see a performance that evening by Alla Nazimova. This Russian-born stage actress and silent film star was famous for her interpretations of works by the Norwegian playwright Henrik Ibsen. Hump was anxious to see her in the flesh, having read much press on her at Brady Sr.'s theatrical offices. It could not have been imagined by Hump at the time that he would one day live at the Garden of Allah in Hollywood which, as "the Garden of Alla," had been Nazimova's home before it was turned into a hotel and colony of bungalows.

But it wasn't a work by Ibsen that Nazimova was performing that night. She was starring in *Bella Donna*, a frothy lust-and-revenge melodrama. Hump would have preferred a more classical introduction to her repertoire. After all, this was the electrifying actress who had brought Chekhov and Stanislavsky to the American theater.

Über-divas
Alla Nazimova

Hump found the diminutive star "shatteringly powerful" and marveled at her "foreign sophistication." This exotic actress would, in fact, pave the way for the likes of silent screen vamp Pola Negri and, in time, Greta Garbo and Marlene Dietrich. In just a few years Nazimova would

and Sarah Bernhardt

31

select Rudolph Valentino as her co-star in the film *Camille* before stealing his wife, the stunningly beautiful Natacha Rambova, as part of a well-publicized and notorious lesbian tryst.

After seeing *Bella Donna*, Bill and Hump headed for a Broadway diner for a plate of ham and eggs for Hump and a hamburger for Bill. His friend told Hump, "Don't go falling for Nazimova. She likes to have sex with women—not men."

This was the first knowledge Hump had of lesbianism, although he would in the 30s and 40s appear with more lesbian stars than any other leading male actor in Hollywood.

He'd heard that boys fooled around together, and had late at night wondered if his own father might have some sort of "unnatural attachment" to the sailor riff-raff he brought to their home. Like Queen Victoria, he'd never given lesbianism a thought.

Bill claimed that Nazimova had fallen in love with his mother, Grace George, and had ardently pursued her, sending her roses every day, even expensive gifts, until Nazimova had tired of Grace's lack of response. By then, Nazimova had moved on, having fallen in love with another actress, Eva Le Gallienne.

Later, Bill promised to invite Hump up to his bedroom where he claimed he would show him some "dirty French postcards" he'd stolen from his father's files. Hump eagerly accepted that invitation. He'd never seen a picture of a man and a woman having sex together.

After a snack, Bill asked Hump to go with him to Coney Island to ride the Ferris wheel. Later the boys planned to shoot out some more bright lights.

On the fast-spinning wheel, something went wrong. The pistol Hump had concealed in his trousers blasted off. The bullet missed his chest, which could have killed him, but blasted into his right wrist. At first Bill thought that Hump was screaming at the thrill of the ride until Hump held up his wrist in agony as the blood gushed out.

Nothing could be done until the end of the ride. Knowing they would have to seek help from the police, Bill took the gun from Hump and tossed it into the night.

At the end of the ride, the manager saw that young Hump had been injured and immediately called the police. Hump, with Bill in attendance, was rushed to the hospital where a doctor discovered that it was a bullet wound. Until then, the police believed that somehow he'd been cut, perhaps by one of the moving parts on the Ferris wheel.

Hump lied to the police and to the doctor, claiming that during the ride a sniper had shot at them, missing Bill but hitting him. The police bought that unlikely story.

When the police drove Hump back home to Manhattan that night, Maud and Belmont were in the foyer waiting for him. After thanking the cops for their assistance, an angry Belmont didn't strike his son in the face this time. What he did do was to forbid him to carry guns any more. He said that he'd gone to his son's room and removed the beloved Daisy Air Rifle.

"It's time to ship you off to the Phillips Academy at Andover to prepare you for Yale," Belmont said.

"And I absolutely forbid you to see that Brady boy again," Maud said. "You were a good boy until you took up with the likes of that Jew."

"I'll go to the academy," Hump said to his parents. "But there's no way in hell I'll give up my friendship with the Bradys." He stormed upstairs to his bedroom, slamming the door behind him.

***

With a bandaged wrist, Hump accepted Bill's invitation to visit his bedroom at the Brady house to view a collection of pornographic French postcards. They had been collected by his father on a visit to Paris and smuggled through U.S. Customs, as was the way in those days of heavy censorship.

Today, in an era when pre-adolescents routinely watch porno on television, it's difficult to imagine the effect back then of a "dirty picture" on young boys at the height of their sexual potency.

Hump was fascinated by the sepia-toned photographs, one showing a young man with a large erection standing up while two bare-breasted women kneeled to service him. Another depicted the same man bedding one of the women. Yet another pictured him plunging down on a woman in the act of cunnilingus.

Bill became so excited by the pictures that he whipped out his penis and began masturbating, urging Hump to do the same. Reluctantly Hump pulled out his penis and he too masturbated to climax.

After putting the postcards back into their folder, Bill asked Hump to kiss him since he hadn't touched him during their sex together.

Hump agreed, providing Bill would swear not to tell anybody. "It's okay," Bill told him. "I've done this to other guys. All the guys at school do it."

Hump kissed him back. As he was to recall years later to his friend, Truman Capote, "It wasn't at all bad. It felt kinda nice. I didn't think anybody in the world loved me at the time, and it was good to know that Bill did. At first I kissed him because I felt I owed him a favor. After we kissed, I liked it a lot. It was the beginning of many kisses we'd exchange over the years. Our relationship never developed much beyond that. Kissing and playing with each other was as far as I was willing to go. I knew Bill wanted to do some of

33

the things in those pictures, but I could never bring myself to it. I loved the guy, though."

***

The marriage between Phillips Academy at Andover, Massachusetts, some twenty miles north of Boston, and Humphrey Bogart was doomed from the beginning, when he arrived there a week late for classes during an unseasonably cool September in 1917. Founded by Calvinists during the American Revolution, it was the finest prep school in the country. One of its stated purposes was to guard young men "against the first dawnings of depraved nature."

The Academy could name-drop like no other school, having historical ties with John Hancock, Paul Revere, John Adams (its fourth principal), George Washington (who gave an address there), and, in time, Judge Oliver Wendell Holmes and, much later, President George Bush Sr.

Belmont had graduated with the class of 1888, having excelled in baseball and football. He'd written his former schoolmate, Alfred Stearns, now headmaster, asking him to admit his son in spite of his poor grades at Trinity.

On the train to Andover, Hump read *Stove at Yale*, Owen Johnson's popular novel which painted a romanticized version of what college life was really like. To Hump, the novel read like a saccharine-laced fantasy. He'd also bought a newspaper that morning, as he always read the front page news carefully. The United States had entered the war on the side of the Allies on April 6, 1917. Before leaving New York, Belmont had told him that many of the students at Andover, along with some faculty members, had temporarily resigned or left the Academy to join the forces on the Western Front in Europe, battling the Kaiser's armies.

Assigned a spartan-looking cell, Number Five, at Taylor Hall, Hump felt that his steel cot evoked a prison cell. Up to now, he'd lived in grand comfort.

Next to Hump's room was the bathroom, shared by twelve other young

men on the floor. A previous occupant of Hump's cell must have had an interest in boys taking a shower, because he'd carved a hole about the size of a baseball between Hump's room and the shower.

Hump discovered that hole in the wall on his second day there when he went to remove

The marriage between Phillips Academy (above) and teenaged Hump was doomed from the beginning

the reproduction of an antique map of Massachusetts. Looking through the hole, he could have a perfect view of the genitalia of the young men showering. Fortunately, no one was in the shower room when he peeked in, or else he would have been embarrassed.

Lonely and sad to be away from Bill and the bright lights of Broadway, the seventeen-year-old Hump found himself facing a Puritan regime that was launched at 7:30 every morning at chapel.

Classes were boring and he wanted to drop out of Phillips Academy after the first semester until he met schoolmate Floyd Furlow, who also lived in Manhattan. The son of the president of Otis Elevator Company, Floyd was a fun-loving guy full of wicked humor.

Although only eighteen years old at the time, Floyd claimed to have had ten affairs with women, three of whom were married to some of his father's best friends. He also stashed away booze in his room and would invite his "favorites" on the floor to come and join him.

Floyd and his friends seemed to know much about the world. All of them had been to Europe and one of them, Philip Burton, had once been taken to Africa on a safari with his father.

Hump couldn't match these adventures, as he'd never been taken even to Canada on one of Belmont's hunting trips.

Frederick Boyce, the stern headmaster of Hump's dormitory, was also a physics teacher. With his white mop of hair, he stuck his eagle's beak into everybody's business. Boyce was known for raining hell and damnation onto anyone who violated house rules.

With his wife, Betty, and their three children, Boyce lived on the dormitory's main floor so he could observe the coming and going of all "my boys." Students were forbidden to use the entrance in the rear.

The only boy on the floor who Hump disliked intensely was a nerd who wore thick wire-rimmed glasses, Charles Yardley Chittick. Chittick wanted to study law at either Harvard or Yale. Hump suspected that he was a spy, reporting every infraction to Boyce.

Charles had the single cell directly opposite Hump's. Whenever they would meet in the hallway, neither spoke to each other. If they encountered each other in the shower room, Hump would turn his back to Charlie and conceal his genitals.

Charles had told Floyd that he considered Hump a spoiled brat, secretly resenting that Hump was invited to Floyd's drinking parties and that he was excluded. Both Floyd and Hump referred to Charles as "a bookworm."

Hump eagerly awaited the Christmas vacation when he could return to Manhattan and take in some Broadway entertainment and resume his friendship with Bill.

Ten days before Hump's anticipated return to New York, Dr. Stearns had written Belmont a bad report. "Your son appears bored in class, his mind dreaming dreams of God only knows what. He is indifferent to the school curriculum. He doesn't participate in sports or any school activities. He doesn't even try to maintain a respectable gentleman's C average. Although we are allowing him to return after the holidays, I must withdraw all off-campus privileges. He will be confined to his room, the library, the dining room, and his classrooms. Despite your earlier assurances to the contrary, I fear that your son is definitely not Andover material. Unless he improves in the upcoming semester, I fear for the continuation of his academic career."

That Christmas, a few days before his eighteenth birthday, Hump was certain of only one thing: he didn't want to be a surgeon like his father, and he didn't want to go to Yale or Harvard.

Home from Andover for the holidays, Hump endured the criticism of his parents and listened to how disappointed they were over his academic record. He promised them he'd buckle down during the second term and make them proud of him, although secretly he had no intention of changing any of his behavior at the academy. None of the teachers inspired him, and their boring recitations of dates and historical events conveyed no drama for him.

On the first night of his return, Hump couldn't wait for the end of his reunion with his parents, so he could sneak out of the house to see Bill Brady. While at the Phillips Academy, Bill had written him almost daily, and Hump had answered every letter. At times Bill's letters were all that kept Hump from wanting to commit suicide.

At the Brady home, Hump was welcomed more lovingly by this Jewish family than by his own dysfunctional and coldhearted parents. Brady Sr. seemed genuinely interested in him, and Grace George and Alice Brady filled him in on all the news of their latest theatrical successes. Hump was particularly intrigued by the silent screen flickers Alice was making, although Grace George considered the movies a passing fancy and not worthy of the attention of a serious actor.

Once alone with Hump in his upstairs bedroom, Bill hugged Hump in a tender embrace and kissed him on the lips. "You're still my best buddy or did you mate with some other person up at Andover?"

"I'm still your best friend," Hump said. "For always. I'm pretty much a loner at school."

In spite of this pledge of devotion, Bill regaled Hump with tales of his recent sexual exploits. Hump was surprised that Bill had never mentioned this in any of his letters. "I met this girl," Bill said. "Priscilla Davenport. I know. A real dumb name. But she was terrific. She let me get into her bloomers any time I wanted. Those secret sessions you and I had together were just kid's stuff. I got the real thing and it was terrific."

"I can't match your record," Hump said. "I pursued a few gals at Andover but nothing happened. A harmless date here and there. Maybe a kiss. Nothing heavy. I'd like to meet this gal of yours."

"Too late for that," Bill said. "She moved to California with her family. Her dad's in the movie business. He thinks Hollywood will one day be the center of films. My dad knows a lot more about flickers than Priscilla's old man. Dad says the heart of the film colony will still be New York and New Jersey."

Hump had mixed feelings about Bill's relationship with Priscilla. He was both happy about his friend's scoring with a woman, yet jealous at the same time. For some reason he resented Bill's intimacy with someone else.

Those feelings of resentment disappeared later that afternoon when Alice Brady introduced Hump to her new beau.

Only slightly younger than Hump, Stuart Rose was the best-looking and most dashing teenager Hump had ever met. In his case, Alice didn't seem to mind that Stuart was younger than herself. She'd treated Hump like a kid, but related to the even younger Stuart like a man of the world.

Precocious for his age, Stuart was a cavalryman in the U.S. Army and was home on leave. The Rose family lived on Riverside Drive, only a ten-minute walk from the Bogart home.

Alice had met Stuart when he'd come backstage to congratulate her for her appearance in the revival of *Little Women*, in which she played Meg, a role she'd first performed on Broadway in 1912.

"Since that first meeting, we've seen each other every day," she told Hump, as she took Stuart's hand and gazed into his eyes.

Caught up as they were in the theatrical productions of Brady, Sr., each member of the Brady family was preoccupied with his newest film, *Love Eternal,* being produced on a sound stage in Queens. Even the dignified Grace George, despite her oft-expressed disdain for "the flickers," was about to appear in her husband's movie, having agreed at the last minute to replace the film's original star, actress Beatrice Lane, who had suddenly fallen ill with pneumonia. Grace was co-starring in the movie with

Doughboy pizzazz: Hump's brother-in-law Stuart Rose

her stepdaughter, Alice Brady, who played the role of the naïve *ingénue,* and young Bill was working as the assistant director to his father.

One evening, when every member of the Brady family was caught up in some aspect of the film's production, Stuart Rose found himself alone for the evening. In the same position, Hump immediately invited him to dinner at Luchow's, the long-established German restaurant on 14th Street so beloved by his father, Belmont.

Throughout the evening, Hump became enthralled with Stuart, who entertained him with stories of his life as a cavalryman. "Women really go for a man in uniform."

Hump was amazed that a teenager even younger than himself had had so many exploits with women. Hump always remembered his introduction to Stuart as "one of the most memorable evenings of my life. With Bill I felt like I was a boy talking to another boy. With Stuart, I felt we were talking man to man. My blossoming friendship with him became a rite of passage into manhood."

When Bill called the next day to invite Hump to a Broadway play, Hump had to turn him down. He'd already accepted an invitation for horseback riding with Stuart, who had a lot of free time because Alice "was shooting some stupid movie during the day and appearing as Meg in *Little Women* at night."

Bill seemed disappointed that Hump had made a "new best friend" so suddenly. Nonetheless, to show what a good sport he was, he invited both Stuart and Hump to a Broadway musical to which his father had given him free tickets. But during the performance, Bill felt a little left out and neglected, as Hump devoted all his attention to Stuart, exaggerating his hell-raising exploits at Andover and his conquests of campus beauties.

Shortly before Stuart had to report back to military service, he came to the Bogart home to retrieve Hump for another afternoon of horseback riding.

Frances (Pat) Bogart was in the living room, and Hump introduced the good-looking Army man to his sister. Frances was almost the same height as her brother and had a shapely figure even then. When Stuart learned that she didn't have an escort for the school dance the following night, he volunteered his services.

Stuart was so captivated with Frances that he asked Hump if he could postpone their horseback ride for another time. He invited Frances to go for a stroll with him in Central Park.

After Hump returned to Andover, Frances wrote to him from St. Mary's School in Peekskill, New York. She informed him that she received a letter from Stuart almost every day. Hump wrote several letters to Stuart himself, but only a brief postcard every now and then came in reply.

Before his departure for Phillips Academy, he hadn't even bothered to call

Bill to tell him good-bye and to thank him for his hospitality. But confronted anew with the loneliness of Andover, Hump started writing Bill again. Hump's temporarily deserted friend responded with enthusiastic letters, and their friendship resumed with only slightly less intensity than before.

***

After his third week back at Andover, Hump's dormitory maniacally celebrated the end of a winning football game. Even the stern headmaster, Boyce, temporarily relaxed his iron-fisted rules and allowed the young men to celebrate the school's victory. Having no interest in sports, Hump had stayed in his room trying to study, hoping for some passing grades.

Some of the men on Hump's floor had slipped beer upstairs and were having a wild party, running up and down the corridor. When this party overflowed into the shower room, it appeared that some of the men were pouring beer over the heads of the others, as they showered.

Anxious to see what was going on, Hump turned off the lamp in his room, removed the antique map, and peered through the hole in the wall at the naked boys in the shower.

That was a big mistake. Somehow Charles Yardley Chittick, even without his horn-rimmed glasses, happened to notice a hole in the wall to the shower room. He detected someone spying on them.

Poking his fingers through the hole in the wall, Chittick encountered the framed map, which had fallen back into position as Hump had jumped back. The wire holding the map came unhooked, the print falling to the floor, its glass frame breaking. Terrified at having been caught peeking, Hump concealed himself in the corner of the darkened room.

"We've got a live one, guys," Chittick yelled to the other boys. "Bogart's spying on our dicks."

As Hump cringed in his darkened room, he heard catcalls and cries of "Sissy, sissy." One of the young men shouted inside the hole, "Look at mine if you want to see a big dick. I'll let you be my gal, Nancy boy."

The next day, humiliated, Hump darted in and out of his classes, hoping not to encounter any of his dorm mates. When he returned to his dormitory, Boyce was waiting for him and asked him to step inside the library. There Boyce appeared to be under reasonable control but his eyes avoided Hump's when he spoke. "Many young men go through certain periods of adjustment in their lives," Boyce said, like a professor giving a physics lecture. "These are natural things. It doesn't mean that these same boys can't grow up to become responsible citizens and loving fathers with a good wife and healthy children. I think you'll grow out of your present behavior. It will take time, though. In the meantime, you're confined to your room after classes let out for the day. You're to leave this building only to go to the dining hall. As for your new room assignment, there is a small one right next to my apartment. It used to belong to a janitor who worked here. You're to take that room. I've had your stuff moved downstairs. Your room upstairs will be assigned to someone else next term. Needless to say, that hole carved in the wall will be sealed up. I'll write Dr. Bogart and bill him for damages. To spare you, I won't tell him why you damaged the wall."

"But I didn't..." Hump stammered in protest but soon realized that it was useless. He'd already been tried and convicted.

After the shower incident, the other young men in Hump's dormitory avoided him, all except one, Floyd Furlow. Catching up with Hump after class one day, Floyd told him that he didn't believe all the stories being spread. "If anyone's a fucking sissy, it's Chittick himself. I wouldn't take a shower with him."

Over a cup of coffee and a hamburger at a local café, Floyd told Hump that the only way he could salvage his reputation at the Phillips Academy was to have an affair. "I've been seeing this older woman regularly. Her name's Medora Falkenstein, and she loves young men. She even likes to do nude drawings of them. I can set up a meeting. When the guys learn you're seeing Medora, they'll forget all about Chittick's dumb gossip."

At first Hump had raised a number of protests, including that he was confined to his room after class. "I'm not even supposed to be here right now," Hump said, looking around the café. "I'll tell Boyce I was studying at the library."

"The Boyce family is sound asleep by ten o'clock every night," Floyd said. "All the guys know that. Your new room is on the ground floor. All you have to do is open your window and slip out after the Boyces are snoring."

Slipping out the next night, Hump was shaking a bit as he knocked on the door of Medora Falkenstein. He was a bit disappointed when she answered the door. A shade past forty, she was garishly made up and wore an artist's smock. He wasn't certain what her body looked like under that ill-fitting garment. But even if he wasn't immediately smitten with her, Medora was enthralled with Hump.

She invited him in and gave him a large glass of Scotch. She also filled him with compliments about "what a beauty you are, far more so than Floyd, although I love that boy dearly."

Hump later told Floyd that he fully expected to get laid that afternoon, and had wanted to get it over with, so he could slip back into the dormitory, letting Floyd spread the word the next day of his conquest.

Medora had her own ideas about sex and how she liked it. On his third drink, when Hump's head was reeling, she showed him nude sketches she'd done of several boys on the campus, especially three of Floyd himself. She claimed that she'd moved to Andover just to be close to campus and "its never-ending supply of good-looking men."

"Who buys this stuff?" Hump asked her.

"I deal exclusively with a private art dealer in Boston," she said. "He has clients all over the country."

"You mean women buy this?" Hump asked.

"Heavens no," she said. "Men who like to be discreet. They pay top prices to see nude sketches of some of the country's most beautiful young men in their prime. Perhaps you'll pose for me one day."

"I couldn't do that," Hump said, no doubt thinking of the time he'd posed nude for Maud's art class.

"There's a hundred dollars in it for you," she said.

He was amazed at being offered that amount of money. It sounded like a fantastic sum. "I'll think about it."

"You don't have something you're ashamed of?" Medora asked, reaching to unbutton Hump's fly. With deft fingers, she removed his penis. "My, oh my, what a big boy you are. Much bigger than Floyd and he's not bad." Before Hump truly comprehended what was happening, Medora skinned back the cap of his penis and descended on him, as he immediately hardened.

In later life Bogie would tell friends that Medora got him addicted to blow jobs. "She was the first person who ever gave me one, and she was also the best. A suction pump. She never allowed herself to be penetrated so she had developed her technique of the blow-job to absolute perfection since that was her only thing." Medora would masturbate herself as she performed fellatio on young men from Phillips Academy who ventured into her studio.

Afternoon visits to Medora became a ritual for Hump, who would go and see her right after his last class of the day. He managed to convince Boyce that he was spending the time in the academy library.

Eventually, since she always plied him with "hooch," as she called it, she didn't have much trouble persuading Hump to pose nude for her. After all, he didn't have anything to hide from her prying eyes that she hadn't seen in intimate close-up. Even buck-naked, he was completely relaxed in her studio, unlike his time in front of Maud's class when he'd been so nervous that he felt he'd shrunk a lot.

That was not his problem with Medora. Sometimes her sketching of him was interrupted when he'd get hard. She'd abandon her drawing and fellate him.

His sessions with Medora continued for nearly a month until one Saturday she invited him to come over around eleven in the evening. "My time with you

41

is too brief. I want to make a night of it. Give you an around-the-world. It drives the boys crazy."

He wasn't certain what an around the world meant, but was intrigued at the prospect. That night a heavy snowstorm descended on Andover, and, anticipating his visit, Hump borrowed a pair of skis from the school athletic room and stored them in his tiny bedroom.

When the Boyces seemed to be deep into their nightmares and snores, he raised his window and slipped out of the dorm, attaching his skis and gliding his way to Medora's studio.

That night there were no nude sketches. Hump quickly learned that Medora's talented tongue could not only tame a hardened penis, but knew how to explore every crevice of a male body.

Regrettably when returning to the dormitory in the pre-dawn hours, Hump was greeted by Boyce who caught him trying to sneak back into his window with the skis. The two men wrestled in the snow. Boyce's coat was ripped, his head injured.

The next morning, Headmaster Stearns called Hump into his office, informing him that he was expelled and was to check out of the dormitory that day, taking the train back to New York. "You are not worthy of the Academy," Stearns told him. "I predict you'll be a miserable failure in life, and have so informed Dr. Bogart."

By three o'clock on that snowy day in 1918, Hump had told Floyd goodbye and was on the train to Boston where he'd catch a larger train bound for New York.

Fearing the wrath of his parents, he decided that before he reached Manhattan he would take charge of his own life. He was going to make some bold career move and announce it the moment he came into the Bogart living room.

Before the train neared the outskirts of New York, Hump had made up his mind. The United States had already joined with the Allies to fight Germany in World War I. He'd join the fray.

Beginning tomorrow morning he was going to enlist in the U.S. Navy and would write his friend, Franklin D. Roosevelt, of his decision. The date was May 28, 1918.

***

If his parents had been cold and distant when he joined the Navy in the closing weeks of World War I, the Brady family was just the opposite. Brady Sr., Alice, Grace, and especially Bill Jr. were saddened to see him go. Each family member, promising to be on shore to welcome him home whenever his discharge might eventually arrive, had hugged and kissed him.

At the Bogart home, Maud would surely have dismissed such a farewell "as cheap theatrics common among Jews." She had given Hump a handshake, as had Belmont. His sisters, Frances and Catherine, had each kissed his cheek and wished him a safe return.

On June 19, 1918, a doctor at the Brooklyn Naval Base found that Hump was free of both syphilis and gonorrhea. In the event of Hump's death while overseas, he was told that his father would collect $35.90 per month for six months.

If he thought life was regimented at Andover, Hump was hardly prepared for the severe discipline of basic training which began July 2 at the Pelham Park Reserve in New York.

By November 9, about four months later, he was pronounced fit for duty and assigned to the USS *Leviathan,* a transport ship with a trio of gigantic funnels and zebra-like camouflage stripes. He came aboard as a helmsman, but even before the ship sailed from Hoboken, New Jersey, news reached the crew of the armistice. Germany had surrendered on November 11, 1918, and World War I was at an end.

There was still a job for the crew of the *Leviathan,* however. Ironically, it had originally been commissioned as the *Vaterland* and assigned to transport the Kaiser's forces. However, when the United States and Germany declared war, the *Vaterland* was in Hoboken and was seized by the United States Treasury Department. After some repairs and alterations, it was rechristened the *Leviathan.* Capable of carrying 14,500 men, it was the largest transport ship in the U.S. Navy.

Although he'd never seen active duty, Seaman No.1123062 put on his sailor's dress uniform with its knotted cravat and white puttees for a victory parade in Brooklyn. The next morning he sailed for Liverpool.

The vessel had been assigned for the next six months to haul U.S. servicemen back from France and England. En route to England, a junior officer, Robert Browne, demanded that Hump carry away some coffee cups and dirty dishes that had been left on deck by the officers. "Not my detail," Hump informed Browne. The officer kicked him in the face,

US Navy Seaman #1123062, Humphrey Bogart

bloodying his nose. "When an officer speaks to you and issues a command, you obey orders, boy."

"Yes, sir," Hump answered. There is no further record of Hump showing insubordination to an officer. Quickly learning that the U.S. Navy was not a democracy, he was a dutiful sailor until his term of duty came to an end.

All those stories, many made up by Bogie himself or his biographers, about the action he saw in World War I were inspired more by the bottle than real life. Bogie was a lot tougher on screen in his trench coat, carrying a gun, than he was in his Navy bell bottoms. Before heading overseas, he was widely quoted as proclaiming, "I'm not afraid of death."

He had no reason to be. The naval historian, Richard Wright, in a report filed with the State Department, wrote, "No troopship coming to the coast of France or England by an American escort was successfully attacked. The U.S. Navy transported two-million troops without losing a single man."

That didn't mean that Hump was freed of all the horrors of war. He was forever scarred by what he'd witnessed when returning soldiers were brought aboard his vessel. The young and the healthy came back from the battlefields "without a scratch." But other, sadder men had lost legs or arms on the battlefields of Eastern France. Some soldiers who'd been the victim of mustard gas were permanently wrecked. "When I saw the suffering of these men, and even though I was just a teenager, the terror of war struck my heart," Bogie was later to say. "War no longer seemed the grand adventure it had when I first sailed."

In later years, it was widely publicized that Bogie had received the famous injury to his upper lip when the *Leviathan* came under German shelling. That was just a fanciful tale conjured up in Hollywood long after the war was over, the U-boat menace itself something for the history pages. In later years, Bogie was embarrassed by his lack of action in World War I, and often invented stories to impress his cronies.

Over the years, Bogie also took particular delight in describing shore leave when he'd take the train from whichever French port where the *Leviathan* had docked, heading for Paris and "all those French dames." Bogie described in detail to John Huston and others how he visited the city's famous *maisons de tolerance*—a graceful term for "whorehouse." Bogie later claimed that he'd spent an entire week at one bordello on the Left Bank, venturing out only for meals. "Everything I learned about sex I learned in that house with about a dozen French-speaking prostitutes including some from Siam and Africa."

The biggest problem with that story is that the crew of the *Leviathan* was never granted shore leave to visit Paris during Hump's entire tour of duty aboard the vessel. He did, however, dock in Southampton, England, and visited the Red Lion Pub which staged drag acts so popular with the English.

Bogie never liked to talk about the most dramatic event of his military career. In February of 1919, he was transferred from the *Leviathan* to the USS *Santa Olivia*, which would be sailing from Hoboken, New Jersey, to Brest, France.

For a final night of fun, he'd gone to The Gilded Cage, a notorious bar in Hoboken that catered to lonely sailors, relieving them of their money and their misery with "some of the most beautiful girls in Jersey."

The bar was run by a German-born lesbian, "Isak Smith," who claimed to be Swedish because of anti-German sentiment in the United States at the time. Apparently her real name was Isak but she changed her last name to Smith because it sounded American. Isak was said to have "auditioned" all the girls who worked in her bar before turning them loose to hustle sailors.

The Gilded Cage was famous for pushing drinks. Each working girl got a commission for every glass of overpriced booze she pushed onto a sailor. By the time many sailors reached a prostitute's bed, they were too drunk to perform although they were charged ten dollars anyway.

Hump had one-hundred dollars in his pocket, and he'd demanded the best-looking woman in the bar. When he left with a beautiful boozy blonde for a room in a nearby hotel, he was falling down drunk.

He had to report to duty at five that morning. As he later remembered it, his new-found girl friend had agreed to wake him up in time. The next morning her clock revealed that it was ten o'clock. The *Olivia* had sailed at seven that morning.

Putting on his trousers, Hump rushed to Naval Headquarters in Hoboken where he turned himself in. He was officially placed in the brig and fed a diet of only bread and water.

Branded a deserter, he very cleverly decided to call in a favor from none other than Franklin Roosevelt, then assistant secretary of the Navy. He wrote Roosevelt, recalling their meeting and their night together at Seneca Point. True to his word and eager to return a kindness, Roosevelt intervened and got Hump's offense changed from deserter to "absent without leave."

Because of Roosevelt's intervention, Hump—despite his status as a deserter—received an honorable discharge at the Brooklyn Naval Yard on June 18, 1919, with a ranking as seaman second class—not the rank of quartermaster that he had hoped for. All that he had to show for his time in the service was twelve dollars in his pocket and a Victory Medal—an award that was routinely given to every serviceman who had completed a term of duty in the Armed Forces.

At the Bogart home on his first evening back, he found the atmosphere even chillier than when he'd left. His sisters were away at school, and all

Maud could manage was another handshake. Belmont was away working as a ship's doctor on a cruise to Florida.

"We can't help you at all," Maud told Hump. Their rich life with a house full of servants was over. "There is no more money, only debts." He learned that the summer home at Seneca Point had finally been sold, the profit having gone to pay off mounting debts. Belmont had invested the family money in a get-rich-quick scheme in Michigan timberland and had lost every penny.

Because of his severe drug abuse, his once-flourishing medical practice had fallen off severely as patients drifted away. That's why he took assignments as a ship's doctor aboard cruises for long periods of time.

Wandering alone on the streets of New York, Hump found himself in the same situation as many returning veterans. He was out of work, relatively uneducated, and not qualified for most professions.

He longed for that overdue reunion with the Bradys, knowing that loving and supportive family might help him decide what to do with his life. He especially missed Bill. But all of the Bradys, including Grace and Alice, were out of town touring with a roadshow.

Hump wrote Bill in Philadelphia. "Hurry back to New York and be my best pal once again. I miss you something awful. My life's a waste. I'm a failure."

***

In desperation and out of cash, Hump tried to find a job. He was hired to work in the mail department of the National Biscuit Company for $25 a week. After a month, and after showing up late for work four times in only two weeks, he was fired. An entire month went by before he found a job with the Pennsylvania Tug and Literage Company, where he was hired to trace shipments reported lost. Part of this job involved inspecting tugboats. Hump had distorted his Navy service record, and had claimed during his job interview that he was qualified as a boat inspector, which he wasn't. After sending in a number of reports that his boss called "nonsensical," Hump was fired.

Out of work and unable to find another job, Hump asked Belmont for help. Belmont's ill-fated investments were handled by the Wall Street firm of S.W. Strauss & Co. Belmont's longtime friend and investment broker, Wilbur Jenkins, was a vice president of the company. After Belmont appealed to Jenkins, the company hired Hump as a "runner" for $30 a week. He was charged with delivering securities and stock certificates to brokerage houses and banks.

When Bill Jr. returned to New York, Hump told him that he "was going to start out like Horatio Alger and work my way up to becoming president one day." Although Hump hated the runner's job, he held onto the position because he needed the money to party with his friends. The post-war era had arrived, and Hump expressed his desire "to become a Jazz Age baby."

As much as he hated his temporary jobs, Hump loved the rediscovery of his old friend. Although both men actively pursued girls, Hump and Bill Brady seemed more bonded than ever. Their boy/boy sexual flirtation with each other was about to enter a new phase. Although Hump was still considered very good looking in an unconventional way, Bill had grown into a remarkably handsome man, eagerly pursued by both girls and older women.

The dashing Stuart Rose had returned from military duty and had resumed his friendships with both Hump and Bill. He spent most of his time dating Frances. When Frances was at school, Stuart joined Bill and Hump on their jaunts to the Playhouse, a theater that William Brady Sr. operated on West 48th Street.

Sometimes, Stuart invited Hump and Bill to one of his equestrian classes at the Squadron A Armory. Originally Hump had been afraid of horses, but he trusted Stuart and responded to his teaching. Stuart pronounced him the best pupil he'd ever had.

Bill was much more interested in "the theater and girls," although he still joined in the rides. On Sunday rides in Central Park, they would sometimes be joined by John Cromwell, the director.

The only problem was that Maud insisted on dressing Hump in fashionable riding gear that she'd seen in English sporting magazines. Hump stood out as a bit of a dandy and terribly overdressed.

It was a time for making new friends and going to social gatherings in Greenwich Village. Bill and Hump learned to love parties in the village where they felt a part of bohemian life for the first time. If given a chance, Hump would sing at these parties. He had made another friend, Kenneth Mielziner, who was an actor using the name "Kenneth MacKenna." Although he could not have known it at the time, Kenneth was to become one of Bogie's closest confidants during his first attempt at a film career in Hollywood. Kenneth shared a brownstone on Waverly Place in Greenwich Village with his brother, "Jo" Mielziner, who was slated for future fame as one of America's leading stage designers.

Kenneth later recalled that he and Hump "liked the same type of woman," although the breed was never specified, since Kenneth's taste ranged from blondes to redheads, from tall, skinny girls to shorter, more fully rounded ones. "When I was through with a girl, I would pass her on to Hump. My attention span with women was short at the time, and I quickly became bored. I picked up girls with greater ease than Hump who was still a bit shy around the fairer sex. He was all too eager to date my discards."

47

By 1938, the situation would reverse itself when Kenneth married one of Bogie's "discards," his second wife, Mary Philips.

Hump was finding it harder and harder to report to work as a runner on Wall Street. Nights were for frequenting speakeasies, listening to jazz, smoking, drinking bootleg hooch, and chasing after pretty women. Stuart remained faithful to Frances, but partly because of their promiscuity, Kenneth, Hump, John Cromwell, and Bill nicknamed themselves "the pussy posse."

If a woman had a choice of these men, she usually opted for Bill Jr., since he possessed great charm and personality. If a girl couldn't get Bill, she settled for one of the other young men. Perhaps because he was smaller and less dynamic around women, Hump was often the last to get picked for a date.

For a very brief time, a young actor, James Cagney, joined the pussy posse. Hump and Bill felt uncomfortable around Cagney but Kenneth insisted on inviting him. Unlike Hump's "sissy" upbringing, Cagney, a man of the streets, had joined gangs as a kid and had learned to use his fists. He was the tough city kid, actually living the role that Hump would play at Warner Brothers when he often vied for the same parts that Cagney garnered, or else co-starred with him. Cagney told Hump that he could not make up his mind: he wanted to be either a song-and-dance man or else a farmer.

Although Cagney exuded masculinity, when he first met Hump he was appearing as a "showgal" in a revival of a production called *Every Sailor*. Originally conceived as a morale-booster for members of the Navy far from

home, its cast included many recently discharged sailors. As in the original, all the female parts were played by men. When one of the cast members got sick, a friend introduced Cagney to the producer, Phil Dunning, who hired him on the spot, providing he'd appear in drag.

"Listen, for $35 a week, I'll come out nude if they want me to," Cagney told Hump. Cagney claimed that he looked great as a gal, especially when he painted his mouth in scarlet red in a "sort of bee sting," like screen goddess Mae Murray. Hump couldn't believe that Cagney could transform himself into a gorgeous dame. Cagney said that he'd show up for their next night on the town in full drag. "The men will flock around me like moths to the flame."

Bogart's friend and competitor
Kenneth MacKenna

Indeed Cagney showed up two nights later dressed as a woman, and the pussy posse was stunned. Bill claimed that he would have asked Cagney for a date if he didn't know he had a dick under that gown.

Cagney demonstrated his skill as a vamp by capturing the attention of the handsomest man at the speakeasy. On a dare, Cagney disappeared two hours later with a young Wall Street broker. What happened later that night remains unknown. Cagney never told the pussy posse how the evening ended, and in his authorized biography, *James Cagney*, he makes no mention of having known Hump in their early days.

The next morning, hung over from an all-night party, Hump showed up late for work and was severely chastised by his boss on Wall Street. He was given documents to deliver to a firm ten blocks away. On the way there, he recalled having a splitting headache. Deep into his hangover, and barely able to continue down the block, he opted for breakfast at a coffee shop, hoping that would cure his pain. Shortly thereafter, three blocks from the scene of his ham and eggs breakfast, he realized with horror that he'd left the valuable documents in a briefcase perched on the coffee shop's coat rack. He hurried back, only to discover that the briefcase had been stolen.

"Knowing I was going to get fired when I returned to the office, I decided not to go back," Hump later recalled.

On an impulse and having given it no thought beforehand, he rode the subway to the theatrical offices of William Brady, Sr. Hump felt that he should have checked with Bill before asking his father for a job but there was no time for that.

Camping it up with James Cagney *(third figure from left)* in drag

William Sr. welcomed Hump into his office as he had remained a family favorite. Telling the elder showman of his plight, Hump found him most sympathetic. "I just happen to have an opening," Brady said. "As an office boy. The pay's $35 a week."

Hump eagerly took the job and was thrilled to be making that much money in 1920. "As you know, sir, Bill and I both love the theater. To be a part of it in some way would make me very happy."

"Cut out all of this I-love-the-theater crap," Brady said. "The Broadway stage is just fine, and I guess it'll go on forever. But the future of mass entertainment lies in the flickers. From now on, I'm a movie producer."

***

Hump found his new job as an office boy exciting, as he would relate to an attractive brunette, Ruth Rankin, who he was dating at the time. He'd given her a handsome picture of himself in his full dress Navy uniform, and she kept the photograph by her bedside, which was always there to greet him during his frequent visits to that much-used bed.

Although Hump humped her frequently, he confessed to Bill that, "I don't really love her." Bill chided him, "You don't have to love a gal to fuck her."

After working for Brady for only a month, Hump was promoted to production manager of the Brady film studio at Fort Lee, New Jersey, his pay raised to $50 a week. His duties included renting props and paying off the actors in cash.

When Brady Sr. saw the first rushes of a film, *Life*, that he'd commissioned, he fired the director, Travers Vale, and assigned Hump to take over the job.

Knowing nothing about acting or directing, Hump found a beret and a pair of black boots in the wardrobe department and showed up the next day, thinking himself a budding Erich von Stroheim or Cecil B. DeMille. The stars of the film were Arline Pretty, Nita Naldi, and Rod La Rocque.

When Bill Brady Jr. visited the set on the second day of Hump's tenure as director, he immediately fell in love with Arline Pretty, launching a hot, torrid affair that lasted exactly three days, until Nita Naldi reported for work. Bill immediately dumped Arline and chased after Naldi. Hump called his friend a "lovesick pup," while denying that he was attracted to Naldi himself. Actually he wanted her and was jealous of Bill for capturing her so soon.

The witty and glamorous Naldi was Hump's first experience with a screen vamp. Ironically, like Alice Brady herself, Naldi had been raised in a convent in New Jersey, where the Mother Superior happened to be her great-aunt. For someone with such a sheltered background, Hump thought Naldi had "street smarts." On the first day of shooting, Naldi informed her young director, "Even though I'm supposed to be a vamp in this pisser of a flick, I don't want to be photographed looking like Theda Bara buried for two-thousand years and just dug up."

After five days of filming, Bill invited Hump to join him after work at a speakeasy in Fort Lee for a private conversation. "I'm in love with Nita and she's in love with herself. I'm having the time of my life, but she says we can't go on unless you get involved."

"What in hell does that mean?" Hump asked.

"She wants you to join us in bed. Otherwise, it's no dice."

"You've got to be kidding," Hump said.

"C'mon," Bill urged. "It's not like we haven't known each other real intimate like. We already know that both of us are made of sugar and spice."

Hump didn't hesitate for long. A few drinks of bootleg gin lowered his inhibitions. He desperately wanted to seduce Naldi. Figuring if this was his only chance, and con-

Bogie's abortive debut as a helmer involved directing silent-film stars
Arline Pretty (*top right*), Nita Naldi (*bottom left*) and Rod La Roque (*bottom right*) in *Life.*

51

sidering that Bill was such a close friend, he agreed to meet that night in Naldi's hotel room.

For the next ten days, shooting on *Life* slowed down considerably, as Bill, Naldi, and Hump spent as much as two hours a day in her makeshift dressing room. For reasons of her own, Naldi could no longer see either man at night.

She'd later confess to her Hollywood comrade and sometimes lover, Natacha Rambova, the second wife of Rudolph Valentino, that she'd let Bill get on her first before allowing Hump to mount her. "I wouldn't let either of them stay on long. When they started getting too excited, I'd make one get off and the other get on. I'd string this out for a long time before letting them have their well-earned climaxes. No woman in New York was more sexually fulfilled than I was."

Born Donna Dooley in New York City two years before Hump, Nita Naldi was the first of many screen vamps Hump would seduce. Fresh from the convent, she'd acquired an immediate job as a clothes model at $15 a week before joining the chorus line at the Winter Garden's Century Roof.

Hump might have fallen for Naldi, but the male star of the film, Rod La Rocque, had fallen for his director.

Born in Chicago of an Irish mother and a French father, Rod had played mainly "boy parts," often at a dollar a performance, before Brady Sr. cast him in *Life*. At the time he met Hump, he was living at a local YMCA with another aspiring actor, Ralph Graves. A closeted homosexual, known for his good looks, elegant profile, and—years later—for a real-estate fortune he developed by buying up then-undesirable California real estate, Rod quickly became a factor in young Hump's life. La Rocque had already appeared in a Brady theatrical production, *Up the Ladder*, with Brady's daughter, Alice. The play had bombed, but Brady Sr. was sufficiently impressed with the actor to give him a chance on film.

As Hump tried to direct Rod, the male star of the film had eyes only for Hump and not the camera. Rod even suggested that Hump direct him privately so he'd know how to play his love scenes with Nita Naldi. "I can play Naldi's part and you can be me in the love scenes."

Fellow sailors during his military duty had put the make on Hump, but he'd never been pursued by a homosexual as aggressively as he was chased by La Rocque.

"The fucker even sends me roses and buys me chocolates," Hump confessed to Bill. "Like I'm his best dame or something. He begs me to go out with him. I'm too nice a guy to punch him out. Besides, he's the star of my picture, and I don't want to mess up his face."

Hump didn't become La Rocque's lover but offered some good professional advice when the actor came to him to discuss screen billings. "Here is my choice of names," La Rocque said. He'd written down suggestions for screen credit on a piece of paper which he handed to Hump.

Roderick La Rock. Rodney La Rock. Roderick La Rocque. Rodney LaRocque or Rod LaRocque. Hump studied the sheet, then wrote, "None of the above. Make it Rod La Rocque. It's catchy."

When Brady Sr. back in New York saw the first footage of *Life* directed by Hump, he was horrified. In several scenes, the drunken cameraman had actually put Hump into the frame, frantically directing his players. "The fucking director is being photographed directing," Brady screamed out in his office.

The news that came in that day was even worse. Two of *Life's* bit players filmed in a speeding car were supposed to be fighting for control of the steering wheel as the vehicle raced toward a stone wall. Hump had instructed the actors, Betty Furnall and Adolf Brunnen, to wait for a signal from him, at which point they were to swerve the car out of harm's way, avoiding the wall. Hump miscalculated.

When he finally signaled, the car had gone beyond the point of no return. It crashed into the wall, and an ambulance was summoned to take the two victims to a hospital. Although injured, they survived the crash and lived to send Brady their medical bills.

The next day Brady drove over to Fort Lee and personally fired Hump, taking over as director himself.

That same day, Nita Naldi informed both Bill and Hump that she couldn't see them any more. While dancing at the Winter Garden in the chorus, she'd been spotted by none other than John Barrymore. She claimed that he had fallen in love with her and was going to cast her opposite him in his flicker, *Dr. Jekyll and Mr. Hyde.*

Sorry to see her go, Hump and Bill agreed that Naldi would be one of the many chorus girls that The Great Profile would pick up and discard. In this rare instance, however, Barrymore did indeed cast her in the role, and Nita Naldi went on to become one of the reigning screen vamps of the Twenties. Her biggest break came in Cecil B. DeMille's *The Ten Commandments*, where she played the Eurasian temptress, Sally Lung, who contracts leprosy as a "wages-of-sin" payment for her evil ways. Her co-star? None other than Rod La Rocque himself.

Brady Sr. went on to salvage *Life*, eventually selling it to Adolph Zukor for $100,000. After he'd purchased the film, Zukor looked at it carefully, deciding it wasn't worth releasing. He assigned it to storage where it managed to disappear.

When Bogie in later life learned there were no more copies left, he said, "Thank the Devil for that."

Out of work, Hump spent the next three weeks writing a scenario for a gory film, *Blood and Death*. He wrote the script at the 21 Club, then one of New York's most famous speakeasies. Thinking that such a costume made him look more like a writer, he wore a tweed jacket and smoked a pipe.

Even though he'd been fired by Brady, Hump showed up at his office with his completed film script. Fearing rejection, Hump was surprised when "Mr. Showman" himself thought the script "could play." He sent it over to a trio of producers he knew, Jesse L. Lasky, Samuel Goldfish (later Goldwyn), and Cecil B. DeMille. All three producers were too busy to read it, and they turned the script over to an office assistant, Walter Wanger. He skimmed it before tossing it into a wastepaper basket.

In later life, when Wanger had become one of Hollywood's biggest producers and Bogie one of its biggest male stars, Wanger always claimed that "Bogart used to write for me."

Wanger went on to produce such classics as Greta Garbo's *Queen Christina* in 1933, John Ford's *Stagecoach* in 1939, and even the ill-fated *Cleopatra* in 1963, co-starring Elizabeth Taylor and Richard Burton.

Walter Wanger with Joan Bennett in 1943

Following a night of tabloid scandal in 1951, Bogie visited Wanger in jail. The previous evening in a fit of jealous rage, Wanger had shot a well-known Hollywood agent, Jennings Lang, in the groin. The agent managed the career of the then famous actress, Joan Bennett. "I was aiming for the fucker's balls," Wanger told Bogie, "but I missed." Bogie's reply: "So what in hell was the matter with my screenplay?"

By 1937, Wanger agreed to cast Bogie in *Stand-In* with his friends, Leslie Howard and Joan Blondell.

Hump wasn't off the Brady payroll for long. Brady Sr. claimed he had no peace at home, because his wife, Grace George, his daughter, Alice, and his son, Bill, kept urging him to give Hump another chance. Brady rehired

Hump at $50 a week and sent him on tour as the stage manager for Grace's play, *The Ruined Lady.*

He toured with Grace for six months in East Coast cities, including Philadelphia and Boston. He did not fall for Grace, who remained faithful to her husband, but she later recalled that he always managed to find a female companion in the seedy hotels her husband had booked them in. Mostly they stayed in fleabags that accepted traveling actors. Many hotels in those days refused to accommodate actors because they gave loud, drunken parties late at night, tore up the furniture, and usually skipped town without paying the bill.

Bogie in later life would view that tour of *The Ruined Lady* as the most sexually liberating period of his life. "Everything I learned about women, I learned then. I'd had sexual experiences with the likes of Nita Naldi and others, but on the road I met all sorts of women—all shapes, sizes, whatever. I learned that some gals will do things to a man that respectable women never do. After that road show, I found a return to New York restrictive."

Co-starring beside Grace was a handsome young actor, Neil Hamilton, playing the *ingénu* lead. Although Hamilton was headed for a big career in Hollywood where he would become one of its most durable actors, Hump as stage manager wasn't impressed with him. He called Hamilton "the stuffed shirt model," because the actor had posed for so many shirt ads in magazines. Hamilton countered by calling Hump "Baby Food." Behind Hump's back, he referred to him as "Baby Shit."

On tour with Hamilton, Hump needled him for "having such a soft job. All you have to do is show up every night, mouth some writer's words, and get your paycheck." Hamilton always protested that there was more to acting than that.

Before sending him out on the road, Brady had insisted that Hump understudy all the male parts in case one of the actors got sick. Before the final performance of *The Ruined Lady*, Hamilton developed the flu and called in to cancel.

The cast assembled that Saturday afternoon for a dry run with Hump as the male lead. He'd memorized all the parts, having heard them week after week. But facing the seats of the empty theater, he was paralyzed and couldn't remember one line of dialogue.

Fortunately for Hump, Grace also developed a fever, perhaps having caught the flu

Neil Hamilton

germs from Hamilton during their love scenes. When members of the prospective audience showed up that night, their money was refunded at the box office.

In spite of what Hump would later call "the disaster that never was," the ever-faithful Brady family continued to believe in his acting talent. In May of 1921, Alice Brady offered him a walk-on part in her play, *Drifting*. It was going to have try-outs in Brooklyn in hope of obtaining backers for a Broadway production.

Its director was John Cromwell, Hump's close friend who was also a stage performer himself. In time, he would become one of Hollywood's leading directors, known for turning out such classics as *Of Human Bondage* in 1934, *Algiers* in 1938, *Abe Lincoln in Illinois* in 1940, and *Anna and the King of Siam* in 1946.

For Hump's stage debut in *Drifting* at Brooklyn's Fulton Theater, he invited everyone he knew. Maud chose not to go see her son on stage, still disapproving of his preferred choice of a profession. But the ever-faithful Bill Brady Jr. showed up, bringing with him Belmont and Stuart Rose. Stuart was still dating Frances. Hump's sister had just seen her husband-to-be march in the Memorial Day parade. All three were eager to see Hump on the stage, hoping it would be a triumph for him.

To Stuart's horror, he discovered that Hump was spectacularly miscast in the role of a Japanese butler. Alice played a *femme fatale*, an archetype that would be perfected by Marlene Dietrich in films of the 30s. In later life, Hump called her role "early Sadie Thompson." Kicked out of her home by her

Puritan father, Alice's character ended up in Singapore "drifting" into a life of depravity before being rescued by a handsome American soldier who falls in love with her.

Bogie made his brief appearance carrying a tray of pink gin fizzes. Trying to imitate a Japanese accent, he uttered the words, "Drinks for my lady and for her most honored guests." Frances and Stuart slid down in their seats in embarrassment, although Belmont later said that he thought his son "did a right fair job."

After he became a star, Bogie always derided the role as "the dumb Jap butler part," as if anticipating the words of

Director **John Cromwell**

56

Erich von Stroheim who called his role in *Sunset Blvd.* opposite Gloria Swanson "the dumb butler part." Von Stroheim made the role the greatest butler part of all time, whereas Bogie's stage debut hardly merits a footnote in theatrical history.

Somewhere between the time the tryouts were held and the play's Broadway opening, Hump and the slightly older Alice began a quiet affair, even though she had married James Crane.

"It's a cordial romance," Hump told Bill, who didn't seem at all horrified that his best friend was sexually involved with his married stepsister. As Hump related to Bill, "We talk theater half the night and then get into bed together. Fortunately, Crane is out of town a lot. I get on top of her, do my job, then roll over and go to sleep,"

It wasn't love, but it was sex. Actually it evolved more into friendship than anything else. Until her death, Hump would remain her steadfast friend.

Drifting did make it to Broadway and ran for sixty-three performances, even though Alan Dale, theater critic for the *New York American*, called the play "strangely protuberant." Its Broadway run at an end, Brady sent Alice and Hump on the road with *Drifting.*

Two months into the run of *Drifting,* Alice announced to Hump that she was pregnant and was going to leave the cast. At first he was petrified, thinking that he might be the father. Alice assured him that the father was her husband.

After she bowed out of the show, she never resumed her affair with Hump, later referring to it as "that brief fling that often happens between actors." For Hump, it would become the role model for a future series of involvements with actresses with whom he appeared on stage or in films.

Brady hired a fast-emerging young star of her day, Helen Menken, to replace his daughter. Arriving at the theater, Helen spotted Hump backstage. She told the theater manager, Glenn Wilson, "Daddy I want a taste of that."

***

A slender, beautiful actress, Helen Menken—because of her temper tantrums—was known as "the Irish Menk" in theatrical circles. She had moppish hair, a sort of auburn red, and her cupid's-bow mouth was just as expressive as her hands, which Richard Schnel, a theater critic, had called "the most expressive on Broadway."

She looked at the world through liquid dark brown eyes that sometimes left the impression that she was misty-eyed. Her face was thin and pale, made even more so by her excessive use of rice powder. She kept her figure because of an extraordinary diet of two boiled eggs a day and perhaps a leaf of lettuce.

That dietary advice had been given to her by the stage actress, Nazimova, who recommended it to all aspiring actresses as a guaranteed way of keeping one's figure. Nazimova, as Hump was to learn later, had introduced young Helen to the delights of lesbian love.

When Helen met Hump, she was already an established star, although not yet at the height of her fame. She'd appeared in Victoria Herbert's play, *The Red Mill*, to critical acclaim.

She'd also scored a success in 1918 in *Three Wise Fools*, a play by Austin Strong. Before her steady employment in the theater, she sold women's hats and also did some clothes modeling at department stores. Prospective employers always commented on her "narrow shoulders," preferring, even then, the more broad-shouldered look that in just a few more years would be popularized by Joan Crawford.

Helen had made her theatrical debut at the age of six when she'd walked out nude in a production of *Midsummer Night's Dream*. It is said that the circumstances that surrounded Helen's true-life stage debut at the age of six inspired the creation of the fictional career of the character of Margo Channing in the 1950 film, *All About Eve*, starring Bette Davis.

Poorly educated and born into poverty, Helen had acquired a gloss of sophistication because of all her years in the theater. Born in New York City, she was the oldest of three children. For some reason of her own, Helen was

Two views of Helen Menken

proud to be a direct descendant of John Wilkes Booth.

Hump was intrigued by her upbringing, which she called "my world of silence." Both of her parents were deaf mutes, although Helen had been born with perfect hearing. She learned to communicate with them in sign language. Whenever her parents would get into an argument, one of them would turn off the lights, ending a fight since they could no longer see each other to communicate.

Helen's mother earned $3.50 a week sewing identification badges for business conventions, but her father had never held down a job for very long. Helen herself had come from a rough-and-tumble background of acting in road shows and sleeping in seedy rooms above drunken saloons.

She remembered when one of these fleabag hotels near Trenton, New Jersey, had caught fire. "I climbed down from the second-floor window since the fire was raging up the only stairway. I raced out into the night and was standing out on the highway before I realized I was stark naked. It was twenty degrees that night."

For years she'd supported her family and had even managed to send one of her brothers to college. Helen herself had had only one and a half years of grade school. She didn't enroll in school until she was twelve years old.

Hump disliked Helen on sight. Because of Alice's sudden withdrawal from the play, he had only twenty-four hours to teach her her lines. He might not have liked her personally but was amazed at how fast she learned the script. Before the curtain went up the following night, she was letter perfect.

Unfortunately the play called for a series of light complicated set changes. Deep into the second act, Hump and the stagehands in their haste had not secured the props. In the middle of Helen's big scene, the wall of a set collapsed on her, burying her in front of the audience. Hump had to pull the curtain before Helen, who had not been hurt, could resume her theatrics.

Helen tried to recoup her dignity but many customers walked out, demanding a refund on their tickets, claiming that they had purchased them to see Alice Brady.

Enraged, Helen rushed backstage to confront Hump. "You asshole!" she shrieked at him. "You little shit."

Because of the abuse suffered at the hands of Maud's ill-mannered and ill-tempered servants, Hump could not stand being called little shit. He kicked her in the rump, sending her sprawling onto the wooden floor. Jumping up, she aimed her sharply pointed high-heel shoe at his groin, scoring a bull's-eye assault on his testicles. Falling to the floor, he doubled over in pain, which is where she left him as she stalked off to her dressing room.

It was the beginning of a beautiful friendship.

Within six weeks Helen was professing her love for Hump. That love was not reciprocated, although he later told his friend Bill that "she's great in the sack." She invited him to come and live with her at her flat at 43 East 25th Street in New York but only for four nights each week. The other three nights of her week, Helen enjoyed the "wild side" of New York with her newly discovered companion, Tallulah Bankhead.

Tallulah was a gorgeous and outrageous Alabama belle, living at the Algonquin Hotel on $50 a week sent to her by her daddy. Her stated ambition for coming to New York was: (1) to become the biggest Broadway star of all time; (2) to seduce John Barrymore, and (3) to "fuck Ethel Barrymore."

Hump had moved in with Helen without knowing much about her. In the first month or so, she kept him like a "toy boy," not introducing him to her friends or making him part of her glittering Broadway world. It was as if she couldn't decide what role he was going to play in her life.

Day by day Hump learned more about his new girl friend. A high strung, nervous woman with a bizarre (perhaps anorexic) diet and a tendency to drink heavily, she worried and fretted most of the day. She read Broadway news with a certain fury, often bursting into violent rages when a rival actress received a part that she felt she was "destined to play."

Although bitterly resentful of the success of other actresses, she encouraged Hump with his theatrical ambitions. "After all, you're no competition to me, darling. Be an actor out in front of the lights, not some God damn prop man. As a stagehand, you stink." She constantly ribbed Hump for that opening night when the scenery fell on her.

Helen had some peculiarities. Long before the world ever heard of Imelda Marcos, Helen spent a good part of her salary buying expensive shoes, even it if meant going without some of life's essentials. She adored her tiny feet, which to Hump evoked memories of Maud's small feet.

The only difference was that Helen demanded that Hump spend as much time in bed kissing, licking, and biting her feet, as well as sucking her toes, as he did in attacking other parts of her body. Helen would spend hours washing, bathing, and caring for her feet, with endless pedicures. She would fret over the right nail polish to use for her dainty toes.

In spite of her lack of schooling, she spoke perfect English. She said she'd learned to speak properly listening to other actresses on the stage, beginning with the star Annie Russell in *Midsummer Night's Dream*. Helen's voice sounded slightly husky, something like that of the future actress, Barbara Stanwyck, Bogie's 1947 co-star in *The Two Mrs. Carrolls*.

Helen was much the same off-stage as she was on, which was very flamboyant. She called everybody "darling," an appellation soon picked up by her protégée, Tallulah.

Almost overnight, Helen became the toast of Broadway. Austin Strong had "loved" her performance in his play, *Three Wise Fools*, and campaigned for her to be cast as Diane in his latest play, *Seventh Heaven*, which opened on Broadway in 1922 and became an immediate hit.

Hump himself was in the opening night audience and was dazzled by her performance. In the role, she played a street urchin in Paris. Her most memorable scene was when she took a bullwhip, and in her rage and despair, drove her mean sister out of the house.

Before meeting Helen, Hump had dated an aspiring young actress, Katharine Alexander. Briefly smitten with her, Hump pursued Katharine for a week or two. He'd never known anyone who'd been born and reared in Alaska, and was fascinated to learn of her experiences in the cold north. "I can take the chill off you," he promised Katharine. She never gave him a chance to prove that.

In spite of her sexual rejection of him, Hump and Katharine would become lifelong friends. She told him that she had never wanted to be an actress, but had studied to be a *concerte artiste.* For some strange reason, she seemed to take the greatest pride in her heritage. She was one-eighth Cherokee Indian.

"I've never had a squaw woman before," he jokingly suggested to her.

"Many conquests are better off dreamed than experienced in real life," Katharine told him. "I'll see you in your dreams."

When he introduced Katharine to the handsomer, taller, richer, better built, and more successful Bill Brady Jr., Hump's romance with Katharine came to an abrupt end. She fell at once for Bill. Hump showed little jealousy, and even suggested at one point that "we should share her," evoking their brief fling with Nita Naldi.

After the third week, Bill would stand for no more talk like that. He'd fallen madly in love with Katharine, and planned to make her "my exclusive property." Within six weeks of meeting Katharine, Bill invited Hump to be his best man at their wedding. Hump asked Helen to accompany him.

Attending the wedding of Katharine and Bill must have given

Tallulah Bankhead

61

Helen an idea. Within weeks, she was urging Hump to marry her. She was proposing to him as if he were the prospective bride and she the groom. Hump didn't turn her down but didn't accept her proposal either.

He turned to his friend Bill for advice. "If I marry Helen," he said, "I'll be repeating Maud's pattern with Belmont. Strong woman, the bread earner, supporting weak husband."

"Forget about that," Bill said. "Marry the bitch. She's a friend of all the critics and knows all the big-name producers. She'll advance your career. Trust me on this one. If you scorn Helen, she'll cut off your balls. She's already kicked them. You may never work on Broadway again."

Hump remained uncertain and confused. At Helen's urging, he went to secure a marriage license, which he would carry around in his wallet for the next four years. In an interview on April 5, 1922, Hump told *The New York Times*, "I plan to marry Helen Menken." Because of Helen's prominence as a Broadway star, the paper gave it a headline. Suddenly, all of Broadway became aware of the struggling actor, Humphrey Bogart. He hadn't even married her yet, and already Bill's advice was proving to be true. Almost overnight, producers started offering Hump parts, no doubt with a little urging from Helen herself.

With the *Times* announcing her engagement, Helen no longer had any reason to keep Hump a secret in the closet. Her toy boy (although men weren't called that then) could emerge into the full theatricality of her glittering world. He would meet for the first time Miss Tallulah Bankhead, whom he had confided in Bill was "Helen's other boyfriend."

CHAPTER TWO

Instead of being threatened or offended by Helen's sexual involvement with Tallulah, Hump was intrigued. He pointedly asked his friend Bill, "Just what do women do in bed together? I understand the kissing part, but the plumbing doesn't seem quite right."

In detail, the more worldly Bill tried to explain lesbian love and how it worked. Even so, Hump didn't quite get it.

That evening, Bill invited him to Harlem's Red Garter, a notorious nightclub that flourished briefly and illegally in the early 1920s until the police shut it down. Patronized only by male customers, the club specialized in presenting live sex acts on its small stage but only between women performers.

The lesbian black actress, Hattie McDaniel, was said to be a frequent patron of the club and was even rumored to have been a performer. Hattie would go on to greater fame playing Mammy to Scarlett O'Hara in *Gone With the Wind*. As a further irony, she was to become the lover of Tallulah Bankhead, as Tallulah in her declining years would readily admit to her homosexual "cunties," as she called her all-male entourage.

It was a wiser and more experienced Humphrey Bogart, man of the world, who escorted Helen to the 21 Club to meet Tallulah.

When Hump was introduced, her hair looked badly combed, yet it was radiant. Her mouse-brown dress, however, should long ago have been sent to the cleaners. "Forgive my appearance, darling," she said, aping Helen's habit of calling everybody darling. "I've just gone down on John Barrymore and haven't had time to make myself into a lady again."

"You look beautiful," Hump assured her. Actually he didn't know what to make of this Alabama bombshell, although he could understand Helen's fascination with her.

"I must ask a tiny favor," she said. "To catch the streetcar home, I need one tiny, little, small penny as I have only four cents in my purse, hardly enough for the five-cent fare."

"I don't understand why you're always broke," Helen said, ordering a martini from the waiter at 21. "You employ a French maid."

"I know, darling," Tallulah said. "Daddy sends me $50 a week, and I have to give the maid half of that. That means I'm penniless for three days a week."

"Fire the maid," Hump said. "My mother did when the family fortune disappeared."

"Perish the thought, darling," Tallulah said. "No respectable lady could live in New York without a French maid. It's simply not done."

Helen was the more established star, but Tallulah dominated the night. Hump concluded that Tallulah was the "man" in her relationship with Helen, his girlfriend the submissive female.

"You must meet my sister, Eugenia," Tallulah said to Hump, reaching over to caress his hand. "She's not a classic beauty like me, but one hell of a woman. Those stories about her being a lesbian are exaggerated. She lives in an apartment next door to Zelda and Scott Fitzgerald. They've been anxious to meet the two of you since the *New York Times* referred to your coupling as a union of two Jazz Age Babies. Scott views himself as the world's expert on Jazz Age babies."

Since Tallulah didn't have any money, Helen invited her to join them for dinner at Sam's Vanity, a popular little restaurant that flourished for three months until its owner, Sam Martin, was fatally shot by his estranged wife.

At table, Tallulah stuffed herself, while claiming that Sam didn't know how to cook Southern fried chicken. After dinner Tallulah invited them for "drinks and drugs" at the apartment of her friend, Napier George Henry Stuart Alington, the third Baron of Alington." She called him "Naps" and claimed a passionate involvement. "John Barrymore for sex," she said, "Ethel Barrymore if I can get her, but for true love, it's Naps. That is, if he isn't too busy fucking Noël Coward."

Naps welcomed them into a plushy furnished Victorian apartment. In his mid-20s, he had a small delicate build, crowned by a mop of blond hair. His most sensuous physically was in his thick lips. He had a nervous habit of constantly licking the roof of his mouth, as if he were tasting honey.

Ushered into the living room, Helen, Hump, and Tallulah were served martinis by an English butler. Spread out on Naps' glass-topped coffee table was a virtual shopping cart of drugs, including cocaine, heroin, and morphine, the substance so beloved by Maud and Belmont Bogart.

The heroin came in little vanity boxes, lined in red silk, evocative of Tiffany jewel boxes. Small hypodermic needles were arranged moonlike around the heroin boxes. For his drug of choice, Hump selected morphine, hoping to understand his parents' infatuation with the drug.

Tallulah claimed that she found morphine boring and chided Hump for not selecting cocaine, which she said was the drug of the moment. Cocaine was enjoying the same type of popularity among New York's jazz babies in the early Twenties as marijuana did among the hippies of the late Sixties. Instead of masquerade balls, "snow balls" were all the rage, and Tallulah said she attended two every week of her life.

The next day, when Hump related the drama of the previous night to Bill, Hump was a little vague on details, not that he was holding back information. He honestly claimed he couldn't remember. "That morphine sent me into another world."

All he recalled was that Tallulah and Helen started kissing on the sofa. "It was like a white girls' show at the Red Garter."

At one point Naps appeared nude in the living room and invited all of them into his bedroom.

"I don't remember anything after that," Hump claimed. "I think I have deliberately blotted out what happened next. I just don't want to recall it."

Somewhere before dawn, Helen and Hump had dropped Tallulah off at some mysterious apartment on West 51st Street, and Helen directed the cabbie to head for her own apartment.

Before stumbling out of the taxi, Tallulah extended an invitation to them for the following evening to meet the reigning literary darlings of the 1920s, novelist F. Scott Fitzgerald and his wife, Zelda.

"I guess I got a real introduction to your world," Hump said to Helen in the taxi.

"Darling," Helen said, "Until tonight I didn't think you were sophisticated enough to handle it. You're a city boy but still a bit provincial."

"Perhaps," he said, "but after that Alabama hurricane and that fucking Naps, I was really initiated. It's a night to remember. Better yet, it's a night to forget."

She reached over and kissed his cheek. "It's only the beginning, my love. Our marriage will be perfect. A shared marriage."

"This 'country boy' has never heard of a shared marriage."

"We must not be selfish," Helen said. "You're a gorgeous man and I'm a devastating female. We'll have to share our marriage with others."

"You mean, carry on like we did tonight?" he asked.

"There will be others, so many others we can invite into our marriage bed. Variety, that's the only way to guarantee that a marriage will stay vital and not become a bloody bore. We'll ask Zelda and Scott tomorrow night what they think about that."

***

The following evening, Helen had to excuse herself because she'd been asked at the last minute to meet with a producer about a change of casting in her play.

Hump was the first to arrive at the Algonquin Hotel where he asked the receptionist to call up to Tallulah's room. She claimed that she'd be down in the lobby quicker than it would take "Ethel Barrymore to slap my gorgeous face." Hump had heard that Ms. Barrymore had slapped Tallulah's face when the grand actress had walked into a party and caught Tallulah doing a devastating impression of her.

He was into his second drink when Tallulah showed up in the lobby in a fur coat borrowed from her much older friend, Estelle Winwood. Hump sat in a corner table. She walked over and kissed him on the lips. "Sorry Helen couldn't make it tonight. I was hoping to be the meat in a sandwich between the two of you."

As Tallulah started to launch into one of her many stories about the men and women pursuing her in New York, she was interrupted by the arrival of Scott and Zelda Fitzgerald, the darlings of the New York tabloids and the embodiment of the Jazz Age. The romantic couple was already deep into a bottle of gin which Scott carried in a pocket of his raccoon coat. In contrast, Zelda wore a thin red woolen coat.

Tallulah jumped up and kissed each of the Fitzgeralds on the lips before introducing them to Hump.

Scott had already written his novel, *This Side of Paradise*, recounting the adventures, romantic and otherwise, of a Princeton man. He'd also published *Flappers and Philosophers*.

Standing in front of Scott and Zelda in the flesh, Hump sensed that they were trying to become public manifestations of the flappers and "sheiks" he had described in his writing.

Shaking Scott's hand, Hump found him rather effeminate. A woman newspaper columnist, Rena Willson, had only recently written a feature story about him. She had claimed that "Scott's face dances between pretty boy and handsome, and his long-lipped mouth virtually cries out for lipstick and belongs more on a girl than a young man."

F. Scott and Zelda Fitzgerald

As Zelda and Tallulah excused themselves to go to the powder room, Scott settled onto the banquette opposite Hump. Watching the women go, he expressed his disappointment that he wouldn't have a chance to meet Helen tonight. "I've seen her latest play and thought she gave a brilliant performance."

"I'll convey that to her," Hump said.

"Before the ladies get back, I've got to ask you something," Scott said. "I read in the papers that you and Helen are getting married. Forgive me, but have you slept with her yet, or are you waiting until the wedding?"

Ever the kidder, Hump startled Scott by looking at him with a deadpan expression and saying, "In all honesty, I can say that I don't recall."

Scott weighed that for a moment then burst into laughter, putting his arm around Hump. "You're my kind of man."

With this trio, Hump hardly could slip in even the smallest observation. Scott, Zelda, and Tallulah had opinions about everything and everybody, and expressed them in such a candid manner as to shock society.

Tallulah went to the reception desk and placed a call upstairs to the room where John Barrymore was temporarily staying. She rushed over to Scott. "I tried to get John to come down and join us, but he's entertaining some lucky gal. But he'll speak to you on the phone."

As Tallulah and Scott departed for their phone dialogue with Barrymore, Zelda slid closer to Hump. "Tallulah claims you're a most satisfying lover, and I'm envious. Scott can't satisfy me sexually. His equipment is too small."

Hump had never heard a woman, much less a wife, make such an observation about her husband.

He studied her face carefully. Her dark honey-blonde hair had been given the world's worst permanent. Her skin was pink and white, a delicate porcelain look. She had a sensual and alluring mouth and deep blue eyes that reflected a sparkling deviltry. If she had any imperfection at all, it was her sharp nose that was a bit beaky.

"The real reason Scott wants to talk to John Barrymore is that he has a crush on him," she said. "Scott's a fairy, you know. I'll prove it." She reached into her purse and produced a photograph, which she said she always carried around to parties.

Staring back at Hump was a stunning looking dame in an off-the-shoulder gown and black high heels.

"It was snapped for The Triangle Club at Princeton," Zelda said. "Scott appeared in a play this way in drag, and his picture was circulated all over campus. He was hailed as the Princeton Play Girl."

"Since there are no women undergraduates at Princeton," Hump said, "men play the female parts. I know this actor, Jimmy Cagney, who launched himself in show business doing drag."

"That may be true, but why was Scott chosen to play the beautiful show-girl?" Zelda asked.

Before he could answer, Scott and Tallulah returned. He seemed thrilled at having talked to The Great Profile himself.

The waiter kept the quinine water flowing to their table, and Scott kept lacing their drinks with gin. Hump was amazed that Zelda seemed to be encouraging Scott to drink. As Scott was engrossed in conversation with Tallulah, Hump leaned over to Zelda. "If you get him too drunk, he won't be able to write in the morning."

"That's fine with me," she said with a smirk on her face.

"But he's a writer. Writers have to write."

"Are you suggesting that I'm jealous of his work and want to keep him from writing?" she asked. "I have no reason to be jealous. In time I'm going to write fiction myself. The world can judge who is the better novelist."

Drunk and out on the street again, Scott dared them to race toward the theater district. With Hump reluctantly trailing behind, Zelda, Scott, and Tallulah darted down the crowded sidewalk, not caring if they bumped into someone. They were like crazed young things without a care in the world.

Even though he ran to keep up with them, Hump felt that all of them were like some incorrigible undergraduates he'd known at Andover. With the wind blowing through his hair, Scott led them right into the dense traffic along Seventh Avenue. "We'll defy death," he shouted back at them.

Shortly after their arrival at a popular dance club, Montmartre, plenty of bootleg hooch suddenly became available. Both Tallulah and Zelda found the patrons "sluggish." Zelda suggested that she and Tallulah take to the dance floor and enliven the joint.

As the orchestra struck up an inappropriate Highland Fling, Zelda whirled around the suddenly emptied dance floor turning cartwheels for the amusement of the crowd. Right on her heels was Tallulah, equally adept at turning cartwheels herself. The only difference between the two performers was that Tallulah had forgotten to put on her bloomers.

At Scott's suggestion, the party moved to the Plaza Hotel. In those days newspaper photographers were always posted in the lobby, hoping to take pictures of celebrities coming and going.

Seeing the cameramen, Scott did a handstand in the lobby, as his picture was snapped. Getting to his feet again, he told Hump. "I'm sure to get my picture in the papers in the morning. I haven't been mentioned for an entire week, so I had to do something."

Zelda suggested to Tallulah that she and Hump join Scott and her in one of their favorite games on the elevator. Once inside the cage, she said that they were to ride up and down. When the door opened to let on new passengers, they were to shock the hotel guests by having Zelda kiss Tallulah on the mouth and Scott kiss Hump on the mouth. Hump didn't much like the idea of the game, but didn't want to live up to Helen's accusation of him as a country boy.

For about fifteen minutes that night, they rode up and down in the elevator with Zelda kissing Tallulah and Scott kissing Hump. And indeed the hotel guests were shocked, many expressing their disapproval with outrageous indignation.

Back in the lobby, one of the photographers approached Scott, telling him that he'd run out of film after the handstand photograph was snapped. He asked Scott to do it again.

"I've got a better idea," Scott said, grabbing Zelda's hand and racing toward the door. Followed by Tallulah and Hump, he ran over to the fountain, dropping his fur coat. "Let's go for a midnight bath," he shouted. "Last one in is an ugly duckling."

Scott jumped into the fountain and began splashing about, as Zelda and then Tallulah followed. Feeling like a fool, Hump jumped in with them as two shutterbugs snapped their pictures for tomorrow's tabloids.

Out of the fountain, cold and dripping wet, Scott raced toward a cab parked in front of the hotel with Zelda trailing him. When she reached it, Zelda turned and kissed both Tallulah and Hump on the lips.

Scott leaned out the window of the cab. "Remember," he said to both Tallulah and Hump. "You two pretty things should know that Oscar Wilde got it right. The only thing worse than being talked about is being forgotten." Zelda jumped in the back seat of the taxi with him, as they headed off into the night.

Still soaked from the fountain, Tallulah screeched for a second cab. "Since Helen and Naps are tied up with other engagements this evening," she said, "I guess that means you're stuck with me as your fuck buddy."

***

Scripts were frequently offered to Hump by Brady Sr. Bill Jr. remained Hump's steadfast friend, and promoted Hump as an actor to his father, despite telling his stepsister, Alice, that Hump "really has no talent." Bill also confessed to her that the only reason he hyped roles for Hump was that he wanted him to have a weekly paycheck. "I'm tired of always picking up the bill at speakeasies."

Brady Sr. had revived *Up the Ladder*, a four-act play presented at The Playhouse on March 6, 1922. Originally, George Le Guere played the part of Stanley Grant. After a respectable run, when Le Guere opted to move on to other venues, Bill talked his father into giving the role to Hump. The play starred Nannette Comstock and George Farren. The original production had featured Rod La Rocque, who still wrote Hump letters, claiming that, "I'm mad about the boy," predating the Noël Coward lyrics.

69

Farren had starred in the 1917 screen version of *The Cinderella Man*. During rehearsals, Farren was always forgetting his lines. "No wonder," Hump later told Bill. "He was born before the Civil War."

It was during his appearance in *Up the Ladder* that Hump befriended the actor, Paul Kelly, who was also appearing in the play, but in a minor role.

When *Up the Ladder* closed, a play called *Swifty* followed. Brady Sr. offered Hump the role of the juvenile lead, Tom Proctor, described by playwrights John Peter Toohey and W.C. Percival as "a young sprig of the aristocracy." John Cromwell, a member of Hump's "pussy posse," was signed on as the director.

The male star was Hale Hamilton, not the more famous Neil Hamilton as many biographers have reported. Throughout their professional lives, the two actors were often confused because of their name similarity. Hump had worked with Neil Hamilton during the ill-fated production of *The Ruined Lady* with Grace George.

The female lead in *Up the Ladder* was played by Frances Howard, and Hump was immediately attracted to her. A flapper, Frances was hailed as one of the great beauties of Broadway. She'd already appeared in *The Intimate Stranger*, starring Alfred Lunt and Billie Burke.

Frances Howard

Frances was slender and well-proportioned with big dark eyes. Her features were so exquisitely chiseled, Hump called her a "fragile doll." Under bobbed raven-colored hair, she had a true peaches-and-cream complexion.

In spite of her strict Catholic upbringing, her years in show business had toughened her. Bill was the first to have an affair with her, calling her a "sexual predator in bed." When Hump pressed him for more details, he said, "You'll have to find that out for yourself."

Frances told Hump that she'd learned "all there was to know about men" when at the age of fifteen she toured with her sister, Connie, in an act billed as "The Howard Sisters." In between stage jobs, Frances doubled as both a fashion model and a chorus girl.

Hump was eager to fill in those three lonely nights a week when Helen was out with Tallulah and a pack of actresses called "the girls." Without telling Frances that he was engaged to Helen, he actively pursued Frances who kept turning him down.

Hale Hamilton

Rehearsals on *Swifty* were going poorly. Brady Sr. wasn't pleased with Cromwell's direction, and had virtually taken over as "co-director." Brady placed himself in the back seat of the theater. During rehearsals, every time Hump uttered a line, Brady would shout, "What? Louder! *LOUDER!*" Handicapped by his lisp, Hump was mumbling some of his lines.

Growing increasingly despondent with what he saw on the stage, Brady brought in Ring Lardner as play doctor to save *Swifty*. But even such a writing talent could not do the job.

In his role in the play as that "young sprig of the aristocracy," Hump was said to have "deflowered" a girl in an Adirondack cabin and then deserted her.

In the play, Hump made his first appearance with a gun, a pose that would eventually become legendary for him. He was directed to rush toward Hale Hamilton, shouting, "I'll kill you! I'll kill you! I'll kill you!"

Moving down to a front row seat for the final rehearsal, Brady had ordered Hump to repeat his big moment in the play a total of twenty times.

When Brady ordered Hump to do the scene yet another time, Hump was exhausted and near tears. Consumed with rage, he gave the role his all. When he'd finished, he looked over the pit at Brady in the front row. The showman was asleep or at least feigning sleep.

Screaming in rage, Hump ran off the stage and tried to attack Brady, but was restrained by both Hale and Bill Jr. The men took Hump into an alley and cooled him down, Bill offering a cigarette and Hale producing some brandy from a hip flask.

Opening night could proceed. What a disaster it was. Hale and Frances were trained professionals, and did the best they could. But Hump's mouth became so dry he disappeared from the stage to get a glass of water, leaving Hale to "vamp till ready." Hale at that point didn't know if Hump would come back on stage or not. Finally, he did and the play proceeded to its dull ending, receiving very weak and only scattered applause.

The only blessing that came out of that night was that Hale wanted to go to a party and not accompany Frances back to her hotel room as she'd requested. Remembering that Hump had been repeatedly asking her out for a date, she agreed to go to the 21 Club with him. She told him, "I hope your performance later in the evening will be better than what you did on stage."

After midnight, Frances invited him back to her hotel room, where he discovered what his friend Bill had already learned. Frances might look like a fragile doll but in bed she was a steel magnolia. "She taught me a trick or two," Hump told Bill Jr. the next day.

When Hump woke up the following morning, Frances was already getting dressed. "You're good," she said. "Almost as good as Bill. But last night was our one and only time."

"What's the matter?" Hump asked. "Last night I had you crying out for more."

"Occasionally I do it for fun," she said, messing with her hair. "I waste few favors on struggling actors, especially bad struggling actors. I'll never get ahead fucking the penniless. I'm determined to go to Hollywood where I'm gonna marry some bigtime producer or director. He'll not only make me a star but I'll become the wife of a millionaire."

To Hump, Frances' ambitions sounded like just so much morning after pillow talk. That's why he was eventually astonished to read on April 23, 1925 that Frances had married her "dream man" in Jersey City.

She had found the perfect role for herself, a part that she would play for almost fifty years. She'd persuaded Samuel Goldwyn to marry her.

When he arrived at the Bogart home the morning after, Maud was waiting with the newspapers and his reviews.

Alexander Woollcott, the leading theater critic of his day, wrote of *Swifty*: "The young man who embodied the aforesaid sprig was what might mercifully be described as inadequate." Bogie would carry around Woollcott's review in his wallet for the rest of his life.

Only Helen Menken urged him to keep trying to become a successful Broadway actor. One day she altered that vision of his future profession. "I've decided you should be on the silver screen."

***

Helen was always vague, even to her husband-to-be, about how she had met Lillian Gish. Tallulah later claimed that she was the one who introduced Helen to Lillian, presenting Helen as "my discard" in the lobby of the Hotel Algonquin.

Discard or not, Helen seemed to mesmerize Miss Gish, who suggested that "a beauty like yourself should also appear in flickers. You'd look lovely in close-ups." Coming from Lillian, the D.W. Griffith star who invented close-ups, that was high praise indeed.

Through her close relationship with the more famous of the Gish sisters, Lillian herself, Helen arranged for a screen test for Hump in Lillian's upcoming film, *The White Sister*.

The film script had been written by F. Marion Crawford and Walter Hackett. It had opened in September 27, 1909 at Daly's Theatre in New York, having only a short run before it closed November 6. Lillian and Henry King hoped to resurrect this tired vehicle, as indeed they would one day as a film.

Two days later, in a barnlike studio in Astoria, Queens, Hump was introduced to the already legendary Lillian, who told him that in her upcoming film she hoped to capture a "spiritual fragility."

Hump remembered that she maintained several quirky "little conceits," which included referring to her Canadian friend as Gladys Smith, even though Gladys was known to the world at large as Mary Pickford. "Griffith used to pay Dorothy and me five dollars a day," Lillian said. "Henry King and I hope to pay you considerably more."

Dorothy, of course, was the other Gish sister, and was also famous as an actress.

King, the director, introduced himself to Hump just before his screen test and explained in rough outline the plot for *The White Sister*. Lillian was to play Angela Chiaromonte, the daughter of a rich Italian count killed in a fall from his horse. Lillian is cheated out of her estate by her older half-sister and is thrown into poverty. She's saved by her engagement to a dashing officer, Captain Giovanni Severini, but he is captured by Arabs in an expedition to Africa. She dedicates her life to her lover's memory by becoming a nun. She's not aware that her lover has escaped and returned to Italy. The climax takes place against a backdrop of the eruption of Mount Vesuvius.

"Just my kind of part," Hump told King, who apparently did not catch the sarcasm in the actor's voice. Hump thought the script ridiculous but agreed to film the final close-up with Lillian minus the volcanic eruption.

He never saw the screen test but felt that he was very wooden with Lillian. "We had all the screen chemistry of yesterday's bathwater." To Hump's surprise, both King and Lillian complimented him on his performance, claiming that they felt he had "real screen presence."

Hump was asked to stay at the studio until after lunch. King was considering asking him to film one more segment of *The White Sister*, depicting when the captain first meets the woman who will become the love of his life.

When Hump returned from lunch, another actor was waiting in the reception room. An Englishman named Ronald Colman was eight years older than Hump. He appeared suave and debonair with a soft cultured voice that contrasted with Hump's lisp. Hump, thinking the role was his, was upset to learn that Colman was also testing for the part. He not only

The White Sister

Two views of Lillian Gish:
(top photo)
with Ronald Colman

73

"spoke pretty," as Hump later recalled, "but he was also God damn good look-ing." Colman, in fact, would in a decade be voted "the handsomest man on the screen." Both King and Lillian had seen Colman appearing in a Ruth Chatterton play and had been impressed with his performance.

Hump and Colman were interrupted when King came into the studio. With Colman's permission, King penciled in a mustache on the clean-shaven actor, a tonsorial touch that would remain with the star for the rest of his life.

Even before the more polished Colman went before the cameras, Hump knew that the British actor had the part. He suspected that King and Lillian had tested him only as a favor to Helen. King called Colman into the studio and dismissed Hump, claiming it wasn't necessary to stick around for that sec-ond scene.

Colman not only won the part of the tragic soldier hero in *The White Sister*, he went on to become one of Hollywood's greatest film stars, pioneer-ing a band of "gentleman heroes" on the screen. As Hump went from one "dumb comedy to another," he watched Colman's meteoric rise to film fame.

For the rest of his life, Bogie would refer to Colman as "that limey bum," blaming the British actor for sabotaging Hump's own screen career in silent pictures.

***

One evening Bill Brady Jr. invited Hump to the opening night of his father's 1923 Broadway production, *The Mad Honeymoon*. They sat next to George M. Cohan.

At the time, any aspiring actor was in awe of Cohan, "the man who owned Broadway." The song-and-dance man of all song-and-dance men, Cohan was celebrated for his hit song, "Over There," for which Franklin Roosevelt would one day award him the Congressional Medal of Honor. Cohan would go on to write such hits as "Give My Regards to Broadway," "You're a Grand Old Flag," and "I'm a Yankee Doodle Dandy." Ironically, Hump's future film rival at Warner Brothers, James Cagney, would win an Academy Award for his impersonation of Cohan in the 1943 film hit, *Yankee Doodle Dandy.*

Fifteen minutes into *The Mad Honeymoon*, both Bill and Hump knew that the show would be a disaster. The only saving grace of the play was when a teenage actress, Mayo Methot, walked onstage as the maid. She had only five lines of dialogue, but brought momentary life to the dying play.

In their front row seats, Hump remembered being intrigued by her cupid's-bow mouth and mass of blonde curls inspired by the MGM screen goddess, Mae Murray. Mayo had big, soulful eyes that looked out across the stage lights, seeming to make direct contact with the audience.

When the curtain went down, Cohan had nothing to say about the play. It received only scattered applause and was lambasted the next morning by all the leading critics of the day.

With his sharp eye for good theater, Cohan said nothing to Bill about his father's opening night disaster, but asked to be taken backstage to meet the maid. "I have just discovered the next Lillian Gish."

Hump was surprised, thinking that a comparison to Mae Murray—not Gish—would have been more apt.

When word spread that Cohan had come backstage, the stars of the play expected that Mr. Showman had come to greet them. They were startled at having been ignored. Cohan sought out Mayo and told her that she was terrific in the role. Mayo reached over with her cupid's bow mouth and kissed Cohan right on his lips.

She shook hands with Bill and Hump but her eyes remained focused on Cohan. That very night he offered her the role of Leola Lane opposite him in his new production, *The Song and Dance Man*. Without even knowing what the role entailed, she accepted on the spot.

Hump remembered Mayo as a cute little blonde, and Bill and he would like to have dated her, even though Bill was married and Hump engaged. But it was obvious that Cohan had seen her first and had a lot more to offer her.

Years later, Mayo recalled her first meeting with Cohan "which changed my life." She also recollected meeting Bill Brady Jr., the son of the producer of *The Mad Honeymoon*. She had "no memory whatsoever" of being introduced to Hump. She later told an interviewer, "If someone had told me then that I would one day become the third Mrs. Bogart, I would have fallen on my cute ass."

***

Hump went back to working as a stage manager for Brady Sr. At night he frequented the speakeasies, spending every dollar he made. Sometimes Helen accompanied him, and often he was joined by Bill and his new wife, the always competent but never exciting actress, Katharine Alexander, who was forging ahead with her career playing wronged wives, society snobs, and respectable women. John Barrymore was in hot pursuit of her, but she claimed she was still faithful to

Mayo Methot *(top photo)* and George M.Cohan

Bill.

Sometimes the director, John Cromwell, would also join the crowd as it made its way from such mob joints in Harlem as the Cotton Club over to Connie's Inn. When they had more money, Hump's party showed up at The Dover Club.

With Stuart Rose, Hump continued to go horseback riding in Central Park. Stuart and Hump also took up ice skating, usually with Hump's sister, Frances. Stuart and Frances were still "an item," as they called it.

Smoking his Andover pipe, Hump went sailing off Long Island whenever he was free from Broadway. He was seen frequently at Mayfair, an actors club, when he wasn't at the Lambs Club, another hangout for actors. Often he took Helen dancing at the Ritz-Carlton Hotel, and the 21 Club remained his favorite watering hole. He was also becoming known for his expert chess playing.

When a year went by and Hump wasn't offered another role, he felt his career as an actor had come to an end. Unexpectedly, Rosalie Stewart, a producer, sent him a script, *Meet the Wife*, a comedy starring Mary Boland and Clifton Webb. Hump was offered the role of a young, fresh-faced reporter, Gregory Brown, in this three-act comedy by Lynn Starling, an up-and-coming playwright of her day.

Mary Boland was already an established stage star when Hump first met her. Born in Philadelphia in 1880, she'd begun her career at the age of fifteen, following the death of her actor father, W.A. Boland. Her film debut in 1914 was in *The Edge of the Abyss*. She'd become a star in 1919 playing the stately scatterbrain, Mrs. Wheeler, in Booth Tarkington's *Clarence* opposite Alfred Lunt.

From the first day they met, Hump was fascinated by the male co-star of *Meet the Wife*. Clifton Webb and Bogie would become friends and remain so for the rest of their lives together. They were an odd couple. Webb was an immaculate dresser and had impeccable manners, but this young dancer turned actor was known along Broadway as "Miss Priss." Born in Indianapolis

Mary Boland

in 1891, he changed his name from Webb Parmallee Hollenbeck to Clifton Webb. Hump both affectionately and jokingly called him Parmallee.

Known as "the Irritable Bachelor," Clifton even then was a notorious homosexual, specializing in seducing young juvenile leads who appeared with him. The still handsome Hump became his chief target during rehearsals for *Meet the Wife*. Hump felt as ardently pursued by Clifton as he had been by Rod La Rocque when he'd directed that actor in the film, *Life*.

One night at a Harlem night spot, Hump decided to confront Clifton. "I'm not going to become your boy, and if you come on to me again I'll punch you out," Hump told him. "But I will be your friend. I like you a hell of a lot. I don't take it up the ass."

"Don't worry, my dear fellow," Clifton said. "I'm a famous bottom." Clifton bent over the table and affectionately kissed Hump on the nose. Somehow this impulsive act endeared Clifton all the more to Hump. Never again did seduction rear its head.

Webb marked the beginning of a series of friendships—not love relationships—that Bogie would have with homosexuals, including the closeted Spencer Tracy and the not-so-closeted Noël Coward and Truman Capote.

Meet the Wife opened at New York's Klaw Theater and would run for 232 performances, with Hump drawing a weekly paycheck of $150, which he spent immediately. A critic for *The New York World* gave Hump the first good notice of his career, referring to the role he played as that of "a handsome and nicely mannered reporter, which is refreshing."

Two nights before the play closed, Hump had been up all night partying in the hot spots of Harlem. When he showed up the next day to perform in *Meet the Wife*, he was hung over and had had no sleep.

On stage during a pivotal scene, he forgot his lines and stood looking glazed against the scenery. Boland was forced to frantically ad lib and even had to feed him some of his lines, hoping he would pick up the rhythm of the play. When the curtain was pulled, she walked backstage and slapped his face real hard. "I'll see to it that you never work again on Broadway."

The next night, at the closing performance, he knew all his lines. However, after Act Two, as if determined to sabotage his career, he disappeared into a dive across the street, claiming he was starved and wanted a plate of ham and eggs. Somehow he completely forgot that he had to stick around to deliver four lines in Act Three.

When he did remember, he raced toward the theater door, just in time to hear the applause as the curtain went down. The stage manager, Bert French, who was also producing the play with Rosalie Stewart, slugged Hump, who struck back, hitting French in the nose just as Boland and Webb were taking their final bows.

Clifton Webb

Chiming in with Boland, French also threatened to end Hump's Broadway days. But Hump was heartened that Maud, without Belmont, showed up that night and praised his acting skill. Being Maud, she had to add a warning. "An actor will spend most of his life starving between parts, and you could have done so much more with your life."

His spirits were lifted when an out-of-town reviewer, Peggy Hill, of Atlanta, saw the play and informed her readers that "Humphrey Bogart is more manly and a lot handsomer than Rudolph Valentino. If I had to be carried away to a Sheik's tent in the desert, I'd much rather be in Bogart's arms than prissy Valentino's."

***

Hump couldn't take Boland's threat to destroy his stage career too seriously. Bill Brady was producing a Broadway play with a part in it just right for Hump. Once again, when all else failed, he could count on the dependable, reliable, and steadfast Brady family.

Less than one month after *Meet the Wife* closed, Hump was offered his biggest role to date, the meaty part of an aviator in a play, *Nerves*, which was being both directed and produced by Bill Brady Jr. The play had been written by Stephen Vincent Benét and John Farrar, and contained only two acts, unusually short for that day. The first act takes place at a Yale house party where several couples, all on the same night, commit themselves to be engaged. The second act occurs in the officers' mess of a squadron of American aviators based in France during World War I. The wartime experience shatters the nerves of one of the aviators—hence, the title of the play.

The star of the show was the now largely forgotten Marie Curtis, who had just completed a run on Broadway in the play, *Time*. Earlier, her attempts at a career in silent films had bombed after she'd appeared as "Lady Dolly" in *Her Greatest Love*.

She played opposite Paul Kelly, only years before his international notoriety and jail term as a convicted man slaughterer.

Bill angered Hump by casting their longtime friend, Kenneth MacKenna, in the third lead over Hump's own fourth billing. Although they would eventually become bitter rivals over the affections of Mary Philips, Kenneth at the time was still a close friend of Hump's, and a faithful member of the coterie that still referred to itself as "the pussy posse," a group that included John Cromwell and Bill Brady, Jr.

Although not officially a member of the posse, Kenneth's brother, Jo Mielziner, signed on as stage designer. It was during rehearsals for *Nerves* that Hump realized for the first time what an immense talent Jo was. Born in Paris

78

two years after Hump, Jo, like Kenneth, was the son of a Jewish and Irish marriage.

The same year Jo designed the sets for *Nerves*, he also created sets for *The Guardsman*. Written by Ferenc Molnar, it was an early Theatre Guild production that brought Jo to the attentions of the moguls of Broadway.

Before his death in 1976, Jo would go on to design the sets for at least 270 stage and film productions. His most memorable stage work included such classics as *Strange Interlude; Death of a Salesman; Carousel; The King and I; South Pacific; Look Homeward, Angel; Tea and Sympathy, Picnic,* and *The Emperor Jones.*

The young actress Mary Philips was cast as one of the supporting players in *Nerves*. Three years younger than Hump, Mary was born in New London and educated in a convent in New Haven. "In those days," as Bogie later recalled, describing his stage career, "I was always deflowering maidens fresh from some God damn convent." Mary characterized herself as a "staunch New Englander but with Irish wit and temperament." When she first met Hump, she later declared, she detected a strong Puritan streak in him.

She'd made her debut as a chorus girl showing off her bosom and her legs in the *Follies Revue of 1919*. It was what playwright James Kirkwood Jr. decades later in *A Chorus Line* would call a "tits and ass" part.

Mary would go on to appear in such productions as *Two Girls Wanted* and *The Old Soak*, which did good business but would hardly merit a footnote in theatrical histories of the 20s.

She had a pretty face with penetrating gray-blue eyes. She would often be compared, to her detriment, to the more successful actress, Ina Claire.

By today's standards of beauty, Mary had a long nose. Hump kidded her, calling it "the beak." "Where do you put that nose when you go to kiss a man?" he asked her during rehearsals. "That's for me to know and for you to find out," Mary told him.

Except for that nose, she had the most perfectly formed lips of all of Bogie's future wives. Her hands were her most attractive feature, and critics often wrote that they were "porcelain like and delicate."

Mary was short and rather small. "Just my

Humphrey Bogart with Mary Philips

type," Hump told Kenneth. She was understanding, sympathetic, and attractive but not flashy, as opposed to the more self-centered and narcissistic Helen. And in definite contrast to Hump's mother, Maud, she was supportive of, rather than critical of, men.

Mary's appearance as a fragile doll was deceiving. She was actually a sports-loving outdoor girl who excelled in tennis and golf. Her Irish temper matched that of Helen's.

During rehearsals, Mary infuriated Hump. In his big scene, when he was to be left alone on the stage, Mary walked toward the wings. "That was what she was supposed to do," Bogie later recalled. "But it was the damn way she walked off. I would have to wait until I saw Marilyn Monroe in the 1951 movie, *Niagara*, before I'd see a walk like that again. I confronted her back stage and accused her of upstaging me. That seemed to piss her off. She slapped my face and told me that she'd walk any way she damn well pleased, and there wasn't anything I could do about it. I wanted to punch her out. I'd hit ladies before and would again. But somehow that slap turned me on. I felt I could really fall for this gal."

The more he worked with Mary, the more intrigued Hump became. Mary told him that she could hold her liquor better than he did. Back then, Hump always said, "I don't trust women who don't drink. They'll betray you every time."

Kenneth was also growing increasingly intrigued by Mary. He even warned Hump to "lay off Mary. She's gonna become my gal, and besides you're engaged to Helen."

"Helen knows I see women on the side," Hump said. "Fuck you, asshole. Helen herself sees women on the side. Maybe I'll take Mary back to Helen's apartment. We could share her."

Kenneth punched him in the mouth. Before a major fight could break out, Bill Brady, Jr. separated the two actors. "You're like two fucking roosters fighting over the prize hen in the barnyard. Don't you guys know there are more than enough women on Broadway to go around? There are at least three showgals for every single male since at least half the men in the theater are fairies. Enjoy! Enjoy! As for Mary, I've taken director's privilege. She got hired on the casting couch. For the duration of the play, she's my private piece and don't tell Katharine."

Both Kenneth and Hump were shocked to learn that Mary was having an affair with Bill. At the Hotsy Totsy that night, Kenneth and Hump repaired their friendship over several tall gin fizzes. "Let's don't let a woman come between us," Kenneth said. "If Bill is fucking Mary, that makes her a slut. We can pick up any slut we want in this club in five minutes. Wanta bet?"

Hump didn't take him up on the bet, knowing that what Kenneth said was true. Midnight found the two men, along with "two sluts," checking into the Hotel Baltimore. They seduced the women on the same double bed, switching partners around two o'clock.

Years later, Mary would rank the sexual performances of the three leading members of the pussy posse in this order: Number one, Bill Brady Jr. "because of his incredible technique"; number two, Kenneth McKenna because "of the sincerity in his eyes when he got on top of you," and, number three, Humphrey Bogart "because he always had a far and distant look in his eyes when he was making love to you, enough so that you always suspected that his mind was somewhere else."

Both Hump and Kenneth feared that Bill was jeopardizing his marriage to Katharine by going out to the speakeasies every night with Mary. "Never fear," Bill assured them. "Katherine specializes in wronged wife parts. I'm just giving her first-hand experience so she'll be a better actress."

One night Bill called Hump to tell him that he'd just bailed Mary out of jail. They had been caught staggering drunk from the speakeasy, Hotsy Totsy. When a cop tried to arrest Mary, she bit his finger down to the bone. She was hauled off to the pokey. Bill had had far more to drink than Mary, but he was not arrested. Brady Sr. posted a five-hundred dollar bail, securing her release.

Nerves opened at the Comedy Theater on September 1, 1924, a date that roughly coincided with the opening of *What Price Glory?*. *Glory* became the biggest hit of any play addressing the issues of World War I, and audiences and critics alike flocked to it instead of *Nerves*. *Nerves* would run for only sixteen performances, as critics ridiculed it and audiences stayed away in droves. Brady, Sr. denounced his son for producing such a flop.

Ironically, Hump received respectable reviews for his role in the play, enough—in Mary's opinion—to give him a "swelled head." Even Hump's nemesis, the critic, Alexander Woollcott, who'd denounced him as the "inadequate sprig" wrote, "Those words are hereby eaten."

Another prominent critic of the day was Heywood Broun, a well-known sports writer and columnist for New York newspapers, and also a leading member of the Socialist Party until he was expelled in 1933. Broun found Hump's performance "most effective." Hump couldn't help but be delighted when Broun faulted co-actor Kenneth's performance, claiming that the actor "suffers from trying too hard

Theatrical, venomous, and bitchy: Alexander Woollcott

to make a feeble play take on the breath of life."

At the play's closing, Helen was preparing to take her own Broadway success, *Seventh Heaven*, to Los Angeles, leaving Hump at her apartment. Before departing, she told Hump that she would marry him but was too busy to fit a wedding into her busy schedule. "I'm at the height of my stardom," she told him, "and I can't let a little thing like marriage stand in my way. Some stars like Bernhardt will last forever. In my case, I fear I will burn terribly bright, then flicker out." Unlike Hump, she spoke in highly dramatic terms, unusual for a person with so little formal education.

As Helen boarded the train to Los Angeles, going via Chicago, she told Hump that he didn't necessarily have to be lonely when she was away in spite of their engagement. She gave him the telephone number of "a young and very beautiful actress that I've been dating. Call her. She's very amusing. She and I are going nowhere fast in our relationship. Women, I fear, are mere playthings for her. She really prefers men. Besides no one can replace Tallulah—that whore—in my life."

Bidding Helen good-bye, Hump returned to the empty apartment. After three hours and drunk on gin, he dialed the number of Helen's actress friend. He was determined to find out the degree to which this mystery woman liked men.

On the other end of the line, a haunting, dramatic voice picked up the receiver. "Hello, this is Louise Brooks. Who's this?"

***

After one night with her, Hump was so mesmerized by Louise Brooks that he told Bill Brady that he wanted to break off his engagement with Helen and propose to "Brooksie" instead. He claimed that she was the best sex he'd ever had with any woman. "She's one earthy broad," Hump said. "We did things I've never even heard of before."

Bill was disdainful of Louise. "She's nothing but a teenage prostitute. She's shacked up with that high roller, A.C. Blumenthal, who's taking over for Ziegfeld. Brooks is a real casting-couch climber. I also hear she's a lesbian."

On their first date together, Hump had shown up at her hotel dressed for dinner, as she'd accepted his invitation to go to a supper club. When she opened the door to her room, she wore a sheer white nightgown with nothing on underneath it. "Come on in, handsome," she said, reaching for his hand. "We'll have room service send us a hamburger. That way, we'll have more time in the sack, as I have to get up early in the morning."

Hump was immediately taken with this "Kansas sunflower," a former Ziegfeld Follies dancer who'd also appeared in George White's *Scandals*. Her raven-black hair was radiant, and she'd styled it in a way that had already led to her reputation as "the girl in the black helmet." She wore it closely cropped in an exaggerated page-boy style.

As she invited him in and offered him some whiskey, he felt that he was encountering the Jazz Age flapper supreme, perhaps someone not real but a creation of F. Scott Fitzgerald.

"Helen tells me you're not rich but I agreed to see you anyway," Louise said. "I have this friend, Peggy Fears, who dances in the Follies. She has a strict rule about dating, 'No ice, no dice.' She thinks I should go out only with rich stage-door Johnnies. But I also like to get plowed, and these old guys are too worn out for my tastes. That's why I turn to guys like you. Trinkets are nice but getting plowed for fun is one of the joys of life, and I want it all."

"I hope I won't disappoint," Hump said.

"I'm sure you won't," Louise said. "Helen has already given me a critique. I asked Helen if you were a redhead. She assured me you were brunette."

"What have you got against redheaded men?"

"I absolutely refuse to go to bed with them," she said. "Based on my experience, I have found that their pricks are always tiny and even misshapen, usually bent to the left and most unappetizing."

"You've lost me there," he said, downing the rest of his whiskey. "I've never done a survey."

"Take my word for it," she said, going over to him and kissing him on the lips as he sat in her sole armchair. When she finally broke away, she said, "You have the most beautiful lips I've ever seen in any man."

"Thanks."

"You've got this little scar on your upper lip. It adds character to your face. I especially like this quilted piece that hangs down in a tiny scallop." She ran her tongue along it. "It's an

Two views of Louise Brooks

imperfection I find terribly appealing."

"Hell," he said, drawing back slightly, not at all comfortable with the conversation. "I should have it surgically removed."

"I disapprove of surgically removing skin from men," she said. "I hope you're not circumcised because I delight in men with foreskins."

"I'm all there," he said, as she reached to fondle him.

"I like the feel of it," she said. "You see I'm a basket-watcher. That's why I spend a lot of time at the ballet watching men in form-fitting leotards. I hate most men's trousers. Except for a few sailors who wear tight pants, they're usually far too baggy."

"You're some gal," he said, "I never heard a woman talk like you."

"Don't get me wrong," Louise said. "An average size prick can offer some satisfaction to a woman but they always leave one unfulfilled. There are three things I like done to me, and only a big prick can do the job."

"Just three?" he said.

"That's right. Unless you can conjure up something new." She rose from his lap, removing her nightgown to stand nude in front of him. "Audition time." With her head she motioned to her empty double bed.

As Hump would later relate to Bill, "It was the wildest ride I've ever had in my life. If Brooksie had a hole somewhere, she wanted it plugged."

After their time together in bed, both Bogie and Louise cleaned themselves up. While he put back on his trousers, she slipped into a red dress. "I've got this fabulous idea," she said. "Get dressed. I want you to walk along Broadway with me. We'll look at all the names up in lights and imagine that one day the names of Louise Brooks and Humphrey Bogart will be up there for all the world to see."

As he was reaching for his trousers, she challenged him. "Edmund Goulding told me that all actresses should be compared to a flower. I can't decide what flower to be? You decide for me."

He looked her over carefully from her tiny feet to her helmet hairdo. "An exotic black orchid."

***

Like many actors of the 20s, including Gary Cooper, Hump went through a period where he tried to model himself after America's reigning heartthrob of the screen, Rudolph Valentino, who had electrified audiences, especially women, with his performances in *The Four Horsemen of the Apocalypse* and *The Sheik.*

Although the men did not really look alike, Broadway writers often cited the physical resemblance between Valentino and Hump. Typical of the com-

84

ments was an interview written by Elita Miller Lenz in 1924. "Humphrey Bogart is one of the few young actors along Broadway that can be classed as a Valentino type in color, which should help much in the matter of future popularity."

Just for fun, Helen acquired a Sheik costume for Hump, which he wore to a masquerade ball at the Plaza Hotel. Helen herself appeared disguised as Agnes Ayres, who had starred opposite Valentino in *The Sheik*. Their photograph ended up in the New York papers.

Helen had even gone so far as to purchase pink silk underwear for Hump, after reading in a fan magazine that Natacha Rambova, Valentino's second wife, insisted that her husband appear "only in pink bloomers."

Whenever Hump pulled off his trousers in the bedroom of many a chorus girl, his partner for the evening often laughed at his "pink powder puff" underwear. However, when Hump slipped off what he called "those sissy drawers," the laughter stopped as he went about his sexual maneuvering for the evening.

As 1924 drew to a close, producer and playwright Barry Connors offered Hump the role of the male lead in a three-act comedy directed by John Hayden. The play was *Hell's Bells*, and it starred two women, the established Broadway actress, Olive May, and also Shirley Booth making her debut at the dawn of a stage and film career that would bring her international fame.

Connors described Jimmy Todhunter, the character Hump would play, as "a regular fellow of twenty-seven, well-educated, ambitious, self-reliant, and industrious." The role would launch Hump into a series of juvenile parts, each of which required the standard costume for an *ingenu* of that era—white duck trousers and a blue blazer. Each of these early roles was radically more wholesome than some of the gangster and tough guy roles (among them Duke Mantee, Sam Spade, Charlie Allnut, and Captain Queeg) that Hump would later play. But at least in the 1920s, Hump became known for playing "young sprigs."

Hell's Bells would hardly be remembered except for one immortal line, which Hump delivered and which would forever haunt him, becoming part of the national vocabulary.

The director, Hayden, needed a device to move some actors off the stage to make way for a scene that focused only on his two leading actresses, Shirley Booth and Olive May. He devised a setup whereby Hump appeared on stage carrying a tennis racquet. Surveying the male actors, he asked of them, "Tennis any-

Shirley Booth

one?" Even today, *Casablanca's* Rick is ridiculed for playing such a toothsome juvenile with such a jejune image.

Although admitting that he had at one time or another delivered some of the most ridiculous lines ever written for the Broadway stage, Hump in later life repeatedly denied that he had come on stage and said, "Tennis, anyone?" in *Hell's Bells* or any other play. Hump claimed the line was, "It's forty-love outside. Anyone care to watch?"

However, Richard Watts Jr., longtime theater critic for *The New York Post*, claimed that he reviewed the opening night of *Hell's Bells* and that indeed Bogart did say that line. "I made a note of it but didn't publish it in my review."

When an attempt at a revival of the play was made in 1934 for a road show tour, Hayden's original script was discovered. The line about it being "forty-love outside" was indeed in the script as Bogie later claimed. But before opening night, Hayden had crossed over the line and written, "Tennis anyone?"

In later life Bogie often spoke bitterly of his early career on the stage. "With my hair slicked back, I'd appear in white flannels with pale blue knit sweaters, always carrying a tennis racquet. Those early parts made me feel silly and girlish. The god damn director would have me come out modeling the latest pinch-back sports coat with pansy neck cloths and a swishy new hairdo."

The star of *Hell's Bells*, Olive May, had been appearing on Broadway since Hump was one year old, introducing herself to audiences in *The Surprises of Love* on January 22, 1900.

During rehearsals Hump met and became briefly attached to Shirley Booth, who was one year older than he was. Those who know her today only as the irrepressible maid on the television series, *Hazel*, which ran from 1961 to 1966, may not understand the physical allure that Shirley had during her youth. In 1925 she was a lovely, gracious, and even beautiful woman. Born Thelma Booth Ford in New York City, she had had an even more miserable childhood than Hump. Her mother, Virginia Wright, was terminally ill, and her father, business executive, Albert J. Ford, was a brutal, stern father. Over her father's objections and at the age of fourteen, Shirley dropped out of school, determined to be an actress on stage.

Interviewed years later at her saltbox house in North Chatham, Massachusetts, she was reluctant to talk about her involvement with Bogie.

"I wouldn't call our first meeting an affair, more like a weekend together," she said. "He was a real gentleman, very polite and respectful of women, although I'd heard that he had a run-in or two with the star, Olive May. We were two frightened kids trying to make our way on Broadway, and we sensed a soulmate in each other, and perhaps turned to each other for a little comfort.

I don't have much to say about that. On the few occasions we talked later in life, we both sympathized with each other about how long it took each of us to become a star."

Hell's Bells opened at the Wallack Theatre on the night of January 26, 1925. It was a flop, running for only fifteen performances. The only consolation for Hump was a claim by Alan Dale, critic for *The New York American*, that "Bogart gorgeously acted his role."

"I don't know how it happened," Bogie later said. "Maybe it was because I'd appeared in three comedies on Broadway, *Swifty, Meet the Wife*, and *Hell's Bells*. All of a sudden I was typecast as a comedy actor on stage. The next few years would offer me nothing but a series of three-act comedies, most of them not funny."

***

Helen was a friend of Woollcott. She felt that Hump's career would be advanced if he actually met some of the critics who would one day review his future plays.

He escorted her to a speakeasy, Tony's, which was patronized by hard-drinking actors and writers. There Hump met the owner, Tony Soma, who loved artists and who welcomed him with great enthusiasm. That welcome would continue for years even when Hump went as long as three months without paying his large and forever mounting bar tabs.

Tony's was the kind of watering hole where Dorothy Parker and Robert Benchley would go with Scott and Zelda Fitzgerald to celebrate Jack Dempsey's four-round victory over Georges Carpentier. When Hump first saw all the celebrated patrons of Tony's, he felt that it was another branch of the famous Algonquin Roundtable. One by one he met all of them.

He was first introduced to Robert Sherwood, who would one day write *The Petrified Forest* which would be Bogie's last stage play, and also his best, and would be made into a film with Bogie and Bette Davis that would become the biggest break of his movie career in the 1930s.

Helen decided she had "to work the room." Before she had finished making the rounds, she introduced Hump to the newspaper reporter, Mark Hellinger, who invited him for a drink at the bar. Even though he couldn't afford it in those days, Mark was known for picking up everyone's bar tabs. Hump and Mark liked each other at once, having no inkling, of course, what important roles they would play in each other's future life.

Tony put his arm around Hump and invited him to frequent his bar and "make it your favorite. You're always welcome here. In return, I want you to marry that Helen. She's one good-looking woman, and I'm afraid some man is going to snare her if you don't tie the knot."

"I'll think about it," Hump said, although he showed up at Tony's the following night without his bride-to-be.

After only two nights, Hump became a regular at Tony's, often dropping in alone and continuing to meet and talk to some of the fabulous personalities of New York in the 1920s.

On nights when Hump drank too much, he'd become quite caustic. One night he insulted Gentlemen Jim Corbett, the boxing champ. He grabbed Hump by the back of the neck and tossed him out onto the rainy street.

Six months went by before Hump dared enter Tony's again. When he did, he always sent a friend ahead of him to see if Gentleman Jim was among the patrons that night.

***

When the newspaper reporter, Mark Hellinger, finally got around to inviting Hump for that night on the town, he made up for lost time. Mark's world, then known as "gay Broadway," was comprised of a square mile of real estate between 40th and 50th streets, bounded by 6th and 8th Avenue. If it wasn't the world's most glamorous mile, it was the most exciting, a district of dime-a-dance joints, speakeasies, chop-suey outlets, cabarets, theaters, movie houses, plush apartments for kept women, panhandlers, Minsky's Burlesque, the Palace Theater, and even Spinrad's Barbershop.

The barbershop was pointed out to Hump by Mark who suggested he should go in there tomorrow and ask for George. "If you're going to be a big Broadway star, you've got to get your hair cut right," Mark said. He also

Mark Hellinger

promised Hump to introduce him to his tailor. "The Jimmy Walker cut is the way to go." Hump had heard about the political aspirations of this fancy dresser, whose career had included stints as a Broadway actor. He was also a talented musician, having written such songs as "Will You Love Me in December As You Do in May?" Rising through the ranks of Tammany Hall, Jimmy Walker was entering the mayor's race.

Hellinger was on a first-name basis with Jack Dempsey, Clarence Darrow, Theodore Dreiser, Ethel Barrymore, Florenz Ziegfeld, W.C. Fields, Eddie Cantor, Jeanne Eagles, Bobby Jones, and even Eleanora Duse and Aimee Semple McPherson. He spent his nights in some of New York's five-thousand speakeasies devoted to drinking "Staten Island or New Jersey champagne" at $35 a bottle or unreliable Bahamian Scotch at $20 a fifth.

During his rounds, Mark was accompanied by another reporter, columnist Walter Winchell. Hellinger eventually evolved into the world's first Broadway reporter, Winchell the first of the Broadway gossip columnists. The two men were seen together practically every night of the week, so much so that they were rumored to be lovers.

Disdaining Winchell's show biz gossip, Mark preferred heart-rending sob stories, filled with laughter and tears, with an O'Henry ending. Mark called his reporting "short stories about the people of Broadway," ranging from the long-legged Ziegfeld girls to the Irish immigrant cop on the block with a nightstick, to the little Sicilian hood who dreamed that he might one day take over Al Capone's crime empire.

Mark had invited Hump to El Fey club, run by bootlegger Larry Fay. (The club was named after him but spelled slightly differently.) Rumor had it that Fay didn't know how to spell his name. The club's hostess was the fabulous Texas Guinan, whose own club had recently been closed by the police for selling bootleg hooch.

Hump was eager to meet Guinan, a name known all over Broadway. The flamboyant show-biz personality and actress was born in Texas in 1884 as Mary Louise Cecilia Guinan. The robust Irish lass grew up on a small ranch near Waco where she became an accomplished horseback rider and roper. She went from there into live Wild West dramas, and in time ended up in the chorus line in such Chicago comedies as *The Gay Musician*.

In Hollywood, cast as the gun-girl heroine in a silent screen western, *The Wildcat* in 1917, this pistol-packing, barrel-riding queen of the West became America's first movie cowgirl long before the likes of Dale Evans. She went on to appear as a gunslinger in *The Gun Woman* in 1918 and *Little Miss Deputy* in 1919 before being lured by the aura of New York in the Roaring Twenties.

Texas Guinan

When Hump entered the bar with Mark, Guinan called out, "Hello, suckers! Come on in and leave your wallet on the bar." On meeting her, Hump liked her free-wheeling, devil-may-care aura. "I'm hanging out at Larry's dump," she said, "because the cops have padlocked my place. I don't have to worry about an automobile ride in New York. Taxpayers foot the bill. Unfortunately, my free ride from the city is always to jail. I've fucked Jimmy Walker six times. He owes me plenty of favors. When he becomes mayor, the cops will get off my back except when they come around to fuck me in the ass."

"You're my kind of gal," Hump said to Texas as Mark lost himself in the bowels of the club.

"I've got some special entertainment planned for you tonight in more ways than one," Texas said.

She ordered Hump a drink, although she always denied that alcohol was sold in her speakeasies. When his drink was served, she told Hump where Fay had stolen the booze. "The other night some of Fay's hoods armed themselves with pistols, sawed-off shotguns, and Tommy guns," she said. "They piled into a large boat and sailed ten miles out to sea where they hijacked a French freighter like a team of God damn pirates. They made off with five-hundred cases of whiskey, wine, champagne, and brandy. Fay didn't go out on the raid himself. He was waiting on shore and paid a measly one-hundred bucks for the whole thing. He'll make thousands off the stuff, especially when my brother, Tommy, waters it down at the bar."

Surveying the club, she said, "I'm not doing too bad. When I was a movie star in Hollywood, I earned fifty dollars a week—those asshole cheats out there. Before the year is out in New York, I expect to earn $700,000."

As the night progressed, she told him that a producer was here tonight, considering casting her in the appropriately titled Broadway review *Padlocks of 1925*. It took a while for the revue to be produced, and the title had to be changed to *Padlocks of 1927*.

"I'm gonna die young," Texas told him. "But I'm gonna have a hell of a lot of fun along the way. What about you, Bogart?"

"I'm gonna die young too but I'm gonna have more fun than you," he said.

"I'll race you to the finish line, sucker," she said before getting up to announce the star act of the evening.

In another one of the strange coincidences in Hump's life, the act being introduced by Texas that night at El Fey was a dance routine by George Raft.

This was the same George Raft that would become the legendary Broadway dancer, the Hollywood tough guy, the gambler, and Don Juan himself with a life-long courtship with the underworld. Hump had read in Winchell's column that Raft had taught the Charleston to Edward, Prince of Wales, later King Edward VIII, and later, the Duke of Windsor.

In his early reviews, Hump was called the Valentino of Broadway. But in Hollywood it was George Raft who'd be billed as Paramount's "replacement" for the long-dead Valentino.

To Hump's regret in the 30s, Warner Brothers eventually signed Raft to a stable of cinema tough guys that included Edward G. Robinson and James Cagney. Hump would often find that whenever he was competing for a choice film role, Raft got the part instead.

***

Future movie stardom was hardly on Hump's mind as he sat mesmerized, watching Raft dance to an audience of patrons consisting of millionaires and bluebloods mingling with nattily dressed hoodlums.

After introducing Raft, the brassy, shoot-'em-up gal, Texas herself, rejoined Hump at table. "Raft is the weirdest, maddest dancer you've ever seen," Texas said in her tough, deep voice. She quickly waved at a couple entering to see Raft dance. "Fuck, I'm starting to attract the literati." Hump recognized Robert Sherwood escorting Dorothy Parker.

"Raft mesmerizes my customers," Texas said. "All eyes shine on Raft as he whirls faster and faster. Every night he stops the show. He's taking in a thousand big ones a week."

Hump didn't need this running dance critique from Texas. He watched in fascination as Raft performed his mongrel dance, called "the Peabody." It was a fantastic speed dance with all kinds of interpolations, a choreography strangely known as "cake-eating." The dance was filled with dozens of twists, turns, and jerks.

The owner of the club, Fay, joined Texas and Hump at table. It was obvious that he'd been quarreling with Texas. Texas was attracting an upper-crust crowd of the Whitneys, the Vanderbilts, and the Astors, whereas Fay was inviting his hoodlum friends from Brooklyn. There was no place with such a mixed clientele in all of New York. An aristocrat like Vincent Astor could be spotted at the bar drinking with five gun-toting and trigger-happy desperados.

Hump was equally fascinated by Raft's incredible speed dance and by Fay himself. Bootlegger Fay looked like a tough hood from Brooklyn, perhaps an unruly labor organizer, more than the owner of a swank night club. Hump later claimed that he used Fay as his role model when he first had to impersonate a gangster in films.

After his performance, Texas brought Raft over to the table to meet Hump. "Here's the actor who's gonna marry Helen Menken." And although they were later to become bitter rivals for the same

George Raft, dancing.....
in this case, with
Carole Lombard

film roles, Hump liked Raft at once. The young dancer was actually the character that latter-day film fans thought Bogie was, even though his background and character were almost the complete opposite of Raft's.

Raft had slicked down his black hair with what appeared to be a whole jar of Vaseline, a hairstyle that had become known as the patent-leather look. Unlike the baggy suits of the day, he wore tight, form-fitting trousers and jackets, along with three diamond rings, one on his pinkie.

He spoke with such brutal honesty and candor about who he was and what he did that Hump was mildly surprised that he'd been so confessional to a stranger. "Listen, unless you're going to fuck Texas tonight, I can get you a hot date," Raft said. "I'll give you the phone number of this go-to-hell pussy, Grayce Mulrooney. She's my wife."

Jazz-age actors, gigolos and roommates George Raft *(top photo)* and *(bottom photo)* Rudolph Valentino

At first Hump thought that Raft was joking until he realized that the dancer was perfectly serious.

"She's alone every night." Raft pointed to a cute little brunette dancing in the chorus line. "That's Ruby Keeler, She's only fourteen and working for Texas and Fay illegally. I'm going to go for her tonight. I'm gonna make the big play. Sometimes I fuck young."

Two men in their twenties passed by their table en route to the men's room. In their tuxedos, each one looked like a twin of Rudolph Valentino. "Everybody's trying to get in on the Valentino act," Raft said contemptuously. "I've even read that about you."

"I don't think I'm going to become another Valentino," Hump said. "We're too different. Besides, I don't look that good in Arab drag."

Raft laughed. "There's talk that I'll be the screen's next Valentino, although it seems like Ramon Novarro has beat me out. I know Rudy very well. We once shared a room together when we were going through rough days back in our taxi-dancing times, long before America knew what a Sheik was."

"I heard he was a gigolo," Hump said.

"You might call it that," Raft said, downing a whiskey. "We were both gigolos, hiring ourselves out on the dance floor for a buck. Rudy's first

92

wife, Jean Acker, keeps writing me to go on the road with her in a dance act, imitating the act that Natacha Rambova and Rudy toured in. Acker wants the billing to read, 'Mrs. Rudolph Valentino and George Raft.' No way. I'm gonna be a star without any help from the Valentino name."

Raft told Hump that after work, and while still dressed in his tuxedo, he ran beer convoys. "I work not just for Fay but for Dutch Schultz and 'Legs' Diamond," Raft said. "Mostly I work for a guy called Big Frenchy. Sometimes we make heists when we raid our competition's booze being trucked into New York. You might think I'm a fantastic dancer, but I'm even better as a truck driver. I can cut corners on two wheels. Turn a truck on a dime and hold the fucker steady going eighty miles an hour, all the time ducking some trigger-happy fool."

He wasn't making this up, although it sounded like a script for one of the films both men would later make at Warner Brothers. Raft also wasn't lying about his driving skills. Because of his expertise learned on illegal booze heists in New York in the Twenties, he would one day save Bogie's life when the brakes gave out on a truck Raft was driving on the set of a film.

Texas returned to the table to warn Raft that she was about to introduce him for his second show of the evening. When Raft excused himself, Texas told Hump that since he had seen Raft dance, she had more entertainment planned for him. "But for the grand finale, you're coming to bed with me," Texas said, leaning over to kiss his lips.

One of the waiters ushered Hump into one of the backrooms where the focused beam of a movie projector revealed a room filled with a blue haze from the heavy smoking of the other male patrons. When the film went on, Hump could understand why these were called blue movies. The star of tonight's porn movie was a dancer who'd been a hit in stag movies and a star at private smokers before going on to Hollywood.

As the actress on film danced the Charleston in the nude, the cameraman told Hump her name was Lucille LeSueur.

Fast forward: It is 1954, and Hump, the "King of Hollywood," is escorting the "Queen of Hollywood" to the Academy Awards ceremony.

More than a decade after Louis B. Mayer had kicked Hump's date for the evening off the MGM lot, she'd bounced back to regain her throne as queen, although not for long.

With a mink stole draped across her shoulder and around her wrinkled neck, Bogie was taking out Joan Crawford, once known as Lucille LeSueur.

***

The Broadway season was ripe for Bogie's women-to-be in 1925, carrying through the spring of 1926. Wife-to-be number one, Helen Menken, was appearing in *Makropoulos Secret*. Wife number two, Mary Philips, was a star in *The Wisdom Tooth*, and wife number three, Mayo Methot, was appearing in *Alias the Deacon*. Wife number four? The one-year old Betty Bacall was in a Bronx nursery in her diapers.

The actress, Mary Boland, had threatened to destroy Hump's stage career because of his unprofessional conduct when he'd appeared with her in *Meet the Wife*. When no suitable young actor could be found for her new three-act comedy, she reluctantly said, "Okay, get Bogart."

Cradle Snatchers was written by Norma Mitchell and Russell Medcraft and directed by Sam Forrest. It was a raucous and bawdy farce about three society women who sneak away with three handsome college men hired as gigolos. The plot thickens when the husbands show up at the same hideaway, thinking that it's a high-class bordello.

It was well-cast, especially with the enormously comical actress Edna May Oliver in a co-starring role. Hump played a minor role, that of Jose Vallejo. Also appearing in a minor role was another actor, Raymond Guion, whom Hump befriended.

Like Rod La Rocque, Raymond wasn't pleased with his name. After several drunken talks in speakeasies, he won Hump's approval for his new stage name. As Gene Raymond, Broadway's so-called "nearly perfect juvenile" would go on to be a successful film career as a handsome, blond-haired actor with a well-toned body.

His greatest fame came on June 16, 1937 when he married MGM's golden singing sensation, Jeanette MacDonald.

Back in 1925, both Raymond and Hump thought they'd found steady employment in *Cradle Snatchers*. Woollcott found Hump's performance "competent," but a visiting theater

The Cradle Snatchers
(Top photo, left to right),
Mary Boland, Edna May Oliver,
and Margaret Dale conspiring; and

(bottom photo)
ensnaring a handsome college
student, Hump *(center figure)*
as a gigolo in their plot.

critic from Chicago, Amy Leslie, was more enthusiastic. She claimed Bogart was "as handsome as Valentino and as graceful as any of our best romantic actors." Opening on September 7, 1925, at the Music Box, *Cradle Snatchers* would run for 332 performances, the hit of the season.

For Hump, the highlight of the play's run was the night Louise Brooks showed up with her new boy friend, Charlie Chaplin. Hump's only regret was that no one in the audience actually watched the play that night, as all eyes were focused on Chaplin. He was, after all, the most famous man on earth. As one stagehand claimed, "I don't know who the president of the United States is, but I sure know who The Little Tramp is."

Louise had taken Charlie to see Helen perform that previous evening, and had even gone with the film star backstage to meet Helen. Louise later claimed that Charlie and she were bitterly disappointed in Helen's performance both on and off the stage. "It's the same show whether the curtain is up or whether she's in her dressing room taking off her makeup," Louise said. "She's so histrionic, so *t-h-e-a-t-e-r*. Her white, thin face is always ecstatically lifted up to her vision of The Drama. I never heard her talk about anything except the art of the theater. She ignored me and was trying to impress Charlie. It didn't work. He couldn't wait to escape from her clutches."

Like an awestruck fan, Hump was delighted to meet Charlie after his performance and even more pleased when Louise invited him to join Charlie, her sometimes girl friend, Peggy Fears, and herself for a tour of some East Side speakeasies. The Little Tramp had developed a fondness for gypsy musicians newly arrived from Budapest. At the final speakeasy visit of the night, Charlie sat enraptured listening to a wild Hungarian violinist, Bela Varga, with an Albert Einstein coiffure, playing nostalgic music left over from the collapse of the Austro-Hungarian Empire.

Invited back to Charlie's suite, the entertainment continued as Charlie did his impressions, the most brilliant being that of John Barrymore reciting the most famous soliloquy of *Hamlet* as he picked his nose. He then rushed into his bedroom and emerged in quick drag, impersonating Isadora Duncan dancing barefoot in a storm of toilet paper. His most comedic impression was left for last—that of how Lillian Gish would achieve orgasm if she ever went to bed with anyone but her sister, Dorothy.

Tired of performing, Charlie offered Louise and Peggy Fears five-hundred dollars if they would strip naked and perform lesbian love on the

Charlie Chaplin:
"A tramp"

sofa in front of his eager eyes. Without hesitation, both women stripped down and got on the sofa, where Charlie, only twelve inches from the scene, played director. The performance must have excited him, as he disappeared inside the bedroom and emerged later totally nude.

Hump was shocked to see that Charlie had coated his monstrous erection with iodine. He proceeded to chase both Peggy and Louise around the living room, finally capturing Louise. As he disappeared inside his bedroom with her, shutting the door behind him, he invited Hump to enjoy Peggy Fears for the night.

After they'd gone, Peggy plopped down on the sofa. "Okay, big boy, show time! Strip down for action. Louise has already told me about you. For a change, I'm gonna lay you for free."

***

Two views of Helen Menken

Four years after taking out the marriage license—it was still valid—Humphrey Bogart wed Helen Menken on May 20, 1926. The wedding took place at Helen's apartment at 52 Gramercy Place.

Hump selected his brother-in-law, Stuart Rose, as his best man. He'd wed Hump's sister Frances two years before. Many of Helen's friends, a regular *Who's Who in the Theater*, showed up. Some one-hundred and thirty guests crammed into the apartment.

Hump invited the Bradys, including Jr. and Sr., Grace George, and Alice Brady. His fellow pussy posse member, Kenneth MacKenna, was also a guest, as was Maud Bogart. Hump's father was at sea at the time.

Stuart was later to recall that the ceremony "was macabre, almost obscene." John Kent, a pastor at St. Ann's Church for Deaf Mutes, conducted the ceremony. He was deaf himself and had been asked to perform the marriage because both of Helen's parents, who were attending the wedding, were also deaf.

Unlike Helen's parents, the reverend had learned to read the service in a kind of warped guttural speech, a sing-song way of talking evocative of Helen Keller. Kent both spoke the words of the ceremony and performed in sign language.

The pastor couldn't hear Hump's "I do," although Helen delivered her "I do" in sign language. After the ceremony, Helen rushed over to Mary Boland where she gushed, "I've been so frightfully busy on Broadway and other stages, I just haven't found time to marry in all these four years, even though Humphrey urged me to do so every day."

When newsmen showed up with photographers, Helen became unstrung. She burst into hysterics. As Louise Brooks would later satirically observe, "For Helen, that wasn't hard to do. She did that every night on stage whether the part called for it or not."

Maud Bogart, Frances, and Helen's mother helped the just-married actress to her bedroom. One of the guests, Dr. Nathan Blomenthal, was summoned to sedate her. Hump did not bother to go into the bedroom to check on the condition of his new bride.

When they'd gone, he turned to Bill Jr. and Stuart. "I think I've made a dreadful mistake."

***

The marriage with Helen Menken began with violence. There was no honeymoon, other than a dinner at Luchow's and a night alone in the apartment. Helen had a fat Cocker Spaniel named "Sam." She insisted on feeding the dog caviar, claiming, "It's his favorite food."

Hump countered that the mutt ate only caviar because there was nothing else in his bowl. Awakening early after their first night as a married couple, Hump went and got the dog a bowl of chopped meat. The animal was in the act of gobbling down the red meat when Helen came into the kitchen. She screamed at her new husband for feeding the dog hamburger and claimed it would give him worms. The fight accelerated until she slapped him severely.

Enraged, he punched her in the face and sent her sprawling on the floor. She couldn't appear on the street for two weeks, and Hump spent the time as a houseguest of Bill Jr. and Katharine Alexander.

When Hump and Helen finally spoke, it was by telephone, when she called to tell him that she was going to appear in a play called *The Captive*.

"What's the plot?" he asked sarcastically. "Do you get kidnapped by African cannibals?"

"Nothing like that," she said. "It's a play about lesbianism."

"Type casting," he kidded her.

"If that God damn drag queen, Mae West, can play a nymphomaniac in some shitty play called *Sex*, then I can play a lesbian in *The Captive*—and if

97

you and the public don't like it, you can all go fuck yourselves." She slammed down the phone.

True to her word, Helen began rehearsals for what would be one of the most controversial plays in the history of Broadway of the 1920s. Deciding to make up with Helen, Hump attended rehearsals.

At the theater, he met the actor, Basil Rathbone, who was seven years older than him. Rathbone had been cast as the male lead in *The Captive.* Rathbone had been born in Johannesburg, South Africa, where his family had to flee to escape the Boers because Rathbone's father, Edgar Philip Rathbone, a mining engineer, had been accused of being a British spy.

He had married Ouida Bergère in April of 1926. His union with this scriptwriter would last until Rathbone's death in 1967, although he told Hump that, "You are and I are destined to love many different women." When he said that, he, of course, was perfectly aware of Hump's marriage to Helen. He also told Hump that, "Helen has told me that she has had many real experiences as a lesbian, so she feels perfectly qualified in the role. When we open, though, I fear the revenge of the bluenoses, who are perfectly capable of tarring us, feathering us, and riding us out of town on a rail."

***

When *The Captive,* starring Helen Menken, opened on September 29, 1926, it shocked and disgusted Broadway audiences. Only Mae West, in her play *Sex*, was generating more newspaper publicity. Unlike Helen, Miss West was enjoying the publicity and notoriety surrounding *Sex*. She was virtually rewriting the script every night, coming up with new and different *double entendres*. Eighty percent of her audience was male, and many of them were returning for a second, third, or even fourth viewing. Because West played it with different nuances and with different scripts and different ad libs every night, it was as if the audience was seeing a different play every time.

As West tried to lure more women into her audiences, Helen wanted more males to attend *The Captive*. Her audiences were nearly eighty percent female. Lesbians from as far away as London and San Francisco flocked to see *The Captive*, the first play on Broadway to deal with the subject of female homosexuality.

New York's district attorney, Joab Banton, was coming under increasing pressure from John Sumner's Society for the Prevention of Vice. Banton made frequent statements to the press, claiming that Broadway wasn't going to become as scandal-ridden as Hollywood. He cited the murder in Hollywood of the director, William Desmond Taylor, and the scandal involving the trial of screen comedian, Fatty Arbuckle, accused of raping the minor actress

Virginia Rappé, causing her death.

Banton found no support from New York's playboy mayor, Jimmy Walker. Walker had attended both plays and claimed he liked them very much. "They're not family entertainment," Walker said, "but there's nothing wrong with having plays for mature audiences." Involved in a torrid affair with his mistress, Betty Compton, Walker was hardly a champion of morality.

When Walker departed for Havana in February of 1927 for a vacation, the acting mayor, Joseph B. McKee—known as "Holy Joe"—seized his opportunity to punish Broadway. He ordered Banton to "banish nudity and obscenity" from the Broadway stage.

An order went out on February 5 to have plainclothesmen from the vice squad monitor the productions of both *The Captive* and *Sex*. On February 9, Holy Joe had his evidence, and he issued orders to have the casts of both plays arrested and charged with offending public morals.

Basil Rathbone and Helen were in the middle of their play's second act when armed policemen stormed directly onto the stage and arrested both of them, along with the rest of the cast. The entire troupe was herded into a Black Maria (an armored paddy wagon used at the time for rounding up, among others, drunks and vagrants) waiting outside the theater. To her shock and surprise, Helen encountered West and some of the cast members of *Sex* within the same Black Maria.

Members of both casts were boiling mad. Each production had been jealous of the other play for the publicity and audiences it was generating. Suddenly, being herded together like cattle and thrown into the smelly, hot Black Maria for a bouncy ride to the police station had the effect of lighting a fuse.

Arguments broke out between the two casts. West felt that she had to defend "my boys," and Helen took it upon herself to champion the cause of the cast of *The Captive*. "We're at least normal," West announced to Helen. "I'm not the one who's up on stage appearing nightly as a sexual deviate."

Unable to withstand such verbal assault, the already infuriated Helen moved toward West, grabbing her by her blonde hair. It was a wig. As the hairpiece fell to the floor, Helen stomped on it. West's own hair was matted down with a protective veil. Fearing she'd have to face newspaper photographers at the jail, West shoved Helen, sending her sprawling down onto the floor of the

Helen Menken, Broadway star and *Captive*, as she's led off to jail for her appearance in a lesbian-themed play

99

Black Maria, as West picked up her wig and began to make emergency repairs to it.

Rathbone graciously lifted Helen from the floor and dusted her off. Helen at this point was furious enough with West to attack her again, but Rathbone restrained her. "I hear you're not a real woman at all," Helen shouted at West. "I hear you're a female impersonator."

"You ugly bitch," West screamed. "If I could get to you, I'd tear every dyed hair out of your ugly head."

At the Jefferson Market Women's Prison, both Helen and West were booked. Hump arrived and rushed to Helen, taking her in his arms. With him were two attorneys from Charles Frohman Productions, Inc.

Before the night was out, the attorneys for *The Captive* had worked out an agreement with the district attorney's office. Helen and the rest of the cast and the producers would accept a proposal of "implied immunity" if they would withdraw *The Captive* from the Broadway stage.

West chose to go the opposite route, preferring to continue with her play *Sex*. Her attorneys would get an injunction from the Supreme Court, barring police shutdown until a trial was held.

The trial itself became a fashion parade for West, who appeared in a different, outrageous, and gorgeous gown for every court appearance. She often wore black satin, some outfits with bugle beads, others with georgette tops. West eventually was convicted for producing *Sex* and sentenced to a ten-day jail term and a fine of $500. She would serve only eight days of her sentence at Welfare Island, getting off for good behavior.

Alone with Hump, Helen remained in seclusion at her apartment, refusing to see anyone and turning down all interviews. In desperation, Hump called Bill Jr. "You know how high strung she is. The arrest has done her in. She's having a nervous breakdown, and I don't know what to do."

"For Christ's sake, call Belmont," Bill advised. "He can shoot her up with morphine, and everything will be okay."

***

When she'd recovered, Helen secured an audition for Hump with the noted director, Guthrie McClintic, to test for the three-act comedy, *Saturday's Children* by Maxwell Anderson. Ironically, Hump knew that the part of Rims O'Neil was up for grabs because he'd already been called by his pussy posse cohort and the play's set designer, Jo Mielziner. Originally the actor, Roger Pryor, had created the role but he had dropped out of the competition after being hospitalized for bleeding ulcers.

McClintic liked Hump's audition and gave him the part. He had only hours to learn the role. Back at Helen's apartment she stayed up all night rehearsing him.

The star of the play, Ruth Hammond, virtually ignored Hump. All she'd said to him backstage was, "Mary Boland has already warned me about you." He thought that Hammond was unprofessional because she upstaged all the other actors.

Hump did not get along with the male star of the comedy either. The Hoosier actor, Richard Barbee, like F. Scott Fitzgerald, had gone to Princeton. Hump felt that Barbee too closely modeled himself after one of Fitzgerald's fictional characters and was not particularly convincing on stage.

Hump struck out with the stars of the play, but was befriended by two members of the supporting cast, Ruth Gordon and Beulah Bondi, both of whom would go on to become celebrated in the theater and in films.

If Hump was known as a kidder and a needler, he met his match when the director introduced him to Ruth Gordon, who was playing a minor role in *Saturday's Children*. Three years older than Hump, she was witty and urbane, known for making such remarks as, "The rich have no friends. They merely know a lot of people."

Despite her ribbings, he was immediately attracted to this daughter of a ship's captain. Their affair, launched the week after their initial meeting, lasted about as long as his romance with Shirley Booth. Gordon later said, "It was over before it even began. I think we had sex. But who remembers so far back, and what difference would it make if I did remember? He's got Betty now, and I've got Garson."

At the time she met Hump, Gordon didn't have playwright Garson Kanin, sixteen years her junior. She was married to actor Gregory Kelly, who would die in 1927.

Before heading for a prolonged run in Chicago, *Saturday's Children* would last for 310 performances on Broadway at the Booth Theatre. The play was not all that Hump was headed for, as his short-term marriage to Helen was rapidly coming to its predictable end.

Newspapers were still comparing Hump's look to that of Valentino, but actually he more closely resembled the newspaper columnist, Ed Sullivan, who at the time wrote a Broadway gossip column for the *Daily News*. A rock-faced Irishman with a hot temper, Sullivan also had a painful shyness and a disdain for phonies.

Sullivan would later achieve international fame on CBS's variety program, *Toast of the Town*

Ruth Gordon in 1920

(1948-55), later called *The Ed Sullivan Show* (1955-71). The show became a national institution, introducing to American audiences such talents as Elvis Presley (Sullivan refused to allow cameramen to photograph him below the hips) and later the sensational appearance of the Beatles.

As he made his rounds across the scope of the Broadway speakeasies, Hump often had gossips come over to him, giving him hot tips for Sullivan's column tomorrow. Since Hump liked to put people on, he never revealed to them that he was an actor, not the newspaper journalist, Ed Sullivan. With a perverted and not altogether kind sense of humor, Hump would often confide some very indiscreet gossip to these strangers. That gossip in most cases got back to its target. Sullivan in the late Twenties found himself in a number of feuds with show biz personalities, never knowing the reason why.

One night, Hump wandered alone into the Mayfair Supper Club, since some of New York's prettiest and most available showgirls frequented the place. He was free to go out on the town because Helen was in Boston. She claimed it was on business, but Hump suspected that it was an off-the-record sexual tryst.

At a red leather banquette and at the best table in the club, New York's handsome and newly elected mayor, Jimmy Walker, was in the company of two long-legged showgirls, one blonde, one a redhead.

The notorious Jimmy Walker, Jazz-Age Mayor (1926-1932) of New York City

Walker was a dapper dresser, though not as flamboyant in attire as Gentleman Jim. Unlike the champ, who preferred to date drag queens, Walker preferred Ziegfeld showgirls when he was not occupied with his mistress.

"Hi, Ed," the mayor called out to Hump. "Loved your column today. C'mon over."

Hump thought that his ultimate coup would be to allow New York's mayor to mistake him for Ed Sullivan. He came over to the mayor's table and was introduced to the two "ladies" of the evening. Hump joined the party not only for dinner but for a round of drinking. Even though booze was prohibited, Walker always said that that law didn't apply to New York's mayor or his guests.

Still impersonating Sullivan, Hump entertained the mayor and his guests with racy stories about Broadway personalities, gossip so hot it couldn't be printed in his column.

Later he joined the mayor heading for the men's room and pissed beside him at one of the club's porcelain urinals. The men did the obligatory pecker-checking, which caused the well-hung mayor to whisper, "Looks like you can take on one of the gals tonight as well as I can." Shaking himself dry, Walker said, "I had planned to sneak away with both of them. But I've had a bad day. I've got a hell of a meeting tomorrow at City Hall. Some farthole is accusing me of being on the take. So please, my good boy, Ed, take one of the bitches off my hands for the night."

"I'd be happy to oblige your Lordship," Hump said.

Back at table, Hump had assumed that the mayor would select the blonde over the redhead, because Walker was well known for liking blondes. Surprisingly, he chose the redheaded stripper, Rhonda Miles, who billed her act—for some strange reason—as "Ringworm." Into her second bottle of Staten Island champagne, Rhonda giggled. "When I first met Jimmy, he told me he only went for blonde fluff. I went and got myself dyed down there, and Jimmy is anxious to see the results. Tomorrow he's gonna pay to have my whole head dyed blonde."

Since he was ordered to do so by the mayor himself, Hump disappeared into the evening with the blonde stripper, who billed herself as Mabel Norman, perhaps in the hope that her audience would equate her stage name with the famous silent screen comedienne, Mabel Normand.

Without ever knowing why, Ed Sullivan found himself uncharacteristically thought of as a stud in the weeks ahead. Mabel Norman, thinking Hump was Ed, had given Hump's performance in bed a rave review.

Sullivan never found out the reason for his sudden popularity with Broadway showgirls.

***

Producer John Turek's decision in 1927 to revive that tired old chestnut, a three-act farce, *Baby Mine*, was a move he'd regret. Turek had seen *Saturday's Children*, and had been impressed with Hump's performance, considering him ideal for the role of the straight-laced juvenile husband, Alfred Hardy, in Margaret Mayo's successful play, which had run for 287 performances when it had originally opened back in 1910.

It was a great year on Broadway and Turek faced stiff competition from other shows, notably Sydney Howard's oedipal melodrama, *The Silver Cord*; Philip Barry's witty *Paris Bound*, and Eugene O'Neill's innovative *The Great God Brown*.

That 320-pound mass of blubber, Roscoe (Fatty) Arbuckle had signed to star as Jimmy Jenks in *Baby Mine*. The screen comedian had arrived in New York hoping for a comeback, following his acquittal on charges of raping and killing Virginia Rappé in a San Francisco hotel suite several years previously.

His once flourishing multi-million-dollar screen career was at an end, as his movies were boycotted in spite of his acquittal. In three trials for manslaughter, all the witnesses and even the district attorney had lied, frequently changing their stories. The first two juries could not reach a verdict but the third acquitted Arbuckle.

From their first meeting, Hump was antagonistic toward Arbuckle. Hump told Turek, "Frankly, I think whale blubber killed that slut, Virginia Rappé. But even sluts deserve to live. I heard Arbuckle is impotent. Can't get a rise out of his little dickie. That's probably why he had to use a milk bottle."

At first, rumors were spread that Arbuckle had raped Rappé with a jagged piece of ice. Later the rumor was changed, the jagged ice story giving way to a milk bottle. The bottle was said to have ruptured Rappé's bladder, causing her eventual death.

On the first day of rehearsals, and to show his contempt, Hump asked the stage manager to deliver an empty milk bottle to Arbuckle's dressing room. Hump had penned a note and attached it to the bottle: "Either call me in to handle your next piece of tail or use this on her."

After that, the fat comedian never spoke to Hump throughout the short duration of the play, except on stage when he had to.

Although Hump detested the star of *Baby Mine*, he told Bill Brady Jr. that he had fallen "madly in love" with the young actress playing the juvenile female lead in the show. She was the very lovely Lee Patrick, a smallish young woman with fair hair, which she wore bobbed like a flapper. Most directors found her face "kind instead of sexy."

Still very young, Patrick had not developed the persona of the brash, sassy blonde she would play in many of her upcoming sixty-five films. She is remembered today for playing the ditsy Henrietta Topper in the Topper television series. She also appeared in a number of film classics, playing second fiddle to Bette Davis in the 1942 *Now, Voyager*; the 1945 *Mildred Pierce* with Joan Crawford, and the 1948 *The Snake Pit* with Olivia de Havilland. Ironically, one of her most remembered roles was as Effie Perrine, the secretary and confidante in the 1941 *The Maltese Falcon* opposite none other than Bogie himself.

Roscoe (Fatty) Arbuckle
Baby Mine

Hump found that his role of a priggish young husband in *Baby Mine* was silly and not convincing. Patrick played the role of his wife, an addictive flirt who maneuvers her way into a lunch alone with Hump's best friend. When he learns of this "transgression," Hump's character walks out on his wife. As part of the intricately contrived plot, Patrick "rents" three babies for an afternoon and, in a dramatic presentation, claims to Hump that all of them belong to her. Finally, Hump learns the truth about these ridiculous episodes, interprets them as minor but adorable quirks of his flirtatious wife's personality, and agrees to let her return to his home and hearth.

Hump's very Victorian role lacked style, grace, and humor, and he was forced to deliver such lines as, "My wife had the effrontery, the bad taste, the idiocy to lunch in a public restaurant with that blackguard." The blackguard referred to was supposed to be Hump's best friend in the play.

Throughout the early rehearsals Hump avidly pursued Patrick, giving her candies and flowers. She repeatedly turned down his overtures until the second week when she agreed to have dinner with him at The 21 Club. After a few drinks, he propositioned her, and she turned him down once again. Finally, she said, "I'll go to bed with you on one condition."

"And that is?" he asked.

"That you'll marry me. I know you're already married to Helen. But everybody on Broadway knows it's not a real marriage. The reason I insist on marriage is that I long ago decided that when I go to bed with a man, it's going to be forever."

Startled, Hump almost left her alone in 21 and fled into the night until his hormones won the battle. He took her back to a hotel room where he seduced her "in the missionary position," as he later confided to Bill Brady Jr. "None of that Louise Brooks kinky stuff—not with a virgin."

After they'd had sex, Patrick cried for what was left of the night. In between sobs, she told Hump that she had fallen in love with him and that there would never be another man in her life but him.

The next day at rehearsals, she confided to him that she had disliked the sex intensely and that it had hurt her. "A friend of mine told me yesterday that the first time always hurts, but it gets better the second and third time until a woman starts to enjoy it."

Hump told her that was true, and round two and round three—each played out in the same hotel bed—soon followed. But by the time the play opened, he was already losing interest in Patrick. As he confided to Brady, "It's too much like fucking a nun."

Baby Mine opened on the night of June 7, and the house was packed. Hump felt that audiences were more interested in seeing Arbuckle in the

Lee Patrick

105

flesh than they were in going to the play. At the close of the final curtain on opening night, Arbuckle appeared before the audience, pleading with them not to believe all the bad press he'd received. He urged them to return again to his play and to bring their friends and relatives.

When Hump from the wings saw the fat comedian shedding tears in front of the audience, he found the act "pathetic." Audiences dwindled during the following nights, and Turek closed the show after only twelve performances.

Hump not only left the play at Chanin's Forty-Sixth Street Playhouse, he also told Patrick that their relationship was over. In her dressing room, she broke down and cried, threatening suicide. He didn't take that threat seriously.

Patrick went on to prove her claim that at heart she was a one-man woman and was "the true blue type." In time she met the writer, Thomas Wood, and married him, their union lasting for forty-five years.

***

After the closing of *Baby Mine*, Hump was out of work for only a week. A sudden call from Chicago and he was asked to get on the next train leaving New York. An actor had taken ill, and the producers wanted Hump to repeat his role in *Saturday's Children* in which he'd appeared with Ruth Hammond and had had that brief affair with actress Ruth Gordon.

Out of work and glad to get another role, Hump agreed to go to Chicago and take over the part. At her apartment, he asked Helen if she'd go with him to Chicago since she, too, was out of work. She flatly refused, claiming she was negotiating to reprise her role in *Seventh Heaven* on the London stage.

Already in London and a sensation over there, Tallulah had written to assure Helen that, "The audiences will adore you, darling. Perhaps you won't create the hysteria I do when I appear in my fancy lingerie, but you'll go over just swell."

Helen's refusal to go to Chicago led to the biggest fight yet between the Bogarts, signaling the final deterioration of their shaky marriage.

"Me, go to Chicago?" Helen shouted at him. "I'm an actress, not a housewife, God damn you if you haven't noticed that. A real actress, not some dumb little actor playing silly walk-ons with a tennis racquet for the mindless. Why in hell do you think I would want to sit in some fleabag Chicago hotel waiting for you to come home at night when the curtain goes down? Why indeed, when I could be the toast of London?"

"Say it like it is," Hump yelled back at her. "What you mean is, you'd rather be licking Tallulah's pussy than getting fucked by me."

"You bastard!" She picked up a vase of flowers and hurled it at him, narrowly missing his face.

"You fucking lez," he yelled at her, as she picked up another object, a silver platter her mother had given her. Before she could hurl this metal missile at him, he grabbed her wrist and forced her to drop it. As a final goodbye, he punched her hard in the face, scoring a bull's eye. The impact was so forceful that he injured his own hand. She fell to the floor as he stormed out of the apartment.

That night in a speakeasy, he told Bill Brady Jr., "I hit her harder than I've ever hit anyone before. At the moment I struck her, I hated all women. I hated the power they've had over me. When I plowed my fist into her face, I was striking back at all women. Even Maud who made me pose nude in that art class. I was hitting every woman who has ever attacked me."

"Maybe you're not the marrying kind," Bill said.

"Maybe I'm not." He looked at Bill, knowing that he had cheated on his wife as many times as Hump had. "You can play the game. Lie to your wife. But I want to be free of any woman. That way I can't be accused of infidelity."

Over a few more drinks, Bill agreed with his friend that a Menken/Bogart divorce was inevitable. "You were completely mismatched," Bill said. "Besides, Helen doesn't need a husband. She needs a string of young and admiring actresses around her, some of whom she will seduce."

"You're right," Hump agreed. "If she'd wanted a real man in her life, she would have stuck it out with me even though I'm not perfect."

Bill's wife, Katharine Alexander, was out of town for the weekend, and he invited Hump to spend the night with him until he was ready to catch the train for Chicago in the morning.

Five hours later at Grand Central Station, Bill had a strange, forlorn look on his face as he embraced Hump in a goodbye. Hump would remember that hangdog expression all the way to Chicago as he rode the rails.

Her face badly swollen, Helen was treated at a clinic in mid-Manhattan. Taking a taxi back to her apartment, she tried to conceal her large black eye from the doorman. She could make no more appearances until her wound healed.

Before signing the contract to go to London to appear in *Seventh Heaven*, she filed for divorce, waiving alimony but demanding that Hump return $2,500 which he'd borrowed from her and had never repaid.

She lied to reporters, claiming that she had been willing to give up her career and "make a real home" for Hump, but had suffered nothing but mental and physical abuse from him. "Sometimes he'd be gone for days at a time, and I never knew where he was or with whom. To him his stage career meant everything. A wife meant nothing to him other than a sometimes convenience."

She found that the press was sympathetic to her fantasies. If anybody valued her stage career more than her home life, it was Helen M herself. She officially charged Hump with "desertion, cruelty, and abuse."

His upcoming divorce was splashed all over the New York newspapers because the names of Helen Menken and, to a lesser extent, Humphrey Bogart, were well known on Broadway. In Chicago neither actor was known.

Fearing that Helen had permanently damaged his professional reputation, Hump wrote Bill Brady Jr. "All this crap that Helen has been tossing at me in the press is going to smell up my career on Broadway. I fear there will be no roles waiting for me when I come back. I'll be blacklisted."

Bill wrote back that Hump need not worry. "What are friends for?" he asked in a letter. "Between Dad, Alice, or me, a job will be waiting for you on Broadway. We'll see to that."

To forget Helen and the divorce mess swirling around him, Hump drank even more heavily than before—and that was a lot. After the curtain went down every night, he headed for the speakeasies of Chicago. He'd never realized it before, but Chicago seemed to have as many good-looking and available chorus girls as New York.

After the first week of making the rounds, he wrote Bill of his conquests. "So far, I've been having auditions nightly. On some occasions, two or three auditions a night. Want to know what I've concluded? There is not one single virgin in Chicago. If I find one, I'll take care of that problem."

***

When Hump returned from Chicago, he continued to make the rounds of the speakeasies with Bill Brady and Kenneth MacKenna. MacKenna wasn't playing around very much, as he was steadily dating that cute little blonde, Mary Philips, who had appeared with Hump and him in *Nerves*.

Married or not, Bill seemed to be free every night after the show to join Hump in a tour of the speakeasies, hitting clubs like Hotsy-Totsy, Chez Flo, the Bandbox, and the Clamhouse.

Hump was staring thirty in the face, and in between booze and chorus girls, he expressed fears about his future to Bill. "How long can I go on playing juveniles? Already I'm getting a little long in the tooth for the roles I'm cast into, some of which would be more suited to a nineteen-year old."

"You need a real meaty part," Bill said, "and I'm sorry I haven't been able to offer you one."

"I'm grateful for the work you've given me," Hump said. "Don't get me wrong. But I need something juicier."

"Have you considered films?" Bill asked.

"What could I play?" Hump asked. "Scarface? This fucking lip of mine would look great blown up on the silver screen."

"Get it operated on," Bill advised. "You'll never remove the scar but you could get rid of that scallop."

"Maybe you're right," he said. "I'll talk to my dad about it. After all, he was the one who gave it to me."

When Hump visited his parents the following day, he found them separated. He hadn't seen either Maud or Belmont for several months, nor had he called them. Belmont had become increasingly addicted to morphine, and had lost their elegant town house because of bad investments. He was forced to move into a small apartment in the East 40s.

Facing failing health and a declining medical practice, Belmont still went out on call as a ship's doctor. When not at sea, he spent most of his time in bed. Maud lived in an apartment next door, and money from her art work supported not only her but took care of most of Belmont's ever-growing number of bills.

Hump was saddened to see both parents in severe decline after having known such prestige and prosperity when they were listed in *Dau's New York Blue Book*.

Hump called on Maud first. Her face was drawn into bitter lines, and she looked dissipated and filled with despair. "I go next door and cook his breakfast every morning. I also go over and see that he has a decent dinner—that is, when I can get him to eat anything. He has these attacks at times, and I have to hire nurses for him, paying out money I can ill afford."

"What kind of attacks?" Hump asked.

"Attacks," she said, dismissing the question. "You always want to know everything."

"Are you guys going to get a divorce?" he asked.

"I have no intention of doing that," she said. "But your father's getting too weak to travel on ships any more. I fear he's going to be bedridden for the few years that remain to him."

"Are you still taking morphine too?" he asked.

"Why don't you go see your father and let me alone this morning?" she said. "I have a job. Not a well-paying assignment but a job, and I need to devote all my time to it—not to your questions."

"I love you," he protested. "I want to know."

"Do I interfere in your life?" she asked, her fury reflected in her stern face. "Did I ask you why you married a lesbian? Why you lay out drunk every night in speakeasies, picking up floozies like your father used to bring home sailor riffraff from the wharves? Do I interrogate you about why you continue in an illicit friendship with that Jew, Bill Brady? The stories spread about him."

"Bill is my friend, and he's going to stay my friend."

"Please leave," she said. "Just leave. My nerves are shattered."

Next door, Hump found Belmont in unusually good spirits, or else he was putting on a brave show for his son. The doctor carefully avoided talk of his failed marriage, his declining career, and his reduced circumstances in life. Unlike Maud, Belmont seemed eager to hear about his son's many "triumphs" in the theater, and Hump exaggerated his achievements and praise.

"The one thing I can't understand," Belmont said, "is why you're always compared to Valentino when there's a write-up about you in the press. I just don't see the resemblance. Besides, he's long dead."

"I don't get it either," Hump said. "There are worse comparisons, though. At least they don't think I look like that rapist, Fatty Arbuckle."

Hump told him that Bill Brady Jr. had suggested a possible career for him in films. He was hesitant to bring up his lip disfigurement since Belmont was to blame for that.

Without ever excusing what he'd done to his son, Belmont said, "I can't remove the scar, but I can do minor surgery and get rid of that scallop. After all, when you become a big-time movie star, and the camera moves in for a close-up, you don't need all that extra skin blown up to giant size on the silver screen. I'll operate this morning."

"You mean, right now?" Hump asked, wondering if Belmont was in any condition to operate on him and fearing that the surgery might lead to greater disfigurement.

"I didn't raise a sissy for a son," Belmont said, rising slowly from his bed. "Go into my clinic down the hall and take off your shirt. We might as well get this over with if you're planning to go to Hollywood one day. Since Valentino died early in life, and no other actor has replaced him, it might as well be my son, Humphrey Bogart. But you'll have to come up with a less sissy name than Humphrey for the marquee."

***

Taking Bill's challenge of going to Hollywood seriously, Hump went alone to see *The Jazz Singer*, that partially talking picture starring Al Jolson. The word reaching New York was that in a year or two recorded human voices would be heard in all future films. Since many stars in Hollywood had awful voices, there was going to be a demand for Broadway actors trained in speaking parts.

Hump still had his slight lisp, but at least he no longer had that scallop on his lip thanks to Belmont.

110

The Jazz Singer had been running for several months before Hump got around to seeing it, and he was impressed, trying to imagine his face on the silver screen. He'd also heard that the pay in Hollywood was much better than it was in the New York theater.

After seeing the film, he went a few blocks down the street to a Manhattan theater where the actress, Mary Halliday, was appearing in a play. On October 26, 1925, Helen had taken him to the opening of Halliday's play, *Easy Come, Easy Go*, and he'd liked the actress and wanted to call on her and wish her luck. He had learned that actresses like Grace George might occasionally recommend him for future roles in their plays, so he felt it was important to keep in touch with some of the many theatrical celebrities he'd met through Helen.

Backstage on the way to see Halliday, he encountered another Mary. Mary Philips, the actress with whom he'd appeared with his "second best friend," Kenneth MacKenna, in the 1924 play, *Nerves*. He'd all but forgotten Mary, but remembered that he'd objected to the sexy way that she'd walked offstage, upstaging his best scene in the play.

To his surprise, Hump saw Kenneth emerging from the men's room, walking toward them. Kenneth approached Mary and kissed her on the mouth, possessively putting his arm around her as if to signal his fellow pussy posse member to back off in case he had any designs on Mary.

After the actors paid their respects to Halliday, Hump invited Mary and Kenneth to join him for "drinks, fun, and maybe a little dinner" at Sardi's.

Over drinks, Mary told Hump how sorry she was to learn of the breakup of his marriage to Helen. "Frankly," Mary said, after a few drinks, "I was surprised she wanted to marry any man. The rumor along Broadway was that you and Helen kept a scoreboard every week to see how many young actresses each of you could seduce. In spite of your reputation as a ladies' man, I was told that Helen beats your score virtually every weekend."

Instead of making him boil, Hump laughed and ordered another drink. What Mary had just said to him was what he might have said to someone. It seemed she liked to kid and needle people as much as he did.

Kenneth remained aloof from their conversation. The more they drank and the more fun they seemed to be having, the more Kenneth resented it. He reminded Hump several times that he and Mary were seriously considering marriage. Although Kenneth could drink as much as Hump could, he ordered only bottled club soda. "Someone's got to keep a clear head. Otherwise the two of you will never find your way home."

When Kenneth got up to go to the men's room again, Mary slipped Hump her phone number and gave him a kiss on the cheek. "Mae West is always telling stage-door johnnies to come up and see her some time. I can't think of a better way to say it."

111

"Invitation accepted." Then, as he was to tell Brady Jr., Mary did something that shocked him. She reached under the table and placed her delicate hand in his crotch, fondling him.

Kenneth was so anxious to return to table that he came back into the dining room still zipping up. Mary discreetly removed her hand from Hump's crotch. She was giving him a hard-on.

She had come a long way since her days in that New Haven convent.

Hump was determined to seduce Mary, even though he knew that his friend, Brady, and obviously Kenneth had sampled the honeypot long before he'd get a taste.

In the weeks ahead, Hump got to know Mary very well. She visited him three or four times a week at his apartment. Since she was unofficially engaged to Kenneth, she didn't want to be seen at any of the Broadway dives with Hump. Sometimes she would arrive a bit disheveled at Hump's apartment, and he knew that she'd just risen from Kenneth's bed. "It's sloppy seconds for me again today," he'd kid her.

Although she didn't have the professional stature of Helen, Mary was an established Broadway star when she met Hump. From that very first night at Sardi's, Hump realized that, especially when a total of five fans stopped by their table to ask for her autograph. Although they were also established actors on Broadway, neither Hump nor Kenneth attracted autograph seekers.

Hump later told Bill that he wasn't even considering marriage, "and if I do it will to be a Roaming in the Gloaming type. And if I marry anybody, it will be Mary Philips. New England and Irish, the perfect combination for me."

Two views of
Bogie's second wife, Mary Philips

"If you do marry Mary, I can vouch that your future wife's not bad in the sack.

112

That's one hot little number."

That provocative remark didn't make Hump mad because he already knew of the affair Bill had had with Mary. He sipped his drink and cast a steely glance at Bill. "Your wife's not bad in the sack either. Dear Katherine. I did have to teach her a few tricks, though."

***

"Kenneth has officially proposed," Mary said one morning when rising from Hump's bed after a night of passionate lovemaking. "He's even bought the ring."

"Did you accept?" Hump asked, rubbing sleep from his eyes.

"I've asked him to give me a month to make up my mind." Completely nude, she towered over Hump who remained in bed. "At the end of the month, if I don't have an official proposal of marriage—engagement ring and every-thing—from one Humphrey Bogart, I'm marrying Kenneth." With that remark, she turned and walked toward his bathroom to repair the damages of the night.

The next few days were agonizing ones for Hump. At speakeasies, he had long, drunken talks with Bill about what he should do. "For God's sake, marry her," Bill advised.

"What about Kenneth?" Hump asked. "He is one of my best friends. I think if I take Mary from him, it will break his heart."

"There are a lot of beautiful women on Broadway who will mend Kenneth's heart," Bill said. "He's one handsome guy. Most women think he's far better looking than we are. He's wildly popular with the gals. A month after your marriage, he will have forgotten all about Mary."

The next night at Tony's, it was painful for Hump to listen to Kenneth's plans for his future life with Mary. "We're not even married yet, and already we're having fights."

"What kind of fights?" Hump asked, more than curious.

"Stuart thinks I'm Hollywood material, and I'm planning to go to the coast."

Hump's brother-in-law, Stuart Rose, had become the East Coast story editor for the Fox Film Corporation.

"When do you think you'll go?" Hump asked.

"As soon as Mary and I get married. I'm taking her to LA with me. A woman's place is beside her husband wherever he goes. Mary believes that the theater is the only true calling for an actor. She thinks movies are for ridicu-lous types like the late Valentino or that daffy blonde, Mae Murray. Or larger-than-life types like Gloria Swanson or Erich von Stroheim."

"You've got a problem, guy," Hump said. "Don't get Mary's Irish up. That's one determined broad."

"So she thinks," Kenneth said. "I'm more stubborn than she is. Within two years, I predict, I'm going to become the biggest male star in motion pictures. When I come home at night, Mary's going to have a pot of Irish stew bubbling on the stove and my slippers waiting at the door."

"Dream on," Hump said, realizing how little Kenneth understood Mary's fierce determination to succeed on the stage.

Exactly one day before Hump's marriage proposal deadline with Mary ran out, he asked her to become his second wife. Remembering his four-year engagement to Helen, he told her he wanted to get married as soon as they could get a license and a minister.

Mary accepted and kissed him long, hard, and passionately. Even so, he was in for a surprise. It would be the beginning of many surprises in their years together. "I want to go and sleep with Kenneth tonight," she said. "A night of grand love-making. I feel I owe him that."

"Fuck that!" Hump protested. "You'll do nothing of the sort. You're my broad now. I've staked my claim."

"What do you think I am?" she asked. "Some Broadway cow you own in your stable? A big tit bovine you've branded with a hot iron? When I agreed to marry you, I didn't say I'd swear off other men. No marriage can work unless a husband and wife are free to have sex with others."

Echoes of his recently failed marital arrangement with Helen resounded in his head. Did all Broadway actresses believe in an open marriage? Not wanting to repeat the mistakes he'd made with Helen, he turned on Mary. "What crap!" he yelled at her. "Many married couples are faithful to each other. Have you ever heard of the vow, forsaking all others?"

"I suppose the next thing you'll throw at me is the perfect marriage of your parents. It was idyllic all right, just so long as Belmont could cruise the waterfront and bring home sailors. Or that Maud could have a discreet affair or two on the side. You told me that yourself."

"My own parents are hardly an example I would want to follow," he said.

"What about your marriage to Menken?" she demanded to know. "Everybody up and down Broadway knows that the two of you slept with everything that had two legs and could spread them."

"My marriage with Helen failed," he said. "I don't want that to happen to us!"

"Maybe there's going to be no God damn marriage," she said. "What are you, some fucking Puritan? I'm not going to agree to marry you unless you let me continue to sleep with Kenneth. And maybe some other good-looking guys I meet. My only promise to you is that these guys will always be actors. That way, we'll keep it in our Broadway family."

"That is the sickest talk I've ever heard," he said, turning from her in disgust.

"Yeah," she said, confronting him. "But it sounds healthy to me. A lot healthier than those three-ways you and Helen had with Tallulah Bankhead. That cozy arrangement had all of Broadway talking. I've heard that you've even had three-ways with Scott and Zelda Fitzgerald."

"That's a God damn lie."

"You were seen kissing Fitzgerald in the elevator of the Plaza Hotel."

"That was just some drunken game we were playing that night," he said.

"When I fuck Kenneth tonight, I'll make sure we're drunk and that it's all a game," she said defiantly. "I don't care what you say. I'm going to do what I God damn please." She stormed out of his living room, heading for the door.

"Forget I ever proposed to a whore like you," he shouted to her departing back. Even when stalking out of the apartment, she still had that same sexy walk she'd used on the stage in *Nerves*. "I wouldn't marry you if you were the last blonde slut on Broadway, which you aren't. Your type is a dime a dozen."

Her answer to that was the loudest slamming of a door he'd ever heard.

***

It was in Hartford, Connecticut on April 3, 1928, that the minor Broadway actor, Humphrey Bogart, aged 28, married Miss Mary Philips, the Broadway star. Whatever differences they had, they had momentarily suppressed them. They'd hardly worked them out.

Arriving two hours before the wedding, Kenneth had gone into seclusion with Mary, pleading with her to, "Marry me, not Hump." Mary had wavered back and forth between the two men, deciding first on Kenneth, then on Hump. Years later, she would sigh and say, "I was really pissed off. Why can't a woman have two husbands? I wanted to marry both of them."

In time, she would.

Kissing Kenneth good-bye and telling him to leave Hartford, Mary turned down his proposal of marriage. She held out a promise to him. "When I get back to New York, I'll still be your wife, but only on certain nights of the week."

Bill Brady Jr. was Hump's best man. The wedding was to take place at the home of Mary's mother, Anne, at 24 Hopkins Street, an apartment in a building across from the old Hartford Public High School.

Only ten minutes before the wedding, Hump told Bill, "I'm a fool to go through with this marriage. It has all the earmarks of a disaster—just like my marriage to Helen. History is repeating itself. She'll probably throw Kenneth

115

a mercy fuck a few minutes before she walks in here to say 'I do.'"

"Maybe the line should be changed to, 'I just did,'" Bill said, joking with Hump and hoping to cheer him up.

After a tearful embrace, Mary finally appeared in front of the justice of the peace, her guilty eyes avoiding Hump's. The couple exchanged marriage vows, even a promise to forsake all others, although Hump knew that was a meaningless promise.

After the ceremony, when he'd put a ring on Mary's finger and kissed her, Hump stood in front of a bowl of punch with the justice of the peace. "We know what a fine star Miss Philips is. Or should I say Mrs. Bogart? But what kind of actor are you?"

"They call me a 'white pants Willy,'" he said.

"What does that mean? I'm afraid I'm not familiar with show business terms."

"A handsome but callow young man who is a staple in many drawing-room comedies."

As they were at the train station heading back to New York, Hump and Mary got caught up in a torchlight parade for Hartford's newest mayor, "Batty" Batterson, who'd just been narrowly elected despite widespread allegations of vote fraud.

After a one-night stopover in Manhattan, during which Mary was gone for two hours for drinks with Kenneth, Mary and Bogart headed for a two-week honeymoon in Atlantic City. "It was the beginning of ten years of deepening misery for me," Bogie in the years to come would say in recalling his New Jersey honeymoon.

When the honeymooners returned to New York, Mary immediately called Kenneth who told her that he was leaving in the morning on a train bound for Los Angeles. He was going to break into the movies and had been promised a "really big part."

Mary kissed Hump good-bye and told him, "I just have to spend this final night with Kenneth. I'm sure you'll understand. After all, I've been with you for two entire weeks."

He wished her a good time. He'd just read in a Broadway column that Helen had returned from her engagement in London. He called her apartment. After receiving her congratulations on his new marriage, he asked her if he could come over and spend the night.

"You're always welcome," she said.

After putting down the receiver, he headed for the shower. He wanted to look handsome and well-groomed for Helen.

That would mark the beginning of an affair with his first wife that would last for the entire duration of his marriage to his second wife, Mary Philips.

***

The next week Hump went to the theatrical agents, Charles Frohman Productions, and signed on with them, telling them he wanted to break into the movies. As Helen's representative, Frohman had secured lawyers for Helen and gotten her out of trouble when she was arrested for appearing in the lesbian play, *The Captive*. Even so, Hump wasn't very cooperative, but one of the staff members, Sheila Crystal, took a liking to Hump and felt that he might photograph well. She'd already seen two plays in which he'd appeared. She was also aware that Broadway columnists still compared his looks to the dead actor, Valentino.

Hump left the agency thinking nothing would come of his signing on. In two weeks, Sheila called him. Even without a screen test, she'd secured him the male lead in a two-reeler, *The Dancing Town*. "The star will be Helen Hayes," Sheila said. "That's Helen Hayes with an s, not Helen Haye. Everybody gets those two gals mixed up."

That night on his tour of the speakeasies with Mary, Hump was thrilled at the offer. He was disappointed in Mary's reaction. "Films are just a novelty," she said. "I think in a few years there will be no films. The theater is the only place for an actor. I told Kenneth that, but the fool wouldn't listen. He's dreaming of seeing himself up on that silver screen."

"You've got it ass backwards," he said. "All the big Broadway stars today will be forgotten a hundred years from now. Films like that crap Valentino made will still be shown."

The day he went to meet Helen Hayes, Hump was excited to be working with her. He'd never met her, but another Helen, his first wife, knew her well. Both of them had gone to see Hayes in the Broadway play, *To the Ladies*, in which she'd appeared from 1922 to 1924. She'd had great success in Oliver Goldsmith's ribald 18th-century comedy, *She Stoops to Conquer*, and she'd followed that by playing Cleopatra in George Bernard Shaw's *Caesar and Cleopatra*.

Hayes had married the same year that Hump had wed Mary Philips. Her husband was the very handsome Charles MacArthur, whom Hump knew casually from their long nights spent drinking at Tony's saloon. Hump was surprised that the demure and ever so elegant Hayes would marry a hard-drinking, hard-living playwright like Charles MacArthur, who was

Helen Hayes

having his big Broadway success with his memorable play, *The Front Page*.

When Hump had first met MacArthur, he was having affairs with both Dorothy Parker and Ned Sheldon, the playwright with whom he had collaborated on the 1926 play, *Lulu Belle*. Hump knew that MacArthur swung both ways, but he didn't know if Miss Hayes knew that, and it wasn't his job to tell her. Bill Brady Jr. always claimed that, "MacArthur will drop his trousers for anybody, male or female, if he's drunk enough." Like his own marriage, Hump didn't give the Hayes/MacArthur union much of a chance.

Hayes was hardly the First Lady of the American Theater the day Hump met her at a studio in Queens. But she was every bit a lady. She was so tiny she made him feel tall. If modern generations have an image of Helen at all, it is of a grandmotherly looking woman with gray hair. But when Hump met her, Helen was "the serpent of the Nile," and she'd appeared in a number of flapper roles, although he felt that she was "too pure" to have any real sex appeal.

Over coffee, and waiting for the cameras to be set up, Helen confessed that she was planning to accompany her husband to Hollywood where he wanted to become a screenwriter for Metro-Goldwyn-Mayer. "Now that the flickers have learned to talk, maybe I'll consider a film career as well. Heaven only knows, I'm no sex pot who can do bathtub scenes like Gloria Swanson."

"I think you're a very sexy lady, and within the hour I expect to be making mad, passionate love to you."

"Heavens," she said, "I'm flattered. You're very handsome, not as much so as my Charles, but a very good-looking man. I'm faithful to my husband, though, even if he isn't to me."

Apparently, she already knew about her husband's extramarital affairs. "I wasn't making a proposition," Hump said. "I've read the script. It calls for us to make mad, passionate love."

"Oh, I see." She looked embarrassed. "It's in the script?"

"I suggest we at least do some heavy kissing before the cameras are turned on us," he suggested. "After all, if you and I are going to become movie stars, we don't want to appear like limp dish rags when we embrace on screen."

"You're probably right," she said. "Lillian Gish has always warned me that the camera—unlike the stage—picks up every facial nuance."

His lips already moist, he wetted them again as he went over to her in her dressing room and took her in his arms. He gently pressed his mouth down on hers. At first she resisted but soon gave in, reaching to put her small arms around him.

The kissing scene was going so well that he inserted his tongue ever so gently into her mouth, not knowing what she'd think of this French kissing. He seemed to be getting to her.

118

Although it was hardly called for in the script, he placed his hand on her thigh and started moving to the North Pole. He'd never know what might have happened because suddenly there was a rude knock on the door. The director wanted both of them on the set.

Hump would later recall that their love-making on the silver screen never matched their warm-up in Helen's dressing room.

Regrettably, there are no known copies of this two-reeler today, which starred two of the most famous actors of the 20th century, Helen Hayes and Humphrey Bogart.

***

"I'm impotent." Hump walked with Stuart Rose along a serene lake near Fairfield, Connecticut where Mary and he were renting a house next to his brother-in-law and his sister, Frances.

"It'll pass," Stuart assured him. "Just give it time."

He took hold of Stuart's arm and confronted him. "Has it ever happened to you and Frances?"

"Can't say that it has, but it happens to a lot of men," Stuart said. "More than they'll tell you. My own father was impotent for two years before he got it back again."

"If only Mary didn't make it worse," Hump said. "When I can't get it up, she mocks me and ridicules me. I should never have married her."

Stuart looked deeply into Hump's eyes. "What's the real problem?"

"It's the kind of marriage we have," Hump said. "I think she's still in love with Kenneth. She sleeps around and tells me about it. She says that what she can't get at home she finds somewhere else. She claims most men don't have my problem."

"Where's Mary now?" Stuart asked.

"She's gone back to New York," Hump said. "We'll probably get a divorce. My reputation will be ruined on Broadway. No gal will want to sleep with me ever again."

The marriage was saved by a three-act comedy, *The Skyrocket*, that was set to open January 11, 1929 at the Lyceum Theatre. It was produced and directed by Guthrie McClintic, who had hired Kenneth's brother, Jo Mielziner, as the set designer.

Mary was cast as the star, with Humphrey playing her husband. After reading the script, he told Jo, "It's another one of those sprig parts. But I need work so I'll take it."

It was like a Broadway homecoming for Hump. Guthrie had directed *Saturday's Children* two years earlier, with Jo doing the sets. The script was one of those rags-to-riches-to-rags stories. Couple strikes it rich but money makes them unhappy. They go broke again and find true love and happiness in their poverty.

Hump's role as "Rims" in *Saturday's Children* had been minor, and he hadn't really gotten to know its director as he'd filled in for another actor after the show was blocked. Both Mary and he were eager to work with the director, Guthrie McClintic.

In their daydreams, Mary and Hump fantasized with each other about becoming the "second Guthrie McClintic and Katharine Cornell." And whereas Woollcott hadn't been impressed with Hump's stage "sprig," he was overwhelmed by Guthrie's wife, Katharine, calling her "The First Lady of the Theater." Helen Hayes claimed that position for herself as well, as did Lynn Fontanne, Cornell's two chief rivals for glory.

Even without Woollcott's usual hyperbole, Cornell was indisputably the reigning Broadway star of the second quarter of the 20th century. When she'd made her debut in 1921 in *Nice People*, her future husband, then a young casting director, saw her performance and recorded in his notebook. "Interesting. Monotonous. Watch."

By the autumn of that year, he'd married her, forming a theatrical union that lasted forty years until his death in 1961, in spite of the fact that she was a lesbian and he was a homosexual. At the time of his death she abandoned the stage. "I can't go on without Guthrie," she told the press.

When Guthrie told his two stars, Mary and Hump, that his wife was going to visit for the final rehearsal, they were thrilled and were glad to have been warned. They planned to give their best performances during the rehearsal even if it left them drained for opening night.

Divas and *grande dames*
Guthrie McClintic and his wife,
Katharine Cornell

Guthrie had also told them that Cornell, following such great theatrical successes as W. Somerset Maugham's *The Letter* and Edith Wharton's *The Age of Innocence*, planned to manage her own productions in the future. Mary told Hump that if Cornell were impressed with them, she might hire them for one of her shows.

On the day of the final run-through, Guthrie delayed *The Skyrocket* for one hour, waiting for his wife. Cornell finally showed up. In a beautifully tailored suit, she took a seat in the final row of the theater. Like an imperial *grande dame*, she signaled her husband that the show could begin.

At the end of the performance, the curtain was pulled shut. When it was opened again,

120

Mary and Hump stepped forward, hoping to hear the applause of Cornell. Guthrie told them that she'd left the theater but had written a note for them. It was addressed to "Mr. and Mrs. Humphrey Bogart."

Dear Aspirant Thespians,

Although you struggled, and I'm sure performed, to the best of your ability, this Skyrocket will never make it to heaven. Actually, the two of you are not to blame. The playwright, Mark Reed, deserves full responsibility. His mother should have smothered him at birth.

All good wishes,

Katharine Cornell

Somewhere during rehearsals, Hump had regained his confidence and his sexual prowess and was once again sleeping with Mary. The attack from Cornell destroyed his confidence once again. On opening night he was jittery and explosive.

To compound his fears of an impending disaster, Mary chose that horrendously inappropriate moment to confess to an infidelity that had been going on right before his eyes, even though he hadn't seen it.

"I've been having an affair with Jo," she said. "I guess I missed Kenneth now that he's gone Hollywood. They say if a gal goes for one brother, she can go for another. Actually I find Jo better in bed than Kenneth. Brothers don't make love the same way."

Hump wanted to slap her, even belt her a good one, but was told that the curtain was going up. He was understandably nervous on opening night, especially after Mary's revelations. Critics pronounced *Skyrocket* a "showy counterfeit." One called it "spurious." Mr. and Mrs. Humphrey Bogart received only faint praise.

An out-of-town critic from Hartford, John Davenport, wrote, "It's surprising that the two stars, Mary Philips and Humphrey Bogart, are in fact newlyweds. There is absolutely no chemistry between them on stage at all."

Of all the critics that night, Davenport was the only one who got it right. *Skyrocket* quickly closed, and both Mary and Hump found themselves out of work once again.

His bouts of impotence continued on and off for several months. He told Bill that his marriage was a "sometimes thing." Mary seemed more excited to get a letter from Kenneth in Hollywood than she did in going out to the speakeasies with her new husband. Sometimes she'd disappear for a week at a time and never tell Hump where she'd been or with whom. "When I'm gone, feel free to date other women," she told him.

No other woman interested him. It wasn't that he wanted only Mary. He didn't want any woman. One night when he'd been alone and drinking heavily in his apartment for three days, Bill Brady Jr. arrived unexpectedly, finding Hump unbathed, unshaven, and almost suicidal.

"I finally figured out what's the matter with me," Hump said, heading to the kitchen to pour himself another drink. "I've decided I'm a homosexual."

"We all go through periods like that," Bill said. "Our own relationship is a perfect example of that."

"It's worse than you think," Hump said. "The other night I was trying to jack off. I willed my mind to think of Mary, but the thing that did it for me—the image that made me pop off—was thinking of what Stuart looked like naked."

"I'm jealous," was all Bill said. "Now come on, big boy, we're going to give you a bath, sober you up a bit, and take you out on the town. Stuart will have to be put on the backburner. You're my date for tonight." Bill winked at him.

As the weeks went by, Hump continued to be filled with loathing of himself and self-doubt about his manhood. It was one of the most morbidly depressing periods of his life, and at times he contemplated suicide. He later told Bill, "I never get beyond the thinking stage of it. I just can't see myself taking a razor to my throat." Bill tried his best to cheer him up and break his mood.

Alone in his apartment on one of the blackest days of his life, Hump saw no future for himself, certainly no career in the theater. His marriage to Mary was rapidly deteriorating, in ways that evoked the earlier collapse of his marriage to Helen.

But ironically, he had resumed seeing Helen again whenever Mary was away. With Helen, he didn't experience impotence, only with Mary. Helen always made him feel like a man.

One night at a speakeasy, when he'd been battling with Mary, he told her, "On those rare occasions with you when I can get it up—that is, when you're not trying to take a razor to my balls—I feel you're thinking about getting plugged by Kenneth and not by me."

"A lady is entitled to her fantasies," Mary had said, rising from her chair and staggering toward the bar to order another drink.

On that dark, rainy afternoon, as he drank alone and grew more despondent in his bleak apartment, the phone rang. Thinking it was Bill, he picked it up to discover Sheila Crystal on the line. His theatrical agent had gotten him another film job.

122

The great singing star of the Twenties, Ruth Etting, had seen Hump's performance in the short-lived *Skyrocket*, and had told her backers that she thought "Bogart would be ideal as my leading man" in a ten-minute short she'd contracted to film for Warner Brothers' Vitaphone Corporation.

Once again and without ever setting foot in Hollywood, Hump found himself cast in a movie opposite a famous woman star.

***

Like Katharine Cornell, the songbird, Ruth Etting, was late on the first day of rehearsals for their film short. She'd been rehearsing for her upcoming Broadway show, *Whoopee!* She was Hump's favorite recording star, and he always proclaimed that she had a "gorgeous voice." He'd seen many pictures of her in the tabloids and had found her a "great beauty."

Etting lived up to her billing. When she finally did show up, Hump was dazzled by the sultry torch singer known as "America's sweetheart of song." Only two years older than Hump, Etting had been born in Nebraska. But, as he later told Bill Brady, Jr. "She looked like no cow gal I've ever seen." When introduced to him, he shook her gloved hand. She reached over to kiss him gently on the lips. "It's good for me to see you in the flesh and up close," she said, still holding his hand. "I found you very sexy and commanding in *Skyrocket* even if the critics didn't."

He looked into her eyes. He'd later say, "I never saw a woman's eyes dance before I met Ruth. We clicked from the very first. After only an hour together, we were confessing intimate secrets. She even told him that her secret ambition was to design clothing. "I design some of my outfits on Broadway," she said.

Later, when the film script called for him to come on to her, he found that his impotence had been miracu-

Two views of Broadway singing sensation Ruth Etting, alone and *(bottom photo)* with Humphrey Bogart

lously cured. Fortunately they were seated at a table. Otherwise, the camera might have recorded one of his biggest erections.

Although he wanted to, Hump didn't put the make on Etting the first day. She gave him several opportunities and seemed to actively encourage him. Hump was afraid—not of Etting, but of her husband. She was married to the Chicago gangster, Martin Snyder, nicknamed "The Gimp" because of a lame left leg. He was promoting her singing career by throwing his weight around Broadway, using tactics he'd learned from a life on the streets in Chicago's underworld.

As work on the short film began, Etting confessed that she'd left "The Gimp" and planned to dump him. She also told Hump that she'd had a very brief affair with showman Florenz Ziegfeld when she'd starred in the *Ziegfeld Follies of 1927*, singing Irving Berlin's "Shaking the Blues Away."

When Hump didn't invite her out that night, she asked him to go on tour of the speakeasies. After a few drinks, she confessed that she was having an affair with the young singer, Bing Crosby. "The Gimp" was supposed to be fanatically jealous, but she seemed to be screwing around a lot, even when she was living with the gangster.

Shortly before midnight, Etting invited Hump back to her apartment. "I thought you'd never ask," he said.

Once in the apartment, she put on a record of one of her songs. She stood in front of her record player and told him to turn off the lights. Not knowing what was about to happen, he turned off the sole light in the room. "Lights," she called out after less than a minute.

When he turned on the light bulb again, Etting was standing nude in front of her record player. She sang "Love Me Or Leave Me" to him. As she sang, he removed his clothing. At the wrap of her song, he moved toward her, his erection guiding his way.

In one of the many ironies of Hump's life, that was not the last time "Love Me Or Leave Me" would figure into his career. Nearing the end of Bogie's life in 1954, Metro-Goldwyn-Mayer considered him for their upcoming picture, *Love Me Or Leave Me* conceived as a vehicle for Doris Day. The studio felt that Hump would be ideal cast as Etting's gangster lover, "The Gimp." Feeling the film was too much a star part for Day, he turned down the role, which eventually went to James Cagney, his longtime rival for gangster roles at Warner Brothers in the 1930s.

***

As it had with so many other women, his affair with Ruth Etting ended almost before it began. "The Gimp" arrived back in New York and had a reconciliation with Etting. Bill Brady Jr. told Hump that "The Gimp" often assigned hit men "to beat up or kill any man who moves in on his lady love." Even with the dangerous gangster back in her life, Etting placed three more calls, hoping to arrange a private assignation with Hump. He was too afraid to return her calls.

Still sleeping with Mary, he had managed a one-night stand with a beautiful actress who had had a brief walk-on in the Vitaphone short, *Broadway's Like That*, in which he co-starred with Etting. Her name was Joan Blondell and her nickname was "Rosebud." To him, she was a blonde bombshell from Texas, and he'd been captivated by her youthful exuberance, expressive face, and popped-out eyes that seemed to devour whatever man they focused on.

Like Kenneth MacKenna, she was heading for Hollywood to star in a picture, *Sinners' Holiday*, with James Cagney.

After their one night of passion, Joan made him promise to "look me up if you ever come to Hollywood." She gave him a phone number where she could be reached in Los Angeles. He wrote it down but didn't expect to see her again.

As he said goodbye to Joan when he went down to see her off at Grand Central, little did he know that this would be "the beginning of a beautiful friendship," and that he would one day be co-starring with her in motion pictures. Not only that, their one-night stand would mark the beginning of one of the most enduring and long-running affairs of his life.

***

Work came in the form of another three-act Broadway comedy, this one a superficial comedy by Laurence E. Johnson, produced and directed by David Belasco at the Belasco Theatre. *It's a Wise Child* was slated to open on August 6, 1929, starring Helen Lowell, Olga Krolow, Leila Bennett, Mildred McCoy, and George Walcott. No longer a co-star as he had been in *The Skyrocket*, with Mary, Hump got fifth billing in yet another juvenile part.

In spite of the many drawbacks of both the play and his role within it, Hump got to work with some of the biggest names on Broadway. First, Guthrie McClintic had been his director. Now, he was being directed by David Belasco, an influential powerhouse sometimes known as "The Bishop of Broadway." The theater, constructed in 1907, in which their play was to open, was even named after Belasco, who had emerged as one of the most influential men in the entertainment industry at the time. He had seemingly done everything in the theater, including the writing of a smash hit, *The Heart of Maryland*, about the Civil War. He had even selected the name "Mary Pickford" for the film actress who would eventually become "America's

Sweetheart."

During the first week of rehearsals, Hump had been disappointed that Belasco, as director, spent so little time coaching him in his role of Roger Baldwin, a part he loathed. The comedy concerned a woman who falls for a young bank clerk as played by Hump. Already saddled with an elderly fiancé, she tells him she's pregnant with another man's child. Hump's role was conceived as that of a "transitional beau," and his character was described as "not one of those silly dancing and drinking men" but as "one of the best-looking men you were likely to ever meet, with the profile of a Greek God." In the final act, the beautiful heroine irrationally dismisses Hump as "just a foolish kid" when he tells her that he cares more about his job than he does about her.

Not particularly attracted to the aging star of the play, Helen Lowell, Hump made a play instead for the enchantingly lovely second female lead, Mildred McCoy, considering her "twice as beautiful as Mary." Mildred seemed fascinated with Hump and invited his amorous attention, even though she constantly refused to go out with him.

Word of Hump's flirtation with Mildred must have reached her beau. As rehearsals began one Monday morning, the stage manager came backstage to tell him that Mildred's lover was sitting alone out front. He was none other than Chief Buffalo Child Long Lance, the most famous "Indian" in America. Hump was even wearing a pair of canvas running shoes, "Long Lance Sport Shoes," named after him.

Long Lance was a darling of the tabloids, which exploited his alleged adventures as an athlete. He was said to have been trained by the legendary Olympic athlete Jim Thorpe and in addition, he was a war hero. He was also a journalist, biographer, public lecturer, pilot, Indian rights advocate, and was heading to Hollywood to become a movie star. Not only that, he was a boxer, having claimed that he had knocked out Jack Dempsey during a sparring match.

In the glittering world of New York society of the 1920s, hostesses vied in sending out invitations to this so-called full-blooded Blackfoot chief, who had captured the imagination of North America with the story of his life and the plight of downtrodden Indians. As a special dispensation, Woodrow Wilson had even appointed Long Lance to West Point.

Not everybody bought his story. There were rumors that he was not a Cherokee from Oklahoma at all. He'd become such a famous fixture on the American landscape that reporters were investigating rumors about his true identity. Reports were turning up from western North Carolina that Long Lance was descended from African slaves. He was dark skinned but not black skinned so he was able to pass as an Indian. Other rumors suggested that his actual father might have been a tobacco planter from England, who had

126

moved to the Winston-Salem area and conceived Lance with a local woman of color, which would account for Long Lance's skin tone.

After the rehearsals, Long Lance went backstage to meet Belasco and other actors. In front of Hump, he kissed Mildred on the lips, asserting his territorial rights. He was an imposing figure towering over Hump. From that day on, Long Lance attended every rehearsal, always coming backstage to rescue Mildred.

After a few days, Long Lance's hostility toward Hump ended as he'd come to view him as no competition for Mildred's affections. "What would she want with that little runt when she's got me?" he asked Belasco one day, "After all, they don't call me Long Lance for nothing."

He even invited Hump to join Mildred and him on a round of the city's speakeasies, where Long Lance dominated the conversation with tall tales of his exploits. Hump listened attentively and seemed enthralled, although later telling Belasco that he too believed that Long Lance was an imposter. "An imposter," Hump said, "but a glorious one."

As he got to know Long Lance better, Hump came to believe that he was indeed black but had assumed the Indian identity to escape the restrictive segregationist policies of the South. Long Lance viewed himself as following in the tradition of what he said was his "remote maternal relative," Kit Carson, and was filled with fascinating tales of his experiences which allegedly ranged from being a rider in a Wild West show to fighting bravely as a Canadian soldier who'd won the Italian War Cross and the French *Croix de guerre.*

One day, Long Lance didn't show up for rehearsals, but cornered Hump when he was leaving the theater in the late afternoon. There was a look of desperation on Long Lance's face. Hump led Lance across the street as a means of talking to him privately. "You can have Mildred," Long Lance said. "She's all yours. In fact, I want you to take her off my hands."

(top photo) Chief Buffalo Child Long Lance; darling of the tabloids, and the most famous Indian in America

(bottom photo) Jazz-Age heiress Anita Baldwin

127

"What's going on here?" Hump asked.

"One of America's most famous women has fallen madly in love with me."

"You mean, the very, very rich Anita Baldwin?"

"Anita and I are through," Long Lance said. "It's someone else. She's big. I can't tell you her name. But I've got to get rid of Mildred. You go after her. Maybe she'll fall for you. If not, she might fuck up this new thing I have going."

Hump said he'd always found Mildred sexy and appealing, and he'd do his best to lure her away from him.

"You're a swell guy, Bogart," he said.

That didn't sound like Cherokee talk to Hump. The two men talked for an hour, pledging eternal friendship to each other. Long Lance even promised to make Hump an honorary Cherokee.

Having been dumped by Long Lance, Mildred finally agreed to go out with Hump after the opening night curtain fell on *It's a Wise Child*. They were in a mood to celebrate when they hit Tony's. Many of the critics also descended on Tony's that night, having already filed their reviews of *It's a Wise Child*. Hump was eager to ask them what they had written but knew that that wasn't proper Broadway protocol.

Mildred and Hump waited for the reviews, which were lukewarm. She was disappointed that only three reviews even listed her, with no comment about her acting. Woollcott wrote that Hump played his role with "more than his usual vigor and sincerity."

Feeling despondent and wanting to be cheered up, Mildred invited Hump back to her hotel room.

The next morning he got one of the worst reviews of his young life. Over coffee downstairs in the breakfast room, Mildred confessed to him. "You and I have no future," she told him. "After enjoying the embrace of Long Lance for many weeks, I realize that you are that inadequate sprig reviewers are always citing."

***

During the run of the play, the Wall Street crash of October, 1929 came tumbling down on the worldwide economy. Miraculously, the play survived the drop-off in business. Many other theaters shut their doors. At first Hump and Mary were unaware of how thoroughly Broadway would eventually be impacted by America's financial crisis. "In bad times, people need to be entertained," Mary told him. "They'll flock to the theater for escapism."

"Yeah," Hump said. "But how in the fuck are they going to afford the tick-

128

ets?"

Even in the midst of the disaster, Hollywood agents had descended on New York, hoping to find "actors who know how to talk." Out on the West Coast the unattractive voices of many silent-screen greats were repositioning them into the dustbin of film history.

Stuart Rose had become good friends with the former Broadway producer, Al Lewis, who ran the New York office for Fox in which Stuart worked. Stuart's job involved reading plays, hoping to find one suitable to be filmed. He managed to persuade Lewis to give his brother-in-law a chance at a screen test. Stuart took Lewis to see *It's a Wise Child*, and Lewis reluctantly agreed, although he wasn't impressed with the scar on Hump's upper lip.

Hump didn't think much would come of yet another screen test for him, but he performed a ten-minute segment from *The Man Who Came Back.*

When Lewis sent Hump's test to Fox in Hollywood, the studio wired him to sign Bogart for $750 a week. If he did well, an option called for his paycheck to go up to $1,000 a week, a virtual fortune at the beginning of the Depression.

Without checking with Mary, Hump signed with Fox. In their apartment that night, he tried to persuade Mary to drop out of *The Tavern*, a play in which she was starring on Broadway. He asked her to go on the train with him to Los Angeles. She refused, and violently so, leading to one of their biggest fights.

"You want to become a big-time movie star," Mary shouted at him. "Well, I want to become a big time Broadway star. Bigger than your lez wife, Helen Menken."

"You're not talented enough to carry the train of Helen's gown on stage," he yelled back at her. "She's a bigger star than you'll ever be. I thought you'd jump at the chance to go to Hollywood. That way you could fuck Kenneth one night, me the next."

She stormed out of their apartment and didn't come back all night. Even if she had returned, Hump wouldn't have been there.

After having farewell drinks with Bill and Stuart at Tony's, Hump called Helen Menken and asked her if he could spend the night with her. She agreed, inviting him to come over right away. With his suitcase already packed, he hugged and kissed both Stuart and Bill good-bye, and took a taxi to Helen's apartment.

Waking up the next morning, he smelled breakfast cooking. Helen was freshly made up and had his favorite bacon and eggs on the table. It was Helen, not Mary, who accompanied him to Grand Central where he caught a train that would take him to Chicago and on to Los Angeles.

On the way to Chicago, drinking heavily, he mixed freely with the passengers, and, like a little boy, even showed some doubters his newly signed contract with Fox. After a few drinks, he told one Kansas City cattleman, who'd never heard of Humphrey Bogart, that those Broadway screen writers were right on the mark. "That screen fob, Valentino, is going to be replaced by me. I'm going to become the biggest movie star Hollywood's ever seen."

Humphrey Bogart

CHAPTER THREE

When the train pulled into Los Angeles, photographers rushed to snap pictures of the most famous passengers. In the confusion, Hump was ignored until he saw Kenneth MacKenna rushing to embrace him at the station. "Welcome to Hollywood," Kenneth said. "Old buddy, old pal."

Hump embraced him warmly. It was good to see someone from New York.

"My apartment's waiting for you," Kenneth said. "I even washed the toilet seat."

Later, Hump read about the death of Long Lance. In 1932 he was found shot dead in the Arcadia, California home of Anita Baldwin. A pistol was by his side. A statement released to the press said that Long Lance, Chief Buffalo Child, had "absented himself from this harsh world by a pistol shot."

But despite the "official" report, up until the day of his death, Hump claimed that Baldwin had killed her black lover, "the great Indian impostor."

***

En route in a taxi to Kenneth's apartment, Hump looked for signs of resentment or hostility from Kenneth, finding none. Even though he'd been in love with Mary and had proposed to her first, he seemed to have forgiven Hump for marrying her instead.

Hump was candid with him, admitting that he and Mary were seeing other people and that the marriage had indeed been a mistake. Hump could have let it go at that, but he was the constant provocateur. He confessed Mary's secret to Kenneth: that she was having an affair with Kenneth's brother, Jo Mielziner. This news seemed to hurt Kenneth, and the moment Hump told his friend that, he regretted the confession.

Even when they got to the apartment, Kenneth didn't say much as he showed Hump around. There wasn't much to see. It was a sparsely furnished one-bedroom apartment—the two men, both lovers of Mary, would be sharing the same bed.

Kenneth was eager to talk about work, not Mary. He said he'd made a film, *Men Without Women*, co-starring Frank Albertson and Paul Page. The 70-minute film depicted the saga of 14 sailors trapped in a sunken submarine with not enough escape gear to go around. It was directed by John Ford.

"That Ford is one tough bastard," Kenneth said. "His first words to me were, 'I run a tight ship. I'm the officer in command and don't forget it!'" He paused to light a cigarette. "I hope you never work with this Ford asshole. He nearly killed all of us."

Eager to share news about his own success in films, Hump told Kenneth that Fox Studios had brought him out as a candidate for the leading role in *The Man Who Came Back*. Kenneth laughed when he heard the news. "You're the fifth actor they've brought out as a candidate for that role. I was the first. None of us is going to get the role. It's going to Charles Farrell, and he's still stuck in the methodologies of the Silent Screen. He can't even talk right."

Hump felt that Kenneth had seemed a little too gleeful in informing him of this, no doubt paying him back for the revelation about Mary having an affair with his brother Jo.

The next day Hump got up early and reported to work at Fox Studios as a contract player. To his painful regret, he learned that Kenneth was right. Not only was silent screen star Charles Farrell already signed to play the lead in *The Man Who Came Back*, Hump had been assigned the job of giving him diction lessons.

Farrell became a big star just as the screen learned to talk, and he'd been famously teamed with Janet Gaynor, especially in their big hit in the 1927 version of *Seventh Heaven*. Ironically, *Seventh Heaven* had been Helen Menken's most successful play a few years previously.

Only a year younger than Hump, Charles Farrell was the Brad Pitt of his day, and with his well-developed physique, had been doing half-clothed scenes on film back in the silent era. When Hump met the hunk in 1930, Farrell was decades away from his future role as mayor of Palm Springs, a position he was elected to in the late Forties.

Hump had seen the film, *Seventh Heaven*, and felt it represented the sappy peak of silent screen romanticism, a gauzy, idyllic romance combined with wholesome vitality. Farrell was wholesome all right, and, in fact, was one of the handsomest actors Hump had ever known. Hump was quickly learning that film actors were required to be more beautiful and photogenic than stage actors.

Kenneth MacKenna posing with Humphrey Bogart on Fox Studios' squash courts in 1930

Even though Hump was forced to work with Charles for six weeks, he took an instant dislike to the star. "I hope you don't teach me your fucking lisp," Farrell said. "You sound like a fairy."

Hump wanted to belt him one, but he feared that Farrell with his athletic physique might flatten him.

On the third day of voice coaching, Farrell became so angry at Hump that he crushed his cigarette out in Hump's palm. Hump winced in pain and rushed into the bathroom to run cold water over his wound. "You fucking conceited bastard," Hump said. "Fox contract or no Fox contract, I'm going to lick you for that."

"I'm sorry," Farrell said. "I didn't mean to do it. I'm mad at Raoul Walsh for making me take diction lessons from some lisping New York actor."

His hand still stinging from the cigarette burn, Hump came out of the bathroom. "You've gone too far."

"I'm really sorry," Farrell said. "I don't know what came over me. When I did that cigarette number on you, I wasn't trying to hurt you. I was standing up for all silent-screen actors who are losing their jobs to Broadway thespians."

"Listen, I need this job, and I want it to work out for me," Hump said. "Let's get on with it. God knows someone should teach you to speak English."

Farrell said, "I still feel sorry about that cigarette thing. The third lead, the juvenile role, hasn't been cast yet. I think you'd be ideal. I know you wanted the lead, but third billing in the latest Gaynor/Farrell film ain't bad."

"You'd put in a plug for me?"

"It's a deal."

When Hump got back to Kenneth's apartment that night, his actor friend was jubilant. "I just got a call from Raoul Walsh. He's cast me in *The Man Who Came Back* after all."

The news stunned Hump. "You mean Farrell's out of the flick?"

"Not at all," Kenneth said, his face radiant. "I've been cast in the supporting part of the juvenile lead."

***

At long last Hump was freed from having to give diction lessons to Farrell. Fox gave him his first major film role, a picture called *A Devil With Women*, based on a novel, *Dust and Sun* by Clements Ripley. It was to star Victor McLaglen and Mona Maris.

His brother-in-law, Stuart Rose, was on a train to Hollywood, bringing with him a series of plays and novels from the New York office, with recommendations of each of them as a pos-

Charles Farrell

sible film scenario. Kenneth had invited Stuart to stay at his apartment, with Hump agreeing to sleep on the sofa.

When Hump met Stuart at the railway station in Los Angeles, he was eager for news from New York. Stuart, though seemingly glad to see Hump, was not forthcoming with much information, as if deliberately concealing what he knew about what was going on back East.

Stuart and Frances had not visited the Bogarts in weeks and didn't know how they were doing. He'd not seen Mary Philips either. Since coming to Hollywood, Hump had written his wife only two letters, neither of which was answered.

In a taxi en route to Kenneth's apartment, Hump detected that something had gone seriously wrong in Stuart's marriage to his sister, Frances. It wasn't anything that Stuart specifically said. That he said almost nothing about Frances left the lingering suspicion that the marriage was on the rocks.

Finally, Hump decided to press the issue. "God damn it," he said. "I want to know. How are my sisters?"

Anger flashed across Stuart's face. "Okay, if you must know. Catherine has become a hopeless alcoholic and is sleeping with every guy in town. As for Frances, she grows more mentally unstable every month. The last time I talked to your dad about it, he held out the possibility that we might have to put her in an asylum."

"My God," Hump said.

"I don't want to talk about it now with Kenneth," Stuart said. "It's too painful. Before I go back east, I'll let you know everything. I figured you had enough on your mind trying to launch yourself at Fox."

Once upstairs, Kenneth and Stuart warmly embraced. Each man's face lit up at the sight of the other. Up to that point, Hump never knew that Stuart and Kenneth were any more than casual acquaintances. But they related to each other like two best friends bonded at the hip.

As if suddenly aware of Hump in the living room, Stuart turned to Hump. "I bet our boy Kenneth has to fight off the beautiful gals out here in Hollywood."

His eyes downcast, Hump headed for the kitchen to get himself a beer. "Something like that."

He heard the phone ring. When he returned from the kitchen, Kenneth told him that he had to report back to the set of *The Man Who Came Back* to re-shoot a scene.

After he'd dressed, Kenneth again embraced Stuart warmly and agreed to meet back at the apartment later when all three of them would go out on the town.

After Stuart showered and dressed, he came into the kitchen and joined Hump at the table, accepting a can of beer. "The publicity department at Fox called me, and they want to begin your buildup. Since the scar on your lip can't be concealed on screen, we've got to invent a cover-up story."

"I got it." Hump said. "But we don't want to implicate Belmont in this."

"No we don't," Stuart said. "The Fox publicist I talked to thinks we can claim that you were injured by a flying wooden splinter from a bursting shell when your naval vessel, *Leviathan*, came under fire from a German U-boat."

"Neat story," Hump said. "If anybody checked, though, I saw no action in the war. The *Leviathan* never came under fire. You're good at embellishing. Can't you come up with a better story, one that can't be checked?"

Stuart excused himself and made some business calls to Fox Studios. When he came back, he said, "I think I've got it. We'll have you stationed in Portsmouth. The Navy had assigned you to take a handcuffed prisoner—let's call him Johnny Ireland—from the naval station to a military prison forty miles away. Ireland, let's say, had been arrested in Boston and charged with desertion. At one point as you're changing trains, let's have Ireland ask you for a cigarette. As you go to light it for him, Ireland raises up his handcuffed hands, smashing you in the face, damaging your lip. We'll then say that Ireland made a run for it. With some skin on your upper lip hanging by a thread, you take out a .45 and shoot the man in his left buttock, grounding him. We'll have some Navy doctor sewing up your lip. Badly."

"That's kinda cute," Hump said. "I like the ring of it. Let's go for it."

That fantasy, conceived by Stuart late one afternoon in a small Hollywood apartment, became, in time, a Hollywood legend.

***

It was Friday night and all of Hollywood seemed to be having a good time except Hump. Mary had said that during their separation he was free to date. So far, he'd met no one.

Joan Blondell

He then remembered that bouncy blonde bombshell, Joan Blondell, with whom he'd appeared in that Ruth Etting flick, *Broadway's Like That*. He searched through his papers until he found her number.

Feeling a bit shy, he went to the phone. It was probably a useless gesture. A woman as sexy as Joan probably had guys lining up at her door, especially on a big date night like Friday in Hollywood. "What the hell," he said, deciding to ring her up anyway.

"Say hello to Miss Dallas, honey," the expressive face with the pop eyes said to Hump as she pulled up in front of his apartment house to find him already waiting on the sidewalk. "Miss Dallas, Texas, and I've got the pictures to prove it."

"Good to see you out here in Hollywood," Hump said, leaning in to kiss Joan on the lips. "Here we are: Two stars of tomorrow."

"Get in, handsome." Her big smile and big blue eyes lured him into the passenger seat of her secondhand 1927

135

Dodge, with its dented fenders and ripped canvas hood tied down with a rope to keep it from flapping. "As you can see, this ain't no Gloria Swanson limousine," Joan said.

She drove toward Santa Monica, where she knew a small and charming Italian restaurant where they could dine quietly. On the way there, he brought her up to date on what was happening—or not happening—to his career at Fox.

With a youthful exuberance lighting up her kewpie doll face, she told him about her own career. "I've been out here long enough to know that Warners has got me pegged as a brassy, gum-chewing, wisecracking blonde floozy. Better that than no work at all."

"I hear that back East a lot of us thespian hacks are out of work," he said. "They call it a depression."

"Jimmy Cagney and me are going to try to make the world forget its troubles," she said. "They signed us both to five-year contracts. He gets the big bills. I get the small change. But it's a job. I'll take any part they want me to play. The only thing I'm fighting is my name change."

"I think Joan Blondell is a great name for a movie star," he said. "What did the Warner friars come up with?"

"Inez Holmes."

He burst into laughter and reached for a cigarette, offering her one.

"Don't laugh too loud," she said. "You don't think Fox is going to let you keep Humphrey, do you? Bogart is okay, but Humphrey. I'm sure they're going to change it to something like Dale or maybe Cary. What about Brad?"

"Hell with that," he said. "It's going to be Humphrey Bogart or nothing. Don't let them rename you Inez Holmes. Warners will take enough from you. Hold onto that name, girl."

Over dinner he got to know her for the first time, as they'd hardly gotten acquainted in New York. Before the spaghetti was served, he'd learned that her father, Ed Blondell, had been one of the original Katzenjammer Kids. Joan was a true "born in a trunk" show biz woman, reared on vaudeville stages, having made her first appearance at the age of three months when she was brought out before the lights as a "carry-on" in the play, *The Greatest Love.*

"I grew up on the stage," she said. "I've taken more baths in train station toilets than anyone."

"How did you get the nickname, Rosebud?" he asked.

"We toured everywhere," she said. "Ed even took the Blondells to China. My big number was called 'In a Rosebud Garden of Girls.' Since then, only my intimates are allowed to call me Rosebud. But before the night is out, I hope you'll be calling me that."

She leaned over and planted a light kiss on his lips.

"Before this night is over, I hope your rosebud and I are on intimate terms," he said.

"Now, now," she said. "No need to get vulgar. Let's keep it clean."

The waiter arrived with the veal parmigiana just as she was telling him how she came to be teamed with Cagney. Hump had told her that he'd known Cagney in New York. "He was a drag queen appearing in cabaret revues back then," he said.

She seemed startled to hear that, and Hump deliberately didn't tell her how Cagney was offered a drag role.

"That big cheese, George Kelly, spotted Jimmy and me trying out this dance number," she said. "He cast us in *Maggie the Magnificent.* Kelly thought Jimmy looked like a fresh mutt, and I, of course, the blonde hooker with the heart of gold."

"I'm hearing real good things about the two of you," he said, reaching for her hand. "I'm just a little bit jealous. Are you guys shacking up?"

"So?" she said, smiling. "Do we really know what Mary Philips is doing in New York tonight?"

"Touché!"

After dinner they went for a walk along the Santa Monica pier, noticing the boats rocking from side to side as the water was choppy. He spotted a drunk throwing up over a rail.

"I'm living with Kenneth MacKenna," he said.

"And I'm living with three broads and sharing the rent," she said. "But there are ways."

"What do you mean?" he asked.

"Have you ever tried it in the back seat of a broken down Dodge?"

***

On the Fox lot Hump encountered his director for *A Devil with Women,* Irving Cummings, for the first time. Hump was startled to learn that if *A Devil With Women* became a hit, the studio planned to co-star him in an ongoing series of adventure stories with the film's big-name star, Victor McLaglen. Cummings seemed very excited at this prospect but Hump managed only a faint smile.

The idea of playing second fiddle to McLaglen, or to any other actor, in an ongoing series of B pictures wasn't part of Hump's dream before he came to Hollywood. He found the prospect so dismal, and the plot line so inane, that secretly he hoped that the picture would fail. Ironically, if the film had been successful, its success would probably have typecast Hump into the

Bogart as a second-tier actor romancing Mona Maris in a movie that almost ended his career, *A Devil With Women*

137

kind of marginal bit player whose consequences might have haunted him for the rest of his career.

Cummings put his arm around Hump and walked him over to McLaglen's dressing room. "You might as well meet the star of the picture. If my gut instinct is right, you'll appear with him in at least twelve films, and I'll direct every one of them. The McLaglen/Bogart films will be my old-age pension."

When Cummings introduced Hump to the British actor, McLaglen had just emerged dripping wet from the shower. At that point an aide summoned Cummings to the set, leaving Hump standing alone with a jaybird naked McLaglen.

"Fix yourself a whiskey, kid," McLaglen said, reaching for a thick towel.

"Pour one for me too, letting it fall from the bottle into the glass like a horse pisses."

Hump poured the actor a drink and said, "I'm happy to be working with you Mr. *Mack-loff-len.*"

"That's *Muh-clog-len*," he said. "Since you can't pronounce my name, just call me Victor."

During their two-hour wait before they were due on the set, Hump got acquainted with this famous and rambunctious star who stood six feet, three inches. His hair was jet-black, and he had a twinkle in his blue-gray eyes. Hump became more comfortable after McLaglen put on his drawers.

The son of the Right Reverend Andrew McLaglen, a Protestant clergyman in South Africa, the young Victor was the eldest of eight brothers. He tried to fight in the Boer War by joining the Life Guards, but the Reverend McLaglen tracked him down and, drawing on his persuasive powers and his political connections, secured his release.

Heading for Canada, he worked only temporarily on a farm devoted mainly to turnips before running off to become a professional prizefighter. That was followed by a tour in circuses, vaudeville shows, and Wild West shows. In these shows, he was billed as a fighter who would take on all comers in the audience. Any young man who could last three rounds with McLaglen was paid $25. He toured with these shows from America to Australia. In Sydney he fought heavyweight champion Jack Johnson, the champ knocking McLaglen out after six rounds.

(top photo) Boxing champ "Sharkey McLaglen," and (bottom photo) his later incarnation as Victor McLaglen, Hollywood actor

When World War I broke out, McLaglen signed up with the Irish Fusiliers and was sent to the Middle East. Eventually he became the Provost

138

Marshal for the city of Baghdad, responsible for the military police.

With his pugnacious nature, he had hoped to resume his boxing career after the war but ended up being cast in the *Call of the Road* in 1920. From that day on, he became a popular leading man in English silents.

By 1924 he'd been lured to Hollywood to appear in *The Beloved Brute*. One role followed another, from *Women and Diamonds*, also in 1924, to *Beau Geste* in 1926. His own glory came to him when he played Captain Flagg in *What Price Glory?* in 1926.

Described as a "British-born Wallace Beery," McLaglen was a two-fisted man of action. Under Raoul Walsh's direction, McLaglen's appearance in the antiwar film was a smash hit at the box office. Audiences delighted in the ribald, gregarious interplay between Flagg and his sergeant, Quirt, as played by Edmund Lowe. Little did Hump know on that first meeting with McLaglen that Raoul Walsh, in about a year, would team McLaglen as Flagg and Edmund Lowe as Sergeant Quirt in a derivative flicker loosely inspired by *What Price Glory?*, *Women of All Nations*.

Hump himself would appear in that movie. No longer viewed as a candidate for a costarring role opposite McLaglen, Hump suffered ninth billing in the screen credits.

In *A Devil With Women*, McLaglen was cast in the role of Jerry Maxton, a soldier-of-fortune at large in a banana republic in Central America. He played a womanizer, romancing "anything in skirts," especially the fair señorita, Rosita Fernandez, as interpreted by Mona Maris.

In contrast, Hump played a supporting role of the clean-cut but wastrelly rich nephew of the country's wealthiest man.

In the film, McLaglen's job involves ending the reign of terror of the notorious bandito, Morloff, who is terrorizing the countryside. McLaglen falls for a woman gun smuggler. Alone with Hump's character, he's lured into the enemy camp, where the two men narrowly escape a firing squad. Maris's character of Rosita provides a refuge for them. The bandits are enticed inside Maris's hacienda where one by one McLaglen, the former prizefighter, knocks them out in a series of one-punch fights.

At the end of the film, McLaglen is ready to claim Rosita as his girl, but she tells him that her heart belongs to Tom Standish, the role played by Bogart. Hump in his first major film gets the girl in the final reel.

Today it appears amazing that Hump was ever cast in another movie after the release of *A Devil with Women*. A financial and artistic failure, with a stupid plot and mismatched actors, it should have ended his career. Fox executives wisely decided not to continue pairing McLaglen with Bogart, abandoning forever the notion of contin-

Director Irving Cummings

uing their original idea about the ongoing series of adventure films. Later in life Bogie threatened to buy up all copies of the film and have them destroyed.

The director, Irving Cummings, was particularly brutal to the neophyte film actor. "McLaglen is biting off your balls and chewing them up on screen. You come off like some rich little twerp repeating one of your Broadway 'Tennis, anyone?' parts."

"God damn it, that's what the role calls for," Hump protested.

"We've got to come up with some business to make your character real," Cummings said.

The director probably gave Hump the worst advice he could. A stage actor unaware of how the camera picked up the tiniest facial nuance, Hump set out to match the almost constant ear-to-ear grin of the burly looking, battered, and brutish British actor.

The writer, Robert Sklar, in reviewing the film, said it best: "Bogart plays a coltish fool, tossing his head, slapping his knees, and laughing with his mouth open so wide you can almost see his tonsils. He looks like an actor who is uncomfortable not only with his part, but also with his body. He employs a few stock gestures that he repeats again and again: arms awkwardly held in front of his body; then pushing back his jacket; then fists at the belt; then into his pockets; then back to the belt, arms akimbo. Smiles, arch delivery of lines, more smiles."

***

Mona Maris with her superb deep-throat technique was taking such good care of Hump on the set that he hardly had enough left for Joan Blondell in the evening. Joan wasn't free every night, only when Cagney could escape from the clutches of his "Willie."

Stuart Rose had left Kenneth MacKenna's apartment to return to the Fox New York office and his unhappy bed with Frances. Hump sensed that Kenneth wanted him out of the apartment so he could conduct his private life with greater secrecy.

When the apartment next door became available, Hump eagerly signed a lease and set out to buy some secondhand furniture. He didn't want to purchase anything too expensive, because he feared that his days as a Fox movie star were about to come to an end.

Kenneth was supportive, but Hump sensed that his host was relieved to see him go. When a phone was finally installed in his own name, he called Joan, only to learn that she was seeing Cagney that night.

"Don't worry," she said. "I ran into an old friend of yours from New York. I gave her your number. You definitely won't be lonely tonight."

"Who is it?"

"And spoil the surprise?" she said. "Have fun, duckie." She put down the receiver.

About an hour later, the phone rang. With some reluctance, he picked up the receiver.

"This is Barbara Stanwyck," the voice said. "Could this be the one and only Humphrey Bogart?"

"Miss Stanwyck," he stammered, fearing at first someone was pulling a trick on him. "I'm honored that you'd call me."

"Joan gave me your number," Stanwyck said.

"She said you were an old friend of mine," he said. "We've never met. Of course, I'd be honored to take you out."

"Never met!" Stanwyck said, mocking him. "In Brooklyn where I come from, when a man fucks a woman, he's met her."

"You and I…" Hump was totally confused.

"I'm Ruby Stevens," Stanwyck said. "That hot Jazz Baby from the chorus line. You told me I was the greatest fuck of your life."

No longer the tough-talking little chorus girl from Brooklyn, Ruby Stevens—a.k.a. Barbara Stanwyck—was now a take-charge movie star. Within two hours of her call, Hump found himself dressing in his best suit.

Stanwyck had shown up at the apartment house as the driver of her own sleek new car. "I know you struggling actors drive around in junk-heaps, and I have my image to think of," she'd said on the phone.

When he opened the door and a stunningly beautiful and elegantly dressed Stanwyck was standing there, he searched for some telltale clue in her face that this ravishing beauty, who was aspiring to become the new queen of Hollywood, was the same chorus girl he'd allegedly bedded. He found none but enjoyed it when she hugged him and kissed him succulently on the lips. He was certain that if he'd ever gone to bed with a dame like this, he would never forget her.

In his apartment, he went into the kitchen to make a drink for both of them. Coming back into the living room, she gulped it down. "C'mon, let's go."

On the way downstairs, she claimed she'd met him one night when he'd stumbled drunk from Texas Guinan's place. "I was working the honky-tonk next door."

Something jolted in his brain, but he wasn't certain. He vaguely recalled picking up some thin girl. Unlike the other ladies in the chorus line, she had few curves and her legs were less well-developed than the others. In years to come, no one could accuse Barbara Stanwyck of competing with the gams of Marlene Dietrich or Betty Grable. With her pretty auburn hair and her blue eyes, he had been attracted to her but he still didn't remember bedding her. Fortunately, there was no motorcycle patrolman on duty that night. She made it to the Cock & Bull for dinner in record time.

Before the first course arrived, she announced,

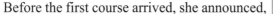

Barbara Stanwyck in 1930

141

"I'm the biggest star in this whole fucking room."

"You're sure as hell a bigger star than me," he said. "I'm not even a star-let."

They ordered steaks from a handsome blond-haired waiter, who was more beautiful than either of them. With his eyes, he made it clear to each of them that, if asked, he would easily be their bed partner for the night.

Stanwyck gave the most "manly" order. "Just sweep it over the brush fire lightly," she told the waiter.

It was one o'clock before they staggered out of the tavern. Although technically, she was too drunk to drive, Stanwyck took control of the wheels of her car anyway. Without anybody saying anything, it was just assumed that she was heading back to his apartment building.

Hump fumbled drunkenly with the key at his own apartment door. "Once again I'm going to get to fuck Ruby Stevens, and I'm drunk as a skunk for the second time."

"When aren't you drunk?" she said with a touch of hostility in her voice. She took the key from him and opened the door right away, entering the apartment before he did.

When he staggered inside, she slammed the door and locked it. "Let's get one thing straight, Bogart. I've got to warn you. When I take you to bed, I run the fuck."

***

In Hump's apartment, it was three o'clock in the morning. Stanwyck was right: she ran the fuck. Twice she'd mounted him. Both times he'd lain on his back as she did her gymnastics over him. He wanted more of that kind of loving, although he didn't plan to abandon his missionary position with Joan Blondell.

Stanwyck stood at his soot-streaked window clad only in a brassière, not bloomers, and looked out into the night, although his view opened onto a brick wall. The room was dark. Propped up in bed, he could only make out the glow of her fiery hot cigarette. She smoked like she acted in movies—with gusto.

Until he would meet Joan Crawford, Stanwyck was the most ambitious actress he'd ever known. It made stars he'd appeared with on Broadway, including Mary Boland and Shirley Booth, look like gentle ladies-in-waiting at the court of some dowager queen.

As Bogie would say later in life, "Ruby Stevens was one tough, sassy broad, but she had class. She was hard-boiled yet soft and vulnerable, a free-spirited woman who took no crap from any man. She was also one of the sex-iest women I've ever known."

Yet, even though she'd seduce many men in her life, including William Holden, Robert Wagner, Glenn Ford, and Gary Cooper, Hump suspected that in her heart she was a lesbian. It didn't appear that passion drove her to men. Stanwyck once told him, "I save my real loving, my gentle side, for women.

142

With men, things immediately revolve around power games."

He bolted up in bed, "My God, I must be sobering up. It's come back to me. I remember you when you were dancing at the Strand."

"Great!" she said in a harsh voice. "So, you aren't a retard. That proves that even as a teenager I can make a lasting impression on a drunk."

"You were one of the Keep Kool Cuties," he said. "You did that number with Johnny Dooley. 'A Room Adjoining a Boudoir,' if memory serves."

"Finally, you know who I am," she said, "even though I had to fuck you twice to jar that pickled brain of yours."

"I miss the Twenties back in New York," he said when she crushed out her cigarette and returned to bed for some pillow talk. "Speakeasies, dirty dances, bootleg hooch, plunging necklines, red hot jazz, flapper clothes."

"And big-dicked New York men," she chimed in. "Don't forget those."

"I didn't know too many of those," he said. "None at all, as a matter of fact."

Since she couldn't sleep, she decided to keep him up too. "It was Mae Clarke who taught me the joy of lesbian love. But, as you also know from tonight, I'm not completely weaned from men either. I don't want to deny myself any pleasure. Too much was denied me as a girl. As a woman, I'll go after what I want. If I want to get fucked by a man, you know I can go for that the way I bagged you tonight. If I want a woman, I'll chase her down and get her. I've already set my sights on that blonde German bitch, Dietrich. Who knows? Marlene, and me might become a thing."

"Invite me over," Hump said. "From what I've seen of Dietrich I'd go for her in a minute. I saw Mae Clarke in *Nix on Dames*. I'd go for her too. You've got good taste. You and Mae still an item?"

"We still are," Stanwyck said. "Me and Mae saw you on Broadway in *It's a Wise Child*. She thought you were kinda cute."

"I'll take you up on that invitation for a three-way," he said.

"You've got a date," she said. "Now let's get some God damn sleep. You'll talk my head off and keep me up all night. I've got to look gorgeous on camera tomorrow."

***

"I heard you taught Farrell how to talk. How about teaching me how to shit? I'm constipated."

Those unlikely remarks launched a friendship that would last to the grave between Humphrey Bogart and Spencer Tracy.

Hump reached to shake the actor's hand on the Fox set of *Up the River*. "Call me Hump."

Bogie with Spencer Tracy in
Up the River

143

"What kind of nickname is that?" Tracy asked. "From now on and henceforth forever more you'll be known as Bogie."

Stocky, round-faced and not particularly handsome, Tracy was hardly a Hollywood hunk like Farrell. A former Jesuit prep-school student who once wanted to be a priest, the Milwaukee-born actor was Bogie's age and, like Bogie, had joined the Navy in the final days of World War I.

Tracy had captured director John Ford's attention on Broadway playing Killer Mears, a convicted murderer in an all-male cast. Tracy was waiting on Death Row in the play *The Last Mile*. Ford thought that he'd be ideal in the role of a character called "St. Louis" in the 1930 prison drama, *Up the River*, opposite the Ziegfeld beauty, Claire Luce.

Bogie was cast as the fourth lead, playing Steve. He'd never met Ford but the director had seen him in a matinee performance of *The Skyrocket* and had decided Hump would be suitable for a role in *Up the River*. Ford later told Bogie in Hollywood that, "I know your wife was the star of that play. But you have the talent. Mary Philips is no actress." Hump decided to use Ford's assessment of her talent in his next big fight with his wife.

On the set, Tracy put his arm around Bogie and led him toward his dressing room. "Ford's in the front office this morning. So in the meantime, let's you and me go have some whiskey. You are a drinking man, aren't you?"

He smiled at Tracy. "I've been known to put away a few."

After the first drink, Tracy delivered the bad news. "There may be no picture. Ford is meeting right now with Winfield Sheehan. In case you're that green around here, Sheehan runs this joint."

"What's the matter?" Bogie protested. "We have contracts. They brought us out from New York."

"That doesn't matter to those fuckers," Tracy said. "Sheehan's been looking at the gross over at MGM on the *The Big House*."

"I saw it," Bogie said. "Great picture. Bob Montgomery and Wallace Beery did a fine job."

"Don't forget my old pal, Chester Morris," Tracy said. "He was in it too. Trouble is, they did too fine a job. Sheehan knows our script isn't half as good. Reviewers would unfavorably compare our picture with *The Big House*. Also, Sheehan has seen screen tests of both of us. And he doesn't want us in the picture, even if he decides to go ahead with it."

"Fuck this!" Bogie said. "I should go back to New York. I'm spinning my wheels out here in this palm pasture."

"Have another drink," Tracy said.

In spite of the bad news he reported, Bogie relaxed in Tracy's presence. The actor had a soothing effect on him. To Bogie, he seemed like a sports loving man's man, with a big head and a boar neck. It was Tracy's well-modulated voice that drew Bogie to him.

As the morning wore on and Ford still hadn't shown up, Tracy and Bogie used the opportunity to drink more whiskey and to get to know each other. Each actor seemed fascinated by the other. There was a restlessness—even a self-destructiveness—about Tracy that intrigued Bogie. He would later claim, "Spence carried around a lot of that Catholic guilt crap."

At that stage in their friendship, Bogie didn't have a clue as to what Tracy had to feel guilt about, but he was determined to find out. Surely it wasn't something as simple as cheating on your wife. All men in Hollywood did that. With all the temptation out here, how could they resist?

Earlier he'd learned that Tracy had been married to a minor Broadway actress, Louise Treadwell, for seven years. "It was love at first sight," Tracy said. Bogie also learned that she'd given birth to a deaf son named John. "His deafness makes me suffer a lot," Tracy said. "Somehow I blame myself. Good, healthy, Irish boy sperm isn't supposed to create a child with birth defects."

"It's not your fault," Bogie assured him as he accepted another whiskey. He feared that if they kept drinking like this, and Ford did show up, having saved the picture from Sheehan, neither of them would be sober enough to appear on camera.

"I was the terror of Milwaukee," Tracy said. "A tough Irish kid. I got into at least three fistfights a day, taking on the Sauerkrauts, the Pollack sausages, and the Dago pizza pies. I was in and out of fifteen—make that eighteen—different schools before I finished the eighth grade."

"You got me beat on that count," Bogie said. "But I was kicked out of Andover. My father wanted me to be a doctor."

"Welcome to the club," Tracy said. "My old man wanted me to be a priest. I still think about it. I used to dream of myself as Monsignor Tracy, Cardinal Tracy, Bishop Tracy. Get this: Archbishop Tracy. Every time I think of what I might have been, I get goose bumps. Of course, I could never have been celibate. Not me. If there's a whorehouse in town, I quickly become the best customer."

Ironically, although Tracy obviously never became a priest, he ended up playing one in four memorable performances—*San Francisco* in 1936 with Clark Gable; *Boy's Town* in 1938, *Men of Boy's Town* in 1941, and a final appearance, *The Devil at Four O'Clock* in 1961.

"Before I agreed to do this picture with you, I saw a rough cut of *A Devil With Women*," Tracy said. "I know you used to do some stupid juvenile roles on Broadway. But I never caught your 'Tennis, anyone?' act. Of course, that fascist, McLaglen, steals the picture from you and that cocksucker, Mona Maris. You bullshit your way through the film. One hammy disguise after another. Some clowns call that acting. I don't. If our damn flick ever gets made, watch how I do it. Don't let the camera see you running around like a chicken with its head cut off. Underplay. That's the way to do it."

Spencer Tracy

145

As insulted as he was by Tracy's advice, Bogie listened to it. He'd never overplay a character again. "There's at least one thing I like about the script. I get the girl."

"So you do," Tracy said, pouring himself another drink. "On the screen you do. In real life, I've already got Claire. She's about to show up here any minute. The moment I introduce the two of you, I want you to get the hell out of here. I'm horny this morning, and that Ziegfeld cutie is one mighty fine piece of tail."

As if on cue, there was a knock on the door. Tracy signaled Bogie to open it.

Standing on the stoop was a stunningly attractive woman, Claire Luce. He recognized her from her photographs. "Can a lady darken these chambers? Or is it strictly a stag party?"

"Come on in. I'm Humphrey Bogart."

"Call him Bogie," Tracy chimed in. "Everybody does."

Bogie stepped back to make way for her.

"Haul that cute ass over here," Tracy said to Luce. "Give your daddy a kiss. I'm in the mood for a big, wet, sloppy one."

Excusing himself, Bogie left the dressing room, shutting the door tightly behind him. Walking toward the set, he encountered for the first time an angry John Ford, the blood vessels on his head looking as if they were about to pop.

***

"I've just got back from the front office," John Ford said to Bogie. "C'mon, let's go for a drive. I've got to clear my head."

As Bogie headed for the studio parking lot with the director, Ford didn't say a word but looked like doom and gloom had cascaded down around him.

Director John Ford

Bogie suspected that he and Tracy had been fired from the cast and had been replaced with two other actors.

"Get in," Ford commanded when they reached his car. He drove out of the studio and headed up into the hills. Back in those relatively traffic-free days, you could actually drive in Los Angeles.

As Ford floored the accelerator and took dangerous curves, almost missing them, Bogie was terrified, his eyes popping out almost as much as Joan Blondell's. Ford kept his eyes glued on the curvy highway. Bogie wondered if Sheehan had fired him too. He even flashed on the possibility that he was playing a secondary role in a suicide run, with Ford planning to take the car, Bogie, and himself over the mountain. That would be like a

146

real life version of *Thelma and Louise* decades before that film was eventually shot.

"For God's sake, man, look out!" Bogie shouted at him. He figured he didn't want to plunge to his death without putting up some protest.

Ford braked the car suddenly, coming to an abrupt stop at a belvedere. When Bogie got out of the car, he noticed that if Ford hadn't applied that brake in time he would indeed have destroyed the car. Ford had allowed himself only a foot of land. Bogie looked back at him. "I'd call that a close shave."

"I'm a bit of a daredevil when it comes to driving," Ford said.

"Could have fooled me," Bogie said, still shaken from the experience. He figured that it would be safer to walk back down that mountain than to get into the car again.

Ford got out of the car and stood next to a still-unnerved Bogie. "I always come up here to clear my head. It's the most beautiful view in Los Angeles."

This was the first time Bogie had looked at the view. It was indeed panoramic. The director had a keen eye for locale.

"I've got a cast and crew waiting back at Fox, but no script," Ford said.

"But I've read the script," Bogie said.

"It's been junked," Ford said, sucking in the fresh morning air. "Fox Studios has decided that we can't compete with *The Big House*. I've been ordered to turn our film into a prison comedy."

"That's a novel idea," Bogie said.

"Get this," Ford said. "I start shooting tomorrow morning."

"Without a script?" Bogie asked, dumbfounded.

"I'll stay up late every night and come into the studio with enough pages written to shoot for the day," Ford said. "The God damn film is only ninety minutes long. I can do it. You'll see."

"From what I've read, it's a pretty grim story to turn into a comedy," Bogie said.

"In its present shape, it's a piece of junk," Ford said, "but I can convert it into a convict comedy. Slapstick and sentiment, that's the way to go. Instead of hardened criminals, you guys can just be naughty boys. It'll be artlessly disarming."

Bogie wasn't convinced.

"Right now I'm writing a scene in my head," Ford said. "In the new version some prisoners stage a theatrical production for the chain gang. In this all-male cast, some of the prisoners can dress in drag. I'll get some discarded gowns from Mae West. Right now I can see Tracy and that actor, Warren Hymer—or is it Hymen?—dressing up like women. They'll make a break for it dressed like gals. Run off to New England to thwart the evil villain's plan. When that mission is accomplished, they'll voluntarily come back to prison and turn themselves in, in time to win the annual baseball game."

"Sounds like a laugh riot," Bogie said.

"Let's go for it," Ford said. "But first I've got to ask you a question. Do you have a pair of balls on you?"

"I'd call them that," Bogie said, "although I'm sure there are a lot of guys in Hollywood with a bigger pair."

"What I mean is, do you like to fuck women?" Ford said. "Most of those Broadway sissies they send over from New York, guys like Kenneth MacKenna, had rather water the pansies in their garden than fuck women."

"I do my share of fucking," Bogie said. "Maybe more than most men."

"I'm glad to hear it," Ford said. "I'm taking you to Louise's. It's the best little whorehouse in the West. All the Hollywood stars go there. Louise has her pick of the most beautiful women in America. All the cute little milkmaids who get off the train here wanting to be stars end up as whores, and the best of them end up with Louise."

"I could always use a good piece of ass," Bogie said.

"Get in the car," Ford said. "We're off."

Committing his life into Ford's hands once again, Bogie reluctantly got in. Ford drove even worse and more recklessly down the mountain than he did going up it. But, finally, they arrived alive at Louise's, a surprisingly elegant bordello.

Louise appeared to be over fifty but it was obvious that she'd been a beauty in her day. She kissed Ford on the mouth. "John and I go way back," she said. "He's one cowboy who sure knows how to take care of a lady." She paused. "If memory serves."

"Meet Humphrey Bogart," Ford said. "He's an actor out of New York. Who knows? He might become one of your best customers."

"I hope so," she said, looking Bogie up and down. "I'd take you on for free."

"He wants something young and cute today, dearie," Ford interjected.

"Maybe some other time," Bogie said, kissing the aging madam on the cheek.

Dawn Night, aka
Glenda Farrell

"Okay, boys," she said. "I hope you like blondes, though. Last night I had a large group of clients from Argentina. Those horny bastards wanted only blondes. I had to order every gal in my joint to dye her hair both on top and down below."

"Blondes will be just fine," Ford said.

Within thirty minutes, Bogie found himself entering a small cubicle of a room. It was dimly lit. But there was enough illumination to accentuate the curves of a very voluptuous blonde lying nude on the bed, wearing only a pair of black stockings and emerald-green high heels. "Come on in, good looking, and lock the door."

"I think I've died and gone to heav-

148

en," Bogie said, feasting his eyes on her luscious body.

She introduced herself as Dawn Night.

"That sounds like a real good name," he said, as he unbuckled his trousers.

After their lovemaking, she became confidential. "My name is not really Dawn Night," she confessed. "I just made that one up. I'm keeping my real name a secret for screen billing. I'm going to become the biggest female star ever to set foot in Hollywood."

He'd certainly heard that line a lot from his previous encounters with chorus gals, except in New York the women always said "Broadway" instead of "Hollywood." "What's your real name? I won't tell. That way, when I see your name up on the marquee, I'll know to go in to see your picture."

"Okay." She giggled again. "If you promise not to tell."

"Trust me, I won't tell."

"Not so fast," she said. "Are you sure I can trust you? I mean, you're an actor and everything."

"Sure I know how to keep my lip zipped," Bogie said. "I sorta dig you, and I'd like to see you again."

"But not in this place. I won't be working here much longer. I've appeared on Broadway. I'm just picking up some quick cash. I'm not really a whore."

"Coming from some other gal I'd doubt that. But I believe you."

"I've already made one film," she said. "It was just a small part and I went unbilled. But I've got this great friend. She's an actress and she's gonna be real big. She's helping me break into Hollywood."

"What's your friend's name?" he asked. "Maybe I've heard of her."

"Joan Blondell."

He was startled but said nothing, masking his shock.

"Only the other day, Mervyn LeRoy was in here with me," she said. "You know, the director? He's promised to put me in a big gangster film. He said it's going to be the biggest film of the year. It's going to star Edward G. Robinson, and it's going to be called *Little Caesar*. Robinson is going to play Rico Bandello, a two-bit hoodlum. Even if he is a star, you can have Robinson. When LeRoy casts me in the movie, I'm going to chase after the co-star. That handsome hunk, Doug Fairbanks Jr., is going to play Tony Massara, Rico's best friend. Before the filming is over, I'm going to take Doug boy away from that whore, Joan Crawford."

"I think a lot of women—maybe a lot of men, too—would like to take that stud away from Crawford. Now tell me your name."

"Glenda Farrell," she blurted out. "Remember that name. Me and you will no doubt appear in some pictures together. You see, I'm going to become Queen of Warner Brothers."

***

On the set of *Up the River* that morning, Bogie sat having bitter black coffee with his co-star, Claire Luce. Even though she was Tracy's temporary mis-

149

tress, Bogie was plotting to see if he could take Luce away from his newly acquired friend. It was the beginning of a one-upmanship that would last until Bogie's death.

In the film, Luce played "Judy," an innocent young girl who was framed by a crooked stock salesman and sent "up the river."

Many chroniclers of Bogie's life have confused Claire Luce with Clare Boothe Luce, (1903-87), the talented, wealthy, beautiful, and controversial New Yorker, best remembered as a congresswoman (1942-46) and playwright who penned *The Women*. She was the first female American ambassador when Dwight Eisenhower appointed her to her post in Italy in 1952. The "Luce" was added to her name when she married magazine tycoon, Henry R. Luce, of *Time-Life-Fortune*.

A much more modest achiever, Claire Luce, the actress sitting across from Bogie, launched herself as a cigarette girl in Rochester, New York, and worked her way to Broadway as a chorus girl. She ended up having an affair with Flo Ziegfeld who cast her in *The Follies of 1927*.

As they sat idly by, Luce told Bogie that she'd fallen madly in love with Tracy and that he had promised to divorce his wife and marry her. Even though Bogie had just launched his friendship with the actor, he suspected that Tracy had used the same line on many a chorus gal.

From where he sat talking to Luce, Bogie spotted John Ford striding onto the set. Bogie would later claim that John Wayne learned his distinctive walk on screen by imitating John Ford.

Ford looked angry and hung over, as he'd been up all night trying to turn "this fucker of a prison drama into a God damn comedy."

Both Bogie and Luce were relieved to learn that they wouldn't have to face Ford's ire that day. Ford's assistant, Tom Hubbard, had told them that they weren't scheduled to go on camera. Nevertheless, Hubbard said that they had to appear at the Fox studio early every morning throughout the entire

Ziegfeld's "Folly"
Claire Luce with Humphrey Bogart

shoot in case Ford decided to use them.

"As long as I get paid," Bogie said.

After a brief conference with Ford, Hubbard approached Bogie and Luce with a concerned look on his face. Always the curious one, Bogie wanted to know what was the matter. Hubbard called Bogie aside, as he didn't want to speak in front of Luce.

"The first scene involves Tracy," Hubbard said, once he was out of earshot of Luce. "And he hasn't shown up this morning. We know where he lives. The front office has a phone number for him. The phone rings off the wall. Ford said that if Tracy doesn't

150

show up on the set by three o'clock at the latest, he's casting Jimmy Cagney in the part. It seems that Cagney is free for two weeks and can play the role."

"God damn it," Bogie said. "This is Spence's first starring role in a feature film. If he fucks this up, he's finished in Hollywood. Word will spread like wildfire. I know he drinks a lot."

"Would you believe that if the Pacific Ocean were alcohol, Spence would have it drained dry in a weekend?"

"Maybe I'd better try to find him," Bogie responded.

Back in those days of lax security, all one had to do was arrive at a hotel's reception desk, ask for a patron's room number, take the elevator upstairs, and knock on the door. That is exactly what Bogie did when he arrived in the lobby of the Hollywood Plaza.

At room 401, Bogie pounded on the door. At first there was no answer. He pounded again. Finally, the door was opened just a bit as it was still bolted to a link chain.

"I'm Humphrey Bogart," he said. "I've got to get in touch with Spencer Tracy. I've come over from Fox."

Although he couldn't see too well, it sounded like a young man behind the door. "Oh," he said. "I've heard of you. You're co-starring with Spence in his movie."

"Let me in," Bogie demanded in his most forceful voice.

"I guess it's okay," the young man said.

"I'm his friend," Bogie said. "Here to help him."

The young man unfastened the latch and let Bogie into the dark room. The light switch came on. Before Bogie stood one of the most beautiful young men he'd ever seen in his life. He was definitely movie star material himself. He wore only a pair of white boxer shorts, revealing his trim athletic build.

"I'm Lew Ayres," the semi-nude man said. Suddenly, Bogie realized who this boyishly handsome man was. Everyone in Hollywood was talking about his success in the role of Paul Baumer in *All Quiet on the Western Front*, Lewis Milestone's World War I masterpiece based on Erich Maria Remarque's novel detailing the horrors of war and its devastating effect on fighting men.

There was talk that the part, his third appearance on camera, might win him the Academy Award for poignantly portraying a young schoolboy thrown into the frenzy of war. In the film he was supposed to be bewildered by his loss of innocence. Bogie wondered how innocent Ayres could possibly be after a night with Tracy.

Without knowing the details, the evidence against Tracy was enough to convict. His new friend was a bisexual. Like all the great "womanizers" of Hollywood that Bogie knew or would know

Lew Ayres

in the future, from George Raft to Errol Flynn, these Romeos seemed to go for boys on the side.

Ayres headed across the suite's living room and put on his trousers and an undershirt. Barefoot, he came back over to Bogie. "Spence was doing fine last night," he said, "but as the night wore on, he drank more and more. He's in the bedroom there sprawled out totally drunk. I've been unable to get him up to go to work. I know he's due on Ford's set."

Bogie crossed the living room and looked into the small, almost alcove-like bedroom. There with the morning light streaming in, Spence lay sprawled nude near the edge of the bed, his mouth open. He was breathing heavily and his head fell over the edge of the mattress and seemed to hang in midair.

"Lew, my good man," Bogie said, turning around to confront Ayres. "Call room service for a big pot of strong black coffee. This here movie star, Mr. Spencer Tracy, and his juvenile lead are heading for the shower. I'm going to wake this drunken sod up if it kills me."

"You think you can?" a hesitant Ayres asked. "I've tried everything already."

"It won't be just the cold shower and the bitter black coffee," Bogie said. "My father's a doctor in New York. I drink a lot myself, and I've stumbled in at five o'clock in the morning when I was due somewhere at eight-thirty. Dad has these pills."

"What kind of pills?" Ayres asked.

"You know I'm not sure they have a name, and I have no idea what's in them. All I know is that when I force Spence here to swallow two of these little mother-fuckers, we're going to have him bouncing on John Ford's set with more energy than those two dancing fools, George Raft and Jimmy Cagney, combined."

When Bogie finally returned to his dressing room after a lengthy ordeal associated with awkening Tracy and hauling him back, in time for his scene,

Body and Soul
Humphrey Bogart with Charles Farrell

to the set, he spotted Ford's assistant walking purposefully_toward him. "The front office has got another script for you," Hubbard said. "You're to start work as soon as Ford is finished with you."

"What picture?" Bogie asked.

"The thing is called *Body and Soul.*"

"Who's got the lead?" Bogie asked. "And what's my billing?"

"You'll get fourth billing," Hubbard said. "The star is Charles Farrell."

***

Long before *Vanity Fair* "outed" Spencer Tracy in the post-millennium, and years before his homosexual dalliances became privately known to the likes of such gossip mavens as Hedda Hopper and Louella Parsons, Bogie was privy to his close friend's darkest secrets.

After the first day's shoot of *Up the River*, Tracy and Ayres invited Bogie to their suite for drinks, to be followed by dinner. From the first, Bogie took an enlightened view about their relationship. He didn't exactly encourage it but he didn't condemn it either. "I say if it feels good, go for it," Bogie told both men as he downed some of their whiskey. "It's no one's God damn business but your own."

"But there's the matter of my faith, my beliefs," Ayres protested. "I don't even like to look myself in the mirror in the morning."

"That's a crock of …." Bogie hesitated, searching for a word. He detested the use of the word "shit." "That's bull. Frankly, you guys are no different from anybody else I've met in Hollywood. Take myself, for instance. Nobody likes a broad better than I do. I've even had thoughts about taking Claire Luce from you." He smiled at Tracy to indicate he wasn't really serious. "But I've done some weird stuff on occasion. Name an actor on Broadway or in Hollywood who hasn't."

Tracy leaned back, his face and demeanor radiating calm in spite of any inner turmoil. "Bogie, unless you were born Catholic, unless you seriously wanted to be a priest, you can't understand Catholic guilt."

"Whatever the fuck that is," Bogie said.

"I understand it," the youthful Ayres chimed in. "It's our faith that drew me to Spence. We actually met in church, not some bar."

Bogie looked at Ayres with that keen eye he used to appraise someone he was meeting for the first time. "I must say, Spence old boy, you sure know how to pick 'em. Lew here is prettier than most gals I know. Put some lipstick on him and a dress and I'd go for him myself."

"All of this seems like one big joke to you," Ayres said, confronting him.

"I didn't mean to get your feathers ruffled," Bogie said. "But I wish you guys would lighten up. I'm just trying to be a supportive friend to the both of you."

Although Bogie's friendship with Tracy would remain steadfast, even when they were fighting over a potential screen billing in a co-starring venture that never happened, or when they were up for the same coveted role, their love for each other never wavered, jealousy or not.

It was two weeks later on the set of his next picture for Fox, *Body and Soul*, that the director, Alfred Santell, introduced him to the film's two leading ladies, each of them gorgeous, charming, and at least in his opinion, available.

They were Elissa Landi and Myrna Loy. He didn't know which woman to look at first: the screen vamp Myrna Loy or the scion of the Habsburg Empire, Elissa Landi. The problem was solved for him, when Santell called Loy to the set for a scene with the picture's star, Charles Farrell. Bogie hoped that Farrell would remember some of his speech training, but seriously doubted if he would.

Landi, in Loy's absence, wanted to discuss the characters they'd be playing, Bogie was struck by her regal bearing, cultured voice, and aristocratic beauty.

Rumor had it that Landi was the secret granddaughter of "Sissi," the Empress Elizabeth of Austria, the beautiful but strong-willed Bavarian-born wife of Emperor Franz Josef, who presided over the final years of the Austro-Hungarian empire.

"How should you be addressed?" Bogie asked, being a little provocative with her because he didn't believe in aristocratic titles.

Landi took him seriously. "Countess would be fine." As he was to learn later, the actress wasn't a real countess. She'd just assumed the title from her mother's second marriage to an Italian nobleman, Count Carlo Zanardi-Landi.

Known for having made a number of British silent films, Landi came to the attention of Fox when she'd appeared on Broadway in *A Farewell to Arms*.

"Just between you and me, I think this flicker we're making is nothing but an old-fashioned hack melodrama," Landi said. In addition to being an actress, Landi was also an acute critic and would go on to write several novels. Together, they tried to make sense out of some dumb, ill-conceived plot by Jules Furthman based on an unproduced and unpublished play called *Squadron*.

After reading the script, another tiresome piece about "The Great War," Bogie told Landi, "At least I know why the play was never staged."

"As I read it, I'm thought to be this German spy named Pom-Pom, but it turns out that Myrna is the real German spy."

"It doesn't really matter," he said. "I understand that Fox is going to open it with a Mickey Mouse cartoon, a Fox Movietone, even a Hearst Metrotone newsreel, and a Mickey Mouse stage act. After all that, no one will notice what a stinker it really is."

(left photo) Countess Elissa Landi with *(right photo)* Myrna Loy

"In the script, you're married to me for only four days before sailing, always wearing your aviator uniform, to France, where you pursue other women," Landi said. "If you were married to me in real life, you'd get such a workout you'd have no time for other women."

"Promises, promises," he said. "Since we're married—it says so right here in the script—I guess that gives me conjugal rights."

"Perhaps," she said enigmatically. "You're rather cute." Getting up, she kissed him and excused herself, heading for her dressing room.

Later, when Farrell invited Bogie to lunch in the Fox commissary, Bogie accepted reluctantly and only because the actor was the star of the picture. There was no mention that Farrell had double-crossed him and pushed Kenneth for the juvenile lead in *The Man Who Came Back*. Perhaps Farrell had forgotten all about it.

As he was leaving Farrell's table, Bogie spotted Elissa Landi coming toward him. "I was told I could find you here," she said. "At 7:30 tonight, I'm giving a dinner party. Black tie. There's been a last-minute cancellation from Chaplin. Please, please fill in for him. I have to have another man to make my dinner party work. Would you pick up Myrna Loy?"

"Sure," he said, wondering where he could come up with a tuxedo on such short notice. "I didn't have anything planned for tonight."

She gave him addresses and some instructions, then hurried off. He was a bit excited to be attending his first formal dinner party in Hollywood.

After renting a well-worn tux for three dollars on Hollywood Boulevard, he drove back to his apartment house.

***

As Bogie drove to pick up Loy to take her to Landi's formal dinner, he fantasized about all the big names who'd be there. Loy was beautifully dressed and waiting out on her front porch when Bogie pulled up at her house. She scanned the sky. "I think it's going to rain tonight."

"That wasn't the forecast," he said.

Noting an ominous cloud rising in the distance, she said, "We Montana belles don't need a radio forecast to tell us when a storm is coming."

In her black velvet gown, she looked lovelier than she did in the movies where she was most often cast as an Asian vamp. She was dressed with a high collar, although he suspected that most of the other women at the dinner would be in plunging *décolletage*.

Noting that he was observing her high-button neckline, she said. "I have to wear this. The other night at a party, Clark Gable and his wife, Ria, offered me a ride home. Clark walked me to my door. As I was fumbling for my key, he gave me a monkey bite. His teeth marks are still on me. Our director, Santell, was furious when he saw that I had been branded like a Montana cow. Naturally, my first appearance on screen called for me to appear in a low-cut gown."

"I hear that when Gable walks into a room," Bogie said, "It isn't a question of if a woman will go to bed with him. It's a question of which one he'll choose for the night."

"Something like that," she said.

As he drove toward Landi's home, he said, "I'm real honored that you're going out with me. If I can believe everything that Louella Parsons writes, I'll be part of a long lineup of distinguished beaux. Let me see. Rudolph Valentino, John Barrymore, Gary Cooper."

"I know all those men, of course, but there's no romance," she said.

"I heard that you and Cooper grew up on the same street together back in Helena," he said.

"We did indeed."

"Surely you must have played doctor," he said.

"Not that," she said. "But I did sneak off with him one late afternoon into the cellar at our house. We didn't conduct any medical examination, however. We were looking for Mother's last jar of apple jelly."

As he drove and talked to her, he found that she was a witty, intelligent, and also beautiful woman. If anything, directors hid her true beauty on the screen with gaudy makeup, usually trying to turn her into an Oriental temptress.

"You look as American as blueberry pie," he said. "Why do they always make you Chinese?"

"Beats me," she said. "I'm just a Montana cowgal. Up against Anna May Wong in that flick, *The Crimson City*, I looked about as Chinese as Raggedy Ann. I've played Burmese, Chinese, a couple of Tijuana vamps, an islander from the South Pacific, and a hot-blooded Creole. The beat goes on. Darryl Zanuck just can't believe that I can play a straight part, and I don't know why."

As he pulled into the driveway of Landi's home, he was amazed at the parade of big and expensive black cars. His battered vehicle looked pathetic. Loy seemed unconcerned with such trivia. She was not a woman of pretensions.

In the golden light from Landi's porch, he was awed by Loy's copper-haired beauty and her delicate, porcelain-white skin. "Once we get inside that party, we'll probably have no more chance to talk," she said in her marvelous voice, which sounded like a hoarse flute.

Her sleek, sassy nose captured his attention. He'd never seen a nose like that, and he thought it was the cutest thing. Impulsively he leaned over and kissed her on the nose.

Little could he have known that in just a few short years, hordes of women across America would be going to the offices of plastic surgeons with pictures of the star, demanding that a "Myrna Loy nose" be carved for them as well.

***

The party was in full swing when Bogie escorted Loy into the foyer where Landi was waiting to give each of them a kiss on their lips and welcome them to her home. She wore a stunning example of Parisian *haute couture*, an emerald-colored silk gown with a large emerald necklace, no doubt looted from the royal treasury of the Austro-Hungarian Empire.

156

As predicted, Loy was swept away, talking to various people she knew. The graceful hostess, Landi introduced Bogie to a circle of her friends clustered around William Randolph Hearst and his mistress, Marion Davies. In front of the other guests, Hearst chastised Marion for ordering another drink. She ignored his command.

The press tycoon returned to relating stories about his annual tour of European spas and was telling the group that while in Germany he'd attacked the Treaty of Versailles in an interview he gave to the *Frankfurter Zeitung*. "I claimed it subjected the Teutonic peoples to the domination of non-German European powers, especially France. If there is one country I loathe above all others, it's France." He looked cautiously around the room. "I hope there are no Frenchman here tonight."

As Bogie made eyes at Davies and the blonde courtesan/actress winked at him, Hearst was reporting on yet another trip he'd made.

Finding Hearst a little too pompous for his tastes, Bogie puckered his mouth in a false kiss to Marion, but only when the media baron wasn't looking.

Some members of the English colony living in Hollywood were at the party. One of them was Basil Rathbone, whom Bogie had met during his appearance with Helen in the lesbian play, *The Captive*.

The two actors reflected briefly, with a tinge of bitterness, on how the New York police had shut down this play because of its strong lesbian theme. "God, if we'd been allowed to continue in that play, we would have been a *cause célèbre* all over America. Every paper in the country featured our predicament. We would have been sold out for months."

"Helen certainly did a lot for the lesbians of America," Bogie said "The last I heard, Helen was still getting letters from the Sappho crowd from everywhere. Young women still send her slave bracelets. And most ironic of all— and probably missing the point completely— the deans of several women's colleges wrote thanking her for warning their students about 'the dangers of a reprehensible attachment.'"

"I was the one who suggested that Helen wear that ghastly white makeup," Rathbone said. "I thought it would convey the severe physical toll a woman must pay for having such 'perverse' thoughts about other women."

Both men laughed at that. "And the violets?" Bogie asked. "Throughout the play, we never saw Helen's pursuer, Madame d'Aiguines. But Helen's character was always getting nosegays of violets."

"We did some research on that," Rathbone said. "Sappho wrote about 'diadems of violets' on the Isle of Lesbos in the Seventh Century B.C."

"I hear *The Captive* and those damn violets have started a fad," Bogie said. "It's the fashion now for women in New York and Hollywood–I'm assuming there are no lesbians in the Middle West–to send violets to each other as a sign of their love." To his dismay, Bogie suddenly spotted the approach of an English actor he'd rather avoid.

Bogie was a bit chilly when introduced a second time to Ronald Colman, remembering with bitterness how his screen test was compared unfavorably to that of the English actor's when they both competed for the male lead opposite Lillian Gish in *The White Sister.*

The talk was of the latest news about George Bernard Shaw, Cornelia Otis Skinner, Grace Moore, Irene Castle, Elsa Maxwell, and Daisy Fellowes. Knowing none of these people, except by their reputation, Bogie grew bored and wandered off.

In a city famed for grand entrances, the latest arriving guest was creating a sensation. All eyes in the room focused on the foyer. Dressed in a man's tuxedo, a blonde goddess stood under Landi's Viennese crystal chandelier, being welcomed by Landi, who kissed her on the mouth.

Right then and there Bogie decided that he was going to divorce Mary and propose marriage to this sultry, alluring Venus de Milo. Her escort was some foreign-looking man, perhaps German.

Bogie's fantasy woman was heading across the room in his direction. He virtually stood in her pathway.

Coming up only two feet from him, she smelled of the most exotic perfume. The scent wasn't overpowering but had great subtlety, a sensation for the nostrils.

He was convinced that her smile was the most provocative since the dawn of time.

"I'm told that God has a talent for creating exceptional women," he said, staring into eyes bluer than any alpine lake on a summer day.

"H-e-l-l-o," she said in her German-accented voice. "You are in my way. Do I have to kiss you or fuck you to make you move?"

"For now, I'll settle for a kiss," he said, standing up to her with more bravado than he actually possessed. His knees were shaking.

"Your wish is granted," she said, leaning in to give him a quick kiss on the lips. The four wettest lips in Hollywood, male and female, exchanged body fluids. He felt the flicker of her tongue. "Since the entire room is watching, including my very jealous director, that is all for now. Catch me later." She

Marlene Dietrich

nodded her head at some people she knew across the big room and headed in their direction.

As he passed by, Josef von Sternberg glared at Bogie. Bogie felt that he'd just blown his chance to get cast opposite the star in any of her future movies.

Before stepping down into the sunken living room, she paused and looked back at him. "Not bad," she said, her tongue darting out ever so slightly as if to taste his kiss, which still lingered on her lips.

"What is your name?"

"Humphrey Bogart," he said.

"Your studio will change that," she predicted. "And, of course, you know who I am. *Marlene Dietrich*. I could be no one else but me."

He watched her go, as von Sternberg followed. Bogie's heart was beating faster, as he'd just fallen in love. He feared that he'd have to join a long line of suitors, both male and female, forming on her left and right.

***

At 1pm on the afternoon of the following day, seated with Myrna Loy and his hostess of the night before, Bogie ordered a plate of ham and eggs in the Fox commissary. Both Loy and Bogie had thanked Landi profusely for inviting them to her dinner party the previous evening.

He'd learned that Landi was an avid equestrian. He told her that "second to sailing," he preferred horseback riding better than anything. After saying that, he smiled awkwardly, looking first at Landi, then at Loy, deciding they were two of the most beautiful women in Hollywood. "Of course, there *is* something I like even better than horseback riding or sailing."

Both women laughed. Loy affectionately stroked his cheek. It was just a flash, and it was quickly concealed, but Landi shot Loy a look that Bogie definitely interpreted as jealousy.

For the second time that morning, he was flattered by a female appraisal of him. Not knowing which woman to ask out first, the issue was solved when Loy went to the powder room to take the shine off Hollywood's cutest nose. After she'd gone, Landi said, "I'm going riding in the morning. If you want to drop by my house at six o'clock, we'll head over to the stables."

"That's a bit early," he said, smiling at her, his eyes twinkling in anticipation, "but I'll be there. Maybe a little hung over. Bleary-eyed or not, I'm ready to race you."

She got up from the table to report back to the set. "You'll find, Mr. Bogart, that your horse can easily overtake mine."

Bogie spotted Loy returning from the powder room. This woman of quick wit showed her acute sensitivity when she looked first at Landi, then at him. "I'm afraid I might have intruded on something."

***

High in the Hollywood Hills, Bogie and Landi brought their horses to rest at a shady spot beside a stream. It was one of those idyllic places that makes a New Yorker glad that he's moved to the West Coast.

Later, they were to learn from a stable hand that they'd stopped at the same spot where the Sheik, Valentino, used to take the screen vamp, Gloria Swanson, to make love to her.

On that far-away morning, as he got to know Landi, he decided then and

159

there she was like no actress he'd ever met on Broadway, in Chicago, or in Hollywood.

Since she was illegitimate, he didn't think she wanted to talk about her relationship with Elizabeth, the Empress of Austria and the Queen of Hungary. To his surprise, he found that was about all she wanted to talk about. After all, "Sissi," as the queen was called, was one of history's most fascinating women, and Landi used her constantly as a role model.

"Sissi is something to aspire to," she said. "A fairy-tale princess and a liberated woman at the same time. Liberated I am, as you'll soon discover. Becoming a princess is not out of my reach."

"How do you plan to go about that?" he asked a little skeptically. "The Habsburg dynasty ended after World War I. There's no empire left—not even a throne."

"Oh, I won't have an empire to preside over like my grandmother, but I will become the biggest star in Hollywood. When that happens, I think many princes around the world will request my hand in marriage. It is not inconceivable for a Hollywood star to marry royalty and become a princess herself."

"A bit far-fetched," he said, "but I could see that happening."

"Sissi was always a dieting fanatic and an expert equestrian," she said. "You've seen this morning when I beat you in our race what a horsewoman I am. As far as the diet is concerned, I follow Sissi's regime, but I don't go on hunger diets like she did trying to obtain that elusive sixteen-inch waist. I eat exactly as Sissi did: a moderate portion of raw steak daily, a glass of milk, and a glass of freshly squeezed orange juice."

"I'll have to try that," he said. "Or else convert you to my diet of ham and eggs."

"How grotesque," she said. "All that animal fat. Sissi also wanted to be a poet modeling herself after Heinrich Heine, whose work she adored. I too will write a great book and win many literary honors. Like Sissi, I too will become an inveterate traveler and see the world, attracting adoring crowds wherever I go. Everyone will want to see the beautiful princess, don't you agree?"

"I'm enjoying seeing the beautiful princess right now, even before she's crowned."

She obviously liked the sound of that, and her porcelain-like arms reached out for him.

"I've never been particularly intimate with royalty before," he said.

"As you seduce me," she said, "I'm going to imagine that I am the young Elizabeth hauled to the bedchamber of the emperor, Franz Josef, I am only sixteen. He is much older. He rapes me on our wedding night. I'm a virgin."

"I've played a few parts in my day," he said. "But never a rapist emperor." He hugged her closer to him. "I think it's a role I can get into."

***

In Landi, Bogie found a woman who was spectacularly satisfying, thereby inspiring thoughts that he should divorce Mary Philips and become deeply involved with Landi, despite the fact that he couldn't give her the fairy kingdom she wanted to reign over as queen. Before four o'clock came on Sunday morning, in her lavish bed, he'd promised her a different kingdom, based on the possibility of their joint reign as the King and Queen of Hollywood.

Although she'd remained tactful, responding passionately to his lovemaking, his comment provoked her first put-down. "It's in my destiny that I'm going to reign as the queen of Hollywood, I just know it. But I've heard from our director, Santell, that the future king of Hollywood won't be our star, Charlie Farrell, or even George O'Brien. I think they carry the stigma of the Twenties with them. John Gilbert is through. Santell claims it'll be one of these up-and-coming rugged he-man types like Gary Cooper or Clark Gable."

Her comments immediately diminished his erection. He turned over with his back to this empress wannabe and fell into a deep sleep.

When he awakened at eleven o'clock Sunday morning, he found her gone without a note. Her fat German maid with a Brunhilde bosom told Bogie, "Miss Landi has gone for a Sunday drive down to Laguna with Mr. Basil Rathbone. She said I should offer you breakfast before I sent you on your way. She made it clear that she doesn't want you here when she gets back."

"Tell Princess Landi thanks for a good time," he said, storming out the door in anger although the ham and eggs the maid was cooking smelled mighty good.

Back at his apartment, a call came in from George Raft, who told him he'd arrived in town and was staying at the Mark Twain Hotel on Wilcox Avenue. He wanted Bogie to meet him in the lobby at eight that night

"It'll be good to see someone from New York," Bogie said. "I'm homesick."

Raft was one Yankee dancer/actor who hadn't gone Hollywood. In black tie he was sitting in an armchair by a potted palm in the lobby of the Mark Twain Hotel, waiting for Bogie to pick him up. The beltline of his trousers seemed to come up to his armpits. He looked like he belonged, not on Wilcox Avenue, but on the corner of Broadway and 42nd Street, waiting for a blonde babe to show up.

Bogie too was in black tie, having never returned the tux he'd rented for the Landi dinner party. He figured he'd go into the shop tomorrow and buy the damn thing.

Raft jumped up from his chair and rushed to greet him. He seemed genuinely glad to see a familiar face from back East. "The prospect of a steak dinner with you brought joy to my heart."

"You're looking good, George," Bogie said.

"So are you, Hump, bigtime movie star."

"Out here they call me Bogie."

"So be it. Out here and back East they still call me George Raft. The one and only."

He glanced at his watch. "We've still got time before dinner. "Let's go up to my room for a drink."

Taking the elevator to the top floor, Bogie was ushered into Raft's cluttered room, which smelled of stale cigarette butts and booze.

"Don't let these sharp clothes fool you," Raft said. "I came out here with a big bank roll. Lost all of it at the track. I ain't got but five bucks in my pocket. Can you lend me something till I get back on top again?"

"Sure thing, old pal," Bogie said. "I just got paid today. Seven-hundred and fifty bucks. I'll split it with you for old time's sake."

"Thanks, big guy," Raft said. "I'll owe you one for this. George Raft never forgets when someone does him a favor."

"If you've got no money, how are you eating?"

"An old friend of mine, Ben Lieberman, owns the Angelus Drugstore downtown. He's letting me run up a tab until my luck gets better. I'm getting fucking tired of BLTs."

"That steak you mentioned will make up for it tonight." He accepted the drink from Raft, bolting it down straight, as Raft poured him another whiskey. "So, good looking, how's your love life?"

"A lot of gorgeous dames out here, even more than in New York," Raft said. "They're throwing themselves at me every night. I had this fling with Molly O'Day. I'm trying to drop her but she's a clinging vine."

"Great looking dame," Bogie said.

"She was a looker," Raft said. "But she got fat and…"

When Raft offered him a third whiskey, he turned it down, remembering that he'd promised Stanwyck he was going to ball her sober for a change.

"I saw that movie, *Patent Leather*, ten times," Raft said. "I want to star in the talkie version of that film. I can just see myself as a cocky prizefighter who learns humility when he's crippled at the end of the picture and can't go to war

George Raft

like he wants. He's a real hero. That scene at the end where he forces himself to struggle out of his wheelchair and stands up to salute the American flag as the band strikes up the national anthem, that's the kind of role I want to play. I've got to get rid of this New York gangster image. Let Edward G. Robinson and James Cagney play the gangsters. From now on, George Raft is going to be playing all-American heroes."

"Hell, I'd love to play a gangster," Bogie said. "I'm tired of these juvenile roles. I'm thirty years old, for Christ's sake."

"Tennis, anyone?" Raft said, bursting into laughter at Bogie's expense, but only after he'd gotten his part of Bogie's paycheck. He looked at his watch again. "By the way, have you fucked with Stanwyck yet?"

"Yeah, first as Ruby Stevens back in New

York although I was too drunk to remember it."

"I haven't fucked Stanwyck as Stanwyck, but Ruby Stevens and I sure got it on. I've also had Mae Clarke. She's one hot piece. Clarke and Stanwyck will fuck anybody out here, male or female. If it's on the hoof and moving, those two broads will go for it."

"My impression is that everybody out here will fuck anybody, in any known combination," Bogie said. "Of course, New York isn't the sticks either."

"Hell, I could be a bigtime movie star right now if I'd put out," Raft said. "Take Rowland Brown, for example. He used to be this hotshot newspaper guy in Detroit. Now he's the hottest young director in Hollywood. I went to the fights the other night and was having dinner at the Brown Derby with my pal, Owney Madden, and some other cronies. I get up to go to the men's room. Brown follows me in. There are five empty urinals. He takes the one next to me as I whip out Blacksnake. He comes on real strong, and I'm about ready to belt him one. Then he tells me he's Rowland Brown, that he saw me dance at this honky-tonk in Detroit, and wants to offer me the second lead in his new film, *Quick Millions*. In New York, only the blonde belles have to be experts on the casting couch. Out here in Hollywood almost as many guys have to shuck their bloomers."

He tried to get Bogie to have another drink but was turned down. "Tell me, hot shot, if you'd been as broke as I am, would you drop your trousers for this cocksucker Brown?"

"Maybe," Bogie said. "I'd certainly consider it. Getting a blowjob is no big deal. All you have to do is whip it out, close your eyes, and let some fag do all the work. While they're at it, you can be dreaming of some beautiful blonde like Molly O'Day."

"I guess you're right," Raft said. "Getting your dick sucked is no big deal. It's not like you're a fag yourself. Maybe I'd better call up Brown and reconsider his offer."

"Maybe you had," Bogie said, "because that's the last paycheck you're getting from me."

"Not even if you saw me panhandling on the street?" Raft said.

"I'm a softie," Bogie said. "I'd let you move into my apartment and sleep on the sofa. I wouldn't let you starve."

"I may have to take you up on that offer the way things are going." There was a loud rap on his door, and he walked over to open it, revealing two large police officers. "You George Raft?" a tall, blond-haired cop asked.

"Yeah," Raft said cockily. "What's it to you?"

Without being invited, both of the policemen walked into the bedroom. "Who's this guy?" the red-haired and equally tall cop asked, looking Bogie up and down. "One of your New York accomplices?"

"Accomplice in what?" Raft demanded to know.

"We'll come clean with you," the blond said. "We've arrested this stick-up artist. Another George like you except he claims his name is George

Roberts. He's being grilled at headquarters right now and is singing like a canary. He's already admitted to a dozen robberies, and claims he had accomplices."

"I'm not a stickup guy," Raft said. "Look at me. Do I look like a guy who would stick somebody up? Look at my clothing—and the way I'm dressed."

"When Roberts was searched, your name was found sewed on to his inner pocket, and he was well dressed too," the blond said. "Real fancy tailor."

"I can explain that," Raft said. "I sold him that suit yesterday for thirty bucks to pay my rent here. I'm an actor. Temporarily out of work. I was forced to sell my suit because I was three weeks behind on my hotel bill."

"You're not fooling me," the redhead said. "The Los Angeles police department has already been alerted to your coming out here. You're a friend of Dutch Schultz."

"Not exactly a friend," Raft said. "He used to come into the club where I danced for Texas Guinan, but I never met him personally."

Bogie knew that Raft was lying, having already been introduced to Dutch Schultz by Raft.

"What about the bootlegger, Owney Madden?" the blond cop asked.

"Owney and I go way back," Raft said. "We grew up on the streets of Hell's Kitchen together. He's a good guy."

"Yeah," the redhead said. "Spent ten years in prison for being such a good guy. I think we're gonna run you in for questioning."

At this point, the manager of the hotel, Robert Parrish, came into the room since the door had been left wide open. "What's going on here? We run a respectable hotel—no drunks, no whores."

Raft looked desperate. "Tell them, Parrish. I sold you my ring last week. I'm having to sell my stuff from New York to raise money."

"He's telling the truth," Parrish said, holding up what looked like a ruby ring encrusted with diamonds. "I've had it appraised. It's worth five-hundred bucks."

"I can vouch for George here," Bogie said. "Squeaky clean, a real good guy. Just because this Roberts guy was caught in his secondhand suit doesn't make George guilty."

"Okay," the redhead said. He turned to Raft. "Let this be a warning to you. We heard about you before you even hit town. This is not New York or Chicago, but Los Angeles, a clean-living town. If you think you gangsters can come out here and take over this town, you've got another thought coming."

"I don't like the look of you," the blond said to Raft. "And I hate those pants of yours. I really hate your guts. We've had another complaint about you. At first we weren't sure about it and our sergeant wanted to drop it, but I'm going back to the station to look into the case personally. Reopen it, so to speak."

"You've got nothing on me!" Raft said. "What sort of complaint? It's a lie."

After some more questions and a few threats, the two policemen left the

164

bedroom. Parrish stayed behind, shaking a finger at Raft. "You have until tomorrow to move out. We don't want your type here. I think I'm going to post a sign in the lobby, 'No New Yorkers allowed.'"

After he'd shut the door, Raft turned to Bogie. "I'd better go for that movie role and quick no matter what Brown wants me to do. It'll look good with the police if I'm a bona-fide film star. I'll do anything but take it up the ass. George Raft doesn't get fucked by anybody. I'm the fucker, not the fuck-ee." Raft looked at his watch again. "Hell, we're running late."

In a taxi on the way to the Roosevelt, Bogie quizzed Raft again about *Quick Millions*.

Raft said that it was the story of a truck driver who'd become a ruthless gangster. "That's the star part," Raft said. "I play his bodyguard."

"What do you think Brown would say if I tried out for the role of the ruth-less gangster?" Bogie asked. "I'd let him suck me off."

"Too late. The lead's already cast."

"Fuck!" Bogie said. "What meathead got the part?"

"This new guy over at Fox," Raft said. "Spencer Tracy."

***

After dinner with Raft, Bogie showed up the next day for the shoot of *Body and Soul*. A messenger brought him a note from Stanwyck. She wanted him to drive over to see her at Universal Studios, where she was starring in *The Locked Door*. Her message didn't explain why she wanted to see him, but no one turned down Stanwyck. When his final scene was locked up, he drove over to Universal where Stanwyck had arranged an entrance pass for him at the gate. Even so, the security guards looked at him suspiciously before let-ting him drive onto the lot.

To his astonishment, the first person he encountered on the set was the picture's male star, Rod La Rocque. "The first and only actor I'll ever direct," Bogie said, embracing La Rocque warmly and not forgetting how the star had chased after him in New York. "Still got a crush on me?" he asked, teasing La Roque.

"Oh, that was so long ago, and I've gone through so many beaux since then. I gave my heart to Gary Cooper but he abandoned me for Lupe Velez. Not before I'd nicknamed him the Montana Mule."

"Sounds like you've been busy," Bogie said. "How's Miss Vilma Banky doing?"

"Talking pictures are not for her," La Rocque said. "Vilma and I make some joint appearances out here. As you might have guessed, ours is a some-what unconventional marriage."

"I thought so," Bogie said. He noticed a handsome, blond-haired actor walking toward them.

"That's William Boyd," La Rocque said. "Even though he's got two inch-es less than Gary, he's all man. What a guy! He goes both ways. Barbara and

165

I are sharing him during the filming of this stinker."

Bogie found himself shaking hands with this former favorite of the director, Cecil B. DeMille, who had cast Boyd as Simon of Cyrene in *King of Kings* in 1927. Before Bogie could become acquainted with America's future Hopalong Cassidy, a messenger came for him, summoning him to Stanwyck's dressing room.

In her dressing room, Stanwyck looked distraught. She told him that Raft had been picked up and arrested by the police "on some trumped up charge." She didn't explain what that charge was, but claimed she'd posted $1,000 bail for his release. "He's been kicked out of the Mark Twain," she said, "and he's got no place to go. He said you agreed to let him move in with you until he gets back on his feet."

"I guess so," Bogie said. "But that wasn't any writ-in-blood commitment."

"He needs our help," Stanwyck pleaded, "and I've got my own private life. I can't become his mother."

"Tell the fucker he can move in," Bogie said. "But I'm afraid I'm going to regret this."

"It'll be just fine," Stanwyck assured him.

Back at his apartment, as Bogie waited for Raft to show up broke but with expensive luggage and clothing, he received a series of phone calls. Far from being lonely and rejected as he had been when he'd first hit town, he suddenly felt like he'd been crowned King of Hollywood.

The first call was from Joan Blondell. Though still in tears at being dumped by Cagney who suddenly favored Mae Clarke, she was still upbeat and hopeful about the future. "He wouldn't be the first man who's dumped me."

Bogie immediately asked her out on a date for the following evening, and she readily accepted.

As he put down the phone, another call came in, this one from Hobart Henley, a director at Universal. Henley told him that since Fox didn't have any immediate roles for him, he'd been loaned out to Universal where Carl Laemmle Jr. had agreed to produce a remake of Booth Tarkington's *The Flirt*. Henley informed Bogie that he himself had already directed a previous version of *The Flirt*—in this case as a silent film back in 1913.

"What's the name of the newest version?" Bogie asked. "Still *The Flirt*? I know you guys retitle everything in the remakes."

"*Gambling Daughters*," he said.

"Which one of the daughters do I play?" Bogie asked. "Who's going to design my gowns?"

"An actor with a sense of humor," Henley said. "Some directors like that. I don't."

Joking aside, Bogie was hoping he'd been cast in the male lead but learned that part had gone to Conrad Nagel. He couldn't help but notice that Henley was delaying telling him exactly what role he'd be playing.

"We have a great cast. Sidney Fox, ZaSu Pitts, Slim Summerville. The second female lead hasn't been cast yet but I expect to get notice from Carl tomorrow."

"And my part?" Bogie asked, fearing the answer.

"You'll play Valentine Curliss," Henley said.

"My character's called Valentine?" It sounded very dubious to him. "And the billing?"

"You get eighth billing," Henley said, "but I assure you your role of Valentine is absolutely crucial to the film. You'll walk away with the picture."

"Yeah, right," he said, feeling despondent. So much for a career in films. After only two pictures, one of them not yet released, he felt that Hollywood stardom was fast eluding him. After assuring Henley he'd show up for work, he put down the phone.

"Valentine," he said out loud, cursing the name of his new character without even reading the script. He wondered whom Fox would cast as the other female lead. "I'll probably get to kiss Marie Dressler," he said to the empty walls of the apartment.

The phone rang again. He thought that in spite of his lack of stardom, he was getting more calls than any star.

It was "Dawn Night" (Glenda Farrell). He'd been meaning to ring her up for a date but had temporarily put her on hold. "You may—just may, I can't promise it—be getting the biggest break of your life."

"Tell me about it," he said. "Right at this moment I could sure use one."

"Mr. Edward G. Robinson—I don't know what the G stands for—has just walked out on *Little Caesar* and Mervyn LeRoy."

"You've got to be kidding," he said. "I hear that's the greatest role in town. What feather got stuck up Robinson's ass?"

"You won't believe this, but Mervyn told me that Robinson had insisted on a scene in which he gets to display his legs."

"His fucking legs? Is this some kind of joke? Does Robinson think he's Marlene Dietrich?"

"The ugly mutt is proud of his legs. He's got this picture of himself in the tights he wore when he played Ottaviano in *The Firebrand*. He hangs it in his dressing room and shows it off to anybody."

"You're putting me on."

"After Mervyn balled me last night, and we indulged in some pillow talk, I suggested you for the role even though he thinks Cagney would be ideal if he can get him."

"Hell, I'd love to play a gangster," he said. "A role like that would get me out of this aging juvenile crap."

"I'll tell Mervyn you're interested, and if he wants me to, I'll set up a meeting," Farrell said. "You've got to strike now before they offer the role to Paul Muni. A lot of other actors will be lining up for the part. I might as well tell you. Mervyn is also thinking about that New York hoofer, George Raft."

"Raft?" he said in astonishment. "The fucker is moving into my apartment. Maybe that's okay. I could drown him in the bathtub."

"Mervyn thinks Raft might be even better in the role than Robinson. After all, Raft *is* a New York gangster."

"I won't mention it to Raft tonight," he said. "Get me in to see LeRoy as soon as we can. Of course, I've got this deal with Fox, but they might lend me out to First National. I'm getting eighth billing to appear in *Gambling Daughters*. A real comedown after my first two pictures."

"I'll call you first thing tomorrow," she said, blowing kisses into the phone.

After he'd gone to the kitchen and had two beers, Raft still hadn't shown up. There were many things he'd like to be doing tonight other than waiting around the apartment for Raft. The phone rang again. It was Kenneth wanting him to come over. Bogie explained that he was waiting for Raft who was going to be staying with him temporarily.

"Sorry, I'd like to see you tonight," Kenneth said. "Since you moved out, I don't see much of you."

No sooner had he put down the phone than it rang again. Bogie welcomed the now familiar voice of Spencer Tracy. But he seemed despondent. Bogie soon learned that Lew Ayres had stopped putting out.

"He still sees me almost every night, but he just wants to hold my hand and talk religion," Tracy said. "I mean, I believe in the church as much as anyone, but I like to work Lew's sweet cheeks when we're not praying together."

"Can't help you on that score, Spence," Bogie said. "Not my scene. So what are you doing?"

"I'm still going to keep seeing Lew," Tracy said. "He's got a changeable nature. He can't last long with this religion shit. He'll get real horny one night and he'll be over begging for me to plug him."

"What you doing in the meantime?" Bogie asked.

"I'll be fucking every woman in town," Tracy said. "The one I'm going after next is Loretta Young."

"I hear her tits are as cold as the Arctic."

"I'm the guy to warm them up."

Raft didn't show up until after midnight. Staggering drunk to his doorway clad only in his underwear. Bogie showed Raft in and pointed him to the sofa. "There's a fresh towel for you in the bathroom and...welcome."

"You look drunk, my friend," Raft said. "I never touch the stuff."

Raft wanted to stay up and talk but Bogie had to get some sleep. He staggered back to bed. After Raft had unpacked the two suitcases he'd brought with him, Bogie was only dimly aware that Raft was making some phone calls. He hoped that they weren't to his gangster friends back East, as he feared that Raft would skip out and leave him with a big phone bill.

Bogie was of two minds about getting some beauty sleep. He knew the role of Rico was not meant for a pretty face. He wondered if when he met Mervyn LeRoy tomorrow he should show up looking a little rough around the edges. That way, he might stand a better chance of getting the part than if he appeared looking young, handsome, and well-groomed, ready for another one of those "Tennis, anyone?" parts.

When Bogie awakened the next morning, he noticed Raft sprawled out nude on the sofa, his blacksnake in semi-erection. Bogie thought that his friend must be having a wet dream.

The phone rang, and he picked it up on the first ring, not wanting to wake Raft. It was his director, Henley, calling again from Fox about his role in *Gambling Daughters*. "The co-star of the picture has been cast, and she wants to meet you. She's seen you on the stage in New York and admires your work."

"That's just great," Bogie said, hung over, his head pounding from the effects of last night's booze.

"Be at the studio at nine," Henley ordered.

After hanging up, Bogie quickly called Glenda Farrell. LeRoy had left her house at six that morning, and had agreed to meet with Bogie about the *Little Caesar* role that afternoon. "He's not promising anything. I happen to know he's testing Raft for the role at nine o'clock."

"Does our friend know that?" Bogie asked.

"Of course, he does. Raft talked with Mervyn yesterday. Anyway, he'll test you at two o'clock. I'm doing the test with Raft this morning. I'll upstage him. Deliberately make him look bad so you'll get the part."

"Thanks, babe," he said. "I'll owe you a big favor for that."

"See you at two, lover."

After he'd hung up the phone, Bogie decided to pull a dirty trick on his new roomie. There was no way he was going to wake up Raft and get him to the studio by nine o'clock to test for the role of Rico.

"The part is mine," Bogie whispered to himself in the shower. He was quiet as could be as he hurriedly dressed, having left the key and a note for Raft on the kitchen table.

At Fox he was anxious to meet the female co-star of *Gambling Daughters*, even though he viewed it as a nothing part. He had his heart set on *Little Caesar*.

Henley greeted him and asked him to be seated. "She'll be here in a minute." An assistant called Henley to the phone. Carl Laemmle Jr. himself wanted to speak to Henley.

Bogie was reading a newspaper but looked up when he heard footsteps walking across the sound stage. In a black and white polka dot dress, with wedge-heeled shoes, a blonde-haired young woman with a ridiculous hat was walking toward him. If he didn't suspect that this was the star of the picture, he would have figured her to be a librarian from a small town in New England.

As he was to recall in years to come, it was a meeting that would forever change his life, both professional and personal.

She extended her hand to him. "I know who you are, Mr. Humphrey Bogart. Nice to meet a fellow actor from back East. I'm told you're going to be one of my supporting players. I'm the star, of course. New England born and bred." She extended her hand. "I'm Bette Davis."

***

He took an instant dislike to Miss Bette Davis. As he was to tell Kenneth and later everybody else he knew, "This high-strung Yankee bitch needs a good fucking. Someone needs to go in there with a stick of dynamite and blast open that squeezed-tight little pussy of hers, and I'm the man to do it."

"So each of us is going to be making our first film, Mr. Bogart," Davis said.

"I've already got three pictures under my belt," he said, slightly angry that she'd obviously not seen any of them and hadn't heard of them either.

Despite his having re-educated Davis in the nuances of his film career, she persisted all her life in claiming that she and Bogie made a joint film debut. That bit of misinformation also appeared in her highly unreliable memoir, *The Lonely Life*.

Before he'd finished his coffee with Davis, the first of many cups to come, Bogie sensed her fierce jealousy of other actresses. "Have you read the script yet?" she asked.

"No one's given me a copy."

"It's about two sisters—one good, one bad," she said. "A story about Midwestern provincialism. At first I thought I'd been cast in the role of the hellion. Imagine my disappointment when Hobart Henley informed me that Sidney Fox is playing the bad sister. I'm ending up in the role of the timid mouse."

"I'm sure you'll be good in the part," he said. "Sometimes you can take a role that's not so flashy and run with it." His first impression of her was that she did look a bit mousy.

Bette Davis

But even at that early stage of her career, she was hardly timid. "Do you know how that whore Sidney Fox got the part?" She didn't wait for his answer. "Miss Foxy is sleeping with the producer, Carl Laemmle Jr. That's why. I'm quickly learning out here that it is who you sleep with that determines which role you get, not how talented you might be as an actress. The juicy parts go to sexual athletes like Joan Crawford. I heard from a very reliable source only the other day that any time Louis B. Mayer wants to be serviced, he calls in Crawford. Mayer sits in his chair, Crawford gets down on her knees and does her job. She's said to be an expert. From what I've been told, she's screwed every male animal in Hollywood except Rin-Tin-Tin, and I'm not so sure she hasn't had that dog too. I wouldn't

170

put it past her."

The only empathy Bogie felt for Davis on that long-ago morning evolved from their shared disillusionment with Hollywood. They both seemed to feel that they'd each made a serious career mistake in coming to Hollywood, and that they'd eventually fail out here and return to the legitimate theater in New York.

"My first assignment was absolutely unbelievable," she said. "It added a new meaning to the term, 'a casting couch.' In one day alone I had fifteen men lie on top of me, pretending to play a love scene with me. They arrived like wooden soldiers, one after the other, each whispering these lines, 'You gorgeous, divine darling, I adore you. I worship you. I must possess you.' Each actor's weight would then rest on my bosom as he kissed me passionately. The director would yell, 'Cut!' The next actor would then descend on me. Only Gilbert Roland had the sensitivity to see how shocked I was. Before he lowered his 170 pounds onto me, he said, 'Don't be upset. This is Hollywood. All actresses have to go through it.' He was the only actor that day who made me feel like a woman and not like some mannequin."

Davis was called away, but before the day ended, he'd meet each of the other actors starring in the film. From Tom Reed, one of the writers of the screenplay, he learned that the title had been changed from *Gambling Daughters* to *Bad Sister*.

Standing before him and measuring four feet, eleven inches tall, Sidney Fox, the film's other female star, might have captured the heart of the producer, Laemmle Jr., but she was way down the list on Bogie's chart of Hollywood *femme fatales*. Certainly she was no Stanwyck, Crawford, or Dietrich, although she looked mighty sexy when stacked up against the rather dull Bette Davis, whose cigarette smoke still lingered as he shook Fox's delicate hand. He'd call her "cute" instead of beautiful.

Ever the needler, he asked her, "Why do you have a man's name?"

"Sure beats Humphrey," she said.

"*Touché.*"

She invited him to join her for lunch, and he accepted but told her he had a very important appointment in two hours. "It'll have to be a short one."

"Most men I've met out here promise me a long one but only deliver short."

Over the lunch table, he looked startled. "You're good."

He liked her brassy way of talking and quickly learned that she was not your typical *ingénue*. She'd studied law at Columbia University before deciding to become an actress.

"So tell me about this guy, Laemmle," Bogie

Sidney Fox with Humphrey Bogart in *Bad Sister*

171

said. "Junior, that is. Is he going to make a big star out of you?"

"Carl's okay but not all that great in the sack. The trouble with Carl is he can't decide if he likes pussy or boy-ass. During the filming of *All Quiet on the Western Front*, he was pounding that cute little butt of Lew Ayres. I took Carl away from Ayres. Now I hear cute-stuff is getting it from your buddy, Spencer Tracy."

"You're a regular Louella Parsons," Bogie said. "If this acting thing doesn't work out for you, you can replace her with a column of your own. Does Carl have big things in store for you?"

"Not really, I fear, in spite of his promises," she said. "Right now he believes that monster movies are going to take over Hollywood. He's all into this Dracula and Frankenstein crap. Mama didn't raise no monster."

He laughed, but as he did he noticed the ominous approach of a messenger boy. Bogie was wanted on the phone. Excusing himself , he went to take the call.

It was Glenda Farrell. "Edward G. Robinson is back in the picture," she said. "He's made up with Mervyn. So you and Raft don't have a chance. I'm sorry. I tried."

He thanked her profusely, concealing his bitter disappointment. As he came back into the Universal commissary, he noticed that Laemmle Jr. had taken his place at Bogie's table and had one arm wrapped around Sidney Fox. Bogie decided to let them eat in peace. He was outranked.

***

With his hope of playing Rico in *Little Caesar* now a distant dream, Bogie walked up the steps to his apartment house. He'd read the script, and focused on his minor part in *Bad Sister*. In it, he'd play the role of Valentine Corliss, a city slicker who comes to a small town to swindle local businessmen.

At first, he was tempted to knock on Kenneth's door, but figured he'd better check in with his new roommate, Raft, instead. The prospect didn't thrill him. After the debacle of the *Little Caesar* casting this morning, Bogie wondered if he'd be competing against Raft in future film roles. Maybe he wouldn't have to worry about that dismal prospect. After the release of *Bad Sister*, he doubted whether Sidney Fox would ever recommend him for another role.

By giving him eighth billing, movie executives had already spoken. Even the prospect of having a hot affair with one of his leading ladies appeared remote. Ms. Fox was already taken by the studio's big brass; and Davis had locked up her pussy and thrown away the key.

He wasn't going anywhere as a Hollywood film actor, but he was scoring with women and that was some compensation for a married man away from his New York wife. He wondered how Mary's own love life was doing. She was a good-looking woman with a charming personality, so he figured she was attracting a string of beaux, all of them actors no doubt.

As he came into his apartment, a man his own age was emerging from his bedroom. He looked startled to see Bogie but extended his hand. "Hi, I'm Rowland Brown."

"The director?" Bogie asked. "Well, tell me, old boy, did Raft get the part."

"He did indeed," Brown said, smiling. "Now I know why they call that handsome devil Blacksnake."

Disgusted with the way business was conducted in Hollywood—Davis had nailed it—Bogie impulsively took Brown's hand and pressed it into his own crotch, where the director took expert measurements. "What part do you have for me?" He pushed Brown's hand away and went to get himself a drink.

"Not bad, not bad at all," Brown said, searching for his pants on the far side of the room. "*Quick Millions* is already cast, but based on what I was just feeling, you're entitled to a role in one of my future pictures."

"Glad to hear that," Bogie said. After pouring his drink, he turned to Brown. "Now get the hell out of here, you faggot. This is where I live. I'm not running a God damn male bordello."

Without saying another word, Brown hurriedly dressed and left. After he'd gone, George Raft emerged from the bathroom stark naked, his blacksnake in repose.

"That Rowland boy is not a bad cocksucker," Raft said. "I needed some relief after my disappointment today. For an hour or two yesterday, I thought I had the part of Rico in *Little Caesar* until I learned that ugly, fat, stumpy-dicked lumphead, Edward G. Robinson, was back in the role."

"You, play a gangster?" Bogie said mockingly. "You told me you wanted to be cast only as an American hero."

"What you want and what you get in life are two different things," Raft said. "I could play Rico in my sleep. Instead of that, I'm appearing opposite your pal, Spencer Tracy, in *Quick Millions*. Brown gave me the part. Sally Eilers is the leading lady. You've heard of her: Hoot Gibson's wife."

"Yeah, I've heard of her," Bogie said, turning from the sight of the naked Raft. "Why don't you put on some clothes? Your audition on the casting couch—or in this case, casting bed—is over."

Raft went into the bedroom and when he emerged, he was dressed as if ready to appear in the spotlight at Texas Guinan's club.

"I've got a date tonight," Raft said. "Jean Harlow. Eat your heart out, babycakes." He headed for the door.

***

On the set of *Bad Sister*, Bette Davis sharpened her nails on her *bête noir*, Sidney Fox, years before she dug into the much-abused flesh of her future rival, Joan Crawford. Even though only twenty-three years old and new to Hollywood, Davis flashed the kind of fierceness that would one day become legendary when she ruled as Queen of Warner Brothers.

Standing with Bogie to the side of the set, she said, "The director is totally insipid, the dialogue sucks. I should be playing the bad sister instead of the good one, and, to top it all, I have to wear this damn microphone in the shape of a corncob concealed in my breasts. They've got this large insulated wire attached to the wall. I virtually can't move in any direction. If I turn to face Conrad Nagel, my voice fades. I guess I'll have to speak all my lines to my stomach."

He laughed at that remark, finding that Davis both fascinated him but still annoyed him with all her whining. "You're taking home a paycheck, aren't you?"

"Christ," she said. "That's one way of looking at it if you care nothing about acting."

At the far corner of the set, Jack Pierce, head of studio makeup, along with two assistants, hovered around Sidney Fox. Barely able to control her fury, Davis said, "All Pierce did for me is to tell me that my eyelashes are far too short, my hair is nondescript, my mouth's too small, my neck's too long, and my face is as fat as a Flanders mare."

"That Pierce," Bogie said, finding that his assessment of Davis had been right on target. "He sure knows how to build up an actor's confidence."

"Instead of offering me some help with my makeup, he hovers around Fox," Davis said. "No doubt on orders from Laemmle. If only I were screwing the boss, things would be different. She's certainly the court favorite. You weren't here for her first scene this morning. Instead of the Hoosier accent the role calls for, her voice reeks of Mayfair. I could be so deliciously wanton and impudent as Marianne, the bad sister, instead of Laura, the good little Miss Two-Shoes." She picked up a copy of *The Flirt*. "Here's how Tarkington describes my character: 'A neutral tinted figure, taken for granted, obscured, and so near being nobody at all.'" She tossed the script down in her chair. "Ain't that a pip?"

Interrupting her diatribe, Bogie abruptly asked her. "I've got to know something. Are you still a virgin?"

She flashed her pop eyes at him. "First off, that's none of your damn business. But if you must know, I am and I'm proud of it. I've never even seen a set of male genitals—not even a picture of what they're like, and I don't intend to until I'm good and ready."

Ever the needler, Bogie came up with his practical joke of the day. He'd learned that in a scene to be shot that afternoon, Davis had to change a set of diapers on a baby rented for the day by Fox Studios.

Since Bogie was playing only a bit part and wasn't needed on the set, he got the permission of the director, Hobart Henley, to go to a local hospital to help the casting director find the right baby. "My father's a doctor," he told Henley. "I grew up with babies. I'll find one that will photograph perfectly and won't cry or take a crap when his diaper comes off."

The rather dim-witted Henley bought that. On the way to the hospital, Bogie told the casting director, Derrick Staunton, his plan. He was going to bribe a nurse to direct them to the baby with the largest genitals in the hospital.

"I thought all little boy babies have pee-pees about the same size," Staunton said.

"Not at all," Bogie said. "The dick on a baby can vary as much as the dick on a grown man. They come in all sizes."

After a fifty-dollar bribe, the nurse said there was a baby in the ward that was "truly remarkable," as she put it. "I can't wait for this kid to grow up. At his age, he's got more than my old man." He found that the blonde-haired nurse looked and acted amazingly like Joan Blondell.

Later, after obtaining the parents' written consent, and even arranging a signed contract stating the terms of the day's work with the child, Bogie drove Staunton and the mother of the baby back to the Fox lot. He hadn't actually seen the baby's genitals, preferring to take the nurse's words for it. To judge from the face of the mother, who sat in the back seat of the car, holding her child, she was right proud of her son.

That afternoon Bogie secretly assembled cast and crew for the unveiling. Henley ordered Davis onto the set and told her that she was to change the diaper of the baby. After being reassured that the diaper was clean, Davis proceeded with the scene, unfastening the safety pins and exposing the genitals of the baby.

A deep blush came over her face, but she was enough of a trouper to see the scene through to its end. Since red turns gray in a black and white film, her face came off as battleship gray when the film was later released.

As Bogie would later relate to Kenneth, "That kid had a set on him that would make some grown men envious."

At the end of the day's shoot with Baby Freddy, Davis stormed off the set where she encountered Bogie, who was laughing as if he'd pulled off the joke of the century. She immediately understood that he was behind the baby plot, and she would forever after refer to him as "that old heckler."

"If you want to see an even bigger one than that," he said to her, "try changing my diaper tonight."

"Mr. Bogart," she said, "you can keep your penis in your pants. You may have experienced the charms of every broad in Hollywood, but my name is not legs-apart Sidney Fox. Humphrey Bogart will never know Bette Davis in the Biblical sense."

"Yes, I will," he said. "Maybe not on this picture, maybe not even within the next few months. But at some time in our futures, Bette Davis is going to get intimately acquainted with Bogie Junior."

"That day will never come," Davis said before heading to her dressing room.

***

There was a hint of desperation in Tracy's voice when he'd called. He claimed that he could not talk on the phone. Bogie had never heard Tracy sounding so flustered. Perhaps his network of romantic liaisons had backfired in some way. In direct contrast to Raft, who attracted trouble like a blonde beauty walking nude onto a construction site, Tracy tended to be very discreet.

When he arrived on the set, Bogie learned that Rowland Brown had summoned all the major players for a night shoot. He spotted Tracy sitting on the far side of the set in a director's chair waiting to be called for his scene. He was talking to an older man. Tracy didn't look desperate the way he'd sounded on the phone. Bogie walked up to him.

Meeting Kenneth in the hallway of their apartment house, Bogie had a brief exchange with him. "Kay Francis wants to marry me," he blurted out.

"You guys would be crazy to get married," Bogie said.

"Would you rather I go back to New York, get Mary to charge you with desertion, help her get a divorce, and then marry me? I'm still in love with Mary."

"Perhaps you are," Bogie said. "In the meantime, Miss Kay Francis herself seems to be keeping you busy. No, I don't want you to take Mary away from me. Marry Kay then. It'll be a good cover for both of you. Two of the biggest tramps in Hollywood pretending to be a loving man and wife."

"I'll marry Kay on one condition," Kenneth had said. "That you'll agree to be my best man."

Bogie crushed out his cigarette and headed for the door. "You got yourself a deal, pal. Name the time and place, and I'll show up. I own a tuxedo now."

At a night club that same evening, he encountered Bette Davis on the arm of Gilbert Roland. The handsome, dashing Roland excused himself to go to the men's room, leaving Davis alone with Bogie at the table.

"You're doing very well," Bogie said. "Gilbert Roland, no less. I understand every horny woman in Hollywood—and at least half the men—are after him."

"He's mine," she said smugly, lighting up one of her interminable cigarettes. "Of all the men I auditioned that day for the kissing scene screen test, he kissed the best and was the gentlest with me."

"You've seen your first set of male genitalia," Bogie said, recalling that well-hung baby on the set of *Bad Sister*. "The question is, have you seen what a real man has hanging?"

"A real man is something you're not, Mr. Bogart," she said. "If you must know, I'm going to surrender my cherry tonight, and I've selected Mr. Roland as the man for the job."

"Happy to hear that," he said. "You're certainly old enough to be deflowered. Personally I think a girl should be broken in well before her sixteenth birthday."

"You're such a prankster and such a juvenile, at least to judge by your antics on the set, that I would think a teenager would be just about your speed, and the perfect date for you. However, I prefer a real man, and I think you'd agree that Gilbert Roland measures up in every way."

"How would I know?" he asked.

"I know you want me for yourself, but you can dream on," she said, smiling as Roland returned to the table.

"Three's a crowd," Roland said to him.

"See you around, pal," Bogie said, hastily departing.

The persistent ringing of a telephone brought Bogie abruptly into his new day. His head was pounding, as he reached for the phone. It was Davis. At first he thought she might be calling to report on the loss of her virginity. That would come later.

"Ruthie has smashed up my car, and I need you to drive me to meet my new director, James Whale."

Later that day he'd learn that "Ruthie" was Ruth Favor Davis, the mother of Bette and a former broad-shouldered girl from Ocean Park, Maine, who'd grown up as an incorrigible tomboy insisting that her family call her "Fred."

"Forgive me," he said. "I'd love to take you. But I have a headache from hell. I've got no work, so I plan to sleep all day."

"Little wonder," she said, considering how much you had to drink last night "Whale is casting *Waterloo Bridge*, and I'm up for the lead. It's the role of a prostitute. Before last night with Gilbert, I couldn't have played the part. For him to get off, he likes to pretend that his girl is a Tijuana whore. In one night, I learned what it's like to be a whore."

"That's good, but I've got to beg off," he said, wanting to get her off the phone.

"The role of the Canadian soldier—the one who falls for me, not knowing I'm a prostitute—is also up for grabs. I'm asking Whale to let you test for the part. It's not that Fox has rushed to offer you another role after *Bad Sister*."

He suddenly perked up. A chance at a part— what every out-of-work actor wanted to hear. "Give me your God damn address, and I'm on my way." He jumped out of bed in search of a pencil. "Fox doesn't have a God damn thing for me. I'll be over at your place in forty minutes."

Heading for the shower, he noticed that Raft hadn't come home last night.

(top photo)
Kenneth MacKenna
(bottom photo) Kay Francis

177

Hoping that the cold morning shower would erase all memories of last night, he put his face up to the spout and cleansed himself. The day didn't hold out too many good prospects—Bette Davis who'd been fucked by only one man in her entire life, and only the night before, and Director James Whale who no doubt had been fucked by a thousand men, maybe more.

Davis was nearly in tears, as Bogie picked her up and drove her over to Whale's set. It wasn't the loss of virginity that seemed to be bothering her. "Laemmle Jr. has seen *Bad Sister*," she said. "I heard him tell someone that I had all the sex appeal of Slim Summerville."

"I didn't know he'd even seen the picture." Bogie said. "Do you know what he thought of my acting?"

She reached for a cigarette and eyed him sharply. "I don't think he even noticed you. He had eyes only for Sidney Fox."

"Sorry to hear that," he said, infuriated at actresses who could only talk about themselves.

"I'd be washed up if it weren't for the cameraman, Karl Freund," Davis said. "He said I had lovely eyes." Thus, the film's photographer became the first to discover "Bette Davis Eyes." "They've got me doing a stinker called *Seed*, with this adorable John Boles. I could really go for him."

"So soon after Gilbert Roland?" he teased her.

"Last night was the most memorable of my life," she said, puffing furiously. "Gilbert is not a man. He's descended directly from the gods. He told me he loved me. Even that he wanted to marry me. But this morning when I called his place, a woman answered the phone. I could swear it was Constance Bennett. Gilbert wouldn't even come to the phone."

"We men are no good," he said with a slight self-mockery in his voice. "You'd better learn that sooner than later."

"Believe you me, Bogart, I knew that before I got on the train to Hollywood."

Davis quickly switched to how excited she was about the possibility of being cast as the lead in *Waterloo Bridge*, a play by Robert E. Sherwood that Bogie had heard about. Mary Philips herself had wanted to play the role on Broadway of the showgirl-turned-prostitute. It was a tragic story. The lead character feels that because she was once a whore she doesn't have the right to her lover's respect. The film ends with her suicide on Waterloo Bridge.

As Davis went to makeup, Bogie met James Whale. "Bette told me that the role of the soldier is still open," Bogie said. "Fox doesn't have anything for me to do and they're paying me by the week. I'm sure they would be happy to lend me to you. Could I test for it?"

"Dear boy," Whale said, patting him affectionately on the arm. "The part has just been cast. You know, it calls for a handsome leading man. The type women will swoon over. I don't see you in such a part. Maybe character roles. A heavy perhaps."

"They said that about Valentino in the old days," Bogie said. "And look what happened."

"My *dear* boy," Whale said. "Trust me on this one. When it comes to casting, I'm never wrong. A natural instinct, I guess."

A fey and vapidly handsome young man emerged from Whale's office. The director introduced him to Bogie. "Meet the male lead in *Waterloo Bridge*. Humphrey Bogart, this is Kent Douglass."

"I'm thinking of changing my name to Douglass Montgomery," he said. "That's Douglass with two Ss."

"Why don't you do that?" Bogie said, giving him a limp handshake. He was resentful of the actor, suspecting that he'd been sleeping with Whale as an incentive to getting the role.

"Would you gentlemen excuse me?" Whale said. "I think Bette Davis is ready for her test." He turned back as if to seek reassurance from Bogie. "I don't know what makeup did to her. But when you brought her onto the set, she looked mousy. Definitely unconvincing as a prostitute. After all, who would pay out good money to go to bed with Bette Davis?"

"Seems to me you've already made up your mind not to cast her," Bogie said. "Why are you even bothering with the test?"

"I was ordered to," Whale said. "You do what a studio boss tells you to do. Actually I saw Mae Clarke the other night opposite Cagney in *The Public Enemy*. Clarke has *prostitute* written all over her." He turned and left, leaving Montgomery standing there awkwardly with Bogie.

As Bogie chatted with Montgomery, he realized that the young actor was making an assumption that he, Bogie, was also a homosexual. At the time, Montgomery was part of the growing influx of young homosexual actors arriving in Hollywood during the late Twenties and early Thirties at the birth of the Talkies. The list of gay, or at least bisexual hopefuls was growing by the day: Anderson Lawler, David Manners, Louis Mason, David Rollins, Richard Cromwell, Alexander Kirkland, Ross Alexander, John Darrow.

"When I came out here, I thought I'd be enjoying one handsome hunk after another," Montgomery said. "It's not been like that at all. I've been sleeping with creatures from the dark lagoon. Charles Laughton. I found him disgusting. When George Cukor's fat lips worked me over, I closed my eyes and dreamed of God, mother, and country. William Haines and Eddie Goulding weren't so bad." He accepted a cigarette from Bogie. "I hear you're a good buddy of Kenneth MacKenna. I certainly wouldn't mind a date or two with him. How's it been with you? What ghouls have you been sleeping with, if you don't mind my asking?"

Eyeing him squarely, Bogie was eager to report this conversation to Kenneth later in the day. "I've decided on another route. For casting-couch advancement, I work the female circuit: Greta Garbo, Marlene Dietrich, Norma Shearer. Dietrich is perfect, but Garbo's feet and especially that pussy of hers are too big. And Shearer has fat ankles. The most disgusting broad I've ever had to fuck? Would you believe Marie Dressler?"

At that point, Montgomery realized that Bogie was putting him on. He excused himself and walked away. It would not be the beginning of a beauti-

179

ful friendship between the two men.

When her screen test was over, and Bogie had delivered Davis back to Ruthie, he hadn't heard the last of her. For some reason, even though it was obvious that she held him in disdain, she'd found a kindred spirit in him and called him with frequent bulletins.

The following morning, Davis phoned him in all her rage and fury. "That God damn faggot, James Whale. Moby Dick, or so he thinks. I'm out of the lead. He's cast me in some dull part as the sister. I'm repeating the part I played in *Bad Sister*. The mouse role. He cast Mae Clarke instead."

"Your day will come."

"Christ," Davis screeched. "Now she's fucking James Cagney. I guess it takes a whore to play a whore. In the film, I'm supposed to be nice to Clarke's character. How can I be nice to her when I hate the bitch's guts?"

"Because you're an actress," he said, "and a damn good one. If the part calls for it, you can do it."

That seemed to please her. The next morning she was on the phone again as if she had to give him a daily bulletin. "Whale is out of his mind," she charged. "There was a scene yesterday that called for a chamber pot to be placed under the bed. For realism, Whale insisted that the pot be half full of the real stuff. Christ, I hope they cut that scene out of the movie."

"You getting on with Mae okay?" he asked.

"I guess," she said. "I stand on the set watching her emote. I mouth her lines, saying them like they should be spoken and acted while she fucks up every scene."

"I hear this Whale is a pretty good director," he said, always wanting to take an opposing point of view.

"Whale is no director. He's a traffic cop. He handles entrances and exits—and that's it."

The next morning, Davis had changed her opinion of Whale. He was not only brilliant, but "one of the greatest directors ever to hit Hollywood."

""What brought this on?" he asked.

"He wants me for the lead in *Frankenstein*."

He laughed. "Now that's a part you can play: The Bride of Frankenstein."

"Remind me never to talk to you again, you son of a bitch." She slammed down the phone.

Forgetting her promise never to speak to him again, she called the following week. "That God damn faggot said I came off horribly in my screen test for *Frankenstein*." She seemed hysterical. "He said I'm totally wrong for the part. What a cocksucker he is. I'm off the picture."

"Who's getting the part?" he asked, genuinely curious.

"Christ, would you believe Mae Clarke? She's so bad in *Waterloo Bridge*, he's giving her *Frankenstein*. If he wasn't a queer, I'd swear he was sleeping with the bitch. Whale can't see talent if it were a roaring truck coming down the road about to run over the slime. Christ, I can't stand queers."

"Now, Bette," he said, "You must learn to co-exist."

"So I do," she said. "But it's God damn hard putting up with them. I dread the day when I'll have to play a love scene with one of them and let them kiss me, considering where their mouths have been. Mae Clarke said that there are men who actually stick their tongues up men's assholes. Have you ever heard of that?"

"Can't say that I have," he said archly.

"Oh, Bogart," she said. "You're such a kidder. You probably do that yourself." For the second time in just a few days, she slammed down the phone on him.

But it wasn't the last he'd hear of Bette Davis.

***

The tough, one-eyed director, Raoul Walsh, called Bogie the next morning, telling him he'd been cast in the new Fox picture, *Women of All Nations*. Bogie was hopeful until Walsh informed him that he was playing the "seventh lead," in a film that would once again team Victor McLaglen with Edmund Lowe. They'd be reprising their roles of Flagg and Quirt which had brought them such acclaim in *What Price Glory?*, which had originally been filmed as a silent in 1926 with Walsh himself as director,

Bogie remembered how the director of *A Devil With Women*, Irving Cummings, had hoped that the team of McLaglen/Bogart would prove so successful that they'd be cast together in several more films. No such luck. With box office revenues down because of the Depression, Fox was dipping into remakes of its past successes to sell tickets—hence, the cameras would be rolling once again on that rugged duo of McLaglen and Lowe.

"Who are the dames in the picture?" Bogie asked Walsh.

"Greta Nissen and Fifi D'Orsay," the director said abruptly before ordering Bogie to report to wardrobe tomorrow at seven o'clock in the morning.

Bogie hoped that his role might have some possibilities. As a fringe benefit, he thought he might be able to seduce that Scandinavian beauty, Nissen, and perhaps that little French cutie, Fifi D'Orsay.

That afternoon he was still hopeful when Fox sent a messenger over to deliver the script to him. He was surprised to see that the screenplay had been written by a man he knew. Barry Conners had also written the three-act comedy, *Hell's Bells*, in which Bogie had appeared on Broadway with Olive May and Shirley Booth. With the latter, he'd performed both on and off the stage, as he so fondly recalled.

After reading the script—he was hardly able to find his part—Bogie was bitterly disappointed. There was virtually nothing for him to do. Any one of a thousand, even 10,000, actors—could have played the part, such as it was. Bogie felt that it was more of "a brief appearance" than a role. It was clearly a showcase for Lowe and McLaglen, but not for him.

"It's nothing but a stupid caper," Bogie told Kenneth when he went next door to have a drink with him. "My career at Fox is nose-diving by the minute.

181

They could get some actor to do this for $25 a week instead of $750."

Bogie's only good luck that day was when he returned to his apartment to find a personal letter waiting for him from New York. At first he thought it was from his Mary. The letter was from Helen instead, informing him that she was coming to Los Angeles where she'd booked a bungalow at the Garden of Allah.

Even though the lesbian play, *The Captive*, had been closed on a charge of "indecency" by the New York police, there was talk of mounting a production in Los Angeles. To Bogie's amazement, Samuel Goldwyn had expressed interest in acquiring the film rights, even though the Will Hays office had forbidden the depiction of any type of "perversion" on the screen.

The next morning after wardrobe had fitted Bogie into a crisp new marine uniform, he stared at his figure in the mirror, thinking he looked rather striking.

When he ran into the director, Walsh, he looked Bogie up and down. "You come off as queer bait—perfect for what I had in mind."

Bogie's part didn't even merit a dressing room. He was assigned a locker room with the rest of the cast, which included the grips and the assistant cameraman. Since his part was so small, Bogie didn't even know why he was needed on the set.

There weren't even any women to flirt with, as Greta Nissen and that cute little Fifi D'Orsay were nowhere to be seen. Perhaps Walsh had them lined up for his casting couch that day.

As Bogie stood idly by with nothing to do, and feeling like a jerk, one of the co-stars of the film, Bela Lugosi, came up to him and introduced himself. "I saw you and Tracy in *Up the River*," Lugosi said. "You guys did a good job."

"Count Dracula himself, I presume," Bogie said. Since neither actor had any work to do that day, Lugosi invited Bogie to the commissary for some black coffee.

Bogie relaxed with this Hungarian actor, born Be'la Ferenc Dezso Blaski in 1882 in the small town—now Romanian—of Lugosi.

When Lugosi ordered coffee from the waiter, Bogie said, "Now you've spoiled my illusion. I thought you drank only blood."

As coffee was served, Lugosi confided in Bogie after he'd promised not to tell Louella Parsons, "I really wanted a career in operettas. I have a remarkable singing voice."

"Blood curdling, I bet," Bogie said, kidding him.

"Actually before I had success as a monster," Lugosi said, "I scored well portraying Jesus Christ. Would you believe I was also a sensation playing Romeo in Budapest in 1911?"

"About you, I could believe anything," Bogie said. "You're a remarkable man. I caught you on Broadway back in '27. I don't care how many roles you've played, you're stuck with that vampire count bit. No one does it better than you."

182

"I know," he said. "It's both a blessing and my curse. I made up a will the other day. In my will, I left instructions that I be buried in my Count Dracula cape."

Bogie laughed. "That means you'll be back! No grave will hold you."

"Speaking of men who are vampires," Lugosi said, "here's one of the stars of the picture coming toward us. Edmund Lowe. I'll introduce you, but make sure your fly is buttoned."

"Don't you look the spiffy marine!" said the slick-haired, debonair screen star.

"Don't you look like something yourself?" Bogie said, pausing to take in the costume of a top-hatted, silk-caped magician.

"With that cape and that hat, are you trying to take over my role as Count Dracula?" Lugosi asked.

"Actually, I'm doing a wardrobe test for this upcoming film, *The Spider*," Lowe said. "I'm being considered for the lead." Lowe would win the coveted role that very year, his character in *The Spider* inspiring the look of the comic-strip character, Mandrake the Magician. "Now I've got to get to my dressing room and slip into my marine drag."

"At least you have a dressing room," Bogie said. "Walsh has demoted me to the men's locker room."

"By all means, share my dressing room," Lowe said. "C'mon," I'm going there now."

The art director on the picture, David Hall, came over to ask Lowe something. He excused himself momentarily to speak to Hall.

"If you guys are going to share a dressing room, watch yourself around that one," Lugosi warned Bogie in a whisper.

"You've got to be kidding," Bogie said. "He's married to the most beautiful woman in Hollywood."

"*Everybody* in Hollywood has to watch himself or herself around Lilyan Tashman." With that enigmatic statement, Lugosi turned and headed

Two Views of *Women of All Nations:*

(top photo, clockwise from lower left), Edmund Lowe, Humphrey Bogart, and Victor McLaglen

(bottom photo) Victor McLaglen, Greta Nissen, and Edmund Lowe

to his own dressing room.

When he'd finished his conversation with the art director, Lowe turned to Bogie. His fingers tightened around Bogie's arm. "Let's head for my dressing room now. I may even find some whiskey there."

"You're my kind of guy," Bogie said.

Lowe's fingers tightened even firmer around Bogie's arm. "And you're my kind of guy too. I always believe that when you need a job done, call out the marines."

***

Edmund Lowe was most solicitous.

After he'd dressed in his own marine uniform, he made a slight suggestion about how Bogie could artfully diminish the impact of his scarred lip with a clever use of makeup. "Believe me, I know more about makeup than Marlene Dietrich," he said. "We actors have to do for ourselves."

Lowe even invited Bogie to accompany him to the set. He said all the things that Bogie had been wanting to hear since leaving New York. "You are a marvelous screen presence. You could be a big star different from all others. It's the directors who are stupid."

"I guess they don't like my ugly mug," Bogie said.

"That's nonsense," Lowe said. "You are very, very handsome, and very, very sexy. I read somewhere that the New York critics considered you as handsome as Valentino."

"They must have had George Raft in mind," Bogie said modestly.

"Actually I don't think Raft looks like Valentino at all," Lowe said. "You've got sex appeal. A heavy dose." He leaned over in a confidential whisper to Bogie. "And from what I hear, you're packing a powerful weapon in that tight uniform of yours."

Bogie was flattered but also a bit embarrassed. "Who in hell have you been talking to."

"I have many credible sources," Lowe said enigmatically. "You've just hit Hollywood and already some of the top stars have fallen for you."

"I wouldn't exactly call it 'fallen,'" Bogie said. "More accurately, they've bedded me and then forgotten me."

"I know Stanwyck went for you," Lowe said, "But now she's chasing after my darling Lilyan."

"With a woman as gorgeous as Lilyan Tashman, I bet I know where you are at night," Bogie said.

"You are a truly adorable, darling man," Lowe said before being summoned to the set. "I'm going to try to get Walsh to make your part bigger on this picture." Before heading off, he paused. "I've got one better. I want you to be the co-star of my next movie."

"Make me your Spider Boy?" Bogie asked.

Lowe seemed amused. "No, not that. I have various roles in mind for you.

I think you can be developed into one of the screen's most romantic leading men."

"You mean, the type who gets the gal in the final reel?" Bogie asked.

"Exactly," Lowe said. "Scar or not, you've got the most sensuous lips. I like the way you always keep them wet. Dietrich knows that trick too."

"With me, it's not deliberate," Bogie said. "I salivate a lot."

"It would be like dying and going to heaven to get worked over by that succulent mouth of yours." As if catching himself, he quickly added. "It would be any girl's dream, I'm sure."

"I was feeling pretty low today until I met Mr. Lowe himself," Bogie said. "I think I'll call you 'High' instead. You've made me feel real good. And thanks for letting me share your dressing room. I don't feel like a third-class citizen any more."

"I've never met an actor in Hollywood I liked instantly like I do you. I've got a great idea. If you're not busy tomorrow night, would you come over and have dinner with Lilyan and me? I know she'll find you as fascinating as I do."

"I'd love to," Bogie said. "Sounds like my kind of evening. No red-blooded man in his right mind would turn down an evening with Lilyan. She's beautiful."

"What about me?" Lowe asked. "Am I chopped liver?"

"Not at all," Bogie said, realizing that no vain actor liked to be slighted. "Not chopped liver at all. More like a juicy T-bone steak."

"You've got that right, baby cakes," Lowe said before heading out to face Walsh's direction.

Marital bliss:
Lilyan Tashman &
Edmund Lowe

***

In his grim and bleak apartment, Bogie found a note from Raft. He'd come into some money and was moving out. He thanked him for his hospitality.

Next day on the set of *Women of All Nations*, in their shared dressing room, Bogie felt uncomfortable stripping off his military uniform under the focused stares of Lowe. But after a few uncomfortable minutes, he decided "what the hell" and stripped down, as needed, anyway. He wasn't really an exhibitionist, but the actor in him appreciated the approval of an audience. Maybe all those stories about Lowe being a homo-

185

sexual were true, and maybe they weren't. He was married to one of the most beautiful women in Hollywood, Lilyan Tashman.

Having gone through a marriage to Helen Menken, Bogie knew that a wedding band didn't mean a God damn thing in the theater or in Hollywood. After the dust had settled on his former marriage, Bogie was convinced that Helen preferred women. Even so, he fully expected to bed her when she reached Hollywood—no doubt at her bungalow at the Garden of Allah.

"Are you sure you don't want me to bring a date to your place tonight?" Bogie asked Lowe, as he buttoned up his fly.

"My Lilyan and I have already arranged a surprise date for you," Lowe said.

"I hope not some dog you're trying to push off on me," Bogie said, almost meaning it.

"Lilyan is a connoisseur not only of *haute couture*, but also of the world's most beautiful women," he said somewhat enigmatically. "Your date tonight one day will take her place alongside some of the world's most enchanting women. The likes of Cleopatra and Helen of Troy."

"You do like to tease a country boy from New York," Bogie said. "I'm sure my date is Marie Dressler."

"Time will tell, my dear, lovely boy," Lowe said. He hovered near Bogie, who at first feared that the actor was going to kiss him. Instead Lowe took his hand and held it gently. "Until tonight, you adorable creature. Lilyan is dying to meet you. She's going to wear her sexiest outfit, a little thing she picked up in Paris."

Lilyan Tashman

"She's your wife," Bogie said. "Why would she wear something sexy for me? Even assuming your marriage is as open as mine, you said I already have a date."

"Listen, pet, let's don't go into logistics right now," Lowe said. "The night hasn't even begun. We must go forward into that good night and welcome its surprises." With that parting comment, he was out the door.

Bogie stood looking confused. He felt that he was heading for either the best or the most disastrous party of his Hollywood life. "Let the night unfold," he said before checking his appearance in the mirror.

As he would confide in Kenneth the next day, he kissed his own image in the mirror. He felt that that kind of self-enchantment qualified him as a narcissist like every other actor in Hollywood. Giving himself a final smooch, he said, "Go for it, you good-looking mother-fucker."

Even though it had been announced as just a small, intimate dinner party, Lowe greeted Bogie at the door in full evening dress.

In his dark suit, Bogie said, "I didn't know it was black tie."

"Come in, dear boy," the slick-haired actor said, taking his hand and guiding him into the foyer. "Dressed, and especially undressed, you're most welcome at the humble Tashman/Lowe abode."

It was actually a Beverly Hills mansion they called "Lilowe."

With the grace of a ballerina, Lilyan moved from her garden into the living room, crossing the parlor to greet Bogie. Her movements were so perfect that they gave the illusion of being choreographed. Even before she'd kissed him gently on the lips, he'd fallen madly in love with her.

"Welcome to our home," she said. "For once Eddie didn't lie about your beauty."

"The only beauty in this room is standing before me," Bogie graciously said. "I'm a regular looking guy."

"Don't be so modest," she said, looking over at Lowe with a smirk. "I never thought I'd ever say that to an actor. I've read in the press that you've been compared to Valentino." As she seated him on the sofa next to her, he was awed by her beauty. She was dressed a little too flamboyantly for his taste, but still exquisite in a Parisian white satin gown with four diamond clasps. When she noticed him checking out her jewelry, she said, "If I happen to wear real diamonds instead of paste, who is to object?"

"Not me," Bogie said, "providing I didn't have to pay for them."

As the maid served drinks, Bogie was eager to learn anything he could about her. He virtually ignored Lowe. Born in New York the same year as himself, she had toiled for years in the Silents, knocking on doors of casting offices and dancing in Ziegfeld's *Follies*.

Eventually, she forged ahead in the Talkies, creating a niche playing sophisticated but sarcastic blondes. The night he met her, she was an acknowledged social leader in Hollywood, consistently cited as the town's best-dressed woman.

Her home was spectacular. "Who's your decorator?" he asked. "He needs to do something—anything—to my rattrap apartment."

"You're looking at *him*," she said. "My hobby is interior decorating."

"She also claims she decorated our Malibu Beach home," Lowe said. "But it was Jetta Goudal."

"Would you shut up?" she said abruptly to her husband before softening her features again when she turned to face Bogie. "Goudal helped, but I did most of it myself." Lowe merely rolled his eyes sarcastically, looking up at the ceiling.

"Oh, I forgot," Bogie said. He reached into the pocket of his suit and removed a small gift package wrapped with red satin ribbon.

Taking the box from him, she deftly opened it, her eyes lighting up in delight. "Miniature hands," she said, fondling the porcelain gift. "Thank you, darling." She reached over and kissed him again on the lips. "I'll add this latest pair to my collection." Reaching for his hand, she guided him into an adjoining room which was lined with glass shelves displaying what must have been the world's largest collection of miniature hands in all shapes and materials.

"I read in some column that you collected these little hands, and I wanted to add my paws to your other ones," he said.

"I will value your hands more than all the others," she said.

She was so convincing that for one brief moment he actually believed her.

As she directed him back into her sumptuous living room, he took in her figure from the rear, finding it slender and slinky. Her throaty voice evoked Garbo with a touch of Dietrich. He'd read that Eddie Cantor had called her face "fox-like."

As Tashman kept the talk bubbly, Lowe became cruder as he drank. As if jealous of his wife, his tone grew bitchy. "I've never known Lil to pay so much attention to a man. Usually it's the women at any party who have to watch out for her. No beautiful gal is safe going to the powder room with Lil at the party."

She patted Bogie's hand. "Eddie does exaggerate so."

"Whether it's a grand dame of the theater or a newly arrived teenage chorus gal from Broadway, Lil chases after them right into the powder room," Lowe said. "Often she seduces them in a private toilet stall. Her technique is amazing, I hear, and it's the talk of Hollywood."

As Bogie looked at her, he found this slander hard to believe. To him, she was the epitome of elegance and taste.

"They don't call her Latrine Lil for nothing," Lowe said.

No longer able to control herself, Lilyan glared at him. "And they don't call you a cocksucking son-of-a-bitch for nothing," she said. Still, to Bogie's surprise, she didn't deny her husband's assertions. When he became too graphic describing her seduction of Louise Brooks, she said, "forgive Eddie. When he's not sucking a big dick—he's a size queen, incidentally—the true feline that lurks in his heart comes out of her cage." To change the subject, she said, "Tallulah's in town looking for movie work and fucking that divine Gary Cooper. But that Montana cowboy has given her gonorrhea, so darling Tallu is temporarily out of commission."

"She told us about your marriage to Helen," Lowe said.

"I'd rather not talk about it," Bogie said, barely concealing his simmering anger.

"It's all right with us," she said. "With Eddie and me, you can let your hair down. After all, you and I have a lot in common. You've both known darling Tallu. I've also enjoyed Miss Helen Menken herself."

At that point Bogie was ready to bolt from the room. What kept him glued to his seat was his utter fascination with Lilyan in spite of her vile talk. She could speak freely of her seduction of women, yet he felt that she also wanted to go to bed with him. All evening, to emphasize a point, she would reach out and touch him. He found her fingers on him thrilling and wanted her to feel more of him. He regretted that Lowe had arranged the surprise date, even though he kept assuring Bogie that an enchantress was on her way.

Even as she continued to touch and feel Bogie, Lilyan still spoke of women. "I've had nearly every major female star in Hollywood, but I struck out with Gloria Swanson, Norma Talmadge, and Billie Dove."

"Better luck next time," Bogie said.

"So, now that you've seen a slice of our domestic life, what do you think of our 'ideal marriage?'" Lowe asked. "That's how all the fan magazines refer to our wedded bliss."

Fortunately for Bogie, he didn't have to answer that direct question. "Only last week I granted *Photoplay* an interview," she said. "About how a woman can hold onto her man." She flashed a look of contempt at her drunken husband." I told the magazine that no man will tolerate a lazy woman for very long. I also told them that a woman has to look good for her man at all times. To quote *moi*, 'I never appear before Eddie looking seedy or badly groomed.'"

"That's a damnable lie," Lowe said. "I've seen my bitch here looking very disheveled after she's worked over some hot pussy and raises herself up with vagina juice dripping down her chin."

"Whenever Eddie drinks, he becomes really vulgar," she said. "You'll find out more about that later." Ideal marriage or not, she looked at him with total disdain. "I call him sewer mouth. But, as I said, you'll see what I mean as the night progresses."

That evening did move on. It was nearly ten o'clock, and Bogie's mystery date still hadn't shown up. He suspected that there was no fourth guest, and that he was here for a three-way.

Enthralled by Lilyan, he wanted her alone, miles removed from her homosexual husband. He couldn't even call up his friend, Tracy, to take Lowe off his hands for the night. Lowe wasn't Tracy's type.

The maid came in and announced that Lilyan was wanted on the phone. She rose gracefully, patted Bogie on the knee, and turned to her husband. "Can I trust you alone with this darling man?"

"I've already seen him jaybird naked in my dressing room," Lowe said. "I restrained myself then, but just barely. I'll be a good boy, although I can't promise that I won't salivate a bit." When

Style-setter
Lilyan Tashman

189

she'd gone, Lowe took Lilyan's place on the sofa beside Bogie.

Uncomfortable seated there, Bogie rose quickly to refill his own drink. Fortunately, Lilyan came back into the room in only a minute or so.

She looked jubilant. "Your surprise date is also doing the cooking tonight. We are so lucky. She makes the best goulash in Hollywood. Instead of cooking in my kitchen, she preferred to cook the goulash in her own home and is bringing it over."

"Prepare yourself for a delightful evening," Lowe predicted to Bogie. "And I don't mean just the goulash."

Growing a little bored with Lowe's fabulous build-up, Bogie said, "Yeah, promises, promises."

In fifteen minutes, the doorbell rang, and the maid went to answer it.

Not knowing what to expect, Bogie was startled when his surprise date came into the living room, after handing a pot of goulash to the maid.

After kissing both Lowe and Lilyan rather passionately on the mouth, she turned to him. He'd met her before, and, as before, he was overcome by her exotic allure and her beauty.

"Mr. Bogie man," she said in her seductively accented voice. "We meet again."

Not wanting to sound like some awed schoolboy, he said, "Did anyone ever tell you you're one hell of a broad?"

"So many, many times," she said, smiling at him before looking around the living room, finally focusing on Lilyan. A slight smirk came onto her face. "Someone in this room is going to get lucky tonight. I don't know...." She paused as if confused about what to say. "What is the damn correct English? On whom I will bestow my charms?"

"If there is a God in heaven," Bogie said, "and at times I seriously doubt it, I am hoping that he is looking with favor on me tonight, Miss Dietrich."

CHAPTER FOUR

Bogie woke up the next morning fully convinced that he was a sexual degenerate. After he'd invited Kenneth over for coffee and conversation, he felt better. Drawing on his experience as a former member of the New York Pussy Posse, Kenneth convinced him that what Bogie was doing in Hollywood—no different from some scenes in which he'd participated in New York—was "just the norm out here."

Long after the world's greatest tasting goulash—"that Kraut sure knows how to cook"—was served, Dietrich and Lilyan had disappeared into her bedroom upstairs.

"My God, the evening turned into a scene out of Arabian Nights," he confided to Kenneth. "I don't remember it, just blurred scenes."

Kenneth was convinced the Bogie remembered everything, but didn't want to supply all the details.

"Before I left that house around four o'clock, I did a trick or two that even I hadn't thought about before," Bogie said.

"Like what?" Kenneth asked. "Tell me. I might be missing out on something."

"When you marry Kay Francis, I'm sure she'll teach you on your honeymoon. I'm saying no more."

"I'm still going to pursue women on all fronts, but I'm going to taper off when Helen comes to town," Bogie said.

"You mean Miss Menken?" Kenneth asked in surprise.

"One and the same," Bogie said. "She'll be staying at the Garden of Allah. I'm sure I'll be spending my nights there."

"Have you all but forgotten Mary back in New York?" Kenneth asked. "I'm still carrying a torch for her."

"Yeah," Bogie said. "Would you have stayed in New York if Mary had married you instead of me?"

"No way," Kenneth said. "I think my future is in Hollywood. But I think I could have convinced Mary to come with me."

"In a way I'm glad she's back in New York, because I'll be returning there soon," he said. "I still want to stay married to her. We'll wipe our slates clean and start all over again."

"Does she have a clue about what you're up to out here?" Kenneth asked.

"Not unless you've written her."

"My lips are sealed," Kenneth said, "I think at this point in our lives, we shouldn't stop to analyze what's happening. Let's just let the good times roll."

Suddenly, a messenger arrived from Fox Studios. Opening the package, Bogie learned that he'd been assigned fourth billing in his final film at Fox. Entitled *A Holy Terror*, it would be directed by Irving Cummings, who had previously guided him through *A Devil with Women*. He'd be appearing with the star of the picture, George O'Brien.

As he read the script, he was even more startled to learn that it was a western based on Max Brand's novel, *Trailin'*. In the film, Bogie was slated to play Steve Nash, foreman of the Drew ranch, who's in love with a character played by Sally Eilers.

The city boy from New York was about to play his first cowboy role.

***

He'd had a lovely evening with Joan Blondell, during which she'd served what she described as one of her favorite dishes—mashed rutabagas mixed with mashed potatoes. Fortunately, she'd also baked a ham as well. That was his favorite. As he related to Kenneth the following morning, "Sex with Joan has become what I imagine it's like between a married couple who's been together for many many years. It's comfortable and safe, but completely without fireworks."

Kenneth seemed relatively unconcerned about Bogie's sex life that morning. He was distracted by plans for his upcoming wedding to Kay Francis. Once again, he secured a promise that Bogie would be there as his best man.

Bogie agreed for a final time, then reminded him that Helen Menken would be arriving in Hollywood soon and checking into the Garden of Allah.

"I adore Helen," Kenneth said. "Bring her to the wedding."

Some of Kay's friends are throwing some parties for us this week. We'd love it if you and Helen could come to any or all of them. I'll slip the invitations under your door."

"That sounds great," Bogie said, "Helen would meet some film people. She already knows everybody on Broadway."

"Wouldn't it be ironic if Helen became a bigger film star than either of us?"

"Things like that happen," Bogie said, lighting up his seventh cigarette of the morning. "But if I make all these appearances at all these parties, people will think I'm back with Helen. Hollywood is a small town. Word will get back to Mary."

"So what?" Kenneth asked. "Mary knows you're sleeping with other gals. And don't kid yourself. Mary hasn't exactly been behaving like a nun recently. I'm sure she has a steady stream of beaux."

"That's our marriage agreement," Bogie said. "It's OK for me to fool around with other women, unless that other woman happens to be Helen.

Mary won't exactly be thrilled by any of this."

"Maybe Mary will divorce you after all," Kenneth said with a wink.

Bogie clinched his fist and pretended to give Kenneth a sock in the jaw. "Still pining for Mary, huh? Here you are about to marry Kay, and you're still trying to steal my wife."

"Hey," Kenneth said, "I've got a sharp eye for a movie plot. How about writing a screenplay together about this romantic entanglement? I bet we could sell it."

"And maybe we couldn't," Bogie said. "About this wedding. Is it going to be a big affair?"

"No. The wedding itself will be very small. The guests include you, Helen, and one or two of Kay's friends. That's why Kay is seeing all of her friends and getting congratulations and, we hope, lots of presents before the actual marriage ceremony."

"Smart thinking," Bogie said, glancing at the clock. "I've got to go to work. Sounds like we'll have a gay old time this week with all the parties and everything."

"It's your chance to score this week," Kenneth said. "You'll be meeting some of the top broads in Hollywood. Too bad you'll be with your wife."

"My former wife," Bogie corrected him. "We're divorced, remember? And besides, even when we were married, Helen and I had an open marriage. And she's likely to be heavily booked during her time out here, spending time with some of her former girl friends, including Tallulah, who's also at the Garden of Allah."

"It's going to be interesting," Kenneth said. "I wish I could follow you around with a camera this week."

"After the marriage, are you still going to be fooling around?"

"Sure. Kay and I both understand that our marriage will be mainly for show. I'm doing it to boost my career in Hollywood. Being married to a major movie star might help. That's why you married Helen—to advance your career on Broadway."

"Something like that," he said. Kenneth's words evoked a sour memory.

"Kay's becoming big out here, really big. She's defined as one of the top five actresses in Hollywood, with lots of attention from the press. Her fans want to see her with a handsome and adoring husband."

"Good luck," Bogie said. "Yours will be just one of many lavender marriages out here."

"No, it'll be a real marriage," Kenneth said. "A complicated Hollywood marriage with lovers of all persuasions coming and going. I like women more than I like men. Just ask your wife. On the other hand, Kay likes women more than she likes men. But she's very attracted to men. The first time I took Kay out, she said, 'I'm not a star. *I'm a woman.* And I want to get fucked.' We'll just have to work out our sleeping arrangements."

***

193

It was a different Helen Menken he met at the train depot. Her immaculate clothes, even her hat, looked more Fifth Avenue than Hollywood and Vine. She had New York written all over her. He could not imagine a woman who looked less Californian.

As he rushed toward her to take her in his arms and kiss her, he encountered a woman no longer in the spring of her life. Her face was still young but it was more mature, a bit harsher, and a bit less forgiving.

She made no effort to probe into his personal life, other than to say, "A handsome devil like you must be the sensation of half the Hollywood cuties out here—that is, the few that George Raft hasn't already subdued."

"Something like that," he said as nonchalantly as possible.

By the time they'd reached the parking lot of the Garden of Allah, Helen had brought him up to date on all the news of Broadway and several mutual acquaintances. No mention was made of his present wife, except one. "I saw Mary the other day," she said. "She's put on a few pounds, but the extra weight is agreeable to her figure. She's getting work, but neither of us is the sensation of Broadway these days, the way we imagined it would be when we were younger. In fact, with so few shows because of the Depression, Broadway is a pretty dismal place."

He wanted to ask Helen if she knew who Mary was dating or perhaps even shacked up with, but he restrained himself. "Sorry to hear about the depressed state of affairs. That's real bad news for me. I'm planning to go back to New York and try for a job on Broadway. Fox isn't going to renew me. They don't know what to do with me. In a few weeks I'm leaving Hollywood for good."

"It's a ghastly place out here," she said. "You and I are New Yorkers. We don't belong outside the civilized world."

"C'mon, let me show you to your new home." He went around to the trunk to get her luggage.

She stood looking at the façade of the Garden of Allah, now functioning as a somewhat rundown colony of rentable cottages.

"I can't believe that this was once Nazimova's private home. I still see her on and off. It's hard to imagine that she was once queen of MGM."

"Garbo seems to have filled her shoes."

"I suppose you're right," she said. "I didn't think Garbo would survive the advent of talking pictures. I guess her audience wants whiskey pronounced *viskey*."

"You talk real pretty," he said, "and look great. I hope to take you around to a lot of parties. Maybe some director will discover you out here and make you a big star like Garbo."

"Oh, Hump," she said, heading for the reception desk as if she already knew where to go. "The Twenties are dead and gone. That was a time for daydreaming. It's the grim Thirties now."

In the privacy of her bungalow, she told him that it was almost certain that a production of her lesbian play, *The Captive*, would be mounted on the stages of Los Angeles. "I'm out here negotiating the deal now." She paused. "That and other things."

For whatever reason, she chose not to tell him what she meant by "other things," which was a signal to him that he would be with her only on certain days, leaving the rest of her Hollywood sojourn a private affair.

"I don't get it," he said. "In New York, that play got you thrown into jail. What makes you think the Los Angeles police won't do the same thing? If anything, they're a lot more liberal in New York than out here. If what they define as perversion is depicted on the screen today, it's got to be hidden. No more Erich von Stroheim. He was the last of that era of decadence, I'm sorry to say."

"We'll see," she said enigmatically. "I have my assurances we're going forward with the project. I can't give you any details until I know more." She waved her arms theatrically. "Here I am installed in my new home in California but with yesterday's husband."

As she twirled around the room, that old sexual stirring came back to him. He still desired this woman.

"I know you just got into town," he said, "and haven't even unpacked. But I've got to know something."

"Whatever do you want to know," she said, coming up to him and kissing him on both cheeks. "You divine, handsome thing you. If anything, in maturity you've grown more beautiful."

"C'mon, Helen," he said. "Even on my finest day no one ever calls me beautiful."

"Handsome then." She kissed him on the lips. "Still keeping those lips moist for me, are you?"

"Yeah," he said. "I've got to know something. When a woman divorces her husband, does said husband have to surrender his conjugal rights, or can he reclaim them at any time?"

"It doesn't matter what the legal restrictions are with me," she said. "If you're talking about that marriage contract between Helen Menken and one Humphrey Bogart, I view the bond as unbroken. Said husband can reclaim those rights whenever he wants to."

"Glad to hear that," he said, taking off his jacket and beginning a striptease in front of her.

"If you're taking off your clothes, I guess you're glad to see me."

En route to the bedroom, she promised him lots of loving before her eight o'clock engagement. "When she heard I was coming to California, Lilyan Tashman wrote me. She wants me to come over for dinner tomorrow night as a means of celebrating my arrival in Los Angeles. As part of your Hollywood rounds, have you met up with the Miss Tashman yet?"

She did not wait for his response, but continued, "Both Katharine Cornell and Nazimova told me Tashman is absolutely divine. Even though married, I hear she has a thing for the ladies. I'll have to be careful that she doesn't seduce me, too."

195

That did it for him. As he mounted Helen and plowed her good, he was more zealous in his efforts because his brain was flashing images of Lilyan Tashman and not the picture of the woman beneath him. From the ecstatic look on her face, Helen was none the wiser.

Later, when he was spent and she too was exhausted, she whispered in his ear. "I don't know who's been letting you fuck them in Hollywood, but your technique has improved."

***

Bogie didn't reach the set of *A Holy Terror* until eleven o'clock that morning. Sucked into the tangled affairs of his roller-coaster private life, he had paid little attention to the script. But when called for a wardrobe fitting, he began to take his role of Steve Nash more seriously. In full cowboy garb, he was to play the foreman of a ranch opposite that handsome, body beautiful stud, George O'Brien.

Greg Brooks had fitted Bogie with a beige-colored Stetson, a six-shooter, a gigantic red handkerchief, which he was to wear around his neck like a tie, a pair of black-and-white striped pants (for some reason), a black shirt, and a battered old leather jacket.

Even Bogie laughed at himself when he saw his image in a full-length mirror. He could never make a convincing cowboy on screen.

After carefully studying his figure, Brooks said, "something's not right. You're just too short to be a cowboy."

"What do you suggest?" Bogie asked. "You got something to make me grow taller?"

Brooks thought for a minute before sending his wardrobe assistant to fetch a pair of shoes for Bogie. When he returned, Brooks insisted that Bogie put on a pair of elevator boots. "That way you can stand up with O'Brien eye-ball to eyeball in your scenes together."

Horrified, Bogie put on the elevator shoes and walked around the dressing room. "I'm walking on God damn stilts. I feel like a fucking dummy."

George O'Brien

"You're getting paid $750 a week, aren't you?" Brooks asked. "That's a lot more than a lot of actors at Fox are taking home. Why don't you just wear the shoes and quit griping?"

"Griping is what I do," Bogie said. "It's my specialty."

"Take off your shirt," Brooks demanded.

"What?" Bogie asked, astonished. "Am I supposed to strip down for you? I've dealt with you little fairy boys from wardrobe before. With me, sweet cakes, you can dream but not touch."

"Don't flatter yourself, Bogart," Brooks snapped. "You're not my type at all. I go for he-men. Now take off your shirt. We've got a real problem here."

Although infuriated, Bogie still wanted to earn that paycheck. He pulled off his shirt. Brooks went over to a drawer and pulled out two strips of white padding. "For some of our insufficiently endowed actors, we fake it. Since you don't have shoulders, I'll create some for you."

As reluctant as he was to do it, Bogie allowed Brooks to apply tape and padding to his shoulders. When Bogie put his shirt back on and stared at his image in the mirror, he was impressed. Unlike the elevator shoes, which he detested, the padding did make him look more like a fully developed man who could be the tough foreman of a ranch.

The person Bogie encountered on the set was Sally Eilers. "I'm sure he's already told you," she said in a low voice. "But when I'm not hooting with Hoot Gibson, I'm seeing your friend, Mr. Spencer Tracy. He's a wild one."

The existence of that liaison had escaped Bogie. When Tracy was with him, he spent more time talking about the men he was seeing instead of the women he was seducing. "He failed to fill me in on that one."

"In the case of Spence, he's got so many women he probably loses track," Eilers said.

"That's our boy Spence," he said

On the set George O'Brien came up to Bogie and invited him for a drink in his dressing room. Minutes later, O'Brien poured him a whiskey before filling a glass most generously for himself. "Love your shoes," he said.

"The less said about them the better. Couldn't they photograph me standing on a rock or on a staircase looking down at you?"

O'Brien pulled off his shirt. As Bogie was to learn during the shoot of *A Holy Terror*, O'Brien took every opportunity to pull off his shirt. Bogie couldn't help but admire his muscles, which reminded him of his own padded shoulders. Brooks was right. O'Brien didn't need any padding.

O'Brien was quick to detect Bogie's interest in his physique. Very bluntly he asked, "Are you a homosexual, like my best buddy, Spence?"

"Like hell!" Bogie said defensively. "I've got a lot of credentials to prove otherwise. I can summon witnesses if necessary."

"Don't get so rattled," O'Brien cautioned him. "I wanted to know who I have to fuck on this picture. I know that Eilers is after me. I've already done Brooks in wardrobe. The director's not a fairy, or at least I don't think so. Who knows? The picture's not over yet."

"Rest assured you can keep your pants on around me."

"It's good to clear the air in the very

George O'Brien, Spencer Tracy

197

beginning," O'Brien said. "When it comes to sex I don't like to beat around the bush. I come right out with it." He laughed at his own remark. That sounds sexually suggestive, doesn't it?"

"I'm beginning to think everything in Hollywood sounds sexually suggestive," Bogie said.

He remained long enough to finish his whiskey, but his presence in O'Brien's dressing room seemed so completely unnecessary that he quickly excused himself and left.

"Mama didn't raise no cowboy," he said to himself as he headed to his dressing room to change out of his uncomfortable Western gear.

After leaving the studio, he drove to the Garden of Allah to take Helen for dinner. He found her still dressing when he came into the room. He took her in his arms and kissed her with more than the usual passion. "I made a big mistake," he whispered in her ear. "We should have stayed together. I should never have married Mary."

"It was my fault," she said. "All my fault that we broke up."

His need for her—his need for any woman, but especially for her—was greater than it had been even when they'd had their reunion in Los Angeles.

Sensing that need, she said in a soft voice, "Dinner will have to wait." She led him to her bed.

***

The next morning on the set of *A Holy Terror*, Bogie, dressed in cowboy drag, had only one scene, after which he was finished for the day.

When O'Brien invited him for lunch, Bogie accepted. Although he wanted to order his typical ham and eggs, O'Brien had insisted that he ask for *huevos rancheros* instead. "The cook in the commissary is Mexican, and they're really good."

For himself, O'Brien asked for four raw avocados. "It's my favorite food. For breakfast, I eat an avocado sandwich on white toast. For lunch I eat them raw with just a little bit of lemon juice. At night I always make guacamole, which I eat as an appetizer before I order a very lean and very rare steak. It keeps my skin young and beautiful." He leaned over to Bogie. "Go on. Feel the skin of my face. Tell me skin like that can only be compared to a baby's ass."

"Hell, man," Bogie said, "I don't want to be seen sitting here in the commissary running my fingers across your cheek. People will think we're a couple of fags."

"Don't be such a sissy," O'Brien urged. "Go on. Rub my skin."

When he sensed that no one was watching them, Bogie ran his fingers across O'Brien's cheek. "That's smooth skin all right, a hell of a lot smoother than mine. I'm not aging well. Starting tomorrow, I'm gonna go on the avocado diet like you." He reached for a cigarette. "Smooth as your skin is, I'd rather be running my hands over the breasts of—say, Jean Harlow."

"Relax, relax," O'Brien told him. "You don't have to assert your heterosexual credentials around me. I'm not going to put the make on you. You're not my type. Either man or woman, I insist they have great bodies. You don't look like you have any physical fitness regime at all. Wardrobe told me they had to pad your shoulders. And those fucking high-heeled boots you wear— that's not my idea of a man who's tall in the saddle like I like 'em."

Blowing smoke toward him, Bogie said, "I guess that means you're not going to ask me out."

Since neither man was needed on the set for the rest of the day, O'Brien invited him to go swimming at Santa Monica. Bogie said that he didn't have any trunks. O'Brien told him that his house was on the way to the ocean, and they could drop off there and change.

An hour later, Bogie found himself in O'Brien's home. Although the actor kept himself incredibly well groomed, he obviously didn't have a maid come in too often to clean his house. It was a pigsty. Dirty dishes piled high in the sink were growing mold, and newspapers and magazines littered the floor. Cups of coffee and platters of half-eaten, long-rotted food were seen about the living room, and the dark wood furnishings looked as if they'd barely survived the Dust Bowl.

When O'Brien emerged from his bedroom, he was stark naked, a most impressive sight. Bogie could only dream of having a physique like the star. "You're not my size," O'Brien said to him. "A buddy left these trunks here. I think you can fit into them."

"I'll let you in on another one of my beauty secrets," O'Brien said, as Bogie stripped down to get into his swim suit.

Observing Bogie's less than perfect figure, O'Brien said, "We've got to get you on a new regime of a sensible diet and vigorous physical exercise to build up your body. You probably drink too much. I take it easy with the booze. I notice you lighting up a cigarette every minute. I confine myself to one after-dinner cigar, and I don't inhale. Your hair too is a problem. You look like a man who is going to loose his hair before he's forty. The trick is you've got to dry your hair thoroughly when you shower or go into the water. Water rots hair. If you keep your hair wet, it'll start to fall out."

Bogart as a cowboy
in *A Holy Terror*

At the beach O'Brien the athlete attracted a lot of attention. Several of his female fans approached him asking for autographs. The actor seemed in his element, and it was obvious that he adored showing off his body. After all, he was called "The Chest."

The beach didn't bring any cheer to Bogie, as he sat watching the adoration heaped on O'Brien by half the women on the beach. The star had made him feel inadequate, and he'd never been proud of his body. "How," he asked himself, "was he ever going to become a leading man in films without a great body?"

As each day went by, he thought more and more about heading back to New York. Of course, that too could be a problem. Helen had told him that there were longer lines at the soup kitchen than at the Broadway theaters.

***

One night at a party honoring Kay Francis and Kenneth, they had arranged for him to meet gossip maven Louella Parsons, claiming she might jump-start his film career and he could remain on the West Coast.

Bogie was ushered into a library. Seated in a large love seat beside the fireplace, Parsons was busy emptying her latest glass.

With his own drink in hand—he'd lost count of how many he'd had—he introduced himself to Parsons. She said nothing but motioned for him to sit down.

As unbelievable as it seemed at the time, Parsons still considered herself one of Hollywood's "glamour gals," although even then she was well on her way toward becoming the hag of Tinseltown.

She had removed a notebook from her purse into which she scribbled some information—probably misinformation—that had gotten trapped in her soggy brain. After that, she reached for her compact and smeared on an extra heavy application of blood-red lipstick, even more of a five-alarm fire tube than Clara Bow wore.

"Bogart," she said, finally staring at him with those steely eyes that had seen too much. "I've been meaning to interview you but have been too busy. With every guy on Broadway getting off the train daily, how can I possibly interview every out-of-work actor who hits town trying to make a buck in Hollywood?"

Gossip maven Louella Parsons

"You've got a point there, pal," he said, reaching for his drink which he'd placed on a coffee table.

"Even when I interview somebody, all I hear is their lies," she said.

"Maybe that's because the real and the illusional in Hollywood are inextricable," he said.

"God damn," she said harshly. "An intellectual. If there's one kind of actor I positively hate, it's an intellectual."

"That I'm not," he said. "You can print in your column that I was kicked out of Andover. Not only for poor grades, but for being a bad boy."

"That's it!" she said. She motioned to a whiskey bottle left on a table beside the French doors. "Pour me some of that and don't be

200

stingy, baby. I'm misquoting a line from that Garbo flick, *Anna Christie.*"

"Yeah, I got that." He also got up to get her that whiskey and to replenish his own supply. When he gave her the drink, he asked, "What did you mean by, 'That's it!'"

"I need a peg to hang a label onto you," she said. "A college dropout. I bet that as the bad boy of Andover, you got into a lot of trouble with girls. Yeah, that's it. I'm gonna call you the bad boy of Hollywood."

"Seems like I have a lot of competition for that title," he said. "George Raft, for instance."

"Hell with him," she said. "He's nothing but a New York gangster. If he gets to play gangsters in movies, it'll be type-casting." Slugging down a hefty swig of that bootleg whiskey, she aimed her eagle eye at him once again. "I've got to ask you something right off the bat. That lisp of yours. It bothers me. I know you're married, but are you a fairy like William Haines? Forgive me, but I have to ask. All the butterflies from Broadway are descending on us out here. It's very hard to make fairies sound manly in my column. Just how many more times do I have to write that Ramon Novarro is still waiting for the right gal?"

They both chuckled at that, and he felt that he'd broken through to her. "I'm strictly a man for the ladies. I find myself having to keep repeating that. But I don't expect you to take my word for that. I'm here with Helen Menken tonight. Otherwise, I'd show you what a man I am."

"Yes, I've met your wife. Charming."

He meant to correct her and say "ex-wife," but he just assumed that the custodian of all gossip in Hollywood was well aware that he'd married Mary Philips. Considering the shaky status of his marriage to Mary, he didn't plan to mention her in the interview.

"What were you saying?" she asked. "About my not taking your word for it. If I can't take your word for it, exactly how do you plan to prove it?"

"I didn't think we'd progress this far so soon into the interview, but I do find you very attractive," he said. "If you have any doubts about my manhood, I'd like to demonstrate otherwise. What I'm saying is you can put me to the test anytime."

She smiled. "You find me attractive, do you? My God, I'm just a working newspaperwoman trying to make a living in journalism. Hearst doesn't pay me enough. I find myself having to fight off half the wolves in Hollywood."

"I didn't mean to insult you," he said. "But you are one good-looking woman. What can I say? In spite of my lisp, I like glamorous women."

"We'll see about that," she said, studying him carefully with a greatly renewed interest. "I've heard a lot of stories about you since you hit town."

"I bet at least one of them is true," he said smiling.

Her face looked puzzled. It was as if she weren't communicating on the same level with him. "I seek the truth but I'm surrounded by lies. People talk lies. They live lies, and with good reason. If the real truth were known about half the stars in Hollywood, the American public would stay away from their movies in droves."

"When we have our interview, I'm going to give it to you straight," he said.

She reached for her notepad again. "Give me your private phone number in case I want to get in touch with you." As he told her the number, she wrote it down in her drunken scrawl.

He felt that he'd carried his flirtatious joking with her far enough and was eager to drop the subject. He was certain that she wouldn't remember his offer the next morning as she nursed her hangover. Even if she did, he knew that she'd never take him up on it.

"I meant to write you a note and thank you for that good review you gave Spence and me in *Up The River.* Mainly Spence, of course. I even carry it around in my wallet along with a review that Alexander Woollcott wrote of my Broadway appearance in *Swifty.* He wrote, 'The young man who embodies the aforesaid sprig is what is usually and mercifully described as inadequate.'"

"Hell with that drunken Woollcott," she said. "What did I write?"

He found her review tucked between some ten-dollar bills in his wallet. He read her own words to her. "Humphrey Bogart, talented New York juvenile, plays the part of Steve straight and does it very well."

"That was very nice of me," she said. "Actually I was very kind to you and Tracy. Frankly, I can skip prison dramas. They're too grim for my taste. America is in the middle of a Depression. We need movies with glamorous women in glamorous settings doing rich, glamorous things. Americans should be treated to a fantasy when they go to the movies. It'll take their minds off their troubles, their empty refrigerators, and all those mortgage foreclosures."

He carefully put the clipping away. "About that juvenile remark."

"What about it?" she asked imperiously, almost defying him to challenge her copy.

"It's the juvenile thing," he said. "I'm trying to get away from that. On Christmas Day, I'm gonna be thirty-one years old. I've played all those 'Tennis, anyone?' roles on Broadway. Out here I'm trying for more adult parts."

"I didn't know you were thirty-one," she said. "You don't look it on the screen. I thought you were much younger. That Helen Menken has literally robbed the cradle. She must be in her late forties or early fifties if she's a day. Women can't lie to me about their age. I can just look at a woman, no matter how much makeup she has on, and tell her exact age."

"And as for men?" he asked.

"They can fool me," she said. She gave him the look of a boa constrictor about to devour a young chicken for its supper. "Now that I know your exact age, I must say I'll have to reconsider that very romantic offer you made me. I have an absolute rule. I never go to bed with a man in his twenties. A lot of young actors proposition me because they think they'll advance their careers by sleeping with me. I've already slept with Clark Gable. With the pick of all the beauties in Hollywood, he went to bed with me. He also went to bed with that bitch, Adela Rogers St. Johns. She's my rival, you know. She thinks she knows so much about Hollywood. I've forgotten more than she'll ever know."

"I heard that Gable was born in 1901," he said. "Did he turn thirty before you guys bedded down?"

"I know I said a man has to be thirty. In Clark's case, I made an exception. In many ways, I wish I hadn't slept with Clark. Now my illusion about him is spoiled."

"I hope I don't disappoint," he said, teasing her.

"I have a feeling you can deliver," she said. "Sometimes one of us glamour gals can only laugh when these He-men take off their trousers. But I've discovered that some of you guys who look like a runt are surprisingly pleasing when you let it all hang out."

She downed the rest of her whiskey and motioned to him that she wanted another refill. "Now let's get down to this God damn interview. I know you're physically attracted to me, but that doesn't mean that I'm going to let you off easy. I don't feel like a candy-ass tonight, believe you me."

After her interview, she reached for his arm. "Escort me back into the party. Before leaving the library, she kissed him on the mouth. Her brewery breath was foul. "I'm flattered by your offer."

He had hoped that she'd forgotten it.

"I'll call you next week." She looked up lovingly into his eyes. "I'm sure we'll have a fine old time when we get together again."

With Parsons on his arm, he came back into the main living room and shuddered at the prospect of facing her again, especially if they were alone.

**

Back on the set of *A Holy Terror*, a message was left for him. "It's important that we get together—and soon!" It was signed "Miss D." He guessed that Miss D was actually Bette Davis.

Since her Hollywood star didn't seem to be shining any brighter than his, he wondered what she wanted with him. He suspected that she didn't really like him, so he doubted if romance were on her mind. Maybe she'd stumbled onto a hot script that would make both of them overnight sensations.

He needed something to happen and fast.

Hung over, disheveled, and burnt out, he headed for wardrobe.

Tapping his foot impatiently, Greg Brooks, known around the Fox lot as "the wardrobe mistress," said, "My, oh my, aren't *we* looking *déshabillée* today."

"Listen, you little faggot," Bogie said, "get out your fucking padding and your high heels and get it over with before I bash your skull in."

"Aren't we the ferocious *tigre*?" Brooks said. "Didn't get any last night? Thank God you didn't call me." He licked his lips. "I was too preoccupied."

At that moment the director, Irving Cummings, came into the department.

Anger flashed across his face as he turned to confront Bogie. "Listen, asshole, and listen good. I can replace you tomorrow with any of about a thousand better actors. You're totally wrong for the part, and Fox is only using you because some idiot signed a contract giving you $750 a week. Actors like you I can get for $25 a week." He backed away from him. "You're hung over and you smell like a brewery. I'm reporting all of this to Carl Laemmle."

"Junior or senior?" Bogie asked provocatively.

The director glared at him and seemed out of control. "After we wrap this picture, you'll never get another job in this town. I'll see to that." Cummings stormed out of the wardrobe department.

Bogie tried to get a grip on himself. He'd wanted to punch Cummings in the mouth.

Later that day, and to punish him, Cummings made him shoot a simple scene forty-five times. The director seemed to be sadistically torturing Bogie and humiliating him in front of cast members.

Fortunately, he'd brought a flask with him. "Instead of becoming the greatest actor in motion pictures, I'm going to become the biggest star on Broadway?"

He stood at a safe distance from the dressing room of Sally Eilers. It was obvious that Tracy had been carrying on with Hoot Gibson's wife since they made *Quick Millions* together. Eilers was the first to leave, since she was due on the set.

After she'd disappeared, Bogie walked up to her dressing room door and knocked on it. In his underwear, with drink in hand, Tracy opened the door. Seeing who it was, he embraced Bogie warmly. "We're supposed to be best friends, and I never get to see you any more. Come on in."

"Aren't you afraid Hoot Gibson will show up with a six-gun?" Bogie asked.

"Not at all," Tracy said. "Sally has told me about the kind of marriage they have. Actually I learned today she plans to divorce him."

"It's probably a smart career move for her," Bogie said, accepting a drink. "Her star is rising. There's talk she's going to become big. Her sagebrush cowboy is riding off into the sunset."

Sally Eilers

"Don't knock sagebrush flickers," Tracy kidded him. "You seem to be making an oater yourself."

"It's George O'Brien's flick," Bogie said with a sigh of despair.

"After I get dressed and have a drink or two with you," Tracy said, "I'm going to head over to George's dressing room. I like George a lot. He's a real loving he-man, unlike that girl, Lew Ayres."

"George and Sally on the same afternoon?" Bogie chided him. "You're more of a man than I am."

"We both know that," Tracy said, smiling to erase the sting from his remark. "George and Sally are both on my plate for the afternoon. Tonight I've got a date with Jean Harlow." When Bogie didn't say anything, Tracy asked him, "Did you hear that?"

"Yeah, I heard it," he said. "You and Harlow must have had one gay old time on the set of *Goldie*, a picture I think should be called *Blondie*."

"Harlow's an okay kid," he said. "Mixed up in the head. A sick family life with her stepfather lusting after her, a mother who's nuts, and an even worse situation emerging with this Paul Bern creature from the dark lagoon."

"Spence, old pal," Bogie said, pouring another drink. "I like you a lot. More than I like Kenneth MacKenna. He's my pal, and I tell him everything that's going on in my life, but I have a special feeling for you."

"Are you coming on to me?" Tracy asked with just a slight touch of mockery in his voice, as if to leave open the possibility he might be joking.

"Cut the crap!" Bogie said. "I have a hard time accepting that part of your life. I mean, I can see you banging Eilers while the grips outside are dreaming of being locked between your spurs. I can see you dating your co-star tonight. Let's face it: Harlow is the sex symbol of Hollywood. All the men want her. What I can't even picture—don't dare picture—is you and guys. George O'Brien, for God's sake. Mr. Avocado Sandwich."

"I love you, Bogie, but I feel you're very limited somehow. Many of the pleasures that God put on this earth for us to partake of, especially forbidden fruit, are not to be enjoyed by you. Your mind's closed off."

"My loss, pal," Bogie said, "and that's how I'm gonna keep it. But if you think for one minute I'm gonna picture you as a pansy like Ramon Novarro and Billy Haines, you're wrong."

"You said it all. I'm a man's man in more ways than one."

"But I hear from people who work with you that you fuck every pretty gal on the set of one of your pictures," Bogie said. "Not just your female leads, but the secretaries, the script gal, the waitress who serves you a BLT in the commissary."

"It's true, I do," Tracy said. "I also fuck beautiful guys. By the way, I'm a top. Screwing a man in the ass is different from fucking a woman. Another kind of satisfaction."

"I know what you're saying," Bogie said "but I'll never understand it. To me, you're the least homosexual male in Hollywood."

"You'll learn as you go through life that we come in the most unlikely packages. The captains of football teams. The heads of industry. Boxers. Weightlifters. Generals. Even one of the presidents of the United States."

"What president was a fag?"

"Abraham Lincoln."

"I don't believe that," Bogie said. "You're putting me on."

"Read your history books," Tracy said. "His lover was Joshua Fry Speed. You fuck too many women at night. You should take a night off and read a history book once in a while."

"You're one to talk."

"I'm serious," Tracy said. "Read about Lincoln and Speed, a handsome young man from Kentucky who slept with Lincoln for three years in a very narrow bed. Speed later wrote that no two men were more intimate than Lincoln and him."

"Why should I doubt your word?" Bogie asked. "After these months logged in Hollywood, I've seen it all."

"If I may correct you, you've seen a bit," Tracy said. "But you haven't seen it all. After another thirty years, you'll have seen it all."

***

Back at his bleak apartment, a sole letter had arrived. It was postmarked from New York, and he tore it open at once, knowing it was from his wife.

Dear Hump,

It's been a long time with no word. Even between good friends, it's been too long without contact. Between a husband and wife, it really marks the end of the marriage. I was prepared to go on in this relationship, at least a little while longer. However, when I read in Parsons' column that you were back with Helen Menken, it was all too much. The bitch even referred to Helen as your wife and not ex-wife. It is as if I didn't even exist. I know that many people still think of Helen as your wife. That's because we did not have a marriage.

As you well know, during the first days of our marriage, I made love to Kenneth far more frequently than I did with you. It may be too late for us, but I realize now that I should have married Kenneth instead of you. He writes every other day, at least, and it is through him that I have had any news of you at all. Of course, Kenneth is a gentleman and leaves out all the bad stuff about you.

I'm sure you've had many affairs in Hollywood with beautiful women, actresses far more beautiful than me. There's even talk in New York about you and Barbara Stanwyck, although I find that hard to believe. Unlike you, I'm no good at playing the field. I'm no saint but I do tend to focus on one man at a time. His name is Roland Young, and I'm sure you know who he is. He's living with me, even though he's married to Marjorie Kummer. He married her in 1921, but I have persuaded him to get a divorce and marry me. That means, of course, that I will soon be filing for a divorce from you. Let's call it the marriage that never was.

Mary

"Roland Young," he said out loud, carefully folding the letter. "A God damn limey." He fully intended to show this letter to Kenneth. The way he saw it, if Mary still felt that she should have married Kenneth, it might affect his imminent plan to marry Kay Francis.

Maybe Kenneth should break off his engagement to Francis and marry his "true love" after all. After reading that letter, Bogie felt that he'd welcome the divorce, and he was ready to tell Kenneth that he didn't have to hold back any longer, and could move in on Mary if he wanted to. But then his old jealousy of Kenneth came back again.

Unaware until he read her letter that Mary even knew Roland Young, Bogie had vaguely followed the actor's career. In the movies and in the theater, other actors kept tabs on their fellow thespians, never knowing when they would become a major competitor for a part.

Young had only recently starred in two films for Cecil B. DeMille—first *Madam Satan*, which co-starred Lillian Roth and Kay Johnson, and *The Squaw Man* with a big-name cast that included Warner Baxter, Lupe Velez, Eleanor Boardman, and Charles Bickford.

Bogie couldn't help but compare himself unfavorably with Young. He'd read in Parsons' column that Young was due back in Hollywood where a string of pictures was being lined up for him. Bogie himself, on the other hand, was facing unemployment in a Depression.

Stepping across the hallway, Bogie knocked on Kenneth's door. When he came to open it, he handed him a letter. "It's from New York. Your girl friend."

"My girl friend?" Kenneth asked, looking astonished. "I no longer have a girl friend in New York."

"You do now," Bogie said, handing him the farewell letter from Mary.

***

When he went back into his apartment, he decided to return Bette Davis's call. When she came onto the line, she told him that she was organizing a cocktail party for some co-workers. "I'm going to kick everybody out by seven-thirty, and I want you to stay on so we can talk privately. It's about our film future."

She'd said the right words, "film future," and he told her he'd be at her house within the hour. He took a wild guess that Davis had come up with a script that would save their fading careers, and he wanted to see what that New Englander had in mind.

As he arrived at the door to the Davis home, it was opened by her mother, Ruth. The look on her Puritanical Yankee face told him that she didn't approve of his coming to her house. To him, she was a

Roland Young

207

tenacious shrew who unduly fussed over her daughter, who was also her meal ticket. He'd heard that she was the stage mother to end all stage mothers.

In a fairly low-cut dress and with no makeup except a "slash" of lipstick, Davis greeted him in her living room. It was a unique party. In her devious mind, the actress had thrown a party for "Hollywood losers," a grouping that included herself. She'd invited some male stars she'd appeared with in unsuccessful films for "tea and sympathy." The sympathy was genuine, but the "tea" was actually whiskey.

She kissed Bogie lightly on the lips. "I think we should celebrate failure this afternoon," she said, appearing a bit unbalanced and giddy. "All of us are being referred to as box-office bombs."

She introduced him to Walter Byron, Pat O'Brien, James "Junior" Durkin, and a very handsome young actor, Frank Albertson.

Bogie found himself standing on the Davis back porch talking to Albertson. He'd appeared with Davis in *Way Back Home*, which had been directed by William Seiter. Originally entitled *Other People's Business*, the film had starred Phillips Lord, who was known across the country for the Seth Parker character he played on his regular radio show for NBC.

"I have to admit it," Albertson said to Bogie, "I'm still carrying a torch for Bette. During the filming, I fell hook, line, and sinker for her. I've asked her to marry me. She's going to give me her answer this weekend."

"Good luck, pal," Bogie said, not really meaning it. For some reason, he felt jealous.

Albertson soon drifted off, his tongue wagging in hot pursuit of Davis. Bogie couldn't believe that Davis would return this young man's affection. And she didn't.

As Bette Davis' star rose in Hollywood, Albertson's twinkled out.

The next failure Bogie tried to engage in conversation was another handsome actor, Walter Byron. He'd appeared opposite Davis in *The Menace*, directed by Roy William Neill. The picture had initially been entitled *The Feathered Serpent*, then *The Squeaker*.

"It should have been called *The Stinker*," Byron said, deep into his booze.

It seemed only months ago that Walter Byron had been hailed in the press as "Hollywood's new John Gilbert." He had landed the male role of the year when he was cast as the roistering German prince opposite Gloria Swanson's shy little Irish girl from the convent in *Queen Kelly*.

"Swanson told me I stood to be the next great male star of Hollywood," Byron said. "Imagine my disappointment when Swanson and Joseph Kennedy pulled the plug on Erich von Stroheim. That film will never be finished. If that nutbag Austrian had had his way, the movie would have been nine hours long and cost millions."

She introduced him to Pat O'Brien. O'Brien would join that exclusive club of James Cagney and Edward G. Robinson as one of Bogie's most frequent co-stars in the future. O'Brien seemed to be a hard-drinking, witty Irishman with an insouciant charm.

As Bogie chatted amicably with O'Brien on that fading afternoon of long ago, the actor told him that he'd been very disappointed with his role in *Hell's House* with Davis and Junior Durkin. "Bette is referring to it as the nadir of her career," O'Brien said, "even before her career gets started."

"Sounds like a great picture, pal," Bogie said. "Remind me to save my quarter and not see it."

As O'Brien drifted away, Davis herself came back, positioning herself next to him. He was having a difficult time getting used to her. She wasn't the mousy actress he'd encountered on the set of *Bad Sister*. This was a new Davis with bleached blond hair. Somehow the new hair made her sexier and more alluring, although Jean Harlow would never have to fear competition.

She held Bogie's hand as she told him, "For about an hour after I saw myself in that horrible movie you and I made, I contemplated suicide. Makeup tried to compensate for my small mouth by exaggerating its size with lipstick. My mouth looked like a tunnel. Crawford can get away with those ridiculously exaggerated lips. I can't. Also, when I'm embarrassed or insecure, and I was both of those things, I smile crookedly."

"My, oh my, aren't we a litany of complaints today," he said.

"That's not all. My outfits stunk. It was obvious I didn't have a hairdresser. Sidney Fox got all the attention. In *Way Back Home*, I looked a little better. I learned that Universal was ready to drop me until Berman—that's Pandro Berman, the producer over at RKO—wanted to borrow me for that cornspun role. A guy named J. Roy Hunt, the cinematographer, actually made me look good for the first time ever on film."

"You're a regular *femme fatale*," he said.

"Don't you put me on, Bogart," Davis said "But actually, I did look rather pretty. A lot of directors in New York called me pretty. Maybe I am a *femme fatale* and don't know it. Carl Laemmle—Junior, that is—thinks I have no sex appeal, but all my leading men fall in love with me."

After her other guests—all losers—had left, Davis invited Bogie to remain behind for "some private conversation." He'd noticed that she'd become more self-assured and poised in the wake of having so many handsome young men, all of them co-stars, falling in love with her.

He too found her the most attractive and alluring he'd ever seen her, which was in direct contrast to his first impression of her. Even so, with her whitened hair and pop-eyed look, she still, at least to him, evoked a dime store Harlow.

It was as if she were still searching for a face and a look but hadn't found it yet, whereas Garbo had burst on the screen, even though very young, with a look and a poise that she'd always keep.

Meanwhile, both Barbara Stanwyck and Joan Crawford, after some awkward beginnings, were finding their "look" and their screen presence. Davis seemed on a desperate and roughly equivalent search, and even without a camera, her intensity to find a screen persona filled the air with electricity.

After the departure of her other guests, when she came out to visit with him on the back porch, she turned off the overhead light, claiming it attracted bugs. But he knew the real reason.

Thankfully, the Wrath of God, Ruth Davis, had gone to bed early, complaining of a headache. For all this stage mother knew, each of her daughter's guests had left. Bogie suspected that Ruth disapproved mightily of the opposite sex, viewing men as "the enemy." She seemed so fiercely protective of her daughter that her behavior reminded him of a butch lesbian, guarding a prized nymphet from the menace of preying seducers.

Once they were seated on the porch swing, and with the warm night air blowing about them, Bogie was in the mood for romance.

Regardless of the outcome of the evening, he'd have a tale to tell Kenneth in the morning. In this case, he no longer cared if Kenneth reported his seductions to Mary. In some perverse part of his mind, he wanted Mary to know that many women, including stars, found him an attractive and a desirable bedmate. Even if he returned to New York, and he was most definitely headed back there, he'd ride the train back East with a proven record of having seduced some of the biggest stars in the movies, even Marlene Dietrich.

On that back porch and to his unpleasant surprise, Davis didn't want to talk about their relationship or even their future career in films, assuming they had one.

She focused her talk on one beau back East, Harmon Oscar Nelson. "I call him Ham," she said, "and he calls me Spuds."

"Ain't that cute?" he said, slightly softening the sarcasm in his voice.

"He wants to be a musician," she said. "He's equally good at playing both the piano and the trumpet. But he'll never become a star doing either. He's also talking about becoming a radio singer like Bing Crosby."

"If he doesn't knock Bing down from the mike," he said, "maybe he'll become the next Rudy Vallée. But what about us? What's gonna happen to Miss Bette Davis and Mr. Humphrey Bogart? Or have you already told me what you think of me by inviting me to this party of losers?"

"Perhaps," she said. "My career seems to be collapsing. So does yours. Stanwyck and Crawford are moving up in Hollywood. You and I seem to be headed the same direction as those silent screen stars. Did you know that Louis B. Mayer was quoted as saying that at least one-third of the stars of 1928 are washed up, and he predicts that in the years to come, even more will fall by the wayside. I think he's right. Look around you. Vilma Banky, John Gilbert, Ramon Novarro, Bill Haines, Gloria Swanson, Pola Negri. Mayer has hated Chaplin since they got into a fistfight at the Hollywood Hotel, and he thinks Chaplin will never really make it in Talkies either."

"So, what are we going to do?" he asked. "I think we're stage actors. Both of us should return to Broadway. Maybe we'll take the train back East together."

"Is that a proposal of marriage?" she asked.

"I'll soon be available. Mary has written that she plans to divorce me. She's fallen for Roland Young."

210

"I know of him," she said. "From what I hear, if a woman manages to keep him close to her bed for three months straight, she's set a world's record."

"I'm not broken up about it," he said. "It wasn't much of a marriage. My friend, Kenneth MacKenna, is in love with her."

"The one marrying Kay Francis?" she said.

"One and the same."

"I'll never comprehend why men out here marry women like that," she said.

Bogie lit a cigarette for her and one for himself, as they sat on that swing going up in smoke, the same way both of them would do later on the screen.

"Ham wants me to give up my career and marry him," she said. "He claims he can support the both of us, and I should be a housewife."

"And how do you feel about that?" he asked.

"I'm not sure what to do," she said. "I'm very confused. I met Ham at the Cushing Academy. He was one year ahead of me. He is a very shy boy, awkward, gangling. I think he brings out my maternal instinct. He's pleasant looking. He'll never be handsome. He has a large nose."

"That can be a promising sign in a man," he said.

"What in hell does that mean?" she asked.

"I'm sure it's not true in all cases, but Joan Blondell told me that a big nose or big feet on a man is a good barometer that something else is big on the man too."

"Really?" she asked skeptically. "I've never heard such nonsense. I note that you don't have a big nose. Nor do you seem to have particularly large feet."

"There are always exceptions to the rule, as I've noted," he said, smiling. "You can put me to the test anytime."

"Ruthie still thinks I'm a virgin," she said. "You know better."

"Not from first-hand experience," he said, putting his arm around her. "Poor Ham. Gilbert Roland is a tough act to follow."

"Roland's taken," she said. "I'm all that Ham has in the world. Ruthie wants me to marry Ham and surrender my so-called virginity to him."

"Too late for that now," he cautioned.

"Indeed. I've already surrendered my virginity to Ham. It wasn't a successful mating."

"How so?"

"It seems that Ham has been a chronic masturbator since he was six years old. He's given to premature ejaculation and can't satisfy a woman. If I marry him, I'll have to work for months—maybe more than a year—to train him."

"I'm already trained," he said. With an arm still around her, he began to feel her right breast. She did not object or pull away.

But she did take note of it. "I'm deliberately letting you have your fun," she said. "I've been told that to be sophisticated, I've got to take up smoking and drinking, which I've done. Apparently, letting a man feel your breasts is another way to be sophisticated. I went to a party the other night. No men clus-

211

tered around me. I felt like the wallflower I did when I attended Newton High. Even the lesbians in the room were clustering around Kay Francis, paying me no mind. Suddenly I looked up into the face of the most beautiful young man I've ever seen. Douglas Fairbanks Jr. I knew I could fall in love with him at once. I've heard that he's breaking up with Crawford. I've also heard he's a great lover. What a headline I could make if he dumps Crawford, divorces her, and marries me. I would install myself at Pickfair with the cream of Hollywood society."

"At first I resented you talking about other men when you've got me," he said, "but I want to hear the outcome of this."

"Oh, he chatted briefly with me. Offered me a cigarette. I was wearing my most low-cut gown. Suddenly, he reached into my dress and fondled one of my breasts. I couldn't believe what was happening. Just like that he did it. The way you're feeling me right now tells me you're not disappointed. Mr. Fairbanks must have been used to bigger and better things. He withdrew his hand rather quickly. He told me I should put ice on my nipples the way Crawford does. And that was that. He just turned and walked away. I've never felt so humiliated."

"I think I can relate to that," he said. "From a man's perspective, it would be like a woman unbuttoning your fly, reaching in to measure the goodies, and then walking away after saying, 'Not enough there to mess up my mouth with.'"

They both laughed at that. "What say we forget the Fairbanks boy, Roland, Ham, and God knows who else?" he said. "You've got a man once billed as the next Valentino, even the next Clark Gable, and you're not taking advantage of the situation. You said yourself, you want to become sophisticated." He took her in his arms and kissed her deeply before reluctantly breaking away. "If you give me a chance, you'll find I don't suffer from Ham's problem. I also find your nipples divine. In fact, I wish to suck both of them."

She offered absolutely no resistance as he moved in on her. He wanted more. He pulled her as close as he could to him, as his hand traveled from one breast to the other. With his other hand, he began the glide up her leg, past her garter belt and along her creamy thigh. He was heading for homeport.

Just before he reached the honeypot itself, the porch light was switched on. In the harsh, unforgiving glare stood Ruth Davis, looking ferocious and clad in her bathrobe.

"Get out of my house!" she shouted at him. "How dare you fondle my daughter like she's some bitch in heat. The loss of virginity before marriage will ruin a woman's life."

He pulled away from Davis but hesitated to get up. His hard-on had risen.

Davis looked down, burying her head on her chest. She began to whimper.

"Get out!" Ruth commanded.

In defiance of her, he rose from the swing with an erection tenting his trousers.

His tumescent state was not lost on Ruth. "You're a slave to your genitalia, Bogart," she said. "A disgusting, perverted creature. My daughter is going to marry Ham Nelson, not you. I'm not going to let her surrender her most prized possession, her virginity, to a sexual predator. I hear you've had half the women in Hollywood. You offer nothing to my Bette but venereal disease and unwanted pregnancy."

"Good night, Bette." he said, adjusting his shirt in his trousers and heading to the door that Ruth held open for him.

Angered and humiliated, he walked rapidly through the living room. He vowed never to see Bette again. The way he figured it, a relationship between the two of them was out of the question.

How wrong he was.

***

He couldn't believe it, but here he was in the Villa Carlotta apartment of Louella Parsons. She'd decided that trying to interview him was too difficult at Hollywood parties because of all the distractions. When she'd invited him over, she'd promised to give him her undivided attention.

Fearing that she might remember his offer of seduction, he could only hope that her husband, Dr. Harry Martin, was home that night. But when he got there, he learned that the doctor was administering to two of his patients, Lew Ayres and Douglas Fairbanks Jr., both of whom had come down with severe cases of the clap, according to Parsons.

"Docky," as Parsons called her husband, had launched his career as a urologist, but Bogie had heard that he was now known as "doctor for the clap" around Hollywood, having treated everybody from Gary Cooper to Tallulah Bankhead. In their case, there was an ongoing disagreement about which party had infected the other. Docky was also the "house doctor," or so it was said, for Lee Frances, one of the reigning madams of her day. Parsons' husband was said to have had more frequent and more intimate contacts with the genitals of stars, both male and female, than any other person in Hollywood.

Inspecting penises and vaginas didn't occupy all of Docky's agenda. Parsons saw to it that he was hired frequently as a technical adviser on films such as *Doctors' Wives* that required some very limited medical expertise. Parsons would then plug the film in her column, lavishing special praise on the technical direction. She'd even gotten Governor Clement C. Young to appoint Docky to the California State Boxing Commission "just for the hell of it."

At this point, a Boston bull terrier came into the living room and immediately jumped up onto Bogie's lap, practically knocking his drink from his hand.

"That's our adorable Pansy Parsons," she said, ordering the dog to get down from the sofa. The dog obeyed her but anchored itself close to Bogie's feet, eyeing him suspiciously as if he might make a tasty snack.

As Bogie sat across from Parsons, enjoying some of Docky's good whiskey, she told him about a startling new development in broadcasting that she and "my Docky" had seen in New York. They'd gone East for a gala dinner, where he'd been awarded an honorary degree at the American College of Surgeons. Bogie was later to learn that William Randolph Hearst and the power of his newspapers were instrumental in securing the undeserved award for Docky.

It seemed that Parsons had been asleep at her typewriter at the advent of the Talkies, and had written that, "Flickers that talk will soon shut up—a mere passing fad."

She didn't want news of such a misguided opinion to ever tarnish her reputation again, so she aggressively embraced the new technology. During their visit to New York, Docky and she had been invited to a television broadcast. "Television is sort of like radio, but with a big difference," she said. "A picture is projected."

"You've got to be kidding," he said.

"It'll be the death of the movies," she predicted. "One day people will sit in their homes watching a moving picture the way they gather today around their radio sets. It'll be like bringing a movie into your own home."

"I don't want to get into an argument with you over this, but, trust me, that day will never happen."

"It's gonna happen sooner than later," she said. "I predict that by 1935 half the homes of America will have a television set. They even told me in New York that it's soon going to be possible to show films on television in color."

"Hey, you're getting carried away. The idea of sitting at home watching a movie is hard enough to take. Watching a color movie on television—that's a bit much."

"No, I mean it," she said, "and they'll do more than just present light entertainment on a home screen," she said. "Football games will one day be broadcast live. Newsreel cameras will photograph late-breaking events and flash them into your home. Presidential inaugurations will be televised. In fact, the whole presidential race will one day be decided by television."

"I don't get that," he said.

"The two candidates will square off on television. The one who photographs best and handles himself better will win the race."

"That means that an actor wanting to be president will have a better chance of becoming that than a non-actor who might be a great politician but lousy in front of a camera," he said.

"Well," she said, signaling him that she wanted a refill of her liquor. "I wouldn't go that far. No actor I've ever known could possibly become president of the United States."

At the urgent ringing of the phone in her library, she excused herself and heaved herself up from her armchair. When she returned, she told him, "It was from Docky. He went with Jack Dempsey and some other friends to Santa

214

Barbara to see a boxing match, and later, Docky and Dempsey had a few drinks together in a tavern. Then Docky and the champ got into an argument. Before it was over, my Docky knocked Dempsey on his ass. What a man!"

Bogie would never know the true circumstances of this barroom brawl, or if Docky had indeed knocked out Dempsey.

"This will show that SOB, Benny Rubin, that low-rent vaudevillian, what a man my Docky really is."

Born the same year as Bogie, Rubin was a famous stand-up comedian and film actor whose career would span fifty years.

"I guess I don't get it," Bogie said. "Why would your husband need to prove his manhood to Benny Rubin?"

"Rubin and Docky were standing next to each other in the bathroom of a hotel at a party we attended recently. Rubin later spread the word around town about Docky. Rubin said he knows why Louella has a constant smile on her face. He claimed that thing hanging out of Docky's fly looked like a baby's arm with an apple in its hand."

"Why did that make you mad?" he asked. "Docky should be flattered."

"A baby's arm," she sputtered, practically spitting out her words. "He could have said a man's arm. I can assure you that Docky, unlike Paul Bern, is a fully grown man."

"We can assume that when your husband put on that show for Rubin, he was soft. I'm sure that when it's hard, a man's arm would be a more appropriate comparison."

"Don't try to pacify me," she warned him. "I'll see that Rubin is finished in this town."

Ever since the episode of Docky vs. Rubin at the hotel urinal, Parsons had been running attacks on Rubin in her column. During his filming of *Marianne* with Marion Davies, Parsons printed the untrue allegation that Rubin got drunk and broke a violin over his wife's head. On the set the next day, Hearst told Rubin that he would "call Louella and dress her down if you want me to." Gallantly, Rubin told the newspaper czar that Parsons' attacks kept his name in front of the public, and that the publicity would boost ticket sales.

Parsons tried to interview Bogie that night, but appeared far too drunk. He was explaining how helpful showman W.A. Brady Sr. had been during the launching of his Broadway career, and how he'd been directed by John Cromwell.

"I know those people," she said, "and even wrote about them a few weeks ago. I said Helen Gahagan, the star of many a Brady play, was visiting Hollywood with her new husband, Douglas Melvyn. I also claimed that not so long ago Miss Gahagan was married to John Cromwell." She held up her drink and looked at him imploringly. "Now what was wrong with that?"

"I don't think Helen appeared in any Brady production," he said. "I know she wasn't married to John, and I think her husband's name is Melvyn Douglas, not Douglas Melvyn."

"Silly me," she said. "I refuse to look anything up. I rely on the old bean. Basically, I was right, though. If it wasn't actually Helen who appeared in Brady plays, it was someone like her. And Cromwell should have married Helen. She should never have married this Douglas or Melvyn, whatever in hell that one calls itself. He has no sex appeal whatsoever."

"Gloria Swanson must disagree," he said. "I read she's cast him in her film, *Tonight or Never*."

"Gloria also thought that that drunk, Walter Byron, was going to become some big shit in Hollywood when she cast him opposite her in *Queen Kelly*. What does she know? I also happen to know that she's trying to hide her pregnancy from the camera. She has to bind herself into elastic underwear."

As the evening and the drinking progressed, it was obvious to him that she wasn't going to write a column about him. She was all too familiar with his lackluster films, and his "Tennis, anyone?" career on Broadway clearly bored her.

Throughout the evening she seemed obsessed with the phone, which never rang again. It was as if she were waiting for some late-breaking story about to happen. Finally, he found out what it was.

"I know the Lombard and Powell marriage is on the rocks," she said, "but I'm after a bigger story that will shake up the world."

"What might this earth-shattering news be?" he asked.

"It's a double story," she said. "The break-up of two marriages, the uncrowned king and queen of Hollywood and Tinseltown's uncrowned prince and princess."

"That could only mean Pickford and Fairbanks Sr. and his son, Junior, and Crawford."

"Who else?" she said, seemingly impatient with him. "How clearly do I have to spell it out?"

As Parsons got drunker, she ranted about various brush-offs she'd received. She claimed that she'd told both Mayer and Irving Thalberg to send Garbo back to Sweden and to cast Jeanne Eagels in her roles. She'd also demanded that the studio give all Jean Harlow parts to Clara Bow, and she'd lobbied to have Blanche Sweet cast in the role of Diane in Fox's *Seventh Heaven* instead of Janet Gaynor. Parsons seemed infuriated that the studios were not heeding her casting advice.

It was after midnight when she, on wobbly legs, rose from her chair. "You've been drinking," she said to him, stating the obvious. "Since Docky won't be home tonight, after having beaten the shit out of Dempsey, I suggest you stay over here at my apartment. Otherwise, I might have to write about your arrest for drunk driving."

His worst nightmare had come true. She'd remembered his invitation to seduction. He'd challenged her to put his manhood to the test.

Faced with the horrific possibility of having to have sex with her, he evaluated her carefully, wondering if he'd be able to get it up.

He'd read somewhere that she was claiming that she was born in 1893, which would make her only about six years older than him. He'd also heard that she'd been born in 1880, maybe even in the late 1870s. That would put her in her fifties.

Figuring that an actor had to do what an actor had to do, he braced himself for the challenge.

She took his hand, leading him to her bedroom.

"I have stage fright," he whispered into her ear.

"What's the matter?" she asked. "You already told me you weren't some lisping faggot. Here's your chance to prove it to America's top newspaperwoman."

"I mean if you objected to Rubin comparing your Docky to a baby's arm—and that was when he was soft—I don't know if I'll measure up to your expectations."

"Don't worry," she said. She suddenly lunged toward him, locking him in a tight embrace. Her lipstick-slashed mouth descended on him, and her tongue darted out like a rattlesnake's. Her alcohol-tainted breath was foul, and he prayed for the strength to get through the evening.

When she finally broke away, she placed her bejeweled hand at his groin. "So, I didn't get a rise out of you yet. I'll have to revert to more drastic measures." She took his hand again, leading the march to her bedroom. "I'm sure you'll please me. Besides, you couldn't possibly be any worse than Clark Gable—and no one could possibly fuck as badly as him."

***

Through Spencer Tracy, Bogie learned that Basil Rathbone had been secretly meeting with Helen about reprising his stage role in *The Captive* if the film, based on the Broadway play about lesbianism, ever made it in a watered-down version onto the screen.

Bogie was doubly hurt that he wasn't being considered for the role of the male lead in *The Captive*. The way he figured it, it would be a cake-walk for him to play the role of a man who falls for a lesbian. He'd had so much experience with that in real life that the part wouldn't be difficult for him at all. He felt that he needed a controversial film to call Hollywood's attention to him, now that Fox was about to dump him.

Helen hadn't been returning his calls, as she perhaps feared that he'd ask her to cast him in her film.

Bogie feared that he might encounter Parsons again. After the previous evening, he wasn't too eager to run into the gossip columnist, and he never intended to have a repeat performance of their sexual marathon at the Villa Carlotta. On the other hand, he didn't have to be ashamed of his performance. If he had to admit it to himself, he'd acquitted himself very well. He didn't know if he were any better than "Baby's Arm," her husband, Docky, but he felt that when he'd left her bed, Parsons was one satisfied woman. After giving her multiple orgasms, he'd shown her what a man he really was.

217

At a Hollywood party, he encountered Tallulah Bankhead again.

"Hump, my darling, I think you and I both are getting a little long in the tooth for Hollywood," she said. "It's for kids in their twenties, not mature adults in their thirties."

"You look more beautiful than ever," he said to reassure her.

"Don't kid a kidder, darling." She brushed back her hair and theatrically gazed at the fading sunset. "The bloom is off this big waxy magnolia. Somehow, film doesn't capture my electrifying personality that I can convey on stage. The critics may be right. On screen, I'm just a pale imitation of Garbo. My face doesn't seem to move right. My eyes don't come alive. I'm not made for the movies."

"Then let's you and me hook up, go back to New York, and become Mr. and Mrs. Broadway," he said, only partially joking.

"That's the best offer I've had all day," she said. "I might take you up on that. But I'll have to get back to you."

"What's holding you back?" he asked, bending over and kissing her lightly on her scarlet-painted lips.

"Since one of my goals—the one about fucking Coop—has already been achieved, I have set two other goals for myself—and two more candidates to fuck before I leave Hollywood."

"Since you've already had me, the best," he said, "who else is there?"

"Garbo, of course. You've not plowed her yet, have you, darling?"

"No, but I got a blow-job from Marlene Dietrich."

"That's no distinction," she said. "Marlene has sucked all of our cocks. My second goal is to bed Johnny Weissmuller with his ten uncut inches."

"The Olympic swimming champ?" he asked. "I didn't think he was your type. I hear he's gonna become the new Tarzan."

Basil Rathbone

"A darling Ape Man if ever there was one," she said. "I met the film's director, W. S. Van Dyke, the other night. Charles Bickford wanted the part but was turned down. Too old. Spencer Tracy's latest flame, Johnny Mack Brown, lost because he's not tall enough, although he seems to satisfy Spence just fine. You won't believe this, but Clark Gable tried out for Tarzan too. Van Dyke decided that Gable wasn't muscular enough and didn't have Weissmuller's inches. Weissmuller is the Ape Man, Gable more a chimpanzee."

She excused herself. "Keep my bourbon chilling for me, darlings. I've got to take a

218

horse piss. Care to watch?"

As he was pouring himself a drink, he turned around to greet Kenneth MacKenna and Kay Francis. "My soon-to-be best man," Kenneth said, kissing him lightly on the lips. Since "going Hollywood," Kenneth had become very theatrical. No sooner had those lips left Bogie's than they were replaced with those of Francis.

"Let's get this God damn wedding over with and soon," Bogie said. "These pre-wedding parties are beginning to wear me out."

***

"Mr. Humphrey Bogart, of New York, meet Miss Ann Dvorak, also New York born."

He was at George Raft's party, and the chorus girl standing in front of him couldn't be more than nineteen years old. She had a lean, sharp face, not altogether to Bogie's liking, yet he was immediately attracted to her. In a red silk gown that clung to her body like a Jean Harlow dress, she was one of the sexiest women he'd ever seen. The cleavage of that gown went virtually to her hips. With the wrong movement on her part, one of her breasts might pop out.

She took his hand and expertly guided him through a sea of gangsters assembled by Raft for the party where the liquor and champagne flowed.

In a corner at a small table, a waiter in a red jacket served them drinks, although Dvorak looked as if she'd consumed far more than her share for one evening. In the dimly lit room, she put one leg up over his. Her gown was split up to a creamy thigh, and he was certain she didn't have on one stitch of underwear. He practically wanted to seduce her on the spot.

As they talked, he found her very direct and outspoken. Even though only a teenager, she didn't seem to embarrass easily. He was convinced that Dvorak had been seducing men at least since the age of fourteen.

The way she kept moving that creamy leg over his thighs was giving him an erection, a movement not lost on her. "So how are things?" he asked rather awkwardly.

"You tell me first," she said.

"Marriage falling apart, career going nowhere," he said. "The usual. What about you?" He'd no sooner asked that question than he wished that he hadn't.

Dvorak revealed a ferocity of ambition matched only by Stanwyck herself. "I'm hot and getting hotter," she said.

At that remark, he put his hand on her thigh and began a massage. "I'm convinced of that."

"I don't mean that way, silly," she said. "I

Ann Dvorak

219

mean, my career, Stud. I owe it all to Joan Crawford. When I was one of the hoofers in *Hollywood Revue of 1929*, I met Crawford. She fell for me in a big way. Howard Hughes had been calling her for a date, and she came up with this idea. Since she didn't want Hughes, she took his call one day and agreed to go over to Hughes' mansion. But instead of Crawford, it was me who arrived on Howard Hughes' doorstep. And the rest is history or will soon be."

"Well, pal," he said, "so you fucked Hughes. What's he going to do for you?"

"He put me under contract," she said.

"He did the same with Harlow, but since then, he seems to be doing nothing for her," he said, deliberately wanting to prick her bubble.

"I know that!" she said, a slight anger flashing. "With me, it's gonna be different. He's putting together this film called *Scarface*. It's based on Al Capone, and Ben Hecht himself is writing the screenplay. Hughes wants Paul Muni to play Capone."

"An Austrian-born actor from New York's Yiddish Art Theater?" he asked in surprise. "Not Cagney, not Edward G. Robinson? What about George Raft himself—even me?"

"Oh, George is in the film. He plays my love interest, Guino Rinaldo. I play Muni's sister, Cesca. I'm told that the scenes between Muni and me will border on incest. There's even a role for Boris Karloff in the film. Hughes wants a lot of sex and violence."

"Sounds like it's headed for trouble with the censors," he said.

"Hughes expects that," she said. "And so does the director, Howard Hawks."

"Two Howards working together," he said. "Which Howard has branded you?"

She giggled and leaned over to whisper in his ear. "I'm balling both of them. To get ahead in Hollywood, Crawford told me it's necessary to fuck both the producer and the director."

"I wish I could fuck someone to get cast in a picture," he said.

"Don't worry, sugar," she said between bouts of tonguing his ear. "When I become the biggest star in Hollywood, I'll insist that you be my leading man."

"Thanks, pal," he said, his hand starting to travel up her thigh to his target of the evening.

She slapped it down and jumped up. "Let's dance."

He didn't want to get up because of his erection but decided what the hell. The room was not well lit, and no one seemed to be paying attention to him.

In the center of the room, she moved her body into his so closely that they seemed to melt into each other. The way she was rubbing up against him, he thought he'd cream in his trousers.

After dancing around, he came face to face with Howard Hawks.

After a rather inauspicious introduction, Bogie sat in the same far corner of the room where he'd previously played seductive games with Dvorak. Across from him sat Hawks, who would play such an enormous role in both his professional and personal life in the years to come.

"Keep your mangy hands off Ann," Hawks was telling him. "She's already got Howard Hughes and Howard Hawks. She doesn't need another 'H' in her life."

"We were just getting acquainted on the dance floor, pal," Bogie said. "Nothing more."

"Don't come within ten feet of her," Hawks said threateningly.

"I'll stay at least twelve feet away," Bogie said jokingly, not taking Hawks' anger too seriously.

I'm balling her," Hawks said. "I find that teenage girls are the only thing that holds my interest. Don't think I'm a pedophile. I only go out with girls in their late teens. No fourteen-year-olds." He paused. "Maybe once or twice, but it's definitely not a pattern with me."

"Glad to hear that," Bogie said. "If I ever have any daughters, I'll keep them far away from Mr. Howard Hawks."

"Listen, I'm not mad at you for trying to move in on Ann," Hawks said. "You're still green in Hollywood. You don't know the ropes yet. I've issued my warning. If after you've been duly warned, you still cross Hughes and me, then I'll cut off your nuts, assuming a little lisper like you has a pair."

"Yeah, I've got a pair," Bogie said. "They're big enough, too. My problem is that I haven't learned how to clank them like you're doing. Or like Hughes is doing. And don't let my lisp fool you."

"Just wanted to be sure," Hawks said. "I can't even go take a piss out here in Hollywood without some queen falling on his knees."

"You should be flattered by such attention," he said. "That means you're a real man. Queens go just for the big studs."

"That's one way to look at it," Hawks said. "Nearly everyone I meet in Hollywood is a dirty little homosexual. There are a few bonafide heterosexuals out here, but not many."

"Name three," Bogie said, challenging him.

"I'll name three guys who've never had their dick sucked by a man," Hawks said. "In order of importance. Howard Hawks, Howard Hughes, Spencer Tracy. The rest I'm not so sure about."

"No contest there," Bogie said. "You're far more of a Hollywood insider than I am."

Hawks surveyed the party of gangsters. "I accepted George's invitation because I knew a lot of New York gangsters would be here since Owney Madden and his boys are in town. I'm soaking up atmosphere for my picture, *Scarface*, that Hughes is producing. I think the film is

Film director Howard Hawks

221

going to be a big success. At least three of my actors are gong to be billed above the title."

"Call me Louella," he said. "I'd really like to know who they are. It's interesting to hear that somebody's making it out here on The Coast."

"Paul Muni, George Raft, and Boris Karloff," Hawks said.

"The fourth?" Bogie asked.

"Ann Dvorak herself," Hawks said. "I've got this incredible instinct for casting. I have a feeling that a lot of movie plots in these Depression days will be about life's losers, and she's perfect for roles like that. After *Scarface*, I think she'll have cornered the market on the portrayal of doomed gangster molls with prolonged death scenes."

"Sounds like a great career," he said. "Since I'm about to be dropped by Fox, what role have you got coming up for me? I'm gonna be in need of a job pretty soon."

"*Scarface* is already cast," Hawks said. "I think my next movie is going to be *The Crowd Roars*. I'm thinking of casting Ann in that movie, too, although I rarely work with the same pussy twice. She might play the second female lead. I want Joan Blondell to play the lead. The second male lead will be played by this faggot kid, Eric Linden."

"I've heard of him," Bogie said. "You said nothing about the male lead. I haven't read the script, and don't even know what the picture is about, but I think I'd be ideal."

"It's not set yet," Hawks said, "but I'm thinking of casting James Cagney."

"I knew Cagney back in my New York days," Bogie said. "He got his start appearing in drag."

"Bullshit!" Hawks said. "You're making that up. If I had to name three men in Hollywood who will never appear in drag, I'd cite Howard Hawks first, Howard Hughes second, and James Cagney third."

"Maybe I was mistaken about Cagney," Bogie said. "Too much rotgut whiskey out here in Hollywood pickles the brain."

"I don't know about you, Bogart," Hawks said. "When I was in New York, I saw you on Broadway in *Cradle Snatchers*. I wasn't impressed. I guess you noticed that when I made *Cradle Snatchers* for Fox, I didn't cast you in your stage part as Jose Vallejo. I cast Joe Striker in the part and changed his character's name to Joe Valley."

"I couldn't help but notice," Bogie said. "Don't judge me by those Broadway days. I've grown a lot as an actor since then. I need one big role and I'll hit it big. A part like *Scarface,* which could make a big name for Paul Muni, as you said. He's playing Al Capone, isn't he?"

"Yeah, but that's not the official word," Hawks said. "I was visited recently by a couple of Capone goons who insisted on knowing who *Scarface* was based on. They'd heard that it was based on their boss."

"How in hell do you get out of that one?" Bogie asked. "I mean Capone has a scarface. I heard someone tried to slit his throat."

"That's right, and the film is based on him," Hawks said. "But I convinced them that *Scarface* has nothing to do with Capone. I told them we're just calling it that to fool the public into thinking it might be about Capone. I said that's known as showmanship. The Chicago boys left me alone with my body intact and went away feeling like Hollywood insiders. Hughes was afraid the boys would go after him, but I assured him that I'd taken care of that too. I told the Capone goons that Hughes was 'just the sucker with the money.'"

Dvorak approached them and reminded Hawks that they had another rendezvous that evening. She smiled at Bogie. "Maybe you'll be my leading man one day in a picture."

Hawks looked back at Bogie. "I don't see that ever happening." A frown crossed his brow. "On another point, I can assure you I'll never cast you in a film I'm directing."

"Sorry to hear that, pal," Bogie said. "Now you two love birds have a good night."

***

Bogie floored the accelerator of his car, heading for the Malibu retreat of Spencer Tracy and his newly acquired friend, the matinee idol, Johnny Mack Brown.

It had been a night he didn't want to remember. Smoking incessantly and badly hung over, he found himself shaking uncontrollably. He felt that he was coming apart. He rarely thought about his wives (former and current), as he was caught up in a whirlpool with an eccentric cast of characters, most of whom he was meeting for the first time.

At Tracy's cottage, he pulled into the driveway. Emerging from the beach in a skimpy, form-fitting bathing suit was one of the handsomest men he'd ever encountered. He figured it could only be Johnny Mack Brown.

After Johnny had shown Bogie to his bedroom overlooking the ocean, and after he'd showered, Bogie joined the actor for a walk on the beach. Tracy was in the bedroom across the hallway recovering from a massive drunk.

Plopping down right on the sands, Bogie accepted a drink from the flask Johnny carried in his beach bag. "Spence told me that you and he have become asshole buddies and that I could tell you anything," he said in a slow Southern drawl.

"I love the man," Bogie said, "but asshole buddies is a bit much. We're more into the handshaking stage."

"Asshole buddies is just a Southern expression," Johnny said. "Let's drop that subject and talk of loftier matters. Like what ol' Spence did yesterday."

"If this is gonna be about what you guys do in bed, pal, I think I'll skip it," Bogie said.

"Nothing like that," Johnny said. "It was at the studio. As you know, Spence is battling Fox about the roles he's been assigned. I mean, a dreadful

223

piece of shit like *Six Cylinder Love,* co-starring that queen, Edward Everett Horton. What a turkey! Yesterday, on the set, Spence had had his fill of the studio and probably the entire film industry as well."

"I don't think I want to hear the rest of this story," Bogie said. He closed his eyes and lay back to get sun. To his surprise, Johnny lit a cigarette for him and placed it in his mouth. "Thanks," Bogie said. "I don't usually let men light my cigarettes, though."

"You'll get used to it," Johnny said enigmatically. "Anyway, Spence showed up on the set of *She Wanted a Millionaire* in evening clothes. He'd been out drinking all night. He was taking out his frustrations with Fox by acting like a rebellious child. He didn't know his lines and he'd have been too drunk to say them even if he had. He went around making lascivious remarks to all the gals on the set, pretty or otherwise. He even went up to the fluttery Una Merkel and asked her if he could play with her pussy. Later he came up to the star of the picture, Joan Bennett, and bluntly asked her, 'Do you want to fuck?'"

"That's understandable," Bogie said. "I'd like a piece of Miss Joan myself. She's even younger and prettier than her older sister, Constance."

"It's more complicated than that," Mack Brown said. "The plot thickens. First, Spence was already furious that Joan got all the best lines in the flick. He told the press he's Bennett's prop, with dialogue best reserved for a wooden Indian. To make matters worse, the director, John Blystone, is in love with Bennett himself."

"God damn it," Bogie said, sitting up and inhaling deeply on his cigarette. "This sounds like a more interesting plot than any of his movies."

"That's not all. Bennett slapped his face. When Blystone rushed over, Spence said to him, 'The script is dishonest.' Then he passed out."

"No wonder our boy is part of The Irishmen's Club in Hollywood," Bogie said. "Those boys sure know how to drink. I drink all the time but I moderate it. Spence, I've noticed, either drinks or doesn't touch the stuff. But

when he drinks, he empties the equivalent of Lake Michigan. My father's a doctor. He calls men like Spence a spasmodic alcoholic."

"Well, he's in one of those spasms this weekend," Johnny said, "so be duly warned. I don't know what Fox is going to do with him. When the crew revived Spence about an hour later, he immediately barged onto the set again, took out his dick, and pissed on an expensive sofa they were using in a scene. The same sofa where Bennett was supposed to sit." He leaned back and eyed Bogie carefully. "There's more. Then he went on a rampage. He turned over lamps, sending them crashing to the floor. There was this bookcase with glass doors. He picked up an ashtray and broke its win-

Football hero and Hollywood actor Johnnie Mack Brown

224

dows. Finally he stood on an armchair and lunged for the crystal chandelier. He was swinging on the chandelier when he fell off, hitting his head against something. That caused him to bleed profusely. The big man himself, Winfield Sheehan, Fox's director of production, had been called to the set. He saw it all."

"Sheehan's gonna can Spence," Bogie predicted. "I just know it. Spence is gonna be on that train back to New York with me. We'll start a club. Two former Fox stars pounding the pavements of Broadway looking for work."

"I agree with you," Johnny said. "Spence is a great actor, probably the greatest in Hollywood. But he's been assigned a series of stupid potboilers, each with really bad scripts. And his pictures are bombing at the box office. Let's face it? His behavior is outrageous. He'll come right up to a woman and fondle her breast. Or he'll reach up her dress. I mean, Spence is not a thigh man, he goes right for the honeypot at the end of the rainbow."

"Maybe Sheehan will tolerate that kind of behavior in a big star cleaning up at the box office," Bogie said. "Someone up there in the Garbo league. But you can't make potboilers that lose money and pull such crap."

"I don't know why Fox hasn't kicked him out on his ass by now. If I acted like Spence, I would have been canned long ago. To make matters worse, Spence will disappear for weeks at a time. He'll lock himself up in a hotel suite and stage a big drunk."

"I hate to see the guy suffer," Bogie said. "He's a real pal of mine, but he seems possessed by some hidden devil that's got his soul."

For the rest of the afternoon, Bogie was content to lie on the beach, drink, smoke, and listen to the sound of Johnny's Southern drawl, which he'd come to find rather soothing. He needed this rest.

Hours later, Johnny said that Tracy had awakened and wanted to see him.

He found Tracy sitting on a narrow balcony overlooking the ocean. He looked sad and depressed.

"Good to see you again, pal," Bogie said, giving him a warm handshake. "I hear you pulled a big one last night."

"I'm glad you could come out," Tracy said. "With all the assholes out here in Hollywood I've been dealing with, you're the only pal that seems real."

"I'm real all right, and fucked up too, but not quite as fucked up as you are," Bogie said, sitting down beside the actor and lighting up another of his cigarettes.

"You'll get no argument with me about that," Tracy said. He looked at the evening waves washing up on the beach. "I don't think I'll ever be at peace with myself until I go to my grave."

"That's a pretty gloomy forecast," Bogie said.

"There's this thing inside me that's like a demon tearing my guts apart," Tracy said. "I can't get rid of it. The only way I can keep it under control is to drink so much I temporarily drown it. But it always comes back. I think this beast within me will live there until my body dies, and then the God damn thing will move into someone else's body."

"If you don't start taking better care of yourself, pal, the morticians will get you sooner than later."

"Sometimes I wish that was true," Tracy said.

***

The following night, after he'd driven back to his apartment and had visited with Kenneth for an hour, relating all the events of the weekend, Bogie felt tired and retreated to his apartment. He planned to cook himself some ham and eggs, but was too short on energy.

No sooner had he stripped off his clothes and piled into bed than the telephone rang. Wearily getting up to answer it, he knew he wasn't interested in accepting any invitations, even if Dietrich herself had called.

It was Helen, filled with remorse about her refusal to take his calls. "I was humiliated at seeing you with the most glamorous women in Hollywood. I felt old and ugly. I felt you didn't love me or need me any more in your life and that you could have your pick of some of the most beautiful women in the world."

"Your beauty is timeless," he said. "Theirs is only of today."

"Thank you, dear heart," she said. I'm sorry I didn't call back. Please forgive me."

"We've done worse things to each other," he said.

"Please come right over" she said, a sudden urgency in her voice.

"At this hour?" he asked. Even for Helen and a reconciliation, he wasn't that interested.

It's only ten o'clock," she said. "Early for Hollywood."

"You're on the west coast now, not New York," he said. "Stars have to go to bed early so that we can look gorgeous on camera."

"Please," she said. "Tonight is so important."

***

After hours spent with Helen, Bogie drove back to his apartment, expecting an early morning call from Fox, announcing that he was needed that day. When no call came in, he showered and dressed, deciding to drive to her apartment since she was not answering her phone. He feared that something might be wrong.

At the Garden of Allah, a young man at the reception desk told him that, "Miss Menken checked out this morning to return to New York." Bogie asked if she'd left a message for him, but was told there was none.

Their night had gone so successfully that Bogie was absolutely shocked at Helen's abrupt departure. Nothing in their time spent together suggested that she was going back to New York so suddenly.

Obviously, she'd decided that she didn't want to wander back into their old relationship, and decided she'd cut it off before it had a chance of grow-ing again. He could never be certain about Helen. She was a woman of impulses, and obviously had acted on her impulse.

Nonetheless, he was angry at her. "After all that love-making," he said in a call to Kenneth MacKenna, "not even a god damn note. Men like us should never marry actresses."

"Maybe she got the part of a lifetime." MacKenna said.

"Maybe." Bogie put down the phone.

Just as he was about to leave, he heard the sound of loud, raucous laugh-ter in the foyer. He spotted those two madcap Alabamians, Tallulah Bankhead and Anderson Lawler, asking the doorman to call them a taxi. Both of them had more in common than a birth state, having just survived separate affairs with Gary Cooper.

Tallulah seemed delighted to see him. "Hump, darling," she called to him. "We're going to Jimmy's Backyard tonight. If you'll go with us, I'll fuck you later and let Andy suck you off."

"An invitation like that sounds irresistible," he said, shaking Lawler's hand and kissing Tallulah on the mouth, feeling the serpentine darting of her tongue.

"Before she checked out," Tallulah said, "I ran into your adorable wife. Helen was furious. She told me about the double-cross. The producers want Barbara Stanwyck to costar in the film version of *The Captive*. They should have asked me." She laughed hilariously at something she was about to say. "Of course, I understand why they didn't consider me. No one would believe me in the role of a lesbian."

"You are the true epitome of ladylike refinement," Lawler said.

"You bet your cocksucking lips I am," she said. She leaned her head over to get a better view of Bogie. "We must get together soon and catch up on the latest Hollywood gossip. I'll tell you my tales. You can tell me your tales. Later, I'll show you my tail, and you can show me your tail. Not that I haven't seen it before, darling."

***

It was late at night as Bogie wandered slightly drunk and alone on the hotel grounds in the aftermath of Kenneth's wedding to Kay Francis. He looked up several times at the windows of their bridal suite. He could only envy Kenneth the wedding bliss he was enjoying with the woman known for some reason as "the trapeze artist" in bed. He wondered if Kenneth would ever fall in love with Francis as much as he loved Bogie's own wife, Mary. Thoughts of her crossed his mind. He imagined that at this very late hour in New York his wife was in the arms of that "God Damn actor," Roland Young.

Bogie looked up one final time at the Francis/MacKenna wedding suite and headed off by himself into the night.

He could not have imagined that within a year Young would be at Warner

Brothers appearing opposite Francis in *Street of Women*, and that Young and Francis would be engaged in a torrid romance.

***

In Joan Blondell's dressing room at Warner Brothers, Bogie had just finished showering after he'd bedded her on the carpet in front of her vanity table. She was his kind of broad. He liked her tremendously, although he wasn't in love with her. She was loyal, dependable, and always there for him when he needed a woman's company. She was warm, loving, and forgiving, and he felt that he could confide anything to her and she'd protect his secrets or else overlook his weaknesses.

He suspected that this former clerk at Macy's Department Store would never make it as a big star, but as an actress she'd always show up for Warner Brothers, taking any part offered, never complaining, never going on suspension, even if they worked her into dizziness, even to the point of making four films at once.

She brought the same vitality to sex that she did to the gold-diggers she played on screen. She was brazen and fun to be with, and she didn't take herself too seriously. After bedding Blondell, he felt ten feet tall. He couldn't understand why James Cagney had dumped her.

After they'd dressed, he drove her over to the first screening of *Night Nurse*, the movie she'd recently made with Barbara Stanwyck and Clark Gable.

On the way to the screening, he asked Blondell, "After we've each gone through two or three more spouses, do you think we'll get married and settle down somewhere in Ohio, growing old and gray together sitting in our rockers on the front porch, watching people go to Sunday morning services?"

"I can see it now," she said. "Right before noon, I'll rise from my chair if my rheumatism will allow it, and head back into our little kitchen with its wood-burning stove. Ham and eggs for you, and rutabagas mixed with mashed potatoes for me. Those will be the diets we'll live on."

As Bogie sat in the theater holding Blondell's hand, he'd seen only fifteen minutes of the 72-minute film when he realized that *Night Nurse*, in spite of its stellar cast, was not going to win Oscars for anybody. Playing a tough, scheming chauffeur, a character called Nick, Gable manhandles the cast, including Stanwyck, but the female members of the audience seemed to like his testosterone-driven violence. He wondered if most women secretly wanted a man to beat them up.

Unlike her usual screen portraits, and in spite of Blondell's appraisal, Stanwyck played her typical dancehall gal on one note throughout. Blondell had exaggerated. Stanwyck not only didn't eat up the scenery, she seemed strangely subdued in her role of Lora Hart, a young woman hired by a rich, drunken widow to act as a private nurse to her children. Bogie felt that Blondell brought the only life and humanity to the film.

228

There was only polite applause at the end of the film. As the manager of the theater slipped the stars of *Night Nurse* out of the rear door, Bogie felt that that was an unnecessary precaution. He thought that Stanwyck, Blondell, and Gable could easily have walked out the front door without being overpowered by screaming fans demanding autographs.

***

Knowing it was going to be his last day on the Fox lot, Bogie arrived three hours before his scheduled meeting with Winfield Sheehan, head of production. He was going to miss his paycheck of $750 a week. Although he'd meant to save most of it, he never got around to doing that, seemingly thinking the money would last forever.

He could only hope that his meager savings would tide him over in Depression-riddled New York until he found a job in the theater.

Maybe once again the Brady family might come to his rescue, as they had when he returned from his term of duty in the Navy. Bill Brady Jr. had been his best friend for many years, and before he left for Hollywood, Bogart had sincerely intended to write to him frequently. But in Hollywood Bogie had turned to Kenneth as his confidant instead. Those letters to family and friends back in New York were meant to be written but never were.

Bogie was uncertain where he would even stay in New York. It seemed hardly likely that Mary, as she prepared to divorce him, would want him living with her and that actor, Roland Young.

Bogie was sitting outside a sound stage on the edge of a curb, his face buried in his hands. He must have looked a pathetic sight when Herb Gallagher approached him. Bogie had seen the elderly man puttering about the studios, but had never spoken to him.

"Everybody knows Winnie is going to fire you this morning," Gallagher said. "But you're a young man. You'll find work at other studios. Maybe Warners. I'd have said Paramount but the smart money says that they're about to go belly-up."

Bogie looked up at the man, squinting his eyes to blot out the morning sun. "You're the janitor, right? I mean everybody here, even the janitor, is in on the details of my getting the boot?"

"I don't mean to get you riled up," Gallagher said, "but your pictures have bombed. You've bombed. Frankly, you were lucky to get that $750 a week. I don't know how you conned them into that."

"Hell, you even know what salary I was drawing," Bogie said. "Are there no secrets in Hollywood?"

"You know the answer to that," Gallagher said, spitting out some tobacco juice only three feet from Bogie. "I was fired myself by Winnie."

"Then why are you still here?" Bogie asked, standing up in hope of avoiding getting hit with the next stream of tobacco juice.

"I was the chief script reader back in 1924," Gallagher said. "When I

229

turned down three scripts that later became hits at other studios, I was canned."

"As I said, why are you still here?" Bogie asked.

"I know too much about Winnie to get the final boot like you're about to get this morning," Gallagher said. "Winnie let me stay on. Instead of reading scripts, I get to sweep up the sound stages. It's a living."

"I once thought Sheehan was going to be my big white hope," Bogie said. "In spite of all the trouble he causes, Spencer Tracy still has a contract, and I don't."

"Maybe Winnie's judgment about you is all wrong," Gallagher said. "From the looks of you, I don't see it, but you could go on to become a big star in spite of your ugly mug, puny body, your lisp, and that scar on your mouth."

"You sure know how to make a guy feel good on the day he's about to be kicked out in the midst of a Depression."

"What the hell!" Gallagher said. "That's how the game is played out here. Look at Pola Negri and Gloria Swanson. The two biggest screen vamps of the Twenties. Now they can't get arrested. Look at John Gilbert. The biggest screen idol of the Silents."

"I know, I know," Bogie said impatiently. "I've read their biographies in the fan magazines."

"In two, maybe three years, Winnie himself will be out the door when a better, more aggressive, and more talented producer comes along. Winnie doesn't know that much about film-making any way. William Fox gave him the job because Winnie blackmailed him."

"What sort of blackmail?" Bogie asked. "Sexual?"

"Nothing like that," Gallagher said. "At one time, Winnie was the secretary to the police commissioner in New York. Fox Studios routinely violated the bylaws of the Motion Picture Patents Company. Somehow, and I don't know how he did it, Winnie covered for them, keeping them two feet in front of the law during their time in New York. When Fox pulled up stakes and headed west, their boy Winnie came with them."

"So that's how you became head of production at a major studio," Bogie said.

"Winnie didn't know a fucking thing about movies when he got to Hollywood," Gallagher said. "He was just a teenager when he joined the Army to fight in the Spanish-American War. After he came back to New York, he was a cub reporter and then a police reporter. He gave that up to work for the police commissioner. Now he's making and breaking stars. In with Spencer Tracy, out with Humphrey Bogart."

Gallagher was called back to duty, and Bogie wandered alone into the Fox commissary where only three tables were occupied. He decided to drink a half-dozen cups of black coffee before facing Sheehan.

In time, Bogie would realize that the janitor knew exactly what he was talking about. By 1935, when the Fox Film Corporation merged with

Twentieth Century Pictures, Sheehan was out, having been replaced by a far more talented and brilliant producer, Darryl Zanuck, who had managed to get rid of Sheehan for $360,000 in severance pay.

As he sat drinking those endless cups of coffee, Bogie came to realize that his whole attempt to become a movie star was a bit ridiculous. At that very moment, he felt that he was the least likely candidate in Hollywood to ever become a movie actor.

When he'd made *Up the River* with Tracy, Bogie had had high hopes of stardom, but it had been a downward spiral ever since. He believed that he was better looking than Tracy, but his friend could act, and Bogie wondered if he even knew what acting was all about. Bogie could snarl and hiss, or even look vapid, but he couldn't be as natural or as convincing on screen as Tracy was. As the director, Raoul Walsh, had once barked at Bogie on the set of *Women of All Nations*, "Footage of actors like you end up on the cutting-room floor."

At eleven o'clock that morning, Bogie, jittery from too much coffee, was ushered into the office of Winnie Sheehan. The studio chief was known for his gregarious style and for some degree of charm, but Bogie found his dapper boss with his "black Irish features" and his legendary "ol' baby blues" rather dour today. At that time, Sheehan was known for chasing skirts and throwing the best parties more than he was celebrated for making great movies. Without looking up at Bogie, he sat at his desk going over some papers, not bothering to greet the actor or shake his hand. Sheehan routinely fired stars, directors, and studio executives every day.

"Bogart," he said in a sharp voice, looking up at him for the first time as he signaled for him to take a stiff armchair in front of his desk. "You're not only untalented, but you're in violation of your contract's morals clause."

"I've bedded a few dames since coming out to the West Coast," Bogie said. "Any law against that?"

"Not against that," Sheehan said. "If there was, I'd be locked away in the dankest cell. No one fucks higher on the list than Winnie Sheehan. Only A-list pussy. When I want a piece of ass, I go only for stars: Jean Harlow, Sally Eilers, Joan Crawford, Elissa Landi, Joan Bennett, Ann Dvorak, Myrna Loy, Sidney Fox. Even Helen Twelvetrees."

"*Even her?*" Bogie said, rather mockingly.

If Sheehan knew he was being ridiculed, he gave no indication of it. "It's this *panz* stuff I'm concerned about." He reached into his top drawer and removed a candid eight-by-ten snapshot which he handed to Bogie.

Bogie studied the picture carefully. He was drunk at the time, and hardly remembered the photograph being taken. It was either at The Fat Black Pussycat or Jimmy's Backyard. In the picture Bogie sat between Edmund Lowe and Lilyan Tashman, with his arm around each of them. Also in the picture was Billy Haines, with his arm around Anderson Lawler. At the far left of the picture Charles Farrell was paying more romantic attention to Kenneth MacKenna than he was to the actor's new bride, Kay Francis.

"You not only go to *panz* clubs," Sheehan charged, "but I heard you

231

attended an all-male lingerie party Richard Arlen threw for Kenneth MacKenna."

"That's true," Bogie said with candor. "I was seen there running around in my Skivvies." He handed the glossy photograph back to Sheehan. "For your bathroom wall," he said, a bite of sarcasm in his voice.

"That overseer of Hollywood morals, Will Hays, has been warning me about using dual-sex boys and lesbos in Fox films," Sheehan said. "If directors like George Cukor had their way, all men in film would be effeminate, flaunting their perversions on screen. I've had a study made of all Fox pictures by my assistant, Sidney Kent. His conclusion is that the sooner we get away from fairies and degenerates in our scripts, and the more family-oriented we become, the bigger the profits for Fox." He picked up a letter on his desk. "Here's what Kent wrote. 'The fairies must be sent packing back to New York where they belong.'"

"Unless I misread the scripts, I wasn't aware that I'd been playing flaming pansies on the screen," Bogie said.

"It's implied in your performances," Sheehan said. "Up against real he-men on the screen, guys like Victor McLaglen or Spencer Tracy, you come across like a lisping queen. I know you played all those faggot juvenile roles on Broadway, coming out in fancy sports dress with a tennis racket and cruising all the handsome men on stage, inviting them for a game of tennis. What the smart people in the audience realized was that you really wanted one of them to join you in the showers after the game."

Bogie chuckled at that preposterous summation of his stage career. "Hey, let's don't get carried away here. I never played any such part. Ask the directors like John Cromwell. And playwrights like Maxwell Anderson."

"It was a subtle thing, and you were able to get away with it on the New York stage," Sheehan said. "But the camera picks up the slightest nuance. For example, *Variety* a few months ago ran an article about all the pansy dancers and chorus boys used in musicals. It demanded that from now on, every studio cast real he-men as chorus boys. During the casting of musicals in the 30s, if a boy is too dainty and pretty, he's going to be out on his ass. And fussy, over-marcelled hair is out too. Film-goers, especially male film-goers, resent seeing effeminate men on the screen. I've seen all the footage you've shot for Fox at the ridiculously overinflated salary of $750 a week. There must have been a typo in your contract. It should have read $75 a week, and even then you would have been overpaid. Let's face the truth: You've got some effeminate mannerisms, and they're even more intolerable because of your lisp."

"So, you're saying that I'm getting kicked out on my ass because I act like a pansy on the screen?" Bogie asked, not concealing his anger, which had flared suddenly.

"You amaze me with your perception," Sheehan said sarcastically. "I think my point is obvious. My recommendation is that you give up acting. You and that co-star of yours in *Bad Sister*, Bette Davis, have no talent. Neither of you have presence on the screen. She looks like a little lost wren, and you look like a sneaky rat. You're not ugly enough to play a villain like Edward G. Robinson, nor handsome enough to be a leading man like Joel McCrea. You've made your last picture for Fox."

"I think I figured that out even before I came into your office today," Bogie said.

"The camera, my boy, is an amazing thing," Sheehan said in worshipful tones. "It creates an illusion of reality so great that it can surpass reality. All studios, not just Fox, have got to show a greater respect for the camera and not parade freaks of nature before it. Guys like John Gilbert, Billy Haines, Ramon Novarro."

"And you're adding the name of Humphrey Bogart to that list of queens?" Bogie asked in astonishment.

"If the shoe fits, wear it," Sheehan said harshly. "Tomorrow's screen belongs to the Clark Gables and the Gary Coopers. You won't find those two out sucking dick or taking it up the ass any more. We've also got to have real he-men directors like Raoul Walsh, not fancy-pantsy George Cukor, directing real men like my latest discovery, Marion Morrison. For *The Big Trail*, I had him get rid of that pansy name and call himself John Wayne. Back in the Twenties, just as a means of getting ahead, Wayne occasionally let one or two of the male stars of his films suck his dick, hoping for a big break. And Clark Gable did the same thing. So did Gary Cooper. Wayne confided to me the names of guys who had gone down on him: Billy Haines in *Brown of Harvard,* John Gilbert in *Bardelays the Magnificent,* Richard Barthelmess in *The Drop Kick,* George O'Brien in *Salute* and again in *A Rough Romance,* and your faggot buddy, Kenneth MacKenna in *Men Without Women.* And now, like Cooper and Gable, Wayne is a star. He won't have to drop his pants ever again for a Hollywood cocksucker."

"When history books are written years from now, I'm sure they'll credit Winfield Sheehan with bringing masculinity to the movies," Bogie said bitterly.

Sheehan took him seriously. "And they'll be right. I did pretty well with George O'Brien in *The Iron Horse*. George is one he-man. I nicknamed him 'The Chest.' In fact, I did all the publicity for *The Iron Horse* in 1924. I came up with the line, 'George O'Brien is not a sheik or a caveman or a lounge lizard. He's a man's man and the idol of women.' Not bad, huh?"

"That sure would have lured me into a movie house," Bogie said, still amazed that Sheehan was taking his sarcastic remarks seriously.

"Just between you and me, Fox is on the verge of bankruptcy, and I've got to save the studio," Sheehan said. "Lisping fairies on the screen won't do the job for us."

"You're telling me that in the new Hollywood big-dicked studs will direct only big-dicked studs. Balls will be clanking so loudly technicians will have to tone down the sound track. John Wayne will come across like a giant phallus spewing semen into the audience."

"Don't disgrace yourself in front of me by getting carried away with too many of your sexual fantasies," Sheehan cautioned.

"Okay," Bogie said, wondering why Sheehan was prolonging this firing. "I'm out the door. Who's next on your list? After you kick out the pansies on their ass?"

"I met with Joseph Breen yesterday," Sheehan said. "As you well know, he works hand-in-glove with Will Hays to safeguard the industry from perversion. Breen is not only against sexual perverts on the screen but lousy Jews like Louis B. Mayer, too. Breen calls Jews the scum of the earth. A Jew will do anything for money. They'll agree to any sexual taboo on the screen if they feel it'll turn a fast buck. These money-grubbers will depict the vilest of scenes. Breen thinks the ultimate aim of the Hollywood Jew is to undermine Catholic morality."

Bogie stood up abruptly. I've heard enough. I'll be off the Fox lot in fifteen minutes. Watch me go. I'm not going to sit here any longer listening to your shit." He actually used the word "shit," which he detested when other people said it. But no word other than shit seemed to describe the garbage pouring out of Sheehan's mouth.

"I'm one cocksucking pansy faggot queer lisping queen, one slimy sissy—a bumbling fluttery butterfly, lipstick-wearing, take-it-in-the-ass, dithery, unmasculine fruit."

"That's how I'd describe you," Sheehan said. "And let me congratulate you on the honesty of your self-portrait. The most accurate I've ever heard."

Bogie walked rapidly toward the door, opened it, then slammed it in Sheehan's face as he headed down the corridor and off the Fox Studio lot.

Amazingly, when Bogie appeared to accept the Oscar as best actor for his role of Charlie Allnut in 1951's *The African Queen*, he singled out Winfield Sheehan specifically for a special thank you for launching him into motion pictures.

***

Bogie walked out onto the rooftop of his apartment building, watching the dawn break across the Los Angeles skyline. As he smoked his tenth cigarette since coming up to the roof, he pondered the Hollywood madness that had driven him here, where he'd actually considered, however briefly, taking a jump off that roof.

Kenneth was due back at his apartment that morning after a short honeymoon with Kay Francis. He too was moving out of the building to live with his new bride under whatever marital arrangements they'd worked out together.

In lieu of Kenneth, he thought he'd call Spencer Tracy and expose himself as a failure, but decided against that. He didn't want Tracy to know how vulnerable he was and preferred for his newly acquired actor friend to maintain the illusion that Humphrey Bogart was tough like Tracy himself.

Back in his own apartment, and safe after his lonely walk on the roof, he received a phone call from Bette Davis, who was demanding to see him. She'd been fired from Universal. Her party for losers had been completely accurate as a harbinger of events to come.

Although within the recent past, he had vowed never to see her again, he invited her over anyway, hoping that two actors, each of them kicked out of Hollywood, might be able to console each other.

The pain associated with his having been fired from Fox was enormous.

Opening the door, he took in the vision of a very distraught Davis, who had been crying. She immediately fell into his arms, sobbing more intensely and violently than she ever would on the screen.

She sat on the sofa across from him, as both of them enjoyed booze and cigarettes, two narcotics that would become lifelong addictions for each of them. Since storming into his apartment, she had talked incessantly about her career, offering only minor condolences about his own dismissal from Fox.

"When I came to Hollywood," she said, "America was in a great depression. It still is. Garbo had learned to talk, and the first thing she said was '*Gimme a viskey.*'" Her imitation of Garbo was right on the mark. "Garbo is still talking. Dietrich had arrived to appear in high heels and expensive gowns running around in the sands of *Morocco*. She's still dressing up, still running around. Norma Shearer had won the Oscar. Norma Shearer is still getting Oscar-winning roles. Hollywood is virtually intact. And it certainly won't miss Bette Davis." She looked over at him. "I'm not movie star material. Like you, Bogie, our faces weren't meant to grace the silver screen."

"If only we'd gotten the right parts," he said defensively. He didn't like admitting failure.

"As far as I'm concerned, both Carl Laemmles, Senior and Junior, can take their so-called 230-acre film factory and give it back to the mustard farmers from whom they took the land in 1915."

"Considering the films those two creeps turn out," he said, "maybe mustard greens would be easier to swallow."

She seemed not to have heard his remark. "'Bette from Boston,' they called me. All the good parts went to that whoring bitch, Sidney Fox. She spent more time fucking Laemmle Jr. than she did on camera. *Frumpy* they called me. Odd-looking. Sexless. Somewhat ugly. Christ. *Somewhat!*" She virtually spat out the word.

"Look at all the guys who've fallen for you," he said. "You're hardly sexless. Why, all the losers at your party had the hots for you. Even me."

She smiled at the remark. "If only that were true."

As he got up to pour her another drink, she too rose to her feet and pranced around the apartment, with the same kind of stalking movement she'd demonstrate in several films. She was a woman with a violent temper and filled with turbulent emotions. "I've failed miserably in films. I can't even stand to see myself on the screen. I'm that bad."

"You came close to getting roles here or there that could have launched you," he said, reminding her.

"Close," she said with a certain contempt. "But miles from the goal. My one hope was that William Wyler would cast me in *A House Divided*. It was my last chance for success at Universal. Even though the women in wardrobe objected, I found this dark plaid cotton dress. The bodice fit real low, and I definitely showed cleavage. After all, let's face it: My breasts are my most alluring physical asset. I'm sure you'll discover that for yourself later."

This was his first indication that he was going to get lucky.

"When I came onto the set showing my major assets pre-packaged in that dress," Davis said, "Wyler took one look at me and dismissed me. I heard him tell his assistant, 'Who in hell do these *ingénues* think they are? They think that if they show off a big pair of tits, they've got the part. Fuck! Hollywood is just one big tit." She sighed before taking a deep drag on her cigarette. "I was so upset by him that I was tongue-tied during the screen test."

Ironically, Wyler would become not only "the love of my life" for Bette, but her best and most favored director, guiding her through her classics, such as *Jezebel*, her consolation prize for not getting cast as Scarlett O'Hara in *Gone With the Wind*, and in Lillian Hellman's *The Little Foxes*, a role that had been created on the stage for her arch rival, Tallulah Bankhead.

"Laemmle Jr. called me into his office to fire me in person," she said. "I think he enjoyed humiliating me, telling me that I had no future in films. After seeing us together in *Bad Sister*, he predicted the same fate for you."

"I know that," he snapped at her. "We've been over all that before."

"I don't know about you," Davis said, "but I'm going to return to Broadway and become the next Lynn Fontanne."

"Can I be your Alfred Lunt?" he asked. Although he'd meant his remark to be facetious, by the time he came to the question mark, it had become serious.

She looked over at him as if sizing him up. "You're not homosexual enough to replace Lunt."

"I'll take that as a compliment," he said. "Maybe we'll be the next Alfred Lunt and Lynn Fontanne, but we'll be more virile. Not as fey."

"Maybe that's not such a bad idea," she said, her pop eyes widening as if the revelation just might be possible. "I could see the names of Bette Davis and Humphrey Bogart in lights."

"We could become the new king and queen of Broadway," he said, daring to hope that such a dream might actually happen.

"You and I are not film people," she said. "We belong on the stage. The theater is in our blood. We'll get the right properties. Get Maxwell Anderson to write a play tailor-made for us. Maybe even Ben Hecht. He'd be great. We'll become the next legendary acting team in Broadway history."

He held his glass up to hers, and she toasted him back, saying, "Of course, your talent will never be as great as mine. But I think you can develop a real stage presence. Sometimes having a distinct personality is more important than acting talent. In my case, I was blessed with both talent and a personality."

He listened patiently, though rather disdainful of her proclamations of her own greatness.

By ten o'clock that night, she'd agreed to go onto the roof with him for his final look at Los Angeles at night.

A wind was blowing in from the ocean, and the night had turned suddenly cold. Wearing only a thin cotton dress, she was shivering. "Hold me!" she commanded. There was desperation in her voice. Without her bravado, she appeared strangely weak and vulnerable, in need of a man's protection.

"I'm here for you," he said, moving toward her. He took her in his arms and kissed her passionately, feeling her quivering response. So great was her need for him that she was moaning softly. She knew that he knew that she was his for the taking, at least for the night.

"I need to feel like a woman again," she whispered seductively in his ear. "Take me downstairs and make me feel like that woman I long to be, but never was."

"You've got yourself a date, lady," he said, kissing her once more. With one arm around her waist, he guided her toward the lone door on the roof, leading down the iron steps to his apartment.

Once inside the apartment, she appeared talked out. There would be no more need for words.

By four o'clock that morning, he'd made more passionate love to her than he had any other woman in his life. He'd made Bette Davis his woman. She hugged him with the kind of desperation a couple faces when they stagger blindly but bravely into a new but uncertain future. Throughout the night they'd clung to each other like two people who, when dawn came, would face the gallows together.

Both of them had convinced the other that their future careers were entwined. Together they could make it as a team, or so they'd told themselves.

Before the night ended, she had begged him to marry her as soon as his divorce from Mary came through. "I didn't know what love-making was until I went to bed with you. I thought sex was something that men did to please themselves with women. Hop on, hop off. You taught me what a thrill it can be for a woman. You've taken me to another dimension, a place I didn't think I could find with any man. You've awakened a desire in parts of my body that I thought

On the air:
Humphrey Bogart with Bette Davis

237

were incapable of a sexual response."

She had obviously regained her articulation. He buried the sound of her voice when he'd moved over her again, giving her a deep, impassioned kiss. Even though he thought his entire body had been fulfilled as never before, he found himself hardening again.

After he'd finished both of them off for the last call of the evening, he urgently pleaded with her, "Get on the train in the morning with me," he said. "Let's go back to New York." Kenneth had agreed to drive him to the depot for his final good-bye to Hollywood.

Like a good New England housewife, Davis rose from his bed and began packing his luggage. But she turned down his invitation to leave with him that morning because, "It's impossible—that's why."

She did commit to him, though, claiming that when, "Ruthie and I shut down our house in the Hollywood Hills, I'll be on the next train east. It'll take about six weeks, but you can count on me to be there. In the meantime, you've got to search for a suitable apartment for us. In New York, we'll pound those sidewalks of Broadway together."

"I'll be in New York keeping the sheets warm," he said, "until your train pulls into Grand Central station." He kissed her on her nose as he headed for the bathroom.

Over breakfast, which included ham and eggs, Davis proved herself to be a capable cook. "You've liberated me as a woman," she claimed to him, her wide eyes popping with a new kind of joy and a dawning reality. "I'll be a better actress because of this night we spent together."

"The first of many such nights," he assured her.

She stood up to pour him some more coffee. "Miss Bette Davis, formerly of Universal Studios and now a Broadway star, will become the third Mrs. Humphrey Bogart. It is her first marriage. For Bogart, it is his third. He was previously married to Broadway actresses Helen Menken and Mary Philips."

"This past night in bed with you will have to last me for several weeks until we're together again in New York," she said. "There can be no other man for me but Humphrey Bogart."

He kissed her one final time, holding her long and close. He made a parting remark before rushing down those stairs where an impatient Kenneth was waiting to drive him to the station.

He turned back and looked with a nostalgic regret at the apartment house where he'd lived during his brief, ill-fated Hollywood career. All he could think about was Davis up there in his bathroom, applying lipstick to her face before she too left the building forever to return to her own home.

Each day for him would be a long one until she was with him in New York and cuddling him in that ample bosom that William Wyler had rejected.

All the way to the station, he wasn't really in the car with Kenneth, but remained still back in that apartment with Davis. His good-bye to her would stab at his memory forever.

238

CHAPTER FIVE

It was a dismal New York that greeted Bogie upon his arrival in 1931. Unemployment was at an all-time high, and the gaiety of Broadway in the Roaring Twenties had roared out. For every acting job, there were more than 3,000 hopefuls who showed up, trying out for a meager part to keep them out of the breadlines.

The great theatrical entrepreneurs, the Schuberts, had gone into receivership. In 1929, two years before, some 250 theatrical productions had been launched for the then-prosperous audiences of Broadway. But in 1931, with America in the throes of a Depression, many of these legitimate theaters had been converted into movie house showcases for hastily produced Talkies being churned out by Hollywood.

The first person he called upon was Mary Philips. Unlike the woman who had written the "Dear John" letter she'd sent him in California, she now seemed to want to save their marriage. At least some of her change in heart derived from the fact that she'd caught Roland Young, her lover, involved in not one, but two affairs with other actresses and had left him.

"I'm just as much to blame for the failure of our marriage as you are," he confessed to her.

"I think we owe it to each other to give it one more try," she told him.

Against his better judgment, he agreed. That night he wrote Bette Davis in Hollywood, telling that he had reconciled with Mary.

Furious at his rejection, she did not respond. "I will never speak to Humphrey Bogart again as long as I live. He treated me like a Saturday night whore." She relayed her feelings to Kenneth MacKenna, hoping he would convey her fury to Bogie back in New York.

Her mother, Ruthie, praised Bette Davis' decision to have no further contact with Bogie. "The man gives me the creeps. He always looks dirty." It would be at the urging of Ruthie that her daughter, with some reluctance, eventually married Harmon Nelson Jr., a no-talent musician, in Yuma, Arizona, on August 18, 1932.

Even though he'd been separated from his family for sixteen months,

Bogie did not want to confront them again, yet nevertheless felt that he had to. He called first on Belmont, whose life had continued down a stairway to some dark gulf. Belmont was paralyzed and had been bedridden for the past four months in a dingy apartment at Tudor City in Manhattan.

His father told him that Maud was living upstairs, within the same compound but in another apartment. The ill-fated couple had not divorced. Instead of functioning as a wife, she'd become a caretaker, providing a hot cooked breakfast for him every morning. Each night at seven, she brought down a nutritious dinner.

After his visit with his father, Bogie called on Maud upstairs. She was living in greatly reduced circumstances, paying her own bills and Belmont's too with the meager earnings from her art work.

During the time Bogie had been away, she seemingly had aged ten years. Her face was drawn and bitter. She was chilly with him, not even extending her hand when she allowed him into her apartment. She didn't want to hear about any of his adventures in Hollywood, and had seen none of his movies. After about forty-five minutes, she asked him to leave because she had developed a migraine headache.

Before he left, she mentioned his sister, Kay (Catherine), whom she claimed had become "a hopeless alcoholic and the town whore."

Kay's drinking led to a rapid deterioration of her health. She died in 1937 of peritonitis after being rushed to the hospital when her appendix ruptured. Before an ambulance arrived, she was screaming in pain.

Frances Rose, his other sister, was in equally bad shape. Ever since she'd suffered through a painful childbirth, the delivery lasting almost 30 hours, she'd become a manic-depressive. She'd been in and out of asylums, and regularly subjected to electric shock treatments.

When Frances was left penniless after her divorce from Stuart Rose, with a young child to care for, she had no one to turn to but her brother. Throughout the rest of her life, Bogie would support her "emotionally and financially."

"The Bogarts are in great shape," he told Mary upon his return to their flat that night. "Each one, in very separate ways, is on the way to hell. Maybe I'm next. It's a family curse."

"We'll make it," she said. "Just you see. It's always darkest before the dawn."

"Stop it!" he shouted at her. "I told you to quit going through life spouting clichés."

Bogie and Mary, "along with the rats and roaches," had moved together into a dismal apartment at 434 East 52nd Street. At night they spent their time listening to the radio and finishing off a bottle of booze. There was nothing else for them to do.

On this marriage's second time around, sex did not emerge as a vital part of their relationship. "I'm too depressed to get it up," Bogie told his friend, Bill Brady Jr.

Even after the first week's anniversary of his reunion with Mary, he had serious doubts that their second attempt at marriage would work out.

One afternoon, he came home to find her writing a letter to Kenneth, now married to Kay Francis. He asked her if he could read it before she sent it, and she refused, tearing the letter into shreds and throwing them into the wastepaper basket.

Not finding any regular work, he sometimes earned as much as five dollars a day playing chess for two bits a round on Sixth Avenue, and bridge at the Players Club, a venue frequented mostly by recently unemployed actors, of course.

After pounding the pavement, Bogie landed a small part in a British comedy called *After All*. It opened to lackluster business at Broadway's Booth Theatre on November 3, 1931.

Helen Haye, who was often confused with Helen Hayes, was the star of this ill-fated play.

Wearing a fake mustache, as required by the role he was playing, Bogie encountered *After All's* British playwright, John Van Druten, who invited him to a tavern on 46th Street, Bogie thought it was to talk about the play, but after a drink or two, Van Druten felt his crotch. Bogie turned down the playwright's offer of sex.

Van Druten, of course, would go on to dazzling success in the theater and in film adaptations, striking gold with such hits as *The Voice of the Turtle* and *Bell, Book, and Candle*. He was not as successful with Hump's play. *After All* closed after only twenty performances.

On the last night of the show, Elliott Baker came backstage. He was one of the many talent scouts working for Columbia, among other studios. He was looking for young actors for talking pictures.

He had seen one of Bogie's pictures and had been impressed with his role in *After All* in which he played an architect married to an invalid.

Invited out for a hamburger, Bogie was expecting another proposition like he'd received from Van Druten. To his shock and delight, the agent offered him a six-month contract at Columbia for $750 a week, a dream salary back then.

Once again, Bogie found himself on the *Santa Fe Chief*, traveling west across the vast expanse of

Playwright
John Van Druten

241

the American continent. This time he knew he was going to make it big.

The big difference was that Mary now sat beside him. In spite of her "beak" nose, she was hoping to get cast in movie roles herself.

Kenneth had secured modest lodges for them at a pretentiously named apartment complex, The Château Elysée. Meeting them at the train station, Bogie appeared dismayed at the extended kiss Kenneth delivered to his wife.

***

Early in 1932, Bogie was awarded the second lead in a romantic comedy produced by Columbia entitled *Love Affair*.

An English beauty, Dorothy Mackaill, four years younger than Bogie, had been cast in the lead. Bogie found her "a stunner, with skin like polished porcelain." A former Ziegfeld Follies dancer, she'd been a bosom buddy of Marion Davies, mistress of William Randolph Hearst.

Love Affair
Humphrey Bogart in a starring role, at last.....with Dorothy Mackaill

Mackaill had made silent films with Bogie's pal, George O'Brien, and had even co-starred with John Barrymore. She told Bogie that she was delighted to have him as a leading man, since the studios wanted young, fresh talent.

"My contract with First National wasn't renewed, and I'm free-lancing. I think if I don't build up a new following in Talkies, I'm through. Help me!"

He didn't know how he could help her exactly. He'd already told friends, "I'm hanging on as an actor by the skin of my left nut."

He worked closely with the director, Thornton Freeland, of North Dakota, who'd started out at Vitagraph back in 1918. "He was more a cameraman than a director," Bogie said, "but he claimed he'd photograph me so I'd look like a matinee idol. That's okay with me, if that's what was needed and wanted. I'd flunked as Fox's answer to Clark Gable, so I needed a new persona."

Love Affair is significant today only because it marked Bogie's first starring role. In it, he played an aeronautical engineer. His

242

lisp is more pronounced in this picture than in later films.

At the end of filming, Mackaill told Bogie, "Here I am, not even thirty years old, and my career is fading fast. Perhaps we'll have a bit hit with this."

They didn't.

Back at their apartment, Mary was often gone until late at night, and he suspected she'd resumed her affair with Kenneth. For some reason he didn't feel particularly jealous. Kay Francis often wasn't home with Kenneth, who was pursuing various affairs with other women, or so Bogie had heard.

Bogie's next job came when Columbia lent him to Warner Brothers, which would eventually become his signature studio. He was given a small part in *Big City Blues* (1932), which "pissed me off—I'm a leading man, not a bit player." The only good news was that he could resume his affair with the star of the film, Joan Blondell.

On the set of *Big City Blues* (1932), Bogie found Joan making two films at a time. She'd have to complete twenty movies before the studio allowed her to take a vacation. Even though both of them remained free agents, Bogie fitted comfortably into the relationship with her as if he'd never left it behind.

Cast as a New York gold digger, Joan had thrived as a Depression-era Showgal. "Chorus girls used to get pearls and diamonds," she wisecracked. "Now all they expect is a corned beef sandwich."

She told Bogie, "My dad always complains about my playing low-life gals of the night, but I seem to fit into those roles better than nun parts."

The San Francisco director assigned to the picture, Mervyn LeRoy, was A-list. His film, *Little Caesar* (1931), had started the gangster craze that Bogie would soon be cashing in on.

Eric Linden was the film's male star. He'd be a leading man in minor Hollywood fare from 1931 to 1941. In *Gone With the Wind*, he'd be cast in a small role.

When he met Bogie, he was cornering the Tinseltown market in portraying artistic, sensitive, smart but weak-willed juvenile males, those who hovered between boyhood and manhood.

"The first time I saw you in *Up the River*, I was totally captivated by you," Eric told Bogie. "You remind me of my father."

"I guess I must be getting old, kid, and I've been told a lot of things in Hollywood, but never that I reminded someone of their father. And, by the way, kid, I'm not an adoption agency."

"I didn't mean it that way," Linden said apologetically. "I hope we can become close friends."

"I've got a lot of bad habits," Bogie said. "Drink too much. I fart in bed. I leave skid marks on my underwear." He lit a cigarette. "And I'm a skirt chaser."

"With all your faults," Linden said, "I want us to become very close friends."

After talking with him for a while, Bogie became dismissive. "It's just not going to happen, kid. You're awfully cute, but it's not for me." He turned and walked away.

There would be a third film before Bogie returned to Broadway. Mervyn LeRoy liked working with Bogie so much he also cast him in *Three on a Match* (1932). Bogie found himself working in a movie that starred four women he'd seduced—Joan Blondell, Ann Dvorak, Glenda Farrell, and once again Bette Davis.

He felt awkward encountering Bette again after dumping her so ungallantly. But when he met her, she shook his hand, "Welcome back to Hollywood, Mr. Bogart." She made no mention of their brief affair, and for that he was grateful.

"I had these big pictures like *Cabin in the Cotton*," she said, complaining to Bogie. "Now I'm the third female lead, working with those two whores, Blondell and Dvorak." She seemed unhappy and couldn't wait for the movie to end.

When her short shooting schedule came to an end, Bogie told her, "I hope we work on another picture soon."

"It is my most fervent wish," Davis said, "that that doesn't happen, Mr. Bogart."

At the wrap, LeRoy told her, "I predict stardom for Blondell, success for Dvorak, and unemployment for you, Bette."

***

Bette Davis (left) with
Joan Blondell

Still in California, before he returned to New York, Bogie appeared in a Broadway-bound comedy, *The Mad Hopes*. It starred Billie Burke, who would later gain screen immortality as the Good Witch Glinda in *The Wizard of Oz* (1939), with Judy Garland. Years before, in 1914, she had generated newspaper headlines thanks to her marriage to the theatrical impresario Florenz Ziegfeld.

The comedy with its giddy goings-on had been specifically written for Burke, but after its run in California, she wisely abandoned it as a means of avoiding the cynical scrutiny of Manhattan audiences. When it finally opened on Broadway on May 28, 1932, it starred Violet Kemble Cooper, and no Bogie. It ran for only twenty performances.

At the end of his stage appearance with the ever pleasant Burke in California, he learned that Columbia was not going to renew his contract. Since there was absolutely no work in Hollywood film studios, he opted to return to his native New York City to see what his chances there might be.

After the train deposited him at Manhattan's Grand Central Station, he headed back to the sleazy apartment he shared with Mary. Relations between them had became increasingly tense. During their obsessive search for work, they had each been leading separate lives. She would often come home late and had little to say. He noticed, however, that she still had time to write one letter a day to Kenneth back in California.

Many Broadway theaters had closed. Most former theater patrons couldn't afford a ticket. Movie tickets were a lot cheaper. Amazingly, Bogie managed to secure roles in five plays in a row, each with long rehearsal periods. Once the plays opened, each of them flopped. He would later remember performances where there were no more than twelve to twenty people in the audience.

His first job came when he was cast as the third lead in a play called *I Loved You Wednesday,* which opened on Broadway at the Sam H. Harris Theatre on October 11, 1932. He was cast as a "sybarite with the morals of a tomcat."

The star of *I Loved You Wednesday* was Frances Fuller, who played Bogie's lover. This Charleston-born actress from a fine American family was related to Secretary of State and U.S. Supreme Court Justice James Francis Byrnes (1882-1972). Frances later became the director of the American Academy of Dramatic Arts and was instrumental in developing the acting style of such

(top photo) Charleston (SC) socialite and film star Frances Fuller

(bottom photo) Ziegfeld Follies star and camp movie queen Billie Burke

245

stars as Grace Kelly and Anne Bancroft.

She was strictly business with Bogie. "No hanky-panky with that stuck-up bitch," Bogie told another young actor in the play, Henry Fonda, who appeared briefly in a non-speaking part which called for him to sit onstage at a bar, wordlessly enjoying cocktails with another future star, Arlene Francis.

Henry Fonda had married Margaret Sullavan in 1931, but his marriage seemed as much a failure as Bogie's marriage to Mary. The two young actors shared their marital and career woes.

Bogie told Fonda one night, "I can play this aging juvenile just so long. My voice is deeper. My beard is darker. Makeup can hide only so much. If I don't get a good role soon, I think I'll be washed up."

"I don't think so," Fonda said reassuringly. "Once you get the right part, you'll be the biggest thing on Broadway, except for me, of course."

Sullavan showed up backstage one night, spending more time checking out Bogie than Fonda.

"I can't stand a man who's lousy in bed," she told him. "Fonda's a fast starter and a lousy finisher."

Bogie had never heard a woman talk in such graphic terms describing her

husband. She seemed like such a castrating female that he shied away from her. He liked his women a bit more demure. Sullavan was far more aggressive, with a more pronounced streak of malice, than Barbara Stanwyck. Bogie genuinely liked Fonda and would encounter him on and off over the years.

Unhappily married:
Margaret Sullavan *(top photo)*,
and Henry Fonda

Years later, in the early 1960s, when Edward Albee wrote the play, *Who's Afraid of Virginia Woolf?*, he had Fonda in mind when he crafted the character of George, the Milquetoast husband who comprised half of an corrosive marital relationship in an outwardly genteel college town.

Fonda's agent arrogantly rejected the choice role without consulting him. When Albee's play became the hit drama of 1962, Fonda was furious.

Before the 1930s came to an end, Fonda would join the A-list of stars in Hollywood, fathering Jane Fonda and seducing Bette Davis, his co-star in *Jezebel*.

246

It came as a total surprise, a ironic shock really, when Bogie found himself cast with Margaret Sullavan in his next job, a Broadway play called *Chrysalis*, which opened on November 15, 1932, running for twenty-three performances at the Martin Beck Theatre.

Bogie's role was defined as "a patent-leather parlor sheik."

The play was a commercial disaster, even though it was cast with some of the most talented actors on Broadway, including Osgood Perkins, a famous actor of his day. He would become the father of an even more famous actor, Anthony Perkins of *Psycho* fame. He and Bogie shared long talks about the theater.

Bogie also befriended Elia Kazan, another actor in the play. He told Bogie he'd rather be directing the play instead of appearing in it.

Elisha Cook Jr., who would appear years later with Bogie in *The Maltese Falcon* and *The Big Sleep*, was also one of the actors in *Chrysalis*.

Cook told Bogie, "When a director wants to cast a cowardly villain or a weedy neurotic, he calls on me."

On opening night, one critic blasted Bogie, calling him "an oily insect, who gets Sullavan drunk and instructs her, through many long and monotonous kisses, in what he refers to as 'the joys of propinquity.'" Brooks Atkinson found the play "astonishingly insignificant" and claimed, rather enigmatically, that "Bogart plays the wastrel in his usual style."

Mary Orr, an actress/writer whose short story, *The Story of Eve*, would eventually evolve into *All About Eve*, Bette Davis's most famous movie, also appeared in *Chrysalis*.

"While the plumbing was being fixed, I had to share a dressing room with Sullavan," Orr later recalled. "What a bitch! She claimed she was going to seduce Bogie that weekend. Sullavan told me, 'He's become a friend of Henry, and I always make it a point to seduce Henry's friends, especially James Stewart. Of course, in the case of Stewart, Henry does far more seducing of him than I do. My husband tries to make it with women, but he's basically a faggot.'"

One night, Sullavan asked Bogie to walk her home, and he reluctantly escorted her. She complained to him that she'd appeared in four Broadway flops in a row. "But I got great reviews," she hastened to add.

She invited him up for some "bootleg hootch," and he readily accepted. He warned her, however, that the U.S. government was deliberately poisoning some bootleg liquor to frighten the public away from alcohol.

She was angry that Fonda had gone off with James Stewart that night. "I can't be tied down to one man, especially a husband that's inadequate."

Before the night ended, Sullavan seduced Bogie. Shortly thereafter, she told Mary Orr, "Bogie's okay in bed. I mean, I've had better. But he's got the proper technique. He makes sure the woman is satisfied before he pulls off her."

Later, Bogie told Osgood Perkins that Sullavan was "one of the Red Hot Dames of 1932 Broadway."

Bogie's next Broadway play was a romantic comedy set in Paris, *Our Wife*. This time, Rose Hobart was the star, with Bogie playing her lover.

A stunning-looking actress, Hobart evoked Marlene Dietrich in appearance and dress. When on occasion Bogie took her out, fans often came up to her table, asking, "Miss Dietrich, may I have your autograph?" She always obliged, signing, "Love, Marlene."

Born into a family of musicians, Hobart had starred opposite Fredric March in his legendary *Dr. Jekyll and Mr. Hyde* (1932). Although he found her an attractive woman, Bogie did not put any moves on her, because the talk of Broadway was that she was involved in a torrid lesbian romance with a big Broadway star, Eva Le Gallienne.

Regrettably, *Our Wife* opened at Manhattan's Booth Theatre on March 2, 1933, the day President Franklin D. Roosevelt declared an emergency bank holiday. Only ten people showed up, each a member of the press. One newsman wrote that the play "is tamely acted and meagerly directed," a blow against Edward Clarke Lilley who helmed it.

Bogie earned fifty-six dollars the first week of the show. Even though the play lasted for twenty performances, the producers ran out of money and couldn't write any more checks after that.

After that, Bogie played a supporting stage role in an Italian comedy, *The Mask and the Face*, which opened on May 8, 1933. Produced by the Guild Theatre, it ran for forty performances. The farce was by Luigi Chiarelli as translated by W. Somerset Maugham. It had first been performed in 1916.

The play also starred Shirley Booth with whom Bogie had had a brief fling back in 1924 during the Broadway production of *Hell's Bells*. The two former lovers worked well together, never mentioning their previous tryst.

Judith Anderson

During rehearsals for *The Mask and the Face,* Bogie came into conflict with the formidable Australia-born lesbian, Judith Anderson. She would make a name for herself playing cold, imperious, or sinister women. When he met her, Anderson was years away from her Oscar-nominated performance as the lesbian housekeeper, Mrs. Danvers, in *Rebecca* with Joan Fontaine. Exasperated during rehearsals when Bogie had not memorized his dialogue, she made a

248

suggestion, "You should seek another profession, perhaps ladling soup to the poor in the breadlines."

The cast also included Leo G. Carroll, who would later appear with Bogie in both *All Through the Night* and *We're No Angels*.

Critics referred to the *The Mask and the Face* as both "a dubious grave-yard lark" and "a grisly farce." Bogie felt lucky that no reviewer mentioned him.

When he thought he'd never see his mug on a movie screen again, a call came in from director Chester Erskine, who was casting *Midnight* (1934) to be distributed by Universal. There was a small role in it for Bogie, and he gladly accepted when he heard it was to be filmed in New York and not on the West Coast. He was familiar with *Midnight*'s star, Sidney Fox, with whom he and Bette Davis had appeared in *Bad Sister*.

This 80-minute film, which also co-starred Henry Hull, would mark Bogie's first appearance on the screen as a gangster.

In the wake of *Midnight*, Bogie returned to the stage once again for a less-than-memorable role in *Invitation to a Murder*.

This play, a melodrama in three acts by Rufus King, opened on May 17, 1934 at Broadway's Masque Theatre, running for only thirty-seven performances.

Bogie played Horatio Channing, a member of a southern California family whose fortune was created by piracy. It was an old-fashioned mystery melodrama, featuring "the usual suspects"—trapdoors, ghosts, and all the other clichés. Critic Pollyanna Garland wrote, "Humphrey Bogart Humphrey-Bogart's his way through the role." The New York *Post* referred to it as "high-voltage trash."

This was Bogie's first stage interpreta-tion of a villain, a part he later referred to as "a gruesome little mishap."

In this murder mystery, Gale Sondergaard was the star, with support from Jane Seymour and veteran character actor Walter Abel.

Bogie admired Sondergaard, who would go on to a Hollywood career as one of the era's most formidable bad women. She became the first winner in the newly estab-lished Best Supporting Actress category in the lavish costume picture, *Anthony Adverse* (1936). Her promising career was later derailed when she became one of filmdom's

Sidney Fox with
Humphrey Bogart in
Midnight (1934)

249

blacklist victims during the Red Scare of the Joseph McCarthy era.

Even though Bogie did not impress the critics in this play, he did attract the attention of Arthur Hopkins, the film's producer and director. A year later, when it came time to cast *The Petrified Forest*, Hopkins would remember Bogie's performance in this otherwise forgotten play.

***

When Bogie couldn't find work as an actor, he was offered a job as a chess player at the sleazy Sportsland on Sixth Avenue in Manhattan's West Forties. He would sit in the window, taking on any member of the public who wanted to challenge him, for a fee of fifty cents, to a game of chess.

When he saved up enough money, he would go over to the "21" for a drink. The owners liked him and let him run up a big tab, which he could not pay until he was cast on stage in *The Petrified Forest* in 1935.

In September of 1934, Mary Philips appeared at the Sportsland Arcade to interrupt Bogie's chess game. She ran up to him. Her message was brief. "Belmont is dying."

At the hospital, Bogie stayed in the same room with Dr. Bogart, watching his life wane. He lived for another forty-eight hours, dying in his son's arms at Manhattan's Hospital for the Ruptured and Crippled on September 8, 1934, at the age of 67.

Belmont expressed no particularly articulate last words. He was unable to speak. However, he did seem to hear his son's last words to him. "I love you, Father." Bogie would tell Mary, "I should have told him that years ago, but I never could."

There was no one to accompany Bogie to Fresh Pond Crematory in Long Island. Mary was auditioning for a Broadway show, and Maud made it clear that she found the idea of cremation, as requested by her husband, "quite ghastly."

After his father was buried, Bogie returned to Maud's apartment. She was going through his papers. "He left $10,000 in debts and $35,000 in uncollected doctor's fees."

She handed him his father's old-fashioned ruby ring. He would wear it until his death, and it can be seen in his films over the years. He told Maud that as a point of honor, he would work to pay off the entire $10,000.

"Then I suggest you find some more profitable line of work than the stage and or B-list movies that no one wants to see."

***

After a string of failures, with a career going nowhere, the "chess player, sometimes actor," as he called himself, had a change of luck. He was plucked from oblivion. Had fortune not shone on him—*finally*—he'd have joined the hundreds of actors, male and female, who enjoyed brief fame in the Silents or had their fifteen minutes of fame in the Talkies during the 30s.

"I would have become a footnote in the history of the theater or the movies," he said. "I would make it as a footnote if that history were summed up in ten volumes. If only one volume, I would have been such an insignificant flea, I would not even have made it as a footnote."

When its producer and director Arthur Hopkins asked Bogie to audition for the coveted role of Duke Mantee in *The Petrified Forest*, Bogie renewed his friendship with Robert Sherwood, who wrote the play. Sherwood actually didn't want him to play Duke, preferring instead that he be cast in another role. Hopkins stood his ground, however.

At Bogie's audition sat Leslie Howard, the English actor, who was to become his friend. Howard agreed with Hopkins. Bogie would be perfect for the part.

After the audition, Sherwood changed his point of view. In *The Worlds of Robert E. Sherwood*, John Mason Brown wrote, "He thought of more than Bogart's masculinity. He thought of his driven power. His anguished eyes, dark eyes, the puffs of pain beneath them, and the dangerous despair which lined his face."

The character of Duke Mantee was inspired mainly by bank robber John Dillinger. Bogie actually resembled the real-life Dillinger.

Cast as an escaped convict, Bogie threw himself into the role and tried to live up to Sherwood's description of the character. "He is well built but stoop shouldered, with a vaguely thoughtful, saturnine face. He is about thirty-five and, if he hadn't elected to take up banditry, he might have been a fine left-fielder. He is unmistakably doomed."

During the course of the play, Duke holds its main characters hostage, including Leslie Howard, who played Squier, the romantic intellectual who believes that "my ilk" is becoming as ossified as the petrified forest in the Arizona Desert. Hostages are held at the Black Mesa Bar-B-Q.

Preview audiences in Hartford gasped at their view of the "new" Bogart. He was no longer a sprig with a tennis racket, but a gangster with a prison pallor and a three-day growth of beard.

Opening on Broadway at the Broadhurst Theater on January 7, 1935, *The Petrified Forest* starred Leslie Howard and Peggy Conklin, who portrayed Gabrielle Maple, the waitress heroine.

At last, praise came from Brooks Atkinson of *The New York Times*, who asserted that Bogie "does the best work of his career as the motorized gorilla."

In a strange coincidence, Kenneth MacKenna had migrated back to New York to pursue his own luck on Broadway. Ironically, he was eventually hired as Leslie Howard's understudy in the Broadway version of *The Petrified Forest*.

Bogie's marriage to Mary Philips continued dysfunctionally, as each pursued his or her respective career in the theater. It was increasingly obvious that their link was held together by a not very sticky glue.

One late afternoon, Bogie told Mary that he was going to stay in the Broadway area for the three hours leading up to the show and wouldn't return home until after curtain.

But when he discovered that he'd either lost or misplaced his wallet, he called her to see if it were left in the apartment. There was no answer, so he made his way back to their apartment. On the floor of the living room, Kenneth was screwing his wife.

Bogie took one look at the coupling and then shouted into the living room. "Carry on, guys. Don't let me stop you." Slamming the door on his way out, he headed back to the theater.

At the theater, he reported the details of the seduction scene he'd just witnessed to Leslie Howard.

Right before the curtain went up that night on *The Petrified Forest*, Bogie received devastating news.

On September 26, 1935, his long-time best friend, Bill Brady Jr., had burned alive while drunk in his country cabin at Colts Neck, New Jersey when the building caught on fire. Ironically, Bogie had been invited to spend that weekend with Bill in his bungalow. "I could have been burned to death along with Bill," he said.

Unusual for him, Bogie burst into hysterical sobs. Howard was going to ask his understudy to go on in Bogie's place. But he pulled himself together in time to face the audience. Howard later asserted that "Bogart gave the best performance of his career."

At Bill's funeral, Bogie stood next to his mentor and long-time friend, Bill Brady Sr. He was now seventy-one years old. The two men embraced, as both of them sobbed for their loss.

Mrs. Brady came up and embraced Bogie. Before leaving that day. Mr. Brady turned to Bogie. "I always knew you'd be a great actor. I was the first to believe in you. I wish to see you return to Hollywood and make your greatest films."

Mr. Brady's wish came true. He sat through a showing of *Casablanca* three times. He saw each and every film Bogie made until 1950, when he died at the age of eighty-six.

With all the rave notices the Broadway version of *The Petrified Forest* received, it was only natural for Hollywood to take notice. Agents for Warner Brothers purchased film rights for the play, with the contractual obligation to cast Leslie Howard in the lead.

In spite of the rave notices generated by his performances in the play, Bogie was not rewarded with a firm contract to play Duke Mantee in the film. Instead, Warner Brothers took an "option" on his services, paying him a small fee to either cast him or not cast him, according to their perceptions and whims, into the movie role. "I was left dangling in the wind," Bogie later said. "Am I getting the part or not?" he kept asking Mary. "According to this god damn option deal," Mary told him, "they can drop you at the last minute and bring in George Raft or Edward G. Robinson. Your option deal means shit."

The play could have run for at least another three or four months but Howard had grown tired of the part. He also nixed a road tour, feeling that an extension might hurt the eventual box office receipts of the movie. Thanks to his role as one of the play's co-producers, along with Gilbert Miller, Howard had such power, and he ordered that the final curtain come down after 181 performances.

During the run of *The Petrified Forest*, Bogie had paid off all of Belmont's debts, and still had two thousand dollars left in the bank.

Since he wanted to save his bankroll, he looked for a job in summer stock. Based on the reputation he'd built on Broadway, he was hired after only two weeks' search, signing a commitment for a series of performances with Will Seabury's Repertory Theatre Company in Skowhegan, Maine.

***

In Skowhegan, in 1935, it was understood that he would appear that summer as a character within three separate plays.

The first was entitled *The Stag at Bay*, a cloak-and-dagger melodrama about the theft of a formula for poison gas. In it he also starred with Keenan Wynn, whom he would often encounter in later years in Hollywood. Keenen was usually seen in the company of Hollywood star Van Johnson, his long-time lover.

Ceiling Zero came next. A drama by Frank Wead, it was said to be the first play ever produced revolving around the life of a commercial airport as its theme. It had starred Osgood Perkins when it was first produced on Broadway in 1935. Bogie's appearance in this summer stock production went unnoticed. But the Wead drama had legs. Warner Brothers optioned it for its 1936 film, also called *Ceiling Zero*, but Bogie wasn't offered any role, the honors going to James Cagney and Pat O'Brien. Just a few years later, in 1941, Warners remade it. Re-titled *International Squadron*, the lead went to the up-and-coming Ronald Reagan.

For his *adieu* to summer stock and to the stage in general, Bogie found himself cast opposite the notorious fan dancer, Sally Rand, in *Rain*. Far more famous as a coyly erotic dancer than as an actress, Sally was noted for her flirtatious ostrich feather dance and her balloon bubble dance.

It was Cecil B. DeMille who had assigned her the name "Sally Rand" years before, back when the now-aging star had first appeared in silent films. DeMille took what became her surname from the Rand McNally Atlas.

Rand became infamous throughout America thanks to the 1933 Chicago World's Fair, an event also entitled *Century of Progress*. She was arrested four times in the course of a single day, charged with "indecent exposure" while imitating a provocatively dressed impersonation of Lady Godiva riding a white horse down the streets of the city.

When she met Bogie, he found her a "stunner," as he later told his pals at Tony's in New York. At the time she was described as a "diminutive (5' 1") damsel with a knockout (35-22-35) figure."

She told Bogie she was tired of burlesque and that "the stage is my destiny."

"It's my destiny, too, when I can find a job that pays at least fifty bucks a week."

Rand had recently agreed to play W. Somerset Maugham's prostitute, Sadie Thompson, in his play *Rain*. A 1928 silent film entitled *Sadie Thompson* had starred Gloria Swanson. In 1935, Tallulah Bankhead had brought the character to Broadway in a revival.

Actually *Rain* was first seen on Broadway in 1922, starring the legendary Jeanne Eagels in a box office success. June Havoc, sister of Gypsy Rose Lee, the stripper, starred in a 1944 Broadway musical, *Sadie Thompson*. In 1932, Joan Crawford appeared in the film version. In 1953 *Rain* would be taken out of mothballs, the character interpreted once again by Rita Hayworth in the film *Miss Sadie Thompson*.

What happened that summer between Bogie and Rand remains a mystery. When he returned to New York, Bogie told his cronies that he had seduced her. "She was my steady piece up in Maine." Later, Rand denied that she'd had an affair with him. Simultaneously, however, she claimed that the impotent Paul Bern, husband of Jean Harlow, was "great in bed." So much for her honesty in reporting.

As far as it's known, there has been only one printed romantic link between Bogie and Rand. A long-ago article claimed, "After the curtain went down on *Rain*, the real action began with the young actor Humphrey Bogart and the aging Sally Rand, the famous fan dancer."

Even that was wrong. Bogie was born in 1899, Rand in 1904.

***

After his immersion in Maine's world of summer stock, Bogie returned to New York City and Mary. She did not ask him what he'd done for private pleasures during his absence. And he chose not to grill her either.

Despite his many previous successes on Broadway the previous season, there were no immediate job offerings. On the slim chance that Jack Warner might take up his option and cast him as Duke Mantee, Bogie decided to take the train to the West Coast.

He asked Mary to go with him. She adamantly refused, devoting her attention instead to starring in a Broadway play, *A Touch of Brimstone*. "My career's about to take off—it's getting hotter and hotter," she told him. "What would I do in Hollywood? Sit around for three weeks waiting for you to finish the shoot? That is, if you even get the role."

Bogie decided to take the train by himself. Incidentally, Mary's co-star was none other than Roland Young. Still sexually involved with Kenneth, she resumed her affair with Young—and "his cheating heart," as she put it.

As Bogie entered the Garden of Allah Hotel in Hollywood, he picked up a copy of *Variety*. Later, by the pool, he read that Edward G. Robinson, a Warner Brothers contract player, had been signed to play Duke Mantee in the film version of *The Petrified Forest*.

Bogie was crestfallen and got horribly drunk that night. Leslie Howard had been vacationing in Scotland when he received a cable from Bogie. "Robinson set to play Duke Mantee. Help me!"

Immediately Howard notified Warner Brothers that if Bogie could not retain the role, that he was also pulling out of the cast. Jack Warner caved in.

Even with Howard as his champion, Bogie still had to get involved in more than a dozen screen tests before he was finally signed to the part.

Bogie was given only a three-week contract at $750 per week. This was the same wage he'd been paid in 1932. Bette Davis agreed to get involved with the film for $9,000, Howard taking in $62,500.

On the first day of shooting, Bogie once again encountered Bette Davis, and once again, previous intimacies seemed to have been forgotten, at least by her.

Smoking a cigarette, she came right up to him and didn't welcome him to the studio. "I was rather looking forward to working with Eddie," she said, referring, of course, to Edward G. Robinson. "I think he would have made a great Duke Mantee."

"What am I?" he asked. "Chopped liver?"

"The trouble with you, Bogart, is that you cannot portray menace on the screen," she said, blowing smoke in his face.

"Since I last saw you, I've learned menace."

She looked at him skeptically. "That's good," she said in a voice already famous to movie audiences.

She told Bogie, "Leslie and I really didn't get along when we made *Of Human Bondage* (1934). But now he's very affectionate. I can show you my arms and shoulders." She pulled back her dress to reveal bite marks across her skin. "At times I think he's a dog. Did you know that he actually enjoys biting women?"

"As you well know, I prefer to plow into them instead."

"No, I don't know that," she said with an imperial air. "You see, I've forgotten all about that."

Bogart as Duke Mantee
in *The Petrified Forest*

Her acknowledgment of these bites and nibbles was an odd admission from Bette. She told several friends, "Did you know that Leslie screwed every female star on every movie he was ever in, with the exception of me? I told him that I was not going to be plastered on the end of a list of his conquests." Of course, what Bette sometimes said and what she did were two different things.

The director of *The Petrified Forest* was Archie Mayo, who on film more or less shot the play as it had been presented on Broadway. He detested "that limey bastard," Leslie Howard, but had praise for Bogie.

With Bette Davis, Mayo established an uneasy truce, having directed her in *Bordertown* in 1935. "I believe in giving that bitch wide berth," Mayo told Bogie.

Ironically, both Bogie and Mayo would work together again on the film, *They Drive by Night,* in 1940, a movie that was inspired by Davis' *Bordertown.*

"Davis and Howard had egos bigger than their talents," he said. "Actually, Bogie was the only actor in a starring part in the film that did what I asked him to do. Later, of course, he became an S.O.B."

256

Mayo said, "Bette seemed pissed off throughout the movie. She constantly complained that she was playing some little field mouse while Howard and Bogie were 'eating up the scenery.' She said she longed for a strong part like the one she'd played in *Of Human Bondage* with Leslie Howard."

At the end of the shoot, Bogie gave Howard his warmest embrace, thanking him for all his support. The two actors agreed to "become friends for life," although for Howard, that would be defined as only a few short years to come.

Before saying goodbye to Leslie Howard on the set of *The Petrified Forest*, Bogie and his mentor had made a vow. Bogie agreed to follow Howard's precedent and seduce each of his upcoming leading ladies. What he didn't know was that he'd occasionally be cast opposite a lesbian. These actresses were certainly beautiful and desirable, but many of them preferred not to share their charms with men.

Bogie would later name his second child Leslie in honor of Howard, who had given him his first big break. A baby daughter was born to Bogie and his fourth wife, Lauren Bacall, on August 23, 1952. *Time* magazine reported that the six-pound, five-ounce baby girl was a boy. But such was not the case.

Movie critics and fellow stars agreed that no man in the history of movies had turned the act of smoking a cigarette into such high drama. The juvenile sprig had become a Hollywood tough guy.

In spite of rave reviews, Jack Warner wasn't all that impressed. He didn't think Bogie had broad appeal.

At the time, Warner Brothers was in the throes of releasing a wave of

The Petrified Forest

(top photo) Leslie Howard kisses Bette Davis
(bottom photo) Bogart frisks Leslie Howard

gangster films, and the studio decided that Bogie would be in a lot of them. There were, in fact, some twenty-nine films released in the five-year span between *The Petrified Forest* (1936), and *High Sierra (*1941). Often he played a jailbird. He died in eight of them, once in an electric chair and once by means of a hangman's noose.

Nine days after shooting on *Petrified Forest* ended in 1936, Jack Warner signed a forty-week contract with Bogie for $550 per week. In signing the contract, Bogie agreed not to "offend the community or ridicule public morals or decency."

The contract contained a complicated series of options, with the understanding that if all of them were activated before the end of 1941, Bogie conceivably could make as much as $1,750 a week.

The moment he signed the contract, Bogie became a tenant along what the studio referred to as "Murderer's Row." Fellow residents included Edward G. Robinson, James Cagney, George Raft, Paul Muni, and John Garfield.

Eventually, Bogie became beloved by the press because he was one of the few actors in Hollywood who spoke what he felt. "Everybody else out here is hiding behind some fake image," he said. "Nobody likes me on sight. There must be something about the tone of my voice, or this arrogant face—something that antagonizes everybody. I can't even get into a mild discussion that doesn't turn into an argument."

Meanwhile, Mary's star as a Broadway actress had dimmed, her latest play not attracting the audience that its backers had anticipated. After it closed after ninety-six performances, there were no more offers. She accepted her husband's invitation to take the train to Los Angeles.

Once there, she spent Christmas of 1935 at the Château Elysée, where they celebrated Bogie's birthday. Her first question upon arrival was, "Which stars have you fucked?"

"No one! I've been celibate. How about you?"

"Just the usual suspects," she said frankly. By that, he knew that she meant Roland Young and Kenneth MacKenna.

Bogie seemed to want to assert his manhood now that he was a contract player, and she was an out-of-work actress. Before, he'd been married to an actress more famous than himself. After *The Petrified Forest* opened to big box office, "I started to clank my balls," he told Spencer Tracy.

A few weeks later, Mary received an offer to return to Broadway to star in *The Postman Always Rings Twice*, adapted from the James M. Cain novel. The property was considered too hot, too steamy for Hollywood. Later it would become one of Lana Turner's most sensational movies. Mary had been cast opposite Richard Barthelmess, the silent screen star who would be making his Broadway debut.

258

Eager to "return to glory," as she put it, she told her husband that she could never settle down, become a housewife, and have children. "I'm afraid, dear, that if that is what you want, you should not have married a Broadway star."

Long after *The Petrified Forest* was distributed and screened around the world, the drama still had "legs." Bogie himself would appear in future manifestations of this play.

In years to come, Bogie contracted to perform in a radio version of *The Petrified Forest*. Produced by the Screen Guild Theater, it was aired on January 7, 1940, starring himself alongside Joan Bennett and Tyrone Power.

The Petrified Forest would also be remade in 1944 as a retitled film called *Escape in the Desert*. This was a second-rate movie, with Philip Dorn in the Leslie Howard role. The gangster role of Bogie was reconfigured into that of an escaped Nazi POW, with Helmut Dantine taking the part.

In a touch of irony, *The Petrified Forest* would be performed again on live television in 1955, with a cast of Bogie and Henry Fonda. The Bette Davis role was played by a young actress named Lauren Bacall.

***

When Hollywood director William McGann called Bogie to tell him that he had been cast as the lead in a 1936 film *Two Against the World,* he was at first delighted. But delight turned to disappointment when he learned that he was actually making a B picture reprise of a five-year-old A-list film, Edward G. Robinson's *Five Star Final,* first released in 1931.

The original 1931 version of *Five Star Final* had been based on a play by Louis Weitzenkorn. But in Bogie's recycled and "watered down" version, scripter Michael Jacoby wrote a much weaker role for Bogie, a role utterly lacking any of Robinson's "fire" from the the original film The setting was switched as well: What had been a newspaper office in the original, became a radio station in Bogie's ver-

Two Against the World (1936)

(lower left photo) our hero
(lower right photo) Beverly Roberts
with our hero

259

sion. As part of the plot motivation, the radio station is hell bent on increasing the number of its listeners by any means it can conjure. Bogie never liked his role.

After Bogie rehearsed his first scene under the scrutiny of director McGann, he was not impressed. "The fucker spent more time watching the clock than in directing me."

Even though the director was aware of his schedule's time restraints, it was still not enough to appease top management.

Hal Wallis was the studio's chief honcho, but Bogie's boss was Bryan Foy, "The Keeper of the Bs," as he was known on the Warners lot. Bryan was the eldest son of vaudeville star Eddie Foy, and he had appeared on stage with his father as one of "The Seven Little Foys." From 1924 to 1963, he produced 214 films, one of which was the distinguished *Guadalcanal Diary* in 1943.

The first time Bogie met Foy, he rushed onto the set accusing McGann of running overtime and over budget. McGann protested that he had forty more pages to shoot. Foy grabbed the shooting script from him and, without reading it, ripped out twenty pages. Before storming off the set, he said, "Now bring this stinker in on time . . . or else!"

That's why *Two Against the World* ran for only sixty-four minutes.

Later, while analyzing that period of his life, Bogie claimed that in a lot of films during the late 1930s, "I was assigned one of two different types of leading ladies—either a star who'd arrived in Hollywood via the casting couch, or else a card-carrying lesbian."

When he met Beverly Roberts, his *Two Against the World* co-star from the latter of those two categories, he immediately recognized her as "one of the boys," from the latter of those two categories. Bogie liked this "tough-talking broad."

Roberts had been spotted singing in a New York City nightclub by a Warner Brothers talent agent and sent to Hollywood to appear with Al Jolson in the 1936 film, *The Singing Kid,* which was followed by her star part with Bogie.

She was signed on at Warner Brothers the same day Errol Flynn became a member of the troupe. Flynn met her that day and also became friends with her. Flynn later told Bogie, "Beverly and I have a lot in common. We both know how to take care of a woman."

Roberts became known for playing "tough-edged dames" on the Warner lot, mainly potboilers. In one film she played it particularly butch during her portrayal of a woman who's running a lumber camp. In another movie, she operated a fleet of buses. "I was women's lib before the term was invented," she said.

Later, Bogie asserted that "Beverly Roberts had more *cojones* than I did."

When Roberts met actress Wynne Gibson during their filming of the 1938 feature film, *Flirting with Fate*, she met "the love of my life," as she told Bogie. She meant that.

Gibson herself was one of the "lovelies" who appeared in the 1930s, making mainly B movies between 1929 and 1956. Roberts and Gibson would live together until Gibson's death in 1987.

Also cast in *Two Against the World* was an actor named Carlyle Moore, Jr. Bogie in the future would appear with the same actor in both *Bullets or Ballots* and in *China Clipper.*

"The last time I encountered this Moore kid, sometime in the late 1930s, all he could talk about was 'Ronald Reagan, Ronald Reagan, Ronald Reagan—he's the handsomest man in Hollywood. He's got a great physique, and he's not stuck up at all. He's the nicest guy.' I let him blabber on. Moore did end up in Reagan's *Knute Rockne—All American*. On Moore's part, I think it was more than puppy love. Good luck to that kid if he thought he was going to get Reagan out of his pants."

When *Two Against the World* was released, none of the cast, including Bogie himself, was pleased with the way the film had been ruthlessly shortened. Beverly Roberts and Carlyle Moore Jr. were among those who complained about how their roles had been cut.

Two Against the World was such a bad picture that Jack Warner delayed its release for months. "We'll release it one day when every newspaper in America is on strike," the studio chief said. "That way, no one will review it."

When the film was finally released, critics slammed it. For television, the movie was more temptingly re-titled *One Fatal Hour.* Today, *Two Against the World* is recommended "Only for diehard Bogie fans."

***

As author Jeffrey Meyers put it, Bogie in the mid-Thirties began a new phase of his career where he'd be "slapped, muddied, shaken, submerged and drenched; bitten, choked, cut, thrown, singed and burned."

He reported early to work to a studio, Warner Brothers, that evoked a prison, with tough security guards at the gate. When he first arrived, he didn't even own a car, so he showed up at the gate in a taxi.

His packed lunch was always the same every day—two cheese and tomato sandwiches, one hard-boiled egg, and a bottle of beer which he had to drink warm.

Unlike plush Metro-Goldwyn-Mayer, Warner Brothers was cost-conscious. In his first year under contract, Bogie would make four films back to back for release in 1936. Each was a B picture, with a minor director. Shooting schedules were tight, sometimes with as little as three weeks allotted.

Bogie often regretted that he'd arrived in Hollywood after the self-regulating Production Code came into effect on July 15, 1934. Strictly forbidden was subject matter which included "profanity, nudity, drug trafficking, sex perversion, white slavery, miscegenation, sex hygiene and venereal diseases, scenes of actual childbirth, children's sex organs, ridicule of the clergy, and offenses against a nation, race, or creed."

Jack Warner was terribly disappointed with Bogie's performance in *Two Against the World,* but decided to give him another chance since he already had him under contract. "Cast him in *Bullets or Ballots,*" he ordered Bryan Foy. "Make Edward G. Robinson the star and give Bogart fourth billing. That way, no one will notice the fucker. Throw in Joan Blondell for the floozy sex appeal."

Bullets or Ballots marked the first picture Bogie made with Robinson, but it was the fourth picture in which he was cast opposite Joan.

Joan Blondell had heard that this hardboiled drama had encountered problems with the Production Code. Joseph Breen, the censor, sent Jack Warner a warning, suggesting that *Bullets or Ballots* was the kind of movie we had "agreed not to make."

Joan introduced Bogie to their director, William Keighley, who had helmed her in *Penny Arcade.* This Philadelphian in *Bullets or Ballots* created a role model of the kind of fast-paced, tightly made film of

Cast members of *Bullets or Ballots*
(top to bottom)

Joan Blondell,
Edward G. Robinson with Bogart,
and Barton MacLane

262

which Warners would specialize in the next few years.

Bogie never liked phonies, and he was put off by what he viewed as the director's "continental manners," perhaps acquired during his tenure on Broadway in the early 20s.

Whenever his name came up in the future, Bogie would mock him, mainly when he cast James Cagney as the lead in the Technicolor epic, *The Adventures of Robin Hood* (1938). Of course, Keighley came to his senses and later cast Errol Flynn instead. Keightly himself was replaced by Michael Curtiz when Robin Hood, Warner's most expensive film of all time fell behind in production.

Bullets or Ballots marked the first of several films Bogie would shoot with Barton MacLane, a native of South Carolina. When directors wanted a furrow-browed tough guy, MacLane was on call. Cameras would move in on his squinty eyes and tightly clamped mouth. He seemed to pose a menace to whomever he encountered.

MacLane's character was modeled on Dutch Schultz, the notorious gangster and main patron of Polly Adler, America's most famous madam.

One afternoon between filming, on a particularly hot day, MacLane went to his dressing room and brought back a violin, and played it for Joan and Bogie.

"Not bad, not bad at all," Bogie said. "For my next party, I'll hire you for a sawbuck."

Bogie was cast as "Bugs" Fenner a mobster. Before the film ends, he will kill a crusader against vice; MacLane's character, and finally Johnny Blake (Robinson). In the final reel, Robinson, wounded by Bogie, finally guns him down.

When Bogie came up to greet Robinson, the shorter man studied him skeptically. Before their careers were over, they would make five films together, with Bogie eventually assuming the lead in *Key Largo* (1948). "I keep reading that you created the movie gangster. I guess you didn't see *Little Caesar*. I do believe that I have become the prototypical movie mobster, and let's get that straight. Did you hear my dying line?"

To Bogie's astonishment, he delivered it again. "Mother of Mercy, is this the end of Roco Bandello?"

Born in Bucharest, Rumania, Robinson was no gangster, but a Renaissance man of great cultivation, a devotee of art and music. He would later collect some $3 million worth of art. At first he didn't want to go to Hollywood, holding movies in disdain, preferring the stage. But after he hit the jackpot as the vicious gang leader in *Little Caesar*, he thought he could put up with all those orange and palm trees after all.

In spite of his charm, Bogie remained leery of him. "Let's face it:

Robinson is the guy to beat."

This good, tough gangster film more or less holds up today. In it, Robinson leaves the police force to crack a city-wide mob run by MacLane.

On April 17, 1939, Bogie signed with the Lux Radio Theater to broadcast a one-hour radio play of *Bullets or Ballots*. Both Robinson and Bogie reprised their roles, but Mary Astor stood in for Joan Blondell.

After his watching himself in his latest film, Bogie said, "I owe it all to Clark Gable with those big ears. Dames go crazy over him. He paved the way for all of us with ugly mugs—Robinson, James Cagney, and my dear friend Spencer Tracy."

***

With Mary still in New York, Bogie resumed his on-again, off-again affair with Joan. She told him she was tired of these dumb, wise-cracking roles and wanted to make it in drama. He worked closely with her and helped her through her scenes. She played a shady Harlem nightclub owner and gave an admirable performance when stacked against Bogie and Robinson.

When Bogie saw how Joan's household was being run, he said, "Hot damn, woman. You've become a movie star at last. Do you need someone to look after your fan mail?"

"Joan was at the peak of her beauty, during the making of this film," Bogie said. "In her wardrobe, she became a fucking garden of flowers. I didn't know whether to water her or not. In spite of Dick Powell beating down her door, she threw me a few mercy fucks so I wouldn't be so tense."

***

After *Bullets or Ballots,* Bogie was cast as the fourth lead in *China Clipper,* a 1936 release from Warners directed by Ray Enright. Bogie played Hap Stuart, a daredevil pilot and wartime buddy of Pat O'Brien, who had been cast as the lead. The screenplay by Frank Wead focused on the creation of the famous *China Clipper,* the plane that made the first passenger run from San Francisco to the Orient. The plot was inspired by Eddie Rickenbacker, the World War I aviation hero who went into the commercial flying business, a career move evocative of Howard Hughes.

Once again, Bogie was cast with Beverly Roberts, who played the female lead.

"We spent a lot of time in my dressing room having a drink," he said. "Beverly could hold her liquor as well as I could. I told her that I hope in the future we wouldn't compete for the same dames."

Ross Alexander and Marie Wilson rounded out the cast. Also appearing in the movie was Wayne Morris, who would go on to greater glory, if that was what it could be called. In *China Clipper*, he had only a bit part.

The son of Irish immigrants, with an ugly mug, O'Brien was an unlikely candidate to become a leading movie star in the 1930s. A friend of both James Cagney and Spencer Tracy, he never bonded as well with Bogie, although they worked together fairly smoothly.

Bogie called him "Hollywood's walking embodiment of Ireland." He once studied to become a Roman Catholic priest, but gave that up, although he often performed as "Father This" or "Father That" in films. If not a priest, he wore a cop's badge in movies. Politically, O'Brien and Bogie were oceans apart. Because of his extreme Right Wing views, Bogie called him "a near Nazi."

In the role of Dave Logan, Barton MacLane played a character inspired by Charles Lindbergh's conquest of the Atlantic on his history-making flight to Paris. In the movie, Logan plans a trans-Pacific airline.

In her usual "Dumb Dora" role, Marie Wilson pursued Ross Alexander. Bogie wasn't living up to Leslie Howard's challenge of seducing all his leading ladies. He found the well-stacked Wilson a sexy number with her ultra-blonde locks, her generous mouth, and her great big eyes.

Wilson had appeared in *Satan Met a Lady* (1936), starring Bette Davis. This was the second film adaptation of the detective novel, *The Maltese Falcon*. Davis would later say, "Marilyn Monroe's on-screen persona was a complete rip-off of Marie Wilson." Wilson would go on to gain national prominence with her hit interpretation of *My Friend Irma* on radio, TV, and film.

Wilson only looked innocent on the screen. In private she wasn't adverse to going to bed with a nice-looking man. Bogie took her out on two dates,

(top photo) Bogie
(bottom photo) Pat O'Brien

265

and perhaps he scored. He obviously told Leslie Howard, but didn't share much information with any of his pals.

***

At long last Bogie came face to face with Ross Alexander, a young actor whose reputation had preceded him. Bogie already resented him for getting star billing over him as the third lead.

Standing 6' 1", he was hailed as the most promising young player at Warner Brothers. With his wavy brown hair and penetrating eyes, the Brooklyn-born actor seemed ideal for those romantic juvenile roles.

Although he'd never met Alexander, he was well known on Broadway. He was what Bogie called a "star fucker" and had seduced several famous actors or directors. He'd been the kept boy of a series of wealthy men, including the renowned John Golden, age 54, producer, playwright, actor, and songwriter.

Alexander was tormented about his homosexuality and tried to conceal it by marrying or else pursuing female stars. His marriage to Aleta Friele in 1934 had ended disastrously. In 1935, despondent over her marriage and career as an actress, she killed herself with a .22 rifle outside the Hollywood home she shared with her husband.

Alexander was also known to many of Bogie's friends or acquaintances, notably Henry Fonda. In fact, other than James Stewart, Alexander was Fonda's best friend. The two actors had met when performing in summer stock together, and on and off had lived together. On the Warners lot, the rumor was that they had been lovers.

It was said that Alexander had caught Fonda on the rebound while still carrying a torch for his former wife, Margaret Sullavan. "I'll always be grateful to Ross Alexander," Fonda said. "He restored my confidence in myself as a man after Margaret de-balled me."

Ross Alexander

"Ideal for those romantic juvenile roles"

Alexander was often photographed with Errol Flynn and his wife, Lili Damita, at swank Tinseltown soirees. The Flynn/Alexander affair intensified when Alexander was cast in Flynn's film, *Captain Blood*.

When Bette Davis heard that Bogie had been cast with Alexander in *China Clipper*, she called Bogie and reported an alarming story.

According to Davis, Alexander had developed an obsession about her. Although married, he

266

kept bombarding her with love letters. "He's not really in love with me," Davis said. "I heard he really wants both of us to divorce our spouses and marry each other. I am told he thinks I'm going to become queen of the Warners lot, and that I'll let him be my co-star in all my future movies."

"Jack Warner may have something to say about that," Bogie told her.

To confirm what Davis had said, Alexander asked Bogie to use his friendship with Davis to advance the actor's cause. "I desperately want to get cast in her next movie," he said. "We'll have a love scene together. Once I get her in my arms, I know she'll respond like a wildcat."

"Probably so," Bogie said. "Claws and all. That's Bette."

Every day a love letter was slipped under Bette's door. She didn't bother reading them, tossing them in the wastepaper basket.

When Davis was filming *Satan Met a Lady*, her husband, Ham Nelson, arrived at the studio for a rare visit. Attached to the door to her dressing room was one of Alexander's latest letters to Davis. It was addressed in large letters "TO MY BELOVED ONE, BETTE." Nelson ripped it off the door, opened it, and read it.

Storming into his wife's dressing room, Nelson confronted Davis, accusing her of having an affair with the young actor.

"That queer is having pipe dreams," Davis shouted at her husband. When she was called before the cameras, Nelson went to find Alexander, discovering him in the studio men's room, where he attacked him, slugging him repeatedly.

In spite of that, Alexander with a black eye did not stop writing love letters to Davis, posting one the very next day.

On the set of *China Clipper*, Bogie met a Boston-born actress, the dark-haired, rather beautiful Anne Nagel. He decided to pursue her only to find that his major competition was Alexander himself. Privately, Bogie confronted him. "What's between this Nagel dame and you?" he asked.

"Anne and I are falling in love, and I plan to marry her," Alexander said.

"What about Bette? Bogie asked. "I thought you were in love with her."

"You of all people should know that it's possible to love two women at the same time,"

Marie Wilson *(left)* with **Anne Nagel**

267

Alexander said. "If Bette responds to my love letters and divorces that monster, Ham Nelson, I will get a divorce from Anne, assuming we go through with the marriage."

"That makes perfect sense to me," Bogie said before walking away to have a drink with Pat O'Brien in his dressing room. "Losing a gal to a bonafide queer," Bogie told O'Brien. "That doesn't say much for me as a man. Of course, Ross is sorta cute. If I get desperate one night, I might ask him to give me a blow-job."

"You're kidding, of course," O'Brien said.

"That's me. Bogart the kidder."

Right after the release of the film, Nagel and Ross were married. Even so, he continued to write those love letters to Davis. His wife discovered some unfinished letters under his desk blotter. He told her, "I can't help myself."

Around Christmastime in 1936, Alexander picked up a handsome male hitchhiker and had a sexual encounter with him. Recognizing him from the movies, the hobo threatened to blackmail him if he weren't given $10,000.

Alexander didn't have the money but persuaded producer Bryan Foy to secure that amount from Warner Brothers. Alexander agreed to pay it back by having the studio deduct it from his future salary.

Growing increasingly despondent, Alexander on January 2, 1937, picked up the same .22 pistol that his former wife, Alete Friele, had used to commit suicide. He went to his barn and shot himself in the temple.

Warners reacted quickly to Alexander's death and within a few weeks had signed another young actor to a seven-year contract. This former sports announcer was to be cast in the roles that the studio had intended for Alexander.

On the studio lot one day, Bogie was introduced to this affable newcomer who spoke in the same clear baritone that evoked Alexander's voice.

"So, you're the new kid on the block," Bogie said. "Welcome to the prison."

"Hi," the young man said, extending his hand. "I'm Ronald Reagan."

"I'm sure we'll be co-starring together very soon," Bogie said.

He never pretended to be a prophet, but in this case he was right.

Chapter Six

Beginning in the mid-1930s, Bogie would establish his professional movie home at Warner Brothers, with whom he'd be associated for most of the rest of his life. He stayed with the studio until the late 1940s. Even after he formed his own production company, Santana, he continued to arrange for his films to be released through Warners, alternating them with less frequent releases through Columbia Studios.

"At Warner Brothers in the 30s, I became a one-man film factory," Bogie later recalled. "I turned out movies so fast that even today the plots are a big blur in my head. Sometimes, I went from one film into another so fast, I forgot what character I was playing. I figured the best way to deal with that was to play Humphrey Bogart, meaning play myself."

During his filming of *The Petrified Forest* for a 1936 release, the Hollywood press once again began to take notice of him. Louella Parsons had already discovered him during his first stint in Hollywood during the early 1930s.

Throughout the 30s, Daniel Mainwaring operated as Bogie's press agent, also functioning privately as both a novelist and screenwriter. His pseudonym was "Geoffrey Homes." With that name, he began to create myths and legends about Bogie, many of which got printed in newspapers as truthful and accurate facts. Perhaps as a means of getting tongues to wag, even though Bogie was playing a tough guy on screen, Homes claimed that during his spare time, the actor painted floral designs on teacups.

Homes continued to pile one myth atop another for processing by the gullible press of the mid-1930s. He spread the word to the press corps that Bogie slept only in Palm Beach suits, never pajamas. Other falsehoods he spread included stories about how Bogie would frequently slip away for late-night music gigs. According to one of Home's PR campaigns, Bogart was said to play the bull fiddle at a roadhouse in the San Fernando Valley, disguised with fake whiskers to avoid recognition from his fans.

When he had any free time from Warner Brothers, which was rare, Bogie, or so said Homes, retreated to an worm farm in Eastern Oregon. Homes told Bogie, "I'm amazed those dummies in the press actually go ahead and print all that shit."

One morning over coffee, Bogie read that "Geoffrey Homes, the noted author, is en route to the Mojave Desert to inspect the rattlesnake farm that he and Humphrey Bogart, the actor, recently purchased.

If Bogie believed that he'd be offered another role as meaty as that of Duke Mantee in *The Petrified Forest,* he was sadly mistaken, at least for the moment. He was ordered to report to work on a movie called *Isle of Fury,* a movie so horrible that Bogie would later deny any involvement in making it.

Jack Warner, on seeing the final product, also realized how truly awful it was, and delayed its release until Bogie had shot two more movies for the studio.

It was only during the first week of shooting that Bogie learned that *Isle of Fury* was a remake of *The Narrow Corner,* which had been a vehicle, released in 1933, for the showcasing of then up-and-coming star Douglas Fairbanks Jr. In some respects, *Isle of Fury* evoked Clark Gable's *Red Dust* (1932).

Released by Warners late in 1936, the sixty-minute tale of tropical adventure co-starred Donald Woods and Margaret Lindsay. With a fake, pencil-thin mustache, Bogie played the lead in a script which was loosely and awkwardly based on W. Somerset Maugham's novel, *The Narrow Corner.*

Its director was Frank McDonald, who had been born only a month before

Isle of Fury
Its props and its octopus
inspired ridicule

Bogie. A former railroad worker, McDonald seemed nervous and unsure of himself. Actress Evelyn Keyes once said, "I've never seen anyone as terrified of directing as Frank McDonald."

In spite of his fears, McDonald churned out more than 100 pictures during the course of his long career, achieving his greatest success at Republic, grinding out popular westerns starring Roy Rogers and Gene Autry.

In a moment of candor, McDonald confided to Bogie, "Let's face it: Both you and me are hacks turning out shit."

"Don't use that word around me," Bogie said. "Why say shit when crap will do?"

Actually, from its inception, the script of *Isle of Fury* had been tailored for Pat O'Brien, who dropped out three days before shooting began.

One scene in *Isle of Fury* got Bogie virtually laughed off the screen. The plot called for him to be attacked by a giant octopus created by the props department. It was suggested that McDonald should have made it a shark attack instead of some ridiculously artificial-looking octopus. The scene just didn't work on screen, and the octopus was such an obvious fake that it provoked ridicule.

Years later, when asked about *Isle of Fury*, Bogie said, "I don't recall making such a movie. Perhaps you've confused me with someone else. If I recall, that movie starred Errol Flynn."

Months before, when shooting had ended on *The Petrified Forest*, Bogie and Leslie Howard had made a bet to see which of them could seduce a greater number of their respective leading ladies. Bogie felt that he was at an unfair advantage since he was often being cast alongside lesbians. An example included the picture-pretty brunette Margaret Lindsay, of Dubuque, Iowa. She was Bogie's love interest in *Isle of Fury*, but her eye was trained on women, not at any man.

Bogie knew that Lindsay had starred on Broadway with Roland Young in *Another Love Story*, and he was interested in picking her brain for any information he could about Young. After all, rivaled by Kenneth MacKenna, Young was a contender for the love of Bogie's wife, Mary Philips. Bluntly, Bogie asked Lindsay, "Is this Roland Young creature still banging Mary?"

Lindsay was equally blunt in her response. "Almost every night from what I hear. You'd better get back to Broadway soon if you expect to hold onto Mary."

Meanwhile, Lindsay was playing an equivalent game of musical chairs. Before filming *Isle of Fury*, she'd been engaged in a torrid romance with actress Janet Gaynor. But when Mary Martin took Gaynor from her, Lindsay turned her romantic affections onto another actress, Mary McCarty.

This time the girl-on-girl romance worked, and Lindsay and McCarty became longtime companions.

Bogie never understood the long enduring success of his co-star, Donald Woods, who was born in Manitoba. "Now I know why he's named Woods,"

Isle of Fury--a "tropical stinker" Bogart tried to forget. *(left to right)* Donald Woods, Bogart, and E.E. Clive

271

Bogie told McDonald. "Donald is the most wooden actor on the screen."

Yet, in spite of that assessment, Woods would have a career that encompassed 75 films and 150 TV shows over forty years. He became known as "King of the Bs."

In the 1950s, long after his appeal as an actor had faded, Woods became a successful real estate broker in Palm Springs, where he tried to sell Bogie a weekend vacation home. His pitch was that Clark Gable had once used the retreat for secret trysts with beautiful young women or—get this—handsome young men.

"That's about the best sales pitch I've ever been offered in my life," Bogie said, facetiously, "but I must turn it down. Gable, huh? Who would have thought that?"

During the spring of 1936, Mary was still on Broadway, appearing in *The Postman Always Rings Twice,* which was doing lackluster business. In marked contrast, Bogie was getting roles in one film after another, and working so hard his friends decided he needed some female companionship to take him out of his frequent dark moods.

Producer Walter Wanger, with some involvement from Henry Fonda, planned a party for Joshua Logan, and he invited Bogie and some actresses from the studio. At the time Wanger was shooting *Vogues of 1938,* a film whose plot revolved around eight of the supposedly most beautiful "models" in the world.

At the party, the girls imported from the cast of the movie looked like cheap hookers, not the "lovelies" that Wanger had promised. Except for a few private talks with Fonda, Bogie sat by himself, although on occasion a gum-chewing cutie encouraged him to join the party, even visit one of the bedrooms upstairs.

A self-satirical portrait of humorist and arts critic Robert Benchley, shaving

At the end of the party, after the models had been driven home, Fonda asked Bogie why he didn't want to "roll in the hay" with one of them.

According to Fonda's biographer, Howard Teichmann, Bogie responded, "Anyone that would stick a cock in one of those girls would throw a rock through a Rembrandt."

The next day, at the Garden of Allah, Bogie paid a visit to the small writing studio of the corpulent Robert Benchley, the actor/humorist who'd been a founding member of the celebrated and gossipy Algonquin Roundtable in New York. Bogie had long been a fan of his, taking special interest in Benchley's sardonic theater reviews.

Through the open door of Benchley's studio walked a slim, panther-like woman with a seductive gamine face. Thanks partly to her distinctive, helmet hairdo, she was as alluring as when he'd seduced her long ago as part of an arrangement set up by his first wife, Helen Menken.

"Brooksie," he said, rising from his chair and giving Louise Brooks a lingering kiss.

"Your lonely nights are over," Brooks said, "at least temporarily." Then she gave Benchley a peck on the cheek.

"Here I am back in Hollywood, a has-been at twenty-nine," she said. "Got anything to drink, fellows?"

Benchley had three bottles of Scotch resting temptingly on his bar. As Bogie remembered it, at least two of those bottles would be finished off "before we heard the wild cackle of Tallulah Bankhead chasing a nude John Barrymore around the pool at three o'clock that morning."

It was at that very moment, 3am, that Bogie and Brooks staggered out of Benchley's studio. They were just in time to see Barrymore and Tallulah jump into the pool, splashing around as if trying to drown each other. Although in need of assistance himself, Bogie half supported Brooks as they made their way back to his own rental unit.

Since he didn't have an early morning call, Bogie slept soundly until eleven o'clock. When he woke up "with the worst hangover of my life," he found a note on the counter from Brooks.

"You're slipping, Bogie boy," it said. "You didn't even fuck me before you passed out last night."

When he encountered Benchley by the pool later that afternoon, his neighbor asked him. "How did it go? I'm all ears."

Not wanting to ruin his reputation, Bogie said, "It's always fun seducing my former wife's girlfriends. I feel closer to Helen that way." He looked over toward Benchley's studio. "Didn't we leave you with one bottle not emptied last night?"

"We did indeed," Benchley said, heaving his heavy body from its position deep within a chaise longue. "I'd always dreamed of becoming a bartender for the great Humphrey Bogart."

Brooks called later that evening to thank Bogie for his hospitality. She was mysterious about her whereabouts, refusing to tell him where she was, even when pressed. "An emergency came up, and I can't explain." He would never learn the reason for her sudden departure.

"You should have stuck around," he said. "I'm much better in the morning."

"I'm sure you are," she told him. "I was tempted to pursue what we never finished in New York, but I decided against that."

"Why?" he asked. "I didn't plow deep enough."

"It's not that, Bogie boy," she said. "I decided we are too much alike. Going to bed with you would be like fucking myself."

In the years to come, he was saddened to see the star of *Pandora's Box*, where Brooks played Lulu, the nymphomaniac, reduced to appearing as a chorus girl in a 1937 Grace Moore musical, *When You're in Love*.

In 1974, Brooks would share her memory of Bogie in her published memoirs *Lulu in Hollywood*. The most controversial piece of her Bogie portrait involved remarks she made about his lips. She alleged that he referred to them as "nigger lips." Instead of viewing his lips as a handicap, Brooks claimed that Bogie decided to take advantage of this "unusual feature," his observations being based on how much publicity Clark Gable had garnered from his big ears.

"Over the years, Bogie practiced all kinds of lip gymnastics, accompanied by nasal tones, snarls, lisps, and slurs," she wrote. "His painful wince, his leer, his fiendish grin were the most accomplished ever seen on film. Only Erich von Stroheim was his superior in lip twitching."

***

From a successful stint in the 1920s on the stages of Broadway, Mayo Methot arrived at Union Station in Los Angeles in 1930, loudly describing her plans to "put the tinsel in Tinseltown." Humphrey Bogart lay in her future, but she had no memory of ever meeting him during the 1920s in New York. That was odd, as she'd previously been introduced to him in the presence of "Mr. Broadway," George M. Cohan, along with Bill Brady Jr.

Years later, defending herself for not remembering her inaugural meeting with the man who eventually became her husband, she said, "With Cohan checking me out, perhaps for a future stage role, how in hell could I remember a two-bit actor with a lisp? The town was full of them in those days."

This Oregon-born actress became known as "The Portland Rosebud," after she became famous for introducing the Broadway show tune, "More Than You Know," which became a standard across the country. She'd introduced the song in the musical *Great Day*, produced by Billy Rose and Vincent Youmans. In Hollywood during the 30s, she would never achieve the celebrity she'd known in New York.

When she arrived in Hollywood in 1930 and signed with Warner Brothers, Jack Warner didn't know quite what to do with her and cast her within roles as either tough-talking dames or as unsympathetic second leads in crime melodramas such as *Jimmy the Gent (*1933).

Directed by Michael Curtiz, who would later helm Bogie in *Casablanca*,

Jimmy the Gent starred Bette Davis and James Cagney. "Thanks to those two super-egos, I broke into Hollywood the hard way," Methot ruefully claimed. "They didn't make it easy for me."

In Los Angeles' Biltmore Hotel in 1936, at the Screen Actors Guild annual dinner, Bogie arrived stag, without an escort. He kept looking at the familiar face of a blonde-haired woman in a scarlet red dress with plunging décolletage. She smiled back at him several times. Finally, he realized that he'd met her before. She was none other than Mayo Methot, the former Broadway star.

Impulsively, Bogie rose from his chair. Plucking a small plaster nude from a nearby decoration, he made his way to her table. "Madam," he said, "I hereby present this Oscar to you as the Most Beautiful Woman in the Room."

It was the beginning of Bogie's most turbulent relationship with any woman. He invited her to dance. As Mayo later related to Bette Davis, "We danced the night away. By two o'clock that morning, I found myself drinking

(left photo) 1933 movie poster for a tough-guy film Bogart envied
(top right photo) James Cagney with iron-fisted director Michael Curtiz
(bottom right) a blonde version of Bette Davis as floozie with "the Gent," James Cagney

a nightcap in his bedroom at the Garden of Allah."

Since Mary was in New York at the time, this tryst was easy for Bogie, but not necessarily for Methot: At the time, she had a husband, Percy T. Morgan, the owner of the popular Cock & Bull, a restaurant and bar on Sunset Boulevard much frequented by the movie crowd.

Soonafter, Methot began spending many of her nights with Bogie, much to the annoyance of Mr. Morgan, who knew his wife was having an affair. But with whom?

Prior to Morgan, Methot had had an earlier husband. At the age of 19, she'd married Jack La Mond, a cameraman for Cosmopolitan Productions. Divorcing him in 1927, she migrated to Hollywood in 1930 and soonafter, she'd married Morgan.

It quickly became obvious to Bogie that Methot was not a fragile and demure hothouse flower. At a bar in Santa Monica, she ordered a vodka and tonic. After the waiter served it, she tasted it and spat it out. This is gin and tonic, you fucker!" she shouted at him.

"It's vodka," he said. "I poured it myself. I'm not taking it back. You can drink it since you're paying for it."

"Drink this, faggot!" she shouted, throwing glass, ice cubes, and gin in his face before storming out of the bar.

"I hate women who are spineless, brainless, clinging vines," Bogie told Edward G. Robinson. "You know the type. They open their eyes wide and their mouths still wider and sigh, 'Oh, you great big wonderful man.'"

On the Warners lot, Methot became known for her heavy drinking. Alcohol had begun to tarnish her former beauty.

"By the time she met Bogie, she was looking the worse for wear," said Bette Davis.

One day, during lunch on the Warners lot, Davis said, "Bogart, you're out of your mind. Mayo is insane. She and her husband staged a knock-out, drag out fight at the Cock & Bull that brought out the police. She was about to kill him."

He smiled. "I adore take-charge women. Whenever I do something wrong, she tells me so. In case I don't listen, she packs a good wallop. I've already nicknamed her Sluggy."

"You know what I've decided," Davis said. "You're as much of a lunatic as Methot is."

A few weeks later, at a Hollywood party, Louise Brooks sat in the corner, skeptically eyeing the drunken antics of Bogart and Methot. In her memoir, *Lulu in Hollywood*, she wrote: "He found her at a time of lethargy and loneliness, when he might have gone on playing secondary gangster parts at Warner Brothers for years and then been out. But he met Mayo and she set fire to him.

Those passions—envy, hatred, and violence, which were essential to the Bogie character—which had been simmering beneath his failure for so many years—she brought to a boil, blowing the lid off all his inhibitions forever."

During the 1930s, Eric Hatch was a well-known writer of screwball comedies, including *My Man Godfrey*. Released in 1936, it starred Carole Lombard and William Powell. That same year, Eric and his wife, Gertrude Hatch, threw a party for Mayo and Bogie.

"It was a wild night," Bogie later said. "Mischa Auer, the Russian character actor, at one point got so drunk on vodka he was crawling nude under the tables. Mayo put on music for an Argentine tango. With a jaybird-naked Auer, they did a burlesque of Rudolph Valentino. Mischa threw Mayo up in the air. That night, the whole room discovered that she'd forgotten to wear her panties."

Suddenly, during one of the party's particularly manic moments, the Hatch family's maid came in to warn that Percy Morgan was at the front door, trying to retrieve his wife.

In her stocking feet, Mayo ran out the back door with Bogie in hot pursuit. They made their getaway. There was a rumor that Morgan was carrying a gun.

The next day, Bryan Foy heard the story and quizzed Bogie about it.

"I want the word to get out," Bogie said. "Tell 'em Humphrey Bogart is in town, and that the only way a man can know that his wife is safe involves strapping a chastity belt on her and locking her in a dungeon."

During the days and weeks ahead, despite her status as a married woman, Bogie openly escorted Methot to private parties and frequently appeared in public with her.

"The final straw came when I invited Bogie to have drinks with me in the bar of the Cock & Bull," Methot told friends. "It was a deliberate attempt to let my husband know that I had moved on, and that Bogie was my new love. Percy sat at the far end of the bar staring at us, but he never came over. I think that signaled him that it was all over except for the actual filing for divorce."

Russian character actor
Mischa Auer
with his pet Dachsund.

"Drunk and crawling, naked, under the tables"

***

On Broadway, fading screen star Richard Barthelmess and Mary Philips, cast into a role as a "gas station strumpet," couldn't generate

277

enough magic to sustain box office for *The Postman Always Rings Twice*. The show closed after its move in April of 1936 to a smaller theater, the Golden. Throughout the run of the play, however, reports filtered through to Mary about how her husband was having a torrid romance with Mayo Methot, whom Mary knew from her Broadway days.

Uncharacteristically jealous, Mary opted to take the difficult air route to Los Angeles instead of traveling by train. That involved several refueling stops across the vast American continent, but she was in a hurry to get to the West Coast.

She notified Bogie that she was on her way, but her plane did not show up on schedule on April 26. He feared it had crashed somewhere. Finally, news reached him that the small aircraft had been grounded somewhere in Oklahoma because of a dust storm.

On the afternoon of the following day, Mary finally landed on the ground in Los Angeles, where Bogie was waiting to meet her.

Only the day before, out of respect for Mary's upcoming arrival, he had gathered together Methot's cosmetics and clothing from his studio, where they had been living together, and sent her packing.

It was not sunny California that greeted Mary as the plane set down. It was one of those cold, windswept days in Los Angeles that sends locals desperately searching for a coat of some sorts.

He embraced her on the runway and kissed her warmly. She would later

tell her lover, Kenneth MacKenna, "The kiss was without passion, more like what a brother would give his sister."

Bogie moved Mary into his rented studio at the Garden of Allah, which Methot had vacated a day or two before. Even though Mary was temporarily back with Bogie, Methot began divorce proceeding against Percy Morgan. He'd been the ideal husband, yet she charged him with mental cruelty. The only cruelty she could cite in her petition involved his refusal to allow her to rearrange the furniture in their living room.

During the first week of Mary's return to Hollywood,

Reviving a faded film star in a Broadway play that later became a Hollywood classic.

(left photo) Richard Barthelmess
in the stage version of
The Postman Always Rings Twice,
an unsuccessful play that co-starred
(right photo) Mary Philips

Benchley, now one of Bogie's close friends, decided to give a welcome-to-Hollywood party for Mary. She wanted to seek work in films at Warner Brothers, and Bogie had set up an appointment for her with Brian Foy, chief of those B movies he'd been making.

"I'm a big Broadway star from a big town hoping to get work in B-pictures in a small town," she told Benchley. "But if I don't stay in Hollywood this time, I know my marriage to Hump is over. Hell, I'm still going to call him Hump. I can't get used to this Bogie shit. And, by the way, don't tell my husband I ever used the word shit."

Mary was not accustomed to the casual style of Hollywood parties, especially on a hot day. Those overcast skies had faded. At three o'clock that afternoon at the Garden of Allah, she emerged from their bungalow on the arm of her husband. As Benchley later reported to Tallulah Bankhead, "Mary looked like she could have headed the Easter Parade along Fifth Avenue. A vision in pink."

At about four o'clock, the thirty-odd guests of the party turned to witness the sudden emergence of Methot, who had appeared suddenly and without warning, seemingly out of thin air. Her hair and clothing were in disarray, and she looked angry and distraught.

Seeing her, Bogie moved to prevent her from entering the pool area, but she slugged him in the face, bloodying his nose. He struck her, knocking her onto the tiles surrounding the pool. She picked herself up and stood before him. Then, she kicked him in the balls. He doubled over in pain.

While he was trying to recover from the agonizing assault, Methot headed toward Mary, who was standing near the edge of the pool.

"We meet again, you little whore," Methot shouted at Mary. Sensing a catfight, the guests moved back. Benchley, as the host, did not inter-

Three early views of Bogie's wife #3, Mayo Methot

279

vene. "I only engage in verbal assaults, nothing physical," He later told Bogie. "I long ago learned not to come between two jealous women who are about to beat each other up."

"I am Mrs. Humphrey Bogart, and I plan to continue to be Mrs. Humphrey Bogart for many years to come," Mary said defiantly.

"He loves me—and not you," Methot shouted. "He told me himself that you're lousy in bed. I can satisfy a man. You can't. Maybe Kenneth MacKenna. But he's mostly faggot anyway."

"Get away from my husband," Mary shouted at her. "I forbid you to see him ever again."

"Forbid me?" Methot said. "Am I hearing right? I can chew a bitch like you for breakfast and spit her out." In an impulsive move, she moved toward Mary and pushed her into the deep end of the pool. In all her New York finery, Mary seemed to be drowning. One of the male guests stripped off his jacket and jumped in to rescue her.

Methot stormed away toward the entrance. Bogie had recovered in time to kick her in the ass as she made a rapid retreat. He rushed over to comfort Mary, who was lying soaked and gasping for breath on the tiles.

"You know how to pick 'em, Hump," she said before Bogie carried her back to his studio.

Bogie turned around and surveyed the astonished guests. "Party's over!" he shouted. "I want each of you to leave a dollar in the kitty. We Broadway actors sure know how to put on a show for you Hollywood types."

***

The next morning, the manager of the Garden of Allah rapped on the door of Bogie's bungalow. Mary was still in bed when Bogie in his underwear answered the summons. "Yeah, what is it?"

"Mr. Bogart, we want you to check out of our hotel as soon as possible," he said. "We're a happy family around here. If you aren't gone by tomorrow morning, I'm summoning the police to have you and Mrs. Bogart evicted."

Thanks to a recent salary increase of fifty dollars a week, Bogie moved Mary into a small Mexican hacienda-style adobe house on 1210 North Horn Avenue, overlooking Sunset Boulevard. It was to be his first real home in Hollywood.

Their marriage was rocky, but both Bogie and Mary seemed to want to give it one final chance. Both of them understood that if they failed this time, their relationship, except for a divorce, would be over.

***

Enjoying a break before shooting on his next picture, Bogie was called to Warners for a script conference. When it was over, he retreated to his dressing room for a Scotch and soda. There was a knock on his door. He opened it to find Methot.

Despite their recent and very public fistfight, Bogie let her in.

"I don't know what went on inside that dressing room that afternoon, but the bitch was in there for four hours," Bryan Foy said. "A grip spilled the beans. They came out looking like lovebirds. We can call that a reconciliation. Where was Mary Philips while all this was going on? No doubt slipping away to fuck Kenneth MacKenna."

Foy revealed to associates that at Bogie's request, he'd arranged a screen test of Mary. "She's awful. She also photographs rather ugly, although she's pretty enough in person. I'll never understand why the camera favors some dames—and not others. My advice to her was to go back to Broadway."

***

With Mary's career at a standstill, Bogie for the first time became the family's only breadwinner. He was elated to learn that he'd been cast as the star of a new movie, a drama, *Black Legion*, to be released in 1937, with co-stars Dick Foran, Erin O'Brien-Moore, and the fast-emerging Ann Sheridan.

Archie Mayo, who had directed Bogie in the film version of *The Petrified Forest*, was the director. This time he'd cast Bogie as Frank Taylor, an embittered factory worker who joins the Black Legion, a Ku Klux Klan-inspired terrorist organization.

Black Legion was a grim picture, marking the first time Bogie played the lead in what eventually evolved into an A-list feature which showcased his talents. Erin was cast as his wife, Foran his best friend.

A publicity still for the grim and gritty *Black Legion* (1937), wherein our hero plays the male lead.
(foreground, left to right),
Erin O'Brien-Moore, Bogart, and Ann Sheridan.
(background figures inspired by the KKK)

The same year, Erin O'Brien-Moore, a fetching beauty from California, appeared opposite Paul Muni in *The Life of Émile Zola*.

Two years later, tragedy struck when she was seriously burned in a restaurant fire. Her recuperation took years of surgery and rehabilitation. When she came back in 1948, she was assigned character roles, her chance for major stardom a forgotten dream.

Ann Sheridan was cast in a small and rather thankless role as the fiancée of Dick Foran, Bogie's co-star in the film. A New Jersey crooner, Foran was known around the lot as Warner Brothers' answer to Gene Autry, the singing cowboy. But occasionally Foran was cast in mainstream dramatic parts, as he was in *Black Legion*.

Bogie had worked with Foran before when he'd been cast as the athlete, Boze Hertzlinger, in the film version of *The Petrified Forest*. He had taken the role that Robert E. Sherwood had originally intended for Bogie (i.e., the role of the athlete, not the Duke Mantee part.)

Meeting him again on the set, Bogie told Foran, "You're much too good-looking and wholesome to have played Duke, although you could have livened that dismal drama by singing 'Home on the Range.'" Foran knew when he'd been insulted.

To complicate his life even more, Bogie, "torn between two lovers," had yet another woman enter his life. She was Ann Sheridan, the so-called "Oomph Girl."

Down to earth and ever so friendly, she approached Bogie on the set of *Black Legion* and introduced herself with, "How in the fuck are you, Mr. Humphrey Bogart?"

"You wanna feel it and find out?" he shot back.

She laughed hilariously. Like Carole Lombard, Sheridan was known for her potty mouth. In fact, around the Warners lot she was called "the hash-house version of Carole Lombard."

Black Legion's on-screen fiancés
Dick Foran *(left photo)* and Ann Sheridan

When Bogie met Sheridan, she, like Bogie, was struggling through a long involvement in Warners B pictures. There was something so frank and honest about her that he fell for her almost immediately.

"She has this come-hither look," he told Archie Mayo. "Show me a real man who can resist that deep, suggestive voice. I've got the hots for her."

"By the way," Archie responded, "isn't it a coincidence that your girl-friend's first name, Mayo, is my last name? And, come to think of it, how's your wife, Mary Philips?"

Bogie got the point and walked away.

During their first luncheon together, Sheridan described her philosophy of life. "What's the use of living if you can't have fun?"

Bogie later said, "There's one thing that dame isn't, and that's a phony. It's well known in Hollywood how I hate phonies, and the town reeks of them."

The following afternoon, when they weren't needed on the set, he invited Sheridan for a drink in his dressing room. Seated across from her, he studied her figure. "I hear you Texas gals are great in the haystack."

"Why don't you find that out for yourself?"

"I just might do that," he said.

"I can be had." As he later related to Mayo, she stood up and began to remove her dress.

At the time, Sheridan was married to an actor, Edward (Eddie) Norris. But, as she claimed, "Why should having a husband prevent a girl from workouts on the side?"

"Why indeed?" Bogie said. "Both of my wives played around on me. Why shouldn't I?"

"If we play this right, we can both have the security of marriage and a lot of fun whenever we're not with our devoted spouses."

"My sentiments exactly. You know what really attracted me to you?" Bogie said. "You smoke three packages of cigarettes a day. My kind of woman."

His meeting with Sheridan that day would mark the beginning of a long friendship, both on and off the screen.

Black Legion remains one of Bogie's best early films. Upon its release, *The New York Post* pro-

"No more B pix for Bogart!"
The New York Post

283

claimed, "No more B pix for Bogart!"

He came to believe the press reports affirming that indeed *Black Legion* would make him a star. Although Bette Davis warned him not to get his hopes up—she'd been disappointed too many times herself—Bogie believed great scripts were on the way. A critic writing in the *New York American* even suggested that "the dynamic Humphrey Bogart would be ideal for the role of Rhett Butler in the coming *Gone With the Wind*, to be produced by David O. Selznick."

Black Legion generated a solid box office return, but not in the league with *The Public Enemy* (1931) which made James Cagney a superstar, or Paul Muni's *I Am a Fugitive from a Chain Gang* (1932).

Nevertheless, Jack Warner was not impressed. His publicity department promoted the film by saying, "There's no Paul Muni in *Black Legion*, but there's Humphrey Bogart."

When the *Black Legion* was released, the KKK sued Warner Brothers, not for libeling their hate organization but for copyright infringement. The studio had used their symbol of a white cross with a black diamond in its center, positioned against a circular red background. The judge wisely tossed the case out of court, but not before ordering the KKK to pay legal costs.

Back at Bogie's house in West Hollywood, Mary was sometimes there, but more often not. During extended periods when she was missing, he called Mayo, who was beginning to frighten him by ratcheting up the pressure to divorce Mary and marry her.

***

When the KKK sued Warner Brothers over *Black Legion*, it wasn't for libel, but for copyright infringement.

The judge threw the case out of court.

Ann Sheridan was the first to hear the news. She and Bogie had been cast together in *The Great O'Malley*, a police drama slated for direction by William Dieterle. The movie would star Pat O'Brien in his familiar incarnation as a cop. "We get third and fourth billing," Sheridan told him.

"Who got the second lead?" Bogie asked.

"Sybil Jason," she said.

He'd heard of this child star. Born in Cape Town, South Africa, she was being groomed by Warner Brothers as a rival to the box office champ, Shirley Temple.

On the set he met this child prodigy, who had learned to play the piano at the age of two. "Would you like to see me do my impression of Maurice

Chevalier?" she asked Bogie.

"Later, kid," he said.

Sybil didn't achieve the success at Warners that Jack Warner had hoped for, and the following year, he didn't renew her contract.

Ironically, her last two films were for Darryl F. Zanuck at Fox. He cast her opposite her rival, Shirley Temple, in *The Little Princess* (1939) and *The Blue Bird* (1940). Sybil abandoned the screen after that. "I had my fifteen minutes of fame," she later recalled.

Born in the Rhineland of Germany, director William Dieterle was stiff and formal with Bogie when they first met on the set. He wore a large hat and white gloves. Throughout the entire course of the shoot, he would remove neither of them. His striking good looks had earned him roles in German films during the 1920s. He'd directed his first film in 1923, *Der Mensch am Wege*, which had co-starred a young Marlene Dietrich.

In 1930, he emigrated to Hollywood, where he took a job directing German versions of American films. His first movie, *The Last Flight* (1931), is today called "a forgotten masterpiece" by critics.

During the span of his long career, he would direct five different actors in Oscar-nominated performances, including Paul Muni, Brian Aherne, Walter Huston, Jennifer Jones, and Joseph Schildkraut. Alas, Bogie would not be a member of that distinguished list.

The Great O'Malley would be one of Dieterle's less distinguished efforts. Bogie wasn't impressed with the script, calling it "another cop picture for Warners. It was terrible, just another of those dramas we turned out at that goddamn sweatshop. Pat O'Brien was very good. But then Pat is never bad."

"My fucking role's too small," Sheridan told Bogie. "Jack Warner said he cast me as a schoolmarm because I'd once studied to become a teacher. My Southern Baptist parents, real zealots, still want me to become a school teacher. They warned me that I'll perish in hell if I play bad women on the screen."

In the film, Bogie played a jobless veteran driven to crime to feed his family. His most dramatic

The Great O'Malley (1937)
An overzealous cop, an adorable tyke, and a war veteran on the brink earn each other's mutual respect. *(left to right, above)*

Pat O'Brien, Sybil Jason, Humphrey Bogart

285

scene occurs when he tries to pawn his war medals for money to buy food. The surly pawnkeeper says, "Ten dollars for this junk? Why don't you go on relief?"

Exploding in fury, Bogie responds, "The only things left to remind me I was once a man and you call them junk!" This is but a prelude to robbery and a vicious attack on the pawnbroker.

Later, the Warners publicity department got it all wrong when they advertised the film as AN IRISH COP VS. A GUN-MAD KILLER!

During the course of the filming, Bogie slipped away with Sheridan for "some Texas gal loving," as she called it. In just a short time, she'd become his *confidante.*

He told her, "My marriage is all but over. Mary can't find work in Hollywood, and she's returning to New York to look for work on Broadway. But the die is cast. Guess who I'll be working with in my next film? Mayo Methot herself. Oh, yes, and the star of this thing is what's her face?"

"Bette Davis," Sheridan said. "I heard the news this morning."

***

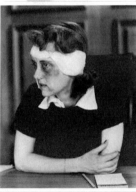

Ever since his childhood days on Lake Canandaigua, Bogie had been devoted to sailing. With his increase in salary, he was able to purchase a 36-foot cruiser that he docked at the Newport Beach Yacht Club.

His "first mate" on these weekend trips, most often a sail to Catalina Island, was Methot. She talked often about marriage, urging him to file for divorce against Mary the way she'd filed for divorce against Percy Morgan. Finally, during a drunken sailing expedition heading back to Newport Beach, Bogie broke down and agreed to marry her.

Just before Christmas in 1937, shooting began on *Marked Woman*, directed by Lloyd Bacon, with Bette Davis getting star billing followed by Bogie in the second lead. The film also starred Lola Lane. Methot was cast into the small role of Estelle Porter, getting seventh billing. Even in such a small role, *Marked Woman* would remain her most famous

Jack Warner claimed that Bette Davis went too far in realistic makeup when she appeared on the set playing an abused woman. "We're selling glamor, Bette. You look like shit!"

film appearance.

After reading the script, Bogie told Bacon, "This movie is about a bunch of whores."

"I know," Bacon said. "But because of the Production Code, we have to call them hostesses at a shady nightclub. But the plot is based on a notorious prostitution ring run by Lucky Luciano, the Sicilian gangster."

For greater verisimilitude, Bacon hired one of Luciano's henchmen, Herman (Hymie) Marks, to play the bit part of a gangster named Joe. Hal Wallis, the producer, objected, claiming that no one would believe Hymie as a hood. "He looks like a Presbyterian deacon."

San Jose-born Bacon was one of the Warners' "work horse" directors during the 1930s. As an actor, he had been known for supporting Charlie Chaplin in such films as *The Tramp* (1915).

Between 1920 and 1955, he directed more than 100 films, and would helm Bogie again in the immediate future.

Bacon is known today for directing *Knute Rockne—All American*, starring Ronald Reagan as "The Gipper." Even during the Depression, Bacon was the highest paid director at Warners, pulling in $200,000 annually when many Americans were in breadlines.

Thomas Dewey, as District Attorney for Manhattan, became a household word in the 1930s when he tackled organized crime in New York City. His greatest achievement was the conviction of Charles ("Lucky") Luciano, the boss of organized crime throughout the entire city. On the side, Luciano ran one of the largest prostitution rings in American history.

Born in Sicily in 1897, Luciano became the father of modern organized crime in America and the first official boss of the modern Genovese crime family. Deported from the United States, he died in 1962.

In the wake of Luciano's convic-

Marked Woman

(top photo) Gordon Hart, as the judge, hears testimony as Bogie quizzes Bette.

(bottom photo) Mayo Methot "comes between" Bette and Bogie.

tion, Dewey became more deeply entrenched in national politics. In 1944, he ran as a candidate for U.S. president against Franklin D. Roosevelt, as he did again in 1948 against Harry S Truman.

Audiences who knew Bogie because of his role as a brooding gangster in *The Petrified Forest* were shocked to see him cast as a district attorney modeled on Dewey in *Marked Woman*. Viewed today, one scene is particularly laughable, when Bogie lectures one of the "hostesses," (in this case, Bette Davis) about what a bad girl she is.

In *Marked Woman,* the role of Johnny Vanning, the pimp, was portrayed by Eduardo Cianelli. In his role, he terrorizes the women who work for him, forcing them into submission at his nightclub.

Ciannelli had a brilliant career in films, some 150 cinematic appearances. In time, he would work with major stars, including Cary Grant, Ginger Rogers, Gary Cooper, Rita Hayworth, Orson Welles, Anthony Quinn, and Marlon Brando. Bogie and he would eventually team again for *Passage to Marseille* (1944).

Meeting Bogie on the set, Davis was eager to tell him about her ongoing lawsuit against Warner Brothers, in which she'd protested the inferior quality of scripts she'd been assigned. In court, Davis had testified that her seven-year contract with Warner's was "a form of slavery."

In fighting the suit brought by their major star, the attorneys for Warner Brothers told the judge that Davis "was a naughty, overpaid young woman."

Even though she eventually lost the lawsuit, she was promised better scripts. The first of these was *Marked Woman*, whose dramatic possibilities appealed to her.

In *Marked Woman,* a young Jane Bryan was cast as Davis' kid sister. As the plot unfolds, Bryan is killed by the mob, which incites Davis to swear vengeance.

During the making of the film, Davis adopted Bryan and protected her as if she was her own daughter. She was worried that a "wolf-like Bogart" might attempt to seduce Bryan. Davis spent all her time with her between shots, talking, eating, or having a smoke. "I have made her my new discovery," she announced to Bogie, "and I want you, and all the other horny bastards on the set, to keep away from Jane."

So mesmerized was Davis by Bryan that she used her influence to secure future roles for her in Davis' upcoming films, including *Kid Galahad, The Sisters,* and *The Old Maid.*

"What? Saving her for yourself? So, those rumors about Barbara Stanwyck and you are true?"

"You are a slimy beast, Bogart," Davis said. "But we have to get through this picture together."

"Your little sister is safe with me," he said. "She's far too demure for my taste. Besides, I have Methot to keep me company."

"Yes, a broken-down old hag with a drinking problem," Davis said. "Just your type. Now get out of my dressing room, I've got to make up my face."

"That should take all day," he said before she shoved him out the door.

Bryan had had a brief fling with Ronald Reagan when they made *Girls on Probation* (1938). But when she met Jane Wyman and they worked together on *Brother Rat* (1938), "I surrendered him to Wyman. They made an ideal couple."

After Bryan met and married the love of her life, Justin Dart, the head of the Rexall drug empire, she left films. Dart made his first million during Prohibition by cornering the market in bourbon and selling it as "prescription whiskey."

Both Bryan and her husband were instrumental in getting Ronald Reagan, the aspirant politician, to run for governor of California and later President of the United States. An ardent Republican, the drug king in time became one of the most trusted members of President Reagan's "kitchen cabinet."

For an actress who once thought of herself as young and beautiful, Mayo Methot in *Marked Woman* was assigned an unattractive role. In the film, the boss of the nightclub where she wants to work eyes her up and down, and is most skeptical. "Kind of old, ain't ya?" he asks her.

Methot's appearance in the film came across as hard and crass, and she looked particularly whorish. She earned $2,500 for five weeks of work on *Marked Woman*, with Bogie, a salaried player, taking in about $3,200.

Davis, in her role of a beaten-up whore attacked by a gangster's goons, decided to make herself look grotesque. She went to her doctor, F. Le Grand Noyes, and asked him to bandage her as if she'd been brutally beaten.

Swathed in bandages, she showed up at Bogie's dressing room. "How do I look, Bogart?"

He looked at her abrasions, swollen black eyes, horribly broken nose, and miles of bloody gauze. "Didn't you used to be the glamorous Bette Davis?"

"Even playing a whore, Bette comes off as a lady," Bacon told Bogie. "Now take your bitch, that Mayo Methot—she's one dame who could play a whore."

Bogie slugged Bacon, but since the two men were under contract, they made up the next day so the picture could continue.

In the film, as a crusading District Attorney, Bogie persuades clip-joint party girl (Davis) to testify against her mobster boss after her innocent sister is accidentally murdered during the course of one of his unsavory "parties."

There is a memorable scene at the end of the picture when Bogie, just for a moment, shows that he might be interested in pursuing Davis's character.

BOGIE:	Where will you go?
DAVIS:	Places.
BOGIE:	But what will you do?
DAVIS:	I'll get along. I always have.

When she saw the movie, Davis told Bogie, "I'm the one to watch. I go full throttle in this one. Frankly, I think as the DA you were a little slow and more than a little dull."

Bacon fell ill during the shoot, and Jack Warner called in Michael Curtiz to fill in. After watching Curtiz at work, Bogie told Davis, "That illiterate is one hell of a pain in the ass to work with. He devours actors and spits out the bones." Unknown to him at the time, Bogie was talking about the future director of *Casablanca*.

One of the stars of *Marked Woman* was Lola Lane, of the famous Lane sisters. Years later at his favorite Hollywood watering hole, Romanoff's, Bogie told Peter Lorre that, "My claim to fame one day will be that I seduced each of the Lane sisters."

Since Bogie was a kidder, he perhaps exaggerated, though Ann Sheridan later claimed that he "might have gotten around to at least Lola and Priscilla." He made pictures with all of these Lanes.

Three of the Lane Sisters—Lola, Priscilla, and Rosemary—achieved success in the 1920s and 30s as a singing act. They later made a series of successful films, including *Four Wives* in 1939.

In *Marked Woman*, Lola played the role of Gaby, a prostitute in a clip joint working alongside fellow prostitutes Davis and Methot.

Lois Lane, the comic book and TV character who evolved into Superman's girlfriend, was inspired by the name of the real-life actress Lola Lane, who played "Torchy Blane," a fictional reporter in one of her 1930s films for Warners.

Although Davis consistently praised *Marked Woman*, particularly her performance within it, Bogie referred to it for years after as "just another Warners potboiler."

***

Bogie put through an early morning call to Bette Davis after he'd received the script for the boxing movie *Kid Galahad,* scheduled for direction by the ferocious Michael Curtiz and starring Edward G. Robinson.

"Have you read this piece of crap?" Bogie asked. "It's a joke. You're to play a woman called Fluff, and I'm to be a guy named Turkey."

"At least I know how to make a silk purse out of a sow's ear," Davis said. "That's something that can never be said for you, Mr. Bogart." She abruptly put down the phone.

Bogie read the script one more time. It was a totally unsympathetic role for him, that of a crooked promoter in the boxing game. To make matters even more difficult for him, word was spreading that Jack Warner did not plan to renew his contract.

Budgeted at $416,000, *Kid Galahad* went into production on January 25, 1937. Robinson had agreed to do the picture for $50,000, with Davis taking home $18,000. The scandal involved the size of the paycheck that went to Wayne Morris.

Desperate for a movie role, Morris accepted a fee of only $66 a week for his appearance in the film, even though he'd been cast into the title role. For the entire picture, he was paid $396. When fan letters started pouring in, he immediately demanded that a raise in pay accompany whatever new roles he'd be assigned. "In *Kid Galahad,* I was green to the business. Back then, even a fifty dollar bill looked like good money to me. But I was a fast learner in the ways of Hollywood. And even though we didn't particularly like each other, Bogie gave me some good advice about money."

On the second day of the shoot, Bogie approached Curtiz and complained about the character he was playing. He felt that as the part was written, it was one dimensional. "Who gives a fuck?" Curtiz said. "I make this film go so fast nobody will notice character."

Later, over coffee with Robinson, Bogie said, "I've got to learn to shoot better."

"Exactly what do you mean?" Robinson asked.

"You see, it's like this," Bogie said. "We kill each other off in another shootout. I die right away, and they put a blanket over me. But my bullet didn't go right into your heart, and you survive for a curtain speech in the arms of Bette Davis. You get to deliver this big Pietà-like death scene, while I'm covered up with a flea-infested blanket."

"That's show business," Robinson said. "I didn't write the script."

"Thank God for that," Bogart quipped, getting up. "If you had, I'm sure your fade-out would have been a fifteen-minute monologue."

Later, as he met Davis going into her dressing room, she said, "I make it a point never to agree with you. But I've read the script. You are right. Warners has recycled the usual clichés of its boxing movies. Except for a few scenes in the ring, we can expect yawns—not excitement, except for what I'm able to generate."

He noted that Davis would at least have cozy company on the set. She'd managed to secure a role for Jane Bryan, her pet. Tired of Davis' barbs, he decided to get even with her.

During a conference with Curtiz, Bogie made a revelation. "You know, of course, that Davis is having a lesbian relationship with Jane Bryan."

"I didn't know that," Curtiz said. "Don't get me excited, Bogart. I've got a goddamn picture to direct. My secret passion is to watch two lesbians go at it."

"Whatever gets to you, man" Bogie said. "Whatever."

"You look like a smart ass," Curtiz said. "You think you know fuck everything. You think I know fuck nothing. Listen to this: I know fuck all!"

"I'm sure you know how to fuck," Bogie assured him.

"Just ask Lili Damita," Curtiz continued. He was referring to the actress wife of Errol Flynn. Curtiz had married her in 1925, the union lasting only a few months. "She told me I was best in the fuck, best than Flynn."

"An impressive credential," Bogie said. "Top of the morning to you."

In *Kid Galahad*, super hunk Morris was being groomed on the Warner lot to become "the next Errol Flynn." Morris welcomed the chance to appear with big stars in his role as a young bellhop transformed into a boxing champ. Many of the women working on the picture, especially extras, made themselves sexually and emotionally available to this blonde Adonis. He didn't seem to want any of them, as he seemed fully booked up when he left the studio to wherever he was going that night.

Wayne Morris *(left)*, configured as the heir to the legacy of Errol Flynn *(right)*

Morris was the kind of California-born stud that Bogie generally detested. Standing 6'2", he towered over Bogie. Morris was remarkably handsome by the standards of the day and had gone through the usual macho roles—football player, forest ranger.

After their initial handshake, Bogie had little to say to him. "Kid, how's it hanging?" Morris looked shocked.

"It's hanging just fine," Morris respond-

292

ed, "but not for Bette Davis. Here she comes."

Davis came up to Bogie and looked disappointed that Morris had fled so quickly. Although she almost constantly attacked Bogie, she became solicitous of him whenever she needed an ally. For now, at least, their shared Enemy No. 1 was their director, Curtiz himself. Over drinks in her dressing room, she related to Bogie the real reason Curtiz hated her so much.

During the early 1930s, Curtiz had tried to seduce her. "I was going through with it," she said, "until he pulled off his pants. I mocked him like Mildred in *Of Human Bondage*. 'A little piece of okra,' I told him. He's hated me ever since."

"Bette, men do not like you to attack their manhood," he warned her. "Fortunately, I never had any complaints from you."

She just couldn't resist delivering another dig. "I was very inexperienced when I first met you. But after I was worked over by Franchot Tone, I know what a real man feels like. There are so few of them around Hollywood. At night, most of you guys are out screwing each other."

Before he could get into a full-fledged bitchfest with Davis, Jane Bryan arrived at the door with tea. "Don't touch the stuff," Bogie said, walking out.

Bogie did not come into conflict with Curtiz during the shoot, because all of the director's ire was directed at Davis. He'd directed many of her pictures and still considered her "a dumb bitch, ugly as shit."

Jane Bryan.
Reagan lay in her future

He'd even objected to her being cast in *Cabin in the Cotton*.

Davis' animosity against Curtiz was so pronounced that she turned down *Mildred Pierce* (1945), the role and the Academy Award eventually going to Joan Crawford. At the time, Davis had said, "I absolutely refuse to do another film with Curtiz." But on Oscar night, watching Crawford,

Kid Galahad.

(left photo) William Haade stands between rivals Bogie and Robinson--both on and off the screen

293

Davis' curses and screams went on until morning, and could be heard down the block from her home.

During the peak of Bogie's lesbian rumors about Davis, she fell big for the muscular Morris, who would later go on to become a naval hero in World War II.

Davis kept inviting Morris to her dressing room, and he kept declining. At one point, he asked Bogie, "How can I get this hot-to-trot mama off my back? I'm not into mothers this year."

Morris was only 23 at the time, Davis 29.

"Why don't you throw her a mercy fuck?" Bogie asked. "After all, she's the star of the picture."

"I get it up only for teenage gals," he said. "Once I get going, I can go all night. Also, I like my gals weak and submissive. That hardly describes Bette Davis."

"You got a point, kid," Bogie said.

In her effort to get to Morris, Davis even went to Curtiz and asked him to write in a love scene between them, which he refused to do.

When Davis called in sick on February 18, Curtiz told Bogie, "She's no good actress. Not really needed on this picture. Maybe with the big hen not protecting the chick, I will get to fuck the chick." He no doubt was referring to Jane Bryan.

Curtiz and Davis weren't the only members of the crew who did not like each other during the period when *Kid Galahad* was being shot. Both Davis and Edward G. Robinson held each other in contempt. She referred to Robinson as "mush mouth" and asserted, loudly and frequently, "pity the poor girls at Warners who have to kiss his ugly purple lips."

Robinson was equally disdainful of Davis, complaining to Curtiz. "This hysterical broad is hopeless. She doesn't belong in the picture." Even though she'd been an Oscar winner, Robinson called her "an amateur."

"I'm this torch singer, the mistress of Robinson," Davis said. "Could any of my fans believe that I'd go to bed with Robinson? It's another cardboard character. I told Jack Warner this morning that he'd better come up with a better script—or else!"

Robinson particularly objected to Davis' hysterics during his death scene. He called a halt to shooting and asked Curtis, "Don't you think Bette is crying too much?"

Robinson saved his final evaluation of Davis for his autobiography. "Miss Davis was and is every inch a lady—polite, mannerly, gracious, even self-effacing. But by today's standards she could never have gotten a job in a high school production of *East Lynn*. I know it's goatish of me to say it, but Miss Davis was, when I played with her, not a very gifted amateur and employed any number of jarring mannerisms that she used to form an image. In her early period Miss Davis played the image, and not herself, and certainly not the character provided by the author."

In contrast, Robinson had a begrudging respect for Bogie and more than a touch of jealousy. "Bogie had a manner, a personality—yes, an immense talent—that has made him almost immortal. Working with him, I think I understood it better than his fans. For all his outward toughness, insolence, *braggadocio*, and contempt (and those were always part of the characters he played, though they were not entirely within Bogie), there came through a kind of sadness, loneliness, and heartbreak (all of which *were* very much part of Bogie the man). I always felt sorry for him—sorry that he imposed upon himself the façade of the character with which he had become identified."

When the film opened to generally respectful reviews, many critics got it wrong. They predicted major stardom for Wayne Morris.

If Bogie ever wished to forget about his appearance in *Kid Galahad,* he would not be so lucky. In 1941, he'd be handed another script entitled *The Wagons Roll at Night.* After reading only ten pages of it, he said, "My God, this is a remake of *Kid Galahad.* The only joy that the remake brought Bogie was that this time, he'd be cast as the lead, playing the role formerly played by Robinson instead of his former supporting part.

As if these rehashes and reprises weren't enough, Elvis Presley starred in a musical remake of *Kid Galahad* in 1962.

Robinson later commented on his shoot-outs with Bogie. "Almost inevitably both of us would get killed at the end of the films in which we worked together. Because we were both rotten, we had to get our just desserts. Will Hays and his successors said so in the motion picture code. The charade followed a precise pattern. When I was the reigning star, Bogie would be slain first, and I'd live another reel before I got it. As the years passed and Bogie became the reigning star and I was demoted to character roles, I'd get the bullet first and Bogie would live out another reel before he was struck down for his sins."

***

"Bogie," came the distinctive voice of Ann Sheridan over the phone. "I've just met with Lloyd Bacon. He's cast us in another movie together. It's called *San Quentin.*"

"I bet it's a pip," Bogie said. He got quickly to the point. "What is it for me? Fourth billing?"

"No, the second lead," she said. "Pat O'Brien is the star, and I'm the love interest."

(top photo) Convict Bogie confronts prison captain Pat O'Brien in *San Quentin*.

(bottom photo) Ann Sheridan, as Bogie's sister, visits him in the pokey.

"That you are, kid," he said. "Don't tell me: I'm a convict and I get shot and killed at the end."

"You've already read the script," she said.

"I didn't have to. What's the name of my character?"

"Joe Kennedy."

"How original," he said. "I think that name has already been used. Any nude love-making scenes between us?"

"Hell, no!" she said. "It's not that kind of picture. You're my kid brother in this flicker."

"Then we'll have to confine our love-making to the dressing room."

"Fine with me," she said. "You know I'm a gal who never turns down a deep dicking. I might as well warn you, though, I'm seeing another actor on the side."

"Don't make me guess."

"David Niven."

"The limey import." Bogie said. "Frankly, I think all British actors should be banned in Hollywood. There aren't enough jobs for home-grown actors."

"Don't send him back home to London yet," she said. "I haven't worn him out yet. There's still life in the old boy."

"He strikes me as a prissy Englishman," he said. "Not my type."

"I know what you mean," she said. "But all Englishmen sound like faggots. In bed, it's another story. His gals have nicknamed him 'beer can.'"

"Don't make me jealous," he said. "See you on the set."

"Incidentally, Barton MacLane has the fourth lead," she said.

"That's the first good news I've had all day," he said. "The last time we appeared together, he was billed over me, and I'm the pretty one. What woman would want to go to bed with MacLane?"

"Actually there are some," she said. "Regardless of what you look like, there's always someone out there salivating over you."

He hadn't seen Bacon since he'd helmed Bogie in *Marked Woman*. On the first day on the set, Bogie came up to greet him, noticing how depressed he looked.

"This is not going to be the film that *Marked Woman* was," Bacon warned his star.

"Let's go for it," Bogie said. "As long as they keep those paychecks coming in, you'll continue to direct, and I'll get by on what is called acting."

Upon the film's release, it was MacLane, in his role as a tough prison guard, who attracted the most attention, some critics calling his performance memorable. One reviewer wrote, "Humphrey Bogart gives a lackluster performance as a con in a lackluster Warner release, another one of the studio's formula prison movies."

Bogie took Sheridan to see the film. At the end and on the way out, she said, "there's one real problem with this stinker other than the obvious. You're playing my kid brother. Don't forget that in real life you're eleven years older than this cutie walking beside you."

***

Long after his intimacy had ended with Bette Davis, she still retained a surface friendship with Bogie, no doubt fearing they'd be cast in another movie together at Warners. Even so, he was surprised when she called him and invited him for lunch on the Warner lot.

She was already at table when he came rushing in. Sitting down beside her, he asked, "To what do I owe this honor, Miss Davis? I assume you don't want to take up where you left off?"

"Count yourself lucky that you were so rewarded," she said. "I'm sure it'll rank as one of your all-time peak experiences."

"My, aren't you self-confident today," he said.

"Today and every day, but that's not why I'm here. I want to talk to you about a script. It's a story set in Africa by C.S. Forester. Jack Warner has acquired it as a vehicle for me. My role is that of a prim, repressed missionary spinster. The male role is that of a Cockney River Rat. Henry Blanke is talking about giving the role to David Niven. When I heard the role called for a River Rat, one who hasn't shaved in days, one who always looks unkempt and maybe a bit dirty, I thought of you."

"I always like to be in the thoughts of a beautiful woman," he said.

"Let's get serious here. I could walk away with an Oscar for this role. The River Rat isn't bad either—in fact, it's perfect for you. Niven is too much of an English gentleman to handle the role. He belongs in a Victorian parlor, not on an old piece of junk sailing along a river in Africa battling the Germans. Let's face it, Bogart. You need a meaty part. So do I, of course. We might eat up the screen with these roles. Will you allow me to advance you as a candidate for the male lead?"

"I've always wanted to play the captain of my own boat," he said, "if that's what the part calls for."

"Of course, your boat is nothing but a piece of shit, hardly able to stay afloat."

"That makes the story all the more intriguing," he said. "I'll keep the old tug floating with spit and guts."

"That's it exactly. If we play this right, I can begin preparing another speech to give on the night of the Academy Awards."

"What about me?" he asked. "Don't I deserve something?"

"That you do. If the competition isn't too rough that year, river rats might be in."

In the weeks ahead, the Warner producer, Blanke, and Bette did not agree on the film. Her major objection was to being photographed outdoors. "But, Bette," he protested, "much of the action takes place outdoors."

In the spring of 1947, Blanke, forgetting their past differences, once again presented her with the script for *The African Queen*. At this point her star was falling, and she had no objections to being photographed outdoors.

"I love the script," she said, "and I want to do it. Do you still have David Niven in mind?"

"Not at all," he said. "I'm pitching James Mason."

"Mason is a fine actor, of course, but what about Bogart? He gets rattier and rattier-looking every day."

"No, he's totally wrong for the part."

Mason may have gone before the cameras in 1947 opposite Bette had she not given birth to a baby girl, Barbara Davis Sherry, and felt in a weakened condition. She also feared location work in a remote corner of Africa, and the actual physical dexterity needed to pull off this role.

The film had not gone into production by the time Davis was kicked out of Warners, a reaction to the dismal box-office receipts generated by her disastrous *Beyond the Forest*.

***

That summer, Bogie learned that he was one of twenty-one members of the Screen Actors Guild listed by the FBI as having "strong Communist Party leanings." He became worried that such a listing would harm his career, as there was no basis for that charge. Although he viewed himself as an outspoken liberal, He had never been a member of the Communist Party and had no leanings in that direction. His appearance on that FBI list did not seem to affect his career.

In summer of 1937, for a change of pace, he agreed to perform a work by Shakespeare, but only on the radio, for the CBS Shakespeare Theater. Along with veteran actor Walter Huston and Brian Aherne, he appeared in *Henry IV, Part One*.

From New York, Mary Philips no longer wrote any letters. He inquired of actors returning to California from Broadway, but no one seemed to have any knowledge of her private life.

He told Ann Sheridan, "My marriage to Mary just needs a divorce."

He continued to see Mayo Methot three and sometimes four nights a week, but he complained to Sheridan that "she's too jealous, too possessive. I'll never marry her in spite of my promises to her."

On Broadway, Samuel Goldwyn had seen Bogie perform as Duke Mantee In *The Petrified Forest*. But when he acquired the rights to *Dead End*, the film adaptation of Sidney Kingsley's Broadway hit play, he told his director, William Wyler, that George Raft would be perfect as the gangster, Baby Face Martin. The romantic leads and the star parts would go to Sylvia Sidney and Joel McCrea.

Raft, however, kept putting off a decision about whether he'd become involved, and he went around town asking other actors, directors, and producers, "Should I take this role—or not?"

When Goldwyn heard about this, he called Wyler. "Get Bogie on a loan-out from Warners. Jack wants Miriam Hopkins for a role at Warners. We want Bogie. Do a trade-off."

Raft's indecision about whether to accept the starring role in *Dead End* would mark the beginning of a series of ill-advised decisions on his part. In every case, Bogie was ready, willing, and certainly able to fill in for his rival. "I took Raft's rejects, and they turned me into a movie star, strictly A-list. Poor, stupid George Raft."

"Who's there to fuck in this movie?" Bogie asked Ann Sheridan in a call to her. "You know everything's that going on."

"I don't know about Sylvia Sidney," she said, but I do know there are two hot little numbers appearing—Wendy Barrie and Claire Trevor. Of course, you could always settle for Marjorie Main, but she's lez."

Wyler, who was roughly the same age as Bogie age, was definitely an A-list director, and Bogie feared he'd be too demanding. He began his career working in the Silents, launching a career that would span nearly half a century and see a record twelve Oscar nominations as Best Director, of which he would win three.

San Quentin. Bogart with *(center photo)* Marjorie Main as his mother, and *(lower photo)* Claire Trevor as hooker.

Firmly established as Goldwyn's director of choice, Wyler tore into the script of *Dead End*, demanding dozens of changes. Bogie had been warned that he might be asked to shoot a take over and over again, as the director was known as "One More Wyler."

Bogie was expecting fireworks on the set with Wyler, but the director reserved his fury for epic battles with Goldwyn. They disagreed over several key scenes.

Once, when Wyler saw Goldwyn coming onto the set, the director said, "Here he comes, clanking balls he doesn't have."

Years later, Wyler recalled his experience of working with Bogie on *Dead End*. "I found him very professional, very easy to work with. His acting was never hammy. It was very simple. Unlike Bette Davis, he also underplayed a scene. I think that's the reason why his films stand up so well today. As an actor he obviously was limited. His range wasn't great, but if he stayed within a certain range he was the best actor around."

Bogie was less eloquent in recalling his work with Wyler. "He directed some of the best pictures ever made in Hollywood, especially if they starred Bette Davis. He did such films as *Wuthering Heights*, *Roman Holiday*, and *The Best Years of Our Lives*. He even directed *Ben-Hur*. When film fans gather to watch Wyler movies, *Dead End* is hardly the first must-see on their list."

Although Joel McCrea became one of the great stars of American Westerns, Bogie remained unimpressed with him. But he did like McCrea's self-appraisal of his own abilities—in fact, McCrea spoke of his modest talents with a certain soft contempt for himself.

And although Bogie did not admire McCrea's acting, he admired his thrift. He told Bogie that Will Rogers once told him, "Save half of what you make, and live on just the other half. I do that and more. I never carry around more than a buck in my pocket. I recommend you do the same. Buy property and more property. Go out into the unincorporated areas. One day that land will be a city suburb of L.A."

That was good advice, although Bogie never took it. "McCrea became a multi-millionaire in the late 40s," Bogie once said at Romanoff's. "My God, didn't he at one time own Thousand Oaks?"

When Bogie met Sylvia Sidney, the female star of the picture, he remembered her for "having the saddest eyes I've ever seen." She was just recovering from a failed marriage to Bennett Cerf, the famous publisher of Random House. Bogie remembered her sitting on the set between takes working on her needlepoint. Her marriage to Cerf technically lasted only three months.

(above photos) Two views of Sylvia Sidney

(lower photo) Random House publisher Bennett Cerf "Never legalize a hot romance"

"One should never legalize a hot romance," Cerf later said.

Referring to this Bronx-born actress, Bogie remembered that "her big, beautiful eyes looked like they were always on the verge of tears. In fact, she jokingly told me that Paramount paid her for every tear shed. Behind that small, vulnerable, long-suffering façade was a tough little number. She practically had 'survival' written on her forehead."

In later life, film critics have cited Sidney's role in *Dead End*, as the best movie role she ever played. She was cast as Drina, a shopgirl, striving to fight her way out of the slums and into a respectable life. She would work again with Bogie in the circus melodrama *The Wagons Roll at Night*.

Playing Bogie's slum mother was Marjorie Main, the daughter of a minister. In the 1920s she had been a hoofer on Broadway. She was to achieve screen immortality in later years as Ma Kettle.

In Hollywood she was repeating her stage role in *Dead End*. "You're good," he said after watching her work.

"Too good," she said, accurately predicting that *Dead End* would lead to a number of slum mother parts.

Bogie had already been made aware of Main's lesbianism as the long-time companion of actress Spring Byington.

In spite of this, she had some deep emotional attachment to her late husband, Stanley LeFevre Krebs, who had died in 1935. The relationship struck Bogie as spiritual, not sexual. In the middle of a scene with him, she stopped and seemed to go into a sort of meditation.

When she'd come out of it, she turned to director Wyler. "It's okay, I can go on." She whispered to Bogie, "I don't want to piss off Wyler, but Stanley was telling me from heaven how to play this scene with you."

A British actress born in Hong Kong, Wendy Barrie was, in the words of Bogie, "a hot tamale, but she didn't inspire lust in me. I held her off. She really wanted my body, though."

Spencer Tracy, still one of Bogie's best friends, had told him to "keep it zipped up" when he starred with Barrie. Tracy had begun an affair with her when they appeared together in a romantic comedy, *It's a Small World* (1935).

"I'm still balling her," Tracy told Bogie. "When I've had it, I'll pass it on to you. Nothing wrong with sloppy seconds—nothing at all."

"You and Claire Trevor are my kind of dames," Bogie told Ann Sheridan. "She doesn't believe in locking up her pussy like some dames," he said. He

The Dead End Kids

loved talking dirty to Sheridan, since she seemed to get off on that. "Trevor is also a solidly professional actress, not great, but way beyond competent." In fact, in all the cast of *Dead End*, Trevor would be the only one who would receive an Oscar nomination.

Cast as Bogie's ex-girlfriend, Trevor had a scene-stealing encounter with him. It is clear to Bogie's character that she has become a prostitute, and a sickly one at that. Some film critics claimed that it was that scene alone that earned the Oscar for Trevor.

He may have avoided Wendy Barrie, but "I scored a home run with Trevor," Bogie later claimed. "It was in my dressing room. I made friends with some of the grips who promised to alert me if Mayo arrived on the set, especially if she was carrying a gun."

At the end of the shoot, Trevor said she wanted to throw him "one good-bye fuck." She suspected they'd work together again one day. "Any time some director needs a floozy, call me. I play floozies in my sleep."

When she was eventually cast as Edward G. Robinson's floozy in *Key Largo* (1948), Bogie and Trevor would meet again. But before that, Trevor, playing a "fence to a gang of safecrackers," would team up with both Bogie and Robinson in *The Amazing Dr. Clitterhouse* (1938).

Bogie would also get to know Huntz Hall, a dopey-looking fidgety teenager, during the shoot. He, along with fellow actors Leo Gorcey and Billy Halop, would become famous as the Dead End Kids (also known as The Bowery Boys), and would continue to work with Bogie in future pictures.

When Bogie last encountered Samuel Goldwyn, he was preparing his acceptance speech for *Dead End*, almost certain that it would win an Oscar as Best Picture of the Year. He was terribly disappointed when the Oscar went instead to Warner Brothers' *The Life of Emile Zola*.

***

Mary Philips drove up to their house late one night after he'd gone to bed. When he heard her turning on the lights, he got up. In his underwear, he confronted her in the living room.

"I've come for my things," she said. "I'm moving out for good."

"Who is the lucky man?" he asked. "Kenneth MacKenna or Roland Young? Perhaps someone else."

"It doesn't matter now," she said, as she headed for the bedroom to start removing her clothing. In the bedroom, she turned to face him. "Don't try to stop me. It's over."

"Who's stopping you?" he asked. "Move out if you want to. I don't believe anybody should stay where they don't want to."

"Let's face it," she said, throwing three dresses on the unmade bed. "Ours was not a real marriage. If we ever had a marriage at all, it was in the 20s in New York."

"We had some good times," he said.

"I remember a few, too, but we've spent most of the 30s in the arms of other people. So it's time for me to move on. I'm very much in love."

"You won't tell me if it's Ken or Roland Young?" he said. "You owe me that."

"I owe you nothing," she said rather harshly. "With me out of the way, you'll be free to marry Mayo Methot, although God knows why. She's an old drunk. She's completely lost her looks."

"She isn't exactly a spring chick if that's what you mean," he said.

"I've got a great idea," she said. "While I finish packing, why don't you go sit out on the patio, breathe the night air, smoke a cigarette, and think about what might have been but can never be."

"I wish you luck," he said. "I know you haven't made the greatest films of all time, but back on Broadway you'll be the brightest star."

"That's very comforting," she said. "I guess I'll return the favor. I know you're getting a bit long in the tooth for a Hollywood matinee idol. As for looks, you're not the romantic type like Errol Flynn, Tyrone Power, or Robert Taylor. But keep at it. When the 1940s roll around, and you're in your own 40s, I think you'll become one of the biggest character actors in Hollywood. I really believe that. It's not bullshit."

"Well," he said awkwardly, "guess it's time for that cigarette."

"When you come back in, I'll be gone," she said.

"I'll miss you," he said, a forlorn quality to his voice. "You were—and *are*—a great gal."

"I'll miss you, too. I'm sorry our marriage didn't work out. Perhaps you'll find someone some day. Ann Sheridan. Claire Trevor. Anybody but Mayo Methot. Please, Hump, reconsider. She's psychotic. If you go on with her, I think she'll kill you one day."

"If that's my fate, so be it." He smiled. It wasn't quite a smile but not a frown either. His face reflected a sense of loss and yet an eagerness to move on into the next adventure. "Good night, sweet Mary."

"Good night, Hump."

He turned and walked toward the patio. The day had been hot, but a sudden chill had come over Los Angeles. The winds were blowing, and there seemed to be crystals of sand in the night air. Surely that's what it was. It must be the sand tearing his eyes.

CHAPTER SEVEN

Spencer Tracy called Bogie to relate details about the latest public opinion poll about the casting of the leading roles in *Gone With the Wind*, the upcoming film adaptation of the best-selling novel by Margaret Mitchell about America's Civil War.

"That big film role you've been dreaming about may actually come true," Tracy said. "Read Lloyd Pantages column, *I Cover Hollywood*."

Over coffee, Bogie smoked a cigarette and read the following item:

"An opinion poll about how *Gone With the Wind* should be cast focuses on the following movie stars: For the role of Scarlett O'Hara, the major contenders include Miriam Hopkins, Bette Davis, Katharine Hepburn, Margaret Sullavan, Claudette Colbert, and Jean Harlow. And for the role of Rhett Butler, Clark Gable is the top choice, and, after that, in rapid succession: Cary Grant, Warner Baxter, Ronald Colman, Edward Arnold, Alan Marshall, Humphrey Bogart, and Basil Rathbone. As for the part of Melanie Wilkes, the unanimous decision falls into the lap of Janet Gaynor."

After reading it, Bogie called Tracy back. "I don't know what the debate is about. The choice is obvious: Jean Harlow for Scarlett O'Hara, Bogie for Rhett Butler."

"Have you actually read *Gone With the Wind*?"

"Not a page, but I hear Gable's a shoe-in."

"Clark told me that he won't accept the role," Tracy said, "so you'd better start practicing a Southern accent. And don't forget to lose the lisp."

A few weeks later, over drinks and dinner, Leslie Howard and Bogie had a Hollywood reunion, thanks to director Tay Garnett having cast them in a Walter Wanger Production, *Stand-In* (1937), a romantic comedy about Hollywood. Joan Blondell would play the female lead. Behind a pair of spectacles, Howard had been cast as a straight-arrow financial analyst who winds up running a movie studio. Bogie, as "Douglas Quintain," plays a boozy producer trying to save a picture called *Sex and Satan*.

Over drinks and dinner, when it came time for the actors to tally their

305

score of conquests of their respective leading ladies, Howard won. Bogie protested that he would have won if some of his leading ladies hadn't been lesbians.

Having just made *It's Love I'm After*, a zany comedy with Bette Davis and Olivia de Havilland, Howard amused Bogie with the details of his campaign to woo both ladies into his much-used bed.

In 1982, when Davis was asked to comment on Howard's pursuit of her, she said, "Leslie Howard was definitely a great ladies' man. His wife used to say that the only leading lady he hadn't gone to bed with was Bette Davis."

"Don't see *It's Love I'm After*," cautioned Howard. "I only made that picture because I wanted to show Warners and its director, Archie Mayo, that I had a flair for comedy. And they paid me $70,000 to make it. I hope to get the same for *Stand-In*."

"Don't ask me what I'm taking home," Bogie said. "Small potatoes."

Howard amused Bogie with the details of his seduction of Merle Oberon, his co-star in *The Scarlet Pimpernel* (1935). "We were in my dressing room having sex, and my wife walked in on us. Seeing us in white heat, she indignantly asked me what I was doing. I blithely replied, 'Rehearsing.'"

Not wanting to be outdone, Bogie related escapades associated with his long-time girlfriend, Joan Blondell.

"I plan to seduce her," Howard said. "Hope you don't mind."

"We don't have any exclusive rights to each other's panties," Bogie said.

Later, during the second week of the shoot, Blondell told Bogie that she found Howard adorable. "He's just a little devil and just wants his hands on every woman around. He would hold your hand while looking into your eyes and rubbing his leg on somebody else's leg at the same time, while having the gateman phone him before his wife arrived on the lot."

As always, Bogie worked smoothly with Howard, as he had in both the stage and screen versions of *The Petrified Forest*. "We both shacked up with Joan," Bogie said. "She's got such a good heart about men and their desires."

"I bet she does," Ann Sheridan said. "I don't know how the poor thing faces the camera. No energy left."

In recalling his late 30s films, Bogie said, "Tay Garnett put Joan, Leslie, and me through our paces more or less well. He'd been an aviator in World War I and a gagwriter for Mack Sennett and Hal Roach. He'd been directing films since 1928. The list of his credits would stretch around the block, yet he's a name almost no one remembers, except when he directed Lana Turner and John Garfield in *The Postman Always Rings Twice*. Garnett did on film what my dear wife, Mary Philips, failed to do on Broadway in the stage version. But, then, Lana Turner's a tough act for any woman to follow."

During the production of *Stand-In*, Howard seemed primarily obsessed with the formation of his own theatrical troupe. Using it as a vehicle, he was planning a new film production of *Pygmalion*, a 1938 adaptation of George Bernard Shaw's play.

Howard was bursting with ideas and creativity, making Bogie slightly jealous, even though he was devoted to the actor. Throughout the shoot, Howard kept urging him to get better roles before he turned forty. "You're a marvelous actor, but they're putting you in crap."

During the course of the shoot, Howard invited Bogie to join him for a screening of a Swedish film, *Intermezzo*, the story of a romantic melodrama about the affair between a famous but married violinist and a student of the classical piano.

"It stars a young actress named Ingrid Bergman," Howard said. "She's the next Garbo. Exquisitely beautiful, soft spoken, intelligent, and sexy in a way that show-gal types like our dear brassy friend Joan Blondell can never duplicate. She brings to the screen a raw emotional power that's hard to find. I'm campaigning to have *Intermezzo* made into an English-language film, with me playing the violinist, Ingrid repeating her role as the pianist. What did you think of her?"

"I'm in awe," Bogie said. "But more than that, I'm in love. Get her to Hollywood as soon as possible. When you finish seducing her, give her to me. Instead of Mayo Methot, I want Ingrid Bergman as my next wife."

"Back in the 1930s and 40s, or even today, it was not unusual for a man to fall in love with a screen image," said Claire Trevor. "Bogie talked about this Swede so much I think he was hopelessly smitten. He knew nothing about her. Maybe she was a lesbian for all he knew. I just knew that Leslie Howard, who screws every woman he meets, would get into Bergman's panties first. Bogie was waiting in the wings, his tongue hanging out like a panting dog. That poor Swedish girl just wouldn't have a chance when faced with those two."

In later years, perhaps to cover her infidelity, Blondell claimed that, "I did not warm to Mr. Bogart. He wasn't a man one ever felt close to—nobody did. But I liked him."

In private with trusted friends, she changed the scenario. "I liked him more than a lot. Perhaps he should have married me instead of Mayo Methot. Of course, there was that problem I was having with Dick Powell. I loved him too."

Joan Blondell
"Here's looking at you, kid."

307

In many scenes from *Stand-In*, Blondell stole the picture from Bogie and Howard, especially when she performed a savage travesty of Shirley Temple singing "On the Good Ship Lollipop." She had snappy dialogue, as when she told Howard, cast as a visitor to the studio, that the star must never be "fatigued or mussed and above all she must never be so vulgar as to perspire. Her stand-in does her sweating for her."

After all his heavy emoting on the stage and screen, Howard was praised by some reviewers for his attempt at comedy. Bogie, to his fury, was completely left out of many reviews. "I might as well have landed on the cutting room floor," he told Mayo Methot.

"I'll break a beer bottle over his head if I encounter Jack Warner," Methot claimed.

"I believe you would," Bogie said, cautioning her. "But that might be taking it a bit far."

"Then I'll break a beer bottle over your head for accepting such a dumb role," she threatened.

"It's love," Bogie shouted, jumping up from his table in the bar. "Let's drink to true love."

***

When *Stand-In* opened, because of its all-star cast, it drew a moderate box office but did little to advance the careers of any of its stars. Bogie told director Tay Garnett, "Every day I go to the mirror and notice another line under my eye. When will that big break come for me?"

"You have to remember that for much of the world there's no such thing in life as the big break."

(top left photo) Bogie and Leslie Howard were no Abbott and Costello in *Stand-In*. On the right, a rare photo showing Bogie without his pants.

"Yeah, don't remind me," he said. "See you

on our next picture, if there's ever going to be one for me."

"There is," Garnett said, smiling.

"Wipe that smile off your face." Bogie said. "Don't tell me. I know already. I'm not even sloppy seconds, but the fourth lead once again."

"No, you have the leading role this time," Garnett said.

"Now you're talking my language," Bogie said.

"Not so fast," Garnett said. "I hear it's a hillbilly musical set in the Ozarks."

"Don't kid a kidder like me," Bogie said, walking away. He'd traversed less than a block on the studio lot before he came to a standstill and lit a cigarette. "Could it be true?"

He put through a call to Joan Blondell. She had a friend in the script department who told her everything going on at Warners.

But when he finally reached Blondell, he found her in the hospital where she was on the verge of a nervous breakdown and also suffering from neuritis. She did indeed know about Bogie's upcoming picture, *Swing Your Lady*, because she'd already been contracted for the role of the romantic female lead.

"It's crap," she said. "Some hillbilly romp. You're supposed to be some low-rent wrestling promoter in the Ozarks. I don't think it's a good idea to jeopardize my health for this cornpone hee-haw."

He agreed with her, remaining with her that afternoon. When she fell asleep, he read the script, detesting his role as the barnstorming promoter Ed Hatch interacting with a dim-witted wrestler, "Joe Skopapoulos," to be played by Nat Pendleton.

Bogie lied to Methot, claiming that he was escorting his mentally ill sister Frances on a boat trip to Catalina Island. Instead he invited Blondell for a short recuperative holiday. It was while staying in a hotel in Avalon, on Catalina Island, that she sent a telegram to Jack Warner, asserting that she was not willing to jeopardize her health by appearing in *Swing*

(center photo) Bogie is the referee between Nat Pendleton *(left)* and Louise Fazenda *(right)* in this Ozark hee-haw.

(lower photo) Bogie striking out with Penny Singleton

309

Your Lady.

She also objected strenuously to working again with director Ray Enright, who'd helmed her in a string of pictures that began in 1933 with *Blondie Johnson*. More recently, Enright had directed her alongside Pat O'Brien in *Back in Circulation*. "I didn't like the picture, and I didn't like Enright," she said. "I'm letting Jack Warner know that I'm tired of getting lousy parts in lousy pictures."

Although shortly after that, the studio placed Blondell on suspension without pay, Bogie showed up on the first day of shooting ready to take the lead. Nagging doubts hung over his head. Several people—not just Blondell—had already told him, "It's a lousy picture—it shouldn't even be made."

Like Blondell, Bogie wasn't impressed with the picture's director, Enright, who had once been a gag writer for Mack Sennett comedies. Three years older than Bogie, this Indiana-born director helmed 73 films between 1927 and 1953. "Fuck," he told Blondell, "Enright first directed Rin-Tin-Tin. From the Wonder Dog to me."

"Don't make an enemy of him," Blondell said. "If I know Jack Warner, Enright will be directing you again." Bogie found that out for himself when he showed up to shoot *The Wagons Roll at Night*.

When Jack Warner asked Enright how he thought Bogie was doing as the lead in *Swing Your Lady*, the director replied, "He shows up on time."

"Talk about damning with faint praise," Warner said. "I'd give Bogie better parts, but what beautiful gal would want to end up with his ugly kisser in the final reel?"

Bogie was shocked to learn that his leading lady was Louise Fazenda, whose husband, Hal B. Wallis, was the top producer at Warners. Behind his back, Wallace had become known as "The Prisoner of Fazenda." He'd married Louise in 1927.

Cast into a comic role in *Swing Your Lady*, Louise had worked with Mack Sennett and had been a rival of silent screen comedienne Mabel Normand. Fazenda created the archtypical country bumpkin, with multiple pigtails, spit curls, and calico dresses, later inspiring both Minnie Pearl and Judy Canova.

Bogie met her near the end of her long and distinguished career. "I found her plain-looking, but a highly gifted performer," he said. "Let's face it: Wallis has his pick of the most beautiful women in America, but for some reason he chose Louise—you figure."

In *Swing Your Lady*, Louise was cast as "Sadie Horn," a mountaineer Amazon who plies the blacksmithing trade.

Based on the script, Bogie interpreted the film as a vehicle for the showcasing of Louise. In one hokey scene, she misunderstands him, thinking he's asking her if she wants to wrestle him. As part of a deft physical assault, she throws him to the ground. Looking down at him, she says, "Now say Hootie Owl."

In the second lead, the always-reliable character actor, Frank McHugh, was cast as "Popeye Bronson." Coming from a theatrical family, this Pennsylvania-born actor, only a year older than Bogie, could always be counted on to deliver a standard but competent performance.

Often cast as a sidekick, providing comedy relief, he would eventually appear in some 150 films and TV productions and work with nearly every major star on the Warner lot. Bogie had worked with him previously in *Bullets or Ballots*, where he'd been billed right after Bogie.

After Blondell turned down the role of Cookie Shannon, the part was shortened and assigned to perky Penny Singleton.

Bogie told McHugh, "To judge from her pictures, she's the only one who looks good enough to fuck on this stinker."

In a previous incarnation of her career, back when she'd been billed as "Penny McNulty," Singleton sang and danced with Milton Berle and Gene Raymond.

Bogie knew that Singleton had recently married. One day on the set, he took a bad fall and chipped his tooth. Singleton drove him over to meet her dentist husband, Dr. Laurence Scogga Singleton.

The following week on the set Bogie doubted how strong her marriage was. He spotted her with a handsome young actor who had been cast as Jack Miller in a minor role in *Swing Your Lady*. Recognizing him, Bogie walked over to shake his hand.

"Mr. Bogart, we meet again," said the fresh-faced Ronald Reagan.

"I don't mean to interrupt you two love-birds," Bogie said, "but I wanted to say hi and wish you well."

Reagan had been cast as a fast-talking sports reporter, which he'd been in real life. He told Bogie, "I don't have much to do but make dumb wisecracks."

"Don't worry, kid," Bogie said. "This is Hollywood. By 1940 you'll be taking home your first Oscar. The good roles will come your way."

"Thanks, Mr. Bogart. Or do you want me to call you Bogie."

The much married Penny Singleton *(top)* also had eyes for Ronald Reagan

"Mr. Bogart will do," he said. He turned to walk away. But he decided to make one final comment. His provocative remarks were already known on the Warner lot as "pulling a Bogie."

As Reagan seated himself, Bogie looked him over carefully and then checked out Singleton as if appraising a heifer on the block. "Look, Penny, if this young and inexperienced guy can't satisfy you, I'll write down my number. Sometimes, in certain matters, experience is better than looks unless you like to break in novices."

"I'm fully booked, Mr. Bogart, but thanks for the offer," she said.

Unknown to Singleton, who was a brunette at the time, she was about to dye her locks blonde and appear as the comic strip character "Blondie" in a popular series that would run from 1938 to 1950.

Later, Bogie was surprised to learn that Singleton wasn't the dumb bottle blonde he'd initially thought she was. She became the first woman president of an AFL-CIO union and led a strike by the Radio City Rockettes.

"The fucking bitch is a rabble-rouser," Bogie told Ann Sheridan. "But the question remains, did Reagan get to fuck her?"

When *Swing Your Lady* opened, Bogie called Blondell. "You were right, babe. Across the country it was hissed off the screen."

Swing Your Lady took in less than $25,000 at the box office, but Jack Warner wasn't willing to let Bogie go. "Taking one more chance on the asshole, I'm upping his salary to $1,100 per week."

In time Harry Medved and Randy Lowell would select *Swing Your Lady* to appear in their book, *The Fifty Worst Films of All Time (and How They Got That Way)*.

Realizing too late that it had been a mistake to make it at all, Jack Warner pulled the plug on *Swing Your Lady* after it had run for only two nights across the country. He quickly replaced it with another Warner feature.

Bogie told the press, "*Swing Your Lady* is the worst film I've ever made." Of course, he had expressed those exact sentiments about some of his other movies.

***

Mary Philips had appeared as Nurse Ferguson in the 1932 adaptation of Ernest Hemingway's novel, *A Farewell to Arms*, starring Gary Cooper and Helen Hayes, but her screen appearances were very limited. However, in 1936 and into the early months of 1937, she decided to give a film career one more chance.

For a few seasons, she worked on several films back to back, appearing in supporting roles but "never as a star," she said. All her films were released in

1937.

Wings Over Honolulu starred Wendy Barrie and Ray Milland. Ironically, that same year Bogie appeared with Barrie in *Dead End*. Later, Mary told her husband that Milland had made a pass at her.

As Good as Married starred John Boles, Doris Nolan, Walter Pidgeon, and Mary. On set Mary spent most of her time talking to a fellow co-star, Katharine Alexander, who had been one of Bogie's first steady girlfriends—that is, until he introduced her to his best friend at the time, Bill Brady Jr., who moved in and stole Katharine's heart. On the set together, Mary and Katharine shared many memories of their days in New York.

That Certain Woman saw Mary and Katharine having yet another reunion when they were cast in a film starring Bette Davis and Henry Fonda. Mary later told Bogie that "Bette and I spent many long hours discussing you, and I must tell you her impression of you isn't exactly favorable."

"Tell me something I don't know," Bogie said.

On the set of *The Bride Wore Red*, Mary hardly got to meet her co-stars, Joan Crawford and Franchot Tone. "They were so into each other, and screwing so much between takes, that they didn't have time for any of us," Mary said.

In her films (top row), Mary Philips was always a minor player. She never made it in Hollywood movies the way she did on Broadway.

In the lower right-hand photo, Mary is remembered when she appeared with Bogie on Broadway in *Nerves* in 1924.

On the set of *Mannequin*, Mary was teamed against Joan Crawford who was co-starring with Spencer Tracy. Bogie felt nervous about Mary discussing him with his best pal, Tracy, and also with Crawford.

Mary was very blunt. "You may think Spencer is your best pal, but he put his hand up my dress."

"I'm not surprised," Bogie said, taking the revelation calmly. "I long ago told Spence that it was you who suggested that we 'date' other people when we worked on different coasts. He probably just wanted to check out what turned me on so long ago. Did you guys do it?"

"That is for me to know and you never to find out. Not only did the male star of the movie come on to me, so did the female star."

"If it's Joan Crawford, I wouldn't put it past her."

During the final months of her marriage, Mary spent far more time in the bed of Kenneth MacKenna than she did with her husband. By the time a hearing was held as part of her divorce proceedings from Bogie, her marriage to him had ended long before.

In the sweltering heat of an August day in Los Angeles, Judge Ruben S. Schmidt called his court to order.

In one corner sat Bogie with his lawyer. On the other side sat Mary Philips in a demure gray dress that made her look far older than her years. She was accompanied by her lawyer, Harry E. Sokolove, and family friend and theatrical agent, Mrs. Mary Baker, who had made several attempts in the past to bring the estranged couple back together.

In the courtroom, Mary Philip's voice was almost inaudible, despite her status as a Broadway actress used to projecting to the balcony. She seemed on the verge of tears, and her testimony was emotional and brief.

"My husband has told me that he doesn't love me," she said.

"How often did he tell you that?" the judge asked her.

"Frequently," she claimed.

"My husband was rarely at home," she continued. "When he came home, he never told me where he had been." She was careful to omit her own infidelities with Kenneth MacKenna and Roland Young.

Mary Baker was called as a witness, and her testimony was brief. "In my presence, as a close friend of the family, I often heard Mr. Bogart tell his wife that he no longer cared for her. I also heard him say that 'married life is too monotonous and does not give me the freedom I crave.'"

The court also heard testimony that the couple spent many months of their married life living apart on different coasts and that they had been separated since January 25, 1937.

The judge granted the divorce. Mary did not ask for alimony. It had been determined that as a working actress on Broadway during most of the span of their relationship, she had earned more money than Bogie did, and that she had often functioned in the past as her husband's sole means of support.

At the end of the courtroom proceedings, Bogie said nothing but shook her gloved hand. Her eyes did not meet his. The first to leave the courtroom, he walked out alone.

Waiting for him across the street in a coffee shop was a very impatient Mayo Methot.

Her first words to Bogie provoked the beginning of what would become hundreds of fights. "Well," she said, "did you finally divorce the whore?"

***

Months before the formal debut of their marriage, Methot and Bogie became known as "The Battling Bogarts." Many of their feuds were carried out at public watering holes. David Niven in his memoir, *Bring on the Empty Horses*, described one such encounter:

He'd met Bogie when he had been loaned by Warner Brothers to Samuel Goldwyn to make *Dead End.*

The two actors agreed to meet for lunch one day at the Formosa Café, since both were aware that the other was, on occasion, dating Ann Sheridan.

"We did not like each other very much," Niven claimed. "I found his aggressively tough and his needling manner rather tiresome. We parted with expressions of mutual respect and a determination from then on to avoid each other like the plague."

Niven, along with other observers, noted that Methot, with "conspicuous cleavage," matched Bogie drink for drink whenever they went out in public. But unlike her escort, she was unable to handle her liquor. It was obvious to many observers that she was becoming deeply entrenched as an alcoholic.

As part of a chance encounter one night at La Maze, a restaurant on Sunset Strip, Niven was seated six tables away from Bogie and Methot. His date for the night was Ann Sheridan. At that time, Methot was

(top) Mayo Methot to Bogie, "Did you divorce the whore?"

(center) David Niven. The ladies called him "beer can."

(bottom) The beautiful Ann Sheridan endorsing Chesterfields. She died in 1967 of esophageal cancer.

315

unaware that Bogie was slipping off to see Sheridan on occasion, usually when they made a picture together. The two couples nodded politely to each other.

Later in the evening from their position across the room, Niven and Sheridan became aware that a burly drunk in a tacky yellow-and-green plaid jacket was trying to pick a fight with Bogie. "You're not so tough," the drunk shouted at Bogie. "I could knock you out flat with one punch."

As a small man, Bogie usually tried not to engage in physical violence with drunks. But the bully kept stabbing his forefinger into Bogie's modest chest.

"Suddenly, all hell broke loose," Niven said. "Bogie threw a full glass of Scotch into his aggressor's eyes, and at the same moment Mayo hit the man on the head with a shoe. Cries of rage and alarm rose on all sides, and the air became thick with flying bottles, plates, glasses, left hooks, and food."

Niven with the Oomph Girl tried to duck under their table. The table was too small so they crawled to the nearest retreat. Within five minutes, Bogie on all fours crawled across the floor to them. Seeing them, he assured them, "Everything's okay—Mayo's handling it. I wish I'd brought a fork, though. I might be able to jab the bastard in the leg."

Sheridan later said, "For David and me, it was a moment of high drama. For Bogie and Methot, it was just another typical night. More fun was on the way. Slashed wrists. An arson attempt by her on their house. Stabbing him with a butcher knife."

***

Bogie told Claire Trevor, Ann Sheridan, Joan Blondell, Spencer Tracy, and any friend who would listen, that, "I hate Jack Warner. The fucker blames me for the failure of *Swing Your Lady*. I hate Warner Brothers; I hate the parts I'm assigned; I detest the studio system itself. *Swing Your Lady* causes a greenish pile to form in my gut."

Finally, over another drink, he asked Tracy, "Are you sure that Clark Gable is

Out on the town and keeping up appearances: "The Battling Bogarts" meet "America's sweethearts" Ronald Reagan & Jane Wyman *(right)*

Mayo *(left)* is fuming. Both marriages were doomed.

not going to play Rhett Butler? What about Gary Cooper?"

With a heavy heart, Bogie awaited his next acting assignment.

No longer a gangster, Bogie found himself cast as the Deputy Commissioner of Correction, running a reformatory school in *Crime School* (1938). His leading lady this time was the unknown Gale Page, with Billy Halop, one of the Dead End Kids, co-starring. Once again, Bogie was appearing with the Dead End Kids, not only Billy but Huntz Hall and Leo Gorcey. Vincent Sherman, who would become an A-list director and helm pictures for Bogie, was the co-author of the screenplay along with Crane Wilbur.

Lewis Seiler, the director, rushed to welcome Bogie to the set as if he were a major star. "At least there's somebody on the Warner lot who respects me," he told Billy.

Bogie sized Seiler up as a lightweight and determined that he would more or less have to direct himself. Seiler had come to Hollywood in 1919 as a gag man and had worked in two-reel comedies before hooking up with Tom Mix during the 1920s in a series of Westerns. Before he left Hollywood, he would attach his name to two A-list pictures, *Pittsburgh* (1942), with Marlene Dietrich and John Wayne, and *Guadalcanal Diary* (1943), with Preston Foster. Between 1923 and 1958, he would direct 88 films, most of them undistinguished.

Heading to Los Angeles from the northwest—Spokane, Washington, to be exact—Gale Page became one of Bogie's less distinguished leading ladies. Her most famous role would be with Ronald Reagan, not Bogie. In 1940 she appeared in *Knute Rockne—All American*.

In a phone call after the first week of shooting, Joan Blondell asked Bogie, "Have

(top photo) Bogie inspects the wounds of reform school's Billy Halop after a flogging.

(bottom) In this picture, Bogie was on the right side of the law.

317

you already fallen in love with your leading lady?"

"Gale's nice enough, a pretty brunette, but much too wholesome for me. Privately, Seiler and I have agreed that she was cast just for decoration in this potboiler. I predict she'll have a short career before retiring to the kitchen as a dutiful housewife rattling pots and pans."

Leo Gorcey was "full of himself" in Bogie's words, especially in the commissary when he was bragging that he'd played Joan Crawford's brother in *Mannequin*. "I'm not gonna be 'Spit' in the Dead End Kids forever."

"Did Crawford seduce you?" Bogie asked.

"Well, not really," Gorcey said.

"Then you're not going to be a star. Before you can become a really big star in Hollywood, you've got to get fucked by Crawford."

Although Bogie had worked previously with Billy Halop in *Dead End*, he didn't really get to know him until they made *Crime School* together. What caught his attention was one reviewer who called Billy "the next Humphrey Bogart." Bogie's response to that was, "the original Humphrey Bogart is still around and isn't going to Forest Lawn any time soon."

When he really met Billy and had some time to talk to him between takes, he actually came to like the kid. "He brought out the father side of me," he told Blondell. "I don't plan to have any kids in life, so Billy is the next best thing."

Billy had been one of the original Dead End Kids on Broadway in that stage hit, *Dead End*, in 1935. Samuel Goldwyn had brought him to Hollywood. In the early 1940s Billy abandoned his association with the other Dead End Kids, seeking a career of his own. To his regret, he could land parts only in B pictures.

Even as early as the period when he met Bogie, when he was still a teenager, Billy was already battling alcoholism. In the decades to come, Bogie would stand on the sidelines, watching his protégé through a series of money problems and marital disasters.

Billy seemed pleased with the salary he was pulling in for *Crime School*: $275 a week. "But they're gonna raise me to $650 a week—at least that's what I was told," he said to Bogie.

One night Billy's car had to be hauled off to the garage. "Damn," he told Bogie. "I've been screwing this hot chick. She's a singer and has a gig tonight at this dance joint in Santa Monica."

"Is it just for teenagers?" Bogie asked.

"No, it's for grownups."

"Well, my girlfriend, Mayo Methot, likes to dance," Bogie said. "Tell you what. I'll take you and your gal to Santa Monica, and we'll have some fun. People seeing us together will think we're your parents serving as chaperones."

"It's a deal."

With Mayo in the front seat with him, and Billy in the back, Bogie drove to the house of Billy's girlfriend.

The girl must have been looking out the window. Billy didn't have to ring the doorbell. She came running out to the car.

Even younger than Billy, this teenager was a bundle of nervous energy. Without waiting for Billy to introduce her, she jumped into the back seat. "Hi, I'm Judy Garland. I know all about you from Spencer Tracy. He took my cherry when I was only fifteen."

"Now that's how I like a gal to introduce herself," Bogie said. He'd never met a teenager like Garland before. Already, even though she was just breaking into Hollywood, she gave the impression of a battle-scarred show business veteran. Later he'd say, "When Judy sang 'Born in a Trunk,' I believed her."

"I lost my virginity to dear old dad," Methot chimed in as a rejoinder to Garland's revelation. "I was only fourteen."

"Now let's keep it cooled down," Bogie said as a warning to Methot. He couldn't help but notice that she was already drunk. She'd taken a flask so they'd have liquid refreshment during the long drive to Santa Monica.

As the evening evolved, neither of "The Battling Bogarts" were able to fulfill their duties as "chaperones" who'd drive their "charges" back home. Billy took the wheel and delivered the smashing drunk chaperones back to Bogie's home, leaving his car parked in front. He and Garland took a taxi back to where they were going.

"That kid's got something," Bogie said about Judy Garland the next morning over coffee with Methot. "I found it thrilling to hear her sing. She really got to me. I think she's going to topple that Deanna Durbin from her throne."

(top photo) Billy Halop with Bogie. "Like a son to me."

(bottom photo) Billy Halop with teenaged Judy Garland. Who stole the cherry? Billy or Spencer Tracy?

"Deanna Durbin," Methot said with contempt. "She may be the favorite singer of Winston Churchill and Joseph Stalin, but I can't stand the little stuck-up bitch."

Later, when *Crime School* was released, Bogie told Spencer Tracy and Joan Blondell that "I am seriously pissed off." Because of the growing popularity of the Dead End Kids, they received top billing over him in *Crime School*. In posters advertising the film, the names of the Dead End Kids appeared in typeface larger than Bogie's in movie posters and newspaper advertising.

***

Most mornings, usually over coffee, Bogie was a faithful reader of Sidney Skolsky's column "The Gospel Truth." In one of its editions he read: "Humphrey Bogart will marry Mayo Methot in September when his divorce

(bottom photo)
Bogie with Priscilla Lane.

Did he really seduce all three of the Lane sisters?

from Mary Phillips (sic) is finalized. She will marry Kenneth McKenna (sic), who was formerly married to Kay Francis, who will marry Baron Barenekow."

"At least Skolsky spelled my name right," Bogie said.

Bette Davis phoned Bogie that week with the news. "I got the news before you did," she said. "Warners has just informed me that you and I will be co-starring in a new film together, with me getting star billing, of course. It's called *Men Are Such Fools*. I haven't seen the script yet, but I just adore the title."

Two weeks later, Bogie still hadn't received a copy of the script. Instead, he got a call from Joan Blondell. "Duckie, it looks like we're going to be starring in a new film together. It's called *Men Are Such Fools*."

"What about a certain Miss Bette Davis?" he asked.

"Oh, she's out the door. I'm in."

By the end of the week, Bogie learned that Blondell was out of the picture too, the lead female role now going to Priscilla Lane.

When Warner Brothers finally contacted Bogie that his next picture was to be *Men Are Such Fools*, and the director was to be Busby Berkeley, his reaction was, "You've got to be

320

kidding. I don't wear feathers and boas, and I don't dance, at least not on camera."

Warners was insistent, however, claiming he'd be with such previous "film mates" as Penny Singleton and Priscilla Lane. The catch was that Bogie was assigned the third lead. The star of the picture would be Wayne Morris. "The big lug," Bogie said. "If you look good on camera, you can be dumb as a carrot but shoot right to stardom."

In addition to Singleton, Bogie's other love interest in the film would be Mona Barrie, playing a sardonic vamp. Before hooking up with Lane and Singleton again, Bogie met the English-born Barrie, who'd begun her career as a teenage ballerina.

He told his director, Berkeley, "Talk about a kid who's going nowhere in pictures. She'll get two or three more film jobs, and it'll be all over for that one. The only woman she can play on camera is the one who loses the man."

It's true that Barrie's career would fade into the setting sun by the early 1950s, but in the meantime she would appear in secondary roles in some fifty motion pictures, earning a star on the Hollywood Walk of Fame.

Morris, as the film's romantic lead, was being groomed as Warner's answer to MGM's Robert Taylor. Newspapers were billing him as "Hollywood's latest hearththrob."

"You've worked with Morris before in *Kid Galahad*," Berkeley said to Bogie. "Do you think he can carry this picture as the male lead?"

"I think if you tossed Morris a football, he could run to the goalpost," Bogie said. "As an actor, he's tall and blond and some say handsome. I also hear he's got a big dick."

"The first qualifications are just fine," Berkeley said. "But I don't get that about the big dick. We can't show that on camera."

"Why not?" Bogie asked. "The day will come in film when you can. Why not be the first? Also showing big dicks on the screen will increase attendance from women and homosexual guys."

"Bogie, you're such a kidder."

Based on a magazine article by Faith Baldwin, the plot of *Men Are Such Fools* was weak. Lane played a woman who wanted both a career and a husband simultaneously, with Morris playing her spouse, an ex-football star. Bogie was cast into the role of a sleazy advertising big shot who will help Lane's career if she'll be "nice" to him.

Bogie had initially thought he'd despise Berkeley on sight. But the two men bonded, each finding that the other was a drinking man. Although he'd reigned as one of the most creative directors in Hollywood, Berkeley was late into his career and deep into alcoholism when he made *Men Are Such Fools*.

"If I recall, and I do, Busby and Bogie drank a lot during the shooting of that picture," said Priscilla Lane.

Although much of Hollywood thought Berkeley was gay because of his outlandish musical extravaganzas, he was a notorious womanizer.

Eddie Cantor said, after seeing *Golden Diggers* in 1937, "Only a flamer would feature 75 helmet-wearing dancers carrying drums and flags with 50 oversized white rocking chairs, each one big enough for three."

Berkeley admitted to Bogie that he went from woman to woman, but had nothing but failed relationships. "I can't satisfy a woman, yet I lust after them."

"Sounds like you got a real problem there," Bogie said, embarrassed at hearing such a personal revelation.

Busby Berkeley directed *42nd Street* (1933).

(bottom photo) Berkeley in a more pensive mood. To Bogie, he confessed, "I can't satisfy a woman."

Bogie told Berkeley he drank because he wanted to, but Berkeley said he did it to control his nervousness. He'd been through several highly traumatic experiences in 1935, his divorce from his fourth wife, Merna Kennedy, being the smallest of his problems.

He'd attended a party thrown by William Koenig to celebrate the completion of *In Caliente* (1935). On the way back home, he crashed into two cars.

Defended by hotshot attorney Jerry Giesler, Berkeley was put on trial for murder, not manslaughter.

Two passengers had been killed and five others seriously injured in the accident. Berkeley was badly cut and bruised. Hauled into court on a stretcher, he heard witnesses testify that they smelled liquor on his breath. They also testified that Berkeley whizzed down Roosevelt Highway, cut out of line, crashed headlong into one car, and then sideswiped another.

After two trials, each ending in hung juries, Berkeley was acquitted in a third and final trial.

"This Giesler sounds like a great phone number to have," Bogie told

Berkeley. "I'm gonna need him when I finally get around to killing Mayo Methot."

On the set, Bogie and Singleton shared their mutual despair over the bomb they'd made, *Swing Your Lady*. She also confessed that, "Ronnie got away from me," meaning Ronald Reagan. "Among others, he's dating a gal named Jane Wyman."

Priscilla Lane came up to Bogie and said, "When you worked with my sister, Lola, on *Marked Woman*, she told me all about you, you wolf."

"Did she also tell you how good I am in bed?" he asked provocatively.

"Watch those come-ons with me," she said. "I look like a sweet and innocent gal, but I'm not. I might take you up on that."

Maybe she did take him up on his proposition. Bogie remains the only source of his claim to his pals that he seduced each of the three Lane sisters.

He was yet to work with Rosemary Lane, but in a few months he'd be co-starring with her in *The Oklahoma Kid*.

During the shoot, Bogie shifted his attention to a young Carole Landis, who got 17th billing.

When he met her, he told her, "You are the most beautiful woman working in movies today."

"A compliment like that will get you anywhere," Landis said.

And so it did.

Landis got the part in the movie because of Berkeley, who was her boyfriend and supporter.

Landis agreed to date Bogie but they had to slip around and conduct a clandestine affair, since Berkeley was hot on her trail, wanting her to marry him, and Bogie had his stalker, the fierce and occasionally violent Mayo Methot.

Without attempting to make Ann Sheridan jealous, Bogie told her that "Carole is my kind of woman. She broke into show business on the casting couch. That's how a gal should do it."

He found Carole strikingly beautiful, but terribly insecure. She seemed to be searching for love and not finding it. He was certain that her extraordinary beauty would win her many men, but not one with whom she could ever build a lasting relationship.

Their affair ended when the shoot was over. "It was brief, but memorable," he said. "Call it *An Affair to Remember*."

Even though he no longer saw Landis, he remained intrigued by her.

When he saw the final cut of *Men Are Such Fools*, producer Hal Wallis said, "I should have junked the whole thing. Let's re-title it *Hanky Panky in an Ad Agency*."

No complete version of *Men Are Such Fools* exists today. In the footage that does exist, Landis does not appear. Just a few months earlier, she'd worked with the same stars, Wayne Morris and Priscilla Lane, on a picture called *Love, Honor and Behave.*

In the years ahead, Bogie often speculated that he should have married Landis instead of Methot. He eagerly listened to any news of her tragic final years in the 1940s and was titillated by the streams of gossip swirling around her.

In 1945, he heard that Landis was appearing in a Broadway musical called *A Lady Said Yes.*

Jacqueline Susann, who later became one of the world's best-selling novelists, had been cast into the same show. The talk of Broadway was that Landis and Susann were sustaining a torrid lesbian affair. When Susann wrote her blockbuster book, *Valley of the Dolls*, she based the character of Jennifer North on Landis.

Bogie was deeply saddened by the death of Landis, presumably by suicide. The date was July 5, 1948, and at the time, Landis was only twenty-nine years old.

Landis had spent her last night with her lover, actor Rex Harrison. On the final evening of her life, he had told her that he would not divorce his wife, Lilli Palmer, that he planned to resuscitate his marriage, and that he was ending his affair. Reportedly, Landis threatened Harrison that she'd reveal the details of their affair to the newspapers.

A maid discovered her dead the next afternoon on the bathroom floor of her Pacific Palisades home. She'd overdosed on Seconal and had left two suicide notes, one for her mother,

Carole Landis entertaining the troops during WWII
(Male figure on left is unknown)

Inset photo: Rex Harrison, "That Limey Bastard"

the second for Harrison. The maid gave Harrison the note, and he destroyed it.

At a coroner's inquest, Harrison denied there was a second note and claimed he knew of no reason why Landis would consider killing herself.

There was underground speculation that Harrison was responsible for Landis' death, faking a suicide when it was actually murder. He apparently feared that a revelation of marital infidelity would destroy his stellar career.

Bogie always maintained that Harrison—"that limey bastard"—had arranged for Landis' death. "No one can convince me otherwise," he said.

***

Since he had no real star power at Warners, Bogie more or less had to take whatever roles he was assigned. Often he found out what role he was slated for by reading the trade papers. Previously known for its black-and-white films, Warners was moving more and more into Technicolor.

He'd heard that George Brent and Wayne Morris were set to star in *Valley of the Giants*, a Peter B. Kyne story about lumber camps in the Northwest.

On March 30, 1938, he picked up a newspaper paper and read an item by Elizabeth Yeaman. Brent was off the picture, having been replaced by Bogie himself. "Oh, no, not Wayne Morris again," he shouted at Methot. "And, to top it off, my puss in Technicolor."

Yeaman predicted that *Valley of the Giants* "will be a bigger opportunity for Bogart, who has plugged along delivering villainous supporting roles, but always turning in a good performance."

Like so many previous casting announcements, this one fell through for Bogie. *Valley of the Giants* (1938) was filmed without him. Morris kept his starring role but Bogie's part went to Frank McHugh, appearing in the film with Claire Trevor taking the female lead.

When director Anatole Litvak sent over a script called *The Amazing Dr. Clitterhouse*, Bogie read it but wasn't impressed. To Methot, he disparagingly referred to this movie as "The Amazing Doctor Clitoris."

"I don't even get to play Dr. Clit," Bogie told Methot. "The lead goes to the ugliest man in Hollywood, Edward G. Robinson. Alongside him, I look like Tyrone Power. Ronald Colman turned down the lead. Smart guy, that Colman. Would you believe my character is called Rocks Valentine? Who makes up crap like this? Some of the other characters include Pat Pal, Rabbit, Tug, and Popus Poopus. One guy, Billy Wayne, plays Candy. If we ever have a son, let's call him Candy. He'll learn to be tough when the bullies beat him up every day in the schoolyard."

This was one of the most bizarre gangster films Warners ever turned out.

As Dr. Clitterhouse, Robinson wants to understand the criminal mind. To gain first-hand knowledge, he becomes a criminal himself, committing several jewelry heists.

He joins up with a "fence," surprisingly played by Claire Trevor, who negotiates deals with a gang of safecrackers headed by Rocks (Bogie himself).

In a weird twist, near the end, Dr. Clitterhouse gives Rocks a poisoned drink so he can study his reactions while he goes into his death throes.

On the set Bogie asked Robinson, "How many times are you gonna kill me in the movies before I die off?"

(bottom photo) "Beauty and The Beast"

Bogie is caught between The Beauty (Claire Trevor) and The Beast, (Edward G. Robinson), whom Bogie called "Dr. Clit."

"I predict you'll have nine lives."

Bogie later claimed that Robinson had his mind on everything but playing the role of Dr. Clitterhouse. "All he talked about was the oncoming war in Europe. He was supporting every group opposed to Hitler and contributing a lot of dough. Because many of the groups he joined were pro-Stalin or pro-Soviet Union, he was later accused of being a Communist."

By late 1949, Robinson was being attacked by such ilk as Gerald I.K. Smith, the moving force behind the Knights of the White Camellia, an anti-Semitic, anti-Black group. "Robinson is one of Stalin's main agents in Hollywood," Smith charged. "A part of the Stalin machine. He should be put in a Federal Penitentiary."

On the set Bogie hoped to resume his warm, cozy relationship with co-star, Claire Trevor, but she was planning to marry CBS producer Clark Andrews, so she had cooled her ardor for him. "Let's be friends," she told him. And so they did.

Born in Kiev, Anatole Litvak, the director, was married to actress Miriam Hopkins when he arrived on the set to direct Robinson and Bogart in *The Amazing Dr. Clitterhouse.*

"Miriam and I just might take your title away from you," Litvak told him. "The Battling Bogarts" might be replaced by "The Battling Litvaks." Miriam and I had a knock-out, drag-out—as you Americans say—the other night. I left her."

"Mayo and I don't need an excuse to fight," Bogie said. "What about you and Miriam?"

"She found out about my affair with her arch rival, Bette Davis," Litvak said.

"That'll do it every time," Bogie said. "Women are so different from men. We're made to have affairs."

"My dear boy, so are women," Litvak said.

Three days later, Bogie was only mildly surprised to encounter Bette Davis slipping onto the set for a rendezvous with Litvak, whom she referred to as "Tola." That same year of the Clitterhouse movie, Litvak would direct Davis in *The Sisters.*

With Davis and Litvak occupied in their torrid love affair, Bogie was left alone on the set to greet Gale Page, with whom he'd made *Crime School,* a film in which he'd been the star and Page his leading lady. Now in *The Amazing Dr. Clitterhouse,* he was reduced to third billing, but she fared even worse, having been demoted to sixth billing in her role as Nurse Randolph.

"I thought *Crime School* was going to make you a big star," he said to Page. "At least, that's what you told me. What happened?"

"You're such a needler," Page said. "I don't need to be reminded about how I'm not setting the world on fire. Perhaps there will be a scene between us in this picture where I, as your nurse, get to stick a very long needle in your ass."

"You'd do anything to see my ass, wouldn't you now?" Bogie asked.

"You don't have one of the great asses of Hollywood, in case you haven't turned backwards for a look in a full-length mirror."

"She turned her back on him and started to walk away. "Actually, I'm an ass man myself, and you've got a set of buns,

Three views of Miriam Hopkins

(top photo) "When I can't sleep, I don't count sheep. I count lovers."

(middle photo) "When I became middle-aged, the phone stopped ringing."

(bottom photo) Hopkins with Bogie's director, Anatole Litvak. "Bette Davis, the greedy bitch, bedded my husband."

baby."

"You'll never get to enjoy it," she said as her farewell greeting.

"An hour later, Litvak emerged from his bungalow, leaving Davis inside, presumably to repair the damage to her makeup. Bogie walked over to Litvak, but decided not to mention Davis. "I just encountered Gale Page," Bogie said. "Leslie Howard and I have this bet to see who can seduce the largest number of our co-stars, but I just struck out with Page."

"Don't bother with her." Litvak said. "I'll give you my wife's phone number. You can call up dear Miss Miriam Hopkins herself. She'd love to get deep-dicked by you. She's certainly not getting it from me."

"Thanks for the offer of your wife's sevices," Bogie said. "Bette Davis must not find out about this. She positively hates Miriam."

"I know," Litvak said. "Now get back before those cameras and try to give me some emotion this time."

As far as it is known, Bogie never revealed to any of his friends, not even Spencer Tracy, whether he took advantage of Miriam Hopkins' phone number—or not.

In the making of *The Sisters*, Davis had fought with her director over how a scene should be shot. She called Litvak "stubborn." He called her "very, very stubborn."

When Davis and Bogie met again, he asked her pointedly. "I heard you and Litvak broke up. What happened?"

"It was more than his being a very stupid director," she said. "I found out that he took Paulette Goddard to dinner at Ciro's and spent most of the evening under the table servicing the bitch."

Bogie had a major fight with wardrobe when he was asked to don a bathing suit and dive off the edge of a swimming pool. "I don't have the kind of body I like to show off," he said. "Get Wayne Morris, maybe Johnny Weissmuller."

Finally, Litvak got him to perform the scene in an old-fashioned "shoulder-to-thigh" suit.

John Huston, the future director of Bogie's *The African Queen* showed up on the set of *The Amazing Dr. Clitterhouse*. He'd written the screenplay with John Wexley, who identified himself to Bogie as "a radical leftist."

That afternoon, Huston would encounter a trio of stars—Robinson, Bogie, and Claire Trevor, all of whom he'd eventually cast in *Key Largo* (1948), along with Bogie's fourth wife, Lauren Bacall.

Billy Wayne played so many bit parts between 1935 and 1955 that he lost track of the number of times he'd been cast as cabbies, sailors, reporters, and photographers. Bogie asked Litvak to introduce him to the boy playing "Candy." He expected him to be effeminate. If so, Bogie would rib him a bit.

"Hi, Candy," Bogie said, coming up to him. "I play Lollipop in this movie. Maybe we can get together and eat each other?"

Wayne studied him carefully. "You know that scar on your lip, Bogart? Would you like another?"

Bogie had several drinks with supporting players John Litel and Ward Bond. They were part of what became known as the "Warner Bros. Stock Company" in the 1930s, assigned to various supporting roles whenever they came up.

"I'm getting old, guys," Bogie told Litel and Bond. "If I don't make it soon as a number one movie star, I'll be playing character roles with you losers."

Always cast in no-nonsense roles, Litel would appear in more than 200 films. A few times he played the lead in B movies. Bogie would work with him again in *They Drive by Night*.

Gruff, burly, Nebraska-born Ward Bond became a familiar face to moviegoers of the 1930s and beyond. A favorite of director John Ford, Bond was John Wayne's best friend.

"What do you guys do all the time hanging out together?" Bogie asked.

"We go to bars, get drunk, and start fights," Bond said.

"Sounds like fun," Bogie said. One afternoon when Bogie was complaining to Bond that Warners forced him to make too many movies in one year, "Don't be a fucking sissy," Bond said "In 1935 I acted in thirty movies."

Bond himself would make at least 175 movies. One drunken night Bond and Bogie made a strange pact. Both of them agreed to die before their 60th birthday. "Who wants to live to be 60?" Bogie asked.

"Not me," Bond replied.

Although they may have forgotten their alcohol-sodden vows by the time of their deaths, both Bond and Bogie kept their promise to each other, each of them eventually dying at the ages of 57 and 58, respectively.

The Amazing Dr. Clitterhouse earned a profit of $10,000, *The New York Times* calling it "sad and aimless," the kindest words they had for this turkey.

Bogie later claimed that the role of

Two views of Ward Bond, the busiest actor in Hollywood and John Wayne's best friend. Bond made a "death oath" with Bogie.

Rocks Valentine was "one of my all-time least favorites."

***

Also cast in the Dr. Clitterhouse movie was Max (Slapsie Maxie) Rosenbloom. Bogie found this former boxer fascinating with his cauliflower ears, fat lips, and punch drunk mug. Instead of chasing women on the set, as he usually preferred to do, Bogie spent long hours talking with Slapsie Maxie, a title bestowed on the boxer by Damon Runyon because of this less-than-classy style of slapping opponents in the ring.

Slapsie Maxie enthralled Bogie with his stories of the ring, but also his tall tales of his gambling and womanizing. He claimed he'd bedded Mae West, and Bogie did not find this unbelievable as Miss West was known to have "this thing" for boxers.

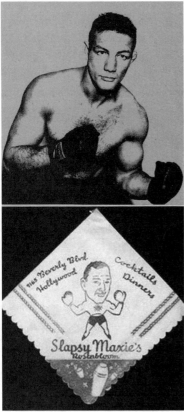

Slapsie Maxie Rosenbloom learned that Mae West had a "thing" for boxers.

(bottom photo) A souvenir from his famous restaurant

Bogie confessed, "I'm a coward. I run from a fight. But since I play a tough guy on screen, every bully goes after me."

Slapsie Maxie agreed to work out with Bogie in the ring to teach him how to defend himself. "I did okay in the ring before I ended up in Hollywood playing Runyon-like thugs and pugs. But I was never a strong puncher in my heyday. I developed this technique of a hit-and-run defensive type of boxing. I'll teach it to you."

"Actually, I wish you would," Bogie said. "Not just to protect myself from bullies, but for another reason. Career advancement. Hollywood is getting ready to make *Golden Boy*. I want the lead role of a boxer."

"Okay, I'll teach you to box," Slapsie Maxie agreed. The ex-boxer kept his promise, with Bogie working out in the ring with the champ, as Mayo stood on the sidelines, screaming, "Kill the fucker, Bogie. Kill him!"

Bogie continued to see Slapsie Maxie over the years.

In 1943, Bogie showed up at Hollywood's newest night club, Slapsie

330

Maxie's. Bogie's date that night was Ingrid Bergman.

In just a few years, the boxer, as Bogie observed, was suffering from Paget's disease, actually *pugilistica dementia*, as a result of continuous blows to his head which he'd endured as a boxer.

"Poor Slapsie Maxie," Bogie later said. "He taught me how to fight. Punch the fucker in the kisser, bloody his nose, and while he's recovering from the blow, run like hell."

***

On the set Bogie encountered Ronald Reagan again. He was complaining about his meager part as a radio announcer. "They are not even letting me show my face in this film—just my voice."

"Would you say that's better than having to show your ass?" Bogie asked. "Listen to me, Reagan, you're a good looking guy—not my type, but good looking enough, I guess, although I prefer men with more kissable tits. I saw a picture of you without your shirt."

"You're kidding me," Reagan said. "I was told you like to put people on."

"You're gonna go to the top," Bogie said. "I've told you this before. You're going to become a bigger star than I could ever hope to be. It'll take a few more Bs for you, then it's Grade A prime rib beef movie roles for you. As for me, with my kisser, I'm stuck in the Bs. Jack Warner has told every director on the lot that I'm not good looking enough for a romantic role. He also considers me a midget. He complains I'm losing my hair. Then there's the question of my lisp."

"Yes, I was wondering about that," Reagan said. "I was told to stay away from guys who lisp in Hollywood."

"Good advice, kid."

"I also got my report card from Jack Warner," Reagan said. "A little bird told me."

"You mean a certain secretary in Warner's office, the one with the shapely legs."

"Something like that," Reagan said. "Warner thinks I'm nice looking—of course, that's damning with faint praise. He says my best quality is my voice, very friendly. As for my acting, he thinks I'm a bit stiff but okay for B pictures. He thinks I have no comic timing, so I can only do drama. But, and here's the rub, he thinks I have 'no heat' on the screen."

"If you and I did a love scene together, we'd burn up the screen," Bogie said.

"You're such a kidder," Reagan said. "I was warned about you. Fortunately, man-on-man kissing scenes will never be shown on the screen—

we can thank God for that."

"As I said, hang in there," Bogie said. "You can play romantic leads throughout the 40s and into the 50s. If you're still around in the 60s, highly unlikely, you'll have to switch to villain roles."

"What about you?" Reagan asked. "You still plan to be a villain in the 1960s?"

"No, not me," Bogie said. "When the 60s roll around, I'll be resting comfortably in Forest Lawn."

"I'm going to hang around for two or three more years," Reagan said. "If I don't make it, I'm going back home, back to radio."

Ronald Reagan in his only role as a villain. Whereas John F. Kennedy seduced Angie Dickinson (depicted with Reagan, above), Reagan, a future president, beat her up, but only on screen.

Of his early roles, including *Swing Your Lady*, Reagan later said, "Remember the guy in the movies who rushes into the phone booth, pushes his hat to the back of his head while the tails of his trench coat are still flying, drops a nickel in the box, dials a few numbers and then says, 'Gimme the city desk. I've got a story that'll split this town wide open!' That was me."

Bogie had met so many young actors like Reagan in Hollywood. As he told Methot, "They start out in bit parts, become romantic stars on the screen, and end up in character roles when the face sags. The hero often becomes an aging villain."

Indeed that was what happened to Reagan in his last movie, *The Killers*, based on a story by Ernest Hemingway. He was cast as a powerful underworld figure who beats up on poor Angie Dickinson. A scene of him, with his face contorted in anger, was used against him when he ran for president in 1980. The head read: HE VIOLENTLY BEAT UP ON ANGIE DICKINSON. AS PRESIDENT, HE'LL DO THE SAME TO AMERICA!

***

As long as Bogie lived, he'd never forget the way Susan Hayward had approached him on the set of *The Amazing Dr. Clitterhouse*. She was appearing in the film in a minor role.

"Hi, Rocks," she said, using the name of the character he was playing. "I'm Susan Hayward, and I've come to Hollywood to play Scarlett O'Hara. It appears we'll be working together, with you as my Rhett Butler."

He was so stunned by her approach that at first he did not have a ready answer, unusual for him. "You certainly have the hair to play Scarlett," he finally said.

"That's not the issue," she said, standing before him with a hand on her hip. "The question is, do you have the balls to play Rhett Butler?"

"Indeed I do," he shot back, "and I'm ready to start clanking them at any minute."

"Ronald Reagan's already beat you to me," she said.

This surprised Bogie, who felt that Reagan wasn't quite enough of a man to handle Hayward. As he would later tell Claire Trevor, "I wonder if *I'm* enough of a man to take Hayward."

"If you can deal with Mayo Methot, you can tackle Hayward."

The details are missing, but it appears that Bogie did have a brief fling with Hayward. It seemed to be a tryst he wanted to break off quickly.

Trevor later said that Bogie came to her one day with a horrible problem. "In bed, Hayward claws a man's back like a tigress. How am I going to explain that to Mayo?"

"I've got an idea," Trevor said. "Take her in the kitchen while she's cooking dinner. You remain fully clothed, with only your pants down. Pull up her dress and go at it. Tell her you were overcome with passion and couldn't wait to get to the bedroom and undress."

"Claire, that's why I love you so," he said. "What would I do without you?"

"Learn to live with it," she said. "I'm fully booked."

"The question was only rhetorical."

In later years, he would say, "Susan Hayward was a stunning beauty. But she had a savage heart. In many ways, her granite-hard Brooklynese, feisty spirit evoked Barbara Stanwyck. Susan made it the hard way. From the slums to the stenographers' pool, from the modeling agency to Hollywood's casting couch. She did it her way. What she lacked in talent, she made up for in fierce determination to become a star. We ended up working for different studios, but I think one of the great screen teams of all times would have been Humphrey Bogart and Susan Hayward. Note the billing, of course."

Susan Hayward

In the final cut of *The Amazing Dr. Clitterhouse*, you don't see Reagan but you hear his voice as a radio

333

announcer, a job he held before becoming a film actor.

As Hayward lamented to Bogie, "My part in the film ended up on the cutting room floor."

"Welcome to Hollywood, babe," Bogie said.

Even though Hayward and Bogie would never work together, she would appear in his life story as a morbid footnote. Bogie and Lauren Bacall were planning on filming *Melville Goodwin, U.S.A.*, a script based on the novel by John P. Marquand.

After Bogie died, Bacall understandably dropped out. Warner Brothers retitled this 1957 release *Top Secret Affair*, giving Hayward Bacall's part and awarding her star billing. Kirk Douglas took the role originally slated for Bogart.

This box office bust was about an aggressive lady publisher seeking to discredit a distinguished war hero. "Too bad Bogie died," Hayward said upon the release of the film. "I wasted my time and energy on this turkey. He should have lived to make his Last Supper."

***

Director Lloyd Bacon called Bogie with the news. "Jack Warner wants you to do another gangster movie. You play the most powerful gangland chief in Manhattan wanting to muscle in on the trucking business."

"It sounds like something from the bio of George Raft, but I guess he turned it down. What's the billing?"

"You're the fucking star," Bacon said.

"At least that's an improvement." Who's the leading pussy?"

"Gloria Dickson," Bacon said.

"Never heard of her."

"It'll be good working with you again, Bogie," Bacon said, "without that Irish drunk hamming it up." The director was referring to Bogie's *San Quentin* picture, in which he'd co-starred with Pat O'Brien and Ann Sheridan.

The film, *Racket Busters,* was based on Thomas E. Dewey's investigations of organized crime in New York City, specifically as they applied to New York City's trucking businesses. George Brent, Bette Davis' frequent leading man, was cast as Bogie's co-star.

Even before meeting him, Bogie had many reasons to dislike Brent, whom he derided as having all the excitement of a tube of paste. His main objection was that Brent had been the lover of Bette Davis ever since the making of *So Big* in 1932. In the years to come they made a series of pictures together including *Golden Arrow* in 1936.

Brent was actually married to the star, Ruth Chatterton, and had little

334

interest in Davis, who was still married to Ham Nelson. But Davis still managed to seduce him in her dressing room whenever they made a picture together.

The same year that *Racket Busters* was released, Brent had been reduced to playing third lead after Davis and Henry Fonda in 1938.

Suddenly, as Davis moved up as the number one star at Warner Brothers, Brent's allure was fading at the box office, although he'd hang on for many years to come.

Gloria Dickson

Bogie had another reason to resent Brent. While casting was being considered by Jack Warner, Bacon had promoted Bogie to play the role of trucker Denny Jordan.

The role of the male lead, an independent truck driver who later rats on the gangland bosses, was clearly the most sympathetic. Bacon cited *Black Legion* in which Bogie had played a similar role, and suggested he'd be excellent as Denny. Warner turned Bogie down, going for Brent instead.

Since Bogie had to work with Brent, he decided to conceal his hostility and accept his invitation for a game, just assuming Brent meant a game of golf.

Arriving at Brent's home, he was directed to a rifle range out back, one which used focused beams of light from photo-electric cells instead of real bullets.

Little tin rabbits painted in rainbow-hued colors raced across the target, but fell "dead" whenever Brent got a "bead" on one of them with the light from the photo gun.

After about fifteen minutes of target practice, Bogie asked Brent, "Got something strong to drink?"

The rest of the afternoon was spent listening to Brent discuss his role in IRA guerrilla fighting during the Anglo-Irish War (1919-1922). He later fled Ireland with a bounty on his head.

To end the day, Brent, a licensed pilot, took

335

Bogie on a sightseeing tour at sunset over the California coast.

On the set the following week, Bogie met his co-star Gloria Dickson. "Where you from, kid?"

"Pocatello, Idaho," she said.

"I thought Pocatello, Idaho, was a joke. I didn't know that somebody actually came from there."

Later he said to Bacon, "The gal looks familiar. I must have seen her in something."

"She made an auspicious debut in *They Won't Forget*," Bacon said.

"Yeah, I caught that one," Bogie said. "But I was too busy watching Lana Turner's tits bounce around in that tight sweater to pay attention to anything else."

Dickson had just gotten married to Perc Westmore, so he gave her wide berth, although he told Bacon that Dickson "is definitely fuckable. But I've got my own bottle blonde at home. Think I'll sit this one out."

Bogie thought Dickson's career would be short but not so tragic. In one of her last performances in *Crime Doctor's Strangest Case*, she played the wife of a man who habitually started accidental fires with carelessly discarded cigarettes. Ironically, within just two short years, she would die in a house fire caused by a carelessly discarded cigarette.

Her footnote in history? Her image was the first natural color photograph in history to be transmitted by International News Pictures from Hollywood to New York.

After she'd died, Bogie was waiting in a dentist office, thumbing through some old movie magazines. He was surprised to find Dickson on the cover. The title of the article was THE LUCKIEST GIRL IN THE WORLD.

Racket Busters almost became Bogie's last movie. His life was saved by the quick-thinking crew. As part of his portrayal of a racketeer in the story, he was instructed to stand on a platform with a bucket of highly toxic sulphuric acid, waiting to throw it over a truck of garden produce as it drove by. The director had ordered that real acid be used because it would raise smoke as soon as it hit the produce.

Just at the moment he was to toss the acid, Bogie lost his footing and fell into the moving truck with the bucket of acid over him. Had it hit his face, he would have been permanently disfigured for life.

Rushing to the scene, the prop men ripped off all his clothes, leaving him jaybird naked. He watched in horror as his clothing seemed to burn to pieces. Someone finally thought to bring him a blanket to cover up his nudity.

The doctor on call at Warners examined him for wounds or damage, but amazingly he had emerged unscathed from the lethal acid.

Instead of allowing him the rest of the day off, Bacon ordered that the scene be re-shot. Dry ice would be used instead of sulphuric acid.

On the set, Bogie couldn't help needling Penny Singleton. "In seventh billing, huh?" he asked. "Just a few months ago you had star billing over me in *Men Are Such Fools*."

"No gentleman would ever point that out to me," she said.

"I'm not a gentleman," he said.

"That was obvious from the first day I met you," she said.

"I hear you just made a movie called *Blondie* where you're the wife of Dagwood Bumstead. And you once told me you wanted to be a serious actress."

"Didn't you set out to be a serious actor?" she asked. "Now look at you. A fourth rate George Raft."

"Okay, Singleton, I think we've traded enough barbs for one day. I've got to hunt up George Brent and needle him. You know, I'm billed over him?"

"Why I'll never know," Singleton said, turning and walking away from him. She paused and looked back at him. "Why can't you be a gentleman like Ronald Reagan."

"Because ladies like a man who treats them rough," he said.

"Then I'm no lady," she said.

"I'd already figured that out for myself."

"Oh, let me out of here," she said. "You just won't let go."

"Not when I've got hold of a hot pair of tits," he said.

"You! You're just insufferable. I don't know how Mayo Methot puts up with you."

"She doesn't."

That day he had lunch with the mustachioed character actor Walter Abel. He had a favor to ask. Abel was married at the time to the concept harpist Marietta Bitter.

Bogie began with an apology. "Of course, there's no money in it but I'd like your wife to play her harp at my wedding to Mayo Methot."

"I'm sure she'd do it," Abel said. "I'll ask her." Bogie ordered ham and eggs, Abel preferring the blue plate special, beef stew. "You know, Bogie, you and I are the same age, but I just don't seem to get the star parts like you. What have you got that I don't have?"

"Three extra inches, your wife tells me."

"You just can't give up that damn needling, can you?" Abel asked. "Not even when you're asking a favor."

"I'm a sicko."

During the course of his long career, Abel would appear with some of the biggest stars in Hollywood, ranging from Bette Davis in *Mr. Skeffington* (1944) to Montgomery Clift and Elizabeth Taylor in *Raintree County* (1957).

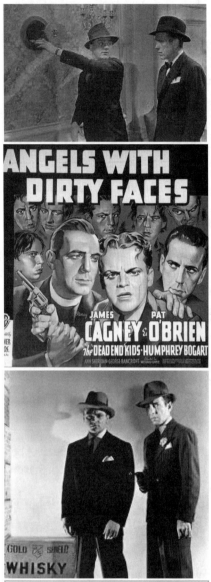

At the end of the shoot, Brent came up and shook Bogie's hand. "It's been real swell working with you. I hope I'll have the pleasure again."

"Perhaps Bette Davis will cast us in her next picture where we'll be two beaux fighting over her honeypot," Bogie said. "Incidentally, speaking of that honeypot—it's ginger if you remember—Bette told me you were a lousy lay."

***

At long last, Michael Curtiz, future director of *Casablanca*, brought Bogie together with one of his three arch rivals on the Warners lot, James Cagney. Thanks partly to his status as a major box office star, Cagney, of course, had been awarded the lead in *Angels with Dirty Faces*, with Pat O'Brien coming in second. Bogie and his friend, Ann Sheridan, had the third and fourth leads.

Bogie was also reunited with the Dead End Kids, Huntz Hall, Leo Gorcey, and Billy Halop. He preferred to spend his time with Billy and not the other boys.

Curtiz, riding the rest of his fame, at first objected to doing a gangster movie. But Hal Wallis insisted. "I know you conflicted with Cagney while making *Jimmy the Gent* with the little fart, but you also have the balls to keep *that one* in line."

As critic Robert Sklar put it, casting Cagney as the lead criminal instead of Bogie gave the menacing figure "a violent comic energy, not a morose lethargy."

During the 1930s at Warner Brothers, Bogie lived in the shadow of James Cagney. Bogie envied Cagney, dismissing him as "a song-and-dance man trying to be a gangster on screen." Both men are depicted in the three images above.

At private parties, Bogie imitated Cagney as a cocky, fast-talking, conceited bundle of dynamic energy.

338

Bogie played James Frazier, a crooked lawyer fronting for the mob. Wallis was hoping with the *Dirty Faces* movie to revive the gangster genre, which had catalyzed a stream of box office hits for the studio throughout the 1930s.

Bogie's first words to Cagney were, "No longer in drag, huh? Don't mess with me or I might spread the word around the lot about how you got your start in show business."

Bogie and Cagney would never be friends—they were far too jealous of each other—but they tried to amuse each other with stories of their work at Warner Brothers.

At one point, Cagney related to Bogie what it was like making the film *Boy Meets Girl* (also set for release in 1938) with sexy, 'dumb-blonde' Marie Wilson.

Cagney knew that Bogie had appeared with Wilson in *China Clipper*. "Marie was required in one scene to sit on my lap, and the director had to shoot and reshoot," Cagney claimed. "I kept getting a hard-on. Marie later told everybody, 'Sitting on Jimmy's lap was like being on top of a flagpole.'"

Bogie was known for delivering the last word before he walked away from a person. "That's a good one, Cagney. But I heard Howard Hughes turned down a loan-out offer from Warner Brothers because he said you're 'nothing but a runt.' As for exact measurements, I guess I'd better ask Noël Coward."

"You know about that, you mother fucker?"

Bogie and Cagney made up the next day. After having recently been suspended by the studio, Cagney was eager to make this picture work. He viewed his role of Rocky Sullivan as a sort of comeback picture for him.

"I told Wallis that I was tired of doing just another gangster picture, and I wanted to make this one something special," Cagney told Bogie.

What Bogie didn't confide to Cagney was that he'd lobbied behind his back to play the role of Rocky himself.

"I haven't read the script yet," Bogie

The Dead End Kids *(top photo)* thought gangster Cagney was a hero until he walked The Last Mile on his way to the electric chair. But Cagney onscreen, during that scene, became a wimp.

339

said. "But I assume you'll kill me in the final reel."

"You got that right, kid," Cagney said.

"I hope you go to the electric chair for it," Bogie said.

"I do, but it'll be the most dramatic last mile in the history of cinema."

Pat O'Brien, in the first of his roles as a fighting priest, played Father Connolly, who struggles to keep the Dead End Kids from pursuing a life of crime. Cagney, a hero to the boys in the neighborhood, is trying to drag them along to hell with himself.

During his direction, Curtiz continued to butcher the English language. Cliff King, the still cameraman, asked Bogie to pose for some publicity stills.

Bogie was a bit fidgety during the shoot, and King asked him to "Please try to keep still while I make the picture."

Curtiz overheard him, "You bum," the director shouted. "When you make the movies you're still, and when you take the stills, you move."

In one explosive scene, real bullets were used, based on direct orders from Curtiz. Regrettably, neither Curtiz nor any of his assistants bothered to tell Bogie. When Bogie found out, he physically attacked Curtiz but two grips pulled him away before he could harm the director.

"I know you don't like the word shit, so I'll say crap." It was Ann Sheridan talking over lunch. "I'm trying to make the best of this part but my character isn't well defined. Rowland Brown [the creator of the original story] spends far too much time cocksucking than he does developing my character. What can I do?"

"Collect your paycheck and go on to your next picture," Bogie said.

As it turned out, Sheridan wasn't the little wren she feared she was. *Angels With Dirty Faces* marked her first big featured role in an A-list picture, and a turning point in her career.

During the making of the film, George Hurrell released his soon-to-be famous photographs of her, and they were published across the country. The publicists at Warners immediately launched a massive campaign, releasing these pictures in magazines and newspapers.

Bogie kept a cheesecake picture of Sheridan posing as the Oomph Girl in his dressing room until Methot visited and ripped it down before hitting him over the head with a liquor bottle, which caused a minor concussion.

During the shoot, the Dead End Kids terrorized the set. One afternoon, they held Bogie to the ground and stripped off his trousers. However, when they tangled with Cagney, he fought back, bloodying Gorcey's nose. After that, they gave him wide berth, "Don't fuck with me," Cagney had told them. "I grew up in Hell's Kitchen."

One day, Judy Garland showed up on the set for a rendezvous with Billy Halop, whom she was still dating infrequently. Bogie generously lent them his

340

dressing room for their tryst.

Afterward Garland came to him, "Oh, Mr. Bogie, a girl can't make up her mind. Should it be Billy? Should it be Mickey Rooney? I just don't know."

"If I was a gal, I'd go for the one with the biggest dick."

"That would be Billy, of course, and he's far handsomer, but Mickey is such a delight to be with."

"Play the field," he told her.

"I've got another problem," she said. "I think Louis B. Mayer actually wants to take me to bed. What can I do? He's the boss."

"Honey, do what every smart gal in Hollywood has done since movies began," he said. "Lie down on that casting couch and endure it. Just five minutes of horror, and it'll all be over. You've got the talent. You might become the biggest star at MGM. So go for it."

"Oh, thank you, Mr. Bogie, for making up my mind for me. I'll let you know how it works out."

"When all these guys have broken you in real good, you come to me for some real loving," he said.

"I will, I will, I promise," she said.

"After these amateurs have worked you over, you can learn how a man does it."

Cagney was right about the movie's final dramatic scene, perhaps the most memorable he ever shot. Just before his execution, Father Connolly begs him to become a sniveling coward on the way to the chair. That way, he'll no longer be a hero to the Dead End Kids.

At first Cagney refuses his old friend. But at the last minute, he breaks down and becomes hysterical. Movie-goers over the years have pondered exactly what was going on in this final scene. Did the character Cagney was playing really turn yellow, and did he decide in the final moments of his life to give in to Father Connolly's last plea to him? Regardless of his motive, he destroyed himself as a role model for the young, potential criminals in waiting.

This is the movie that inspired Cagney impersonators. He twisted his neck, lifted his shoulders, and bit his bottom lip which became his signature act. He said he learned these ticks from a pimp in Hell's Kitchen who used to stand on his street corner.

Reviewer Harrison Carroll claimed that *Angels With Dirty Faces* "is the most grimly realistic gangster film that has come out of Hollywood since the early days of the cycle."

After the film opened, Cagney walked off with honors, winning the 1939 New York Film Critics Circle Award for Best Actor. In addition, he was nominated for an Oscar.

One film critic claimed if there was only one Cagney film to place in a time capsule, it should be *Angels With Dirty Faces*.

Somehow Bogie got lost in all the buzz over Cagney. But Bogie was left with a steely determination to star with Barbara Stanwyck in *Golden Boy*. To do that, he had to renew his relationship with the Steel Magnolia herself.

***

As she made preparations to marry Kenneth, Mary opened on Broadway in the comedy *Spring Thaw*. Appearing opposite her was her long-time lover, Roland Young.

One drunken night, Bogie called his old friend, Kenneth, when he found out he was making plans to marry Mary. "I keep hoping Mary will change her mind and come back to me before our divorce becomes final."

"Surely you don't mean that," Kenneth said in protest. "You never really loved Mary. I should have married her back in the 20s in New York. Tell me you don't mean what you just said."

"Of course, I mean it," Bogie said. "Have you ever heard me say something I don't mean?"

"Yeah," Kenneth said, not concealing the anger in his voice. "You didn't mean it when you told me I was your best friend." He put down the phone.

Bogie's best friends continually speculated that he was not in love with any of his three wives. Spencer Tracy once said that "in Helen Menken he found a mother figure. Young boy dominated by a strong mother ends up marrying mother. Classic case."

"If Bogie were in love with any woman in the 1930s, it was Mary Philips," Leslie Howard once said. "But they spent much of their time on separate coasts sleeping in the beds of other people."

No one could accuse Mayo Methot of being anybody's mother. Bogie once admitted to Ann Sheridan, "I don't love Mayo. But I'm fascinated by her, and I love to beat her up, especially when she beats me back."

On August 12, 1938, the Associated Press carried a notice that "Mary Phillips Bogart, known professionally as "Mary Philips," whose divorce from screen actor Humphrey Bogart became final two days ago, and Leo Meilzinger, former husband to Kay Francis, also a film prominent, were married today at the office of the Justice of the Peace J. Fred Collins."

The article noted that Meilzinger was known in the theatrical world as Kenneth MacKenna, a film editor for MGM in New York City. Kenneth was 38, Mary 37.

In some long-forgotten fan magazine of the 30s, Bogie gave a surprisingly candid interview on the dawn of his marriage to Methot.

"I love a good fight," he claimed. "So does Mayo. We have some first-rate battles. Both of us are actors, so fights are easy to start. Actors always see the dramatic quality of a situation more easily than other people and can't resist dramatizing it further. For instance, I come home from a game of golf. Maybe I've been off my drive. I slump into my chair. 'Gosh, I feel low today.' I start. She nods meaningfully. 'Low, hmm, I see. You feel low. You come to see me and it makes you feel low. All the thrill has gone and . . . you feel low.' And we go right on from there. We both understand that one of the important things to master in marriage is the technique of the quarrel."

As an ominous sign, there were threatening storm clouds across Los Angeles on the morning of August 20, 1939. But by eleven the highly unpredictable skies cleared in time for the wedding of Humphrey Bogart, age 38, to Mayo Methot, age 35.

Bogie and Mary Philips had long been a friend of Mary and Mel Baker, who had agreed to host the wedding of Bogie to his third wife, Mayo. Mel was a comedy writer and Mary Baker a theatrical agent to both Mary Philips and Bogie. He had long forgiven her for testifying against him in Mary's divorce case against him. Judge Ben Lindsay had agreed to perform the ceremony marrying Bogie to Mayo.

Methot arrived at her wedding to Bogie in a housedress that looked as if she'd slept in it. Her hair was ratty, needing to be washed and set.

"I've got nothing to wear," she told actress Gloria Stuart. "I spent all my money on liquor, and that tightwad Bogart, the fucker, wouldn't give me money to buy a new dress."

"What a great way to start a marriage," Stuart said. She went to see Mary Baker, the hostess, who claimed she had something appropriate. She emerged with a beaded dress and a matching hair band that Joan Crawford might have worn in *Our Dancing Daughters*. Right before her, Methot pulled off her dress, revealing that she wore no under-

Wedding bells for "The Battling Bogarts." A marriage made in hell almost didn't make it through the first day.

343

wear.

Appraising herself in the mirror, Methot turned to Baker, "Aren't you supposed to wear something borrowed at a wedding? Well, look at me now."

"What about some panties, darling?" Mary asked.

"Who needs them?" she asked. "If a man wants to fuck you, you should make it easy for him and not make him have to take off a lot of garments. Just pull up your dress and tempt him with your cooze."

Marietta Bitter and her harp provided the event's high point in culture, but another performer, Mischa Auer, stole the show. He attracted the most attention by crawling naked under the tables, putting an experienced hand up several of the women's dresses.

During the actual marriage ceremony, Bogie cried through the entire service. "If I were marrying Mayo Methot, I would cry too," said Spencer Tracy.

Long before the sun set that day, "The Battling Bogarts" were at it. After downing nearly half a bottle of Scotch, Methot in front of the guests, filled her hands with great globs of creamy wedding cake, walked up to her new husband, and crushed the gooey mess into his face, rubbing it in. Some gossip at the party had told her that her new spouse was having a torrid affair with Claire Trevor.

Bogie punched her back, knocking her down. She fell backward, crashing into a table of four enjoying the wedding buffet.

Bogie ran back into the house, and within an hour he and Mel Baker were driving down the coastal road toward the Mexican border. Methot spent her wedding night sobbing in the bed of Mary Baker, who tried to offer the new bride whatever comfort she could on her "honeymoon."

Two days later Bogie sent Methot a rubber plant, and "The Battling Bogarts" made up, at least for a few hours.

Methot told Mary Baker, "We managed to screw for a few hours before we started in again. It was over the Tijuana whores I suspected he'd sampled during our honeymoon."

CHAPTER EIGHT

Back from a real honeymoon in Oregon, where Bogie met his in-laws, he arrived in Hollywood with a steely resolve.

Over breakfast with his new bride, his face tightened into knots of determination. "God damn it, I'm gonna be a big-time movie star in spite of Jack Warner. It's now or never. I'm seeing Barbara Stanwyck today."

"I don't have to be jealous of that bitch," Methot said. "Bette Davis told me she's lez. Her romance with Robert Taylor is just for show."

"I want to star with her in *Golden Boy*," Bogie responded. "Babs and I can heat up the screen with that film. If she doesn't think I can quite handle the part, I'll throw you in as the party favor for Stanwyck."

Bogie ducked just in time to miss a flying plate that crashed into the wall behind him.

If Bogie had known how many young actors wanted to play the role of the boxer, Joe Bonaparte, in the screen adaptation of Clifford Odets' Broadway play, *Golden Boy*, he might never have gone out for the role. Everyone from matinee idol Tyrone Power to newcomer Alan Ladd was competing.

Director Rouben Mamoulian estimated that some 5,000 actors, including a 17-year-old Dale Robertson, wanted the part. "My God," Mamoulian said, "more guys wanted to play Joe Bonaparte than gals wanted to be Scarlett O'Hara." [In all, 1,400 candidates for the role of Scarlett were interviewed. Of these, ninety were given screen tests.]

Methot reminded Bogie that he was nearly forty years old and didn't have the figure for an appearance in boxing trunks. She accurately predicted that some twenty-year-old brat would get the part—"and it'll probably make him a star."

As payment for her forecast, she got a plate of unfinished ham and eggs thrown in her face. The last thing Bogie wanted was to be reminded of how old he was.

He was convinced that if Stanwyck would just return his calls, he could use his former connection to her to get the director to cast him. In preparation, he took boxing lessons every day and also violin lessons. In the play,

Bonaparte wanted to be a violinist before he was lured into the ring.

Unknown to Bogie at the time, a future co-star of his, William Holden, was also taking boxing and violin lessons.

THE ROMANTIC STAGE
SUCCESS THAT CAPTURED
A NATION... IS NOW A
GREAT MOTION PICTURE

Bogie tried to get two of the most coveted roles in Hollywood--that of the violinist/boxer in *Golden Boy* and also that of Rhett Butler in *Gone With the Wind*.

He lost the roles to William Holden (depicted in all three images above) and Clark Gable, respectively.

Barbara Stanwyck *(bottom photo)* wanted Holden--and not just on the screen.

Finally, the call came in from Stanwyck, whose star was rising rapidly in Hollywood. It was not the kind of call he expected. At first she didn't even mention *Golden Boy*.

"Bogie, how's it hanging?"

"It's grown three inches longer since the last time," he said. "Wanna swing on it again?"

"No, I'm perfectly satisfied with Robert Taylor's four inches," she said. "Let cut the crap, Bogie. You know why I'm calling."

"I hear Samuel Goldwyn has signed you for *Golden Boy*," he said.

"That's the least of my concerns right now," she said. "The publicity people are pushing me for the role of Scarlett O'Hara. Can you believe such nonsense?"

"A gal from Brooklyn. I'm surprised. If you get it, you've got to sound like you have magnolia juice dripping down your chin."

"That's not all," she said. "I hear David Selznick wants us to do a screen test together. You, of all the actors in Hollywood, for the role of Rhett Butler."

"As dumb as it sounds, let's go for it," he said. "If we could pull this one off, we might become the biggest stars in Hollywood since Rin Tin Tin."

"They're going to get in touch with you," she said. "Now, more business. What's all this talk I hear that you want to play Joe Bonaparte. Are you out of your mind?"

"It's a great role, and I could do it."

"But you're forty years old," she said. "Almost. The kid in the movie should be in his early twenties."

Before she hung up, he convinced her to come to his gym the following day and watch him work out in the ring with Slapsie Maxie.

346

"I don't want that retard," she said. "I want to see you in the ring with a real man. I'll bring along someone to get into the ring with you and duke it out."

"You've got yourself a deal, Babe, or is it Babs?" he said.

"Miss Stanwyck will do," she said after jotting down the time and place.

Stanwyck showed up with a stunningly handsome actor whom she introduced as William Holden.

While Holden was in the changing room getting into his trunks, Bogie said, "I've never seen a boxer that good looking before. Where did you find him?"

"He's not a boxer," Stanwyck said. "He's an actor. He's also up for the role."

At this point Holden returned, looking even younger and more gorgeous without his clothes. Like some boxing manager, Stanwyck ushered Bogie and Holden into the ring together. "May the best man win."

The bout was short, not sweet. After only four minutes of sparing, Holden threw Bogie a punch that knocked him out.

When he came to, he was sitting on the sidelines, with a gym attendant and Stanwyck hovering over him. Holden had disappeared.

Bogie had a splitting headache, and Stanwyck appeared rather blurred before his eyes. "I didn't quite come clean with you," she said. "Holden was assigned the part yesterday. Better go back to those gangster roles, sweet cheeks."

"You are an incredible bitch," he said.

"There are side benefits from casting Holden," she said. "In case you haven't noticed, twenty-year-old cock tastes better than forty-year-old cock."

***

Two days prior to the screen test with Stanwyck and Bogie for the Rhett and Scarlett

In *The Two Mrs. Carrolls*, Bogie marries Barbara Stanwyck *(top photo)* but falls for a neighbor, as played by Alexis Smith *(bottom photo)*.

The solution? Bogie plans to poison Stanwyck.

347

roles, Selznick's office sent Bogie a message, notifying him that the screen test had been cancelled.

Bogie didn't expect any romantic fireworks when he was cast opposite Alexis Smith *(top photo)* in *The Two Mrs. Carrolls*. The same with Barbara Stanwyck *(bottom photo)*.

Bogie told his pal, Sydney Greenstreet, "I don't have the right equipment for these two lesbians."

Not only was Bogie's screen test cancelled, but the following week he received a memo from Selznick.

"Mr. Bogart, although I admire your talent in gangster roles, you are not a serious candidate for the role of Rhett Butler. Although some polls list you as a candidate, you are not. As you should know, the role is completely unsuitable for you. You'd be laughed off the screen. In case you and Barbara Stanwyck haven't read the novel, it's set in Georgia—not Brooklyn. I have not determined who will play Scarlett, but I am more or less set on Gary Cooper for Rhett Butler. Kindest personal regards, David O. Selznick."

With a certain bitterness, Bogie watched newcomer William Holden and Barbara Stanwyck appear in one of the greatest films of 1939, perhaps the single greatest year in the history of motion pictures.

He vowed never to speak to Stanwyck again. Methot warned that if she encountered her at a party or in a public place, "I'll pull out every hair in her head."

Bogie watched in amazement as Stanwyck became the highest paid female star during World War II. At the end of the war, and after *Casablanca*, his own star had risen so high that he was offered star billing over her in *The Two Mrs. Carrolls*, slated for a 1947 release. For the opportunity to co-star with her, with his name above hers, he decided to forgive her and go ahead with the picture.

He told its English director, Peter Godfrey, that he could definitely honor his marriage vows while making this movie. "You've cast me opposite two lezzies-Stanwyck and Alexis Smith. Maybe the gals will connect—not me."

Bogie had already co-starred with Alexis

Smith in the 1945 *Conflict*, which included backup support from Sydney Greenstreet.

During the filming of *The Two Mrs. Carrolls*, Bogie and Stanwyck each realized they were miscast in this adaptation of Martin Vale's play that had brought such success on Broadway to the great Elisabeth Bergner and Victor Jory.

During the shoot, reporters provocatively asked Bogie how she could hook up with him on the screen when she had "pretty boy" Robert Taylor waiting back home at the ranch.

"I'm not good looking, and I admit that," Bogie responded. "I used to be quite pretty, but not in the league of Robert Taylor. But I've got character on my face. It takes an awful lot of late-night drinking to put it there."

Godfrey allowed Bogie to mug shamelessly as the psychopathic artist who paints wives as "Angels of Death," then kills them with poisoned milk.

Warners held up the release of the film for two years. When it finally hit screens across the country, critics ridiculed and mocked it. The public cast its vote by staying away. The film would find new life in the 1960s when it was rediscovered by the French New Wave.

Stanwyck and Bogie made a valiant attempt to appear together one final time on the screen in *The Fountainhead* based on Ayn Rand's best-selling 754-page novel. This Russian-born philosopher novelist stood for "muscular capitalism and a disdain for the common herd." Stanwyck wanted to play the lead

role of Dominique Francon who marries the book's villain but loves the hero, architect Howard Roark of unbounded ego. Bogie saw himself in that part of a rugged individual.

When Mervin LeRoy signed to direct, it was with the understanding that the stars would be Bogie and Stanwyck. Before shooting began, he was forced to leave the picture.

Called in to direct, King Vidor wanted Gary Cooper for the part of Howard Roark. "Stanwyck's too old to play Dominique. Not sexy enough. I want Ida Lupino."

In the end, Cooper retained the lead, appearing opposite the "new love of my life," Patricia Neal.

Bogie survived the rejection, but Stanwyck virtually "fired herself" on June 21, 1948, by sending a blistering communication to Jack Warner, expressing her wish to end their con-

Kay Francis had once reigned as the highest paid female star in Hollywood, but when she made *King of the Underworld* with Bogie, she was on the way out the Warner Brothers' gate.

349

tractual obligations to each other. At the time, the studio was in financial trouble and was glad to see her go. *The Fountainhead* had marked her first defeat to a younger actress. "I had Gary Cooper long before this Neal bitch," Stanwyck told Bogie.

***

It was a bittersweet reunion Bogie had with Kay Francis when director Lewis Seiler cast them together in the 1939 release, *King of the Underworld*.

Seiler had helmed him in *Crime School*, and the two men worked easily together. George Bricker, co-authored the screenplay with Vincent Sherman, who would direct some of Bogie's future pictures.

Sherman later admitted, "I was not proud of my work on this film." It was a remake of *Dr. Socrates*, a Paul Muni film in 1935.

Bogie hadn't read the script until the first day of the shoot. "I'm supposed to be a dumb gang leader who fancies himself as the next Napoleon," he protested to Sherman.

"Don't blame me. It wasn't my idea. I just work here."

"Kay," he said, coming up to kiss her on the first day of the shoot. "Great to see you again. It looks like we couldn't hold on to our mates, so they ended up marrying each other."

He was, of course, referring to Kenneth MacKenna and Mary Philips.

"Mary's welcome to Kenneth," she said. "I've moved on."

"True, true," he said. "But at times I miss Mary, especially when Mayo is beating me over the head with a beer bottle. Mary was such a gentle person."

"Then she won't make it in this town," Francis predicted. Over lunch that day, she shared her woes.

Francis told Bogie that her career was in serious decline, and she was hoping that their co-starring venture would pull her up again.

The offscreen Kay Francis *(center figure in bottom photo)* confessed to Bogie that she suspected her real-life husband of being a Nazi agent. The actor on the right is James Stephenson.

350

"Even though my pictures end up in red ink, I still have a contract," she said. "In 1936, I took in $227,500, the highest paid star on the lot."

"Don't remind me," he said.

"But I've been moving from one flop to another," she said. "Jack Warner personally told me that I'm not worth my paycheck."

"I fear he's gonna tell me the same thing one day," Bogie said. "Sooner than later."

"I had a lavish dressing room, but they moved me out to give it to John Garfield," she said. "You better watch that kid. He might take your roles. Right now they're paying me $4,000 a week to do screen tests with unknown actors. I'm the only actress doing B pictures for a six-figure income."

"Don't worry, babe," Bogie said. "I hear your latest beau is rich." He was referring to Baron Raven Erik Barnekow, with ties to the aviation business.

"He's rich and handsome," she said. "But there are problems. He's so jealous, he's a psycho. And, get this, he told me the other night that if I don't stop wearing makeup he will leave me. Imagine an actress without makeup."

"I shudder at the prospect," Bogie said mockingly.

She leaned over to him to whisper something. "I know I can trust you. My husband makes secret trips to Mexico. He refuses to discuss where he's been. I think he's a secret Nazi agent."

"Sounds like a good plot for your next movie," he said. "I could play the baron."

The third star of the movie was James Stephenson, a British actor who was ten years older than Bogie. "Pretty late to be breaking into films, don't you think, kid?"

"Better late than never," he said. "Forgive the cliché. Jack Warner has signed me to play urban villains and disgraced gents. Incidentally, you're my favorite star."

"Good God, a newcomer to Warners with some taste," Bogie said. "I'm not used to that."

Bogie and Stephenson never

Bogart, Methot, and their friend

351

became close friends, but Bogie was happy for him when William Wyler cast him in the sympathetic role of the family attorney in Bette Davis' *The Letter* (1940). In "my role of a lifetime," he was nominated for Best Supporting Oscar.

With regrets, Bogie read in the paper that Stephenson had died at the age of 53 in 1941. He'd suffered a heart attack, and death was sudden.

He turned to Methot, "I fear I'm gonna die young too."

"Impossible," Methot said. "You're already too old to die young."

"I'm gonna get you for that, you broken down drunken hag," he said, rising to chase after her.

Methot later told Bette Davis, "Our epic battles always end in hot sex, so starting a good fight is usually worth it."

"How odd," Davis said. "My battles with my husbands or lovers always begin after sex."

Months later after filming on *King of the Underworld* came to an end, Bogie encountered Francis at a party. She looked awful and had gained at least twenty-five pounds.

Used to needling people, he resisted mocking her. Her last two years at Warners had been hellish enough.

"I was right about my baron," she said. "He left me without a note and returned to Germany. He wanted to be by Hitler's side during the invasion of Poland."

Francis ended her career working on Poverty Row turning out undistinguished pictures for Monogram. "Poverty Row" was the name applied at the time to the low-rent, marginal studios that churned out cheapies.

Bogie never saw her again but was saddened to hear that she'd attempted suicide while traveling in a road show, *State of the Union*, in Columbus, Ohio.

She survived, and Bogie was relieved. "No one should choose Columbus, Ohio, as the place to die."

***

Heavy drinking destroyed many a career in Hollywood of both men and women. Regardless of how much Bogie drank the night before, he always showed up promptly for work the following day. He arrived at the studio in time to be made up, and he had always memorized his lines.

Nathaniel Benchley, in his portrait of Bogie, tried to put his heavy drinking into the context of the day, noting that if a man didn't drink "he was considered some sort of fairy. It was a sign of masculinity to get drunk—a sign of a free man who did as he pleased—and it also fitted the tough guy image that was his trademark."

Benchley later noted that Bogie "could be enchanting when sober, but savage when drunk. Since he didn't show drunkenness in the usual manner, the only way to tell if he was sober was by what he was doing. He didn't slur his words or stumble, but he did things that catalyzed an acute remorse the next day. The sober Bogart bled for what the non-sober Bogart had done."

One example of his outrageous behavior occurred one night at the Café La Maze when Bogie spotted John Garfield at another table with a very young and very beautiful blonde actress, who looked somewhat like Lana Turner did years later when Garfield would appear with her in *The Postman Always Rings Twice.*

With a sense of despair, Bogie heard that Garfield would soon be replacing him in many of those bad boy roles at Warner Brothers. Bogie rose from his table with his glass of Scotch, approaching Garfield's table. He tossed the liquor in the young actor's face.

Garfield handled the scene with such style and sophistication that he amazed the other patrons, who thought he would attack Bogie. "Tastes good, man," Garfield said. "Let me call the bartender to order another one since your glass is empty."

Bogie had so embarrassed himself that he turned and walked out the door.

On some nights he was seen out drinking with Clifton Webb. Ever since his early days on Broadway, he and Webb had been friends—Bogie called him "Webby." Often they would be seen leaving bars together with their arms around each other.

Since Webb was a notorious homosexual in Hollywood, rumors were spread about Bogie and the actor. But there is no evidence that the relationship ever became sexual.

On weekends, Bogie and Methot sailed on a small powerboat he'd purchased. Their destination was always Catalina Island, twenty-one miles west of Los Angeles. He nicknamed the craft "Sluggy," as he and Methot staged some of their epic sea battles aboard the aptly named boat. One night Bogie tried to drown her, and she fought him viciously, scratching and bloodying him. Fortunately, he was between pictures.

Whenever she wasn't beating the hell out of Bogie, Methot was a decent housekeeper at "Sluggy Hollow," a nickname for 1210 North Horn, in Greater Los Angeles. Bogie was making enough money to hire a black woman, the

When Bogie encountered John Garfield, "tomorrow's competition," he tossed a glass of Scotch into the young actor's face.

353

very overweight May Smith, as their "cook and bottle washer."

He didn't like much variety in his diet, but the cook provided a lavish spread for guests.

Beryl Evelyn Wood Methot, his mother-in-law, was a frequent visitor from Oregon. Bogie called her "Buffy," and got on with her rather well considering that she was Methot's mother. One of the leading newspaperwomen of her state, Buffy enjoyed the respect of her daughter. Methot became rather docile whenever Buffy was living with them. Unlike Methot, Buffy could handle her booze and finished off many a bottle with Bogie long after Methot had gone to bed.

At one point, Bogie was heard at a party saying, "Buffy, old gal, I should have married you and not Mayo."

Ann Sheridan once visited the Bogarts when Bogie's mother, Maud, was there. "It was amazing," Sheridan said. "Bogie related to Buffy, but Mayo gravitated to Maud."

Disappointed at how her life had gone, Maud had moved to the West Coast where Bogie had secured a small apartment for her. That way, Maud could be not only with Bogie, but with her mentally ill daughter Frances. Maud earned a meager living by drawing sewing patterns for a company, her $50,000 annual salary a distant memory.

Maud told her son, "Belmont and I used to have our arguments. An argument, not a fight to the death. I really believe you and Mayo will one day kill each other." Maud was referring to a past evening when Bogie had taken a rope and chased Mayo into the garden, threatening to hang her from a tree.

On Sunset Boulevard, Maud lived only two blocks from Schwab's Drugstore, the center of social activity for Hollywood actors in those days. Bogie said his mother started hanging out there "and picking up all the gossip, which she later confided to me. This proper Victorian woman was treated like Lady Maud, because everyone knew she was my mother. One day I came to get her and caught her talking to Bob Hope. On another occasion she met Betty Grable."

In New York, Maud had been contemptuous of her son's attempt to become an actor. But at Schwab's Drugstore, she often approached gossip columnists like Sidney Skolsky, and introduced herself. "I'm Humphrey Bogart's mother. Would you like to hear what 'The Battling Bogarts' did last night?" Suddenly, after decades, she came to understand that her role as Bogie's mother was something to be flaunted.

At some point during the final years of her life, Maud began to lose her mind. On many a night, the police brought her back from Sunset Strip to Bogie's home after they came to know who she was. One night they found her chatting with about six prostitutes who worked the corner.

During one of her more rational moments, she confessed to Methot, "I think I'm going crazy like Frances Bogart Rose."

At times, Maud would say something to Bogie that made him fear that she was losing her mental stability. One example among countless others included:

MAUD: "I just can't believe that Frances has been confined and her husband hasn't come to see her."

BOGIE: "Mother, Stuart Rose divorced Frances years ago."

Whenever Frances recovered from one of her straight-jacketed seizures, she was allowed to go free again. But insanity would soon after seem to overtake her.

Like her mother, Frances too would get arrested in public places. One night she went out into the city topless, wearing only her panties. The headline the next morning read: BOGART'S SISTER ARRESTED ON SUNSET STRIP.

The Hollywood columnist and writer, Joe Hyams, who knew both Bogie and Frances, later claimed that Bogie loved his sister "who was tall and slender and had a short waist and long legs like Betty. In fact, they looked very much alike. And I think that was one of the reasons he fell in love with Betty."

The columnist, of course, was referring to Lauren Bacall, whose name at the time of her birth on September 16, 1924, in New York was Betty Joan Perske.

There were many dangers inherent whenever Maud wanted to sit out in the garden at the Bogart home. California was filled with butterflies, and whenever she saw one, she would scream and become hysterical. It would take hours for Methot to calm her down.

***

A familiar voice came over the phone. It was director Lloyd Bacon. "I'm teaming James Cagney and you in a Western called *The Oklahoma Kid*."

"Am I the Oklahoma Kid?" Bogie asked.

"No, Cagney is. You play a black-clad guy named Whip McCord who is a gang leader. You guys hold up the stagecoach carrying government money to the Indians for their land. You'll also be working with Ward Bond."

"I don't have to kiss Ward, do I? Who's the pretty one?"

"Rosemary Lane," Bacon said.

"I have had the other two Lane sisters," Bogie said. "Might as well spread my goodies around to the third."

355

Only moments before he's fatally shot on screen, Bogie tries to strangle Cagney *(top photo)*.

After the release of this oater, no one ever compared Cagney and Bogie to Roy Rogers and Gene Autry

"You may not get so lucky this time."

"By the way, I assume I get killed in the final reel," Bogie said.

"You got that right."

"It's my first Western," Cagney said, greeting Bogie on the set. "And we're going to make it a good one. I just knew you'd be my evil adversary, since that's about all you know how to play."

"Compliments from such a big-time box office attraction like you are always appreciated," Bogie said. He noted that Cagney looked like a midget standing alongside his horse. "I hear you own a lot of horses. I bet you're an expert rider."

"Well, not really," Cagney said. "Don't tell anybody."

Cagney was assigned a horse who'd made dozens of Westerns. After the star straddled the animal and was taking in the sun the following day, the horse heard the assistant director's clapper and apparently thought it was a call to action. Taking off at break-neck speed, the horse raced toward the distant camera.

"I grabbed his neck and held on," Cagney said. "He came to a ditch and jumped it—about six to seven feet. I don't know how the hell I stayed on, but I did. We worked well together after that, once the horse found out I could hang on."

"Lola Lane, Priscilla Lane, and now Rosemary Lane," Bogie said, coming up to the female co-star of the movie.

"I hear you're telling everybody in town you seduced Lola and Priscilla, which I find hard to believe," Rosemary said. "Priscilla might have flirted with you, but she's a deeply religious woman. So is my older sister Lola."

"What about you?" he asked.

"I can be had for the price of a drink."

Bacon was aware of Bogie's claim to have

356

seduced all three of the Lane sisters, "but I don't think he made it with either one of them. Maybe he seduced them in his mind."

Years later Cagney recalled working with Bogie. "He and I never became friends, and we never saw each other after work, maybe only one time. We didn't hate each other. We just didn't care for each other that much. I don't think he had any real friends—maybe Spencer Tracy. Nobody at Warners really liked him. Bogie said, 'I beat 'em to it. I don't like them first.' He hated just about everybody, but that was his aim—to hate them first. When it came to fighting, he was about as tough as Shirley Temple."

As a hobby, Cagney liked to write poems. As he was driving along Coldwater Canyon Drive, he stopped for a traffic light, spotting Bogie in a sleek red sports car in the lane next to him. He was busy picking his nose, waiting for the light to turn green. "He wasn't just picking, but really going for the big ones."

The next day, Cagney left a poem tacked to the door of Bogie's dressing room.

In this silly town of ours,
One sees odd primps and poses;
But movie stars in fancy cars,
Shouldn't pick their fancy noses.

At the end of the shoot, Bogie as Whip and his gang try to kill Cagney, who was playing the Robin Hood desperado. With Bacon directing, Cagney walks into the ambush set by Bogie and his men.

When Bacon called a wrap, Bogie sauntered over to him. "That scene should give audiences a laugh. Up to now in the picture my gang and I—all supposed to be dead shots—have fired 172 times at Cagney and haven't hit him yet."

"It's called movie-making," Bacon snapped back.

Viewed today, *The Oklahoma Kid* is pure camp, especially when Cagney sings "I Don't Want to Play In Your Yard," a number interrupted by gunfire. In another scene, he croons "Rockabye Baby" in Spanish to an actual baby.

Bogart and Cagney as Oklahoma Kids: NYC boys camping out in the Wild West

357

The film is often remembered for a scene of Cagney rubbing the thumb and forefinger of his hand together and exulting, "Feel that air!"

When he saw the final print, Jack Warner said, "What were we thinking? Cagney is a street kid from Hell's Kitchen. He's no Hopalong Cassidy. Don't put him in a Western ever again. As for Bogie, let's cast him in 'The Lisping Cowboy.'"

When Bogie sat through the final cut, he said to Bacon, "In that ten-gallon hat, Cagney looks like a mushroom."

***

Dark Victory, starring Tallulah Bankhead, had been a rather unsuccessful Broadway play during the 1934-35 season. David O. Selznick had once optioned it, hoping to cast Greta Garbo in the role of socialite Judith Traherne, who is dying of a brain tumor. She turned him down, as she was occupied making *Anna Karenina* at MGM.

When Warners took over the property, the studio briefly considered it as a role for fast-fading Kay Francis.

Davis told Bogie that she had "begged, cajoled, and pleaded for months to get Jack Warner to buy the property. His answer, 'Who wants to see a picture about a gal who dies?' But he finally gave in to my demands."

After Garbo bowed out, Gloria Swanson tried but failed to get the movie role.

Bogie even heard from Barbara Stanwyck, who was calling everybody she knew to get the role for herself. "I really hated missing out on the part," Stanwyck told Bogie. "I was encouraged when I heard Selznick had optioned it, and I told my agents to do *anything* go get it for me. Then I learned that Selznick, the fucker, was preparing it for Merle Oberon. When I played Judith on Lux Radio Theater, I thought I had it wrapped up. Then in stepped Miss Bette Davis."

Bogie played the third lead under George Brent. "I've been demoted," Bogie said to Brent. "When we made *Racket Busters*, you were my second stringer."

"The vagaries of casting at Warners," Brent said.

Bogie's old pal, Spencer Tracy, had turned down the role that eventually went to Brent.

Bogie couldn't help but notice that even though Davis' marriage to Harmon Nelson was crumbling, that didn't prevent Brent from visiting her dressing room for an hour in the afternoon between takes.

Edmund Goulding, directing Bogie and Davis, was "Hollywood's genius bad boy." The reputation of this London-born director had already preceded him. He was known for his heavy drinking, homosexual liaisons, and orgies. In fact, he was the most notorious director in Hollywood.

Goulding wisely cast the Irish actress Geraldine Fitzgerald in her American debut in a role where her character was "to act as a sort of one-person Greek chorus, so that the central doomed figure would not have to cry for herself."

Bogie never bonded with Fitzgerald, but met her at the peak of her career. This fine, passionate actress would go from *Dark Victory* to a star role in *Wuthering Heights*, where, as Isabella, she is the best thing in the film. Laurence Olivier, as Heathcliff, marries her on the rebound.

Bogie was so impressed with both of Fitzgerald's stellar performances that he called her and seriously urged her to reconsider starring with him in *The Maltese Falcon*, which she'd turned down. "I'd rather face suspension," which is what happened to her. The part, of course, went to Mary Astor.

Cast in the movie was the inexperienced Ronald Reagan as Alex. He clearly did not like his role, preferring the part of Michael O'Leary, the stable hand, that was slated for Bogie. Someone on the set told Reagan that he was actually playing a homosexual, although such "perverted" characters could not actually be depicted on the screen at that time.

The gay producer, David Lewis, said Reagan "could not distinguish between playing a homosexual and being implicated as one. He clashed several times with Goulding. It was not only the role but personal. The director had come on to him."

Later, recalling making *Dark Victory*, Reagan said, "It wasn't the rewarding experience it should have been. I was playing the kind of young man who could dearly love Bette but at the same time the

(middle photo, center figures)
Bette Davis with Ronald Reagan

(bottom photos)
Two views of director Edmund Goulding

359

kind of fellow who could sit in the girls' dressing room dishing the dirt while they went on dressing in front of me. For myself, I want to think if I stroll through where the girls are short of clothes, there will be a great scurrying about and taking cover."

Even as shooting began, Reagan was still pleading with Goulding to give him Bogie's role. "He's already got the lisp," Reagan said.

When Bogie heard what Reagan had said, he decided to play one of his many practical jokes. The following day before lunch, he saw Reagan heading for the men's toilet on the Warner lot.

Although there were eight urinals lined up in a row, Bogie stood immediately next to Reagan, who was already urinating.

"To get even with the fucker and to frighten the hell out of him, I stared down at his dick," Bogie said to Goulding. "I leaned over close to him and whispered in his ear, 'I can take care of that thing for you.' Reagan didn't even finish pissing before he was zipping up and out of that toilet."

Throughout the remainder of his life, and despite overwhelming evidence to the contrary, Reagan always insisted in private that Bogie was a bona fide homosexual.

However, when it came time for Reagan to write his memoirs, *Where's the Rest of Me?*, he had only kind words for Bogie. "I've always been glad that some of my pictures teamed me with Humphrey Bogart. Here was a pro, an affable, easy person, fond of gentle ribbing. At this time he was yet to reach his ultimate potential, which came about during the war years in *Casablanca*—a part he was given after George Raft turned it down."

Originally, *Dark Victory* was to end on an anticlimactic scene with Bogie. According to the movie plot, after Judith's death, her horse was seen winning a race while its trainer, Michael

(Bogie) was seen crying. Sneak preview audiences in Pasadena mocked Bogie's tear-filled moment, and Goulding cut his scene.

Dark Victory became a hit at the box office, and marked Davis' third Oscar nomination in five years, although it did little for Bogie's career. "I spent most of the movie shoveling horse shit," he said mockingly, finally bringing himself to use the word shit.

One reviewer noted that Bogie played his role with a "creepy kind of sexuality and seemed terribly miscast and out of place. As for Reagan, he doesn't do much of anything but guzzle vast quantities of alcohol and generally embarrass himself."

Time Out London critic Tom Milne pronounced it "a Rolls-Royce in the weepie world."

Davis would lose the Oscar to Vivien Leigh that year for her portrayal of Scarlett O'Hara in *Gone With the Wind*, a role Davis had coveted.

***

As a boost to his career, Bogie eagerly wanted to play the male lead in *The Old Maid*, which had been tailored as a vehicle for Bette Davis with a script based on a novel by Edith Wharton. Budgeted at $778,000, shooting on *The Old Maid* began on March 15, 1939, with Edmund Goulding directing.

Bogie was scheduled to begin working five days later, even though both Goulding and Davis would have preferred Alan Marshall. With a dapper manner and a mustache, he was suave and sophisticated. He was often described as the poor man's Ronald Colman or perhaps the discount version of David Niven. Bogie had met Marshall briefly and thought this Aussie-born actor was "a complete phony."

Hal Wallis, the producer of the movie, told Goulding he wanted "a George Brent or David Niven type" for the role. That Bogie was offered the part has never been fully explained, since no one seemed to want him.

On his first day, Bogie went to call on Davis and found her furious at Goulding. He'd cast Miriam Hopkins, her dreaded scene-stealing enemy as the second female lead. "I should cut off Jack Warner's balls," Davis told Bogie. "That's not all. I, the star, am getting paid $35,000 for this picture, while dear Miriam is hauling in $50,000."

In his first scene, Bogie knew he was bombing. Davis later recalled that unhappy Monday at Warners. "One of the funniest miscastings I remember was Humphrey Bogart playing a nineteenth-century romantic lover opposite me in *The Old Maid*. In the opening scene, he appeared in a flowing black cloak, running through a railroad station trying to catch up with me. As he pursued me along the platform, he looked so sinister that he seemed for all the

361

world like a thug trying to kidnap me—rather than a hero trying to express his devotion."

"After watching him for a while, the entire cast became hysterical with laughter," Davis said. "When we finally subsided, Bogie said to Goulding, 'I guess you'll have to get yourself another lover boy.'"

Jack Warner interpreted Bogie's first day on the set with comtempt. "He's far too old and too ugly. Far too unconvincing to play the role of a man who wins the love of two women, especially two pussies like Hopkins and Davis. He's fired."

"Hal Wallis was the first to suggest George Brent," Warner said to Goulding. "Get Brent."

Goulding did just that.

"Maybe I'm lucky," Bogie told Methot. "Miriam and Bette will probably stage the biggest catfight in Hollywood history."

Privately, Bogie was furious, as his drinking increased and his fighting with Methot intensified.

When director Edmund Goulding cast Bogie as the romantic lead in *The Old Maid,* he was laughed off the screen when his first scenes were evaluated. Bogie was fired, leaving Bette Davis *(left)* to face her arch rival, Miriam Hopkins

***

Bogie reunited with director Lewis Seiler, who had helmed him in *King of the Underworld*. Cast as a petty crook, Frank Wilson, Bogie also reunited with his friend Billy Halop of the Dead End Kids.

The picture was *You Can't Get Away With Murder*. On the first day on the set, he met up again with Gale Page, playing the female lead. "It's old home week," he said to her, having worked with her in *Crime School*.

"I detest Bette Davis," she said.

"The line forms on the right," he told her.

"Jack Warner was set to give me my big chance," she said. "Then Miss Jezebel intervened at the last moment. The greedy bitch took the role from me in *Dark Victory*. Now I may never become a big movie star."

"You weren't the only actress left out

in the cold," Bogie said. "Even Tallulah Bankhead called me—she used to be my first wife's girlfriend. She wanted to repeat her stage role in the film."

"What chance does a gal have up against such dragons as Bankhead and Davis?"

"Not much," he said. "They chew and devour little guys like us for breakfast."

Minus the Dead End Kids, Billy was cast as a hood from Hell's Kitchen who idolizes a small-time gangster as played by Bogie.

Years later, Bogie recalled very little about the film. "I played one nasty son of a bitch. Not a shred of humanity. Henry Travers, who played Pop in the movie, the Sing Sing librarian, got it right when he said my character is the kind of guy who's so crooked if he tried to go straight he'd crack. The only good thing I could say about the movie was that it didn't have Reagan or Bette Davis in it."

All he remembered later on was, "I got to meet Betty Grable, who I think had had an affair with Reagan—or was about to have one. Judy Garland had dropped Billy, and he'd taken up with this lady with the million dollar legs. I could go for Grable myself. She was one hot blonde. But I didn't put the make on her since she had eyes only for Billy, and, of course, Jackie Coogan and Mickey Rooney and Desi Arnaz."

Grable had been kicked around Hollywood for more than a decade. Even today it is hard to understand why she became the hottest female box-office attraction of the 1940s. Maybe it was those array of pin-up pictures of hers that lined footlockers from Bataan to Okinawa.

Bogie never got to know Grable, but he said he would have liked to. She married Jackie Coogan, the child actor and her co-star in *Million Dollar Legs* in 1939. Later she'd marry bandleader and trumpeter Harry James.

"Honey," she said to Bogie, "Coogan taught me more tricks than a whore learns in a whorehouse."

Playing a petty crook, Bogie threatens Billy Halop to keep him from "squealing." In real life, Bogie said, "I love the kid like he was my own son."

He'd already heard that when she was only fifteen, George Raft had taken her virginity. After that, she seemed to be giving it away—not only to Reagan, but to Tyrone Power, Victor Mature, Robert Stack, Artie Shaw, and lots of drivers she liked to fellate at truck stops.

Reflecting on Grable, Bogie told his director, Seiler, "That's what Mayo Methot should look like but doesn't. If she keeps letting herself go, people are going to take her for my mother. As for George Raft, he gets all the good roles that I should be playing, and gets to the fifteen-year-old virgins like Grable before I've had my chance to deflower them."

When Bogie saw the ad for *You Can't Get Away with Murder*, he was taken back. It read: SIXTY-THREE CENTS WORTH OF ELECTRICITY WOULD END THIS MENACE FOREVER!

***

When Bogie heard he'd been cast as the third lead in *The Roaring Twenties*, to be directed by Raoul Walsh, he called his old friend from New York, Mark Hellinger. His short story, *The World Moves On*, had become the basis for *The Roaring Twenties*. "Listen, pal," Bogie said.

"I love you. But..."

"But what?"

"Let's get together for a wet lunch at Romanoff's."

When Hellinger entered Romanoff's, all eyes turned to him. A nationally syndicated columnist, he looked like he'd somehow landed directly from Times Square. At table, Bogie was already deep into his second martini.

Hellinger had always been proud of his links to the mob on both coasts, and he seemed trapped in some time capsule from the 1920s. Unlike the other men of his day, Hellinger wore a tight-fitting suit with a midnight blue shirt and sunflower yellow tie. He could easily have been mistaken for either a gangster or a pimp. He'd arrived in a chauffeur-driven, bullet-proof Lincoln that had previously been owned by the notorious gangster, Dutch Schultz.

Two views of the ultimate WWII pinup, Betty Grable

(top photo) as a child star with what would become "million dollar legs"

Seated at table opposite Bogie, Hellinger told him he'd just come from his doctor's office. "I don't have long to live. This burly doctor told me that this morning. As you know heart disease runs in my family. My parents died young. Since I last saw you, I lost my brother. I really loved him."

"I'm real sorry, pal, to hear this," Bogie said.

"Anything I can do?"

"Sure there is," Hellinger said. "Help me celebrate life. I'm doing so with three packages of cigarettes a day, a quart of brandy before the cocktail hour, and all the barbiturates I can get my hands on. There's a lot to be said for dying young. There's also sex, lots and lots of sex. You know I married this hot-to-trot showgal, Gladys Glad. She wants it morning, noon, and evening, and always a blast-off at midnight. She's not satisfied until all three holes are plugged."

Glad was a beautiful, ex-Ziegfeld showgirl he'd married in 1929, divorced in 1932, and would remarry a year later.

When their dialogue finally focused on the script for *The Roaring Twenties*, Bogie said, "I haven't read it yet. I know James Cagney is playing Eddie Bartlett, with me playing this guy called George Hally. I'm sure before the final curtain, Cagney will kill me like a buzzard, and perhaps die himself in a long extended death scene."

"You *must* have read the script," Hellinger said.

"No, I didn't," Bogie said. "I didn't have to."

"It's a bit of a gangster picture cliché, I admit that," Hellinger said.

"I can't believe how many more times in how many movies Cagney will be killing me," Bogie said. "Just once, can't I shoot the creepy little guy himself and give myself an extended, histrionic death scene?"

"Your day will come," Hellinger said.

"You play a ruthless bootlegger."

"The part should have gone to George Raft," Bogie said. "Let's face it, he *was* a ruthless bootlegger in the 1920s when I was a 'young sprig' on Broadway with a tennis racket, wearing a blue blazer and white shoes."

In the plot set at the end of World War I, Army buddies Cagney, Bogie, and Jeffrey Lynn, find their lives intertwining dramatically in this largely hackneyed script.

It had been a long time since Bogie had met the colorful director Raoul Walsh, who had voted against casting him in *The Man Who Came Back* way back when. Instead of giving Bogie a star role, he had assigned him the job of giving diction lessons to silent screen star Charles Farrell.

"So, we're working together once again," Walsh said. "When I first met you, I didn't think you'd go far or go anywhere for that matter. Now you're the leading male co-star in a Cagney movie. Who would have thought that?"

"Not you," Bogie said sarcastically, angry that

Mark Hellinger
"Live Fast, Die Young"

365

many years ago Walsh had not given him the break he so desperately wanted when he'd first arrived in Hollywood.

"Let's put bygones behind us and get on with the job of the day," Walsh said.

"Looks like I don't have much choice if I want to get paid at the end of the week."

"I'll go easy on you," Walsh said. 'Just be on screen the vicious son of a bitch you are in real life. It takes one to know one."

The director still had a patch over his eye, perhaps the same patch he wore back when Bogie first met him. He claimed that a jackrabbit crashed through the windshield of his car, permanently injuring his eye with the broken glass. Walsh's eye patch had become almost as synonymous as the jodhpurs worn by Cecil B. DeMille. To other listeners, he claimed that a buzzard in Arizona descended and plucked out his eye one scalding hot afternoon.

Years later, Walsh reflected on shooting a movie with both Cagney and Bogie. "I learned that a director must never kill off Clark Gable, Errol Flynn, Gary Cooper, or Gregory Peck," he said. "But when we 'shot' Cagney or Bogart, the audience and the box office loved it."

It was said that Walsh never let the truth get involved in a great story. He later claimed, "I was the one who made Bogie a star when I cast him in *The Roaring Twenties*. He was going nowhere until I put him in some of my other films. He was referring to *They Drive by Night* (1940) and *High Sierra* (1941). I also saved James Cagney's career."

Priscilla Lane had star billing over Bogie, much to his regret. "Well, well, well," he said sarcastically, "Little Miss Priscilla is rising fast. Who are you fucking?"

"You do reduce things to their most vulgar level," she said. "I'm not a casting couch kind of girl. Talent, Mr. Bogart—that's what I have. Right now I'm getting the most fan mail at Warners except for Miss Bette Davis. No one can touch her."

Raoul Walsh
"A son of a bitch directing a son of a bitch."

"Who would want to?" he asked, ignoring his own past experience with the star. "Well, my advice to you is to keep it up. You look like Ginger Rogers. Can you dance?" He did not wait for an answer. "I hear you and Wayne Morris are shacked up."

"We are dating on occasion—nothing serious," she said.

"Well, keep him out of any future movies with me," Bogie said. By the way, ever since I've known you, you've worn the same brown leather shoes. Want me to buy you another pair?"

"Not at all," she said. "I wear these shoes in every scene of every movie. They're my good luck charm. What's your good luck charm?"

"My dick."

"You do know how to say the most enchanting things to a lady."

"You were lucky with your hit, *Four Daughters*," he said. "I didn't bother to see it, but I heard that Fannie Hearst tearjerker was meant to star Bette Davis and Errol Flynn. They turned it down."

"If you go to see it, and I hope you will, pay special attention to John Garfield. He's from the New York theatre, and I predict he's going to become the biggest male star at Warner Brothers. Jack Warner told me that he plans to make a screen team of John and me. He wants to make the two of us the biggest stars at Warner Brothers in the 40s. As for you, Cagney, Raft, and Edward G. Robinson, it's time you gave up those gangster roles and started playing father parts."

He just couldn't let her get away with that.

"Walsh told me your role as the singer Jean in *The Roaring Twenties* was inspired by the real Ruth Etting," he said. "I knew her in New York. Now that was a torch singer. What a woman! Perhaps Walsh can get Etting to dub your voice for such songs as 'Melancholy Baby' which you sing in this movie."

"You really can't help needling people, can you? Have you ever considered it as a mental illness instead of a virtue. I assure you I can do my own singing in any movie I'm cast in. Get it? I'm a singer. Got that?"

***

Although there was nothing romantic going on between them, Bogie bonded with character actress Gladys George who blazed across Hollywood films in the 1930s and 40s. She was cast as Panama Smith. "She's my kind of broad," he told his director Walsh. "She worked in vaudeville since she was three years old," Bogie said. "No one plays a bad girl like Gladys. She's a gal who knows how to party, how to hold her liquor, and how to have a romance in a dark alley."

When he more or less shared this point of view with Methot, she hit him over the head with a beer bottle in a bar. "The God damn part had my name written all over it—not Gladys George. I can play a role like that in my sleep. Listen, you better get me a job—or else. No one seems to want to cast me in anything. Living off your dough these days, I'd even work for free."

Ann Sheridan had originally told Bogie that she was up for the role of Panama Smith, which was clear-

Gladys George
"My kind of broad"

ly based on the notorious nightclub hostess Texas Guinan. But at the last minute Sheridan was assigned to another picture.

Cagney's character was based on the bootlegger Larry Fay. Bogie knew Fay and Guinan, and the movie sparked many memories of his life in the speakeasies of the 20s.

The real-life Fay didn't end as glamorously as Cagney in the movie. Fay was shot and killed on New Year's Day of 1932 when he told his doorman that he was forced to reduce his pay. The doorman pulled out his revolver and fatally shot his boss four times.

One scene between gangster Cagney and speakeasy queen Gladys George became legendary. She confronts a fatally wounded Cagney staggering up the steps to a church. He's just been rubbed out by Bogie. In his usual death scene manner, Cagney staggers back down diagonally and falls professionally face up and camera ready.

Kneeling next to him, George tells the police, "He used to be a big shot."

This line from Gladys George was inserted into the script at the last

minute and was interpreted at the time mainly as a fade-out remark, nothing special at all. But somehow it caught on with movie audiences who remembered and often repeated it. At the begining of the 21st century, the line was still remembered. Members of the American Film Institute ranked George's last line as the number one most famous remark ever uttered in a gangster movie. Bogie would work with George again when she was cast with him in *The Maltese Falcon*.

In *The Roaring Twenties,* Gladys George had fourth billing, with fifth billing going to Jeffrey Lynn. Along with Bogie and Cagney, Lynn was cast as the third doughboy in the movie. A handsome, mild-mannered actor, he had been a former schoolteacher in Massachusetts. Unlike Cagney and Bogie, Lynn was completely without menace on the screen.

Before being cast in *The Roaring Twenties,* Lynn had had a notable success in 1938 when he had appeared with the

More *Bête Noirs*: Cagney with Bogart in *The Roaring Twenties*

368

Lane sisters--Lola, Priscilla, and Rosemary--in *Four Daughters.* That film had been so successful it had spawned three sequels.

Bogie had only a few encounters with Lynn on the set. Either kidding or not, he asked Lynn, "Well, how do you score, pal? I've worked with all the Lane sisters, and screwed each one of them."

"I didn't even try," Lynn honestly claimed.

"Well, Priscilla's in this movie," Bogie said. "Here's your last chance."

"Not interested." Lynn said.

"You a homo or something?"

"I like the gals. But . . ." he hesitated. "If you must know, I'll let you in on a secret. I'm having this thing with Paulette Goddard, but I don't want Charlie Chaplin to find out. I met her when we tested together for *Gone With the Wind.* It's almost definite that Paulette is going to play Scarlett, and I'm going to appear as Ashley Wilkes, Scarlett's true love. In fact, every time Selznick wants to test a new actress for the role of Scarlett, he calls me in to make a screen test with the hopeful. These gals don't have a chance. Paulette's got it sewed up."

In a touch of irony, the role of Ashley Wilkes, of course, would ultimately go to one of Bogie's best friends, Leslie Howard.

Like many male stars of the late 1930s, who entered World War II, Lynn never recouped his former stardom when he returned from the battlefields. His career stalled and went into such a decline he took a job selling homes to baby boomers.

At the world premiere of *The Roaring Twenties*, Bogie escorted a drunken Methot to the gala affair, which brought out even Louis B. Mayer and Darryl F. Zanuck to the glittering event.

As the curtain was about to go up in the theater showing *The Roaring Twenties,* Bogie noticed that Hellinger was missing from his seat. He asked Gladys Glad where her husband had gone.

"He's a nervous wreck," said Glad, "Mark is sitting it out at the Cafe La Maze next door."

Leaving the theater as the picture began, Bogie went next door to find Hellinger deep into his second glass of brandy.

"All those fucking guys in their penguin tuxedos and their whores in their glittering gowns—all of them judging me," Hellinger said.

"They're loving it," Bogie assured him, getting him to agree to walk back to the theater next door.

Later he wished that he hadn't. "We'd gone no more than ten steps before Hellinger threw up all over

Jeffrey Lynn
"Dreams of playing Ashley Wilkes"

369

my shiny new tux," he told Methot.

At the end of the screening, Bogie accepted congratulations, but Cagney got most of the attention that evening. Bogie was eager to retire to La Maze for drinks with Methot. She'd washed most of Hellinger's puke off him.

At La Maze, Bogie seated Methot in a chair just warmed by the brandy-drinking Hellinger. Bogie had dim hopes for *The Roaring Twenties* they'd just seen in its final cut.

Bogie reflected on the movie's plot. "You know, it's all long-gone crap—bootlegging, beer drop-offs, the Stock Market crash, Wall Street ticker tapes going beserk, burly men in tuxedos pushing around big tit blondes in Art Deco speakeasies. It's all so pointless now. Much of the world is at war, and we Yanks will be in it soon. Instead of gangster pictures, like the one Cagney and I just did, I think *Confessions of a Nazi Spy* will be more what the public wants to see."

In spite of Bogie's dire assessment for the success of *The Roaring Twenties,* it was a big hit and drew rave reviews. *The Hollywood Citizen-News* joined the chorus, claiming "this is not just another Warner Brothers gang war drama."

The strangest review appeared in a small Long Beach newspaper. The "critic" wrote: "It's worth the price of admission just to see Joan Blondell's new, laughable haircut." The problem with that review involved the fact that Blondell was not in the movie.

Although Bogie didn't see any future for *The Roaring Twenties,* the film in 2009 would be cited in *Empire Magazine* as number one in a poll of the "Twenty Greatest Gangster Movies You've Never Seen."

The Roaring Twenties would be the last film Bogie ever made with Cagney, and would be Cagney's last gangster film for a decade.

***

Over breakfast the next morning, Bogie choked on his coffee when he read that Cagney had become the second biggest wage earner in Hollywood, topped only by Gary Cooper. Cagney had taken home $368,333 the previous year, which made him one of the highest wage earners in an America drifting down the long road into World War II.

***

His agent, Mary Baker, known as Bogie's "eternal fairy godmother," hooked him up with a super-agent, Sam Jaffe, a tiny man with a gift for securing first-class roles for his clients. What Bogie couldn't do on his own in the

30s, Jaffe did for him in the 40s when he shot up to become the highest paid actor in Hollywood.

"I had a real challenge when I took on Bogie," Jaffe recalled in an interview in London where he had gone into "exile" after his career in Hollywood faded. "Bogie was balding; he didn't have a great physique; he was aging prematurely. His boozing and wild living with Methot was beginning to show on his face. Middle age was not only advancing on Bogie, it was overtaking him."

The agent, Sam Jaffe (1901-2000), is not to be confused with the famous character actor with the same name.

Beginning as an office boy at Paramount, the agent had worked his way up through the ranks to become that studio's executive in charge of production. Then, after a brief stint at Columbia in the early 1930s, he broke away to launch his own talent agency.

In time, he would represent some of the biggest names in the business, not only Bogie and Lauren Bacall, but Peter Lorre, Fredric March, David Niven, Zero Mostel, Richard Burton, and Stanley Kubrick. Jaffe's career declined when he came under suspicion by the Red-hunting demons of Joseph McCarthy during his search for suspected Communists in the film industry.

"At one time I was the only man in Hollywood who believed that Bogie had a future in the movies," Jaffe said. "Most people thought he was just an aging drunk who beat up his wife in bars. But there was great intelligence and ambition there. I sought the help of Leland Hayward. What I couldn't do for Bogie, Leland could. But it was a formidable challenge. Of course, it didn't come easy. Before *High Sierra*, there were still some turkeys Bogie had to make for Warner Brothers."

When Jaffe confronted Jack Warner about his client's stalled career, the studio honcho said: "Here's how I see Bogie. Give him the lead but only in B minus films, sorta Barton MacLane roles. Make him the third or fourth lead in A-list films. Maybe a great film every now and then like *Dark Victory*. Bette Davis is A list, Bogie is B list. But in that big film, keep him in a minor role like the stable hand he played. Of course, if any film calls for a gun-toting killer who dies in the last reel, then that script has Humphrey Bogart written all over it."

"Throughout the entire 1930s, Warner never realized the potential of Bogie," Jaffe claimed. "But other producers and directors were taking notice, especially after seeing Bogie's performance with Bette Davis in *Dark Victory*. We got several offers for star parts for Bogie in A-list pictures. But Warner always said no, preferring to keep his low-paid contract player churning out those B-list potboilers."

Jaffe recalled some tantalizing offers that came in, including *Of Mice and*

Men (1939), based on the novella by John Steinbeck. The star role went to Burgess Meredith. Directed by Lewis Milestone, the film was nominated for four Oscars.

Bogie was also offered the star role in a remake of *The Valiant*, the 1929 film that had starred Paul Muni, a role that garnered that actor an Academy Award in the Best Actor category.

The American film producer, Walter Wanger, wanted Bogie to co-star with Joan Bennett, his newly married wife, in *The House Across the Bay*, a 1940 film directed by Archie Mayo, who had worked with Bogie before. He was to appear in the role of Steve Larwitt, an imprisoned gangster set to be released from Alcatraz. The part seemed perfect for Bogie. Ironically, George Raft was given the role. Usually it was the other way around, with Bogie taking parts that Raft turned down.

In time Bogie and Joan Bennett would become friends and make a picture together for Michael Curtiz. Paramount didn't want to cast Bennett as the female lead in *We're No Angels* (1955), but Bogie, who still had star power, interceded on her behalf. She was retained in her role of Amelie Ducotel. There were very few film offers for her after that.

"Even John Garfield, a newcomer to the Warners lot, was taking home a bigger weekly paycheck than Bogie," Jaffe said. "Garfield got $1,500 a week, Bogie $1,250. That contrasted with James Cagney taking in $12,500 a week; Edward G. Robinson pulling in $8,500, and George Raft $5,500."

"It was no, no, no from Jack Warner," Jaffe said. "Many of these roles could have sparked Bogie's diminishing career years before *Casablanca*. He had to stand in the shadows while others took the spotlight. Mistreated and mishandled by Warner Brothers, Bogie had a contract that seemed more like a jail sentence than anything else. We referred to Warner Brothers as 'the prison,' with Jack Warner as the warden."

Bogie's future director, Vincent Sherman, summed up Bogie's position at Warners as 1939 came to an end. "If it's a louse-heel you're looking for,' Jack Warner shouted, 'Get Bogart!'"

The most bizarre offer Bogie received was to co-star with Mae West and W.C. Fields in *My Little Chickadee* (1940). He was tempted to accept it, if Jack Warner would go along with the deal, which he doubted. Even so, at Jaffe's urging, Bogie decided to check it out.

He told Methot that it would be a "hoot" to appear with West and Fields—"a total change of pace for me. Maybe it would bring out my comic side. As you of all people know, I'm a laugh riot."

As later revealed to columnist Jim Bacon, Bogie claimed he went to the office of the producer, Lester Cowan. "I was handed a script. I had a few lines, then the next thirty pages would be blank except for the notation—'Material to be supplied by Miss West.' Another few lines for me and then thirty more blank pages. 'Material to be supplied by Mr. Fields.' The whole damn script was like that. I left quietly through an open window."

West heard that Bogie had bolted. She called Jaffe, whom she knew, and asked him to invite Bogie to her all-white apartment where she would explain his role to him and her part as Flower Belle Lee.

Bogie accepted the invitation, more to see Mae West than for any other reason. He had no plans to take the role. He told Jaffe, "Fields and West would chew me up in one bite."

Apparently, West did not hold a grudge against Bogie based on the long-ago catfight she'd had with his first wife, Helen Menken.

For reasons never fully explained, both West and her writing partner, Fields, wanted Bogie to play the romantic lead in *My Little Chickadee* (1940). He was offered the role of the "Masked Bandit," which eventually went to Joseph Calleia.

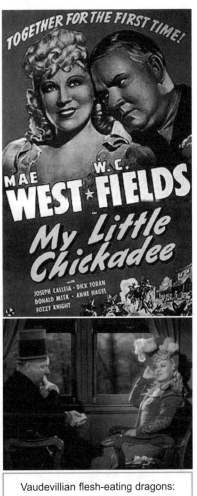

As Bogie recalled, West had arranged herself regally on a sofa in her immaculate living room. She had almost nothing to say about the film but covered a wide range of other subjects.

Obviously she had heard that he was a compulsive drinker, and she shared with him her views on liquor. "If you've craving a drink," she said, "it means your nerves are screaming out for B-Complex vitamins, calcium, and other elements. It's best to refrain. If you get offered a drink—say, at a party—just tell the hostess that you're allergic to alcohol."

"I'll keep that in mind," Bogie falsely claimed.

"I'm a great believer in a star maintaining his health," she said. "I wanted you to play my lover in the film, but we may have to do something about your hair—perhaps a hairpiece would be in order. Of course, it's better to have natural hair," said the woman famous for her wigs. "To save your hair, tell your wife—Mayo Methot, if I can

Vaudevillian flesh-eating dragons:

W.C. Fields, Mae West

believe the papers—to put you on a special diet. We'll draw up a list of what you can eat. Beef heart, beef brains, lamb kidney, plenty of oysters, turnip greens, mustard greens, cabbage, raw wheat germ—and plenty of buckwheat and cornmeal."

"Stop it!" she said. "You're making me hungry."

When not discussing health and regeneration, West talked about her favorite subject—herself. "Let's face it, after all these years, I'm outrageously sexy, unlike all those lez actresses you've appeared with. We won't even mention that older woman you married. The less said about that number the better. I'm an immortal sex symbol. I would never play a role that harmed my image. You've got to build an image like mine, but of a different sort, of course."

"Like what kind of image?" he asked.

"First, you've got it all wrong. You've patterned yourself after the wrong guys in films. Take George Raft for instance." She smiled amusingly at her own wit. "I've already had him, and you can definitely take him. You've got to come up with a different role model. I know back in the 20s they were talking about you being the next Valentino. Today, it's different. Gary Cooper is the biggest thing at the box office. Tell Warners to start billing you as the next Gary Cooper."

"But Coop is two years younger than me," he said. "How can I be the next Gary Cooper?"

She thought for a minute. "We've got a problem here. Give me some time to think that one through."

Methot and Bogie slugging away aboard the Sluggy

374

"Also, my dick isn't as big as his—or so I hear."

"Well, Mother Nature wasn't always fair when she dispensed the goodies. Take me for instance. I'd venture to say that every woman on Earth would want to look like Mae West. But not one can match me. A man can't do a lot about the actual size of his dick, but he can do something about what he thinks is the size of his dick."

"I don't understand that."

"The trick is, select the right kind of woman. Go to bed with her. The right kind of woman can make a man with a four-inch dick feel like he's got ten inches."

"You've got a point there," he said. "In other words, stop going to bed with Mayo Methot, who makes me feel I've got only an inch with nothing to spare."

"Exactly," she said. "Incidentally, Mr. Bogart, I'm just the kind of woman you need to make you feel like a big man in bed."

"I'm sure you are," he said. "But I didn't mean to give you the wrong impression. I mean, I'm not small—in fact, I'm rather large, especially for a man of my size."

"I'm sure that what you say is true, but Mae never accepted a man's word for the size of his dick. I'm from Missouri by way of Brooklyn. Show me. As men from coast to coast can testify, a night in the bed of Mae West will rank as the most memorable of your life. When you die—say, around 1975,—your last memory will be of me and what we did in bed together."

The next day, Sam Jaffe could not pry the final details of Bogie's night with Mae West from him. Future film historians are left with a baffling puzzle.

Did Humphrey Bogart seduce Mae West that night—or did he not?

When he returned home the next morning, Methot had already answered the question for her husband. As he walked inside the door, a ceramic living room lamp sailed past his head, shattering on the ceramic tiles of the hallway's floor.

***

The year 1939 is still hailed for having produced some of the greatest movies of Hollywood. That year witnessed the release of such instant classics as *Gone With the Wind*, *Wuthering Heights*, *Stagecoach*, *The Wizard of Oz*, and many other memorable films.

Bogie would remember it as one of his least favorite years.

He suffered through the release of both *The Oklahoma Kid* and *The Return of Doctor X*. *Dark Victory*, of course, became a classic, except nearly all reviewers drew attention to two particularly inept miscastings within that Bette Davis film—Ronald Reagan's part as the disguised homosexual companion of Davis, and Bogie as the Irish horse trainer who longs for her love.

In *The Return of Doctor X*, Bogie's first and only horror movie, Bogie received bad reviews for a role that had originally been intended for Boris Karloff. In the decades to come, thanks to Bogie's chalky makeup and streaked hair, he evoked a punk rocker.

In the film, Bogie played a criminal who died in the electric chair, and then was brought back to life by the doctor, John Litel, who revived him.

The film's director, Vincent Sherman, remembered Bogie's first reaction to playing third lead in *The Return of Doctor X* (1939). "It's my first horror movie, Vince baby," he said. "I hear I play the living dead, lusting after Rosemary Lane in my ceaseless search for blood to sustain my second life beyond the grave. Wayne Morris as the lead! Why in hell do I have to play second fiddle to that stuck-up, no-talent, big-dick creep!"

"On orders from Jack Warner," Sherman said. "We are just the working stiffs on this turkey. It's movie hokum, but I've got to start out as a director with the first picture Jack Warner assigns me. Stick around and watch me go. We'll do some great pictures together in the 40s. Of course, with the way the world is, those will no doubt be war pictures."

Years later, in 1990, Sherman claimed that Bogie did not complain about getting trapped in *Dr. X*. "He was cast into one villain role after another. He came from the theater, as I did, and even if it was a cornball, crappy part, you tried to do the best you could with it. I was the one who suggested the white streak in his hair because he had been electrocuted. That's

(middle photo) Bogie, one of the "living dead," struggles with Rosemary Lane in his search for fresh blood.

(bottom photo) Bogie appears in chalky white makeup in his first horror flick.

right, he was electrocuted and not hanged. And I got the idea of him walking around with a rabbit and stroking it because that was life—that was blood. We gave him that pasty look because he had been executed and brought back to life."

"When I was assigned Bogie as one of the leads in *Dr. X*, I was told by the honchos at Warners 'to get him to play something besides Duke Mantee,'" Sherman said. "That was a reference, of course, to his role in *The Petrified Forest*. The thinking was that Bogie should always be cast as a heavy, not as a romantic leading man. I bought into that. It was inconceivable to me that he'd ever be cast as a romantic lover, appearing opposite Ingrid Bergman in *Casablanca*. But he became the idol of millions, more dashing to some fans than Errol Flynn himself."

"When I directed Bogie, I never knew if he'd show up beaten, stabbed, or bloody," Sherman recalled. "He was married to this vixen named Mayo Methot. She showed up on the set one day looking for her man. She rightly suspected that Bogie was having an affair with the script girl."

"I was ahead of her," Sherman said. "I sent Bogie to my studio office to fuck the girl, because the first place Methot looked was in Bogie's dressing room."

"To get one up on Bogie, who thought he was so damn smart, I came up with an idea," Sherman said. "Since she couldn't find her straying husband, I invited the bitch for a drink. Before the night ended, I screwed the hot-to-trot harridan. Bogie was none the wiser. He showed up the next day, looking like the cat who swallowed the canary. But I was the one who got his whore. I went back to directing him in his cornball role in this hokey picture, and no one was ever the wiser. What Bogie didn't realize was that Methot was getting as much on the side as he was."

"Bogie's claim to fame in the boudoir was that he had seduced all three of the Lane sisters when he worked with them in movies," Sherman said. "I can't vouch for that, but I did see Rosemary Lane, who had the female lead in *Dr. X*, emerge on two different occasions from his dressing room. Maybe they were just holding hands or going over the script together. But I doubt that. I really do."

"Wayne Morris, the lead, looked good only when he had a hard-on, or so I was told," said Sherman. "Since we didn't show hard-ons back then, he did-n't look good on camera, certainly not as an actor. He tried to be funny in the film, once or twice. He fell into a room by leaning against a supposedly locked door which suddenly opened. That was really hilarious. Huntz Hall was the funniest thing in the movie except for Bogie risen from the grave as a leftfield mad doctor."

***

As Bogie moved deeper into middle age, a new and younger crop of stars was being groomed for the leading roles of the 1940s.

Although he'd worked briefly under the name of Stanley Morner, the newly emerged "Dennis Morgan" had been assigned three pictures for release in 1939, one of which was *The Return of Dr. X*. Although he'd be first and foremost a singing star, he would go on to do straight drama, Westerns, light comedies, and even war movies. He'd scored a hit when he sang "A Pretty Girl Is Like a Melody" in *The Great Ziegfeld* (1936), using his Stanley Morner name. Sometimes he was billed as Richard Stanley.

"I hear you're the latest sensation," Bogie said, coming up to Morgan and extending his hand. "But what name will you be using next year?"

"From now on, it's Dennis Morgan to the grave," the handsome young actor said.

"I hope you're not gonna take any jobs from me," Bogie said. "I have a lot of people to support."

"That will never happen, Mr. Bogart," Morgan assured him.

Bogie didn't believe him. "He was an ambitious actor with a gleam in his eye. I think he would have sold me down the river the first chance he got."

Although some film historians deny it, Morgan admitted later in life that he, along with Ann Sheridan and Ronald Reagan, were briefly considered for the star roles in *Casablanca*. "I shudder to think what would have happened if I had fucked up a classic like that," Morgan said.

"I don't give a damn what all these so-called historians say, I was approached to play Rich Blaine in *Casablanca*," he said. "Jack Warner himself talked over the role with me. Ronald Reagan was originally slated to play the Paul Henreid role before Warner considered him for Rick. Ann Sheridan was originally set to play the Ingrid Bergman part. Instead I made *Thank Your Lucky Stars*—Bogie was in that one too—and *The Desert Song*, that creaky operetta that was updated to include Nazis. My greatest regret in life was I didn't get to play Rick. By the 50s, I was on the way out. At least I was remembered for a role in *Won Ton Ton, the Dog Who Saved Hollywood* in 1976."

In the last months of her life, Maud recalled hearing a sound truck blaring along Hollywood Boulevard hawking *The Return of Doctor X*.

Dennis Morgan
"I, not Bogie, should have played Rick."

WHO IS THE VILEST FIEND IN HISTORY? WHO IS THE MONSTER WHO LAUGHS AS HE KILLS? WHO IS THE VAMPIRE WHO DESPOILS A WOMAN FOR HIS PLEASURE?

She called her son to complain. "At least they could have told the world they're talking about my son, Mr. Humphrey Bogart. If only Belmont had lived to see this cursed day."

When the film was released, and as his marriage to Methot crumbled, Bogie was at his most despondent about his career.

Within a year or so, his luck would change. But first he had to survive a string of upcoming screen disasters. Only his most diehard fans would ever remember those films.

As Methot herself said, "I sat through two of them, saw only twenty minutes of the third one he made, and didn't bother to see the final two."

***

Director Lloyd Bacon, who'd just helmed Bogie and Cagney in *The Oklahoma Kid*, cast him once again in *Invisible Stripes*, a film about the ethical struggles of ex-convicts on parole.

Bogie found his billing in fourth position behind George Raft, Jane Bryan, and William Holden humiliating. Jack Warner had decided to give Holden the lead over Bogie because of his success in *Golden Boy*, a role Bogie himself had desperately wanted.

"Guess who I really wanted to play Raft's brother?" Bacon said. "Not Holden. Wayne Morris."

"Why in the fuck is it, that every picture I'm in the director wants to hire this no-talented big prick?" Bogie asked.

Bacon told Bogie that he was sorry he'd cast Holden in the film. "He's just too damn inexperienced. But Raft seems to have taken him under his wing. Betty Grable told me that Raft is a

(lower photo) A very "noir" shot of William Holden ("the object of George Raft's affection") in *Invisible Stripes*

379

switch-hitter."

"I can confirm that," Bogie said. "Back in the golden days of Broadway, Raft was banging his roommate, Rudolph Valentino."

"Personally, I think Raft has the hots for Golden Boy," Bacon said.

"I haven't read the final pages of this script," Bogie said to Bacon. "But let me guess. Both Raft and I are bumped off in the final reel?"

"You don't even have to ask me that question," Bacon said. "You already know it's true."

Bogie made his hostility to Holden obvious. One scene called for Holden, with Bogie riding on the seat behind him, to drive a motorcycle into a wall. "That S.O.B., he'll crack it up!" Bogie shouted at Bacon. Bacon insisted, and Holden aimed the cycle head-on into a wall. Fortunately, both stars escaped unharmed.

Encountering Raft again, Bogie said, "Me and you old guys are slowly being replaced with studs like William Holden. They call them stars of tomorrow. What are we? Stars of yesterday."

"You weren't a star of yesterday," Raft said. "I was. Not only that but Jack Warner personally told me that he'll be lining up a whole string of pictures in the 40s and plans to star me in most of them."

"That's wonderful," Bogie said, "not that Warner's promises mean a damn rat's fart. But don't count on anything. They may not be making gangster movies in the 40s. Only war pictures."

The female lead, Jane Bryan, was polite but reserved with Bogie. They'd last appeared together in the Bette Davis/Edward G. Robinson film, *Kid Galahad*. In *Invisible Stripes*, Bryan played "Peggy," Holden's girlfriend.

"Not only does Holden get third billing over me, but he gets the girl while I end up with a bullet," Bogie said.

Bacon was tired of listening to Bogie complain. In a cutting dig, he said,

From *Invisible Stripes:*
Two views of George Raft with Humphrey Bogart, "working together but hating each other."

380

"There are stars in the making like William Holden, already established stars like George Raft, and stars that will never be."

Bogie resented the close bond that quickly formed between Raft and Holden, both on and off the set. "George was my big brother in and out of the movie," Holden said. "In fact if he hadn't helped me, I might have been thrown out of the picture. He told Bacon to go easy on me."

In one scene, though, Holden, straight from the boxing ring of *Golden Boy*, accidentally rammed his head into the socket of Raft's left eye, causing damage to Raft that included bruises and stitches.

"He forgave me," Holden said, "and I ended up sitting with him all night, applying cold compresses on his eye."

Unlike his rather formal reunion with Jane Bryan, Bogie had a warm reunion on set with one of the supporting players, Lee Patrick. She came up to him and gave him a long, passionate kiss. "I have a right to do that," she said. "Don't forget you were my husband."

"I don't remember us getting married," he said. "I drank a lot in those days. Still do, as a matter of fact."

"No, you silly goose, you were my priggish young husband on Broadway in *Baby Mine*."

Later over lunch, she said, "I know you know how old I am, but don't tell anybody.

"Actually, I don't remember," he said.

"I'm only two years older than you, but in Hollywood I claim I was born in 1911. A gal's got to earn a living, right, and I'm not ready for grandmother parts yet."

"Your secret is safe with me." He looked at her intently. "Are you happily married—or shall we resume our shack-up?"

"I'm married to a great guy, Tom Wood. We're really suited to each other."

"Are you and I gonna be second bananas in film for the rest of our careers?" he asked.

"I'm afraid so in my case,"

Behind the scenes of *Invisible Stripes*: George Raft *(left)* and Bogie nude in the shower together. Raft showered with his shoes on. "We compared cock sizes with each other," Bogie said.

she said. "I'm resigned to it. My last big chance came when I was considered for the lead in *Stella Dallas*. Alas, *Miss* Barbara Stanwyck snagged the role from me. So, whenever Jack Warner has a potboiler, and he needs someone to play a nurse, a floozie, whatever, he can call on me. I specialize in hard-bitten dames." At the end of the lunch, she kissed him long and hard. "After going to bed with you, I know why they call you Hump."

"I'm now called Bogie."

Invisible Stripes played for a week in movie theaters along Hollywood Boulevard. During its run, Bogie invited Methot to go with him to see it after dinner at the Brown Derby. The meal went off smoothly, without any physical violence, even though patrons at the other tables waited for The Battling Bogarts to break into a fight.

But they left the restaurant without any altercation. As Bogie drove up to the Warners Hollywood Theater, he noticed that the marquee read: GEORGE RAFT AND WILLIAM HOLDEN STARRING IN *INVISIBLE STRIPES.*

Immediately, Methot accused Bogie of being a wimp for not demanding billing instead of Holden. "Next thing I know, Jack Warner will demand that you lick off Holden's dingleberries on camera."

That started it. The Battling Bogarts launched America's entry into World War II before the Japanese attack on Pearl Harbor.

***

Fast forward to September of 1953: The feud between William Holden and Bogie was still percolating when they appeared together on the set of *Sabrina*, a movie that starred the enchanting Audrey Hepburn. Bogie was the star this time, with Holden billed third. Soonafter, hostilities between "the two roosters" [director Billy Wilder's words] bubbled over.

Bogie admitted that "I always knew Wilder wanted Cary Grant for the part, but the faggot turned it down."

"Bogie's face was so weathered at this late hour in his life, I felt audiences would not believe that a cute little number like Audrey would go for this grandfatherly type," Wilder said.

In *Sabrina*, Bogie played a boring, workaholic tycoon, Larry Larrabee, with Holden cast as his playboy brother, David. Both are vying for the prize, young and beautiful Sabrina Fairchild, the daughter of their chauffeur.

When he made *Sabrina*, Bogie was fifty-four years old, but Wilder thought he looked "at least sixty-five, maybe more so."

Bogie staggered through *Sabrina* as best he could, but it was obvious to Hepburn that his many years of hard drinking had made him dyspeptic and ill. Unknown to the cast, Bogie was beginning to show the first symptoms of the cancer that four years later would claim his life.

"Paramount has given me a real problem," Wilder said. "I have to make the audience believe that Audrey would prefer weathered old Bogie to the handsome, dashing, and gorgeously blond Bill Holden, who was thirty-five but looked twenty-eight.

Bogie and Wilder feuded right from the beginning, with Bogie calling *Sabrina* "a crock of crap." He still didn't use the word shit. At one point, studying his new lines of dialogue, he asked Wilder if his young daughter had written it.

Between takes, Bogie reminded Holden that he was earning $300,000 for the picture, as compared to Holden's $125,000.

Directly to his face, Bogie called Wilder "a Prussian German with a rid-ing crop." On other occasions, he called Wilder a "Kraut bastard" or "Nazi." When Wilder issued an instruction, Bogie mocked him by saying "*Jawohl!*"

When Hepburn flubbed her lines, Bogie said, "Have you considered staying home and learning your lines instead of going out every night?"

Holden later complained that on many a day on the set, he almost came "within an inch of knocking Bogie's teeth out because of the insulting way he was treating Audrey and Wilder, too."

As he moved closer to death, Bogie became more and more insecure. He mocked Holden as "Smiling Jim," and ridiculed his good looks. "More matinee idol than a man." He even mocked his hair, whose color had been lightened for the role.

Holden snapped back at Bogie in the press. "He's an actor of consummate skill, with an ego to match."

At one point during a scene, Holden blew smoke in Bogie's face, making him ruin his lines. Bogie stalked off the set, shutting down production.

When Bogie's long-time friend, Clifton Webb, visited the set and asked what it was like working with Hepburn, Bogie replied,

(left to right in images above)

Bogie, Audrey Hepburn, and William Holden. Bogie may have won Audrey on screen, but Holden got her when the cameras stopped rolling.

383

"It's okay if you like to do thirty-six takes."

Bogie recalled passing in front of Holden's dressing room at the end of the day, where, in the words of author Bob Thomas, "he could hear the rattle of ice cubes and the tinkle of Audrey Hepburn's laughter and Holden's hearty guffaw as they listened to Billy Wilder's witticisms."

"Those Paramount bastards didn't invite me," Bogie claimed. "Well fuck 'em."

Toward the end of the shoot, Bogie learned that Holden had fallen in love with the film's female star. "I really was in love with Audrey," Holden told Wilder. "But she wouldn't marry me. So I set out around the world with the idea of screwing every woman in every country I visited."

Irving ("Swifty") Lazar, who was Bogie's agent at the time, summed up the tense condition on the set of *Sabrina*. "Bogie thought that Wilder must humble himself before Bogie. But on a Billy Wilder picture, there is no star but Billy Wilder."

At the end of the shoot, Bogie dismissed Hepburn, Wilder, and Holden. "I'd rather drink a quart of rat's piss than work with either of them again. In fact, I've decided *Sabrina* is going to be my last picture."

That was just a drunken vow Bogie made at Romanoff's to Clifton Webb. Even on his death bed, he was planning to make another picture and another picture.

***

Back in Hollywood in 1939, Bogie was given his latest assignment, a Western called *Virginia City*, to be directed by Michael Curtiz, whom he met at Romanoff's for a wet lunch to discuss its details. Both men were just a few short war years from making *Casablanca* together.

"I want you to wear a mustache," Curtiz said.

"Whatever Herr Director wants," Bogie replied. "More to the point, what's the billing?"

"You're the fourth lead," Curtiz said. "It's an Errol Flynn picture. You'll absolutely hate the fucker. He's nothing but a big piss."

"I can work with Flynn providing you write in some love scenes between us," Bogie said.

"You're such a kidder," Curtiz said. "Always make the joke."

"Who are the other co-stars?" Bogie asked.

"Miriam Hopkins and Randolph Scott."

"Oh, goodie-goodie, a super bitch and a cocksucker."

384

CHAPTER NINE

The dashing star of *Virginia City*, Errol Flynn, was remarkably different from Bogie. Self-destructive, sexually wanton, and reckless in his private life, Flynn, like Bogie, had started out at Warners at about the same time, although their careers would follow remarkably different paths. Whereas it would take years for Bogie to reach the top, Flynn burst like a dynamo upon the American public, a strikingly beautiful, romantic figure with enough charisma to obscure his limited acting talent.

Flynn was a swashbuckler, excelling at swordplay both on and off the screen. "I'm a devil-may-care ladykiller," he said of himself, leaving out mention that he had a great fondness for young boy ass too.

"Robin Hood," Bogie said to him on the set. "I almost didn't recognize you without your green tights."

"They were far too tight to hold my big bundle of goodies," Flynn claimed.

"This is no reflection on working with you, but I hope this is my last western," Bogie said. "I'm a big city boy who hates getting cactus in his ass and sleeping with rattlesnakes."

"I hear you keep fighting for better roles," Flynn said. "Not me. I keep fighting Jack Warner for more money. Miriam Hopkins is getting the same paycheck as me, $50,000. Randolph Scott is taking home $35,000. How about you?"

"Would you believe $10,000?" Bogie said.

The hard-driving Michael Curtiz, of the short fuse, was furious at being assigned to helm another Western. "I know no God damn thing about Westerns," he said. "Why choose me? All I know is that all that horse riding makes cowboys impertinent."

"Don't you mean impotent?" Bogie asked.

"Call it what name you want," Curtiz said. "Let's don't fight over words. It means cowboys after all those years in the saddle become no good in the saddle. Get my river gush?"

A handsome, self-destructive rogue: Erroll Flynn

"You mean drift, don't you?"

"What are you?" Curtiz asked. "Some fucking English teacher? I know English better than you. That's why dialogue's my specialty. But you dumb actors can't say words right."

When not fighting with Flynn during the shoot, Curtiz directed most of his hostility toward Hopkins. "Cunt can't ride horse," he told Bogie. "Says it's the time of month for her period. Cunt too old to have period, but claims her vagina's bleeding."

In the final days of 1939, the unit manager wrote Warners: "It grows more difficult each day for Curtiz to handle Miss Hopkins. They have utter contempt for each other. I have never seen such hostility. Perhaps you can fire her and hire Bette Davis instead. The last line is a joke, of course."

"Oh, God," Bogie told Ann Sheridan who came to visit him. "In the future I'll have a rule. No more mustaches. I'm dressed in black to let the audience know I'm a villain. I play this half-breed outlaw with a Spik accent."

"At least it's not that Irish brogue from *Dark Victory*," she said.

"Curtiz is always the same directing Flynn," Bogie said. "His fists are clenched, his face red with rage, and his voice constantly shouts 'You bum, you bum' to Flynn. Some of the hostility between the two is because they'd both married Lili Damita."

Bogie with Randolph Scott
A *faux* cowboy in black
vs. the real thing

Bogie told Sheridan that she should be playing the saloon girl and Confederate spy, not Hopkins. "You could give it a sexy, comic touch," he said. "Hopkins is playing it like a *grande dame*."

On November 13, 1939, Sidney Skolsky revealed to the public what was happening on the set of *Virginia City*. "There are plenty of feuds in the *Virginia City* company. Errol Flynn and Humphrey Bogart are feuding, Errol Flynn and Miriam Hopkins are feuding, and Mike Curtiz and Miriam Hopkins are feuding."

When Bogie encountered Ronald Reagan on the studio lot, the two actors agreed to break for a cup of coffee, with Bogie smoking a cigarette, of course. "I was set to play the Randolph Scott role, but another project kept me from it," Reagan said.

"Sorry we didn't get to work together," Bogie said. "But you might not have had time to learn your lines. That Jane Wyman is one hot little cutie."

"No, it's not like that," Reagan said. "She's not a nympho like Betty Grable. Jane and I believe in moderation."

"Good to hear that, pal," Bogie said. "I wish another project had come up for me instead of my playing a *bandito mexicano*. Talk about type-casting. Now I understand why you were cast as a latent homosexual in *Dark Victory*. You look like a latent homosexual."

"I could get insulted by that, but I know you're a ribber," Reagan said. "Actually I heard that Olivia de Havilland was set to take over the Hopkins role. Something went wrong."

"Maybe Flynn got tired of fucking her in all those pictures and wanted a change of vaginas," Bogie said.

"You're something else, Bogie," Reagan said, slightly embarrassed. "I don't think you're housebroken. If you don't improve your manners, how can Jane and I invite you over for dinner?"

Bogie told him, "I was raised with politeness and manners. That's the way I was brought up. But in the goldfish bowl of Hollywood, it's impossible to use them. Do you think politeness and manners would work on Michael Curtiz, much less Jack Warner? Dream on."

Flynn was mostly involved with his gang that included Alan Hale, Guinn "Big Boy" Williams, Bruce Cabot, William Lundigan, and Patric Knowles. Curtiz called them "raisers from hell."

"Don't you mean hell-raisers?" Bogie said.

"Whatever," the director said. "The key word is hell."

One night when the Flynn's entourage didn't show up, Flynn invited Bogie for a night of boozing, not womanizing. He later told Cabot, "I am amazed at the whiskey Bogie can drink and still stay on his feet. He drank me under the table."

If any revelation emerged that night, it came from Flynn, who drunkeningly informed Bogie that Mayo Methot, a wife Bogie hated but couldn't live without, had been "royally screwed" [Flynn's words] not only by himself, but by his pals Bruce Cabot and Knowles. All this had occurred when Methot was cast in a bit part in *The Sisters* (1938), a film that had starred Bette Davis, Flynn, and Knowles.

Bogie's reaction to this revelation is not known. Perhaps it led to another fight between "The Battling Bogarts," or perhaps he never brought it up. Considering his own record, he could hardly attack her for infidelity.

Far from seeming angry at Methot, he gave her a $15,000 diamond necklace for Christmas, the most expensive gift he'd ever presented to anyone. That piece of jewelry could be split up into various combinations of brooches, clips, and bracelets.

Jack Warner more or less ordered Bogie to attend the world premiere of *Virginia City* in Nevada. He told Methot, "I found myself drowning in a sea of rhinestone-studded cowboy suits, ten-gallon hats, and six-shooters."

***

With his fake mustache removed, Bogie rushed from the set of *Virginia City* to take the third lead in *It All Came True.*

After Bette Davis turned down the role, Ann Sheridan was cast as the star of the picture, playing a sexy nightclub entertainer described as "teasing, tempting, and a manhandler." It was a good showcase for her, as she also got to sing "Angel in Disguise" and "The Gaucho Serenade."

The ardor between Sheridan and Bogie had cooled, but they remained close friends and confidants. Playing Sheridan's boyfriend was Jeffrey Lynn, who had second billing. Bogie, who had appeared in titles above him in *The Roaring Twenties*, was sorry to see himself demoted. "I think Jack Warner is gradually shoving me out the door," he told Sheridan.

The director, Lewis Seiler, was not a temperamental Michael Curtiz, but a working professional who had helmed Bogie in *You Can't Get Away With Murder*. Bogie expected to encounter no problems with him.

During the first day of the shoot, Seiler told him that James Stewart had originally been set to star in the film. Stewart had a one-picture commitment to Warner Brothers.

When that didn't work out, Jack Warner conceived a new screen duo of George Raft teamed with John Garfield. "Garfield can do all those gangster roles that I used to give Bogie in the 1930s," Warner said.

But both Garfield and Raft pulled out at the last minute. With an undisguised contempt, Raft dismissed the role of the gangster in the film, *Chips Maguire*. "It's a Humphrey Bogart part," he told Jack Warner.

Bogie's close friend, the writer Louis Bromfield, came onto the set to bond with Bogie. He'd sold his story, "Better Than Life," for

Bogie with Sheridan in
It All Came True
"A teasing manhandler"

388

$50,000, which is the exact amount that David Selznick had paid Margaret Mitchell for her rights to *Gone With the Wind*.

Bromfield attacked screenwriters Michael Fessier and Lawrence Kimble. "They couldn't decide if Bogie was a villain or a good guy." When he saw the final cut, Bromfield praised Bogie's excursion into comedy. He played a mobster who was a sort of guardian angel to some aging vaudevillians, including ZaSu Pitts, in a rundown boarding house."

In fact, Bromfield was so pleased with Bogie's work that when the time came for Bogie to wed Lauren Bacall, he invited him to conduct the ceremony at his Malabar Farm in Ohio.

***

Mark Hellinger, Bogie's pal and the associate producer, brought him the script for the next Edward G. Robinson film, *Brother Orchid*. Robinson had contracted to play Little John Sarto, with Bogie in the third lead as Jack Buck.

The female star of the picture, Ann Sothern, had been cast as Robinson's ever-faithful girlfriend. In this far-fetched yarn, Robinson goes from racket chieftain to a monastery.

James Cagney was originally set to play the Robinson role, but bolted at the last minute. Producer Hal Wallis had wanted Bogie's long-time friend, Lee Patrick, to play the female lead as Flo, and Bogie was looking forward to working with her. At the last minute Hellinger, against Bogie's wishes, appealed to Jack Warner to cast Sothern, and he agreed.

When Bogie read the script, he told Hellinger, "Of all the films I've made with that runt, Robinson, this is the only one in which neither of us is killed."

Once again Bogie found himself working with director Lloyd Bacon, who had last helmed him in *Invisible Stripes*.

Bacon was anticipating tension between Bogie and his rival, Robinson. But Robinson said, "Everybody thought we'd be at each other's throat. Not at all. He was a pro in the best meaning of the word. Between takes we talked ominously about America's entry into the war. We saw it coming."

In the fifth lead was dependable Ralph

top photo: Robinson with Bogart
bottom photo: 1940s glam with Ann Sothern

389

Bellamy, best known for playing second leads who invariably lose the girl in the final reel.

"When you need an actor to play *anything*, get Ralph Bellamy," Robinson said. "His range is limitless; his abilities unparalleled; his ego barely ever ruffled. He is the kind of star that made it possible to make pictures. Never getting the girl is a difficult role; it enables an actor to grow old gracefully. I cherish Ralph. I could not say the same about *Brother Orchid*."

Bogie had a lot of respect for the British film actor, Donald Crisp, who would go on to win an Oscar as Best Supporting Actor for his performance in the 1942 *How Green Was My Valley*. Bogie had worked with him before on such pictures as *The Great O'Malley* and *The Amazing Dr. Clitterhouse*.

When Bogie met him again, he'd just appeared with Laurence Olivier in *Wuthering Heights* (1939).

"We're 19th century men," Bogie said to Crisp, welcoming him to the set. "Tell me what it was like fighting the Boer War the year I was born?"

Crisp's answer startled Bogie as it was so earthy. "All I remember was crossing pathways with the Prime Minister of Britain. A very young Winston Churchill and I took a horse piss together. I can assure you that if the PM had whipped out his dick in front of him, Hitler would have declared the war lost."

Over a drink later that night, Crisp confided, "I'm not English, really Scottish. We Scots know the value of a pound."

He did, indeed, becoming at one time in later life chairman of the Bank of America.

Bogie was introduced to Ann Sothern. From the cold winds of North Dakota, this sexy, good-looking, wisecracking blonde had originally appeared on the screen as Harriet Lake, her real name. She had wanted to be a singer, but movie producers had other plans for her, viewing her mainly as a comedienne.

When Bogie met her, she had just finished filming *Maisie* in 1939. The film proved so popular she would be appearing as Maisie in sequels up to 1947. She'd also been teamed with Gene Raymond in a series of films which, among many others, included *The Smartest Girl in Town* (1936).

"How is it working in picture after picture with the same guy?" Bogie asked.

"Gene Raymond is a jerk."

"Thank you for confirming what I already know," he said. Since you're a married lady, and because I'm a New York gentleman who respects marriage vows, I won't be pursuing you on this picture."

"Are you talking about that jerk I'm married to, Richard Pryor?" she asked. "Me and him will be heading for the divorce courts one of these days. No doubt I'll meet you and Mayo Methot there too."

"Perhaps," he said. "I'd leave her, but I'm afraid she'd hunt me down and kill me."

"At any rate, drop by my dressing room late this afternoon," she said, "and I'll see if you're man enough to handle me."

The next day, Bogie told Hellinger, "I don't think Sothern enjoyed me so much in the sack. As a consolation prize, she told me I'd be just the right fit for her old MGM cohort, Lucille Ball. It seems that Ball is alone for weeks at a time whenever Desi Arnaz is on the road."

***

It was once again Mark Hellinger, its associate producer, who brought Bogie his next film script, *They Drive by Night.* Based on A.I. Bezzerides' novel *Long Haul,* it was a drama about the rough-and-tough trucking industry.

"Who am I playing second lead to this time?" Bogie asked. "It has to be either George Raft or Edward G. Robinson."

"You're right on the mark," Hellinger said. "It's Raft. He plays your brother. You're only the fourth lead. Ann Sheridan, your old gal pal, is the second lead, and Ida Lupino is in third position."

"That Lupino is one hot dame," Bogie said. "It gives me an incentive to work on this stinker."

"You're judging the script before you even read it?" Hellinger asked.

"Hell, I could play the role without even reading the script."

Raoul Walsh, the testy director with the eyepatch, was called in to helm the stars. He'd last worked with Bogie in *You Can't Get Away With Murder.*

Arguably, Walsh was the one who nicknamed Bogie as "Bogie the Beefer," because he was always complaining about roles he received. "His acting experience resembled that of John Barrymore," Walsh said. "Both hated, or appeared to hate, every part of the motion-picture industry. John damned it because of the long hours and Bogie echoed him: 'They get you up before daybreak and work your ass off all day until sundown. In the theater I went to work at eight in the evening and was

bottom photo:
Bogie, Ida Lupino and George Raft
Driver Raft saved their lives that day.

391

through by eleven; all the rest of the night and next day to play and catch up with my drinking. Working in pictures is for the birds.' Bogie could go on like this indefinitely, and his invective never faltered."

Tiring of his gripes, Walsh confronted him. "You like that fat paycheck at the end of the week, don't you?"

With a scowl, Bogie said, "That's the only kick I get out of this lousy business."

The film version of *They Drive By Night*, at least in terms of some aspects of the plot, is derivative of *Bordertown* (1935), that had starred Bette Davis as the predatory wife alongside Paul Muni and Margaret Lindsay. In *They Drive by Night*, Ida Lupino took over the Bette Davis role, Raft was cast in the Paul Muni part, and Sheridan won the role previously played by Margaret Lindsay.

The plot was recycled once again in 1953 in a film, *Blowing Wild*, starring Barbara Stanwyck, Anthony Quinn, and Gary Cooper.

Ironically, during the casting discussions for *Blowing Wild*, Lauren Bacall had been the first choice to play the tempestuous wife of an oil baron, the role that eventually went to Stanwyck, but Bacall turned down the offer.

On the set of *They Drive by Night,* Bogie once again came into contact with Gale Page, with whom he'd previously starred in *Crime School.*

"My parts are getting smaller with each picture," Page said. "I'm still hanging in there, but just barely. Jack Warner told me I look like an ordinary 1940s housewife. So any time a script calls for a drab but dependable housewife, I can do it."

"Not all women were made to be the Oomph gal," Bogie said. "Since not all women in the audience look like Lana Turner, the public will identify with you. You're the type of gal a man brings back to meet his family before he marries her."

"Thanks, Bogie," she said. "I think I was just insulted but in the nicest way."

Veteran actor John Litel, was also upset by his role with an eighth billing. "You know I've starred in movies. The *star*, carrying the whole fucking picture. You know that's true."

"Not really," Bogie said. "The only pictures of yours I've ever seen were those you did with me."

Although he was attracted to her, Bogie had only a passing relationship with the British/American actress Ida Lupino. The young star was too busy trying to get her role of Lana right, since this was her first picture for Warners. She announced to Bogie that "Bette Davis is a tough act to follow."

"Even Bette Davis finds Bette Davis a tough act to follow," he said.

Sheridan and Lupino clashed. It wasn't a feud to equal Bette Davis and Miriam Hopkins, but it was nonetheless lethal. "That two-bit British whore is stealing my thunder," Sheridan complained to Bogie in his dressing room over drinks. "I could pull out every hair in the bitch's head. Howard Hughes should have fucked me when I was fifteen years old—not that tight little pussy."

Sheridan's rivalry with the British import dated back to a 1934 Paramount film, *Ready for Love*. Ida Lupino had been the star of that movie, and Clara Lou Sheridan—Ann's original name—had a walk-on.

"When the camera is on you, no one can steal the scene from you," Bogie said, gallantly.

"Thanks for being so reassuring," she said.

Sheridan was correct, however, in her belief that she was being upstaged. In a July 9, 1940 review in the *Hollywood Reporter*, a critic observed: "Ann Sheridan is in a tough spot because of little Ida Lupino. Annie looks great, and before Miss Lupino comes on the screen with so much the better of the parts, the redheaded Sheridan stands out. But after Ida gets working, she steals all the attention. But Miss Oomph is okay."

The highlight of *They Drive by Night* involved Lupino's scene in the courtroom where she went berserk, confessing to the murder of her husband, who had been portrayed by the veteran actor Alan Hale. The way she played it made her a star, landing her a seven-year contract at Warner Brothers.

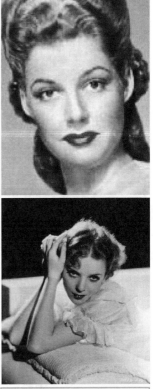

In the 1920s, George Raft had driven a truck along Third Avenue in Manhattan, delivering bootleg liquor for the notorious gangster and bootlegger, Owney Madden. During his portrayal of a gangster on the set of *They Drive By Night*, Raft's real-life experience paid off.

In one scene he was called upon to drive a truck down a steep California mountain road, with Bogie and Sheridan as his passengers.

Halfway down the hill, as the cameras were rolling, the truck went out of control, the brakes not working. Sheridan screamed and covered her eyes. Bogie shouted, "You're gonna kill us!"

The speedometer reached eighty miles per hour. Spotting an embankment which was being dug out for another road, Raft swerved the truck up that embankment. Halfway up the embankment, the truck skidded to a stop.

Jumping out of the truck, Sheridan kissed him on the mouth. "I owe you the fuck of your life for

Upstaged by a younger ingenue: Ann Sheridan *(top photo)* and Ida Lupino

that."

Bogie merely said, "Thanks, pal," perhaps embarrassed at all his screaming and cursing.

"Don't thank me," a shaken Raft said. "Write a letter to Owney Madden."

They Drive By Night was completed in thirty-three working days for a
budget of $500,000. According to the preview audiences at theaters on
Hollywood Boulevard, it seemed unanimous that Lupino had stolen the picture from Bogie, Raft, and Sheridan. One writer asserted Lupino projected a
"fascinating blend of beauty, danger, and deceit."

***

On March 13, 1940 Warner Brothers bought the screen rights to W.R.
Burnett's crime novel *High Sierra*, with a plan to star Paul Muni as its male
lead. In 1936 Muni had won the Oscar for *The Story of Louis Pasteur*, and
since then, he had reigned as Warner's number one male star, even at age 45.

A decade earlier, Burnett had become famous for his crime novel, *Little
Caesar*, based on the life of Al Capone and brought to the screen in a sensational performance by Edward G. Robinson.

John Huston was called in to tweak the script, but
Muni rejected the first version. Warner then decided to
ask Burnett himself to work on a screenplay for *High
Sierra*. When Burnett's version was submitted to the
censors manning the Production Code, they objected
to the "illicit" sexual relationship spinning around Ida
Lupino with unmarried partners. They also found the
words "damn," "tramp," and even "punk" objection-
able.

Ida Lupino was cast as the female lead playing Marie
Garon, a dime-a-dance tramp willing to run off with
whatever man came along.

In the wake of Muni's rejection and the perception by
the studio that he wasn't really right for the role anyway, a revised script was submitted to George Raft. He
turned it down, claiming he was not going to be killed
off in any more films. Huston and Burnett then resub-
mitted the script to Muni who rejected it once again,
even though he thought it had been vastly improved.
He rejected it this time because it had been turned
down by Raft.

Studio autocrat
Jack Warner *(top photo)*,
and *High Sierra* script doctor John Huston

Next in line, Edward G. Robinson said "no way,"

394

before the script was shopped to John Garfield. Even though he had no real star power at the time, he, too, rejected *High Sierra*. Exasperated, Jack Warner said, "Who else but Bogart? He's a son of a bitch, but what actor isn't?"

Even at the last minute, Warner almost didn't cast him. As he told his friend, Raoul Walsh, "Bogie's going around telling people I'm a fairy. But if you want to take a chance, go ahead."

Why Bogie spread the story that Warner was a homosexual is not known, perhaps in revenge for Warner's long ago taunting him about his lisp.

Hard at work on the screenplay, Huston was contemptuous of Raft. "*Everything* was intended for Raft at the time. I was not one of his great admirers. I thought he was a clown, walking around in his white suit with those padded shoulders and form-fitting hips, protected by bodyguards. He was very much a Mafia type and liked to display it. And it turned out the poor devil came to nothing. He refused everything that was thrown at him. And he refused *High Sierra*. You know, he was really an ignorant man. And I was delighted he didn't do our script because Bogie then got to play it. And I knew Bogie was a fine actor."

Huston said that what made *High Sierra* different from other gangster films was the way Bogie played Roy Earle. "We had seen bad guys, hundreds, maybe thousands of them before, but the bad guy Bogart played was a decent man. He had a sense of loyalty, a code of ethics. He could feel sorry for a neglected dog or a crippled girl and go out of his way to help them. He was essentially a loner, a man up against a system, and even though he knew how to use a machine gun and was on the wrong side of the law, he was likable. The way Bogart played him, you couldn't help rooting for Roy Earle."

Although they knew each other before, it was during the making of *High Sierra*, that Bogie bonded with Huston. For some reason, Bogie

bottom photo:
Ida Lupino with Bogart

395

called his future director "The Monster & Double Ugly."

Author Axel Madsen said, "John was Bogie's kind of snake charmer, a natural-born anti-authoritarian, a guy with panache and style. Bogie thought John had more color than ninety percent of Hollywood's actors. In the future when John would call and say, 'Hey, kid, let's make a picture,' Bogie knew he was being conned but he also knew he would have a great time."

On the set of *High Sierra,* Bogie found every excuse he could to complain about the working conditions. He even attacked the packed lunches the crew was served. "I wonder when this sandwich was made? Last year? Christ, they feed the cons at San Quentin better than this."

"In spite of his eternal beefing, Bogie turned in a top performance, jerking tears when he paid for the young lame girl to have successful surgery and setting the audience on the edges of their seats during the robbery and long chase before he died," Walsh said. "This performance made Bogart a star. He would never have to play bit parts again. He only grunted when he read the good things the critics had to say. His mind seemed to be busy with other things. I think he was still blaming Jack Warner for sending him that lousy lunch."

At first, Lupino and Bogie appeared almost hostile to each other on the set. "I have a way of kidding with a straight face," she later said. "So does Bogie. Neither of us recognized the trait in the other. Each thought the other was being nasty, and we were both offended."

Detroit-born Joan Leslie got her first major role in *High Sierra*, playing a crippled girl. She would soon star with Bogie again. Bogie told Walsh, "I can never relate to good girls like Leslie. They're so wholesome, so pure, like professional virgins. I don't think she'll go far in films. We need Lana Turner, Bette Davis, Ann Sheridan, Claire Trevor—you gotta be a bitch to make it big in Hollywood. This town is full of sweet, perky, young things like Leslie." Later he said, "Imagine being little Joan Leslie, and peaking in your career at the age of twenty-one."

Bogart--Very, very noir

As *High Sierra* was being filmed, Walsh came to Bogie with some good news. Muni and Jack Warner had had a violent argument and Muni was out the Warner door.

Warner had been on the verge of green lighting a film for Muni about Ludwig von Beethoven. When Warner told him the movie had been canceled, Muni exploded. He severed his relationship with Warners and tore up his seven-year contract. At last, the road opened for

Bogie to get better scripts.

Barton MacLane appeared in *High Sierra*, but with a tenth billing. Bogie had worked with MacLane before in such films as *San Quentin*. He would appear with Bogie again in the Forties—in fact, MacLane's name is kept alive to future generations because of his appearance in three of Bogie's big movies of the Forties.

Bogie stayed mainly to himself during early filming. But he did meet and talk with some major actors in the supporting cast, including Alan Curtis. His role as Babe Kozak in *High Sierra* remains perhaps the most memorable of his career.

At the time Bogie met Curtis, he was on the dawn of marrying the Hungarian actress Ilona Massey, that shapely operatic blonde from Budapest.

Curtis discussed his marriage plans. "Massey is not a woman you marry," Bogie said. "She's a woman you have make you goulash and then you fuck her." Curtis seemed insulted but Bogie was giving good advice. The marriage was virtually over in three months, although officially it lasted a year.

Perhaps the best actor in the supporting cast was a Kentuckian, Henry Hull, a thin man with a furrowed brow who specialized in playing practical oldsters or crotchety types. Over a drink, Bogie told him, "It's great talking to one of the real pros in the business, *The Werewolf of London*." He was referring to Hull's 1935 hit. Both Hull and Bogie recalled their 1934 appearances in the film *Midnight* with Sidney Fox.

By this time, Bogie had been around the Warner lot so long that it became increasingly obvious that he was working with much younger "stars of tomorrow," some of whom he held with a certain disdain. He was resentful of Arthur Kennedy, because he'd been discovered by James Cagney, who'd cast him in *City for Conquest* (1940) as his younger, piano-playing brother. When Kennedy brought up the name of James Cagney four times in different conversations, maintaining that Cagney was the best actor in Hollywood, Bogie finally interrupted. "You're out of your mind, fucker. Cagney can do only one thing well. Dress up in drag and pick up sailors to bed. I hear he's great at fellatio. Don't tell me he didn't put a good-looking guy like you on the casting couch."

Kennedy and Bogie would get along better when they starred together in William Wyler's *The Desperate Hours* (1955), where Kennedy played a policeman trying to capture Bogie.

One star of tomorrow who Bogie interacted with was Cornel Wilde, who had only a small role in *High Sierra*, but would go on to stardom. When Bogie encountered this bisexual actor from Hungary, he was

Joan Leslie

397

fresh from having taught fencing lessons to Laurence Olivier for his 1940 Broadway production of *Romeo and Juliet.*

Bogie had already heard the rumors about Olivier and Wilde. "What else did you teach Mr. Olivier?" Bogie asked.

"How to handle his sword," Wilde said.

"I can take that two ways," Bogie said with a smirk.

Years later, when Bogie was appearing in *Battle Circus* (1953) with June Allyson, he ran into Wilde in a restaurant. "How's it hanging, kid?" he asked.

"Haven't you heard?" Wilde said. "I'm in beefcake bondage. I've become the darling of the S&M crowd. In *At Sword's Point*, I was stripped and bound at the waist in a torture chamber where my chest was burned with a hot iron. In *California Conquest*, my next picture, I was again stripped to the waist and bound to a tree. I was lashed across my beautiful, golden chest with a whip."

"Sounds like kinky fun to me," Bogie said. "I'll have to hire some whore to do that to me."

As filming progressed, according to Walsh, Bogie was clearly falling in love with Lupino. At first they stayed clear of each other, but as the days passed they became cozier and cozier, taking lunch together, spending time in each other's dressing rooms, having drinks after work and delaying a return home to their spouses.

"Bogie knew such an affair could mean nothing but trouble for them," director Raoul Walsh said. "It was like they couldn't help it. As for Ida, I don't think she really loved Bogie, at least not as much as he loved her. She cared for him; she liked him. But I wouldn't call it love. Several members of the crew disagreed with me, and told me that Ida looked at Bogie with love in her eyes. I think the sex between them was good. Methot was no longer the sex

Cornel Wilde

object that she used to be. Also, like many men his age, Bogie wanted someone much younger and prettier on the hoof. Ida was in the relationship for sex. For Bogie, it either love or temporary insanity. If Methot caught him, I truly believe she would have shot him dead, just like Edward G. Robinson used to do on screen."

Deeper into the shoot, Lupino and Bogie were drawn even closer to each other. "Too close," in the words of Huston.

Somehow Mayo Methot got word of this and began showing up on the set. "If I see that little limey floozy make one move toward my husband, I'll yank out every hair in her overworked pussy."

Dialogue director Irving Rapper said, "Mayo

398

was so jealous of the younger, more beautiful Lupino that she was in a boiling rage. We expected violence on the set."

Louis Hayward, Lupino's husband, also showed up on the set. He'd seen a picture of Bogie in a bathing suit on his knees looking adoringly at Lupino as she rested on a chaise longue by a pool.

Born in South Africa, but reared in London, Hayward was sophisticated, urbane, and a light second lead that made him one of the less memorable leading men of his day.

Fearing a fist fight, and often reluctant to engage in battle, Bogie remained in his dressing room until Walsh told him that "the coast is clear. I ordered Hayward to go home."

Methot hawkeyed what was going on when *High Sierra* was shot in a studio. But for seven weeks, the film was shot on location, including a fishing camp and the Arrowhead Spring Resort. The final scene, which included Bogie's death on film, was in the Sierra Nevada of Eastern California, with Mt. Whitney looming in the distance.

Location shooting allowed Lupino and Bogie to spend their nights together, living almost like man and wife in full view of the crew. "They did little to conceal their relationship, which surprised me since both of them had jealous spouses," Walsh claimed.

In September, the filming of *High Sierra* came to an end, and under its budget of $455,000. Bogie earned $11,200, with Lupino taking home $12,000. Walsh got $17,500.

At the end, Lupino and Bogie decided to go their separate ways. In later interviews, she treated him with respect, but denied that any affair ever took place between them. "He was the most loyal, wonderful guy in the world."

Critics hailed *High Sierra* as the last gangster film of the Depression Era. Others called it "the most memorable of the twilight-of-the-gangster pictures."

When Lupino went on to make *The Sea Wolf* (1941), the other stars included Edward G. Robinson and John Garfield. Bogie sent her a note: "Hanging out with my competition. Traitor."

***

Just as his career was starting to ascend into super stardom, Bogie was labeled a Communist. He likened the accusation to "a bolt of lightning hitting me." His only political activity had been in the mid-1930s when he backed the striking, underpaid lettuce harvesters in the San Joaquin Valley, and when he had contributed $200 to the strike fund of another underpaid group of workers, the reporters on some Seattle newspapers.

A witch hunt, evocative of that led by Senator Joseph McCarthy in the early 1950s, had been launched by Congressman Martin Dies, a blond-haired bully who had been appointed head of the Special Committee on Un-American Activities of the House of Representatives. His claim to fame today is that he ordered his staff "to prove that Shirley Temple was a Communist." Somehow he found Red propaganda in her motion pictures.

Dies opposed Franklin Roosevelt's New Deal, labor unions, Jews ("especially those of New York"), and all black people. The latter he privately told supporters "should be shipped back to Africa where these jungle bunnies belong." He didn't particularly oppose homosexuals since he did not believe "that such perversion" ever took place on American soil.

Testifying before the Dies Committee in July of 1940 was John L. Leech, who called himself "chief functionary" of the local Communist Party in the Greater Los Angeles area. Before the committee, he named names of the leading Communists in Hollywood. Heading the list was Humphrey Bogart, followed by Fredric March, Melvyn Douglas, James Cagney, and Franchot Tone. On August 15, 1940 in a front-page story, Bogie was cited for attending Communist study groups and contributing $150 a month to Communist causes.

He issued a statement: "I have never contributed money to a political organization of any form. That includes Republican, Democratic, Hollywood Anti-Nazi League, or the Communist Party. Furthermore, I have never attended the school mentioned nor do I know what school that may be. I dare the men who are attempting this investigation to call me to the stand. I want to face them myself and not by a proxy to whom I am only a name."

Only the year before, a trial examiner had labeled Leech "a pathological liar." Even so, a newspaper head proclaimed HOLLYWOOD STARS ACCUSED AS REDS BEFORE GRAND JURY.

Congressman Martin Dies
"Shirley Temple is as red as her panties!"

In a suite at the Biltmore Hotel, Bogie confronted Dies, who year round wore a piss-stained suit the color of eggnog ice cream with a red, white, and blue polka dot tie. Under extensive questioning, Dies could not find one iota of evidence that Bogie was or had ever been a Communist.

After the meeting, the Dies Committee exonerated Bogie, claiming that he was a patriotic American. However, unlike the front-page accusations, that item appeared on page 18 of the *Los Angeles Times*. The report stated that "the link of

400

one Mr. Humphrey Bogart to the Communist Party does not appear to be founded in fact."

All this did not escape the attention of Jack Warner. He was set to give Bogie star billing in his most important picture to date, *High Sierra*. At the last minute, he called his publicity department. "On all the posters, make it IDA LUPINO AND HUMPHREY BOGART STARRING IN HIGH SIERRA."

***

During the closing months of 1940, Maud Bogart was battling cancer at the age of seventy-two. On November 23, she lost the battle.

Methot called Bogie at the studio, telling him that his mother was dead.

Since she moved to her small studio on Sunset Boulevard, she still hadn't become intimate with her son, but they had come to respect and admire each other.

He would later regret that they had not developed a more intimate relationship. He also regretted that she did not live to see him ascend to become the major star on the Warners lot. "When she died," he told Methot, "I was still playing third or fourth leads in crappy movies." She never lived to see me in *High Sierra*."

That landmark movie opened in January of 1941, weeks after her burial.

Methot, who remained close to Maud, even though fighting with her son, handled the funeral arrangements. She was interred at Forest Lawn, which would see the burial of Bogie himself in the 1950s.

He cried as Maud was buried. All he could manage to say was, "She died as she had lived. With guts!"

***

After *High Sierra*, Bogie expected Jack Warner to offer him the best scripts floating around the studio. To his disappointment, he was presented with *Carnival*, which seemed to be a cheap rip-off of *Kid Galahad*. The boxing ring of *Kid Galahad* had been changed to a circus setting.

Instead of a top-notch director, Bogie was assigned Ray Enright, the same guy who'd directed him in one of his worst movies, *Swing Your Lady*.

Amazingly, the sluggish director had assembled a first-rate cast. Bogie would co-star with Sylvia Sidney with whom he'd appeared in *Dead End* in 1937. Joan Leslie was once again appearing with him, as was a charming and very talented young actor, Eddie Albert.

Bogie sarcastically told the director, "Great script. Instead of getting mowed down by Edward G. Robinson, I get killed by an insane lion in the final reel."

"All in a day's work," Enright said.

To add to his humiliation of starring in *Carnival*, Bogie was "the sloppy second" choice [his words]. Hal Wallis had at first offered the role to George Raft. Usually Raft was a poor judge of scripts, but not this time. He rejected it, but did not do so in a diplomatic way. "Go fuck yourself," he notified Warners.

Before going into general release, the film's original title, *Carnival,* was changed to *The Wagons Roll at Night*. The plot called for Bogie to play a traveling carnival owner Nick Coster, with Sidney as his girlfriend, Flo Lorraine. Eddie Albert played a lion tamer, Matt Varney, who falls for Nick's sister, Joan Leslie, cast as Mary Coster.

Bogie is the definite loser in this film, and it did nothing to establish him as the romantic hero he was about to become. Not only does his girlfriend, Sidney, fall for Albert, but so does his sister, Joan Leslie.

Bogie hated the film and did not want to see the final cut. He did encounter a fan while he was buying a new suit at a men's store on Hollywood Boulevard. "I didn't think you were *that* bad," the salesman told him.

Many articles have claimed that *The Wagons Roll at Night* was the first film in which Bogie got first billing. Actually, he'd had top billing in such 1930s features as *Racket Busters*, *King of the Underworld*, and *You Can't Get Away With Murder*.

On a trip with Methot to New York, "the battlers" had seen Irwin Shaw's hit play, *The Gentle People*. Bogie had gone backstage to chat with its star, Sylvia Sidney, who had gotten the best notices for *The Wagons Roll at Night*.

Franchot Tone, trying to escape the label of "Mr. Joan Crawford," was cast as the male lead, Geoff, a waterfront extortionist who is the terror of his neighborhood.

After the show, Bogie told Methot that he was "itching" to play the role in the screen version. He personally telegraphed Hal Wallis that he wanted the part.

Upon his return to Hollywood, he learned that Wallis was going to cast James Cagney. Cagney balked, and, once again, so did George Raft, who completely rejected the script.

Anatole Litvak, its director, pleaded with both Raft and Cagney to change their minds, but each of the actors adamantly refused. In desperation, Litvak turned to Edward G. Robinson, who in one afternoon read the script and immediately turned it down.

Bypassing Wallis at this point, Bogie shot off a telegram to the boss man himself, Jack Warner. IT SEEMS TO ME THAT I AM THE LOGICAL PERSON ON THE LOT TO PLAY GENTLE PEOPLE. I WOULD BE GREAT-

LY DISAPPOINTED IF I DIDN'T GET IT.

While in New York, Hal Wallis received a telegram from the coast. Ida Lupino had been cast as the female lead with script approval and arguably approval of her choice of leading man as well. Wallis read the wire. LUPINO REFUSES TO PLAY IN PICTURE WITH BOGART.

In later years Lupino denied that she had refused to work with Bogie. "We parted on the friendliest of terms," the actress claimed. "Hal Wallis, and perhaps Jack Warner, just did not want Bogie in the role. But they blamed me. Both of them preferred John Garfield. Even when Bogie was trying to get the role, the department had come up with what they thought was a novel idea. They were going to promote John and me as a new screen team. That never happened, of course. Ironically, pictures original-ly intended for John and me, such as *To Have and Have Not* or *Key Largo,* went to Bogie and his new bride, Lauren Bacall."

One morning over Methot's too black coffee, Bogie picked up a trade paper. The headline read: BOGART OUT, GARFIELD IN.

Bogie took a small delight when *The Gentle People*—its title by now changed to *Out of the Fog*—opened to mixed reviews and dwindling box office returns.

He was out of work for only two weeks, most of which he spent battling with Methot, when the studio told him they were putting him back to work in *Manpower,* the latest George Raft movie. Each of them would play a power lineman vying for the affections of Marlene Dietrich, who had been lent to Jack Warner in a deal with Universal.

The powers behind the movie were well known to Bogie—Raoul Walsh as director, Mark Hellinger as producer. He'd also known Dietrich, but hadn't seen her in years.

When he read the script, he realized that it was a rip-off of Howard Hawks' 1932 film *Tiger Shark*, in which Edward G. Robinson had played a Portuguese fisherman.

Raft's bitterness and jealousy toward Bogie reached a boiling point on the set of *Manpower*. He even called Bogie's agent, Sam Jaffe, telling him "the role is completely absurd for your

Merrily They Rolled Along

(upper photo) Bogie with Sylvia Sidney *(lower photo)* Bogie, Cliff Clark, Joan Leslie, Eddie Albert

client. If he continues in this picture, it will ruin his career." Raft complained daily to Walsh and to the co-stars, including Dietrich.

Finally, Raft stormed into Jack Warner's office and told him bluntly: "I will walk off the lot today if Bogart stays in the picture."

After an hour of cajoling, pleading, and threatening, Raft got his wish. "I'll tell Walsh to fire Bogart this afternoon," Warner claimed. "Eddie is free."

He was, of course, referring to Raft's other rival, Edward G. Robinson.

Walsh went along with orders, but told Warner, "Your boy Raft is really stupid. He was offered *Manpower* last year when the script was called *Danger Zone*. He turned that down. The fucker doesn't know it's the same damn script."

Before leaving the set, Bogie called on Dietrich in her dressing room for a final *adieu*. She stood at the door and didn't let him in, as she was obviously entertaining someone. Was it George Raft himself? "I'm sorry you didn't stay longer," she whispered. "We could have gotten together and shared our goodies." She gave him a wet-lipped kiss and then shut the door. He heard a man's voice calling to her.

In the second week of the shoot, Raft was so furious at Robinson he asked Walsh if he would hire Bogie back. He and Robinson clashed every day. Not only were they vying for top gun on the screen, but battling offscreen for the affections of Dietrich. At one point they were caught by a *Life* magazine photographer punching each other out. After *Manpower* wrapped with a minimum of violence, Robinson wouldn't speak to Raft for the next fourteen years.

As Bogie was being laughed off the screen for his performance in *The Wagons Roll at Night*, he received an unexpected call from his new friend, John Huston. "My dream has come true. I'm going to direct a picture, and I want you to star in it."

"What character do I play?"

"You play a private detective named Sam Spade. It's based on a novel by Dashiell Hammett."

"What's this stinker about?"

"Well, it's about a bird."

"That sounds okay with me," Bogie said. "A bird I can handle. In my last picture, I got bumped off by a lion."

"My picture is called *The Maltese Falcon*," Huston said.

"Are you recycling that old Bette Davis movie, *Satan Met A Lady*?"

"Indeed I am, but with a different twist,"

John Garfield

404

Huston said. "This is serious drama. Actually Ricardo Cortez was the first Sam Spade back in those bad old Depression days of 1931."

"Listen, I need a hit," Bogie said, "I can't keep appearing in all this recycled crap."

"Perhaps, you'll change your mind when I tell you who your leading lady in *The Maltese Falcon* is going to be. Miss Ingrid Bergman, late of Sweden."

Bogie paused for a long moment. "Ingrid Bergman. Leslie Howard told me a lot about her. Ingrid Bergman, you say. OK, I'll star in your fucking picture."

***

There are various stories as to what caused Methot to stab Bogie with a butcher knife in their kitchen.

John Huston later claimed that Bogie told him the true story, or at least his version of what happened one night when Methot and her spouse were sitting in their living room drinking. At first, the talk was about politics. Bogie was a Roosevelt Democrat but Methot was politically conservative.

As related by Bogie, the evening got off to a bad start when Bogie suggested that Ingrid Berman "is the only true lady in Hollywood." They had just returned from seeing Bergman play a French governess in *Adam Had Four Sons*.

"Well, what do you think I am?" a drunken Methot asked.

"You did play a prostitute in *Marked Woman*," he said. "Type casting."

Within moments she'd gone to the bar and picked up a whiskey bottle, bashing it into his skull.

Getting up from the sofa bleeding and with a splitting headache, he made his way to the kitchen to get an ice pack.

Furious at her, he called back. "Jack Warner called me in the other day. He said with the release of *High Sierra*, I'm gonna be a big star, and I can no longer be seen around town with a blousy matron long past her peak—that is, if she ever had a peak. He said I need to have a young, beautiful wife more appropriate to my new status as a star. Someone like Ingrid Bergman or Ida Lupino."

Methot came into the kitchen and picked up a butcher knife. In a fit of madness she lunged toward him. Seeing her coming, he ducked. Instead of his heart, she missed, stabbing him in his back.

Bleeding profusely, he ran out the door and called on a neighbor in a house nearby. An ambulance was summoned, and he was taken to a hospital. As it turned out it was only a flesh wound but had bled so much it seemed more serious.

Unless Bogie was putting on Huston, he claimed that after he left the hospital he went to a nightclub and later spent the night in a Turkish bath.

He enjoyed seeing the state Methot was in when he took a taxi home the next morning. She had not slept all night and had been frantically calling all over Hollywood to locate her husband.

"She was a model wife for forty-eight hours," Bogie told Huston.

The following Sunday night, Bogie invited Methot to La Maze for dinner and drinks, lots of drinks. He was usually more modest, but as of late he preferred to believe the press generated by *High Sierra*, not *The Wagons Roll at Night*.

"You know what, your old man is going to become the new idol of American women," he told her. "All the hot tamales will be shaking it at me, telling me to climb up for the wildest ride of my life. I'm gonna be bigger than George Raft and Edward G. Robinson. The dames will adore me. You should read my fan mail. Half the women of America, or so it seems, are begging me to fuck them. I'm adored by my public."

"You fucking ham actor," she shouted at him, throwing her glass, filled with alcohol, in his face. She raced toward the door and started down the street. One of her high heels came off, and she stumbled, falling drunk onto the sidewalk. She managed to pick herself up and stepped off the curb, hoping to summon one of the cabs that lined up in front of nightclubs in those days.

In the meantime, Bogie, who had driven to the restaurant, summoned the valet to get his car, even though he was in no condition to drive. Behind the wheel, he headed down the street. Spotting Methot, he stepped on the accelerator, and the car lunged toward her.

As he later told Huston, "I think I wanted to kill her at that moment. If ever I were psychotic in my whole life, that was it. I was heading right toward her. But at the last minute, I swerved and narrowly missed her, although I felt my car sideswiped her body. I braked but the pavement was wet and I skidded right into a parked car."

Both Methot and Bogie spent the night in the same hospital room. A policeman came to investigate. Fortunately, he was a fan of Bogie's, and no charges were filed.

"As you know, I once made a movie called *San Quentin*," Bogie told Huston. "Had I not swerved that night, I would have ended up in that prison. And if I hadn't seen Mayo coming at me with that knife, she'd be in prison too, and I'd be lying next to Maud at Forest Lawn."

"Kid, my advice to you is to file for a divorce from this bitch," Huston said. "She brings out the worst in you. I want to become a director, and I want you to star in my biggest films. That can't happen if you're dead. I know you rose from the dead in *The Return of Doctor X*. But we're talking real life here. Divorce her! You're going to sooner than later. Why not now? Don't postpone it—or it may be too late."

"You're right!" Bogie said. "I'm gonna go home tonight and kick the bitch out of my house."

That was a promise he'd keep, but not right away. Even more spectacular wars would be raged between "The Battling Bogarts" before the final curtain.

***

Huston later recalled that, "I got one of the most disappointing calls of my life when Jack Warner told me that he was going to offer the part of Sam Spade to George Raft. I had to call Bogie and tell him he was off the picture. No Ingrid Bergman. No Bogie."

Since Huston didn't want Raft anyway, he was delighted when he turned down the role. He called Bogie right away with the news.

By now Bogie felt he was a star and, although he wanted the part of Sam Spade, he regretted that he was still second choice—"still a sloppy second," he told Huston.

Raft had told Jack Warner that he did not think the movie "would be an important picture." He exercised a clause in his contract that stated that he did not have to work on remakes.

He also objected to Huston. "I'm too nervous to entrust my career to a director's first assignment, this young John Huston. He's far too inexperienced to direct me."

After Raft turned down *The Maltese*

Portraits of a marriage: Three views of Humphrey Bogart with Mayo Methot

Falcon, "Warner began to see him as a jerk," according to Huston.

Bogie heard that the studio owed Raft $75,000 but that Raft nonetheless bought out his contract for $10,000 "just to get the hell off that Warners' lot."

Warner told friends he "practically ran to the bank to cash the check before Raft changed his mind."

The long battle for roles between Raft and Bogie had at last come to an inglorious ending.

In the aftermath of the Bogart vs. Raft conflicts, Raft would make only one more movie for Warner Brothers, *Background to Danger* (1943), in which he was directed by Raoul Walsh with Peter Lorre and Sydney Greenstreet as his co-stars.

Background to Danger, ironically, was conceived as a spin-off of *Casablanca.* Because of the spectacular success of *Casablanca,* every studio in Hollywood was trying to duplicate its ambience.

***

Bogie came off a two-month suspension to appear as the lead in Huston's *Maltese Falcon.* He'd refused to do *Bad Men of Missouri,* which was rare for him, as in the 1930s he'd more or less done what Jack Warner told him to.

Bogie's intended role in *Bad Men of Missouri* went to fast-rising Dennis Morgan, who vowed that he'd never take a part away from Bogie.

When Bette Davis ran into Bogie on the Warner lot, she'd already read that he'd be starring in *The Maltese Falcon.* "That tired old thing," she said provocatively. "You tell everybody you don't want to take Raft's sloppy seconds. Now you're taking mine."

Released in 1931, *The Maltese Falcon,* the original version, had starred Bebe Daniels with Ricardo Cortez cast as the detective. In the first version, Cortez played it much more as a ladies' man than Bogart in his version of 1941.

Davis was referring to her failed film, *Satan Met a Lady,* which was the second recycling of *The Maltese Falcon.* In 1936, she starred in the most unsuccessful adaptation of the drama, appearing in the Brigid role opposite Warren William. Within the Davis movie, detective Sam Spade had been turned into a lawyer.

Bogie was very disappointed to learn that Ingrid Bergman had only been considered, and that no firm offer had ever been extended to her.

"I will give you the world's greatest consolation prize?" Huston said.

"*Who dat*?" Bogie asked. "Marjorie Main?"

"No, Rita Hayworth."

"That's great, pal," Bogie said. "If her father has stopped fucking her,

408

maybe Rita will share some of her goodies with me. Send her on."

Before Bergman or Hayworth were considered for the role of the female lead, Brigid O'Shaughnessy, it had originally been pitched to 27-year-old Geraldine Fitzgerald, with whom both Bogie and Bette Davis had worked in *Dark Victory*. Wanting to play sympathetic parts, she turned it down. "Let Bette do those bitch roles," she said.

Huston then had to call Bogie with more bad news about the female lead. "Rita Hayworth is off the picture. But, get this, how about Olivia de Havilland?"

"First you give me Raft's sloppy seconds," Bogie protested. "Now you offer Errol Flynn's sloppy seconds."

Finally, a contract for the female lead was finally signed, with Mary Astor, whom Bogie knew only slightly, having performed a radio drama with her.

Originally a child star, Astor had had a checkered past. As a teenager she'd been seduced by John Barrymore, and she'd even had an affair with Walter Huston during the filming of *Dodsworth* (1936). "She went first for the father, then for the son," Bogie said.

Her first husband, Kenneth Hawks, the brother of Howard Hawks, had died in a plane crash.

During her divorce from her second husband, Dr. Franklyn Thorpe, in 1935, her scandalous diary was entered into evidence in the custody fight for their daughter, four-year-old Marylyn Thorpe.

Among other revelations, it included juicy insights into her notorious affair with playwright George S. Kaufman. She confessed that the playwright was "the kind of man I'd go over a cliff for."

The diary also revealed her struggle with alcoholism and her various suicide attempts.

Usually, off-screen notoriety would be a detriment to a star's career. But in Astor's case, Huston hired her for the

Scenes from the 1941 version of
The Maltese Falcon:
(middle photo) Mary Astor with Bogie
(bottom photo) Bogie, Peter Lorre,
Mary Astor, Sydney Greenstreet

409

role because of her adulterous reputation. Astor described her role of Brigid as a "bitch cauldron" and a psychopathic personality.

"I'm a director at last," Huston said, rushing to embrace Bogie when he showed up on the set of *The Maltese Falcon*. "It sure beats sleeping on park benches in Hyde Park when I was a struggling scriptwriter in London. To keep from starving, I even sang cowboy songs to people waiting in line to get into the theater."

It was Bogie who welcomed Walter Huston, John's father, to the set. As a good luck gesture in honor of his son's debut as a director, Walter had agreed to appear in an uncredited camco. John had promised Jack Warner, a tightwad, that he would not charge Warners for his father's appearance.

In his cameo, Walter, a sea captain sieved with bullet holes, appears in Spade's office. Mumbling a word or two, he delivers the falcon before falling dead.

During the first week of the shoot, Huston came to Bogie. "Let's talk man to man, kid," he told his star. "During the filming, Mary Astor is off limits to you. I'm taking director's privilege, and I'm the one who fucks the female star."

Scenes from the 1931 version of
The Maltese Falcon

(bottom photo)
Ricardo Cortez with Bebe Daniels

"That's okay with me, pal" Bogie said. "I don't want to end up in some sex diary."

Bogie had several talks with Astor on the set. In spite of her scandalous life, he found her a sensitive, caring woman. He confided to her that he "hated the marriage trap."

"I don't like to be used, the feeling that another human being possesses me, that I always have to buckle down, turning out all those crap pictures to bring home the bacon."

When Astor, years later, heard about his upcoming marriage to Lauren Bacall, she approved completely. "The remarkable Bacall knew who he was and let him be who he was and what he was. In return, he was at last able to give something no other woman could grab from him— certainly not Mayo Methot or Mary Philips—and that was his total commitment."

410

In recalling her work with Bogie on *Falcon*, Astor said, "He wasn't very tall; vocally he had a range from A to B; his eyes were like shiny coal nuggets pressed deep into his skull, and his smile was a mistake that he tried to keep from happening. He was no movie hero. He was no hero at all."

***

Bogie had fond memories of making *The Maltese Falcon*, and either was a friend or became a friend of some of the supporting players.

On the set, he invited "two of my all-time favorite" broads—Lee Patrick and Gladys George—to his dressing room for drinks. Patrick, a former girlfriend from the 20s, was cast as Effie Perine, the loyal, quick-thinking secretary of Sam Spade. This small role became one of her most enduring film characterizations. Patrick had been called in at the last minute. Eve Arden had been the first choice for the role of the secretary.

Years later, Patrick's final acting role was a reprise of the Effie Perine character she developed for *The Maltese Falcon*. In a reworking of the Sam Spade story, *The Black Bird* (1975) starred George Segal as Sam Spade Jr. In that movie, he was forced to continue his father's work and to retain his father's increasingly sarcastic secretary.

Gladys George, who had worked with Bogie before in *The Roaring Twenties*, received third billing, even though she played a relatively minor role. In *The Maltese Falcon* she was cast as Iva Archer, the faithless wife of Spade's partner, Miles Archer. The role became her most remembered.

According to Huston, Jerome Cowan was perfectly cast as Miles Archer, Sam Spade's sleazy partner.

In *The Maltese Falcon*, Bogie would be forever linked in the public's mind to two of his supporting players, Peter Lorre and Sydney Greenstreet.

Working with Lorre on the set of *The Maltese Falcon* marked the beginning of a beautiful friendship between Bogie and the Hungarian-born actor, who had made a name for himself in the German theater before fleeing to America to escape the Nazis. Lorre was known as Warner's "resident pervert with an accent."

Like Belmont Bogart, Lorre was a morphine addict, having developed his addiction in the wake of a horrendously painful gallbladder operation during the late 1920s. He first achieved fame as the psychotic child murderer in Fritz Lang's *M* (1931).

Lorre and Bogie became "close pals," in Bogie's words and would work in four more films together, not only the memorable *Casablanca* but the controversial *Beat the Devil*.

Lorre, incidentally, became the friend who would urge Bogie to marry

411

Lauren Bacall in spite of the vast difference in their ages. "Five good years are better than none," he told Bogie.

The Maltese Falcon marked the first pairing of Lorre and Greenstreet, who would go on to make nine more movies together. "They became more famous as a couple than Romeo and Juliet," said Huston.

"I will always remember Peter Lorre and Sydney Greenstreet moving through some fog-laden street on the back lot of Warners," Huston said. "You could be sure that both of them were up to some heinous deed. I'd call them the Laurel and Hardy of crime. Even though they appeared in many films without each other, they are forever married as a pair of disreputable but fascinating evil-doers that won a place in our hearts forever. They may, in fact, become immortal long after we've forgotten Lana Turner and Rita Hayworth."

From the start, Lorre was Huston's first choice to play the role of Joel Cairo. "You will know that you're playing a homosexual," Huston said. "I will know that, and Bogie will know that. But according to the Production Code, we're not supposed to depict homosexuals openly on the screen. Those blue noses think that sucking cock or taking it up the ass isn't what men should do. So let's keep it our little secret, okay?"

Lorre defiantly played the role of Cairo as effeminate. In the movie, both his calling cards and handkerchiefs are scented with gardenias; he fusses about his wardrobe, and becomes hysterical when blood from a scratch spoils his shirt. He also virtually fellates his cane during an interview with Sam Spade.

In Hammett's novel, the character is more blatantly homosexual, and is called "queer" and "the fairy."

Greenstreet made his first on-screen appearance as Casper Gutman or "The Fat Man" in this picture. The 357-pound, 60-year-old British actor would forever be associated with Bogie's screen image.

The scene where Greenstreet tries to get Bogie to take a drink which is drugged was the performer's first appearance in front of a Hollywood camera.

Greenstreet fit Hammett's description—"flabbily fat with bulbous pink cheeks and lips and chin and neck, with a great soft egg of a belly that was all his torso."

Before making his first appearance on camera, Greenstreet turned to Astor, "Mary, dear, hold my hand; tell me I won't make an ass of myself!"

During his previous forty years, Greenstreet had been a prominent stage actor. Two decades Bogie's senior, Greenstreet had once been a tea planter in Ceylon before going on what he still called "the wicked, wicked stage" in London.

Suffering from diabetes and Bright's disease, Greenstreet made films for a period of only eight years, but he is among the best remembered and the most recognizable of all film actors. Greenstreet's film career ended not in a Bogie movie but in *Malaya* (1949), in which he had third billing after Spencer Tracy and James Stewart.

Lorre wasn't the only actor evoking a homosexual in the film. Elisha Cook Jr., who had appeared on Broadway with Bogie in the 1932 *Chrysalis*, was cast as the punk, Wilmer Cook.

In the movie, Sam Spade refers to Wilmer as a "gunsel." The censors thought that meant a gunman. The Yiddish term gunsel, literally "little goose," was a vulgarism for a homosexual, similar to the Yiddish word "faigle" or "little bird." Gunsel usually meant a young man involved in a homosexual relationship with an older man.

Cook later claimed, "I was forever cast as a pimp, an informer, or a cocksucker."

The characters of Casper Gutman (Greenstreet) and Wilmer (Cook) were referred to in the *Falcon* film as "Fat Man" and "Little Boy." These were the names used for the two atomic bombs that were dropped on Nagasaki and Hiroshima in 1945, ending World War II.

***

Arguably, *The Maltese Falcon* included more scenes wherein its principal actors smoked cigarettes onscreen than any film of the 1940s, surpassing even movies made by Bette Davis. Jack Warner hated to see actors smoke on the screen, claiming it would prompt smokers in the audience to leave their seats and walk out into the lobby to light up.

But the excessive smoking in *Falcon* actually contributed to the atmospheric tension of the convoluted story.

Faces and a sense of *film noir* from the 1941 version of *Maltese Falcon*

(top photo) Humphrey Bogart
(middle photo) Elisha Cook
(bottom photo) Peter Lorre, Mary Astor, and Sydney Greenstreet

Jack Warner wanted to entitle the movie *The Gent from Frisco* because *The Maltese Falcon* had been the name of the 1931 version. But Huston insisted that the original title be used, and he eventually

413

won the battle.

In thirty-four days, Huston ushered the filming of *The Maltese Falcon* (1941) to completion, one of the world's most classic films. If *High Sierra* didn't quite put Bogie on the A-list in Hollywood, *The Maltese Falcon* did the trick.

"Bogie was a second-class star who then became a big star after *The Maltese Falcon*," Huston said.

Or as Otto Friedrich claimed, "Bogie was released from his gangster roles and won audiences over by playing a good guy anti-hero. *The Maltese Falcon* was the movie in which he created the persona that not only made him famous for the rest of his life but gradually became his own permanent identity."

The climatic confrontation in the movie lasted for almost twenty minutes, taking up one-fifth of the 100-minute running time. All five principal stars were on camera, the shoot taking an entire week with a day off to celebrate July 4.

The closing line, "The stuff that dreams are made of," was voted as the 14th most famous piece of movie dialogue of all time by the American Film Institute. It was Bogie who suggested that Huston use this paraphrase of a line from Shakespeare's *The Tempest*.

In 2007, the American Film Institute also ranked *The Maltese Falcon* as #31 among The Greatest Movies of All Time.

On May 18, 1950, the Screen Guild Theatre broadcast a thirty-minute radio adaptation of the movie, with Bogie as Sam Spade. His fourth wife, Lauren Bacall, performed the Mary Astor role.

After *The Maltese Falcon*, Huston would have only admiration for Bogie as an actor. "There was a devil in the kid, and Bogie made audiences aware of his demons. The devils were so obvious that it was like unzipping your pants and putting your dick on public display. When Bogie was uncaged, he was one of the most exciting creatures in the history of movies."

Bogie's acceptance of Huston as a director and his acceptance of the role of Sam Spade consolidated their life-long friendship and set the stage for collaboration on such later films as *The Treasure of Sierra Madre* (1948), *Key Largo* (1948), *The African Queen* (1951), and *Beat the Devil* (1954).

The Maltese Falcon was nominated for Best Picture Oscar in 1941, but lost to John Ford's *How Green Was My Valley*.

When he saw the finished cut, Bogie proclaimed, "I'll no longer have to be a punching bag for guys like Cagney, Robinson, and Raft. The world is starting to discover what drives Mayo Methot crazy—and that is Humphrey Bogart has sex appeal. I've been denied love in nearly all my films. It's time from now on that I get the gal in future movies. Old guys like me need love, too."

CHAPTER TEN

Bogie was always getting a call, either from another actor or a director, which indirectly transmitted details about his next starring role. Jack Warner or Hal Wallis never contacted him personally, the way they did with George Raft.

The last time he'd seen the producer, Wallis, Bogie had reminded him, "I'm the new George Raft. Let's not forget that when assigning roles in the future. When did Raft last deliver a hit like *The Maltese Falcon*?" He paused a few seconds. "You don't have to answer that."

This time around, it was director Vincent Sherman who called to tell Bogie he'd been cast in *All Through the Night* (1942) to be produced by Jerry Wald.

"Who are my co-stars?" Bogie asked.

"Conrad Veidt and Kaaren Verne," Sherman said.

"You've got to be kidding. "With a war nearly upon us, you put me in a film with Krauts. Don't you know there's anti-German sentiment out there? Who else?"

Listen, I had to settle for Verne," Sherman told Bogie. "I really wanted David Selznick's new discovery, Ingrid Bergman, but she wasn't available. At one point Warner wanted Olivia de Havilland."

"John Huston has his eye on De Havilland, so she's off-limits to me," Bogie said. "No use spoiling a great friendship. But that Swedish icicle, the Bergman dame. I bet I could melt her down."

"In addition to the leads, we've got an amazing supporting cast," Sherman claimed. "Some of the best supporting talent in Hollywood. Your new friend, Peter Lorre. But also Jane Darwell. She was marvelous in *Grapes of Wrath*. Frank McHugh. Barton MacLane. Wallace Ford. Phil Silvers. Jackie Gleason, William Demarest. Fucking comics they give me. And, for the lezzies, Judith Anderson."

"What's my character called?"

"Gloves Donahue, a bigshot Broadway gambler."

"Gloves?" Bogie asked. "What about Mittens?"

"Listen, the picture is all about Nazi agents," Sherman said. "It's very timely and all. Part of the film involves a Nazi attempt to blow up the Brooklyn Navy Yard. You're not going to bolt, are you?"

"I'll do the goddamn picture, providing you sign a blood oath that you didn't offer it to Raft first."

Unhappy with the script of *All Through the Night*, Bogie placed a private call to Irene Lee, the West Coast story editor for Warner Brothers. Contract players weren't supposed to do that, but Bogie said, "What the hell!"

"What's the hottest property you've got cooking on the stove?" he asked Lee, who was a fan of his.

"I've read a copy of this play that never got produced," Lee said. "It's called *Everybody Comes to Rick's*. It's set in Morocco. I sent it to Wallis, and he liked it. But he didn't like the title, though. *Algiers* was such a big hit that he wants to call it *Casablanca*. The lead role, Rick, owns a bar. There's this gal. They met in Paris."

"Could I play Rick?"

"The role was made for you," Lee said. "But there's a problem. Wallis and Jack Warner see George Raft doing it."

"See you, kid," Bogie put down the phone.

By now, Bogie was openly telling anyone who wanted to listen, "Raft is a complete asshole. The day is coming, and it's coming very soon, when Raft will be taking my sloppy seconds. Mark my words."

Peter Lorre called Bogie to meet him for drinks at Romanoff's, where he was introduced to his female lead, Kaaren Verne. This Berlin-born actress had fled the Nazis in 1938. Bogie had never heard of her, and she explained why.

(center photos) Conrad Veidt, Kaaren Verne
(bottom photo) Humphrey Bogart,
film noir movie star

"The studio changed my name to Catherine Young," she said. "But since

416

Jack Warner thinks war with Hitler is inevitable, he told me to call myself Kaaren Verne again. He thinks there's publicity to be gained by a Teutonic actress who turned her back on Hitler and fled to America."

Before the second drink, Bogie had decided that Verne and Lorre had fallen in love. It didn't seem to matter that Verne was married to musician Arthur Young, and Lorre had wed Celia Lovsky in 1934.

Ever his provocative self, Bogie, now into his fourth martini, asked Verne, "What does a dame like you, a member of the superior race, want with this little Jew gnome?"

"There's more to Peter than meets the eye," she said.

"I hope so," Bogie said. "Judged from the outside package, he looks like a shrimp."

The affair between Lorre and Verne began during the making of *All Through the Night*, but neither of them would divorce their spouses until 1945, at which time they married each other.

Verne had played the lead for Vincent Sherman in *Underground* (1941), and they worked well together. "Finally," Sherman told Bogie, "you get the girl but only on screen. Our little Jew boy [a reference to Lorre] is pounding that Kraut pussy every afternoon in his dressing room before she goes home to hubbie."

Meeting Jane Darwell, Bogie virtually fell into her bosom. "You're my mommy on screen but I want you to be my mommy off screen too. I'm a new orphan, and I need my mommy."

"You can place that lovely head of yours in my bosom any night you want," Darwell told him.

Bogie's first greeting to Gleason was, "You look like the man who came to dinner and ate the guests."

On the first day of the shoot, Sherman complained to Bogie that Warner was giving him only $300 a week to direct the picture with a budget of $600,000. "Other directors are getting so much more."

"Maybe you just ain't worth it," Bogie said just to rile him.

Bogie fitted easily into his role as a Damon Runyon New York type who has to outwit a ruthless pack of Nazi sympathizers.

All Through the Night was one of the first anti-Nazi films. Once war against Germany was declared, Hollywood began turning out such pictures by the hundreds.

Sherman explained to Bogie that he was forced

Jane Darwell
"My bosom for you."

to use "this fat guy," Jackie Gleason, because he was pulling in $250 a week, and Warners had no role for him. The same problem was faced by Phil Silvers. Since there was no work for them at Warners, the studio let them both go soon after they'd appeared in *All Through the Night*. As comics in the years ahead, Gleason and Silvers, of course, became household names.

Both Sherman and Bogie had seen Conrad Veidt in *The Cabinet of Dr. Caligari*, as had most of *tout* Hollywood.

In the film, Veidt delivered his usual "iron-fist-in-velvet glove" performance as a Nazi agent.

He told Bogie, "With America about to enter the war, I think I have a whole new career ahead of me in playing dreaded Nazis. Actually, I fled the Nazis. My wife is Jewish." By that time Bogie was calling Veidt "Connie."

He was accurate in his prediction. Predating *Casablanca*, Veidt's next film was entitled *Nazi Agent*.

Over drinks, Veidt told Bogie that there was another reason to leave Germany. "I was known as a staunch anti-Nazi," he said. "As such, I attracted the scrutiny of the Gestapo. A decision was made to assassinate me. I found out about the plot in time. I was able to escape from Germany before the Nazi death squad got to me."

One drunken night when Veidt had had too many beers, he asked Bogie if he could sing a song in his ear. Very quietly he sang "Where the Lighthouse Shines Across the Bay."

"It was the song I sang in my last German film *F.P.I.* in 1933," Veidt said. "My record was a flop."

"Yeah, my songs haven't been hits either," Bogie said jokingly.

Ironically Veidt's song became a hit in England fifty years later when it was discovered by disc jockey Terry Wogan.

Filming of *All Through the Night* went smoothly except on six different occasions when Mayo Methot showed up. She suspected that Bogie was having an affair with Kaaren Verne.

On the set of Veidt's previous picture, *Above Suspicion*, he had told Joan Crawford, "When I made *All Through the Night* with Bogie, I was shocked at the fighting that went on between him and his wife, Methot. I heard screaming one afternoon, and I opened the door to my dressing room in time to see Bogie chasing Methot across the sound stage. At the top of his voice, he was screaming, 'You dirty bitch! You filthy bitch! I'm gonna kill you, you broken-down old hag.'"

"I went to Sherman to see what was going on," Veidt said. "He told me, 'Get used to it. One day, sooner than later, one of them is going to kill the other. I hope it's Methot who bites the dust. I need Bogie.'"

All Through the Night came under fire from isolationists, but Warner and

Bogie, too, did not back down. Bogie's response to such isolationists as Senator Gerald Nye was, "Go stick a fat dildo up your crusty ass." Senator Bennett C. Clark charged Bogie with "creating war hysteria with such anti-German propaganda movies."

At long last Bogie and Jack Warner were united in a common cause, fighting censorship and undue influence from Washington politicians who wanted to silence them.

Warner denounced isolationists, claiming, "I may be charged with being anti-Nazi, but no son of a bitch is going to call me anti-American."

Bogie chimed in, telling the *Hollywood Reporter* that censorship "is the number one enemy of a free democracy. Let Josef Goebbels stay where he is in Berlin, licking the dingleberries off Hitler's asshole." The first part of his statement was printed, the second part was censored.

Bogie was not a joiner. But he did join the Fight for Freedom Committee, urging the entry of the United States into World War II.

He knew that an attack of some sort on American soil was imminent. He volunteered his thirty-eight foot, diesel-powered *Sluggy* for the war effort.

Southern California, with all its defense plants and refineries, was vulnerable to attack. After qualifying for the U.S. Coast Guard Auxiliary, he piloted his *Sluggy* along the coastline one weekend, looking for enemy ships. Larger vessels had already been called up by the U.S. Navy.

All Through the Night was wrapped around the middle of October in 1941.

Ironically in the weeks preceding December 7, 1941, Warners was developing an action thriller for Bogie called *Aloha Means Goodbye*, involving a Japanese plot to attack military installations in Hawaii. It had been serialized in the *Saturday Evening Post*.

Bogie was due December 10 in St. Louis to appear at a Fight for Freedom rally with Melvyn Douglas and his politician wife, Helen Gahagan Douglas. Linda Darnell, a rising film star, was also slated to appear with Bogie and Mr. and Mrs. Douglas, whose career would later be ruined by a Red-baiting young politician named Richard M. Nixon.

All plans were cancelled on December 7. Peter Lorre telephoned Bogie so that he'd switch on a radio for news about the Japanese attack on Pearl Harbor.

In January of 1942, *All Through the Night* opened across the country and did better business than *The Maltese Falcon*. By then both Franklin Roosevelt and the Congress had declared war against both Germany and Japan.

There were no more protests against Warner Brothers for its anti-Nazi films. The America First organization, which had opposed the entry of the United States into World War II, had become history once Pearl Harbor was attacked.

Bogie specifically requested that Jack Warner star him in more anti-Nazi films.

He made another call to see how that play *Everybody Comes to Rick's*—tentatively entitled *Casablanca*—was coming along.

In the meantime, Sam Jaffe negotiated a new contract for Bogie with Warners, a seven-year deal at $1,750 a week.

He had high hopes for his wartime future in films. Having already served in the military during the closing days of World War I, he was too old for the draft.

Expecting bigger and better pictures, he was immediately disappointed when he learned that the leading role in *The Big Shot*, his next film, had been previously rejected by George Raft. "Another sloppy second," he told his director Lewis Seiler, who had helmed him before.

When Bogie read the script for *The Big Shot* (1942), he interpreted it as just another aging gangster clinker. He told director Seiler that, "I thought we stopped making crap like this in the 30s."

Bogie was disappointed that Mary Astor, his co-star in *The Maltese Falcon*, had turned down the role of the female lead.

"I saw a secret memo that Jack Warner sent to his directors," Astor confided to him. "After this war is over, there may be no more pictures for either

one of us to turn down. That's why I'm desperate to take only the right roles. Warner has urged his staff to find new stars. To quote him directly, he said, 'We just cannot go on being satisfied with the old ones because each day they become more unmanageable and less box office.'"

"What you're really saying is for me to avoid turkeys—or else," Bogie said.

"Perhaps we'll work again some day," she said.

"Maybe in Grandpa and Grandma roles," he said, before ringing off.

During the shoot of *The Big Shot*, Bogie was sleeping with Methot only on special occasions, whatever that was. He was looking to begin an affair. For a while he settled on his female co-star, the beautiful, sultry Irene Manning, an actress-singer from Cincinnati.

(lower photo)
Bogart with Irene Manning
"I took a bullet for him."

420

He recognized her from her appearance in *Yankee Doodle Dandy* (1942), as Bogie never missed a James Cagney movie. "I need to see what the drag queen is up to," he told Methot.

Manning had been around since the mid-30s, appearing with Roy Rogers and Gene Autry. She quipped, "I left light opera for horse operas."

Bogie may have seduced Manning—or maybe not. Neither party ever spoke of the matter. It was obvious to those on the set that he was attracted to her, but whatever there was between them was not recorded by any eyewitnesses.

"Instead of hot love scenes with Bogie in the film, I had to take a bullet for him in the final reel," Manning said.

Bogie was even more attracted to the second female lead, a Spokane-born "starlet with promise," the lovely and luminous Susan Peters.

But he backed away when he heard this young girl was dating Howard Hughes and also getting serious with actor Richard Quine, whom she would marry in 1943.

She'd been nominated for an Oscar as Best Supporting Actress for her appearance in the 1942 *Random Harvest*. Bogie realized that Peters was one of those stars of tomorrow that Mary Astor had been talking about.

Bogie liked Peters and had several long talks with her between takes. He told Seiler she "treats me like a father. After all, I can't expect a nineteen-year-old gal to fall for me."

Obviously Bogie wasn't very good at prophesying his own future, as Lauren Bacall waited in the wings.

He was very saddened to pick up a newspaper on New Year's Day in 1945 to read that Quine and his bride, Peters, on a duck-hunting trip outside San Diego, had had an accident. Her rifle had discharged accidentally, the bullet lodging in her spine, leaving her permanently paralyzed from the waist down.

Peters would hang on to life until October 23, 1952, when she died. She'd lost her will to live and had literally starved herself to death, having not eaten in weeks.

***

Bogie was in the doldrums, his marriage to Methot all but over except for the divorce. Three or four times a week, he went to the Finlandia Baths on Sunset Boulevard. Methot became convinced that it was a brothel. She was right, at least in one aspect. It was a brothel but not filled with women.

It was patronized by young actors, many of whom were gay. There is no evidence that Bogie ever participated in any of these gay activities going on at the baths, which in the 1950s would draw such actors as Rock Hudson.

Methot's ire at Bogie's Finlandia visits grew so pronounced that one night she set their home on fire. With the aid of the studio police at Warner Brothers, the flames were put out, and there was no newspaper publicity.

His wife's drinking, violence, and mental instability grew worse. On several occasions, he tried to get her to seek psychiatric help. "There's nothing wrong with me that a stiff drink and a stiff dick won't cure." In a bizarre touch, she went around all day and half the night humming "Embraceable You."

Bogie's depression was relieved when a call came in from John Huston. "How about being in my next movie, playing a character called Rick?"

At long last Bogie showed some excitement. "I've been waiting for months to play Rick. Jack Warner is finally green-lighting *Casablanca*."

"Not so fast," Huston warned him. This is a different Rick. Rick Leland. It's a war movie. The good news is you'll be reunited with Mary Astor and Sydney Greenstreet, minus Peter Lorre.

Huston sent over the script that afternoon, and Bogie immediately recognized the screenplay by Richard Macaulay as a rewrite of *Aloha Means Goodbye*, which he had been up for before December 7. It involved Rick's attempt to prevent a Japanese attack on Pearl Harbor. Since he failed to do that, the plot was reworked to have Rick save the Panama Canal from a Japanese bomber.

As a title, *Across the Pacific* had been used by Warners for a silent feature in 1926, starring Monte Blue. For his own personal amusement, Huston gave Blue a small role in the 1942 version.

In a role originally slated for Ann Sheridan, Astor was cast as Alberta Marlow, a mysterious, sophisticated lady with whom Bogie has a light-hearted romance. Greenstreet was cast as Dr. Lorenz, an urbane spy for the Japanese.

Not only Bogie, but Astor, Greenstreet, and Huston claimed, "We miss Peter."

"One afternoon Peter donned a white coat and walked through a scene in which Sydney, Bogie, and I were being served breakfast on the ship," Astor recalled. "We didn't know John had made the switch with the actor who was playing the waiter. Peter was behind us, so we couldn't see him, and he served us, making tiny mistakes—holding a platter a bit too far away, just touching Sydney's arm as he lifted a cup of coffee. Finally, he leaned down and kissed me on the back of the neck, and we all broke up."

Peter Lorre

Having scored a hit with *The Maltese Falcon*, Jack Warner was eager to repeat the success of that film. He used not only part of the same cast—Bogie, Astor, and Greenstreet—but similar dialogue, especially that spoken between Bogie and Astor.

Right from the beginning, Huston created a "deliberate ambiguity" in the character of Rick. Was Bogie a renegade? A gangster? Or ultimately the hero who saved the Panama Canal?

Before filming began, Huston warned Bogie that at any minute he might have to leave the movie. He was set to be called up for active duty, as he was close to being commissioned in the signal corps.

At the most crucial point in the film, Huston got his marching papers. In the plot, Bogie had been roped to a chair, and he was surrounded by a small army of Japanese soldiers with machine guns. There was virtually no way he could escape from that trap.

Huston had come to a stumbling block in the script, and he couldn't solve it. He told Bogie on the set that he'd been called up. "I'm out of here. Off to war."

"How in the fuck am I going to get out of this Jap trap?" Bogie asked.

"Don't worry about it," Huston assured him. In a call to Jack Warner, Huston said. "I'm off to the Army. Bogie will know how to spring himself from that trap."

Bogie's friend, Vincent Sherman, was called in to complete the picture.

In a talk with Warner that morning, the studio chief told Sherman, "It's not just the Army. Huston is having female trouble. His wife comes in one door, and Olivia de Havilland goes out the other. The guy sometimes doesn't know what he's doing. Take over for him in the morning and finish the damn picture. I'm running out of money."

(middle photo) Bogie, in a jam, facing Sydney Greenstreet.

(lower photo) Bogart with Mary Astor

In the film, Bogie manages to overpower a guard and take over his machine gun station in time to shoot down a Japanese plane taking off to bomb the Panama Canal. Bogie shouts, "I'm not easily trapped."

When someone pointed out to Sherman that this plot development was not believable, the director shot back. "If you ask me, we were lucky to get the bastard out of there at all."

As one reviewer noted, "The characters in *Across the Pacific* never got to the Pacific, much less crossed it."

Long after completing her last movie with Bogie, Mary Astor reflected on the man himself.

"I have heard people say he wasn't really a good actor," she said. "I don't go along with that. It is true that his personality dominated the character he was playing—but the character gained by it. His technical skill was quite brilliant. His precision timing was no accident. He kept other actors on their toes because he listened to them, he watched, he *looked* at them. He never had that vague stare of a person who waits for you to finish talking, who hasn't heard a word you said. And he was never 'upstage center,' acting all by himself. He was there. *With you.*"

***

After Huston volunteered for Army duty and abruptly abandoned the film he'd been directing, there was a glitch. He was assigned an Army desk job with nothing to do. When Jack Warner heard that Huston was just waiting around for an overseas posting to the war front, he sent him the script of *The Killers* to work on.

The Killers was an adaptation of a short story by Ernest Hemingway. The

film was to star two exciting new personalities, both of whom were gorgeous. They were Ava Gardner, who had became famous when she'd married Mickey Rooney, and the new sensation, muscular, strikingly handsome Burt Lancaster.

Huston did not accept screen writing credits for *The Killers* because he did not want the Army to find out that he wasn't devoting his full attention to his do-nothing job, which consisted of just waiting every day for his orders.

One evening, after Huston had finished coaching Ava Gardner for her part in *The Killers,* the lady herself showed up on his doorstep. It was after midnight. He'd been having his ninth drink of

Director Vincent Sherman
"Saving Huston's ass"

the evening on his outdoor patio, and he asked her to join him.

"She was jaw-dropping beautiful," Huston told Bogie. "Still with her North Carolina accent. The Tarheel farm gal has become a Hollywood goddess."

"Did you fuck her?" Bogie asked.

"She seduced me. She stood in front of me and pulled off her clothes and jumped in the pool. When she emerged wet, I had a towel waiting. I don't think I got to dry her off before we did the dirty deed."

Bogie was anxious to meet this goddess, and soonafter, a private dinner for three was arranged way out in the San Fernando Valley, presumably where no one in the film industry would see them.

Bogie remembered that drunken evening, where Gardner called him "honey chil'." He found her beguiling and wanted to take her away from Huston and have her just for himself.

When Huston went to the men's room, Gardner provocatively said, "I saw a picture of you and your wife. Miss Mayo Methot. Is that really your wife or your mother?"

"You're good, kid," he said.

"I'm not just good, I'm the best."

At the end of the evening, Gardner succulently kissed Bogie right on the lips in front of Huston. "Some day let's make a picture together. Perhaps John will direct it."

"Considering how you look and how I look, I could only play your father," Bogie said.

***

Fast forward to Rome in January of 1954. Joseph L. Mankiewicz was set to film *The Barefoot Contessa*, based on the tumultuous life of Rita Hayworth, who had turned down the role. "Too close to home," she said.

Mankiewicz had cast Bogie in the lead, with Gardner playing Maria Vargas. Cast as a loud-mouthed press agent, Edmond O'Brien had the third lead, for which he would win an Oscar as Best Supporting Actor.

Bogie played the world-weary writer-director Harry Dawes. He arrived on the set with his wig maker and long-time mistress Verita Peterson. In the first weeks of the shoot, Lauren Bacall had not yet arrived in Rome.

The wonderful camaraderie that had flourished between Bogie and Gardner during the war years did not exist on the set of *Contessa*. He got top billing, but he was drawing only half the salary that she was.

As a founding member of the Rat Pack, Bogie was a close friend of Frank Sinatra's. Gardner had just separated from him.

425

"I'll never figure you broads out," Bogie told her when they met on the set. Half the world's female population would throw themselves at Frank's feet, and here you are flouncing around with guys who wear capes and little ballerina slippers."

He was referring to Luis Miguel Dominguín, the celebrated Spanish matador with whom she was having an affair.

Although Gardner was putting away a massive amount of alcohol every day, Bogie told her he knew why she drank so little. "That's because when you're drunk you revert to your cornpone-and-molasses Southern accent. Then all your fancy friends will know you're just a hillbilly gal."

"That's what attracts them, honey chil'."

Mankiewicz was forced to shoot many takes of their scenes together. Either Gardner would flub her lines because of her "stage fright," or else the scene would be interrupted by Bogie's racking coughs, an early sign of the cancer that would eventually kill him.

Bogie would often halt production, "God damn it, Mankiewicz, can you tell the dame here to speak up? I can't hear a God damn word she's saying."

When he was actually speaking to Gardner on the set, he told her, "I think I'm good for another decade or so. Then maybe Betty will support me. She'll carry on for at least another forty years." He was, of course, referring to his fourth wife, Lauren Bacall.

Gardner was well aware of his affair with Verita Peterson. Bogie was also aware of her awareness. He told her, "When Betty arrives in Rome, I've got to stash Verita somewhere. We can't go carrying on right in front of Betty."

"I'll take her off your hands," Gardner said.

"Then those rumors about you are true," he said.

"That's for you never to find out, honey chil'. Now get out of here. I need a bullfighter's fuck now. To go on camera having just been fucked makes my skin more radiant."

"It makes my dick limp," he said, exiting her dressing room.

"Mr. Bogart didn't make my life any easier," Gardner said. "He was always needling me, calling me the Grabtown Gypsy, and complaining that he needed a running start toward the set if he wasn't going to be trampled by my entourage."

Gardner also didn't endear herself to Bogie after *The Barefoot Contessa* opened. Having learned that he didn't like the word shit, she

Ava Gardner

426

penned the following note: "Bogie, just seen *Contessa*. I'm sure you'll agree that I looked the most gorgeous I've ever been photographed. But, honey chil', you looked like shit! Love, Ava."

The review from Pauline Kael didn't help much either. "*The Barefoot Contessa* is a trash masterpiece: a Cinderella story in which the prince turns out to be impotent. It's hard to believe Mankiewicz ever spent an hour in Hollywood; the alternative supposition is that he spent too many hours there."

***

In January of 1942 Bogie was disheartened to read an item in the *Hollywood Reporter*, claiming that Ronald Reagan and Ann Sheridan, the lovers in *Kings Row*, had been selected to head the cast in *Casablanca*, with Dennis Morgan as the third lead in this romantic triangle.

This may have been a trial balloon. Years later Reagan claimed that he was made no serious offer to play Rick. Speculative casting was a common practice to attract publicity for a forthcoming film.

The producer Hal Wallis wanted to cast Bogie in the lead, Jack Warner preferring Raft. Warner prevailed.

Raft at the time was trying to escape the taint of gangster roles. In the films of the 40s, the Nazis had become the gangsters of the 1930s. Raft felt that Rick Blaine, an ex-smuggler, was really a gangster. "The script doesn't make clear why Rick can't return to America," Raft said. "Obviously he was involved in some illegal activity. I won't do it."

But after turning it down, he had second thoughts. He then notified Wallis that he would accept the role. It was too late. Warner had agreed to let Wallis cast Bogie.

"I had many regrets after I gave Bogart the role of Rick, the slick casino owner, in *Casablanca*," Raft said. "But the part caught up with me in Cuba. In *Background to Danger*, the movie I shot in Havana, I starred in a real-life drama that was more exciting

The Barefoot Contessa ("Trash Masterpiece") *(upper photo)* Bogart romancing Ava Gardner *(lower photo)* Vincenzo (Rosanno Brazzi) tells Bogie that Maria Vargas (Ava Gardner) is dead.

427

than *Casablanca*. It had a live revolution as a background, and the bullets in the machine guns pointed at my head were real."

The screenplay for *Casablanca* was based on an unproduced play, *Everybody Comes to Rick's*, written by Murray Burnett and Joan Alison.

Lisbon was the major port of embarkation for refugees from Nazi-occupied Europe. The playwrights in their first draft set the scene in Portugal, but later transferred it to Casablanca, which was also one of the key stops for refugees on the run.

Samuel Marx had pitched the property to Mayer as an ideal vehicle for Clark Gable. Alison had envisioned him for the role. "Gable as Rick was my concept of a guy that I would like. I hated Humphrey Bogart. I thought he was a common drunk."

Warners did not immediately get first dibs on the play *Everybody Comes to Rick's*. Samuel Marx of MGM wanted to offer Burnett and Alison $5,000, but Louis B. Mayer vetoed the idea.

The script of the play arrived on the Warner lot on December 8, 1941, one day after the Japanese attack on Pearl Harbor.

The first script analyst at Warner who read the play, Stephen Karnot, called it "sophisticated hokum." In his words, "It will play." He sent it up to Irene Lee, head of the Warner story department. She liked the script and shot it at once to Jack Warner, who also liked it. He agreed to pay $20,000, the highest amount ever paid for an unproduced script.

Thinking of the success of the film, *Algiers* (1938), Warner had already ordered that the play be retitled *Casablanca*.

After several attempts to get a workable screenplay, Hal Wallis had long talks with Julius J. Epstein and Philip G. Epstein, two brothers. These writers were known on the lot as "The Boys" or else "Phil and Julie."

Identical twins, they were both bald and rather lanky, but each of them was known for their snappy dialogue, as demonstrated when they were called in "to fix" *Yankee Doodle Dandy* for James Cagney in his role of George M.

Cohan.

In its simplest format, the Epsteins created their romance/drama set in unoccupied Morocco during the early days of World War II. An American expatriate, Rick Blaine (Bogie), meets a former lover Ilsa Lund (Ingrid Bergman), with unforeseen complications. She is in essence torn between two lovers. Paul Henreid, as Victor Laszlo, would later be cast to fill the triangle.

To bail out the brothers, screenwriter Howard Koch was called in to develop a screenplay from scratch.

As a writer, Koch had already had a moment of notoriety. He was known for his dramatization of H.G. Wells' *The War of the Worlds*. That broadcast had convinced thousands of Americans that the country was being invaded by Martians.

Later, writers Casey Robinson and Lenore J. Coffee were asked to read both the Koch version of the play and the Epstein version. These two new writers found merit in both scripts. But Robinson beefed up the romantic angle.

Wallis considered casting Hedy Lamarr as Ilsa, because of her success in the film *Algiers*. In the final negotiation, MGM refused to release her. Hedy also objected to the unfinished script.

Months later, when both Bergman and Bogie were overseas entertaining the troops, Hedy, along with Alan Ladd in the Rick role, agreed to perform the screen drama in a 1944 radio show for the Lux Radio Theater.

A classic French beauty, Michèle Morgan was a serious contender for the role of Isla. Her enigmatic features and gloomy allure invited comparisons to a young Greta Garbo. Although she would be cast opposite Bogie in his upcoming *Passage to Marseille*, she did not click with American audiences. After the war, she'd go home to France where she became one of her country's most popular leading ladies.

"We'll always have Paris"

Her asking price of $55,000 was too high, since it was more than twice what Warner would have to pay Bergman.

Years later, when asked how she felt losing out on the pivotal role of Isla Lund in *Casablanca*, Morgan issued an enigmatic statement: "A woman can always deceive a hundred men but not a single

429

woman."

The Epstein twins were sent to meet with David Selznick to persuade him to lend the services of Ingrid Bergman, whom he had under exclusive contract. Although the twins were articulate on paper, they bumbled the plot, which had not really been worked out in their minds, when they had to deliver it face-to-face to Selznick.

"*Casablanca* is going to have a lot of schmaltz—lots of atmosphere, cigarette smoke, guitar music," Julius Epstein told Selznick. After nearly half an hour of describing the movie to a seemingly bored Selznick, Julius finally gave up and said, "Oh, what the hell! It's a lot of shit like *Algiers*."

"When Selznick stopped slurping his luncheon soup and nodded, I knew we had Bergman," Epstein later claimed.

Selznick agreed to lend Bergman to Warners for $25,000. It was a barter agreement. To sweeten the deal, Selznick agreed to lend Bergman for eight weeks in return for eight weeks of services from Olivia de Havilland. Selznick never used De Havilland but lent her to RKO to make the lackluster *Government Girl* instead.

"I didn't want to be Ilsa in *Casablanca*," Bergman said. "There wasn't that much for me to do."

But since she was under exclusive contract to Selznick, she had to go through with the deal; otherwise she'd face suspension. To prepare for the role and to understand Bogie's acting style, Bergman watched *The Maltese Falcon* six times.

Selznick wasn't as dumb as this exchange with the Epsteins made him appear. At the time, there was fear that Sweden might be joining forces with the Axis to fight the West. A Swedish actress might be viewed as an anathema to American audiences.

Off and on-screen views of *Casablanca* with Bogart, Rains, Bergman, and Henreid

"...a 'B' picture soon forgotten."
---Ingrid Bergman

Greta Garbo had already retired and didn't face that problem.

Bergman was a politically naïve young woman when she filmed *Die vier Gessellen* (*The Four Companions*) in Germany. One of her biographers, Charlotte Chandler, claimed she at first interpreted the Nazis as only "a temporary aberration—too foolish to be taken seriously."

"Germany will not start a war," Bergman claimed. The actress later had a life-long guilt because she had so horribly misjudged the situation and was so slow to see the evils of Hitler.

Her estranged first husband, Petter Lindstrom, in a later attempt to embarrass his wife, claimed that she had been taken to a Nazi rally in Hamburg and later praised Josef Goebbels, the Third Reich's minister of Enlightenment and Propaganda, for giving "a fantastic speech." That was corroborated in another Bergman biography, Laurence Leamer's *As Times Go By*.

Amazingly, even after Germany invaded Poland and launched World War II in 1939, Bergman turned down a movie role in *So Ends Our Night*, which was based on an Erich Maria Remarque novel. Allegedly, the actress claimed that the script was "too anti-German."

Selznick wisely suspected that Bergman was a public relations time bomb waiting to explode. If word of her pro-German sentiments got out, it would no doubt have seriously damaged her career. As it turned out, the script for *Casablanca* was perfect for her, portraying her as the supportive wife of a resistance fighter.

Weeks later, an anti-Nazi like Bogie told Peter Lorre, Michael Curtiz, and others that he was the one who "turned Ingrid's head around politically" during their time together.

"I educated her and warned her never to be heard speaking German again," Bogie claimed. "I told her, 'If it's called for you to speak German in a script, turn it down. And don't wear one of those new bathing suits seen at the North Sea resorts, where a Fraülein has the image of a swastika covering her vagina.'"

Warner and Wallis assigned their temperamental Hungarian director, Michael Curtiz, to helm *Casablanca*. "Curtiz has tamed Bogie before," Warner told Wallis. "I'm sure he can do it again. After *The Maltese Falcon*, Bogie is getting a little

Two views of Ingrid Bergman
"She'd do it with doorknobs"
--Alfred Hitchcock

too big for his breeches."

Bogie had long wanted to work with Bergman, and in *Casablanca* at long last he had the opportunity. He asked Geraldine Fitzgerald, who had appeared with him in the Bette Davis picture, *Dark Victory*, to set up a luncheon, since she knew Bergman.

The cover-up of what actually went on between Bogie and Bergman may have begun at that luncheon. Fitzgerald would later claim that the two stars of *Casablanca* rarely spoke to each other off camera, which suggested that they were feuding, which they were not.

Bergman herself may have asked Fitzgerald to spread that false story. At any rate, Fitzgerald was not in *Casablanca* and was not privy to what went on privately among the actors.

During the luncheon, Bergman confessed that the role she really wanted

was that of Maria in *For Whom the Bell Tolls* (1943), which she eventually won, appearing with Gary Cooper, who became her temporary lover.

At the luncheon, Bergman pointedly asked Bogie, "How can I play Ilsa in *Casablanca*? I'm supposed to be the world's most beautiful woman. I look like a Swedish milkmaid."

"If that's what you think you look like, I'm taking up a new profession—that of milking cows."

"Don't be vulgar," Bergman cautioned him. "I hardly know you."

"When you get to know me, we can get down and dirty together."

According to Fitzgerald, "The whole subject at lunch was how both Bogie and Ingrid could get out of making that movie. They thought the dialogue was ridiculous and the situations were unbelievable. I knew Bogie very well, and I think he wanted to join forces with Bergman, to make sure they both said the same things."

There's another problem here. Fitzgerald's summary of the lunch with Bergman and Bogie may have accurately stated her position, but it left out the fact that Bogie had campaigned for months to play Rick Blaine. Why would he suddenly want to bolt from *Casablanca*?

Because Paul Henreid was not available at

Three views of infidelity:
Bogart with Berman

the time shooting began, Wallis and Curtiz considered Herbert Marshall, Dean Jagger, and Joseph Cotten for the role of Victor.

Henreid did not want to play Victor Lazlo, fearing that being placed in a secondary character role would ruin his burgeoning career as a romantic lead.

With a cast not fully decided, but with Bogie and Bergman in tow, principal photography began in May of 1942 on *Casablanca*.

The film's scriptwriting team, which was composed of five writers, had not yet come up with a suitable script. Many problems in the plot had not been worked out. Some loopholes in the plot were never answered even after the film was released—for example, why had Rick been banished from America?

***

On the first day of shooting, Curtiz received a telegram from Warner. "These are turbulent days and I know you will finish *Casablanca* in tops seven weeks. I am depending on you to be the old Curtiz I know you to be, and I am positive you are going to make one great picture."

Bogie was rushing through the film because he had agreed to star in *Sahara* for Columbia in return for a Cary Grant commitment.

"Bogie told Curtiz, "The audience won't believe that a looker like Ingrid would fall for a guy with a mug like mine."

Later, after viewing the first rushes with her, he changed his mind. "When the camera moves in on that Bergman face, and she's saying she loves you, it would make anybody look romantic."

Spencer Tracy advised Bogie, "This is the first time you've played the romantic lead against a major star. You stand still and always make her come to you. Curtiz probably won't notice it. If she complains, you can tell her it's in the script. You've got something she wants, so she has to come to you."

The Blaine in the name of Bogie's character came from Amory Blaine, the romantic hero of *This Side of Paradise* (1920), the first novel of F. Scott

Desperately trying to get out of town

(top photo) Greenstreet, Henreid, Bergman
bottom photo: Henreid, Bergman, Bogart

Fitzgerald.

In spite of his initial complaints, Bogie was actually pleased with the role, yet didn't want to admit it to anybody. In the first draft script sent to him, a reader had made this notation about the character of Rick Blaine. "Two parts Hemingway, one part F. Scott Fitzgerald, a dash of Christ."

Bogie did demand that his character be made stronger. "The world is at war, and Rick is crying in his champagne about some whore he dumped in Paris."

The difference in height between his stars caused some problems for Curtiz. Bergman towered over Bogie, who stood on a box in some scenes or else sat on a pillow. In one scene which was shot while Bogie and Bergman were sitting together on a couch—the famous "franc for your thoughts" moment—Curtiz directed Bergman "to slouch down." Bogie also had to wear platform shoes in some scenes.

Rick's *Café Americain* in the movie was modeled after the Hotel El Minzah in Tangier, former retreat of such vacationing stars as Errol Flynn and Marlene Dietrich.

Because of wartime restrictions on building supplies, Rick's Café was one of the few original sets custom-built for the film. The rest of the sets were recycled from previous Warner Brothers films. As an example, the set which depicted the Paris train station was recycled from *Now, Voyager* (1942), which had starred Paul Henreid and Bette Davis.

Wartime restrictions also made it impossible for an actual airport to be used after dark because of security reasons. To solve that problem, Curtiz had a small cardboard cutout airplane made, which he filmed in forced perspective. To create the illusion that the craft was full-sized, he hired midgets to portray the crew preparing the plane for the famous take-off with Ilsa's immortal goodbye to Rick.

A *film noir* legend
"By the time I was twenty-seven, I knew not to marry an actress, so I married four of them."

At last, Bergman came together with her director, Curtiz, former circus juggler, strongman, and trampoline artist. His directional advice about how to play Ilsa was simple: "Just be yourself, Ingrid Bergman. Bogie will be himself, like the asshole could be anything else."

But when she showed up the next day for filming, she encountered a very different personality. "Fortunately," she later recalled, "I'd already made *Dr. Jekyll and Mr. Hyde*, so I knew about dual personalities."

When Bergman appeared on the set, Curtiz

attacked her. "You're playing a decent woman, not a whore from 10th Avenue. Take off pounds of makeup. No lipstick."

Bergman pestered Curtiz, asking him, "Which man am I in love with?" Since the director hadn't decided, he told her to "play it in between."

Until deep into the shoot, Curtiz and the writers could not make up their minds about how the film should end. Bergman later said, "I never knew from day to day which man I was in love with, Rick or Victor."

Curtiz discussed with his writers the possibility of having Rick run away with Ilsa. But he was warned that the censors might object. After all, Ilsa was married to Victor. Finally it was decided that Ilsa, although still in love with Rick, would remain with her husband.

The third lead, Paul Henreid, reluctantly showed up on the set long after shooting had begun.

He was about to enter the pantheon of film history for his portrait in *Now, Voyager*. In the film, he had put two cigarettes at once to his lips, lit them, and passed one on to Bette Davis. A legend was born.

Rivals on the screen, Bogie and Henreid did not get along. Bogie told Peter Lorre that Henreid was a "prima donna." Both Bogie and Henreid were

gentlemen and managed to conceal their contempt for each other, although denouncing each other privately. On the surface, they seemed like friends and even played chess together between takes.

Henreid told Bogie that when he'd appeared in a 1940 British thriller, *Night Train to Munich*, he got a lot of fan mail from women asking "Who was that cute Nazi in the movie?" It is believed that Henreid had some Jewish ancestors, hence his flight from Nazi-occupied territory.

Although Bogie was all smiles playing chess with Henreid, when the actor disappeared into his dressing room, Bogie attacked him to Curtiz. "Henreid is the biggest case of self-idolatry since I last fucked Hedy Lamarr. After lighting that cigarette for Bette, he pictures himself a matinee idol."

"Wait a minute, you slimy son of a bitch," Curtiz said. "You fucked the Austrian bitch? I saw *Ecstasy*. When she ran bare-assed naked, I got a hard-on."

"Play It Again, Sam"
Two views of Dooley Wilson

435

"She called me one night, and we got together," Bogie said. "At the time, as you know, she was up for the role of Ilsa. She wanted to see if we had any sexual chemistry together. We did. And how! Her pussy is top of the line. I heard she once fucked both Hitler and Mussolini—not at the same time, of course. With Hedy, it may be the only time in my life where I had sloppy seconds after the *Führer*."

"You asshole," Curtiz obviously infuriated said. "The Lamarr cunt should have come to me. After all, I'm the director of this silly fairytale. How did it happen? An ugly guy like you born when Lincoln was president. Hedy Lamarr and Ingrid Bergman. Who's next? Betty Grable? Lana Turner? Veronica Lake? Rita Hayworth?"

"If you brag to me you fuck one of these cunts, I'll cut off your dick if I can find it," Curtiz threatened. You may be great with women off-screen, but you are lousy on screen. When you go to kiss Bergman, you look like you about to throw up. You're no homosexual, are you? Errol Flynn told me you were always looking at his crotch. Ronald Reagan told me you made a pass at him in the men's toilet."

"That was just a joke," Bogie protested.

"Don't speak to me rest of day," Curtiz said. "Just for fucking Hedy Lamarr, I'm gonna make you do one take thirty-two times."

Lamarr had made *Ekstase* (*Ecstasy*) when she was fifteen. She'd met the

Fascist dictators during the course of her marriage (1933-1937) to Fritz Mandl, a Vienna-based arms manufacturer and multi-millionaire. In those days she always appeared in public wearing a fortune in jewels, especially diamonds.

For *Casablanca's* supporting players, Curtiz had rounded up the usual suspects: Claude Rains, Conrad Veidt, Sydney Greenstreet, Peter Lorre, S.Z. Sakall, Joy Page, Dooley Wilson, and Helmut Dantine.

Claude Rains, in a brilliant screen portrayal, was cast as Captain Louis Renault, a corrupt Vichy opportunist who claims, "I have no convictions. I blow with the wind, and the prevailing wind happens to be from Vichy."

Two views of Paul Henreid

(top photo) Night Train to Munich (bottom photo), Now, Voyager, with Bette Davis

Freelancer Rains, arguably the single most talented actor in the cast, certainly had a lot to smile about in his role, as he'd jacked up his salary from Jack Warner to $4,000 a week.

"Let the shoot drag on forever for all I care," he told Bogie.

Rains would go on to appear in *Notorious*, the Alfred Hitchcock film that also starred Bergman.

The bulky Sydney Greenstreet played the small but pivotal role of Signor Ferrari, the jovial but sinister fez-wearing owner of the Blue Parrot, chief rival of Rick's Café. That was his day job. At night he was Casablanca's leading black marketer. Everything was for sale for a price, even a passport to get a refugee out of Casablanca and on the plane to Lisbon and freedom.

Conrad Veidt, on loan from MGM, was paid the same amount that Bergman was, $25,000. Originally Curtiz had wanted Otto Preminger for the role of Major Strasser, but at the time, he was under contract to Darryl F. Zanuck, who demanded a salary of $7,000 a week. Jack Warner turned Preminger down.

Veidt delivered his usual brilliant performance as the icily cold but elegant Gestapo major, Strasser, who likes vintage champagne and very cold caviar.

Many of the actors who played Nazis in *Casablanca* were in fact German Jews who had escaped from Hitler's Nazis. Veidt himself had hurriedly escaped Germany when he learned that the SS had sent a death squad after him because of his anti-Nazi activities.

Peter Lorre was cast as the creepy petty criminal Ugarte, selling "letters of transit," which he obtained through the murder of two Nazi couriers.

In a key moment, Lorre as Ugarte asks Rick, "You despise me, don't you?

Rick answers, "If I gave you any thought, I probably would."

The defining moment occurs when Lorre is trapped by the police in Rick's Café. He rushes to Rick, his eyes bulging with fright. "Rick," he cries. "Do something! You *must* help me!"

Rick shares his personal credo with Lorre. "I stick my neck out for nobody."

The unfortunate Lorre is hauled off by the police and assassinated.

S.Z. Sakall, cast as Carl the waiter, was from Hungary. Although he had fled from Germany in 1939, each of his three sisters died in a concentration camp.

Chubby-jowled Sakall had such rotund cuteness that he was nicknamed "Cuddles." Bogie is claimed to have given him that nickname, but that doesn't appear to be true. Sakall hated the part of the head waiter in *Casablanca* and turned it down. He finally took the role when he was guaranteed four weeks of work for $5,250. Sakall actually had more screen time than either Greenstreet or Lorre.

Wallis had considered hiring female musicians such as Lena Horne, Ella Fitzgerald, or Hazel Scott for the role that was eventually awarded to Dooley Wilson, who played Sam. Warners feared a backlash, especially in Southern theaters, for giving such a pivotal role to a black woman.

Wilson was a professional drummer who had to fake his piano playing. Since the music was recorded at the same time as the film, the piano playing was actually by Elliot Carpenter who performed behind a curtain. He was positioned so that Dooley could watch—and copy—his hand movements.

Curtiz was not without female companionship on the set. As Henreid revealed, "Curtiz, befitting the reputation of most Hungarians, was a practiced womanizer and was known to hire pretty young extras to whom he promised all sorts of things, including stardom, just to have them around and make passes at them at any odd hours when there was a break in shooting. He would choose any private place on the set, usually behind some flat in a secluded area. He'd have the grips move a piece of furniture there, a couch, or even a mattress—almost anything to soften his lovemaking."

"But I didn't go for Bergman," Curtiz recalled. "I decided to give Bogie a chance. I had plenty of other broads to fuck on this picture."

At one point Lorre secretly hooked up a mike to Curtiz's dressing room. The whole crew heard a script girl screaming. "Oh, God! No! No! I can't take it! More, more, more!"

For all the cast to hear, Curtiz shouted "Take it all, take it all—my balls too!"

One of the emotional highlights of the film was the "duel of the anthems," between the French singing *La Marseillaise* and the Nazis warbling *Die Wacht am Rhein*.

Censorship continued to plague the film. Ilsa says, "Victor is my husband, and was, even when I knew you in Paris." This was almost cut, as it suggested adultery. However, at a later point, she claimed that she thought Victor was dead at the time of her affair with Bogie. The censors then agreed to let the line stay.

As he stated in *Love and Death in Casablanca*, author William Donelley

claimed that "Rick's relationship with Sam, and subsequently with Renault, is a standard case of repressed homosexuality that underlies most American adventure stories."

That's why one of the most famous of all straight love stories, the celluloid romance of Bogart and Bergman, always ends up on a list of most famous gay films.

Gays claim that the real love story is not between Rick and Ilsa, but between Rick and Captain Louis Renault, as played by Claude Rains.

One viewer claimed that for him, the most

Hungarian S.Z. Sakall

438

interesting relationship in the movie is between Rick and Louis. "Theirs is a relationship of almost perfect cynicism, one-liners, and claims of neutrality that provide much humor, as well as gives a necessary display of Rick's darker side before and after Ilsa's arrival."

Many famous movie reviewers, including Roger Ebert, knew that Rains was playing a "subtly homosexual police chief."

Rains as Louis is obviously besotted with the super-butch Rick. In Rick's presence, Rains becomes almost like a school girl. Gays picked up on such lines as when Louis says to Rick: "You were never interested in any woman."

Louis also tells Rick: "She [Ilsa] was asking questions about you earlier, Rick, in a way that made me *extremely jealous*." Rains said "extremely jealous" in such a way that only a redneck homophobe could not have picked up on what he meant.

At the end of the film, after Ilsa, accompanied by her husband, is airborne, the captain walks away with his man. Bogie famously drawls, "Louis, I think this is the beginning of a beautiful friendship." World War II audiences didn't get this homoerotic overtone.

The line, "Louis, I think this is the beginning of a beautiful friendship" was voted No. 54 among "The 100 Greatest Movie Lines" of all time.

Wallis came up with this line after the film was finished. Bogie was called back to the Warner lot to dub it in.

In fact, *Casablanca* ended up having more famous one-liners than any other movie in history.

One of the most famous lines of the movie, "Play it again, Sam," was never uttered. The actual dialogue was, "You played it for her, you can play it for me. Play it!"

Ilsa says, "Play it, Sam, play 'As Time Goes By.'"

In name recognition, "Round up the usual suspects" came in No. 32, with "We'll always have Paris" voted No. 43.

Casablanca
On the tarmac, in an artificial fog, an inspector confronts Claude Rains, Paul Henreid, Bogart, and Ingrid Bergman

Reportedly, the line, "Here's looking at you, kid," was improvised by Bogie when he appeared as a star in the little-seen film *Midnight* in 1934. The movie's line was voted the fifth most famous movie quotation of all time by the American Film Institute.

Bogie fell in love with the word "kid" when describing his screen women. In *Dead Reckoning* (1947), he called Lizabeth Scott "kid" twice. Again in *Tokyo Joe* (1949), he called the Czech-born actress Florence Marly "Hello, kid." Finally, in *Sirocco* (1951), he tells Marta Toren, "You're a sweet kid!"

Bogie added another line to the script other than the "kid" reference. He was given the line, "Of all the cafés in all the cities in all the world, she walks into my café." He changed it to, "Of all the gin-joints in all the towns in all the world, she walks into mine."

When the Allies invaded Casablanca on November 8, 1942, Jack Warner went into a tizzy, as he was urged to incorporate the invasion into the film's storyline. Hal Wallis thought the invasion could be presented as an epilogue for the spring release of *Casablanca*. The producer was prepared to shoot a sequence in which Bogie and Claude Rains hear about the invasion. However, Warner eventually nixed the idea, thinking the invasion worthy of a film all on its own and not just as an epilogue. It was decided to release *Casablanca* as a pre-invasion story.

Bogie had his greatest moment on film when he stood on the gray tarmac with those fog machines blasting away. In his rumpled trench coat and fedora, he looked into Bergman's eyes welling with tears.

"You're saying this only to make me go," Bergman says.

"I'm saying it because it's true. You belong with Victor. If that plane leaves the ground and you're not on it, you'll regret it. Maybe not today, maybe not tomorrow, but soon, and for the rest of your life. I'm not good at being noble, but it doesn't take much to see that the problems of three little people don't amount to a hill of beans in this crazy world. Here's looking at you, kid."

***

Rick (Bogart) sending Ugarte (Peter Lorre) to his doom

As Laurence Leamer, Bergman's biographer, put it: "For Bogie, it was booze, blood, and brawls, a butcher knife in the back, a fistfight in the living room, pistol shots in the ceiling. It was a wife so jealous of Ingrid that he didn't dare get near his co-star. It was life as a forty-two-year-old balding actor with an alcoholic wife, a drinking problem of his own, and a co-star so beautiful, so irresistible, so shrewdly professional, that he was likely to lose the movie to her."

Night after night, Methot fought bitterly with Bogie over his alleged affair with Bergman. Finally, Bogie had had it. He told Curtiz, "If you have the name, why not play the game? I'm going after the Swedish broad. I'm an ass man myself, and that gal's got ass."

As a Hollywood insider, Mrs. Humphrey Bogart, his third wife, knew much of what was going on, especially off camera. From the very beginning of her marriage, she'd suspected that Bogie was a "whoremonger" [her words], and she never changed that opinion. She'd known many actresses personally with whom he'd had brief flings in the 1930s.

Methot also knew that Ingrid Bergman's screen image had nothing to do with the private woman. Alfred Hitchcock, who directed her in several later films, claimed "She'd do it with doorknobs."

She was "Notorious" (the name of one of her movies) for having affairs with her leading men. They included Leslie Howard, co-star in *Intermezzo* (1939); both actor Spencer Tracy and director Victor Fleming on the set of *Dr. Jekyll and Mr. Hyde* (1941); Gary Cooper in *For Whom the Bell Tolls* (1943) and *Saratoga Trunk* (1945); Joseph Cotten in *Gaslight* (1944); Bing Crosby in *The Bells of St. Mary's* (1945); Gregory Peck in *Spellbound* (1945); Yul Brynner in *Anastasia* (1956); Anthony Quinn in *The Visit* (1964), and Omar Sharif in *The Yellow Rolls-Royce* (1964), plus numerous other actors and directors, including her "sponsor," David Selznick himself.

Why should Bogie be exempt?

The homosexual actor, Anthony Perkins, claimed that Bergman tried to seduce him on the set of *Goodbye Again* (1961). She did not succeed.

Spencer Tracy was quoted as saying, "Ingrid worked best when she was in love with her leading man. Beginning with Leslie Howard in *Intermezzo*, she seduced all of us." He'd made *Dr. Jekyll and Mr. Hyde* with her in 1941.

Larry Adler, the world's most famous harmonica player, whom Ingrid met on a USO tour in 1945, was egocentric and a political leftist. Bergman's long talks with him turned into an affair.

Adler later said, "I think she needed to show her power over men. She wasn't coquettish or a tease. Ingrid wasn't interested in sex all that much. She did it like a polite girl."

In that opinion, Adler was a minority of one.

Bergman was wise not to allow any of the details of her affairs with her leading men of the 1940s to be revealed. Her virginal image as a model of propriety was shattered when her affair with the Italian director, Roberto Rossellini, was revealed in 1949. The affair and her subsequent pregnancy

441

Views of Ingrid Bergman with her leading men/lovers *(top to bottom)*:

Leslie Howard, Spencer Tracy, Gary Cooper, and Joseph Cotten

shocked her fans and sent her into exile from America for seven long years.

Although it seems silly today, her affair caused national outrage and she was denounced for her "immorality" on the floor of the U.S. Senate. In the wake of that, the press tore her reputation to shreds. She was temporarily "soiled" among puritanical moviegoers who refused to even tolerate her image on the screen.

One of Bergman's most famous off-screen remarks about Bogie was when she said, "I kissed Bogie. But I never got to know him."

Later among her friends in Sweden, when she had nothing more to lose career-wise, she admitted, "I did say that. Can't a woman say something that is not true? That happens all the time. Why should the world at that time have known about my private relationship with Bogie? I didn't announce any of my other affairs with leading men. Why should I have with Bogie? It would not have helped either of us. Besides, what went on between Bogie and me is our own personal business."

In an interview in her native Sweden in later years, she recalled, "What could I say? That we were carrying on passion-ately and had a brief but torrid fling? We were both married at the time. An adul-terous affair—look at what happened to me later—could have destroyed my career. It probably would not have affected Bogie's own career that much."

There is no real proof that Bogie and Bergman had an affair. Likewise, there is no proof that they did not. Eyewitnesses claim they did, notably

Michael Curtiz, who had his finger on the heartbeat of every member of the cast.

When Curtiz found Bogie becoming "love sick," he warned him, "Ingrid's trapped in a bad marriage. For her fun, she fucks her leading men, then forgets them. Don't fall in love with her. She's poison. Other men fall for cunt, then regret it. She'll break your heart."

"After marrying Mayo Methot," he said, "I no longer have a heart to break."

He confided to Ann Sheridan that he'd fallen in love with Bergman and had asked her to marry him, after both of them had gotten divorces from Methot and Bergman's Swedish doctor husband, Petter Lindstrom.

Bogie even gave Sheridan a review of Bergman in bed: "She's great but won't fellate me."

Rossellini, Bergman's future husband, had much the same complaint, claiming that his new wife would not perform fellatio on him, one of his major sexual pleasures. "She doesn't do the things a whore does. For that, I have to go to a bordello."

Claude Rains later told Bette Davis that when he dropped by Bogie's dressing room for a drink, Bergman was adjusting her dress and Bogie zipping up. "I assumed that they had been rehearsing their love scenes," he said sarcastically. "What else could it have been?"

Henreid also told Davis that Bogie and Bergman were having an affair.

"I'd heard that she 'auditions' all her leading men," Davis snorted. "No doubt she's trying to rival Joan Crawford in

Views of Ingrid Bergman with more of her leading men/lovers *(top to bottom):*

Bing Crosby, Gregory Peck, Yul Brynner, and Anthony Quinn

443

that department." Davis looked skeptically at Henreid. "Do you think you and Bogie will share her during the shooting?"

"I think I'm out in the cold," Henreid said. "She told me I look too much like Petter." He was referring, of course, to Bergman's husband, Petter Lindstrom.

Spencer Tracy, Bogie's pal, told George Cukor that Bogie and Bergman were having an affair, and gossipy Cukor spread the word.

Bob Williams, Bogie's publicist on *Casablanca*, later claimed. "I think Bogie fell in love with Ingrid. He was so jealous that if I brought anyone on the set, especially another man, to see her he was furious at me. He would sulk. I had a feeling he wanted Ingrid for himself."

Jack Warner seemed to know about the affair. When Bogie showed up late on the set two days in a row, Warner fired off a memo to Curtiz: "Tell Bogart to quit fucking the Swedish broad all night long and report on time. In one of the rushes, he looks sixty years old. Tell him to clean up his act. The Swedish pussy can wait until picture's end. Then he can have a whole fucking smörgåsbord."

Vincent Sherman, Bogie's sometimes director, claimed that Bogie told him that he had an affair with Bergman all throughout the shooting of *Casablanca*. "Forget all those stupid biographies that claimed Bergman and Bogie didn't have an affair. He fucked her during the entire making of *Casablanca*, and fell madly in love with her. In spite of that saintly look, that cold Swede was hot to trot once you got her pants off."

Methot frequented the set for confrontations with Bogie. She accused him of having an affair with Bergman. In this case she was right.

That chemistry was undeniable both on and off the screen, although biographers for years have perpetuated a myth, spread by Bergman herself, that she had almost no contact with Bogie off camera. Methot knew better.

Emotionally deranged even without provocation, she allowed her fury to bubble over one afternoon. Halfway through the shooting of *Casablanca*, the picture came close to not being finished, at least with Bogie and Bergman in the leads.

An anonymous letter had been sent to Methot. It read:

"When your errant husband isn't needed on the set, he disappears into the dressing room of Ingrid Bergman, the Swedish cow. The sounds coming from that dressing room can be heard all over the sound stage. Your husband can be seen leaving Bergman's room zipping up his pants. They are engaged in a torrid affair. How many nights does he come home late? You answer that question for yourself."

The next afternoon Methot showed up on the set. Somehow she'd obtained a pistol. It was later revealed that she planned to shoot both Bogie and Bergman, hopefully after she'd caught them together.

When she got there, from a distance, she saw Bogie innocently playing chess with Lorre. She asked the script girl to direct her to Bergman's dressing room.

The script girl rushed to tell Bogie what was going on. Sensing trouble, he jumped up, according to Lorre, and raced to Methot. Confronting her, he discovered that she packed a pistol. He fought with her to wrest it from her tightly clenched fingers. The gun went off. Instead of shooting him, the bullet was fired into the air, alerting the entire crew.

Bergman emerged from her dressing room. Rather calmly she walked over to Methot.

"Mrs. Bogart," she said, "I recognize you from your photographs which do not do you justice. Your devoted husband here has told me what a wonderful person you are. It's an honor to meet you. I'm sorry they didn't find a role for you in this picture. I saw you in *Marked Woman* with Mr. Bogart. You stole that picture from both your husband and Bette Davis." Then Bergman, showing enormous grace under pressure, turned and walked away.

Methot seemed stunned and didn't know how to react. At this point Curtiz arrived with two stagehands. Lorre had told him what had happened. Curtiz ordered that Methot be forcibly removed from the set and barred from entering the studio gates again until *Casablanca* was wrapped.

Bogie's reaction to this drama taking place off camera is not known. He didn't want to speak about it to Curtiz, to Lorre, or to anybody.

Under the cloak of darkness. Bogie came and went from the place where Bergman was staying, since her husband was back on the East Coast with her daughter, Pia Lindstrom.

On the final night Bogie saw Bergman, he invited her to an out-of-the way restaurant to celebrate the end of filming.

It was on that fateful night that Bergman gave Bogie "the worst news of my life." She rejected his proposal to marry him after their respective divorces from Lindstrom and Methot.

She explained to him that she was going back to her husband in "dreary, boring" Rochester, New York. "There is no great romance there, but I have a daughter, Pia. I owe it to her to go back and be a mother. I can't leave either of them."

Bogie was said to have cried that night, and he was a man who didn't cry very often.

Although it may be apocryphal, Ann Sheridan later claimed that Bergman, as a final goodbye, told Bogie, "We'll always have Paris."

***

Curtiz brought the film in just eleven days over schedule. Problems arose along the way. He constantly fought with Bogie over script changes, which delayed production. As shooting began, the actors did not have a working script. Curtiz handed them new pages of dialogue on the morning of each day's shoot.

Max Steiner complained to Curtiz about the song, "As Time Goes By." It's got to be cut from the final score," Steiner demanded.

"Like hell!" Curtiz shouted at him. "I love that song. You're an idiot!"

Casablanca, budgeted at $950,000 ran over budget, going $100,000 into the red, much to the fury of Jack Warner.

In one of his final interviews, Henreid revealed what had never been told before.

One night he was called back for "still" sittings with Bergman. Warners planned to use these photographs for publicity purposes.

Bergman seemed heartbroken. Henreid assumed that it was because her affair with Bogie was going badly. "I knew that she had broken it off with him, and she looked very sad," he said. "I was completely mistaken when she revealed what was really wrong. She went in and out of affairs with her leading men so quickly it did not seem to phase her."

She was actually heartbroken over the loss of the role of María in Ernest Hemingway's *For Whom the Bell Tolls*, the part having gone to Vera Zorina.

"Those idiots," Bergman told Henreid. "Picking Zorina of all people. She can't act. She just can't, and I'm good. I'm really good!"

Bergman with Roberto Rossellini
"an international scandal"

Born in Berlin, Zorina was an American ballerina, musical theater actress, and choreographer. At the time she was considered for *For Whom the Bell Tolls*, she was married to the famous choreographer George Balanchine.

When word got out that Zorina had been fired from *For Whom the Bell Tolls,* and replaced by Bergman, her film career was more or less destroyed in Hollywood. She never recovered from the blow. Although she tried for other major roles, she failed to find them. In 1946, she said good-bye to Hollywood.

In the middle of the photography session,

446

Bergman was called to the phone. During her conversation, she let out a yell that Henreid compared to that of "a tigress who has made a kill, a yell of such joy and triumph that I was stunned."

Returning to him, she kissed Henreid on the lips. "I got it! I got it! Zorina is out. I'm María. I got it! Paul, we've got to celebrate!"

It was at this point in his memoirs that Henreid drew the curtains, the way movie directors in the 1930s did when a man and woman faded into the bedroom to make love.

"That night," I learned what Bergman meant by celebrate," Henreid said. "It wasn't just the champagne. In spite of her cool demeanor, she was that tigress in bed, the same blood-curdling scream I'd heard on the phone when she got the part of María. Over pillow talk, as you Americans say, she told me that I was a much better lover than Bogie—much smoother in bed, more suave, more capable of making a woman feel like a real woman. She also told me that in spite of all the experiences he'd had with women, Bogie still approached a woman in bed with a certain schoolboy awkwardness."

Suave, sleepy-eyed Henreid, whose acting style was "as rigid as a board" in *Casablanca*, enjoyed only a passing vogue in the 1940s, mainly as a continental lover. Decades after his appearance in *Casablanca*, he expressed a bitterness against the movie. He especially disliked its director and Bogie himself.

Many of Henreid's fans assumed he was French born. Actually, the actor was Austrian, having been born in Trieste (now part of Italy) when that city was part of the Austro Hungarian Empire.

"Mr. Bogie Man was a nobody," he claimed shortly before he died in 1992. "That is, before *Casablanca* he was a nobody. He was the fellow Robinson or Cagney would say, 'Get him!' He was always a very mediocre actor with an extremely limited range. He was so sorry for himself in *Casablanca*. Unfortunately, Michael Curtiz was not a director of actors; he was a director of effects. He was first rate at that, but he could not tell Bogart he should not play the role of Rick like a crybaby. It was embarrassing, I thought, when I looked at the rushes."

Those negative comments about Bogie were deleted from his 1984 autobiography called *Ladies' Man*. Henreid's editor at St. Martin's Press felt it might harm the potential sale of the book.

"I would much prefer that I be remembered for my role opposite Bette Davis in *Now, Voyager*," he claimed. "If I had it to do over again, I would never have accepted the role in *Casablanca*."

The stories that Henreid spread in the interviews he gave during his later years did not appear in his memoirs and cannot be verified at this late date. Perhaps he was getting some long-delayed revenge on Bogie. Or perhaps the incident he described that night with Bergman really was true.

Much of the initial success of *Casablanca* resulted from the sweeping historical events that had inspired its plot. In November of 1942, Allied forces landed in Morocco, forming a beachhead at Casablanca. Then in January of 1943, the famous Casablanca Conference took place between Franklin D. Roosevelt and Winston Churchill in a suburb of Casablanca. It was at this conference that Roosevelt announced that "unconditional surrender" would be demanded of the Axis powers.

Casablanca premiered at the Hollywood Theater in New York City on November 26, 1942. It was timed to coincide with the Allied invasion of North Africa and the capture of Casablanca. But it didn't go into general release until January 23, 1943, when it took advantage of the publicity generated by the Casablanca Conference.

After President Franklin D. Roosevelt returned from the war-time conference in Casablanca with Sir Winston Churchill, he asked for a screening of *Casablanca* at the White House ["Casa Blanca" in Spanish].

During its initial run, the film was a solid but not spectacular success. The legend would come later. In time, its characters, dialogue, and music would become iconic.

In its aftermath, many bizarre legends arose about the movie, including one that claimed that Jack Benny had appeared briefly in it.

Not all the reviews were raves, *The New Yorker* referring to it as only "pretty tolerable." *The New York Times*, in contrast, asserted that it "makes the spine tingle and the heart take a leap." *Variety* claimed that Bogie was "more at ease as the bitter and cynical operator of a joint than as a lover," and Bogie himself agreed with that review.

When Julius Epstein saw the final script, on which so many others had labored, he said, it contained "more corn than in the states of Kansas and Iowa combined. But when corn works, there's nothing better." He later expressed grave reservations about the script, calling it "slick shit."

"Casablanca is one of my least favorite pictures," Epstein said. "I'm tired of talking about it after thirty years. I can explain its success only by the Bogie cult that has sprung up after his death. I can recognize that the picture is entertaining and that people love it. But it's a completely phoney romance, a completely phoney picture. For instance, nobody knew what was going on in Casablanca at the time. Nobody had ever been to Casablanca. The whole thing was shot in the back lot. There was never a German who appeared in Casablanca for the duration of the entire war, and we had Germans marching around with medals and epaulets. Furthermore, there were never any such things as letters of transit around which the entire plot revolved. . . . the movie is completely phoney!"

Actually, there were some Nazis in *Casablanca* during the early 1940s. These Germans were arrested when the Allied invasion occurred. Those "letters of transit" were actually visas and exit papers which were eagerly bought by European refugees wanting to escape to Lisbon where they could subsequently arrange transport to New York.

Both Bogie and Bergman later claimed that they were wrong about the impact and the importance of *Casablanca*. "We thought we were making a B movie, and that was how it was viewed at the time," Bogie said. "I was used to making B movies. To me, *Casablanca* was just another assignment. It took me years to realize that it was a picture that ranked up there with *Citizen Kane* as one of the greatest movies ever made."

Bergman later said, "Regardless of how many more movies I make, or how many Oscars I win, when I die *The New York Times* will give me a front page headline that says 'CO-STAR OF CASABLANCA DIES.'"

Movie buffs have long pondered why Bergman and Bogie never made another film together, given their on-screen chemistry.

The success of *Casablanca* led Warner to plan a sequel. It was to be called *Brazzaville*. However, Bergman was not available. Geraldine Fitzgerald, whom Bogie had appeared with in *Dark Victory*, was considered for the role, before the project was killed. In the late 1990s, Michael Walsh's novel, *As Time Goes By,* was published as the sequel.

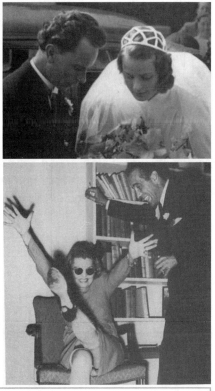

For his role as Rick, Bogie took home exactly $36,667, in contrast to Lorre, who made only $2,333. Curtiz was the highest grosser, earning $73,400.

Following the release of *Casablanca*, Bogie would become the highest paid actor in Hollywood, and in the world for that matter. He would reign as Tinseltown's biggest star from 1943 to 1949.

After hitting it big in *Casablanca*, Bogie was no longer Duke Mantee, gangster at large, or Sam Spade, detective at large. After the release of *Casablanca*, he could

Portraits of two marriages:
(top photo) Petter Lindstrom with Ingrid Bergman
(bottom photo) Mayo Methot with Humphrey Bogart

virtually play any character part he wanted, ranging from the seedy captain of *The African Queen* to the psychotic Captain Queeg in *The Caine Mutiny*.

The date was March 2, 1944, the setting Grauman's Chinese Theater. When it was announced that *Casablanca* had been designated as Best Picture of 1943, the audience gasped. It had not been a heavy favorite.

Paramount's *For Whom the Bell Tolls* or Warner Brothers' *Watch on the Rhine* were considered the major contenders. Bogie lost his chance for the Oscar, as Paul Lukas walked off with the Best Actor prize for *Watch on the Rhine*, in which he'd co-starred with Bette Davis. Claude Rains, nominated for Best Supporting Actor, lost to Charles Coburn for *The More the Merrier*.

Accepting his Oscar as Best Director, Curtiz said: "So many times I have a speech ready, but no dice. Always a bridesmaid, never a mother. Now I win, I have no speech."

Casablanca was nominated and won the Oscar as Best Picture of the Year.

Wallis rose to accept the Oscar until he noted Jack Warner hurrying down the aisle. It was an Academy tradition that the producer of the film accepts the Best Picture Oscar, not a studio head.

Wallis was so incensed that he never forgave Warner. Up to then Wallis had been regarded as the *Wünderkind* of Warners, but he left the studio shortly after that slight at the Academy Awards ceremony.

***

Bogie invited Ann Sheridan to the *Casablanca* wrap party. Ironically, Sheridan was to have been the award-winning film's female star. With her was her newly minted close friend, a demure little brunette.

"Bogie," she said, "I want you to meet a good friend of mine and the best hairdresser in Hollywood. She can do wonders for that toupée of yours. Meet Verita Peterson."

CHAPTER ELEVEN

"Who is this good-looking broad?" Bogie asked of Ann Sheridan.

"Those words were the first I ever heard from Bogie," Verita Peterson recalled. "Romantic, don't you think?"

"After that intro, Annie wandered off and threw herself at Michael Curtiz, so we figured we'd seen the last of her," Verita said.

Verita Bouvaire Peterson, locked into an unhappy marriage to Robert Peterson, a studio technician, met a middle-aged but rising star, Humphrey Bogart, who was also locked into an unhappy marriage to Mayo Methot.

At the wrap party for *Casablanca*, she later recalled, "No one on the set, including Bogie and Michael Curtiz, knew they'd made a classic."

"Bogie didn't like to dance, but, honey, we danced the night away," she said in an interview in 1998. "From that night on we were lovers."

The attractive little brunette who would become his mistress and the "custodian of his toupée" was a hard-drinking beauty who could match Bogie drink for drink. "I liked to down the booze. He liked to down the booze. I could match him cuss word for cuss word, shot for shot. We did a lot of crazy things together, some of which I'd rather forget. It got a little kinky at times, but so what? The war was going to end one day, although when I met Bogie I thought we might lose it."

"From the very beginning, Bogie told me he'd never marry me," she said. "'Marriage is a trap,' he said. 'I've been trapped too long. When I escape from Mayo, I never want to be trapped again. But we'll have a lot of fun, and having fun is what life is all about.'"

"I couldn't agree with you more," she whispered into his ear as he whirled her around the dance floor.

Half-Irish, half-Mexican, Verita arrived in Hollywood straight from Arizona. "I didn't know a God damn thing about acting, but I felt a gal like me could have a hell of a good time in Hollywood. When I won a beauty contest, Miss Arizona, I decided to try to capitalize off it. In fact, after a few auditions on the casting couch, I got a job at Republic."

"I was cast in a Western and fell off my horse the first day and broke my arm," Verita said. "I was soon out of Republic but got to fuck John Wayne and Forrest Tucker."

"Then I got picked up by the pool one day by this Frenchman who'd come to America with a huge amount of French lace and a lot of beautiful hair from the convents of Europe," she said. "Believe it or not, French lace is one of the best foundations for making great wigs and toupées. Because France had been invaded by Hitler's armies, the lace was not available all during the war."

"I'd inherited a lot of money from my grandfather who had died, and I agreed to stake this guy," she said. "I bought a brand new car, figuring it would be the last one made until the war was over. I filled it with his wigs, toupées, and falls and started making the rounds of all the studios. That's how I met Bogie's pal, Ann Sheridan. They'd had this little fling, but once they got the fucking out of the way, they found they really liked each other and became pals."

"I did wigs for women, but a lot of the men were having problems with

Verita Peterson

their hair too," Verita said. "I'd become a licensed hairdresser. I found the men more fun to work with than the ladies. Within a year, I'd been fucked by Ray Milland, Charles Boyer, and Gary Cooper. Not bad."

"When I met Annie at Max Factor, she was just coming down from a fling with Ronald Reagan," Verita said. "He wasn't my type at all. He had to have his flings during the day because Jane Wyman kept him locked in a cage at night—just joking."

"Gary Cooper was at the wrap party for *Casablanca*," Verita said. "I'd already had him, so Ingrid Bergman was welcome to him. She was obviously making a big play for him, and they were about to make a movie together. Having dumped Bogie, she was pursuing her next leading man."

That evening Bergman broke from Cooper long enough to come over and pay her respects to Bogie. He was seat-

452

ed with Verita at a makeshift table while the orchestra hired by Warners took a break.

"She came to our table and shook Bogie's hand," Verita said. "She pointedly ignored me, and Bogie didn't bother to introduce us. He also didn't rise to his feet. It was all very cold. She called him 'Mr. Bogart' and told him how much she'd enjoyed making *Casablanca* with him. It was total bullshit!"

"Annie had told me that Bergman and Bogie had had an affair, and that the Swedish bitch had broken Bogie's heart," Verita said. "I really think that's why he turned to me so suddenly. He didn't want to show up at the wrap party stag, looking rejected with tears in his eyes. I don't know where Methot was. Bogie almost wanted to show Bergman that he, too, had moved on with his life. In a matter of days, Bergman was in Cooper's bed and I was in Bogie's, or rather Bogie was in my bed. Of course, all of us in this quartet had spouses, even Bergman, but what the hell. This was Hollywood!"

"It was one o'clock and we were still dancing," Verita said. "In front of the whole cast and crew. Fortunately, Jack Warner had left. Bogie began kissing my neck. For the last thirty minutes, he hadn't taken his hand off my ass."

"You've got a great ass on you, ol' gal," he told her. "I'm an ass man myself."

"That's the most romantic thing a man has ever said to me," she told him. "My brains must be in my ass, or otherwise I wouldn't be dancing around the floor with you at this hour with everybody looking on."

"Bogie was pressing hard against me," she said. "I really felt him and more or less knew how this night would end. He kept kissing my neck."

Finally, they left the studio's wrap party. Bogie walking her to her car in the parking lot. "I thought he was gonna take me home and fuck me in the ass," she recalled. "But he didn't. At my car, he gave me a long, lingering French kiss and told me he'd call me tomorrow after I gave him my phone number. I never expected to hear from him again. Nor did I expect him to take advantage of that subtle invitation to sex I gave him—that is, if you call grabbing his crotch subtle."

***

To her surprise, Bogie did call the next day, and they agreed to meet for lunch at the Smoke House, a popular actors' hangout across from Warner Brothers. He was already into his second martini when she came in, sliding

Ingrid Bergman with Gary Cooper

453

into a booth alongside him. They talked only briefly of the night before, as he placed an order for his typical ham and eggs.

He got to the point quickly. "Where do you live and how do I get there?"

She explained that she and her husband, Robert Peterson, lived on Roselli Street in Burbank, and that he was away until six o'clock in the evening.

Within an hour of her return home, she spotted Bogie arriving at her house in his Jaguar XK-120.

"He walked so briskly to my door that he looked like an eager schoolboy about to lose his virginity," she said.

Within fifteen minutes inside the house, he had ushered her into the bedroom. It was the beginning of an affair that, with some interruptions, would last until 1955.

After that successful debut—"Bogie was a great lover"—he slipped off to see Verita whenever he could. "I feared the neighbors would spot him coming to see me and tell my husband about it," she said. "After all, *Casablanca* had made him one of the most recognizable faces in the world."

Indeed her worst nightmare came true. "No, it wasn't my worst nightmare. My greatest fear was that Mayo Methot would catch us. She was a stick of dynamite waiting to explode."

One afternoon after love-making, Verita feared that Bogie was too drunk to drive home. She put on a pot of coffee and led him into the shower. They both got into the booth together, and she turned on the cold water.

"At that moment my husband Bob came home early and caught us," she said. "He'd been tipped off by a nosey neighbor."

Still drunk under the cold shower, Bogie started attacking Bob for being "a son of bitch barging into a ladies' toilet."

"Bob didn't exactly see it that way," Verita said. "After all, I was his naked wife showering with not just another man, but *the* Humphrey Bogart, world famous movie star."

"Fortunately Bob wasn't a violent man," she said. "After storming and yelling, he barged out of the house. My marriage was over at that point. Actually, it'd been over for a long time."

She later claimed that "Bob could have ruined Bogie's divorce by getting us some unwanted front-page headlines, but he didn't."

Before the Petersons could file for divorce, Bob was drafted into the Army. They would remain married in name only until the end of World War II, at which time he filed for divorce, never naming Bogie as the reason why.

"My affair with Bogie continued," she said.

***

In the wake of Pearl Harbor, with Nazi U-boats taking a horrible toll on Allied shipping, especially on the run to Murmansk, Russia, Jack Warner had an idea. "Let's make a movie about our Merchant Marines."

He called in producer Jerry Wald who assigned John Howard Lawson to write the script based on a novel by Guy Gilpatric.

Bogie's long-time director, Lloyd Bacon, was assigned to help the picture, to be called *Action in the North Atlantic* (1943).

Bogie had accepted the assignment before filming *Casablanca*. Like so many of his pre-*Casablanca* assignments, he was a second choice.

Bogie went into a rage when he picked up a copy of the *Hollywood Reporter* and read that Edward G. Robinson and George Raft were to star in the picture. When both stars pulled out, the role went to Bogie—"sloppy seconds again"—and Raymond Massey.

Bogie was very avant-garde in casting, telling *The Pittsburgh Courier* on September 26, 1942 that he felt an African American should play the ship's captain. Most WWII films rarely gave lead roles to blacks. "In the world of the theater or any other phase of American life," Bogie said, "the color of a man's skin should have nothing to do with his rights in a land built on the self-evident fact that all men are created equal."

Bacon directed Massey as Captain Steve Jarvis, with Bogie as his chief executive officer, Joe Rossi. For Bogie's love interest, Julie Bishop was assigned.

Bogie was surprised that Warners didn't assign him a bigger name. Colorado-born Jacqueline Wells acted under her real name until 1941 when she changed it to Julie Bishop. She'd been a child actress in silent movies, appearing with Mary Pickford and Clara Bow.

Reasonably attractive, though not stunning in any way, she intrigued Bogie at first. "I made a pass at her but she didn't receive it," Bogie told director Lloyd Bacon.

Perhaps the reason for that was that she'd met her second husband, Clarence Shoop, a pilot, while filming the 1943 *Princess O'Rourke* with Olivia de Havilland.

"I thought while hubbie was up there in those blue skies, wifie would want a little

Bogart with Raymond Massey

455

male companionship down here on the ground," Bogie said. "Where have gals like Ann Sheridan and Claire Trevor gone? Some of these actresses today at Warners are too tightly wound."

Ruth Gordon, Bogie's friend from "way back when," was cast as Massey's wife. Seeing her after a long time, Bogie came up to her, "Ruthie," he said, "you look younger than the day I meet you. But I've always wanted to ask you something. Did we ever have sex back in the 1920s?"

"I'll never tell," she said, kissing him on the mouth.

Those future stars of tomorrow that Bogie feared as he neared fifty were popping up. He met Bernard Zanville who had the seventh lead.

Bogie liked Zanville even though at one point the lowly actor shouted at him, "You son of a bitch! You just don't know your lines!"

Bogie not only forgave him for his outburst but suggested that he change his name to Dane Clark, and not "Brick Bernard," as Warners had wanted. As Dane Clark, future movie star, the actor became known as "the poor man's Bogart."

Robert Mitchum, a future superstar, had one line of dialogue in the movie. Since he couldn't support himself, he was hustling Clifton Webb on the side. Webb kept his private homosexual life from Bogie.

"Webby and I never spoke of such things," Bogie told Verita Peterson.

Warners built a replica of a ten-thousand ton tanker on its sound stages. Wartime security restrictions would not allow movies to be filmed on vessels on the open seas.

Bacon had been the head of the U.S. Navy's photo unit during World War I. In *Action in the North Atlantic*, he used real live war combat footage.

At one point Bogie and Massey were drinking and watching stunt men rehearse their escape from a burning vessel after it was torpedoed by the Germans.

Dane Clark
(aka Bernard Zanville)

As Massey later related, "Bogie, after his fourth martini, faced me with that 'Play it again, Sam' look and said, "come to think of it, I guess I'm braver than you.'"

"Maybe so," Massey said. "Are we going to let two men risk their lives to make us look good?"

"Are we men or mice?" Bogie asked.

Bacon warned them, "If either of you idiots gets fried, it'll be your fault and I'll rewrite the script."

The shot was potentially dangerous to its stars. As Massey later recalled, "The

456

burning tanker was really terrifying, to actors as well as audiences. The effect was achieved by dozens of gas jets controlled through a set of valves which looked like an organ console. This was operated by the so-called "smokebun," who could play his valves with such skill that the actors seemed to walk through the flames. And that's what Bogie and I did. I got through the flames, but Bogie got his pants caught on fire, and we had to rip them off him. The director got what he wanted, even though Bogie was almost turned into a human torch."

Midway through the filming, Bacon's contract expired, and Jack Warner didn't renew it. Bacon walked off the job, and Jerry Wald hastily hired Byron Haskin to finish the shoot.

Franklin D. Roosevelt introduced the movie in a prologue, declaring "DAMN THE TORPEDOES, FULL SPEED AHEAD."

Massey would make one more picture with Bogie, *Chain Lightning* in 1950, co-starring Eleanor Parker. In that one, Bogie was cast as a WWII bomber pilot, with Massey playing a jet manufacturer loosely based on Howard Hughes.

***

In a 1943 release, *Thank Your Lucky Stars*, Bogie appeared as himself in a "Calvacade of Stars" benefit. It reunited him with many Warner stars with whom he'd worked before—Bette Davis, Errol Flynn, Joan Leslie, Ida Lupino, Dennis Morgan, and even S.Z. Sakall from *Casablanca*.

Bogie's friend, Mark Hellinger, produced this WWII distraction, which included appearances by John Garfield and Olivia de Havilland, both of them playing themselves.

In a patriotic skit, "tough guy" Bogie is intimidated by roly-poly "Cuddles" Sakall.

***

At long last Bogie was able to fulfill his commitment to Columbia when he starred in *Sahara* (1943), a World War II action picture supposedly depicting the battlefields of the Sahara in North Africa. Actually, it was

Bogie with "Cuddles"
(S.Z. Sakall)

(middle photo)
Bogart with Bruce Bennett
bottom photo:
Bogart in command

filmed in the desert of California. Originally *Sahara* had been cast with Melvyn Douglas and Glenn Ford in the lead roles.

Saying good-bye to Verita in Burbank, Bogie headed for what he called "a God forsaken hellhole," a reference to Brawley, California, which lies in the harsh Borego Desert of the Imperial Valley north of the Mexican border. The temperatures and the terrain evoked conditions in the Sahara desert, the setting for this war-time drama.

The script was based on a 1937 Russian film, *The Thirteen*, and it evoked another film, John Ford's *The Lost Patrol* (1934). That film had starred Victor McLaglen and Boris Karloff.

Bogie's action picture showed a British-American unit stranded in the Sahara in the path of the oncoming Nazi infantry. Bogie, cast in the lead, played Sergeant Joe Gunn. The picture was directed by Zoltan Korda, who was the middle brother of filmmakers Alexander and Vincent Korda, all born in Hungary.

A former cavalry officer, Korda specialized in military action and adventure films, many of which were filmed in Africa or India. His greatest cinematic triumph was the 1939 *The Four Feathers*, starring Sir Ralph Richardson. He both directed and wrote the screenplay for *Sahara*, which was produced by Bogie's pal, Mark Hellinger.

Bogie bonded with most of the cast, whom he invited to his suite at night at the seedy Planter's Hotel for some heavy drinking.

Bogie found his co-star, Bruce Bennett, fascinating. "He was my kind of guy," Bogie later recalled.

Growing up in the rugged lumber camps of Washington State, Bennett built up his physique. After playing football in the 1926 Rose Bowl, Herman Brix (his original name) won six national titles in the 1928 Olympics in

458

the shot put category, eventually earning a Silver Medal.

He had been a screen Tarzan in the 1930s but had changed his name to Bruce Bennett when he wanted to escape the serials and become a legitimate actor.

In Gabe Essoe's book, *Tarzan of the Movies*, he wrote: "Brix's portrayal was the only time between the silents and the 1960s that Tarzan was accurately depicted in films. He was mannered, cultured, soft spoken, a well-educated English lord who spoke several languages—and didn't grunt."

Although she hated the blistering desert heat, Mayo Methot showed up on the set with a thermos of chilled martinis for her husband. Bennett and his wife, Jeannette, spent many nights with the Bogarts, even driving down to Mexicali with them for a picnic.

In later years, Bennett said, "We had a room next to Bogie's suite. Sometimes they'd fight all night. Many a night we heard the sounds of broken glass. Mayo was very unhappy. I think she knew she was losing her man but didn't know how to keep him. She would literally drink all day and night. Bogie did tell me that Mayo wasn't anything like the woman he'd married.

'She was very witty, very intelligent, and possessed a remarkable charm when I fell in love with her,' he said. 'Now she's turned into a possessive, overbearing harridan.'"

"She interrupted many a shoot," Bennett claimed. "She fought on the set with Bogie and even used her fists. She'd throw bottles at him. She gave him a big black eye and inflicted cuts on him. Korda often had to shoot around these damages that makeup couldn't hide. It became obvious to me that Mayo was mentally ill. Bogie confided to me that he thought his wife was 'a schizo'—his words—and I agreed."

"Finally, when we were alone, I asked Bogie: 'why in hell do you stay married to someone like Mayo?'"

"I leave her for a week or so at a time," Bogie told Bennett. "But I go back to her. On several occasions, she's attempted suicide, and I don't want to be responsible for her death."

Bennett and Bogie became pals, and Bogie was instrumental in getting John Huston to cast Bennett in *The Treasure of Sierra Madre* (1948).

"Bogie was king of the hill at this time in his

Two views of Bruce Bennett (then known as Herman Brix) as Tarzan in the early 1930s

459

career," said Bennett. "For the most part, he was very cooperative and friendly to the workers. But he just loved to drink. Every morning when the director came on the set, Bogie wanted to argue. Sometimes he would argue about something for an hour. It was really frustrating Korda. Finally I said to Korda, 'Don't you know what's going on? Bogie drinks every night, and he needs to buy some time in the morning to get his head clear and learn his lines.'"

Born on the Mississippi River, the son of a steamer fireman on the riverboat *Robert E. Lee*, Rex Ingram was an African-American actor. When he met Bogie he'd finished his best known film appearance as the genie in *The Thief of Baghdad* (1940). He is also remembered for playing Jim, the fugitive slave, opposite Mickey Rooney in *The Adventures of Huckleberry Finn* (1939).

To Bogie's surprise, he found that Ingram was a licensed physician, like Bogie's late father.

In 1949 Ingram pleaded guilty to a charge of violating the Mann Act when he transported a teenage girl to New York "for immoral purposes," and drew an eighteen-month jail sentence.

Bogie liked Ingram and visited him in prison, telling him, "It's too damn bad when a guy gets sent up the river for liking young pussy. I've been known to go for teenage pussy myself."

The German-born actor Kurt Kreuger was befriended by Bogie who called him "The Kraut." A strikingly handsome "blond God," as the press called him, Kreuger was the third most requested male pinup at 20th Century

Two views of Rex Ingram
(lower photo) as the
Genie of the Lamp in
Thief of Baghdad

Fox, after Tyrone Power and John Payne. He complained to Bogie that he was going to have to go through all the war movies of the 1940s being typecast as a Nazi.

"Don't complain," Bogie told him. "It beats a concentration camp."

As quoted in the *San Francisco Chronicle*, Kreuger said, "I was running across the dunes when Tambul [Rex Ingram] jumped on top of me and pressed my head into the sand to suffocate me. Only Korda forgot to yell cut, and Ingram was so emotionally caught up in the scene that he kept pressing my face harder and harder. Finally, I went unconscious. Nobody knew this. Even the crew was transfixed, watching this dramatic 'killing.' If Korda hadn't finally said cut, as an afterthought, it would have been all over for me."

That's not the story Bogie told when he got

460

back to Los Angeles. He said he came onto the set and immediately saw what was happening. "I was the one who called cut. If I hadn't, The Kraut would have bit the dust in more ways than one."

Another member of the cast, Dan Duryea, who had graduated from Cornell University in 1928, had made his name on Broadway in the play *Dead End*. Ironically, Bogie had starred in the film version.

Duryea was one of those "stars of tomorrow" that Bogie dreaded to meet, but he got along with him. The actor would go on to demonstrate a certain villainy on the screen.

When he had a brief fling with actress/girl about town Liz Renay, Duryea said, "I looked at my nude body in a full-length mirror. Ugly puss. So-so dick. A 155-pound weakling. No leading man. So I decided right there and then to become the meanest SOB in movies."

Like other actors such as Dane Clark, Duryea also became known as "the poor man's Bogart."

Bogie also bonded with Lloyd Bridges, the California-born actor who is best known today for his role of Mike Nelson in *Sea Hunt*, which was the top American TV series in 1958. "He was no dumb actor," Bogie said. "You could have a real conversation with this fucker,"

Shortly after making *Sahara*, Bridges left Columbia to enlist in the U.S. Coast Guard.

Near the end of the shoot, Methot was back in Los Angeles, as was Bridges' wife, Dorothy Simpson, whom he had married in 1938. Bogie invited him one night to drive across the Mexican border to sample the wares in a bordello.

"I picked the wrong chick," Bridges later said. "I got the clap. Bogie got a clean one and emerged unharmed. Perhaps he had so much alcohol in his body it killed all VD germs."

Bogie also liked character actor J. Carrol Naish, who, although of Irish descent, always ended up playing Latin, Arab, or East Indian characters. The year Bogie met him, he was also cast as

Veteran Character Actors

(top photo) Dan Duryea
(middle photo) J. Carrol Naish
(bottom photo) Kurt Kreuger

461

Dr. Daka, the first villain to go up against Batman on the silver screen in the serial *The Batman* (1943).

For his appearance in *Sahara*, Naish would be nominated for an Academy Award as Best Supporting Actor, losing as did Claude Rains himself (*Casablanca*), to Charles Coburn in *The More the Merrier*.

When Bogie and Bennett had their final drink together at the wrap party for *Sahara*, Bogie said, "I'm a professional. I've done pretty well, don't you think? I've survived in a pretty tough business."

Bennett claimed that, "Part of his survival was due to his great talent and his determination to pay the price, any price, for success. But certainly some credit must be given to Dame Fortune and timing, as well."

Shooting ended in April, and Bogie returned from the desert to Los Angeles. Since he didn't have to go to work until May, he spent most of his time aboard his boat, *Sluggy*. He developed a technique. Right before leaving for days at sea, he'd stage a big fight with Methot, then storm out of the door.

Sailing *Sluggy* in the Pacific, he'd spend the nights in the arms of Verita.

***

(top photo) Bogie getting cosmeticized by Verita Peterson

(bottom photo) Cover of *Harper's Bazaar,* March 1943, introducing "Betty Bacal"

Events were spinning around Bogie's future in 1943. Often he didn't know what they were, although his life would be affected by them.

While he was in the Imperial Valley shooting *Sahara*, the March issue of *Harper's Bazaar* fashion magazine came out. Its cover featured "Betty Bacal" an eighteen-year-old blonde from New York, who had a sultry, come-hither look. The magazine generated inquiries from Howard Hughes, who probably wanted to seduce her, David O. Selznick, and Columbia Pictures. But it was Howard Hawks, a Warner Brothers director, who ended up putting her under personal contract.

In the closing days of the shoot of *Sahara*, Betty Bacal (later changed to Lauren Bacall) arrived in Hollywood.

As Bacall settled into a new life, Mary Baker, still Bogie's agent and "guardian angel," negotiated a new contract for him at Warner Brothers that paid him $3,500 a week.

Production was set to begin in May on Bogie's next film, *Passage to Marseille* (1944). For some odd reason, the "s" was left out of the name of this Provençal city, and no one caught it.

Back in Burbank and with Robert Peterson away at war, Bogie spent many a night at Verita's home. His separation from Methot often stretched out for a week at a time. Sometimes she'd chase him from the house with an iron skillet.

"There was many a night he would arrive drunk on my doorstep at two or three o'clock in the morning, having fled from Methot," Verita said. "Once he escaped his house wearing nothing but his underwear. He always kept his keys in his car in case he had to make a fast getaway."

Inevitably the talk was of marriage. "He told me that he wanted to marry me as soon as I divorced Bob and he divorced Methot. I had reservations, but planned to go through with the marriage. We were in love with each other. I thought that once married to him I could straighten him out."

"All during the war, I couldn't file divorce charges against Bob," Verita said. "What could I do? Charge him with adultery? I also feared a scandal that would damage Bogie's career. Also I didn't want to call Methot's attention to me. If I did, she might show up at my doorstep with an ax. I was in a real dilemma. Bob thought I'd get over Bogie and would settle down to become his *hausfrau* when he came marching home."

"Bogie was talking with lawyers about divorcing Methot, and he urged me nightly to divorce Bob," Verita said. "Still, I held back. We began to fight and argue about our mutual

Three views of Bogie as a resistance fighter: *(second from top)* with Michelle Morgan *(third from top)* with Claude Rains

divorces—not the brutal fights he and Methot had. All this fighting was putting a serious strain on our romance, except when we were sailing aboard *Sluggy*, as we did every weekend."

As Verita related in her memoirs, she claimed that one night they were sitting and drinking at her kitchen table. She said, "I told him he had lousy taste in wives, and that he chose them as a fighter would choose sparring partners. I also told him that he drank too much and that I drank too much when I was with him, and I told him that maybe our fiery natures were too combustible for marriage. I wasn't sure I could live with some of his characteristics, such as needling people to the brink of fight or flight."

The end result of that night in the kitchen led to an agreement between the two of them not to see each other until their divorce papers were filed. That way, she claimed, there would be no chance of her being named as a correspondent in his divorce proceedings against Methot.

Bogie agreed but in the weeks ahead he called several times and wanted to renegotiate their agreement. But she remained steadfast, and he respected their deal.

Years later in New Orleans, Verita claimed, "It was the worst mistake of my life. I almost set up a situation where he'd meet some other dame. Separation seemed right at the time, but I was wrong. I blew my chance to become the fourth Mrs. Humphrey Bogart, and I have no one else to blame but myself. For Bogie and me, it was the final curtain. Or so I thought at the time. But life moves in very unpredictable ways. I never dreamed that what would happen between us would actually happen."

***

Actor Leslie Howard Reported Lost With Big British Airplane

LONDON, June 2.—(*P*)—British overseas transport plane, with actor Leslie Howard reported among its 13 passengers, was officially declared overdue and presumed lost today after reporting in a final message yesterday that it was being attacked by enemy aircraft while enroute from Lisbon to England.

Leslie Howard

Although Bogie hadn't seen Leslie Howard in many months, the two actors still wrote each other. "I loved the man and would always be grateful to him," Bogie said.

On June 2, 1943, Bogie received the shocking news.

On a KLM/BOAC flight from Lisbon to Bristol, England, the plane carrying Howard had been shot down by a German Junkers-JU 88 aircraft over the Bay of Biscay. All passengers aboard had lost their lives.

There were rumors that the Nazis believed that Winston Churchill, who had been in Algiers, was on board. In his autobiography, Churchill expressed that a mistake about his activities might have cost Howard his life.

Subsequent research does not verify Churchill's belief. Other authors have concluded that the Germans wanted to shoot down the plane in order to kill Howard himself. His intelligence-gathering activities had come to their attention. It is also believed that the Nazis wanted to demoralize Britain with the loss of one of its most outspoken and patriotic figures.

The Nazi high command knew the whereabouts of Churchill at the time of the attack on Howard's plane. Also, they were hardly naïve enough to believe that the war-time prime minister would be traveling alone aboard an unescorted and unarmed civilian aircraft when both the secrecy and the air power of the British government were at his command.

It is believed today that the order to liquidate Howard came from Josef Goebbels himself. He had denounced the actor for "being the most dangerous propagandist in the British service."

On hearing the news, Bogie went into a deep depression. He had his own theory as to why he thought Howard was assassinated in the air crash.

He claimed that Howard was on a top secret mission at the bequest of Churchill to dissuade Francisco Franco, Spain's dictator, from joining the Axis with Benito Mussolini and Hitler.

Bogie may have been right. Long after Bogie's death, a Spanish writer, José Rey-Xieman, in his book *El Vuelo del Ibis* (*The Flight of the Ibis*) documents Bogie's claim of the secret mission in convincing detail.

***

Bogie was thrilled as he prepared to film *Passage to Marseille*. He would be reunited once again with "the gang"—or at least most of them—from *Casablanca*. But suddenly Jack Warner changed his mind and sent him a script called *The Pentacle*. This was a story of a man who kills his wife after their fifth wedding anniversary. At the time Bogie was trying to establish himself as a romantic hero on the screen or else an action hero.

(lower photo)
Bogart conflicting with
Alexis Smith

465

He did not want to return to the role of a villain, especially one who murders his wife.

Steve Trilling had become Jack Warner's executive assistant, and Bogie called him to denounce both the storyline and his part in it.

Trilling reminded him that he had promised "greater cooperation" after signing a fat seven-year contract. "This part has George Raft written all over it," Bogie said. "Give him *my* sloppy seconds."

Trilling promised rewrites. Bogie told him if they met his specifications, then he would agree to postpone *Passage to Marseille* and film *The Pentacle*.

When the rewrites arrived, Bogie discovered that it was still basically the same script with him playing the wife killer "with no motivation."

"I won't film this fucker," Bogie told Trilling. "You're an asshole to send it to me." He slammed down the phone.

Bogie's new contract had brought him a huge financial gain, but it did not bring him script approval. Jack Warner had refused to grant that.

Warner dug in his heels and got tough with tough guy Bogart. The studio had changed the film's title from the God-awful *The Pentacle* to the more commercial *Conflict*, but the weak plot remained unchanged.

Warner issued a threat to Bogie that he'd replace him in *Passage to Marseille* with French actor Jean Gabin.

Even a threatening call from Jack Warner refused to make Bogie change his mind. It became a battle of wills between a gigantic star and a studio head.

Exasperated, Warner slammed down the phone on Bogie but not before issuing a warning: "You'd better watch it that you don't get your left ball caught in a wringer."

One clever telegram from Warner evoked the song from *Casablanca*.

> *Dear Rick,*
> *You must remember this. As time goes by, you must remember your contract. Or else Ilsa may not be the only person you're telling good-bye on the tarmac.*
> *Jack Warner.*

Soonafter, Warner fired off a telegram to super-agent Charles K. Feldman, who represented Gabin, who was known at the time "as France's answer to Spencer Tracy." Gabin was made a firm offer to star in *Passage to Marseille*.

Warner called the next day. "Bogart, I've made stars and I can break them. Only the other day a star from way back when was trying to get me to cast him as an extra in one of our upcoming movies. You've got no hair; you've got bags under your eyes, and you've got the physique of a Nazi general who's been held in a Russian prisoner-of-war camp for two years."

Willingly agreeing to go on suspension, Bogie told Warner, "Unleash your mad dogs on me."

But by now, Warner was harboring second thoughts about the box office allure of Gabin, who was being asked to carry a $2 million picture. His box office draw, strong in his home country, was virtually nil with American audiences.

Hal Wallis was the producer of *Passage to Marseille*, and Bogie was caught up in a battle of egos going on between Warner and his greatest producer, Wallis. Secretly Warner had been tipped off that Wallis was in secret negotiations with Darryl F. Zanuck to move to 20th Century Fox.

Warner fired off a telegram to Wallis, warning him that, "I, Jack Warner, am in charge of production at Warner Brothers, and I do not want any executive producer taking undue credit for my achievements."

Two weeks later, the agent, Feldman, responded to Warner's offer. "Gabin has refused the role in the Marseille picture. He did suggest that an S be added to the spelling of one of his favorite French cities."

Because of his loyalty to Bogie, Sydney Greenstreet announced that, based on the studio's bad treatment of Bogie, that he was considering pulling out of both *Passage to Marseille* and *Conflict*, as he'd been cast in each of them.

At the last minute, Bogie caved in. Shooting began on *Conflict*, starring Alexis Smith.

Originally Joan Crawford was slated for the female lead, that of Bogie's first wife. She read the script and sent word to Warners: "Joan Crawford never dies in her movies, and she never loses her man to anyone." She wrote that before *Mildred Pierce*, of course, in which she loses Zachary Scott to her own daughter, played by Ann Blyth.

Greenstreet came back on board when Bogie agreed to do the film.

Once again Bogie was reunited with Rose Hobart, with whom he'd worked before. She recalled that Methot arrived on the set to celebrate the fifth anniversary of her marriage to Bogie. "There was a certain irony here," Hobart said, "since the plot concerned a man plotting to kill his wife on their fifth anniversary. I found it amazing that the Bogarts had not killed themselves a long time ago."

Bogart with Methot in 1944

As soon as Bogie completed *Conflict*, he rushed to the set of *Passage to Marseille* (1944), where he was reunited with many of his *Casablanca* stars, including director

Michael Curtiz.

Missing was Ingrid Bergman. The French actress, Michèle Morgan, who had originally been asked to play Ilsa, was his female co-star. Although a stunning beauty, she and Bogie did not make sparks on the screen in this lackluster gathering of the clan.

Casey Robinson, one of the scripters for *Casablanca*, worked on the screenplay with Jack Moffitt, based on a novel *Men Without Country*. This was another World War II drama, depicting a Devil's Island escape marred by a flashback-within-flashback confusion. As WWII films go, it was not bad, but a disappointment considering the collective talent of its *Casablanca* stars that included Claude Rains, Sydney Greenstreet, Peter Lorre, and Helmut Dantine.

"Bogart was a difficult man to relate to," Morgan said. "He was polite, but always seemed to have his guard up. I knew he was in an unhappy marriage. He appeared every morning on the set with an awful hangover. He was very hard to direct, and argued constantly with Curtiz."

Director Howard Hawks, who had cast Bogie in the lead for *To Have and Have Not*, his upcoming picture, brought his new discovery, Betty Bacal (to be billed as Lauren Bacall) to the set of *Passage to Marseille*.

She would recall the moment in her memoirs, *Lauren Bacall By Myself*. Hawks wanted to determine if there was any chemistry between his star and the young actress. He introduced Bacall to Bogie.

She wrote: "There was no clap of thunder, no lightning bolts, just a simple how do you do. Bogart was slighter than I imagined—five feet ten and a half, wearing his costume of no-shape trousers, cotton shirt, and scarf around neck. Nothing of import was said—we didn't stay long—but he seemed a friendly man."

Lauren Bacall
Young, so very young

Bacall may have had visions of appearing opposite Cary Grant, Tyrone Power, or Charles Boyer. Reportedly, she had not been impressed with Bogie on screen.

Biographer Joe Hyams quotes her as saying, "When Hawks said the star would be Bogart, I was disappointed and thought, 'How awful to be in a picture with that mug; that illiterate. He must not have a brain in his head. He won't be able to think or talk about anything.'"

Hawks had acquired the rights to the Ernest Hemingway novel, *To Have and Have Not*. He had long wanted to make a movie out of it, which he planned to both produce and direct.

He hoped to introduce Lauren Bacall to

movie audiences, along with a supporting cast that included crusty old Walter Brennan and even Hoagy Carmichael.

The upcoming release of *Passage to Marseille* sparked controversy before it was shipped around the world. The domestic version showed footage of Bogie, in an act of vengeance, shooting down unarmed Nazi pilots escaping from their downed plane. The U.S. Office of War Information asked Jack Warner to cut this violent footage before sending the film abroad. Warner agreed, but told the office that Warner Brothers would retain the scene for domestic consumption within the United States.

Because of its broad similarities to *Casablanca,* including a recycling of most of its cast, *Passage to Marseille* did mediocre business, although most reviewers concluded, "It is no *Casablanca.*"

Conflict, as Bogie had predicted, was a disaster of a film, as reflected by the poor box office. On viewing the movie, Jack Warner realized he'd made a mistake by forcing Bogie into the role. He delayed *Conflict*'s release for two years.

***

An early morning call came in for Bogie, who was staying anonymously at a small hotel in West Hollywood. It was from Methot, who had somehow found out where he was lodging. "I've cut my wrists," she shouted to him when he picked up the phone. "I'm bleeding to death."

In his pajamas and a robe, he drove to their home where he rushed upstairs to the bedroom. She hadn't lied to him. Her wrists had been slit. He called immediately for an ambulance.

No one knows the exact details of what happened next, and neither Bogie nor Methot volunteered any information. It was an embarrassing incident that the Warners publicity department rushed to suppress from the newspapers.

The end result of that suicide attempt led to Bogie moving back in with Methot, much to the chagrin of Verita.

After Methot recovered, Bogie told Michael Curtiz, "The old men declare the wars, then send the young men off to get killed. I want to do something for the war effort."

He asked Jack Warner if he could apply to the

(top photo) Methot
bottom: Bogie with Bacall

469

Hollywood Victory Committee and take his month-long vacation entertaining the troops overseas. Seeing the publicity value of such a tour, Warner agreed to it, not realizing that Bogie planned to take along the emotionally unstable Methot.

After an investigation from the F.B.I. cleared him of any Communism connections—once again—he was scheduled to travel abroad with his wife.

Bogie told Peter Lorre, "Here we are fighting Hitler and the Japs, but all the War Department is concerned with is do I have any Communist connections. Russia is our ally in this war. Why don't they ask if I'm a Nazi spy? There's word out there that Errol Flynn is flirting with some Nazis, although I find that hard to believe."

In November of 1944, with the war still raging in Europe, Bogie, along with Methot, began a ten-week tour of North Africa, West Africa, and Southern Italy. Their itinerary would transit across 35,000 miles of war-torn terrain.

Along with the unhappily married couple were actor Don Cummings and accordionist Ralph Hark. Bogie dubbed them "The Filthy Four." Guest appearances before thousands of GIs began with a local band playing "As Time Goes By." The *Casablanca* legend was already in the making.

Onstage during some of the troop entertainments, Bogie apologized for not being "a dancing fool" like James Cagney in *Yankee Doodle Dandy*. "Edward G. Robinson claims he had the most beautiful legs at Warners in the 1930s," Bogie told the audience. That line always got a big laugh. "Not having gams like Robinson, I can't show off my toothpick legs, but I'll bring out my wife who was a Broadway stage beauty. Mayo Methot."

"She's the only real entertainer here," Bogie said, knowingly or otherwise insulting Cummings and Hark.

Methot usually got heavy applause, and she sang some blues numbers and

Bogart and Methot
Offstage and rowdy during a USO tour

show tunes from Broadway of the 1920s. Her favorite song for entertaining the battle-weary troops was "More Than You Know."

From Berlin, Joseph Goebbels broadcast an attack on Bogie, referring to him as one of America's most noted gangsters before he entered into films, perhaps confusing his past with that of George Raft's. "That Humphrey Bogart is the best that America has to send abroad clearly demon-

470

strates the complete breakdown of American morals," Goebbels charged. "Under the dire command of Franklin D. Roosevelt, the whoremonger in the White House, the Americans are destined to lose the war."

When Bogie landed in the actual city of Casablanca, GIs recognized him, each one demanding, "Show me the way to Rick's. Is my first drink on the house?"

An officer in charge of their tour wrote back to his home in Pennsylvania. "The Battle of North Africa took on new meaning with the arrival of The Battling Bogarts. They are a disaster. They're polite to each other on stage, but off stage they're killers."

One infantryman insulted Bogie by asking him, "Couldn't Warner Brothers have sent Ann Sheridan instead of you and that wife of yours?"

"See that scar on my lip?" Bogie asked the soldier. "Do you want one for yourself? Back off!"

Freezing in the cold and in his long johns, Bogie with Methot arrived in newly liberated Naples to perform their show in the San Carlo Opera House, which had been spared during the many Allied bombing raids which rained destruction down around it.

Looking like a combat veteran himself, Bogie appeared on stage, hawking his tough guy image. "Listen, you guys, I'm formin' a gang to take back to Chicago. Any of you guys wanna go back with me?"

No one laughed. The audience was filled with troops who were surviving on "inhuman rations" and often freezing in the winter cold. On a brief four-day leave, they were going to be sent back to fight Germans, and many expected the only way they'd see Chicago, or their hometown in America, was feet first.

When their supply of liquor ran out, the Bogarts switched to cognac, which Methot likened to rancid olive oil. "But we guzzled

Methot and Bogart
Hung over and on tour with the USO

471

the stuff."

Methot later claimed that "I fell in love with Bogie all over again when we were visiting wounded soldiers in a hospital outside Naples. One guy had had both legs and an arm amputated."

"The soldier from his hospital bed looked into Bogie's eyes and asked him, 'Will my gal still accept me like this?'" Methot said.

"She'll not only accept you but love you more than ever," Bogie assured the twenty-two-year-old.

In letters back home, Methot said, "We slept in blankets on the floor; we bounced in Jeeps for endless hours over incredibly rough roads; we trudged through mud, and we still did our stuff."

Bogie virtually had to offer a bribe to get a bed for Methot and himself in the Army's VIP Hotel in Naples. One officer reported that the Bogarts, back from an all-night party with the troops, had guns and started shooting up the hotel in the early morning hours. The sleeping officers at first thought it was an attack from the Nazis.

One general in his boxer shorts removed the guns from the Bogarts and asked them to check out.

Northeast of Naples in Caserta, the Bogarts had a reunion with Captain John Huston. Bogie renewed his friendship with the director, who was always contemptuous of Methot. He called her "The Rosebud."

Jealous of the camaraderie between Bogie and Huston, Methot tried to take over the reunion. She rose to sing.

"She was drunk," Huston recalled. "She couldn't sing. Everything off key. It was humiliating for Bogie to sit through it and have me sit through it."

Later in his film, *Key Largo*, starring Bogie, Huston would insert a similar scene, when he had Edward G. Robinson force Claire Trevor to sing off key.

When they returned to Naples, Bogie and Methot checked into a seedy hotel, where they staged a raucous all-night party for enlisted men. The noise was so loud that a general, lodging in a room across the hallway, knocked on their door. He ordered Bogie and Methot to go to bed and tell their guests to leave.

When Bogie refused, the general politely asked him again.

This time Bogie told the general to "fuck off." The next morning Bogie and Methot received a notice to leave Naples at once on the next available Army transport.

***

They reached New York on the cold, rainy morning of February 15, 1944.

472

Arriving exhausted after a grueling flight, the Bogarts checked into the Gotham Hotel on Fifth Avenue. Jack Warner himself stayed there on his visits to New York. A wire was waiting for Bogie to report to Warners for the start of *To Have and Have Not*.

Bogie was in no condition to return to the Warner sound stages in California. He was also drinking heavily and needed a vacation. Instead of responding to the urgent request from Warner Brothers and Howard Hawks, he sent a telegram to Peter Lorre instead. "Mayo and I have the distinction of being thrown off two continents," it said.

Beginning at around midnight, the Bogarts wrecked their hotel suite, tossing lamps and furniture around. They woke up everyone on their floor. The manager was summoned from his bed to confront them. He asked them to check out at once and pay damages.

Bogie refused. The bill for damages was later sent to Warner Brothers. The studio chief ordered that the amount be deducted from Bogie's weekly salary.

Leaving an angry, confrontational Methot to face the hotel manager, Bogie fled the building without telling his wife where he was going. She was alarmed that in his drunken state, he might get run over in New York's wartime traffic.

Returning, eventually, to the Gotham the following morning in time to check out at nine o'clock, Bogie faced Methot. She demanded to know, "What whore did you sleep with last night?"

For the first time in his relationship, Bogie decided to tell her the truth. "Helen Menken," he said calmly. "I asked her to remarry me after my divorce from you comes through." At that point, what remained of their hotel suite was wrecked.

Word arrived once again from Jack Warner, demanding that Bogie return to Burbank at once, since shooting on *To Have and Have Not* could not be delayed any longer. The studio chief threatened to hold Bogie personally responsible for the cost of any further delays on the picture.

Defiantly, Bogie sent word that he planned to remain in New York "with my divorced first wife, Miss Helen Menken, Broadway star."

Warner even threatened the Army that it would no longer send stars on USO tours if Bogart wasn't returned immediately. Then the studio chief was informed that Bogie was still under military jurisdiction. The Army issued orders for Bogie to fly immediately to Los Angeles.

Because of wartime conditions, there were no flights available. Bogie, along with Methot, was booked on the train, the Twentieth Century Limited. The reservations were for Thursday night. At the last minute Bogie bolted. No one could find him.

A call from the Army to Menken's apartment brought her to the phone. She denied having any knowledge of his whereabouts. Of course, she could have been covering for him, and no doubt was.

Methot was waiting at Grand Central Station Thursday night hoping Bogie would appear. Extreme manipulation and endless phone conversations had transpired behind the scenes. At one point Warner had threatened to sue him for breach of contract.

Two minutes before the train was set to leave the station, Bogie appeared without any explanation to Methot about where he'd been.

In Chicago, Howard Hawks, the director of *To Have and Have Not*, had a telegram delivered to Bogie's compartment on the train.

"We have an exciting new girl I want to appear opposite you in our film," he wrote. "Anxiously awaiting your arrival at Union Station when the train pulls into Los Angeles."

On the train heading west, Bogie was grumpy. He complained to Methot, "Hawks has lined up what he calls his protégée. We know what protégée means. He's cast some unknown teenage pussy opposite me. God damn, the bastard. That means I'll have to carry the picture on my own. He wants some of my major stardom to rub off on his latest crush."

When I agreed to do this God damn picture, I was told that Ann Sheridan was to be my co-star," Bogie said. "Now I get this schoolgal and clothes model. Just my fucking luck. Warner is sticking it up my ass once again."

***

Co-starring Bogie and Methot, a three-minute short film, *Report from the Front* (1944), was released in theaters across the country. Its sponsor was the Red Cross Drive Committee of the Motion Picture Industry, and the distributor was National Screen Service. The film begins with the arrival in North Africa of the Bogarts on December 11, 1943, for their three-month tour entertaining the troops. They are shown visiting Army camps, military bases, hospitals, and field units.

Bogie handled the narration and issued an appeal for donations for the war effort.

Report from the Front marked the last screen appearance of Mayo Methot.

***

Before a final casting decision was made about who would play the female lead in *To Have and Have Not*, Howard Hawks asked Lauren Bacall to do a screen test. It was with the actor John Ridgely, who was under contract for Warners.

Hawks wanted the scene "to be special" in his words, and he had written it himself. It became known as "the whistle scene." In time it would become her most famous scene among her many screen appearances.

The lines were provocative.

At the doorway, as she is about to leave the room, she asks the main character.

"You know how to whistle, don't you, Steve? You just put your lips together and blow."

Days after filming her screen test, she was told that Bogie had seen it. She feared his reaction.

Called to lunch with Hawks, she headed for his bungalow at the appointed time. Just as she was heading for the door, it opened. Bogie appeared. Having met with the director, he was just leaving.

This was her second meeting with the star. He appeared to evaluate her more carefully this time, taking in her tawny blonde hair, her triangular cat-like face, and her penetrating green eyes.

Finally, he spoke, "I saw your test. We'll have a lot of fun."

***

And so they did.

475

AMERICAN ICONS:
BOGIE AND BACALL

EPILOGUE

William Faulkner, "out of print and out of work," was hired by Howard Hawks to work on the script of Ernest Hemingway's *To Have and Have Not*. To the chagrin of his rival, Hemingway, Faulkner contributed greatly to the snappy dialogue, much of it emerging from the beautiful lips of Lauren Bacall, who was cast as Marie ("Slim") Browning.

Critics claimed that *To Have and Have Not* was Hemingway's worst novel. When the Bogie/Bacall movie was released, other critics called it Hawks' version of *Casablanca*.

Cast as a tough skipper-for-hire guy named Harry Morgan, Bogie in the plot reluctantly becomes involved with the French Resistance. He also woos an equally tough character, as played by Bacall.

Hawks would later claim, "It wasn't Bacall that Bogie fell for; it was the character of Marie. She had to play Marie for the rest of her life. She should have fallen for me."

In their love scenes, you can practically see Bacall and Bogart falling in love for real. When she saw the movie, Methot agreed with that assessment. "Bogie's no good on the screen in love scenes. But in *To Have and Have Not*, it was clear to me he wasn't faking that kissing just for the camera."

Dolores Moran, who had fourth billing, had been cast as the lead actress, but her part was reduced to give Bacall more screen time.

Moran, along with Bacall, was promoted as a new screen personality. Bacall made it; Moran did not. A popular pin-up girl, she never struck it big in movies, although she appeared in major films such as *Yankee Doodle Dandy* with James Cagney and *Old Acquaintance* with Bette Davis.

Moran languished in Hollywood, working sporadically. Near the end of her life in 1982, she claimed, "Had it not been for Lauren Bacall, I too might have become a screen legend. She stole not only Bogie, but my thunder. Had she not come along, I know Bogie would have fallen for me. I was his type."

In 1944 as February (a leap year) moved into spring, the forty-four-year-old Bogie fell in love with the nineteen-year-old Bacall. They didn't mean to—it just happened.

During the shoot, Methot turned forty, but her beauty had disappeared somewhere in a bottle of Scotch. She'd gotten fat and no longer went to the hairdresser. Often she appeared without make-up, making her look even older than she was.

The immaculately groomed Bacall, in contrast, was the epitome of New York chic, looking for the most part as if she stepped from the pages of *Harper's Bazaar*.

During the early days of her courtship with Bogie, Bacall met him in the shadows, keeping their love affair a secret, although Hawks was aware of it from the very beginning.

Jack Warner told his colleagues, "In Bacall, we have another Marlene Dietrich in the making. After all, The Kraut isn't getting any younger. I hear she spends two extra hours painting her face before appearing in public."

In the wake of the success of *To Have and Have Not*, and Bacall's stunning screen debut, Howard Hawks cast the lovebirds in *The Big Sleep* (1946), with dialogue also written in part by William Faulkner, and music by Max Steiner. The third lead was played by John Ridgely, who had starred with Bacall in her screen test.

This *film noir* was the first movie version of Raymond Chandler's 1939 novel, featuring the character of detective Philip Marlowe. The plot was convoluted, and many fans did not fully understand it but went to see it because of the "Bogie and Bacall" phenomenon. Even the original author, Raymond Chandler, couldn't figure out who the murderer was.

Because of Bogie's ongoing affair with Bacall and his marital problems, his drinking became even heavier during the shoot and on some days he was unable to work.

When Chandler saw the finished cut, he claimed that Martha Vickers had delivered such an intense performance that she overshadowed Bacall. That led to much of Vickers' work ending up on the cutting room floor. She never forgave Hawks for that.

A stellar supporting cast was lined up for *The Big Sleep*, including Dorothy Malone and Regis Toomey. Bogie was reunited with Elisha Cook Jr.

If such a thing were possible, Methot increased her own consumption of alcohol. During one fight with Bogie, she fell down and broke her foot. Recovering in bed, and furious at the news of Bogie's affair with Bacall, she called her rival at three o'clock one morning in October. "Listen, you Jewish bitch—who's going to wash his socks? Are *you*? Are *you* going to take care of him?" At this point her marriage to Bogie was over except for the divorce.

On October 10, 1944, Warners announced the separation of Bogie and Methot, but, almost unbelievably, they had a reconciliation two weeks later.

On December 4, Bogie, following one of their most violent fights, ran out of the house for the final time.

At the wrap of *The Big Sleep* in January of 1945, Bacall returned to New York, and Bogie was hot to trot on her trail. That month he announced to columnist Earl Wilson that he and Bacall would marry.

Back in Hollywood, he filmed *The Two Mrs. Carrolls* (1947) with Barbara Stanwyck. This was followed by a May 10 divorce from Methot, in which she got two-thirds of his cash.

At long last, on May 21, 1945, Bogie and Bacall were married in Lucas, Ohio, on Malabar Farm, belonging to Bogie's friend, the writer Louis Bromfield, a descendant of Daniel Boone. Their honeymoon was spent cruising in *Sluggy* along the California coast.

By August 15, World War II was over, a Cold War about to begin. It appeared that Bogie had settled into a happy marriage. But there were complications.

It wouldn't be quite the storybook romance that publicists or even biographers have suggested.

***

Back in Burbank, Verita Peterson had read in the papers that Bogie was seeing a young actress named Lauren Bacall. She didn't realize the seri-

(bottom image}
Martha Vickers
"an on-screen nymphomaniac"

479

ousness of the romance.

When his divorce from Methot came through, she thought, or at least hoped, that he might resume his relationship with her. News of his marriage to Bacall came as a shock to her.

"I was furious at first, then I cried for several days at the news," Verita said. "I took it so hard. I felt I'd been betrayed. I raged against Bacall, whom I viewed as an opportunistic Jane-come-lately. Perhaps irrationally, I did not blame Bogie for his action. It appeared that I had removed myself from the race too long. I was sick, and I hated myself for what I'd done. Now, thanks to me and my damned dispassionate reasoning, it was over. At least I thought it was over."

Three months later, a call came in from Bogie, asking her to lunch at the Smoke House where it all began. He told her he was glad to see his "sassy li'l

bitch again."

Before they could resume their old relationship, she had to needle Bogie the way he needled other people. "Who is this bitch anyway? Someone who just *drifted* into your life! A total goddamned *stranger*!"

Then Bogie said an amazing thing. "Pete, I've told you a hundred times. You're the only woman in my life."

Verita later said, "I started to walk out of the restaurant at that point. What did he mean that I was the only woman in his life? What about Lauren Bacall? She seemed like a woman in his life."

He tried to explain his marriage. "Okay, I did it again. I got drunk and I got married. I don't even know how the hell it all happened. But now I'm locked in again, and I gotta figure a way out of it."

She bluntly asked him, "Do you love her?"

"What the hell's love?" he asked. "We haven't a damn thing in common, and she's young enough to be my daughter."

By his third martini, Bogie made his pitch. He wanted Verita back as the keeper of his toupée. "Listen, Pete, how the hell can you go off and just leave me at the mercy of those fags over at Warners in makeup? I mean, they're prancing in and fluffing up my muff between every goddamn

(upper image) Hollywood promotes Bogie and Bacall
(lower image) Verita Peterson

480

take."

"I knew what was coming," she later recalled. "He wanted me back to fluff his muff, but that could be taken two ways, and he meant it two ways. What surprised me was not that he pitched the ball at me but that I caught it. Without thinking I said, 'Of course, we can take up right where we left off.'"

Bogie and Bacall purchased Hedy Lamarr's secluded house called Hedgerow Farm at 2707 Benedict Canyon Road in Beverly Hills in January of 1946. At first Bogie liked the isolation of it, but in time he began to feel that "it is too remote."

Verita turned down the hairdresser job on *The Big Sleep*, perhaps because Bacall was in it, but she was back on board for the filming of *Dead Reckoning* (1947) for Columbia Pictures.

Bogie's *film noir* had been intended for Rita Hayworth but, because of a commitment to Orson Welles, she was not free. A sultry blonde, Lizabeth Scott, was cast instead by the director John Cromwell, Bogie's long-time friend dating back to the 1920s.

Bogie traded in his beloved *Sluggy* for the *Santana*, paying Dick Powell $50,000 for the fifty-five-foot championship racer which had once been owned by George Brent and Ray Milland.

Verita bowed out as hairdresser to Bogie on the film, *Dark Passage* (1947), for which he returned to the Warner Brothers lot to star with Bacall again. There, he was reunited with Bruce Bennett, who had remained one of his favorite people, and Agnes Moorehead, who had never been one of his favorite persons.

Cast as Vincent Parry, Bogie is framed for the murder of his wife. He escapes from San Quentin and alters his face with plastic surgery. The film is unusual in that the audience does not see Bogie's face until sixty-two minutes into the feature.

This is the first film in which Bogie wore a full hairpiece. It was designed by Verita, although she did not appear on the set.

For a while, Bogie was miffed that John Huston had walked out at a crucial moment during the filming of *Across the Pacific*. But he had to forgive him. After all, Huston was putting his life on the line to join the Army to defend his country during a time of peril. "And what were the rest of

(lower image)
Bogart with Lizabeth Scott

481

us doing?" Bogie asked. "Making bad movies about the war."

Their friendship had been renewed when Bogie and Huston met up on the battlefields of Italy. Huston had always held Mayo Methot in utter contempt, but he had nothing but praise for Bogie's fourth wife, Lauren Bacall. The Bogarts became friends with Huston and his new wife, actress Evelyn Keyes, or "Scarlett O'Hara's Younger Sister" as she called herself in her memoirs.

Upon his return from the war, Huston and Bogie would make their greatest pictures together.

For the 1948 release of *The Treasure of the Sierra Madre*, Huston hired his father, Walter Huston, as Bogie's co-star in a picture that became a classic.

Ronald Reagan had desperately wanted to work with Bogie, in spite of certain reservations, but he was told that Bruce Bennett had been cast as "Colt," the role Reagan coveted.

The Treasure of Sierra Madre was John Huston's first film since his return to Hollywood. The plot concerned three Americans who set out into the depths of Mexico's mountainous country to search for gold. Bogie had never looked so disheveled. A critic wrote that by the end of the film he "became frighteningly inhuman—little more than a black mask, with white eyes, and a wolf grin."

Bogie's appearance in *Sierra Madre* was a far cry from that "sprig of aristocracy" on Broadway who invited guests out for tennis.

For his appearance on screen, Bogie needed Verita more than ever. By the time he arrived in Mexico to shoot scenes for *Sierra Madre*, he was almost completely bald. He'd been taking vitamin B shots to make his hair grow back, but it never really did. He'd opt to wear a wig for the rest of his screen life.

Huston put Verita on the payroll. She fitted his toupées in Burbank, but did not go on location to Mexico to fit them on Bogie's bald head.

A mistress who endured two of Bogie's marriages: Verita Peterson Thompson

When he saw the final cut of *Sierra Madre* with John Huston as director and Walter Huston as co-star, Bogie said, "One Huston is bad enough, but two are murder."

Bogie heard he hadn't been nominated for his magnificent performance of Dobbs in *Sierra Madre*. He claimed, "I wuz robbed!"

Laurence Olivier won that year for *Hamlet*, competing against Lew Ayres in *Johnny Belinda*, Montgomery Clift in *The Search*, Dan Dailey in *When My Baby Smiles at Me*, and Clifton Webb in *Sitting Pretty*.

"All those guys are homosexual," Bogie said.

"Don't get me wrong. I think Webby is a great guy, but everyone nominated, according to my sources, can perform fellatio better than Nancy Davis." He was referring, of course, to starlet Nancy Davis, who would later marry Ronald Reagan.

At Oscar time, it was Walter Huston who walked off with an Academy Award for best performance of the year in a supporting role in *The Treasure of the Sierra Madre*.

For his next film, *Key Largo* (1948), John Huston teamed Bogie and Bacall again in this *film noir* set in the Florida Keys. Huston also reunited Edward G. Robinson with Bogie, casting Robinson as a gangster once again, this time playing Johnny Rocco, based on Al Capone.

Originally Huston had wanted Charles Boyer for the role, but Jack Warner had screamed at him that the French actor was box office poison.

In supporting roles, Huston hired Lionel Barrymore, who performed in a wheelchair. Bogie also had a reunion with Claire Trevor, with whom he'd had a brief fling years before.

Bogie was cast in a sympathetic role—no longer a gangster. He played Frank McCloud, who visits a small backwater Key Largo hotel run by Barrymore and his daughter-in-law, Nora, the widow of Frank's WWII friend. Once there, he becomes trapped n the motel which Rocco and his gang have taken over.

Although major talent was involved, Trevor would take home the Oscar as Best Supporting Actress for playing Robinson's boozy moll. Her singing "Moanin' Low" *a cappella* was probably the scene that won her the Oscar. The Trevor character of Gaye Dawn was based on the real-life moll, Gay Orlova, of gangster Lucky Luciano. *Key Largo* would mark the fourth and final pairing of Bacall and Bogie.

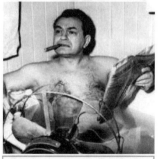

2nd, 3rd, and 4th images above, each from *Key Largo*,

Bogart, Claire Trevor, & Bacall; Bacall with Bogart; Edward G. Robinson.

483

Despite the fact that he was deep into its shooting, Huston had not yet conceived of a logical conclusion to *Key Largo*. Howard Hawks came to the rescue. During the filming of *To Have and Have Not* with Bogie and Bacall, he had produced goodly amounts of celluloid depicting a shootout on a boat. That footage did not make it into the film's final cut.

Hawks met with Huston and showed him how the unused *To Have and Have Not* footage could be spliced into the footage of *Key Largo* for a logical conclusion. When both directors saw the final cut of *Key Largo,* Huston said,

"My God, your half-baked idea has popped out of the oven fully baked. I love you. Thanks, pal! I'll let you kiss me with tongue to thank you."

In lieu of marriage, Bogie and Verita formalized their relationship as a business contract. In the future he'd have her written in as his personal hairdresser on all his movies. Agent Sam Jaffe drew up the contract. Beginning in 1949, she would work on all but four of Bogie's last eighteen pictures.

The contract gave her a reason to be seen in public with Bogie. Up to then, they'd had to slip around in shadows to see each other. In the future, she'd go on trips with him, arriving, for example, in New York with Bogie at her side.

When reporters inquired who she was, Bogie always said, "My hairdresser and my mistress." The newsmen thought he was joking about the mistress angle and never reported on that part of their relationship.

On December 20, 1947, Mark Hellinger had died, which ended Bogie's plans to join with him to co-produce films. Without Hellinger, he forged ahead to set up his own production company. As such, he was the first post-war actor to form his own production company, calling it Santana Productions after his boat.

By mid-year in 1948 Santana films produced *Knock on Any Door* for Columbia. Bogie starred with John Derek, then at his most beautiful.

The film was directed by Nicholas Ray. Bogie was cast as a lawyer, Andrew Morton, taking the case of Nick Romano (Derek), a troubled

(center photo)
Bogart looking scruffy
(lower photo, left to right)
Bogart, Walter Huston, Tim Holt

young man from the slums.

Right before his death, Hellinger had purchased the rights to *Knock on Any Door* and planned to star Bogie and a young Marlon Brando.

In the movie, Derek says the line that would become the clarion call for a generation of disenfranchised youth—"Live fast, die young, and leave a good-looking corpse."

Bogie referred to Nicholas Ray as "a lightning rod," and was impressed with him. The director, who would go on to helm *Rebel Without a Cause* with James Dean, was openly bisexual and a heavy user of drugs and alcohol. Bogie told him, "Listen, pal, I'll join you in the alcohol, but I'll have to skip out on the bisexual stuff and the drug use."

At the time Bogie meet Ray, he was married to the sultry blonde Gloria Grahame, with whom Bogie would appear in *In a Lonely Place*.

That same year Santana also produced *Tokyo Joe* co-starring Alexander Knox, Florence Marly, and Sessue Hayakawa, the silent screen actor.

Tokyo Joe was the second of two films that Bogie would make with director Stuart Heisler. The other was *Chain Lightning* with Eleanor Parker and Raymond Massey. Although it was wrapped in 1949, it wasn't released until 1950.

On January 6, 1949, at the age of forty-nine, Bogie became a dad. At the Cedars of Lebanon Hospital, Bacall gave birth to a six-pound, six-ounce boy, Stephen.

Bogie had wanted to star with Bacall again in the next Santana Production *In a Lonely Place*, a 1950 *film noir*, but Warner Brothers refused to lend her out. Instead, director Nicholas Ray cast his wife, Gloria Grahame.

In the film, Bogie stars as Dixon Steele, a cynical screenwriter suspected of murder. The movie, not fully appreciated at the time of its release, later became a classic.

During the shoot, Ray and Grahame became

(center photo)
Bogart with John Derek

(bottom photo)
Director Nicholas Ray

485

(two images above)
Bogart with Florence Marly

(bottom image, below)
Bogart as aviator

estranged. Ray came home one night and found his wife in bed with his teenage son. Later, when he came of age, Grahame married her former stepson, Anthony Ray, with whom she had two children.

Bogie did not like the script for Warner Brothers' film, *Murder Inc.*, and told director Bretaigne Windust that he felt it was "old fashioned." He was cast with such veteran actors as Zero Mostel, Ted de Corsia, and Everett Sloane. The title was later changed to *The Enforcer* (1951).

Windust, a French-born theater, film, and TV director, became ill. Raoul Walsh took over, but insisted that he not be credited, wanting Windust to take the honor.

No longer a gangster, Bogie played a district attorney, Martin Ferguson, in this one.

In another film produced by his own studio, Santana, Bogie signed to star in *Sirocco* (1951), with one of his best array of character actors, including Lee J. Cobb, Everett Sloane, and Zero Mostel (once again). Cast as Harry Smith, Bogie plays a gun runner in French-occupied Damascus in the year 1925.

His female lead was Marta Toren, the Swedish-born actress who joined the pantheon of exotic European stars that Bogie appeared with in the late 40s and 50s.

Bogie found Toren intriguing because she was secretly dating Dr. Petter Lindstrom, the former husband of Ingrid Bergman. When a reporter visiting the set asked her about her romance with Lindstrom, Toren claimed, "I met him only once at a party."

After the reporter left, Bogie told her, "That's the way to tell 'em, gal. When a reporter asks me about my mistress, I always claim she's my hairdresser."

"Petter told me you were once in love with Bergman," Toren said. "Is that true?"

486

Ever the provocateur, Bogie said, "No, that was just a smokescreen. I was in love with Petter himself. I always felt that getting fucked by a Swedish doctor is one of the world's greatest thrills, and I'm sure you agree."

"I don't know," she said. "Howard Duff is not bad."

"But don't you think Ava Gardner is a tough act to follow?"

"Perhaps she is, but Duff prefers me."

"You sound like a genuinely bad girl." He said.

"Didn't you read the *Sirocco* script?" she asked Bogie. "That's the role I'm playing."

Although born in 1926, as opposed to Bogie's birth in 1899, they would die the same year in 1957. Toren succumbed to a brain hemorrhage.

The German director, Curtis Bernhardt, had helmed *Conflict*, one of Bogie's least popular films. He came back to direct him in *Sirocco*. When Bogie saw the finished cut, he said, "Curtis, dear old pal, you failed again. *Sirocco* is too set bound."

On his next film, Bogie scored a bull's eye, arguably his greatest movie, even better than *Casablanca* in the view of some critics.

It began with a call from John Huston, who told Bogie that "I have one hell of a script. The lead is a low life. As you are the biggest low life

left: Sirocco
Bogart with Lee J. Cobb

Above, top to bottom
In a Lonely Place
Bogart with lonely hands, and
Gloria Grahame with Bogart

487

in Hollywood, you'd be perfect for it."

Over lunch at Romanoff's, Huston revealed the title. It was a screen adaptation of C.S. Forester's novel *The African Queen* (1951).

"That tired old thing," Bogie said. "Bette Davis has been hustling that script for years."

"I've read the book, and I know the role," Bogie told Huston after two martinis. "You and I both know I can do it. But working with Bette Davis in the wilds of Africa. That's a bit much even for me."

"Would you believe Katharine Hepburn?" Huston asked.

"Katie's a friend of mine. Spencer Tracy's mother. She's a fragile-looking thing but tough as nails. She'll de-ball us before the last reel."

Within weeks, Hepburn, Bogie, and Bacall were sailing on the *Liberté* to the port of Le Havre in France. Bogie and Bacall would visit London and Paris before flying to Rome. From Italy, they would fly to Léopoldville in the Belgian Congo (now Zaire).

Arriving in darkest Africa, Bogie said, "At least this film gives me a chance to get out of a trench coat. It is my destiny to play Charlie Allnutt, and destiny is not a word I go around using."

"Here I am," he told Huston, "just where you wanted us. On the banks of the Ruiki River, deep in the Congo, a hundred miles from nowhere. Heat, soldier ants, and poisonous snakes—my kind of place."

Huston warned him that the river itself, which was black because of decaying vegetation, was filled with crocodiles. "Even worse than the crocs are parasitic worms. They're called *bilharzia*. They penetrate your skin and live off your flesh."

Of all of the stories told about the making of *The African Queen*, and there were hundreds of them—Katharine Hepburn even wrote a book about her adventures—Bogie topped them all.

(center and bottom images)
Two views of
Bogart with Katharine Hepburn

"John had to recruit natives for crowd scenes in the jungle. The tribal chief got the idea that we were white cannibals and planned to eat his peo-

488

ple. Huston asked for two hundred natives. But at first the chief gave us only ten. He sent some women—perhaps former wives—he was bored with and some unwanted children. He charged sixpence for the small kids, but a whole shilling for the larger kids. When he saw we didn't boil them in a pot, he allowed more natives to come and work for us."

In mid-June the mail from American brought some sad news. In a June 9 dispatch from Portland, Oregon, appeared this headline: MAYO METHOT, STAGE AND FILM ACTRESS, DEAD.

After Bogie dumped her, Methot went through her money quickly, as she sank deeper and deeper into alcoholism and depression.

Returning to Oregon to live out her final years, she died in a seedy motel room on the outskirts of Portland. Her body wasn't discovered until two days later.

In the jungles of Africa, Bogie read her obituary. His only comment was, "Such a waste."

Near the end of the shoot, Bogie's patience with Africa and with Huston was running out. "I hate the fucking jungle," he told his director. "The blistering heat, and those bugs, those awful, never-ending bugs," Bogie said. "The only way to beat the bastards is to burn 'em, kill 'em. After you've done that, reward yourself with three double Scotches. I wanted to turn Hepburn onto Scotch, not the water. She didn't listen and spent most of two weeks sitting on the makeshift can."

The crew, at great expense and difficulty, moved to Uganda with the final scenes shot in a studio outside London.

Through it all, Hepburn kept her cool. "Damn Hepburn!" Bogie shouted at Huston. "Damn her! She's so God damn cheerful. She's got killer ants in her bloomers, a fungus-like mildew in her shoes, and she's so God damn cheerful."

The Best Actor Oscar competition for 1951 was the toughest in years. Bogie faced Marlon Brando in *A Streetcar Named Desire*, Montgomery Clift in *A Place in the Sun*, Arthur Kennedy in *Bright Victory*, and Fredric March in *Death of a Salesman*.

Broderick Crawford, who sat next to Bogie at the Pantages Theater in Hollywood, later revealed, "Bogie was a nervous wreck. He jumped up and

(lower image)
Bogart with Kim Hunter

489

down and out of his seat a hundred times. When his name was announced, he was sweating blood. He was so flustered he fluffed his ad-lib, stammered a polite thank you, and stepped on Greer Garson's toe as she handed him the statuette."

(two lower images) Bogart as an army surgeon in Korea

with Keenan Wynn
and
with June Allyson

"Later, backstage, Bogie regained his nerve and became Bogie again," Crawford claimed. "He said that all this Oscar business was just bunk. He also said if the Academy wanted to know who the best actor of the year was, they should put each guy in costume and have him play Hamlet."

Fresh from his triumph in *The African Queen*, Bogie signed with 20th Century Fox to star in *Deadline—U.S.A.* (1951), directed by Richard Brooks, who also wrote the screenplay.

Bogie's leading lady this time was Ethel Barrymore, the grand dame of the theater. Bogie had already appeared with her brother, Lionel Barrymore in *Key Largo*.

A personal friend of Bogie's, Brooks had lined up a stellar cast that included Kim Hunter, who had famously appeared as Stella opposite Marlon Brando in *A Streetcar Named Desire*. Rounding out the cast were such veteran actors as Ed Begley, Paul Stewart, and Martin Gabel.

Bogie was cast as Ed Hutcheson, a crusading managing editor of a large metropolitan newspaper called *The Day*.

To get the feel of what it would be like to work for a real newspaper, Bogie hung out at the city room of *The New York Daily News*.

Years later when James Dean started to receive such acclaim, Bogie said, "I once made a movie with Dean," He was referring, of course, to *Deadline—U.S.A.* Cast as an extra, Dean appears only briefly in the movie.

Shooting had already begun when Brooks, Bogie's longtime friend, told him that Darryl Zanuck had wanted either Gregory Peck or Richard Widmark for the lead. "Here I am, a fucking Oscar winner, and still I'm getting sloppy seconds," Bogie said.

Brooks later claimed that *Deadline—U.S.A.* marked "the beginning of the end of Humphrey Bogart. He had a few good pictures left, but he wasn't the same man we knew and loved. He was arrogant, grumpy during the entire shoot, argumentative, and he never knew his lines. He was very sarcastic and snapped at the other actors, although he treated Miss Barrymore with the greatest of respect. How could he not?"

Richard Brooks immediately cast Bogie in *M.A.S.H. 66* (later changed to *Battle Circus*, 1953). As his co-star, June Allyson played opposite him. She'd been known as America's Sweetheart back in the 1940s. Keenan Wynn played the second male lead in this Metro-Goldwyn-Mayer production.

When Brooks viewed the final result, he had to admit, "There is no on-screen chemistry between Bogie and June at all. When he had to kiss her, it was like he was kissing his maiden aunt."

Bogie already knew Allyson, as he'd purchased his beloved *Santana* from her husband, Dick Powell.

Set behind the front lines during the Korean War, the picture is not to be confused with the Robert Altman film *M*A*S*H* in 1970 or the long-running TV series of the same name (1972-83). Neither the TV series for CBS nor the Altman film would ever want to be associated with the lackluster *Battle Circus*, one of Bogie's lesser efforts.

The highlight of the film? Bogie accidentally set his left thumb on fire with lighter fluid while filming the scene in which his character of Major Jeb Webbe

Marrying profitably:

(top row) Bacall, Marilyn Monroe
(third photo from top)
MM, Bacall, and Grable
(lower photo) Attending the premier in 1953: Bacall, Bogart, and Monroe

491

accidentally burns some documents.

The accident is clearly visible on screen, as Brooks decided to keep it in. He later said, "The thumb burning was the most exciting thing in the movie. At least I got some real pain, not fake pain."

At the end of *Battle Circus*, Bogie told his friend Brooks, "Let's not make any more movies together."

On August 23, 1952, Bacall gave birth to a six-pound, five-ounce baby girl. Bogie named her "Leslie" in honor of his long ago friend, Leslie Howard, who had given him his first big break in *The Petrified Forest*.

Around the same time the Bogarts moved from their rustic Benedict Canyon house to a $175,000 roomy, whitewashed brick colonial manse in chic Holmby Hills next to Beverly Hills. David Niven arrived to see the new mansion and immediately told Bogie, "I thought it'd never happen. The ol' rebel himself has gone Hollywood."

For his final film with John Huston, *Beat the Devil* (1954), the director had assembled an all-star cast of Jennifer Jones, Gina Lollobrigida, Robert Morley, and Peter Lorre. *Beat the Devil* was intended as a tongue-in-cheek spoof of his early masterpiece, *The Maltese Falcon*.

Huston told Bogie that if Sydney Greenstreet had still been acting, "I would have cast him instead of Morley."

Many actresses were considered for the role of Gwendolen Chelm before it went to Jennifer Jones. Huston suggested either Jean Simmons or Audrey Hepburn. Bogie recommended an actress named Lauren Bacall.

Finally, the name of Ingrid Bergman was proposed. She was living in Italy at the time and could have easily played the role.

Bacall had a more intriguing offer. Coming out of retirement after three years, she had agreed to play one of the trio of gold diggers in *How to Marry a Millionaire* (1953), starring

(top photo) After the premier of *How to Marry a Millionaire* Bacall, Bogart, Monroe

(bottom photo) Truman Capote

492

Betty Grable and her "replacement," Marilyn Monroe.

In an automobile accident along the Amalfi Drive in Italy, Bogie knocked out three of his front teeth, which hindered his ability to speak. He already had a lisp. Huston in an emergency hired a young British actor noted for his mimicry skills. He re-recorded some of Bogie's spoken lines in post-production looping. That actor was Peter Sellers.

Peter Lorre came to realize that *Beat the Devil* "was the fifth and last movie that I'd ever make with Bogie. He was ill at the time. In the hotel where we stayed, I heard him coughing. Some nights he seemed to stay up half the night coughing. I think cancer was already eating his body."

Lollobrigida was a star in Italy, but not in America. On meeting her, Bogie told Huston that "she makes Marilyn Monroe look like Shirley Temple." Huston countered, "Gina is built like an apartment house with balconies."

Bogie noted that "Jennifer Jones, when not getting marching orders from her husband, David Selznick, in Morocco, spent most of her free time running around the Amalfi coast trying to escape from the clutches of a tall, aggressive lesbian."

Morley didn't like any of the cast, calling Bogie "a man with no brain." He said Lorre "is an unlovely man in every way."

The convoluted plot tells of the adventures of a motley crew of swindlers and ne'er-do-wells, trying to lay claim to land rich in uranium deposits in Kenya. They are stalled in a southern Italian port hoping to travel aboard an ill-fated tramp steamer to Mombasa.

To hammer some sense into the disorganized script, Huston, on the recommendation of David Selznick, hired Truman Capote, who was living in Rome at the

Beat the Devil

(middle photo) Robinson with Lollobrigida
(bottom photo) Jennifer Jones, Bogart, Lollobrigida

time. Capote arrived in Ravello in a red overcoat that came down to his ankles with a ten-foot lavender-colored scarf. He was openly homosexual, and Huston feared he might conflict with Bogie, who always called everybody "a fag" if he didn't like them. To his surprise, Capote and Bogie bonded. After two days Bogie was calling him "Caposy."

Bogie told Huston, "He's the kind of guy you want to put in your pocket and take home with you."

"He's mine, you bitch," Huston shouted at Bogie so the entire cast and crew could hear him. The onlookers actually believed that Huston and Bogie were having a "gay catfight" over Capote.

For years Capote dined out on stories about the filming of *Beat the Devil*. "Everybody thought John and I were having an affair since we shared the same bedroom. Bogie spread the story, claiming the sounds coming from our bedroom were clearly of my screaming as John fucked me."

Capote also claimed that "I gave Bogie a blow job one drunken night. It was to settle a bet. I told him if I could beat him at arm wrestling three times in a row, he'd had to submit to a blow-job. He agreed. When I beat him, he went upstairs with me and unbuttoned his pants and took it out for me. He allowed me to blow him but warned me 'not to swallow.'"

Capote later claimed that he alone was the author of the screenplay. "All Huston did was play cards and drink while I wrote. He was like Irving Berlin, who had the little nigger boy in the trunk writing all his songs."

Back in Hollywood, Huston privately screened *Beat the Devil* for Bogie. Heavily invested in it financially, Bogie did not like it. "Only phonies will like it," he told Huston.

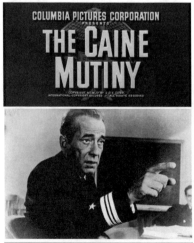

"a pathetic, babbling ruin"

Beat the Devil was the only movie Bogie ever made where audiences across the country lined up at the box office, demanding their money back.

Critic Roger Ebert later said that *Beat the Devil* was the first camp movie. In later years, Capote claimed, "When I wrote the script for *Beat the Devil,* I invented camp." Huston thought so little of it he did not renew the copyright, and today *Beat the Devil* is freely available to anyone to distribute.

Bogie had long been a friend of Dick Powell, who'd married June Allyson. But relationships between actors, even when they're friends, tend to become stormy

494

when they're maneuvering for the same part. For a long time Powell had wanted to play Captain Queeg, the cruel and paranoid skipper in *The Caine Mutiny*.

The producer, Stanley Kramer, had arranged for Columbia to release the film. He had a production schedule of fifteen months. Powell went to him and practically begged for the role of Queeg.

"No way!" Kramer said. "Bogie was just in here, and I think he'd be a hell of a lot better as Captain Queeg than you."

Before settling on Bogie, Kramer considered Richard Widmark for the role of Queeg. Bogie demanded his usual top salary, and Kramer was reluctant to pay it.

"This never happens to Cooper, Grant, or Gable—only to me," Bogie told Bacall. He was actually too old for the role. He was fifty-five at the time of filming, but the captain was supposed to be in his early thirties.

Based on a novel by Herman Wouk, with music by Max Steiner, the screenplay had been written by Stanley Roberts.

Director Edward Dmytryk had lined up an impressive all-star cast headed by José Ferrer, Van Johnson, Fred MacMurray, Tom Tully, May Wynn, E.G. Marshall, Arthur Franz, and Lee Marvin. An up-and-coming actor, handsome, blond-haired Robert Francis had been cast as Ensign Willie Keith.

Kramer later said of Bogie, "He has the damnedest façade of any man I've ever met in my life. He's playing Bogart all the time, but he's really a big, sloppy bowl of mush. I believe that the façade is a defense mechanism "

Bogie gave one of his most stirring performances as Queeg, especially in the courtroom scene where he rolls around those steel marbles in his hand. Of his character, Bogie said, "I don't know if he was a schizophrenic, a manic depressive, or a paranoiac—ask a psychiatrist—but I do know that a person who was any one of these things works overtime at being normal. In fact, he's super normal until pressured. And then he blows up. I personally know a Queeg in every studio."

Film critic Tim Dirks called Bogie's role "his last great film performance" although he would go on to make *Sabrina* (1954) and *The Barefoot Contessa* (also 1954).

The picture was a huge success, and Bogie found himself competing with Marlon Brando for the Best Actor Oscar. Brando had delivered a memorable performance in *On the Waterfront*. Bogie had competed and won against Brando for his role in *The African Queen*, triumphing over Brando's *A Streetcar Named Desire*. But this time around, Brando's role in *On the Waterfront* beat Bogie.

Ava Gardner, who had previously appeared with Bogie in *The Barefoot Contessa*, told Frank Sinatra, "I think he's dying. Sometimes we had to stop a scene when Bogie was gasping for air."

At the end of the summer of 1954, filming began on *The Desperate Hours*, which would be released by Paramount in 1955. Produced and directed by William Wyler, the thriller co-starred Fredric March. The role of Glenn Griffin would be Bogie's last as a screen villain.

When the play was presented on Broadway, it was miscast with a young actor named Paul Newman in the Bogie role. Later Bogie called his role "Duke Mantee comes of age."

Bogie had a reunion with Arthur Kennedy, and the cast was rounded out by Martha Scott, Gig Young, and Mary Murphy. Dewey Martin, famous for a while as "Mr. Peggy Lee," was also in the cast.

When Bogie saw the final cut of *The Desperate Hours*, he called Wyler. "I think I'm too old to play gangsters."

With tongue in cheek, the director said, "I'm thinking of casting you as a priest in my next movie. If that whore-mongering friend of yours, Spencer Tracy, can get away with playing a priest, so can Mr. Humphrey Bogart."

Right before Bogie's Christmas birthday in 1954, he signed a deal with Harry Cohn, the chief honcho of Columbia Pictures. With a stroke of Bogie's signature, his production company, Santana, became history, at least for him. The sale netted him a million dollars.

Verita Peterson had remained a constant in Bogie's life up until 1955. Since she had become an employee, he brought her into his family life, introducing her to Bacall. There is a photograph of her cutting the hair of Bogie's son, Stephen.

"It seemed hypocritical as hell for me to have anything to do with Bogie's home life, and while Bogie agreed with me in principle, he pointed out that it would raise suspicions if I didn't act as an employee of his normally would. And so I became more familiar with Betty and the

The Desperate Hours

Bogart terrorizing
(middle image) Martha Scott and
(lower image) Fredric March

496

two children than I wanted to under the circumstances."

Verita's affair with Bogie finally came to an end—with his full approval—when she married the producer Walter Thompson in 1955. But she would remain Bogie's friend and occasional companion to the end.

Verita remained married to Thompson until his death in 1975. A few months later she opened Verita's La Cantina on Sunset Boulevard. In 1982 she wrote *A Love Story, Bogie and Me*, revealing what much of *tout* Hollywood already knew.

In the 1990s she moved to New Orleans and opened a piano bar, naming it "Bogie and Me." When Hurricane Katrina was roaring down on the city, she refused the offer of a private jet to escape the storm's fury. "Lauren Bacall failed to chase me out of Hollywood. Katrina won't force me out of New Orleans."

Writer Larry Cone encountered Verita in 2005 and wrote: "Verita Thompson, a woman in her late 80s—dressed to the nines in fishnet stockings and high heels—swirled to music with the rest of us. She once had an affair with Humphrey Bogart, we were told. She's a regular at the clubs and is treated with reverence by everyone."

Verita died in New Orleans on February 1, 2008. Under her pillow a maid found Bogie's long ago toupée.

In the spring of 1955, the Holmby Hills Rat Pack was born when Bacall surveyed the wreck of a four-day party in Las Vegas. "You look like a god-damn rat pack!" she told the boys.

A legend was born. After Bogie's death, Frank Sinatra not only became the leader of the Rat Pack, but he filled Bogie's shoes in another way, becoming the temporary boyfriend of Bacall.

From the set of *The Desperate Hours*, Bogie began filming *The Left Hand of God* for 20th Century Fox. His beautiful co-star was Gene Tierney, former mistress of John F. Kennedy.

Bogie worked again, with Edward Dmytryk, with a supporting cast of familiar faces, including Lee J. Cobb, Agnes Moorehead, and E.G. Marshall.

In the film, Bogie managed to be convincing posing as a clergyman with diverting results in this

Hardcover and paperback editions of Verita Thompson's autobiography

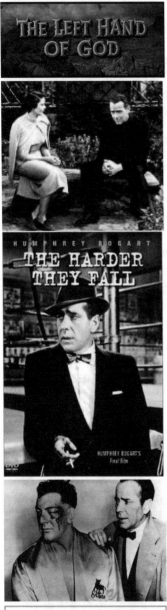

drama set in post-WWII China. He called William Wyler, "At last I got to be a priest, even if a fake one."

At first he attacked Tierney for not knowing her lines. But when he came to realize how emotionally fragile she was, he softened his stance and began to help her in any way he could. He told Dmytryk that Tierney reminded him of his mentally ill sister, Frances.

Tierney was emotionally shattered at the end of her relationship with Prince Aly Khan. She would soon suffer a nervous breakdown and be sent to a mental ward for almost two years.

In spite of declining health, Bogie was convinced he could play Joseph in *We're No Angels* released in 1955. On the set he was reunited with his *Casablanca* director, Michael Curtiz. Age had only embittered Curtiz, who told Bogie, "I want to tell Hollywood to go fuck me."

"Don't you mean, you want to tell Hollywood to go fuck itself?" Bogie asked.

"I know what I mean." Curtiz snapped at him, "especially when it comes to fucking."

Curtiz had assembled an all-star cast, including Aldo Ray, Peter Ustinov, Joan Bennett, Basil Rathbone, and Leo G. Carroll. The film would prove to be only mildly entertaining, as it told of three escapees from Devil's Island who find refuge with a French family. Once there, the convicts extricate the family from their various dilemmas.

Robert De Niro and Sean Penn would remake the movie under the same title for a 1989 release.

In the autumn of 1955, Bogie would begin work on *The Harder They Fall*, his last motion picture. In this swan song, Bogie starred in a drama by Budd Schulberg in which he played a cynical sportswriter turned press agent. He realizes for the first time how badly prize fighters are managed.

Left Hand of God
(2nd photo from top)
Gene Tierney with Bogart

The Harder They Fall
(Bogart's Last Film)
Doomed boxer
(Mike Lane) with Bogart

498

The *film noir* was directed by Mark Robson. Two talented actors, Rod Steiger and Jan Sterling, backed up Bogie in his final appearance in this brutal, disagreeable story.

Bogie would soon be diagnosed with esophageal cancer. Robson found that his voice was not clear in some of the takes. Paul Frees, who appeared in the film as a priest, dubbed some of his lines in post-production. He could perfectly imitate Bogie. This re-dubbing was later denied by the studio.

In January of 1956, Bogie and Bacall reported to Warner Brothers for wardrobe tests on an upcoming film, *Melville Goodwin, U.S.A.* But before production began, Bogie entered the hospital, where he learned that his cancer had invaded his esophagus and spread throughout his entire body.

Bogie called producer Milton Sperling. "I can make our film, but I've got to tell you, pal, I'll be dead in six months." His coughing spasms grew more pronounced and of longer duration. Warners was reluctant to go ahead with the film.

On February 29, 1956, Bogie checked into Good Samaritan Hospital in Los Angeles, where Dr. John Jones operated on him for nearly ten hours.

His esophagus was removed, along with two—maybe more—lymph nodes and one of his ribs. Bacall was told the cancer had been detected too late. The suggestion was that Bogie would not live to see Christmas and his birthday.

Weeks of chemotherapy followed. When his friend Joe Hyams asked how the treatments were going, Bogie said, "It's shit!" He'd never been known to use that word.

Bogie still went to Romanoff's, though he had no interest in food. He was literally a walking skeleton.

Verita Peterson Thompson came for a final *adieu*. He secretly told her, "I think Betty has fallen in love with Frank Sinatra. If she's not in love with him, then he's in love with my wife."

Bogie was furious when the press learned of his illness. He hated reading about his upcoming death. He claimed, "I'm down to my last martini. The only thing I'm fighting is to keep my head above the press."

In spite of his denial in an "Open Letter to the Working Press," he checked into St. John's Hospital in Santa Monica on November 26, 1956. His cancer had metastasized. Bacall was warned that her husband had only weeks to live.

Bacall and Sinatra in the late 1950s

Friends such as Spencer Tracy and Katharine Hepburn, knowing he was dying, dropped by to pay their final respects in Bogie's home. Brave to the end, Bogie came down each afternoon to his living room to greet old friends like Raymond Massey at the five o'clock cocktail hour. When he could no longer walk, he was brought downstairs in a dumbwaiter.

John Huston was one of the last friends to see Bogie, flying into Los Angeles early in January of 1957. He was shocked to see the condition of his former star, whose weight was down to sixty-five pounds.

"His eyes seemed to bulge from his head," Huston said. "They were giant eyes. He looked at me, and I looked at him. If ever I wanted to cry, that was the moment. But I figured if he could be brave, so could I."

Bogie's last visitors were Tracy and Hepburn. They arrived at five o'clock on the evening of January 12. After chatting briefly with him, Hepburn kissed him on the lips. "I didn't say anything to him," she later said. "The kiss stood for it all."

Tracy bent down over him and also kissed him on the mouth. "Good night, Bogie."

With those haunting eyes, Bogie looked into the face of his decades-long friend. "Good-bye, Spencer."

An onscreen view of Spencer Tracy with Katharine Hepburn

The following day Bogie drifted into a coma. He would not come out of it.

Attended by two nurses, Bogie died at 2:25am on January 14, 1957.

Bogie's body was cremated, his ashes taken to the Gardens of Memory section of Forest Lawn Memorial Park in Glendale.

On January 18, a memorial service was held at All Saints Church on Santa Monica Boulevard in Beverly Hills.

John Huston delivered the eulogy.

"He was endowed with the greatest gift a man can have—talent. The whole world came to recognize it. His life, though not a long one measured in years, was a rich, full life. We have no reason to feel any sorrow for him—

only for ourselves for having lost him. He is quite irreplaceable. There will never be another like him."

Mary Astor, Bogie's co-star in *The Maltese Falcon*, attempted to explain the Bogie cult that grew by the thousands in the wake of his early death.

"The Bogart cult that has emerged is very understandable. There he is, right there on the screen, saying what everyone is trying to say today, saying it loud and clear. 'I hate hypocrisy. I don't believe in words or labels or much of anything else. I'm not a hero. I'm a human being. I'm not very pretty. Like me or don't like me.' We who knew him well liked him. *Bogie was for real.*"

***

One of the nurses who attended Bogie in his final hour revealed to the press his final words:

"I should never have switched from martinis to Scotch."

HUMPHREY DEFOREST BOGART
1899-1957

REST IN PEACE

ABOUT THE AUTHOR

Darwin Porter began his career writing about politics and the entertainment industry for *Knight Newspapers* and *The Miami Herald*. Today, he's one of the most prolific biographers in the world. His portraits of Paul Newman, Merv Griffin, Steve McQueen, Marlon Brando, Humphrey Bogart, Katharine Hepburn, and Michael Jackson have generated widespread reviews and animated radio and blogsite commentaries worldwide. Some of his biographies have been serialized to millions of readers in *The Sunday Times* of London and *The Mail on Sunday.*

He's also the co-author, along with Danforth Prince, of *Blood Moon's Babylon Series*, Volumes One and Two.

Darwin is also the well-known author of many past and present editions of *The Frommer Guides*, a respected travel guidebook series presently administered by John Wiley & Sons Publishers.

Scheduled for upcoming release in 2010 are *Damn You, Scarlett O'Hara,* co-authored with Roy Moseley, exploring the secret lives of Laurence Olivier and Vivien Leigh; and *The Kennedys, All the Gossip Unfit to Print*, about the peccadillos of America's most scandalous political clan.

Scheduled for release in the spring of 2011 are *Sinatra, The Boudoir Singer, All the Gossip Unfit to Print from the Glory Days of Ol' Blue Eyes,* about the 20th Century's most controversial and politically connected singer; and a biography of FBI Directors *J. Edgar Hoover and Clyde Tolson*, a story about celebrity worship and the dark side of the American saga.

When he's not traveling, Darwin lives with a menagerie of once-abandoned pets in a Victorian house in one of the outer boroughs of New York City.

BIBLIOGRAPHY

Agustí, P. *Vidas de Cine—Humphrey Bogart*. Madrid: Edimat Libros, 1998.

Allyson, June. *June Allyson*. New York: Berkley Books, 1983.

Andersen, Christopher P. *A Star, Is A Star, Is A Star!—The Lives and Loves of Susan Hayward*. New York: Doubleday & Company, Inc., 1980.

Astor, Mary. *A Life on Film*. New York: Delacorte, 1967.

_____ *My Story—An Autobiography*. New York: Doubleday, 1959.

Bacall, Lauren. *Lauren Bacall By Myself*. New York: Alfred A. Knopf, 1978.

_____*Lauren Bacall Now*. New York: Random House, 1994.

Bacon, James. *How Sweet It Is—The Jackie Gleason Story*. New York: St. Martin's Press, 1985.

Baxter, John. *Hollywood in the Thirties*. New York: Paperback Library, 1970.

Benchley, Nathaniel. *Humphrey Bogart*. Boston: Little, Brown and Company, 1975.

Bergman, Andrew. *James Cagney*. New York: Galahad Books, 1973.

Bergman, Ingrid and Burgess, Alan. *Ingrid Bergman—My Story*. New York: Delacorte Press, 1972.

Bogart, Stephen Humphrey. *Bogart—In Search of My Father*. New York: Dutton, 1995.

Bret, David. *Errol Flynn—Satan's Angel*. London: Robson Books, 2000.

Brim Crow, Jefferson III. *Randolph Scott—A Film Biography*. North Carolina: Empire Publishing, Inc., 1994.

Bubbeo, Daniel. *The Women of Warner Brothers—The Lives and Careers of 15 Leading Ladies*. North Carolina: McFarland & Company, Inc., 1958.

Capua, Michelangelo. *William Holden—A Biography*. North Carolina: McFarland & Company, Inc., 2010.

Chandler, Charlotte; *Ingrid—Ingrid Bergman A Personal Biography*. New York: Simon & Schuster, 2007.

Chapman, Mike. *Please Don't Call Me Tarzan—The Life Story of Herman Brix/Bruce Bennett*. Iowa: Culture House Books, 2001.

Clarke, Gerald. *Capote—A Biography*. New York: Simon and Schuster, 1988.

Coe, Jonathan. *Humphrey Bogart—Take It & Like It*. New York: Grove Weidenfeld, 1991.

Cunningham, Ernest W. *The Ultimate Bogart*. California: Renaissance Books, 1999.

Dale-Harris, Leslie Ruth. *A Quite Remarkable Father—Leslie Ruth Howard*. New York: Harcourt, Brace and Company,1959.

Donati, William. *Ida Lupino—A Biography*. Kentucky: The University Press of Kentucky, 1996.

Duchovnay, Gerald. *Humphrey Bogart—A Bio-Bibliography*. Connecticut: Greenwood Press, 1999.

Easton, Carol. *The Search for Sam Goldwyn—A Biography*. New York: William Morrow and Company, Inc., 1976.

Eells, George & Musgrove, Stanley. *Mae West*. New York: William Morrow and Company, Inc., 1982.

Flamini, Roland. *Ava*. New York: Berkley Books, 1983.

Fleming, E.J. *A Tragic Life in Hollywood—Carole Landis*. North Carolina: McFarland & Company, Inc., 2005.

Flynn, Errol. *My Wicked, Wicked Ways—The Autobiography of Errol Flynn*. New York: Cooper Square Press, 1959.

Fonda, Henry with Teichmann, Howard. *Fonda My Life.* New York: New American Library, 1981.

Frank, Alan. *The Screen Greats—Humphrey Bogart.* London: Optimum Books, 1982.

Gardner, Ava. *Ava—My Story.* New York: Bantam Books, 1990.

Godfrey, Lionel. *The Life and Crimes of Errol Flynn.* New York: St. Martin's Press, 1977.

Goodman, Ezra. *Bogey—The Good-Bad Guy.* New York: Lyle Stuart, Inc., 1965.

Gordon, Ruth. *Ruth Gordon—Myself Among Others.* New York: Atheneum, 1970.

Greenberger, Howard. *Bogey's Baby.* New York: St. Martin's Press, 1978.

Grobel, Lawrence. *The Hustons.* New York: Charles Scribner's Sons, 1989.

Hamann, G.D. *Humphrey Bogart in the 30's.* California: Filming Today Press, 1995.

Hanna, David. *Bogart.* New York: Leisure Books, 1976.

Harmetz, Aljean. *Round up the Usual Suspects—The Making of Casablanca—Bogart, Bergman, and World War II.* New York: Hyperion,1992.

Henreid, Paul. *Ladies Man—An Autobiography.* New York: St. Martin's Press, 1984.

Henry, William A. III. *The Great One—The Life and Legend of Jackie Gleason.* New York: Doubleday, 1992.

Higham, Charles. *Errol Flynn—The Untold Story.* New York: Dell Publishing Co., Inc., 1980. *Hollywood in the Forties.* New York: Paperback Library,1970.

_____*Warner Brothers—A History of the Studio: Its Pictures, Stars, and Personalities.* New York: Charles Scribner's Sons, 1975.

Howard, Leslie Ruth. *A Quite Remarkable Father.* New York: Harcourt Brace and Company, 1959.

Hyams, Joe. *Bogart & Bacall—A Love Story.* New York: David McKay Company, Inc., 1975.

_____*Bogie—The Biography of Humphrey Bogart.* New York: The New American Library, Inc., 1966.

Kennedy, Matthew. *Edmund Goulding's Dark Victory—Hollywood's Genius Bad Boy.* Wisconsin: The University of Wisconsin Press, 2004.

____ *Joan Blondell—A Life Between Takes.* Mississippi: University Press of Mississippi, 2007.

Laguardia, Robert & Arceri, Gene. *Red—The Tempestuous Life of Susan Hayward.* New York: Macmillan Publishing Company, 1985.

Leamer, Laurence. *As Time Goes By—The Life of Ingrid Bergman.* London: Sphere Books Limited, 1986.

Leff, Leonard J. and Simmons, Jerold L. *Dame in the Kimono.* Kentucky: The University Press of Kentucky, 2001.

Linet, Beverly. *Portrait of a Survivor—Susan Hayward.* New York: Berkley Books, 1981.

Madsen, Axel. *John Huston—A Biography.* New York: Doubleday & Company, Inc. 1978.

_____*Stanwyck—A Biography.* New York: HarperCollins Publishers, 1994.

_____ *William Wyler—The Authorized Biography.* New York: Thomas Y. Crowell Company, 1973.

Marchant, William. *The Privilege of His Company—Noël Coward Remembered.* New York: The Bobbs-Merrill Company, Inc., 1975.

Mast, Gerald. *A Short History of the Movies.* Indiana: The Bobbs-Merrill Company, Inc., 1981.

McCarthy, Todd. *Howard Hawks—The Grey Fox of Hollywood.* New York: Grove Press, 1997.

McCarty, Clifford. *Bogey—The Films of Humphrey Bogart.* New Jersey: The Citadel Press, 1965.

_____*The Complete Films of Humphrey Bogart.* New York: Carol Publishing Group, 1990.

McClelland, Doug. *Susan Hayward—The Divine Bitch.* New York: Pinnacle Books, 1973.

Mellen, Joan. *Big Bad Wolves—Masculinity in the American Film.* New York: Pantheon Books, 1977.

Meyers, Jeffrey. *Bogart—A Life In Hollywood.* New York: Fromm International, 1999.

Niven, David. *Bring on the Empty Horses.* New York: G.P. Putnam's Sons, 1975.

O'Brien, Pat. *The Wind at My Back—The Life and Times of Pat O'Brien.* New York: Doubleday & Company, Inc., 1964.

Oller, John. *Jean Arthur—The Actress Nobody Knew.* New York: Limelight Editions, 1997.

Paris, Barry. *Louise Brooks.* New York: Alfred A. Knopf, 1989.

Parish, James Robert. *The Cinema of Edward G. Robinson.* New Jersey: A.S. Barnes and Co., Inc, 1972

._____The George Raft File.* New York: Drake Publishers, Inc., 1973

._____The Great Gangster Pictures.* New Jersey: The Scarecrow Press, Inc.,1976.

Quirk, Lawrence J. *Child of Fate—Margaret Sullavan.* New York: St. Martin's Press, 1986.

_____*The Films of Ingrid Bergman.* New York: The Citadel Press,1970.

_____*Fasten Your Seat Belts—The Passionate Life of Bette Davis.* New York: William Morris and Company, Inc., 1990.

Riese, Randall. *All About Bette—Her Life from A to Z.* Illinois: Contemporary Books, 1993.

Roberts, Jerry. *Robert Mitchum—A Bio-Bibliography.* Connecticut: Greenwood Press, 1992.

Robinson, Edward G., with Spigelgass. *All My Yesterdays—An Autobiography.* New York: Hawthorn Books, Inc., 1973.

Rose, Frank. *The Agency—William Morris and the Hidden History of Show Business.* New York: Harper Collins, 1995.

Ruddy, Jonah and Hill, Jonathan. *Bogey—The Man, The Actor, The Legend.* New York: Tower Publications, Inc., 1965.

Schickel, Richard & Perry, George. *Bogie—A Celebration of the Life and Films of Humphrey Bogart.* New York: St. Martin's Press, 2006

Schlesinger, Judith. *Bogie—A Life in Pictures.* New York: Metro Books, 1998.

Schultz, Margie. *Ann Sheridan—A Bio-Bibliography.* Connecticut: Greenwood Press, 1997

Scott, C.H. *Whatever Happened to Randolph Scott?.* North Carolina: Empire Publishing, Inc., 1994.

Sealy, Shirley. *The Celebrity Sex Register.* New York: Simon and Schuster, 1982.

Sennett, Ted. *Masters of Menace: Greenstreet and Lorre.* New York: E.P. Dutton, 1979

Server, Lee. *Ava Gardner—Love is Nothing.* New York: St. Martin's Press, 2006.

_____ *Robert Mitchum—"Baby I Don't Care".* New York: St. Martin's Press, 2001.

Sherman, Vincent. *Studio Affairs—My Life as a Film Director.* Kentucky: The University Press of Kentucky, 1996.

Sikov, Ed. *Dark Victory—The Life of Bette Davis.* New York: Henry Holt and Company, 2007.

Sklar, Warren. *City Boys—Cagney-Bogart-Garfield.* New Jersey: Princeton University Press,1992.

Soister, John T., and Wilks Battle, Pat. *Conrad Veidt on Screen—A Comprehensive Illustrated Filmography.* North Carolina: McFarland & Company, Inc., 2002.

Spada, James. *More Than a Woman—An Intimate Biography of Bette Davis.* New York: Bantam Book, 1993.

Sperber, A.M., and Lax, Eric. *Bogart.* New York: William Morrow and Company, Inc., 1997.

Spoto, Donald. *Enchantment—The Life of Audrey Hepburn.* New York: Harmony Books, 2006.

_____ *Notorious—The Life of Ingrid Bergman.* Massachusetts: Da Capo Press, 1997.

Springer, John & Hamilton, Jack. *The Had Faces Then—Hollywood in the '30's—The Legendary Ladies.* New Jersey: Citadel Press, 1974.

Thomas, Bob. *Golden Boy—The Untold Story of William Holden.* New York: Berkley Books, 1983.

Thompson, Verita with Shepherd, Donald. *Bogie and Me*. New York: Pinnacle Books, 1982.

Tomkies, Mike. *The Robert Mitchum Story—"It Sure Beats Working"*. New York: Ballantine Books, 1972.

Vogel, Michelle. *Marjorie Main—The Life and Films of Hollywood's "Ma Kettle"*. North Carolina: McFarland & Company, Inc., 2006.

Wallace, Stone. *George Raft—The Man Who Would be Bogart*. Georgia: BearManor Media, 2008.

Walsh, Raoul. *Each Man in His Time—The Life Story of a Director*. New York: Farrar, Straus and Giroux, 1974.

Warren, Doug with Cagney, James. *James Cagney—The Authorized Biography*. New York: St. Martin's Press, 1983.

Weatherby, W.J. *Jackie Gleason—An Intimate Portrait of the Great One*. New York: Pharos Books, 1992.

Wise, James E. and Collier Rehill, Anne. *Stars in Blue—Movie Actors in America's Sea Services*. Annapolis: Bluejacket Books, 1997.

Yablonsky, Lewis. *George Raft*. New York: McGraw-Hill Book Company, 1974.

Index

Abe Lincoln in Illinois 56
Abel, Walter 249, 337
Above Suspicion 418
Academie Julian (Paris) 10, 11
Across the Pacific 422, 424, 481
Action in the North Atlantic 455, 456
Adam Had Four Sons 405
Adams, John 34
Adler, Larry 441
Adventures of Huckleberry Finn, The 460
Adventures of Robin Hood, The 263
Affair to Remember, An 323
AFL-CIO 312
African Queen, The 234, 298, 328, 414, 450, 488, 490, 495
After All 241
Age of Innocence, The 120
Aherne, Brian 285, 299
Albert, Eddie 401, 402
Albertson, Frank 131, 208
Alexander Hamilton 3
Alexander, Katharine 61, 75, 81, 97, 107, 313
Alexander, Ross 265, 266, 267, 268
Algiers 416, 428, 429, 430
Algonquin Hotel (NYC) 66, 72
Algonquin Roundtable, The 87, 272
Alias the Deacon 94
Alington, George Henry Stuart 64
Alison, Joan 428
All About Eve 58, 247
All Quiet on the Western Front 151, 172
All Through the Night 249, 415, 416, 417, 419
Allyson, June 398, 491, 494
Aloha Means Goodbye 419, 422
Altman, Robert 491
Aly Khan, Prince 498
Amazing Dr. Clitterhouse, The 303, 325, 326, 327, 329, 332, 333, 390
America First 419
American College of Surgeons 214
American Film Institute 414, 440
American Tragedy, An 16
Anastasia 441
Anderson, Judith 248, 415
Anderson, Maxwell 100, 232, 236
Andrews, Clark 326
"Angel in Disguise" 388
Angels With Dirty Faces 338, 340, 341
Angelus Drugstore (Los Angeles) 162
Anglo-Irish War, The 335
Anna and the King of Siam 56

Anna Christie 201
Anna Karenina 358
Another Love Story 271
Anthony Adverse 249
Arbuckle, Roscoe ("Fatty") 98, 103, 105
Arden, Eve 411
Arlen, Richard 232
Arnaz, Desi 363
Arnold, Edward 305
Art Students' League (NYC) 10
Artists and Models Studio (NYC) 20
As Good as Married 313
"As Time Goes By" 439, 446, 470
As Time Goes By (by Michael Walsh) 449
As Times Go By (by Laurence Leamer) 431
As Ye Sow 29
Astor, Mary 264, 359, 409, 410, 411, 412, 420, 421, 422, 424, 501
Astor, Vincent 91
At Sword's Point 398
Atkinson, Brooks 247, 251
Auer, Mischa 277, 344
Autry, Gene 270, 282, 421
Ayres, Agnes 85
Ayres, Lew 151, 152, 153, 168, 172, 204, 482
Baby Mine 103, 104, 105, 381
Bacall, Lauren 94, 257, 259, 328, 334, 355, 371, 389, 392, 410, 412, 414, 425, 426, 462, 468, 474, 477, 478, 479, 480, 481, 482, 488, 492, 497, 499
Back in Circulation 310
Background to Danger 408
Bacon, Jim 372
Bacon, Lloyd 286, 289, 334, 335, 355, 356, 357, 358, 379, 380, 389, 455, 456, 457
Bad Men of Missouri 408
Bad Sister (see *Gambling Daughters*) 171, 172, 173, 176, 209, 232, 236, 249
Baker, Elliott 241
Baker, Mary 314, 343, 344, 370, 463
Baker, Mel 343, 344
Balanchine, George 446
Baldwin, Anita 128, 131
Baldwin, Faith 321
Balkan Princess, The 29
Ball, Lucille 391
Baltimore Hotel, The 81
Baltimore Morning Herald, The 17
Bancroft, Anne 246
Bankhead, Eugenia 64
Bankhead, Tallulah 60, 62, 63, 64, 65, 66, 67, 68, 69, 72, 82, 115, 188, 193, 213, 218, 227, 254, 273,

509

279, 358, 363
Banky, Vilma 165, 210
Banton, Joab 98, 99
Bara, Theda 51
Barbee, Richard 101
Bardelays the Magnificent 233
Barefoot Contessa, The 425, 426, 495
Baring, Maurice 30
Barnekow, Baron Raven Erik 320, 351
Barrie, Mona 321
Barrie, Wendy 300, 302, 303, 313
Barry, Philip 103
Barrymore, Ethel 60, 64, 66, 490, 491
Barrymore, John 60, 63, 64, 67, 75, 95, 242, 273, 391
Barrymore, Lionel 483, 490
Barthelmess, Richard 233, 258, 277
Batman, The 462
Batterson, Mayor "Batty" (Hartford, CT) 116
Battle Circus (aka *M.A.S.H. 66*) 398, 491
Baxter, Warner 207, 305
Beat the Devil 411, 414, 492, 493, 494
Beatles, The 102
Beau Geste 139
Begley, Ed 490
Belasco, David 29, 125
Bell, Book, and Candle 241
Bella Donna 31
Bellamy, Ralph 390
Bells of St. Mary's 441
Beloved Brute, The 139
Ben-Hur 300
Benchley, Nathaniel 352
Benchley, Robert 87, 272, 279
Bennett, Bruce (aka Herman Brix) 458, 459, 481, 482
Bennett, Constance 178, 224
Bennett, Joan 54, 224, 231, 259, 372, 498
Benny, Jack 448
Bergère, Ouida 98
Bergman, Ingrid 307, 331, 377, 405, 408, 415, 429, 430,
    431, 432, 434, 435, 440, 441, 442, 444, 445, 446,
    449, 452, 453, 468, 486, 492
Bergner, Elisabeth 349
Berkeley, Busby 320, 321, 322, 323
Berle, Milton 311
Berlin, Irving 494
Berman, Pandro 209
Bern, Paul 254
Bernhardt, Curtis 487
Bernhardt, Sarah 29, 30
Best Years of Our Lives, The 300
Beyond the Forest 299
Bezzerides, A.I. 391
Bickford, Charles 207, 218
Big City Blues 243
"Big Frenchy" 93
Big House, The 144, 147
Big Shot, The 420
Big Sleep, The 247, 478, 479, 481
Big Trail, The 233
Biltmore Hotel (Los Angeles) 275
Bishop, Julie (aka Jacqueline Wells) 455
Bitter, Marietta 337, 344
Black Bird, The 411
Black Legion 281, 282, 283, 335
Blaine, Amory 433

Blanke, Henry 298
Blomenthal, Dr. Nathan 97
Blondell, Ed 136
Blondell, Joan 54, 125, 135, 140, 149, 166, 192, 222,
    228, 243, 244, 264, 305, 306, 307, 309, 310, 316,
    320
Blood and Death 54
Blowing Wild 392
Blue Bird, The 285
Blue, Monte 422
Blumenthal, A.C. 82
Blystone, John 224
Blyth, Ann 467
Boardman, Eleanor 207
Body and Soul 152, 153, 165
Bogart, Adam Watkins 10
Bogart, Catherine 4, 11, 12, 134, 240
Bogart, Cornelius Edward 10
Bogart, Dr. Belmont DeForest 1, 4, 6, 8, 9, 10, 11, 13,
    19, 20, 23, 24, 25, 33, 34, 40, 46, 56, 62, 100,
    109, 110, 114, 240, 250, 253, 379, 411
Bogart, Frances (Pat) 4, 11, 24, 38, 56, 76, 97, 134, 240,
    354, 355, 498
Bogart, Julia 10
Bogart, Leslie 257, 492
Bogart, Maud 1, 2, 6, 7, 9, 11, 12, 13, 16, 20, 22, 24,
    26, 27, 33, 43, 46, 56, 59, 62, 72, 78, 80, 97, 107,
    109, 240, 250, 354, 378, 401, 406
Bogart, Stephen 485, 496
Bogie and Me 497
Boland, Mary 76, 77, 94, 97, 101
Boland, W.A. 76
Boles, John 178, 313
Bond, Ward 329
Bondi, Beulah 101
Booth Theater (Manhattan) 248
Booth, Shirley 85, 86, 181, 248
Borderson 256, 392
"Born in a Trunk" 319
Bow, Clara 216, 455
Boy Meets Girl 339
Boy's Town 145
Boyce, Betty 35
Boyce, Frederick 35, 39, 42
Boyer, Charles 452, 468, 483
Brady, Alice 29, 54, 56, 57, 96
Brady, William Jr. 14, 27, 30, 32, 33, 36, 42, 47, 50, 54,
    56, 61, 63, 69, 71, 74, 75, 78, 80, 81, 96, 104,
    107, 115, 122, 229, 252, 274
Brady, William Sr. 14, 28, 29, 42, 49, 69, 71, 75, 81, 96,
    97, 215, 252
Brand, Max 192
Brando, Marlon 288, 485, 489, 490, 495
Brazzaville 449
Breen, Joseph 234, 262
Brennan, Walter 469
Brent, George 325, 334, 335, 337, 358, 362, 481
Bride Wore Red, The 313
Bridges, Lloyd 461
Bright Victory 489
Bring on the Empty Horses 315
Broadhurst Theater (Manhattan) 251
Broadway's Like That 125, 135
Bromfield, Louis 388, 479
Brooks, Greg 196, 203

510

Brooks, Louise 82, 84, 95, 97, 188, 273, 274, 276
Brooks, Richard 490, 491, 492
Brother Orchid 389, 390
Broun, Heywood 81
Brown of Harvard 233
Brown, John Mason 251
Brown, Johnny Mack 218, 223, 225
Brown, Rowland 163, 176, 340
Brunnen, Adolf 53
Bryan, Jane 288, 291, 293, 379, 380
Brynner, Yul 441
Bullets or Ballots 264, 311
Burke, Billie 70, 244
Burnett, Murray 428
Burnett, W.R. 394
Burton, Philip 35
Burton, Richard 54, 371
Bush, George Sr. 34
Butterick Pattern Co., The 15
Byington, Spring 302
Byrne, Jane 8
Byrnes, James Francis 245
Byron, Walter 208, 216
Cabin in the Cotton 293
Cabinet of Dr. Caligari, The 418
Cabot, Bruce 387
Caesar and Cleopatra 117
Cagney, James 48, 49, 67, 74, 91, 124, 125, 136, 137,
      151, 220, 222, 228, 258, 263, 265, 275, 284, 338,
      339, 340, 341, 355, 356, 357, 358, 365, 366, 367,
      372, 389, 397, 400, 402, 428, 470, 477
Cain, James M. 258
Caine Mutiny, The 450, 495
California Conquest 398
Call of the Road 139
Calleia, Joseph 373
Camille 32
Canandaigua Gazette, The 1
Canova, Judy 310
Cantor, Eddie 188, 322
Capone, Al 220, 223, 394, 483
Capote, Truman 16, 77, 493, 494
Captain Blood 266
Captive, The 97, 98, 99, 157, 182, 194, 217, 227
Carmichael, Hoagy 469
Carnival 401, 402
Carousel 79
Carpenter, Elliot 438
Carpentier, Georges 87
Carroll, Harrison 341
Carroll, Leo G. 249, 498
Carson, Kit 127
Casablanca 252, 274, 338, 348, 360, 377, 378, 384,
      408, 411, 416, 420, 422, 427, 428, 431, 432, 433,
      437, 439, 440, 444, 445, 447, 448, 449, 450, 451,
      454, 455, 465, 466, 468, 487
Casablanca Conference, The 448
CBS Shakespeare Theater 299
Ceiling Zero 253
Cerf, Bennett 301
Chain Lightning 457, 485
Chandler, Charlotte 431
Chandler, Raymond 478
Chaplin, Charles 95, 96, 210, 287, 369
Charles Frohman Productions, Inc. 100, 117

Chatterton, Ruth 334
Chekhov, Anton 31
Chevalier, Maurice 285
Chiarelli, Luigi 248
Chicago World's Fair (1933) 254
China Clipper 264, 266, 267, 339
Chips Maguire 388
Chittick, Charles Yardley 35, 39
Chorus Line, A 79
Chrysalis 247, 413
Churchill, Winston 319, 390, 448, 465
Cianelli, Eduardo 288
Cinderella Man, The 70
Ciro's Restaurant (Los Angeles) 328
Citizen Kane 449
City for Conquest 397
Claire, Ina 79
Clarence 76
Clark, Dane (aka Bernard Zanville) 456
Clark, Senator Bennett C. 419
Clarke, Mae 143, 163, 181
Cleopatra 54
Clift, Montgomery 337, 482, 489
Clothes 28
Cobb, Lee J. 486, 497
Coburn, Charles 450, 462
Cock and Bull Restaurant (Hollywood) 276, 277
Coffee, Lenore J. 429
Cohan, George M. 74, 75, 274, 429
Cohn, Harry 496
Colbert, Claudette 305
College of Physicians & Surgeons (Columbia
      University) 7
Collins, J. Fred 342
Colman, Ronald 73, 74, 157, 305, 325, 361
Columbia Studios/Columbia Pictures, Inc. 769, 455,
      462, 481, 496
Comrade (the yacht) 12
Comstock, Nannette 69
Cone, Larry 497
Conflict 349, 466, 469
Conklin, Peggy 251
Connie's Inn (NYC) 76
Connors, Barry 85, 181
Coogan, Jackie 363
Cook, Elisha Jr. 247, 413, 479
Cooper, Gary 84, 142, 165, 213, 233, 288, 312, 317,
      348, 349, 366, 374, 392, 432, 441, 452, 453, 495
Cooper, Violet Kemble 245
Corbett, "Gentleman Jim" 14, 88
Cornell, Katharine 120, 121
Cortez, Ricardo 405, 408
Cosmopolitan Productions 276
Cotten, Joseph 433, 441
Cotton Club, The (Harlem, USA) 76
Cowan, Jerome 411
Cowan, Lester 372
Coward, Noël 77, 339
Cradle Snatchers, The 94, 222
Crane, James 57
Crawford, Broderick 489
Crawford, F. Marion 72
Crawford, Joan 93, 149, 170, 209, 212, 220, 231, 254,
      293, 313, 314, 318, 343, 402, 443, 467
Crime Doctor's Strangest Case 336

Crime School 317, 318, 320, 327, 350, 392
Crimson City, The 156
Crisp, Donald 390
Cromwell, John 47, 56, 70, 71, 76, 78, 215, 216, 232, 481
Cromwell, Richard 179
Crosby, Bing 124, 210, 441
Crowd Roars, The 222
Crystal, Sheila 117, 122
Cukor, George 232, 233, 444
Cummings, Don 470
Cummings, Irving 137, 140, 181, 192, 203
Curtis, Alan 397
Curtis, Marie 78
Curtiz, Michael 263, 274, 290, 291, 292, 293, 294, 338, 340, 372, 384, 385, 386, 387, 388, 431, 433, 434, 435, 436, 438, 443, 444, 445, 446, 447, 449, 450, 451, 468, 469, 498
Cushing Academy, The 211
D'Orsay, Fifi 181
Dailey, Dan 482
Dale, Alan 57, 87
Daly's Theatre (NYC) 72
Dame aux Camélias, La 30
Damita, Lili 266, 292
Dancing Town, The 117
Daniels, Bebe 408
Dantine, Helmut 259, 436, 468
Dark Passage 481
Dark Victory 358, 359, 360, 361, 362, 371, 375, 386, 387, 409, 432, 449
Darnell, Linda 419
Dart, Justin 289
Darwell, Jane 415, 417
Dau's New York Blue Book 22, 109
Davenport, John 121
Davenport, Priscilla 36
Davies, Marion 157, 215, 242
Davis, Bette 58, 87, 104, 170, 171, 173, 175, 178, 180, 203, 207, 209, 232, 235, 236, 237, 238, 239, 244, 246, 255, 259, 265, 266, 275, 288, 289, 290, 291, 294, 297, 300, 305, 306, 320, 327, 328, 334, 337, 352, 359, 361, 362, 363, 366, 367, 371, 387, 392, 396, 409, 413, 434, 443, 445, 447, 450, 457, 477, 488
Davis, Nancy 483
Davis, Ruth Favor ("Ruthie") 177, 210, 212, 213, 238, 239
Day, Doris 124
De Corsia, Ted 486
De Havilland, Olivia 306, 409, 415, 423, 430, 455, 457
De Niro, Robert 498
Dead End 299, 300, 301, 302, 303, 313, 315, 318, 401, 461
Dead End Kids, The 303, 317, 318, 320, 340, 34, 362
Dead Reckoning 440, 481
Deadline—U.S.A 490, 491
Dean, James 490
Death of a Salesman 79, 489
Delineator Magazine 12, 15
Demarest, William 415
DeMille, Cecil B. 50, 53, 54, 166, 207, 254, 366
Dempsey, Jack 87, 126, 214
Der Mensch am Wege 285
Derek, John 484

Desert Song, The 378
Desire (the motorboat) 12
Desperate Hours, The 397, 496, 497
Devil at Four O' Clock, The 145
Devil With Women, A 133, 137, 139, 145, 181, 192
Dewey, Thomas E. 287, 288, 334
Diamond, "Legs" 93
Dickinson, Angie 332
Dickson, Gloria 334, 336
Die vier Gessellen (The Four Companions) 431
Die Wacht am Rhein 438
Dies Committee, The 400
Dies, Martin 400
Dieterle, William 284, 285
Dietrich, Marlene 31, 141, 143, 159, 190, 191, 210, 218, 235, 248, 285, 317, 403, 404, 434, 478
Dillinger, John 251
Dirks, Tim 495
Divorçons 28
Dmytryk, Edward 495, 497
Doctors' Wives 213
Dodsworth 409
Dominguín, Luis Miguel 426
Donelley, William 438
Dooley, Johnny 143
Dorn, Philip 259
Douglas, Helen Gahagan 419
Douglas, Kirk 334
Douglas, Melvyn 215, 400, 419, 458
Douglass, Kent 179
Dover Club, The (NYC) 76
Dr. Jekyll and Mr. Hyde 53, 248, 434, 441
Dr. Socrates 350
Dreiser, Theodore 15, 16, 18
Dressler, Marie 167
Drifting 56, 57
Drop Kick, The 233
Duff, Howard 487
Duncan, Isadora 95
Dunning, Phil 48
Durbin, Deanna 319
Durkin, James ("Junior") 208
Duryea, Dan 461
Dust and Sun 133
Dvorak, Ann 219, 222, 231, 244
Eagels, Jeanne 216
East Lynn 294
Easy Come, Easy Go 111
Ebert, Robert 494
Ebert, Roger 439
Ed Sullivan Show, The (aka Toast of the Town) 101
Edge of the Abyss, The 76
Edward G. Robinson 367
Edward, Prince of Wales (aka King Edward VIII of England, aka the Duke of Windsor) 90
Eilers, Sally 173, 197, 204, 231
Ekstase (Ecstacy) 435, 436
El Fey Club, The (NYC) 89
El Minzah Hotel (Tangier) 434
El Vuelo del Ibis (The Flight of the Ibis) 465
Elizabeth, Empress of Austria ("Sissi") 154, 160
"Embraceable You" 422
Emperor Jones, The 79
Enforcer, The (aka Murder, Inc.) 486
Enright, Ray 264, 310, 401

512

Epstein, Julius J. 428, 430, 448
Epstein, Philip G. 428
Erskine, Chester 249
Escape in the Desert 259
Essoe, Gabe 459
Etting, Ruth 123, 124, 125, 135, 367
Every Sailor 48
Everybody Comes to Rick's 416, 420, 428
F.P.I. 418
Fairbanks, Douglas Jr. 149, 212, 216
Fairbanks, Douglas Sr. 28, 216
Falkenstein, Medora 40, 41
Farewell to Arms, A 154, 312
Farrell, Charles 132, 152, 155, 161, 167, 231, 365
Farrell, Glenda 167, 169, 172, 244
Farren, George 69
Fat Black Pussycat (Los Angeles) 231
"Fat Man" 413
Faulkner, William 477, 478
Fay, Larry 89, 90, 91
Fazenda, Louise 310
Fears, Peggy 83, 95
Feldman, Charles 466
Ferguson, Beth 3
Ferrer, José 495
Fessier, Michael 389
Fielding, Mary 11
Fields, W.C. 29, 372, 373
Fifty Worst Films of All Time, The 312
Fight for Freedom Committee, The 419
Finlandia Baths, The (Hollywood) 421
Firebrand, The 167
Fitzgerald, Ella 437
Fitzgerald, F. Scott 64, 65, 66, 67, 68, 69, 87, 101, 115, 434
Fitzgerald, Geraldine 359, 409, 432, 449
Fitzgerald, Zelda 64, 65, 66, 67, 68, 69, 87, 115
Five Star Final 259
Flappers and Philosophers 66
Fleming, Victor 441
Flirt, The 174
Flirting with Fate 261
Flynn, Errol 152, 260, 266, 271, 292, 304, 366, 367, 384, 385, 386, 434, 436, 457, 470
Follies of 1927, The 150
Follies Revue of 1919, The 79
Fonda, Henry 246, 259, 266, 272
Fonda, Jane 246
Fontaine, Joan 248
Fontanne, Lynn 236
For Whom the Bell Tolls 432, 441, 446, 450
Foran, Dick 281, 282
Ford, Glenn 142, 458
Ford, John 54, 131, 144, 146, 147, 148, 150, 152, 329, 414, 458
Ford, Wallace 415
Forester, C.S. 297, 488
Forrest, Sam 94
Foster, Preston 317
Fountainhead, The 349, 350
Four Daughters 367
Four Feathers, The 458
Four Horsemen of the Apocalypse,The 84
Four Wives 290
Fox Studios (aka Fox Film Corporation) 132, 134, 135,
140, 147, 174, 192, 230, 233, 234
Fox, Sidney 167, 170, 172, 174, 175, 209, 231, 235, 249, 397
Fox, William 230
Foy, Brian 268, 277, 279, 281
Frances, Lee 213
Francis, Arlene 246
Francis, Kay 176, 191, 192, 193, 207, 211, 212, 227, 231, 234, 243, 320, 342, 350, 358
Francis, Robert 495
Franco, Francisco 465
Frankenstein 180
Frankfurter Zeitung 157
Franz-Josef, Emperor of Austria 154, 160
Franz, Arthur 495
Freeland, Thornton 242
Frees, Paul 499
French, Bert 77
Fresh Pond Crematory (Long Island, NY) 250
Freund, Karl 178
Friedrich, Otto 414
Friele, Aleta 266, 268
Front Page, The 118
Fuller, Frances 245
Fulton Theater, The (Brooklyn, NY) 56
Furlow, Floyd 35, 40
Furnall, Betty 53
Gabel, Martin 490
Gabin, Jean 466, 467
Gable, Clark 155, 202, 217, 218, 228, 233, 242, 272, 274, 305, 316, 366, 428, 495
Gable, Ria 155
Gahagan, Helen 215
Gallagher, Herb 229, 230
Gambling Daughters (also see *The Bad Sister*) 166, 168, 169
Garbo, Greta 31, 54, 194, 209, 216, 235, 358, 429, 431
Garden of Allah Hotel (Los Angeles) 255
Gardner, Ava 424, 425, 426, 487, 495
Garfield, John 258, 306, 351, 353, 367, 372, 388, 395, 399, 403, 457
Garland, Judy 319, 340, 363
Garland, Pollyanna 249
Garnett, Tay 305, 306, 308
Garson, Greer 490
Gaslight 441
Gaucho Serenade, The 388
Gay Musician, The 89
Gaynor, Janet 132, 216, 271, 305
Gent from Frisco, The 413
Geoffrey Homes (aka Daniel Mainwaring) 269, 270
George White's Scandals 82
George, Gladys 367, 368, 411
George, Grace (aka Mrs. William Brady, Sr.) 28, 29, 32, 36, 54, 55, 70, 96, 111
Gershwin, Ira 25
Gibson, Hoot 173, 197, 204
Gibson, Wynn 261
Giesler, William 322
Gilbert, John 210, 230, 233
Gilded Cage, The 29
Gilded Cage, The (Hoboken, NJ) 45
Gilpatrick, Gil 455
Girl of the Golden West, The 14
Girls on Probation 289

Gish, Dorothy 73, 95
Gish, Lillian 72, 95, 118, 158
"Give My Regards to Broadway" 74
Glad, Gladys 365
Gleason, Jackie 415, 417, 418
Goddard, Paulette 328, 369
Godfrey, Peter 348
Goebbels, Josef 419, 431, 465, 471
Golden Arrow 334
Golden Boy 330, 345, 346, 379, 381
Golden Diggers 322
Golden, John 266
Goldie 205
Goldwyn, Samuel 54, 72, 182, 299, 303, 315, 346
Gone With the Wind 63, 236, 243, 284, 305, 361, 369, 375, 389
Good Samaritan Hospital (Los Angeles) 499
Goodbye Again 441
Gorcey, Leo 303, 317, 318, 340
Gordon, Ruth 101, 106, 456
"Gospel Truth, The" 320
Gotham Hotel (New York) 473
Goudal, Jetta 187
Goulding, Edmund 84, 179, 358, 359, 361
Government Girl 430
Grable, Betty 141, 363, 364, 379, 387, 436, 493
Grahame, Gloria 485
Grant, Cary 288, 305, 382, 433, 468, 495
Grapes of Wrath 415
Grauman's Chinese Theater (Hollywood) 450
Graves, Ralph 52
Great Day 274
Great God Brown, The 103
Great O'Malley, The 284, 285, 390
Great Ziegfeld, The 378
Greatest Love, The 136
Greenstreet, Sydney 349, 408, 411, 412, 422, 436, 437, 467, 468, 492
Griffith, D.W. 73
Guadalcanal Diary 317
Guardsman, The 79
Guinan, Texas (aka Mary Louise Cecilia Guinan) 89, 91, 93, 141, 173, 368
Gun Woman, The 89
Hackett, Walter 72
Haines, William ("Billy") 179, 205, 210, 231, 233
Hale, Alan 387, 393
Hall, David 183
Hall, Huntz 303, 317, 377
Halliday, Mary 111
Halop, Billy 303, 317, 318, 338, 340, 362, 363
Hamilton, Hale 70, 71
Hamilton, Neil 55, 70
Hamlet 95, 482, 490
Hamlin, Frank and Arthur 2
Hamlin, Mary 2, 13
Hammett, Dashiell 404, 412
Hammond, Ruth 101, 106
Hancock, John 34
Harder They Fall, The 498
Hark, Ralph 470
Harlow, Jean 205, 209, 216, 231, 254, 305
Harper's Bazaar 462, 478
Harrison, Rex 324
Haskin, Byron 457

Hatch, Eric 277
Hatch, Gertrude 277
Havoc, June 254
Hawks, Howard 220, 403, 409, 462, 468, 473, 474, 477, 479, 484
Hawks, Kenneth 409
Hayakawa, Sessue 485
Hayden, John 85
Haye, Helen 241
Hayes, Helen 28, 117, 119, 241, 312
Hays, Will 182, 232, 234
Hayward, Leland 371
Hayward, Louis 399
Hayward, Susan 332, 333, 334
Hayworth, Rita 254, 288, 408, 425, 436, 481
Hazel 86
Hearst, Fannie 367
Hearst, William Randolph 157, 214, 242
Heart of Maryland, The 125
Hecht, Ben 220, 236
Heine, Heinrich 160
Heisler, Stuart 485
Hell's Bells 85, 86, 87, 181, 248
Hell's House 209
Hellinger, Mark 87, 88, 89, 364, 389, 391, 403, 457, 458, 484
Hellman, Lillian 236
Hemingway, Ernest 16, 312, 332, 424, 446, 468, 477
Henley, Hobert 166, 174
Henreid, Paul 429, 432, 434, 435, 443, 444, 446, 447
Henry IV, Part One 299
Hepburn, Audrey 382, 383, 384, 492
Hepburn, Katharine 305, 488, 489, 500
Her Greatest Love 78
Herbert, Victoria 58
Hertzlinger, Boze 282
High Sierra 258, 366, 371, 394, 395, 396, 397, 399, 401, 405
Hill, Peggy 78
Hitchcock, Alfred 437, 441
Hitler, Adolf 419, 431, 436, 465
Hobart, Rose 248, 467
Hodgins, Eric 19
Holden, William 142, 346, 347, 379, 380, 381, 382, 383, 384
Hollywood Reporter, The 393, 419, 427, 455
Hollywood Revue of 1929 220
Hollywood Victory Committee 470
Holmes, Oliver Wendell 34
Holy Terror, A 192, 196, 198, 203
Hope, Bob 354
Hopkins, Arthur 250, 251
Hopkins, Miriam 299, 305, 326, 328, 361, 362, 384, 385, 386
Hopper, Hedda 153
Horne, Lena 437
Horton, Edward Everett 224
Hospital for the Ruptured and Crippled (Manhattan) 250
Hotsy-Totsy (NYC) 81
House Across the Bay, The 372
House Divided, A 236
How Green Was My Valley 390, 414
How to Marry a Millionaire 492
"The Howard Sisters" 70
Howard, Connie 70

514

Howard, Frances 70, 71, 72
Howard, Leslie 54, 251, 255, 257, 266, 305, 306, 307, 308, 328, 342, 369, 405, 441, 464, 465, 492
Howard, Sydney 103
Hubbard, Tom 150, 152
Huckleberry Finn 17
Hudson, Rock 421
Hughes, Howard 221, 339, 393, 421, 457, 462
Hull, Henry 249, 397
Humphrey, John Perkins 10
Hunt, J. Roy 209
Hunter, Kim 490
Hurrell, George 340
Hurricane Katrina 497
Huston, John 11, 20, 44, 328, 394, 404, 405, 407, 414, 415, 422, 423, 424, 425, 459, 472, 481, 482, 483, 487, 488, 489, 492, 493, 494, 500
Huston, Walter 285, 299, 409, 410, 482, 483
Hyams, Joe 355, 468
I Am a Fugitive from a Chain Gang 284
"I Cover Hollywood" 305
"I Don't Want to Play in Your Yard" 357
I Loved You Wednesday 245
"I'm a Yankee Doodle Dandy" 74
Ibsen, Henrik 31
In a Lonely Place 485
"In a Rosebud Garden of Girls" 136
In Caliente 322
Ingram, Rex 460
Intermezzo 307, 441
International Squadron 253, 254
Intimate Stranger, The 70
Invisible Stripes 379, 380, 382, 389
Invitation to a Murder 249
Iron Horse, The 233
Isle of Fury 270
It All Came True 388
It's a Small World 302
It's a Wise Child 125, 128, 143
It's Love I'm After 306
Jacoby, Michael 259
Jaffe, Sam 370, 371, 373, 375, 403, 420, 484
Jagger, Dean 433
James Cagney 49
James, Harry 363
Jason, Sybil 284
Jazz Singer, The 110
Jefferson Market Women's Prison (NYC) 100
Jeffries, Jim 14
Jezebel 236
Jimmy the Gent 274, 275
Jimmy's Backyard (Los Angeles) 227, 231
Johnny Belinda 482
Johnson, Jack 138
Johnson, Kay 207
Johnson, Laurence 125
Johnson, Owen 34
Johnson, Van 253, 495
Jolson, Al 110, 260
Jones, Dr. John 499
Jones, Jennifer 285, 492, 493
Jory, Victor 349
Julian, Rodolphe 10
Kael, Pauline 427
Kanin, Garson 101

Karloff, Boris 376, 458
Karnot, Stephen 428
"Katzenjammer Kids, The" 136
Kaufman, George S. 409
Kazan, Elia 247
Keeler, Ruby 92
"Keep Kool Cuties, the" 143
Keighley, William 262
Keller, Helen 97
Kells, Dr. John 26
Kelly, George 137
Kelly, Grace 246
Kelly, Gregory 101
Kelly, Paul 70, 78
Kennedy, Arthur 397, 489, 496
Kennedy, John F. 497
Kennedy, Joseph 208
Kennedy, Merna 322
Kent, John 96
Key Largo 263, 303, 328, 403, 414, 472, 483, 490
Keyes, Evelyn 482
Kid Galahad 288, 290, 291, 294, 295, 321 401
Killers, The 332, 424
Kimble, Lawrence 389
Kind Lady 28
King and I, The 79
King of Kings 166
King of the Underworld 350, 352, 362, 402
King, Lillian and Henry 72, 73, 74
King, Rufus 249
Kings Row 427
Kingsley, Sidney 299
Kirkland, Alexander 179
Kirkwood, James Jr. 79
Klaw Theater (NYC) 77
Knights of the White Camellia 326
Knock on Any Door 484
Knowles, Patric 387
Knox, Alexander 485
Knute Rockne—All American 287, 317
Koch, Howard 429
Koenig, William 322
Korda, Alexander 458
Korda, Vincent 458
Korda, Zoltan 458, 459, 460
Kramer, Stanley 495
Krebs, Stanley LeFevre 302
Kreuger, Kurt 460
Ku Klux Klan (KKK) 281, 284
Kummer, Marjorie 206
Kyne, Peter B. 325
La Marseillaise 438
La Maze Restaurant (Hollywood) 315, 353, 406
La Mond, Jack 276
La Rocque, Rod 50, 52, 53, 69, 165
Ladd, Alan 345, 429
Ladies' Man 447
"Lady Godiva" 254
Lady Said Yes, A 324
Laemmle, Carl Jr. 166, 171, 174, 209, 235, 236
Laemmle, Carl Sr. 235
Lake Canandaigua 1
Lake, Veronica 436
Lamarr, Hedy 429, 435, 436, 481
Lancaster, Burt 424

Landi, Elissa 153, 154, 156, 159, 231
Landis, Carole 323, 324, 325
Lane Sisters, The 290, 377
Lane, Beatrice 37
Lane, Lola 286, 290, 356
Lane, Priscilla 290, 320, 321, 323, 356, 366
Lane, Rosemary 323, 355, 356, 376, 377
Lang, Jennings 54
Lansing, Grace (aka Mrs. Gerald Lambert) 13, 14, 15
Lansing, Mrs. Harry 13
Lardner, Ring 71
Lasky, Jesse L. 54
Last Flight, The 285
Last Mile, The 144
Laughton, Charles 179
Lauren Bacall By Myself 468
Lawler, Anderson 179, 227, 231
Lawson, John Howard 455
Lazar, Irving ("Swifty") 384
Le Gallienne, Eva 32
Le Guere, George 69
Leamer, Laurence 431, 440
Lee, Gypsy Rose 254
Lee, Irene 416, 428
Lee, Peggy 496
Leech, John L. 400
Left Hand of God, The 497
Leigh, Vivien 361
Leland, Rick 422
Lenz, Elita Miller 85
LeRoy, Mervyn 149, 167, 168, 243, 244, 349
Leslie, Amy 95
Leslie, Joan 396, 401, 402, 457
Letter, The 120, 352
Leviathan, U.S.S. (aka *Vaterland*) 43, 44, 135
Lewis, Al 129
Lewis, David 359
Lieberman, Ben 162
Life 50, 52, 53, 404
Life of Emile Zola, The 282, 303
Lilley, Edward Clarke 248
Lincoln, Abraham 18, 205
Linden, Eric 222, 243
Lindsay, Judge Ben 343
Lindsay, Margaret 270, 271, 392
Lindstrom, Dr. Petter 431, 443, 444, 445, 486
Lindstrom, Pia 445
Litel, John 329, 392
"Little Boy" 413
Little Caesar 149, 167, 169, 172, 173, 243, 263, 394
Little Foxes, The 236
Little Miss Deputy 89
Little Princess, The 285
Little Women 37, 38
Litvak, Anatole 326, 327, 328, 402
Locked Door, The 165
Logan, Joshua 272
Lollobrigida, Gina 492, 493
Lombard, Carole 277, 282
Lonely Life, The 170
Long Haul 391
"Long Lance, Chief Buffalo Child" 126, 127, 131
Look Homeward, Angel 79
Lorre, Peter 290, 371, 408, 411, 412, 414, 415, 416, 419, 422, 431, 436, 437, 438, 445, 449, 468, 470,
473, 492, 493
Los Angeles Times, The 400
Lost Patrol, The 458
Louise's Brothel (Los Angeles) 148
Love Affair 242
Love and Death in Casablanca 438
Love Eternal 37
"Love Me Or Leave Me" (the song) 124
Love Me Or Leave Me (the movie) 124
Lovsky, Celia 417
Lowe, Edmund 139, 181, 183, 184, 185, 186, 187, 189
Lowell, Helen 126
Lowell, Randy 312
Loy, Myrna 153, 155, 156, 159, 231
Luce, Claire (the actress) 144, 146, 149, 153
Luce, Claire Boothe (NY Congresswoman and Ambassador to Italy) 150
Luce, Henry R. 150
Luchow's German Restaurant (NYC) 11, 38, 97
Luciano, Charles "Lucky" 287, 483
Lugosi, Bela 182
Lukas, Paul 450
Lulu Belle 118
Lulu in Hollywood 274
Lundigan, William 387
Lunt, Alfred 70, 76, 236
Lupino, Ida 349, 391, 392, 393, 394, 398, 399, 403, 457
Lux Radio Theater 264, 429
Lynn, Jeffrey 365, 388
M (the 1931 Fritz Lang film) 411
M*A*S*H 491
MacArthur, Charles 117
Macaulay, Richard 422
MacDonald, Jeanette 94
Mackaill, Dorothy 242, 243
MacKenna, Kenneth 47, 78, 80, 81, 96, 111, 114, 121, 125, 129, 131, 133, 137, 148, 175, 192, 193, 205, 206, 207, 210, 219, 227, 231, 233, 234, 238, 239, 241, 252, 271, 278, 303, 314, 320, 342, 350
MacLane, Barton 263, 265, 297, 371, 397, 415
MacMurray, Fred 495
Mad Honeymoon, The 74, 75
Mad Hopes, The 244
Madam Satan 207
Madden, Owney 163, 164, 221, 393, 394
Madsen, Axel 396
Maggie the Magnificent 137
Main, Marjorie 300, 302, 408
Mainwaring, Daniel (aka Geoffrey Homes) 269
Maisie 390
Major Barbara 28
Makropoulos Secret 94
Malabar Farm (Lucas, OH) 389, 479
Malaya 413
Malone, Dorothy 479
Maltese Falcon, The 104, 247, 265, 359, 404, 405, 408, 410, 411, 413, 414, 415, 419, 422, 430, 431, 492, 501
Mamoulian, Rouben 345
Man Who Came Back, The 129, 132, 133, 134, 155, 365
Mandl, Fritz 436
Mangam, Liam 8, 26
Mangam, Joseph L. 425, 426, 427
Mankiewicz, Joseph L. 425, 426, 427
Mannequin 314, 318
Manners, David 179

516

Manning, Irene 420
*Manpower (*aka *Danger Zone)* 403, 404
March, Fredric 248, 371, 400, 489, 496
Marcos, Imelda 60
Marianne 215
Maris, Mona 133, 139, 140
Mark Twain Hotel (Los Angeles) 161, 166
Marked Woman 286, 288, 289, 290, 297, 323, 405, 445
Marks, Herman (Hymie) 287
Marly, Florence 440, 485
Marquand, John P. 334
Marshall, Alan 305, 361
Marshall, E.G. 495, 497
Marshall, Herbert 433
Martin, Dewey 496
Martin, Dr. Harry (aka "Docky" Parsons) 213, 215
Martin, Mary 271
Marvin, Lee 495
Marx, Samuel 428
Mask and the Face, The 248
Mason, James 298
Mason, Louis 179
Masque Theater (Manhattan) 249
Massey, Ilona 397
Massey, Raymond 455, 456, 485, 500
Mature, Victor 364
Maugham, W. Somerset 248, 254, 270
Max Factor 452
May, Olive 85, 86, 181
Mayer, Louis B. 93, 170, 210, 216, 234, 341, 369
Mayfair Supper Club, The 102
Mayo, Archie 256, 257, 281, 282, 306, 372
Mayo, Margaret 103
McCarthy, Joseph 371, 400
McCarty, Mary 271
McClintic, Guthrie 100, 119, 120
McCoy, Mildred 126, 127, 128
McCrea, Joel 233, 299, 301
McDaniel, Hattie 63
McDonald, Frank 270
McGann, William 259, 260
McHugh, Frank 311, 325, 415
McKee, Joseph B. (aka "Holy Joe") 99
McLaglen, the Rt. Rev. Andrew 138
McLaglen, Victor 133, 137, 138, 181, 232, 458
Medcraft, Russell 94
Medved, Harry 312
Meet the Wife 76, 87, 94
"Melancholy Baby" 367
Melville Goodwin, U.S.A. 334, 499
Melvyn, Douglas 215
Men Are Such Fools 320, 323, 337
Men of Boy's Town 145
Men Without Women 131, 233
Mencken, H.L. 15, 16, 17
Menken, Helen 15, 57, 59, 60, 62, 63, 65, 72, 80, 85, 87, 91, 94, 95, 96, 97, 98, 99, 106, 108, 114, 115, 116, 129, 182, 186, 188, 192, 194, 195, 202, 206, 226, 227, 273, 342, 373, 473, 474
Meredith, Burgess 372
Methot, Beryl Evelyn Wood 354
Methot, Mayo 74, 75, 94, 274, 275, 276, 278, 279, 280, 284, 286, 289, 290, 299, 303, 304, 307, 308, 309, 315, 316, 318, 319, 320, 323, 330, 333, 337, 342, 343, 344, 345, 348, 352, 353, 355, 364, 367, 369, 372, 373, 375, 377, 379, 382, 387, 390, 398, 399, 401, 405, 406, 410, 414, 418, 420, 421, 425, 441, 443, 444, 445, 451, 453, 454, 459, 461, 462, 463, 467, 469, 470, 471, 472, 473, 474, 477, 478, 479, 480, 482, 489
Metro-Goldwyn-Mayer (MGM) 261, 429, 491
Meyers, Jeffrey 261
Midnight 249, 397, 440
Midsummer Night's Dream 58, 60
Mielziner, Jo 47, 78, 100, 119, 131
Mildred Pierce 104, 293, 467
Miles, Rhonda 103
Milestone, Lewis 151, 372
Milland, Ray 313, 452, 481
Miller, Gilbert 253
Million Dollar Legs 363
Milne, Tom 361
Minsky's Burlesque 88
Miss Sadie Thompson 254
Mitchell, Margaret 305, 389
Mitchell, Norma 94
Mitchum, Robert 456
Mix, Tom 317
"Moanin' Low" 483
Molnar, Ferenc 79
Monroe, Marilyn 80, 493
Montmartre Dance Club (NYC) 68
Moore, Grace 274
Moorehead, Agnes 481, 497
Moran, Dolores 477
"More Than You Know" 470
More the Merrier, The 450, 462
Morgan, Dennis (aka Stanley Morner, aka Richard Stanley) 378, 408, 457
Morgan, Michèle 429, 468
Morgan, Percy T. 276, 277, 278, 286
Morley, Robert 492, 493
Morocco 235
Morris, Wayne 292, 293, 294, 295, 321, 325, 328, 366, 376, 377, 379
Mostel, Zero 371, 486
Mr. Skeffington 337
Mulhouse, Jonathan 1
Mulrooney, Grayce 92
Muni, Paul 220, 258, 282, 284, 285, 350, 372, 392, 394, 396
Murphy, Mary 496
Murray, Mae 74
Mussolini, Benito 436, 465
My Friend Irma 265
My Little Chickadee 29, 372, 373
My Man Godfrey 277
Nagel, Anne 267
Nagel, Conrad 166
Naish, J. Carrol 461
Naldi, Nita (aka Donna Dooley) 50, 52, 53
Narrow Corner, The 270
National Biscuit Co., Inc. 46
Nazi Agent 418
Nazimova, Alla 31, 32, 58, 194
Neal, Patricia 349
Negri, Pola 31, 210, 230
Nelson Oscar Harmon Jr. ("Ham") 210, 211, 239, 267, 335, 358
Nerves 78, 79, 115

517

New York American, The 57, 87, 284
New York Daily News, The 101, 490
New York Post, The 283
New York Times, The 62, 64, 251, 329, 448, 449
New York World, The 77
New Yorker, The 448
Newman, Paul 496
Niagara 80
Nice People 120
Night Nurse 228
Night Train to Munich 435
Nissen, Greta 181
Niven, David 296, 298, 315, 316, 361, 371, 492
Nix on Dames 143
Nixon, Richard M. 419
Nolan, Doris 313
Norman, Mabel (the NYC stripper) 103
Normand, Mabel (the Hollywood actress) 103
Normand, Norma 310
Norris, Edward (Eddie) 283
Notorious 437
Novarro, Ramon 92, 201, 205, 210, 233
Now, Voyager 104, 434, 435, 447
Noyes, Dr. F. Le Grand 289
Nye, Senator Gerald 419
O'Brien-Moore, Erin 281, 282
O'Brien, Edmond 425
O'Brien, George 161, 192, 196, 197, 198, 199, 204, 233, 242
O'Brien, Pat 208, 264, 268, 270, 285, 295, 310, 334, 338, 340
O'Day, Molly 163
O'Neill, Eugene 103
Oberon, Merle 306, 358
Odets, Clifford 345
Of Human Bondage 56, 293
Of Mice and Men 372
Oklahoma Kid, The 323, 355, 357, 375
Old Acquaintance 477
Old Maid, The 288, 361
Old Soak, The 79
Oliver, Edna May 94
Olivia, U.S.S. 45
Olivier, Laurence 359, 390, 398, 482
"On the Good Ship Lollipop" 308
On the Waterfront 495
"Open Letter to the Working Press" 499
Orlova, Gay 483
Orr, Mary 247
Otis Elevator Co., The 35
Our Dancing Daughters 343
Our Wife 248
Out of the Fog (aka The Gentle People) 402, 403
"Over There" 74
Padlocks of 1925/1927 90
Page, Gale 317, 327, 328, 362, 392
Page, Joy 436
Page, Paul 131
Palace Theater, The (NYC) 88
Palm Springs (CA) 132
Palmer, Lilli 324
Pantages Theater (Hollywood) 489
Pantages, Lloyd 305
Paramount Pictures, Inc. 383, 496
Paris Bound 103

Parker, Dorothy 87
Parker, Eleanor 457, 485
Parrish, Robert 164
Parsons, Louella 153, 156, 172, 182, 200, 203, 206, 207, 213, 215, 216, 217, 269
Passage to Marseille 288, 429, 463, 465, 466, 467, 468, 469
Patent Leather 162
Patrick, Lee 104, 105, 381, 389, 411
Payne, John 460
Pearl, Minnie 310
Peck, Gregory 366, 441, 490
Pendleton, Nat 309
Penn, Sean 498
Pennsylvania Tug and Literage Co., Inc. 46
Penny Arcade 262
Pentacle, The 465
Percival, W.C. 70
Perkins, Anthony 247, 441
Perkins, Osgood 247, 253
Peters, Susan 421
Peterson, Robert 451, 454, 463
Peterson, Verita (aka Verita Thompson) 425, 426, 450, 451, 453, 454, 456, 458, 462, 463, 464, 469, 479, 480, 481, 482, 484, 496, 497, 499
Petrified Forest, The 87, 250, 251, 252, 253, 256, 257, 258, 259, 269, 270, 271, 281, 282, 288, 299, 306, 377, 492
Philips Academy (Andover, MA) 33, 34, 35, 38, 41, 42
Philips, Anne 115
Philips, Mary 48, 78, 79, 80, 81, 94, 108, 113, 114, 115, 116, 119, 120, 121, 122, 129, 131, 134, 137, 161, 178, 198, 206, 210, 239, 240, 250, 252, 253, 258, 271, 272, 277, 279, 280, 283, 299, 303, 304, 306, 312, 313, 314, 342, 343, 350, 410
Photoplay 189
Pickford, Mary (aka Gladys Smith) 73, 125, 216, 455
Picnic 79
Pidgeon, Walter 313
Pierce, Jack 174
Pitt, Brad 132
Pitts, ZaSu 167
Pittsburgh 317
Pittsburgh Courier, The 455
Place in the Sun, A 489
Players Club. The 241
Plaza Hotel (NYC) 68
Postman Always Rings Twice, The 258, 272, 278, 306
"Poverty Row" 352
Powell, Dick 264, 307, 491, 494
Powell, William 277
Power, Tyrone 259, 304, 345, 364, 460, 468
Preminger, Otto 437
Presley, Elvis 102, 295
"Pretty Girl Is Like a Melody, A" 378
Pretty, Arline 50
Princess O'Rourke 455
Pryor, Richard 390
Pryor, Roger 100
Psycho 247
Public Enemy, The 284
"Pussy Posse, The" 48, 78, 191
Pygmalion 307
Queen Christina 54
Queen Kelly 208, 216

518

Quick Millions 163, 173, 204
Quine, Richard 421
Quinn, Anthony 288, 392, 441
Racket Busters 334, 358, 402
Radio City Rockettes, The 312
Raft, George 90, 91, 92, 152, 161, 162, 163, 164, 167,
    168, 176, 194, 201, 219, 220, 253, 258, 299, 334,
    360, 364, 365, 367, 372, 374, 379, 381, 382, 388,
    393, 394, 395, 402, 403, 404, 407, 415, 420, 427,
    455, 466, 470
Rain 254
Rains, Claude 436, 438, 440, 443, 450, 462, 468
Raintree County 337
Rambova, Natacha 32, 52, 85, 93
Rand, Ayn 349
Rand, Sally 254
Random Harvest 421
Random House, Inc. 301
Rankin, Ruth 50
Rappé, Virginia 99, 104
Rapper, Irving 398
Rat Pack, The 425, 497
Rathbone, Basil 98, 99, 100, 157, 217, 305, 498
Ray, Aldo 498
Ray, Anthony 486
Ray, Nicholas 484, 485
Raymond, Gene (aka Raymond Guion) 94, 311, 390
Ready for Love 393
Reagan, Ronald 254, 287, 289, 311, 317, 323, 331, 332,
    333, 337, 359, 360, 363, 364, 376, 378, 386, 427,
    436, 452, 482, 483
Rebecca 248
Rebel Without a Cause 485
Red Dust 270
Red Garter Nightclub, The (Harlem, USA) 63, 65
Red Mill, The 58
Reed, Mark 121
Remarque, Erich Maria 151, 431
Renay, Liz 461
Report from the Front 474
Republic Pictures 452
Return of Dr. X, The 375, 376, 377, 378, 407
Revere, Paul 34
Rey-Xieman, José 465
Richardson, Ralph 458
Rickenbacker, Eddie 264
Ridgeley, John 478
Rin-Tin-Tin 170
Ripley, Clements 133
RKO 430
Roach, Hal 306
Roaring Twenties, The 364, 365, 366, 367, 388
Roberts, Beverly 260, 264
Roberts, Stanley 495
Robertson, Dale 345
Robinson, Casey 429, 468
Robinson, Edward G. 91, 149, 162, 167, 172, 173, 220,
    233, 253, 255, 258, 263, 276, 290, 294, 295, 303,
    325, 326, 372, 389, 394, 398, 399, 401, 402, 404,
    455, 470, 472, 483
Robson, Mark 499
"Rockaby Baby" 357
Rogers, Ginger 288, 366
Rogers, Roy 270, 421
Rogers, Will 301

Roland, Gilbert 176, 211
Rollins, David 179
Roman Holiday 300
Romanoff's Restaurant (Hollywood) 290, 301, 364, 384,
    416, 488, 499
Romeo and Juliet 398
"Room Adjoining a Boudoir, A" 143
Rooney, Mickey 341, 363, 424, 460
Roosevelt, Eleanor 4
Roosevelt, Franklin Delano 3, 4, 5, 24, 42, 45, 74, 248,
    288, 400, 419, 448, 457, 47
Roosevelt, Sara Delano 24
Roosevelt, Theodore 24
Rose, Billy 274
Rose, Stuart 37, 38, 56, 76, 96, 113, 119, 129, 133, 135,
    240, 355
Rosenbloom, "Slapsie Maxie" 330
Rossellini, Roberto 441, 443
Roth, Lillian 207
Rough Romance, A 233
Rubin, Benny 215, 217
Ruined Lady, The 55, 70
Runyon, Damon 330, 417
Russell, Annie 60
Sabrina 382, 384, 495
Sadie Thompson 254
Sahara 433, 457, 458, 461
Sakall, S.Z. 436, 437, 457
Salute 233
Sam's Vanity (NYC) 64
San Francisco 145
San Francisco Chronicle, The 460
San Quentin 334, 397, 406
Santana Productions, Inc. 269, 484, 485, 496
Santana, The 481, 491
Santell, Alfred 153, 155
Saratoga Trunk 441
Satan Met a Lady 265, 267, 404
Saturday Evening Post, The 419
Saturday's Children 100, 101
Scarface 220, 222
Scarlet Pimpernel, The 306
Schildkraut, Joseph 285
Schmidt, Frank 1
Schmidt, Judge Ruben S. 314
Schmidt, Lars 23, 24
Schnel, Richard 57
School for Scandal, The 28
Schuberts, The 239
Schulberg, Budd 498
Schultz, "Dutch" 93, 164, 263, 364
Schwab's Drugstore (Hollywood) 354
Scott, Hazel 437
Scott, Lizabeth 440, 481
Scott, Martha 496
Scott, Randolph 384, 386
Scott, Zachary 467
Screen Actors Guild 275
Screen Guild Theater, The 259, 414
Sea Hunt 461
Sea Wolf, The 399
Search, The 482
Segal, George 411
Seiler, Lewis 317, 350, 362, 364, 388, 420
Seiter, Walter 208

Sellers, Peter 493
Selznick, David O. 284, 346, 348, 358, 369, 389, 430,
    431, 441, 462, 493
Sennett, Mack 306, 310
Seventh Heaven 61, 82, 106, 107, 132, 216
Sex 97, 99
Sex and Satan 305
"Shaking the Blues Away" 124
Sharif, Omar 441
Shaw, Artie 364
Shaw, George Bernard 28, 307
Shaw, Irwin 402
She Stoops to Conquer 117
She Wanted a Millionaire 224
Shearer, Norma 235
Sheehan, Winfield 144, 225, 230, 231, 233, 234
Sheik, The 84
Sheridan, Ann 281, 282, 286, 290, 295, 297, 299, 302,
    304, 306, 312, 315, 316, 323, 334, 338, 340, 342,
    354, 367, 378, 388, 391, 393, 394, 396, 422, 427,
    443, 445, 450, 451, 452, 456, 471, 474
Sherman, Vincent 317, 350, 372, 376, 377, 415, 416,
    417, 418, 423, 444
Sherry, Barbara Davis 298
Sherwood, Robert 87, 178, 251, 282
Shoop, Clarence 455
Sidney, Sylvia 299, 300, 301, 401, 402
Silver Cord, The 103
Silvers, Phil 415, 418
Simmons, Jean 492
Simpson, Dorothy 461
Sinatra, Frank 425, 495, 497, 499
Singing Kid, The 260
Singleton, Dr. Laurence Scogga 311
Singleton, Penny 311, 312, 321, 323, 337
Sinner's Holiday 125
Sirocco 440, 486, 487
Sister Carrie 16
Sisters, The 288, 327, 328, 387
Sitting Pretty 482
Six Cylinder Love 224
Sklar, Robert 140, 338
Skolsky, Sidney 320, 354, 386
Skyrocket, The 119, 125, 144
Sloane, Everett 486
Smartest Girl in Town 390
Smith, Alexis 348, 467
Smith, Gerald I.K. 326
"Smith, Isak" 45
Smith, Mary 354
Smoke House Restaurant (Los Angeles) 453, 480
Snake Pit, The 104
Snyder, Martin (aka "The Gimp") 124
So Big 334
So Ends Our Night 431
Society for the Prevention of Vice 98
Sokolove, Harry E. 314
Soma, Tony 87
Sondergaard, Gale 249
Song and Dance Man, The 75
Sothern, Ann 389, 390
South Pacific 79
Spellbound 441
Spencer, Lady Diana (aka Princess Diana of England) 9
Sperling, Milton 499

Spider, The 183
Spinrad's Barbershop 88
Sportsland 250
Spring Thaw 342
Squaw Man, The 207
*Squeaker, The (*aka *The Feathered Serpent)* 208
St Ann's Church for Deaf Mutes 96
St. Davids, Dwight 4
St. Davids, Peter 4, 15
St. Martin's Press 447
St. Mary's School (Peekskill, NY) 38
Stack, Robert 364
Stag at Bay, The 253
Stagecoach 54, 375
Stalin, Joseph 319
Stand-In 54, 305, 306, 308
Stanislavsky, Constantin 31
Stanwyck, Barbara 60, 141, 142, 163, 166, 209, 227,
    228, 342, 345, 347, 348, 349, 358, 382, 392, 479
Starling, Lynn 76
State of the Union 352
Staunton, Derrick 174
Stearns, Alfred 34, 36, 42
Steiger, Rod 499
Steinbeck, John 372
Steiner, Max 446, 478, 495
Stella Dallas 382
Stephenson, James 351, 352
Sterling, Jan 499
Stewart, James 247, 266, 388, 413
Stewart, Paul 490
Stewart, Rosalie 76, 77
Storer, Doug 11, 18
Story of Eve, The 247
Story of Louis Pasteur, The 394
Stove at Yale 34
Strange Interlude 79
Strauss, S.W. & Co. 46
Street of Women 228
Streetcar Named Desire, A 489, 490, 495
Striker, Joe 222
Strong, Austin 58, 61
Strunsky, Leonore (Lee; aka Mrs. Ira Gershwin) 25, 26,
    27
Stuart, Gloria 343
Sullavan, Margaret 246, 247, 266, 305
Sullivan, Ed 101, 102
Summerville, Slim 167
Sumner, John 98
Sunset Blvd. 57
Sunset in the Old West 14
Surprises of Love, The 86
Susann, Jacqueline 324
Swanson, Gloria 57, 118, 159, 208, 210, 216, 230, 254,
    358
Sweet, Blanche 216
Swifty 70, 71, 72, 87, 202
Swing Your Lady 309, 310, 312, 316, 332, 401
Tarkington, Booth 76, 166, 174
Tarzan of the Movies 459
Tashman, Lilyan 183, 184, 188, 190, 191, 196
Tavern, The 129
Taylor, Elizabeth 54, 337
Taylor, Robert 304, 321, 345, 346, 349
Taylor, William Desmond 98

Tea and Sympathy 79
Teichmann, Howard 272
Tempest, The 414
Temple, Shirley 284, 285, 308, 400, 493
Ten Commandments, The 53
Thalberg, Irving 216
Thank Your Lucky Stars 378, 457
That Certain Woman 313
Thelma and Louise 147
They Drive by Night 256, 329, 366, 391, 392
They Won't Forget 336
Thief of Baghdad 460
Thirteen, The 458
This Side of Paradise 66, 433
Thomas, Bob 384
Thompson, Verita (see Peterson, Verita)
Thompson, Walter 497
Thorpe, Dr. Franklyn 409
Thorpe, Jim 126
Thorpe, Marylyn 409
Thousand Oaks (CA) 301
Three Wise Fools 58, 61
Tierney, Gene 497, 498
Tiger Shark 403
Time Out London 361
To Have and Have Not 403, 468, 473, 474, 477, 484
To the Ladies 117
Tokyo Joe 440, 485
Tone, Franchot 313, 400, 402
Tonight or Never 216
Tony's (NYC) 87
Toohey, John Peter 70
Toomey, Regis 479
Top Secret Affair 334
Toren, Marta 440, 486, 487
Touch of Brimstone, A 255
Tracy, Spencer 77, 143, 144, 145, 147, 152, 165, 168,
    189, 197, 205, 221, 223, 224, 225, 232, 265, 302,
    305, 314, 316, 342, 344, 357, 358, 413, 433, 441,
    444, 488, 496, 500
Trailin' 192
Tramp, The 287
Treadwell, Louise 145
Treasure of the Sierra Madre, The 414, 459, 482, 483
Trevor, Claire 300, 302, 304, 307, 316, 325, 326, 333,
    344, 396, 456, 472, 483
Triangle Club, The (Princeton) 67
Trilling, Steve 466
Trinity School, The (NYC) 18
Truman, Harry S 288
Tucker, Forrest 452
Tully, Tom 495
Turek, John 103, 106
Turner, Lana 258, 306, 336, 353, 392, 396, 436
Twelvetrees, Helen 231
20th Century Fox/20th Century Pictures 231, 460, 467,
    490, 497
21 Club, The 54, 63, 71, 105
Two Against the World 259, 260
Two Girls Wanted 79
Two Mrs. Carrolls, The 60, 348, 349, 479
U.S. Office of War Information 469
Underground 417
Up the Ladder 52, 69
Up the River 144, 149, 153, 182, 202, 231, 243

Ustinov, Peter 498
Vale, Martin 349
Vale, Travers 50
Valentino, Rudolph 32, 52, 78, 84, 93, 159, 277, 374,
    380
Valiant, The 372
Valley of the Dolls 324
Valley of the Giants 325
Van Druten, John 241
Van Dyke, W.S. 218
Vanity Fair Magazine 153
Varga, Bela 95
Variety 232, 448
Veidt, Conrad 415, 418, 436, 437
Velez, Lupe 165, 207
Verita's La Cantina (Hollywood) 497
Verne, Kaaren 415, 416, 418
Vickers, Martha 478
Vidor, King 349
Virginia City 384, 385, 386, 388
Visit, The 441
Vitaphone Corp. 123
Vogues of 1938 272
Voice of the Turtle, The 241
Von Sternberg, Josef 158
Von Stroheim, Erich 50, 57, 208, 274
Wagner, Robert 142
Wagons Roll at Night, The 302, 310, 402, 404
Wald, Jerry 415, 455, 457
Walker, Jimmy 88, 90, 99, 102
Wallis, Hal 310, 323, 338, 361, 389, 402, 403, 415, 427,
    439, 440, 450, 467
Walsh, Michael 449
Walsh, Raoul 133, 139, 181, 231, 233, 364, 365, 391,
    395, 396, 403, 408, 486
Wanger, Walter 54, 272, 305, 312
War of the Worlds, The 429
Warner Brothers, Inc. 3, 27, 48, 90, 93, 124, 253, 261,
    268, 269, 270, 274, 288, 298, 306, 315, 325, 349,
    367, 371, 372, 394, 416, 422, 430, 434, 463, 469,
    471, 473, 479, 481, 485, 499
Warner, Henry and David 2
Warner, Jack 255, 257, 284, 285, 290, 291, 308, 310,
    312, 316, 331, 334, 351, 358, 361, 362, 367, 371,
    372, 376, 378, 382, 385, 387, 388, 395, 401, 402,
    404, 405, 407, 410, 413, 415, 419, 420, 422, 423,
    424, 427, 428, 436, 437, 440, 444, 446, 450, 455,
    457, 465, 466, 469, 473, 478, 483
Washington, George 34
Watch on the Rhine 450
Waterloo Bridge 177, 178, 180
*Way Back Home (*aka *Other People's Business)* 208, 209
Wayne, Billy 325, 329
Wayne, John 150, 233, 317, 329, 452
We're No Angels 249, 372, 498
Wead, Frank 253, 264
Webb, Clifton 76, 77, 353, 383, 384, 456, 482
Weissmuller, Johnny 218, 328
Weitzenkorn, Louis 259
Welles, Orson 288, 481
Wells, H.G. 429
Werewolf of London, The 397
West, Mae 29, 97, 98, 99, 330, 372, 373, 375
Westmore, Perc 336
Whale, James 177, 180

Wharton, Edith 361
What Every Woman Knows 28
What Price Glory? 81, 139, 181
When My Baby Smiles at Me 482
When You're in Love 274
"Where the Lighthouse Shines Across the Bay" 418
Where's the Rest of Me? 360
Whistler, James McNeill 10
Whistler's Mother 10
White Sister, The 72, 73, 158
Who's Afraid of Virginia Woolf? 246
Whoopee! 123
Widmark, Richard 490, 495
Wilbur, Cranc 317
Wildcat, The 89
Wilde, Cornel 397
Wilde, Oscar 69
Wilder, Billy 382, 383, 384
Will Seabury's Repertory Theatre Company
    (Skowhegan, ME) 253
"Will You Love Me in December As You Do in May?"
    88
William Brady, Jr. 313
Williams, Bob 444
Williams, Guinn ("Big Boy") 387
"Willow Brook" 2, 12
Willson, Rena 66
Wilson, Dooley 436, 437
Wilson, Earl 479
Wilson, Glenn 57
Wilson, Marie 265, 339
Wilson, Woodrow 126
Winchell, Walter 89
Windust, Bretaigne 486
Wings Over Honolulu 313
Winwood, Estelle 66
Wisdom Tooth, The 94
Wizard of Oz, The 244, 375
Wogan, Terry 418
Women and Diamonds 139
Women of All Nations 139, 181, 185, 231
Women, The 150
Won Ton Ton, the Dog Who Saved Hollywood 378
Wood, Thomas 106, 381
Woods, Donald 270, 271
Woollcott, Alexander 72, 81, 87, 128, 202
Wong, Anna May 156
World Moves On, The 364
Worlds of Robert E. Sherwood, The 251
Wouk, Herman 495
Wright, Richard 44
Wuthering Heights 300, 359, 375, 390
Wyler, William 236, 238, 299, 300, 302, 352, 397, 496,
    498
Wyman, Jane 289, 323, 387, 452
Wynn, Keenan 253, 491
Wynn, May 495
Yankee Doodle Dandy 74, 421, 428, 470, 477
Yeaman, Elizabeth 325
Yellow Rolls-Royce, The 441
You Can't Get Away with Murder 364, 388, 391, 402
"You're a Grand Old Flag" 74
Youmans, Vincent 274
Young, Arthur 417
Young, Gig 496

Young, Governor Clement C. 213
Young, Roland 206, 210, 227, 229, 239, 255, 271, 303,
    314, 342
Zanardi-Landi, Count Carlo 154
Zanuck, Darryl F. 285, 369, 437, 467, 490
Zanville, Bernard (aka Dane Clark) 456
Ziegfeld Follies of 1927 124
Ziegfeld, Florenz 124, 150, 244
Zorina, Vera 446, 447
Zukor, Adolph 53

BLOOD MOON PRODUCTIONS

Publishing that Applies the Tabloid Standards of Today
to the Tinseltown Scandals of Yesterday.
IT'S A TOUGH JOB, BUT SOMEBODY'S GOT TO DO IT!

Blood Moon, a publishing enterprise based in New York City, researches, indexes, and preserves the previously unrecorded oral histories of America's entertainment industry. Reorganized with its present name in 2004, Blood Moon originated in 1997 as The Georgia Literary Assn., a vehicle for the promotion of obscure writers from America's Deep South.

Since 2004, Blood Moon has generated at least ten different literary awards. They've included both silver and bronze medals from the IPPY (Independent Publishers Assn.) Awards; four nominations and two Honorable Mentions for BOOK OF THE YEAR from Foreword Reviews; and Honorable Mentions from both the New England and the Hollywood Book Festivals.

For more about us, including access to a growing number of videotaped book trailers, click on www.BloodMoonProductions.com, or refer to the pages which immediately follow.

Thanks for your interest, best wishes, and happy reading.

Danforth Prince, President
Blood Moon Productions

And its affiliate, the Georgia Literary Assn

A DEMENTED BILLIONAIRE:

From his reckless pursuit of love as a rich teenager to his final days as a demented fossil, Howard Hughes tasted the best and worst of the century he occupied. Along the way, he changed the worlds of aviation and entertainment forever. This biography reveals inside details about his destructive and usually scandalous associations with other Hollywood players.

Howard Hughes:
Hell's Angel by Darwin Porter

Set amid descriptions of the unimaginable changes that affected America between Hughes's birth in 1905 and his death in 1976, this book gives an insider's perspective about what money can buy--and what it can't.

"Darwin Porter's access to film industry insiders and other Hughes confidants supplied him with the resources he needed to create a portrait of Hughes that both corroborates what other Hughes biographies have divulged, and go them one better."
-*Foreword Magazine*

"Thanks to this bio of Howard Hughes, we'll never be able to look at the old pin-ups in quite the same way again."
-*The Times* (London)

A BIG comprehensive hardcover,
Approx 814 pages, with photos
$32.95
ISBN 978-1-936003-13-6

Hughes--A young billionaire looks toward his notorious future

Billie Dove--duenna of the Silent Screen. She gave him syphilis.

Did Howard Hughes murder David Bacon?

"The Aviator flew both ways. Porter's biography presents new allegations about Hughes' shady dealings with some of the biggest names of the 20th century"

New York Daily News

The Secret Life of the U.S. Emperor
LOVE! SEX! POWER!
"The Aviator flew both ways."
New York Daily News

The Richest Man in America
**SEXUAL PREDATOR
LUSTFUL VISIONARY**

PAUL NEWMAN

The Man Behind the Baby Blues
His Secret Life Exposed
by Darwin Porter

The most compelling biography
of the iconic actor ever published

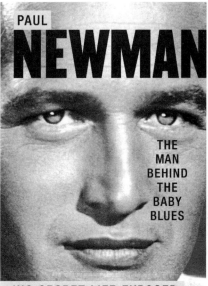

Drawn from firsthand interviews with insiders who knew Paul Newman intimately, and compiled over a period of nearly a half-century, this is the world's most honest and most revelatory biography about Hollywood's pre-eminent male sex symbol, with dozens of potentially shocking revelations.

Whereas the situations it exposes were widely known within Hollywood's inner circles, they've never before been revealed to the general public.

If you're a fan of Newman (and who do you know who isn't) you really should look at this book. It's a respectful but candid cornucopia of information about the sexual and emotional adventures of a young man on Broadway and in Hollywood.

One wonders how he ever managed to escape public scrutiny for so long...

A pioneering and posthumous biography of a charismatic icon of Tinseltown. His rule over the hearts of American moviegoers lasted for more than half a century--a potent, desirable, and ambiguous sex symbol, a former sailor from Shaker Heights, Ohio, who parlayed his ambisexual charm and extraordinary good looks into one of the most successful careers in Hollywood. It's all here, as recorded by celebrity chronicler Darwin Porter--the giddy heights and agonizing lows of a great American star.

Paul Newman, The Man Behind the Baby Blues
His Secret Life Exposed
ISBN 978-0-9786465-1-6 $26.95
Hardcover,   520 pages, with photos.

BLOOD
MOON
Productions, Ltd.

MERV GRIFFIN
A Life in the Closet

by Darwin Porter

Merv Griffin, A Life in the Closet

Merv Griffin began his career as a Big Band singer, moved on to a failed career as a romantic hero in the movies, and eventually rewrote the rules of everything associated with the broadcasting industry. Along the way, he met and befriended virtually everyone who mattered, made billions operating casinos and developing jingles, contests, and word games. All of this while maintaining a male harem and a secret life as America's most famously closeted homosexual.

In this comprehensive biography--the first published since Merv's death in 2007--celebrity biographer Darwin Porter reveals the amazing details behind the richest, most successful, and in some way, the most notorious mogul in the history of America's entertainment industry.

Most of his viewers (they numbered 20 million per day) thought that **Merv Griffin**'s life was an ongoing series of chatty segués--amiable, seamless, uncontroversial. But things were far more complicated than viewers at the time ever thought. Here, from the writer who unzipped **Marlon Brando**, is the first post-mortem, unauthorized overview of the mysterious life of **the richest and most notorious man in television**

HOT, CONTROVERSIAL, & RIGOROUSLY RESEARCHED

HERE'S MERV! Hardcover, 566 pages with photos

ISBN 978-0-9786465-0-9 $26.95

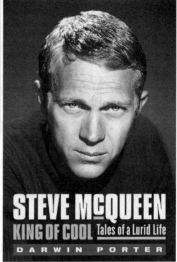

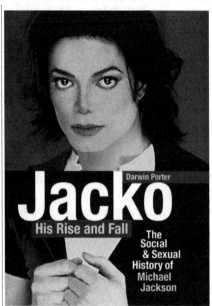

This "entertainingly outrageous" (FRONTIERS MAGAZINE) biography provides a definitive,
blow-by-blow description of the "hot, provocative, and barely under control drama" that was the life
of America's most famous Postwar actor.

Brando Unzipped

by Darwin Porter

"Lurid, raunchy, perceptive, and certainly worth reading...One of the ten best show-biz biographies of 2006."　　*The Sunday Times (London)*

"<u>Yummy</u>. An irresistably flamboyant romp of a read."
Books to Watch Out For

"Astonishing. An extraordinarily detailed portrait of Brando that's as blunt, uncompromising, and X-rated as the man himself."
Women's Weekly

"This shocking new book is sparking a major reassessment of Brando's legacy as one of Hollywood's most macho lotharios."
Daily Express (London)

"As author Darwin Porter finds, it wasn't just the acting world Marlon Brando conquered. It was the actors, too."
Gay Times (London)

"*Brando Unzipped* is the definitive gossip guide to the late, great actor's life."
The New York Daily News

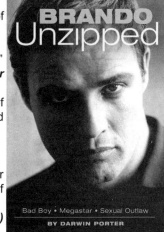

Hardcover, 625 indexed pages,
with hundreds of photos.

ISBN 978-0-9748118-2-6.
$26.95

This is one of our most visible and most frequently reviewed titles. A best-seller, it's now in its fifth printing, with French, Portuguese, and Dutch editions selling briskly in Europe. Shortly after its release, this title was extensively serialized by THE SUNDAY TIMES in the UK, and in other major Sunday supplements in mainland Europe and Australia

Katharine the Great (HEPBURN)

A Lifetime of Secrets Revealed, by Darwin Porter

A compelling biography of the most phobically secretive actress in Hollywood

Katharine Hepburn was the world's greatest screen diva--the most famous actress in American history. But until the appearance of this biography, no one had ever published the intimate details of her complicated and ferociously secretive private life. Thanks to the "deferential and obsequious whitewashes" which followed in the wake of her death, readers probably know WHAT KATE REMEMBERED. Here, however, is an unvarnished account of what Katharine Hepburn desperately wanted to forget.

"Behind the scenes of her movies, Katharine Hepburn played the temptress to as many women as she did men, ranted and raved with her co-stars and directors, and broke into her neighbors' homes for fun. And somehow, she managed to keep all of it out of the press. As they say, *Katharine the Great* is hard to put down."
The Dallas Voice

"The door to Hepburn's closet has finally been opened. This is the most honest and least apologetic biography of Hollywood's most ferociously private actress ever written."
Senior Life Magazine, Miami

"In Porter's biography of Katharine Hepburn, details about the inner workings of a movie studio (RKO in the early 30s), are relished."
The Bottom Line, Palm Springs

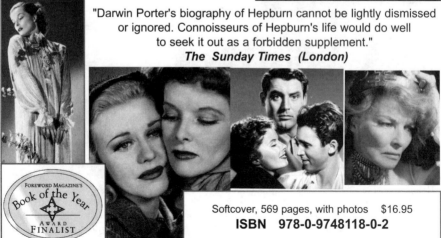

"Darwin Porter's biography of Hepburn cannot be lightly dismissed or ignored. Connoisseurs of Hepburn's life would do well to seek it out as a forbidden supplement."
The Sunday Times (London)

FOREWORD MAGAZINE'S
Book of the Year
AWARD
FINALIST

Softcover, 569 pages, with photos $16.95
ISBN   978-0-9748118-0-2

The Revealing, Tempestuous Lives of the 20th Century's Most Flamboyant Theatre Couple, as recorded by people who knew them intimately.

Damn You,
Scarlett O'Hara
The Private Lives of **Vivien Leigh** and **Laurence Olivier**

by **Darwin Porter** and **Roy Moseley**

The scandalous love affair of "The Royal Family of the British Stage" was second in fame and notoriety only to that of the Duke and Duchess of Windsor. Co-authors Roy Moseley (the couple's adopted godson, long-standing friend, and personal assistant) and Darwin Porter tear away the velvet curtain previously draped over the reputations of this famous team, exposing with searing insights the depths of their sexual excess and interpersonal anguish. Some of the most iconic figures of the 20th century move through chapters that highlight a revelation on every page

Available November, 2010.   Hardcover   435 pages with photos
978-1-936003-15-0. $27.95

GET READY FOR WHAT'S GOING TO ROCK THE COUNTRY JUST BEFORE CHRISTMAS OF 2010

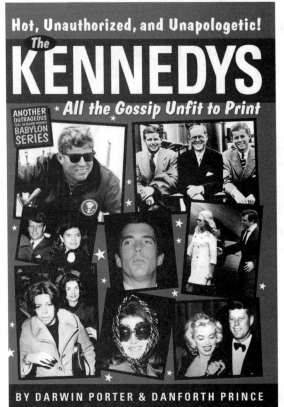

FROM THOSE WHO KNEW THEM:

THEIR POWER, THEIR PECCADILLOS, THEIR PORN.

OK, we appreciate their politics, but what about their sex lives? Read all about it in Volume 3 of Blood Moon's award-winning Babylon series, an inter-generational archive of embarrassments showcasing the libidinous indiscretions and extramarital romps of America's horniest political tribe.

Available in December, 2010
Hardcover, 425 pages
with hundreds of photos
7"x 10"
978-1-936003-17-4
$25.95

"So, with many hundreds of books about the Kennedys published over the years, you think you've heard all the deep dish, sizzling gossip and sexual intrigue surrounding America's royal family of politics and power? **Think again.** *This buzz-rich exposé, culled from decades of intense research by Kennedyphile Darwin Porter, carefully documents the mind-boggling chain of triumph and calamity that has dogged generations of a dynasty both idolized and reviled by a nation. Pick it up and you'll be hard-pressed to put it down."*

RICHARD LABONTÉ, BOOK MARKS AND Q SYNDICATE

FRANK SINATRA, THE BOUDOIR SINGER

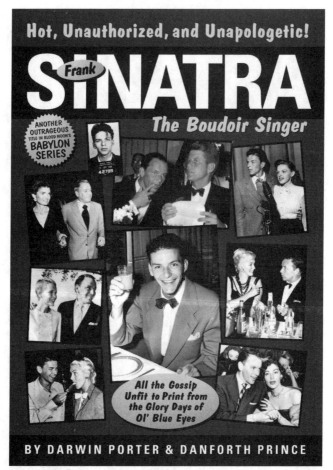

50 Years of Queer Cinema
500 of the Best GLBTQ Films Ever Made

An indispensable reference source for films about
The Love that Dare Not Speak Its Name

As late as 1958, homosexuality couldn't even be mentioned in a movie, as proven by the elaborate lengths the producers of Tennessee Williams swampy *Cat on a Hot Tin Roof* took to evade the obvious fact that its hero, Paul Newman, was playing it gay. And in spite of the elaborate lengths its producers took to camouflage its lavender aspects, in-the-know viewers during the late 50s realized all along that Joe E. Brown was fully aware that Jack Lemmon wasn't a biological female ("nobody's perfect") in *Some Like it Hot* (1959).

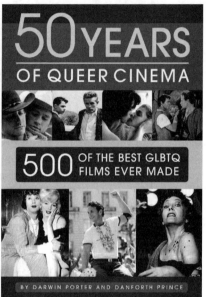

That kind of baroque subterfuge ended abruptly in 1960, when cinema emerged from its celluloid closet. With the release of *Boys in the Band* in 1970, gay cinema had come of age—It was queer and here to stay. Decades later came *Brokeback Mountain, Transamerica,* and *Milk.*

This comprehensive anthology documents it all, bringing into focus a sweeping rundown of cinema's most intriguing Gay, Lesbian, Bisexual, Transgendered, and "Queer Questioning" films that deserves a home next to the DVD player as well as on the reference shelves of public libraries. Crucial to the viability of this book is the fact that new DVD releases have made these films available to new generations of viewers for the first time since their original release.

More than just a dusty library reference, this book shamelessly spills 50 quasi-closeted years of Hollywood secrets—all of them in glorious Technicolor.

A comprehensive paperback designed as a reference source for both private homes and libraries.   524 pages, with 500 photos
ISBN 978-1-936003-09-9 $24.95

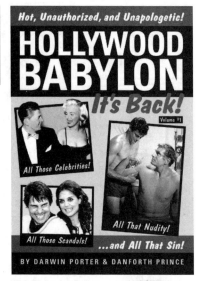

Wild, orgiastic nights in pre-code Hollywood

Hollywood's
Silent Closet
by Darwin Porter

ISBN 978-0-9668030-2-0   Trade Paper 7" x 10"
746 pages. 60 photos $24.95

Hollywood's Silent Closet

a novel by
Darwin Porter

An anthology of star-studded scandal from Tinseltown's very gay and very lavender past, it focuses on Hollywood's secrets from the 1920s, including the controversial backgrounds of the great lovers of the Silent Screen.

Valentino, Ramon Novarro, Charlie Chaplin, Fatty Arbuckle, Pola Negri, Mary Pickford, and many others figure into eyewitness accounts of the debauched excesses that went on behind closed doors. It also documents the often tragic endings of America's first screen idols, some of whom admitted to being more famous than the monarchs of England and Jesus Christ combined.

The first book of its kind, it's the most intimate and most realistic novel about sex, murder, blackmail, and degradation in early Hollywood ever written.

"The *Myra Breckenridge* of the Silent-Screen era. Lush, luscious, and langorously decadent. A brilliant primer of **Who Was Who** in early Hollywood."
-*Gay London Times*

A banquet of information about the pansexual intrigues of Hollywood between 1919 and 1926 compiled from eyewitness interviews with men and women, all of them insiders, who flourished in its midst. Not for the timid, it names names and doesn't spare the guilty. If you believe, like Truman Capote, that the literary treatment of gossip will become the literature of the 21st century, then you will love **Hollywood's Silent Closet.**

Millions of fans lusted after Gary Cooper (background) and Rudolph Valentino (foreground) but until the release of this book, **The Public Never Knew**

BLOOD MOON PRODUCTIONS ANNOUNCES THE RELEASE of the 75-minute documentary it filmed in late May from the floor of America's world-famous and most important bookselling event, BEA 2010.

BOOK EXPO 2010: BLOOD MOON'S VIEW FROM THE FLOOR, represents history's first attempt to capture—close, in-your-face, uncensored, and personalized—the interactions, alliances, scandals, and dramas that explode for a small book publisher during a bookselling mega-event devoted to the marketing, pricing, and sale of its literary products.

Defined as a hybrid between a documentary and an infomercial, the film was conceived as a publicity and promotion piece by Blood Moon's founder and president, Danforth Prince: "Book publishers operate in a state of barely controlled hysteria, especially in this economic climate," he said. "Within this film, we've captured some of the drama of how books are promoted and hawked at a highly competitive event where everyone from Barbra Streisand to the Duchess of York was shaking his or her bonbon to sell something."

"At BEA 2010, enemies, competitors, and authors evoked Oscar night in Hollywood before the awards are announced," Prince continued. "This film is the first attempt to depict, on video, how a small press swims in the frantic, shark-infested waters of the book trade. It's a documentation of a specific moment in America's mercantile history, with implications for America's reading habits and how consumers will opt, sometimes through digitalization, to amuse and entertain themselves in the 21st century."

During the footage he shot from within and near his booth #3784 at BEA, Mr. Prince was assisted by members of Blood Moon's editorial staff, and directed by Polish-born Piotr Kajstura, winner of several filmmaking awards and grants for his work with, among others, the tourism board of South Carolina.

BOOK EXPO 2010, BLOOD MOON'S VIEW FROM THE FLOOR.
© Blood Moon Productions, Ltd. Available now, electronically and without charge, from the home page of **BloodMoonProductions.com**

WHAT BOOK-INDUSTRY CRITICS SAID ABOUT THIS FILM:

Blood Moon Productions, which specializes in books about Hollywood celebrity scandals of the past--many of which were hushed up at the time--offered a feature-length video on BookExpo America 2010, which aims to give "nonprofessional book people an insight into book fairs"--while highlighting some Blood Moon titles. The narrator is Blood Moon president Danforth Prince, who interviews, among others, Carole Stuart of Barricade Books, Philip Rafshoon, owner of Outwrite Bookstore and Coffeehouse, Atlanta, Ga., Graeme Aitkin of the Bookshop in Sydney, Australia, Eugene Schwartz of ForeWord Reviews, and a what seems like half of the staff of National Book Network, Blood Moon's distributor.

Shelf-Awareness.com August 3, 2010 (volume 2, issue #1247)